INDIANA UNIVERSITY BASKETBALL ENCYCLOPEDIA

JASON HINER

FOREWORD BY DICK VAN ARSDALE

SP

SPORTS
PUBLISHING
L.L.C.

www.SportsPublishingLLC.com

"History is a guide to navigation in perilous times.
History is who we are and why we are the way we are."
—*David McCullough*

ISBN: 1-58261-655-8

Publishers: Peter L. Bannon and Joseph J. Bannon Sr.
Senior managing editor: Susan M. Moyer
Acquisitions editor: Mike Pearson
Developmental editor: Doug Hoepker
Art director: K. Jeffrey Higgerson
Book layout: Krista King
Dust jacket design: Kenneth J. O'Brien
Project manager: Greg Hickman
Imaging: Heidi Norson and Dustin Hubbart
Bracket design: Dustin Hubbart
Photo editor: Erin Linden-Levy
Vice president of sales and marketing: Kevin King
Media and promotions managers: Dan Waldinger, Randy Fouts (national), Maurey Williamson (print)

Printed in the United States

Sports Publishing L.L.C.
804 North Neil Street
Champaign, IL 61820

Phone: 1-877-424-2665
Fax: 217-363-2073
Web site: www.SportsPublishingLLC.com

The Indiana University Basketball Encyclopedia *is dedicated to Everett Dean, Branch McCracken and Bob Knight—three men who dedicated so much of their lives to making college basketball players into better young men, and to making IU basketball a tradition that the people of Indiana could be proud of.*

Coach Everett Dean
IU Archives

Coach Branch McCracken
IU Archives

Coach Bob Knight
IU Archives

CONTENTS

INDIANA UNIVERSITY BASKETBALL ENCYCLOPEDIA

FOREWORD

When my twin brother, Tom, and I were recruited by Indiana University coach Branch McCracken in 1960 to play basketball for the "Hurryin' Hoosiers", they didn't have to worry about us selecting another school. Indiana had always been our team. Tom and I began watching Branch and the Hoosiers in 1953 when they won the NCAA title. I was 10 years old and a big fan. My parents would also take us to a Big Ten football game in Bloomington each year. That's when I also fell in love with those beautiful fall days on the IU campus and in neighboring Brown County. My uncle John had also attended Indiana and was friends with Branch and assistant coach Lou Watson. He helped persuade us to choose IU, but no urging was really needed.

I remember Coach McCracken as a big man with a full head of silver hair. He had a great personality and commanded respect. I didn't enjoy the pre-season mandatory two-mile runs, but I would have run through a wall for Branch. He really cared about his players. I am also grateful to Branch that academics were so important to him, and I graduated in four years with a degree in economics.

The student support for the IU basketball team was tremendous. Most of my S.A.E. fraternity brothers attended the games, as well as my future wife, Barb Fenton, who was a Pi Phi at IU. There was a real closeness between the students and the athletes during that time. The fact that athletes were just part of the student population and not isolated in athletic dorms made my college experience much more enjoyable. I lived in the S.A.E. house all four years. That was a period in my life I will cherish forever.

My days at IU prepared me well for my 12-year career as a player in the NBA, three years with the New York Knicks and nine years with the Phoenix Suns. I had experienced many tough practice sessions at IU, and the Big Ten games were very physical and competitive, so I was ready for the contact in the NBA.

I continued to follow the fortunes of IU basketball after graduation, and was thrilled at the success the teams achieved under Coach Bob Knight. Branch had won two NCAA titles, and Coach Knight contin-

ued the tradition by adding three more. Bob Knight has also become a longtime friend and fishing companion. He's an excellent fisherman, and I don't believe there has ever been a better collegiate basketball coach.

After Coach Knight left Indiana, Mike Davis took the reins, and IU advanced to the NCAA Finals in 2002, losing to Maryland. I watched intently, praying my old school would win another title. It wasn't to be, but that game reminded me that I will always be rooting for the Cream and Crimson.

I'm really glad to see that the rich history of IU basketball is being documented in Jason Hiner's book, the *Indiana University Basketball Encyclopedia*. I'm looking forward to giving copies to my kids so that they can see that their old man was a part of that great tradition.

Dick Van Arsdale

Senior Vice President, Player Development
Phoenix Suns

Dick Van Arsdale shared the 1960 Indiana Mr. Basketball award with his brother Tom. The two 6'5" forwards were both three-year starters at Indiana, and after graduation, they both went on to successful careers in the NBA.

Dick Van Arsdale, current day.
Courtesy of the Phoenix Suns

Dick Van Arsdale as a member of Branch McCracken's "Hurryin' Hoosiers". IU Archives

ACKNOWLEDGMENTS

When I first discovered that no one had written a comprehensive book on the full history of Indiana University basketball, I was very surprised. With the enthusiasm that so many IU alumni and people throughout the state of Indiana have for the IU basketball team, I figured someone would have written a book that offers details on the different eras and provides team photos, season results, and statistics for each of the seasons. When I realized that a book like that didn't exist, I thought to myself, "Hey, I'm a writer, maybe I'll write the book myself." Eventually, I signed a book contract with Sports Publishing to write the *Indiana University Basketball Encyclopedia*. Then, in the course of almost three years of working on this project (on a part-time basis), I quickly came to realize why no one had ever taken on this task—because the huge scope of the information involved meant that it would take a ton of work to bring it all together into a single volume. That also meant that there were a lot of logistical hurdles to overcome. Thus, it would have been impossible to pull off a project like this without a lot of help from many different people.

First, I am greatly indebted to the many journalists and authors who have written about Indiana University basketball in the past. As my bibliography testifies, I have benefited from the chronicles of a lot of different writers. However, most of my primary source material came from the newspaper reports of the *Indiana Daily Student* and the various Indianapolis and Bloomington newspapers that have served Indiana throughout the past century. For the early years prior to 1940, I am deeply indebted to many nameless *Indiana Daily Student* and *Arbutus* (the Indiana yearbook) reporters, who provided invaluable recaps of various games and seasons. For the modern era, I am indebted to Bob Hammel and Ray Marquette, especially Hammel. It's tough to say anything new or original about the Bob Knight era, because if it was important, then Bob Hammel's already covered it—and done it with precision and eloquence.

I also benefited from the many detailed managers' reports that were compiled and recorded for posterity between the early 1920s and the early 1970s, so I am indebted to a long line of former IU managers that gathered this information. Of course, I wouldn't have had access to these or any other materials in the Assembly Hall archives without the assistance of IU's Media Relations contact for basketball, Pete Rhoda. Pete was always very professional and very responsive to my requests, even when he was obviously very busy.

For the photos in this book from the period of 1990 to 2004, I must thank Beth Feickert in the IU Media Relations office for gathering the requested photos. For the period before 1990, I owe a huge thanks to Brad Cook in the IU Archives. Brad had to scan 90 years worth of team photos and then had to go back to the archives again and again to look for photos of players, games and events that I requested. I'm grateful that he never got annoyed by my many requests. Brad also gathered a lot of valuable documents and materials from the archives for me to study during one of my trips to Bloomington, and many of those materials turned out to be unique and valuable for my research.

Another big-time assist came from the librarians in the periodicals section of the Allen County Public Library. During a period of four months, I spent two nights a week at the Allen County Public Library looking up and copying newspaper articles on IU basketball games throughout the 20th century. The librarians had to repeatedly go down to the storage facility and haul up huge stacks of microfilms for me. Then, they often had to repeatedly refill the toner or paper for the microfilm machines that I used to copy the articles. They always provided service with a smile and never acted put out. The staff of the GIMSS (Government Information, Microforms and Statistical Services) department at the IU Main Library was also very helpful when I was in Bloomington to make copies of old *Indiana Daily Student* articles. Likewise, the staff members in the

Newspaper Microfilm Room of the Indiana State Library in Indianapolis were very helpful when I went there to copy articles from newspapers that I couldn't find anywhere else.

I'd like to give a note of thanks to the numerous eBay sellers who sold me old IU Media Guides, books that were out of print, memorabilia, original copies of newspapers and magazines, and other materials—almost all of which became an important part of my research.

Another individual that I'd like to tip my hat to is John Decker at *Inside Indiana*. John gave me the regular Hoosier History column in *Inside Indiana*, where I was able to explore many of these IU basketball history topics, including some events and individuals that I was able to cover in more depth than I was able to do in this book. It has been a column in the truest sense, as John has allowed me a lot of editorial freedom in pursuing different topics, for which I am very thankful. I'd also like to thank all of the former IU players that I have interviewed for Inside Indiana as well as for this encyclopedia. Special thanks go to Dick Van Arsdale for agreeing to write the foreword for this book. Of all the former players whom I interviewed, Dick was one of my favorites. He's just a terrific human being. The same goes for Hallie Bryant. He's another great guy I really enjoyed talking to.

Of course, I have to thank Sports Publishing and its acquisitions director Mike Pearson for believing that I could write this book and do justice to this expansive topic. I also must give a big thanks to my developmental editor, Doug Hoepker. Doug was great to work with and provided some excellent feedback and suggestions that have undoubtedly made this a better book.

Finally, in the tradition of "the last shall be first", I must thank my wife, Heather, and my son, Noah. They sacrificed a lot of nights and weekends with me while I was working on this project, but they never showed any resentment about it and were always very encouraging. Their love and support sustained me during a lot of long hours of researching and writing this book. As cliché as it may sound, I'd also like to thank God, whom I turned to for inspiration during some of the toughest stretches of this project. He never let me down.

INTRODUCTION

In the opening scene of the movie *Hoosiers*, as Coach Norman Dale drives across the state of Indiana, he sees basketball hoops wherever he looks, most of them attached to barns or mounted to poles with young men shooting baskets to a backdrop of cornfields and farmland. That scene, along with the ones with Jimmy Chitwood shooting jump shot after jump shot by himself, portray some of the most traditional and enduring images of basketball in the Hoosier state.

I experienced something similar, but with a modern twist, when I moved back to Indiana at the age of 14 after living on the east coast for eight years. When I returned to Fort Wayne, Indiana (where I was born and lived until I was six), I noticed an interesting phenomenon as we drove by different neighborhoods. It seemed like there were basketball hoops in nearly every driveway. In reality, there were probably just several basketball hoops on every block, but that was a lot more than I was used to. Back on the east coast, basketball had become one of my favorite sports growing up. However, there were usually only one or two basketball hoops on most streets (and sometimes only one or two in the whole development), and all the kids in the neighborhood simply congregated there when they wanted to play some hoops.

Back in the Hoosier state, I quickly discovered that a lot more people play basketball, and many of them play by simply going out and "shooting some buckets" by themselves, just like Chitwood in *Hoosiers*. Thus, all of those extra hoops were put to good use. I also learned that Indiana folks not only play basketball, they know basketball, and are often eager to debate the merits of particular styles of play or analyze the results of basketball games from the grade school level up to the NBA.

I also soon realized that their favorite subject is college basketball (with high school ball a close second). In many ways, college basketball is viewed as the pinnacle of the sport in Indiana. While the NBA is dominated by one-on-one play and superior athleticism can trump the best game plan, college basketball

remains the venue where teamwork and solid basketball fundamentals are still valued and still determine the winners. At least, that's the prevailing opinion in the Hoosier state.

For that reason, the most popular basketball team in the state is not the NBA's Indiana Pacers (although there are lots of Pacer fans). It is the Indiana University Hoosiers. When you drive through just about any Indiana town, it is the interlocking "I" and "U" logo that you see most often on bumper stickers, caps, flags, t-shirts, and painted on backboards. You'll occasionally see some Pacers paraphernalia, or even some items bearing the logo of the Indianapolis Colts' NFL franchise, but those two teams aren't even a close runner-up in popularity to IU. That honor goes to another college basketball team, the Purdue University Boilermakers—IU's traditional in-state archrival.

Of course, I was always well aware of the popularity of IU basketball, even if I wasn't totally conscious of it. Some of my family's earliest pictures of me as a toddler usually show me wearing either a white IU t-shirt in the summer or a red IU sweatshirt in the winter. Even when I lived out east, I was a loyal IU fan who watched the Hoosiers whenever they played on national TV.

I also have first-hand experience with the intense IU-Purdue rivalry. In my extended family, we have a mix of both IU and Purdue alumni, and the issue of bragging rights is a very serious matter. After a particularly important victory or an especially convincing blowout, the IU fans will often call (or e-mail) the Purdue fans to do a little gloating, and vise versa—and if they don't call right after the game, you can bet it will be a hot topic at the next family gathering. Once I decided to go to Indiana and then became an IU alum, my lot was squarely thrown in with the IU camp.

As an adult, I've further realized the full extent to which the IU basketball squad is really the most popular sports team in the state of Indiana, as well as being the state's most high-profile representative to the rest of the world. For example, one of my former neighbors who is a pilot in the U.S. military, told a story of a trip he made to Bahrain in the late 1990s. One of the locals asked him where he was from in the United States and he told the guy that he was from Indiana. The guy responded, "Oh, Indiana—Bobby Knight!" When my neighbor returned to Bahrain a couple of years later, after Knight's dismissal in 2000, he saw the same guy, who immediately exclaimed, "They fired him!"

Having a highly successful and high profile coach like Bob Knight definitely helped to spread and reinforce the view of Indiana as America's "basketball state"—even beyond the borders of America. However, Indiana also has a storied basketball tradition that preceded Knight's arrival in Bloomington, and precious little has been written about it. Even for the Knight era, which has been covered in great depth, the information is spread out in a lot of different sources. That's why I decided to write this book—to gather the information from the beginning of IU basketball during the 1900-01 school year up to the present day and put it all in a single book with lots of photos, statistics and commentary. In my experience, the only thing Hoosier fans like to debate and discuss as much as IU basketball games is the history of IU basketball and how it compares to what's currently happening with the IU squad. My hope is that this book provides a central resource of material for Hoosier fans to further explore, compare and debate the teams and heroes of Indiana's great basketball tradition.

I have organized the book by seasons and divided them by different eras—usually related to the different coaches. In the process I have tried to tell the story of each season and also portray the feelings of the time, including expectations going into the season, elation over big wins, disappointment over bitter losses, and the Hoosiers' progress in the conference race during the season. In the season commentaries, I have also tried to pull out some of the details and experiences that you can't see in the box scores and season results, such as the fact that IU rallied from a 10-point deficit in the final five minutes of a game or that a player had a great performance even though he was fighting through an injury or an illness. The hard-est part has been condensing all of the information into a book of this size. For almost every season, I had a lot more stories and details that didn't make it into the book. Because I was covering 104 seasons, I had to put a limit on what could be covered. I'm sure there will be facts, tidbits and stories that some Hoosier fans will feel should have been included. If so, you are welcome to e-mail me your feedback at jhiner@iub-ballencyclopedia.com.

Some particularly diligent IU fans will also notice that there is information in this book that conflicts with some other sources of information on IU basketball history—even some of the official sources. This is especially true in regards to information from before 1940. For the early years, there is sometimes conflicting information about names, dates, games, numbers and other stuff. As a result, I had to make an historian's judgment call in some cases as to which information is the most likely to be correct. Thus, I think you can be fairly confident that the information in this book is the most accurate information based on the available sources. That being said, sometimes new sources come to light that change the picture. If you believe that there is an error in any of the information in this book, or you have new information that can help fill in some of the gaps (such as a player's first name or uniform number, which are sometimes missing for players in some of the earlier seasons), then please e-mail me at jhiner@ihoosiershistory.com.

I hope that this book will provide IU fans with palpable information on some of the famous names and teams of IU lore, so that they are no longer just vague names and numbers to the average fan. I also hope that this book sheds some light on some of the great moments and accomplishments that have faded from the public memory.

And of course, as an Indiana alum, I would encourage all IU fans to make good use of this book as ammunition in their friendly debates with Purdue fans.

Jason Hiner
May 2004

PART I

THE TEN GREATEST SEASONS OF IU BASKETBALL

CHAPTER 1

TOUGHNESS, GREATNESS, AND PERFECTION

1975-76

OVERALL RECORD: 32-0

CONFERENCE RECORD: 18-0 (FIRST PLACE)

TEAM HONORS:

NCAA CHAMPION, BIG TEN CHAMPION, INDIANA CLASSIC CHAMPION,

HOLIDAY FESTIVAL CHAMPION

INDIVIDUAL HONORS:

BOB KNIGHT—NATIONAL COACH OF THE YEAR (CONSENSUS)

SCOTT MAY—NATIONAL PLAYER OF THE YEAR (CONSENSUS), ALL-AMERICA,

ALL-FINAL FOUR, ALL-BIG TEN (FIRST TEAM), BIG TEN MVP

KENT BENSON—ALL-AMERICA, FINAL FOUR MOST OUTSTANDING PLAYER,

ALL-FINAL FOUR, ALL-BIG TEN (FIRST TEAM), ACADEMIC ALL-AMERICA,

ACADEMIC ALL-BIG TEN

QUINN BUCKNER—ALL-AMERICA

TOM ABERNATHY—ALL-FINAL FOUR

Sports—like life—is filled with shortcomings and disappointments. That is why people are so thrilled when they get a rare glimpse of perfection. While countless other events are destined to become discarded memories, these moments of perfection become almost immediately immortalized and destined to be relived time and again by future generations. And witnessing perfection involves a sense of touching something eternal, something higher; something that transcends the normal limits of life.

Indiana's 1975-76 basketball team gave us one of these perfect moments by coming from behind to defeat Michigan in the 1976 NCAA title game. That victory sealed the national championship along with an unblemished 32-0 season for the Hoosiers. Interestingly, at the time, IU's undefeated season wasn't exactly a unique feat. It was the fifth time in 13 years that a team had made an undefeated run to the national championship. However, the other four times were all accomplished by one school—UCLA. Before that, San Francisco in 1956 and North Carolina in 1957 were the only other teams to reach the mystic mountaintop of an undefeated campaign

capped off with an NCAA title. During the first 17 years of the NCAA tournament, no team made it to the pinnacle undefeated. Then, all seven of the undefeated national champions were crowned in a 21-year stretch leading up to 1976. In the 28 years following Indiana's magical 1976 run, no team has been able to scale that mountain again. In fact, with each year that passes without an undefeated champion, the feat itself becomes more and more mythical. It has become something akin to the .400 hitter in major league baseball or the Triple Crown in horse racing. It hasn't happened in so long that many people have begun to wonder if it will ever happen again.

Now, for nearly three decades Indiana has reigned as the last example of perfection in college basketball. However, during the 1976 season itself, the entire college basketball world was essentially waiting for the other shoe to drop, so to speak, in regards to the Indiana team. The Hoosiers began the season ranked No. 1 in the nation as they returned four starters (including three All-Americans) from a 31-1 season in 1974-75. But, they lost All-America forward Steve Green and "Super Sub" guard John

The 1975-76 team. First row (left to right): Bobby Wilkerson, Jim Crews, Scott May, Quinn Buckner, Tom Abernathy, Kent Benson; Second row: manager Tim Walker, Rich Valavicius, Mark Haymore, Scott Eells, Wayne Radford, Bob Bender, manager Chuck Swenson; Third row: head coach Bob Knight, assistant coach Harold Andreas, Jim Roberson, Jim Wisman, assistant coach Bob Donewald, assistant coach Bob Weltlich. IU Archives

Laskowski, and there was a general feeling throughout the season that, as good as the Hoosiers were, they still weren't as good as the season before. As a result, everyone kept waiting for the Indiana squad to lose. They kept waiting for the inevitable off night when someone would sneak up and knock off the Hoosiers. They kept waiting … and waiting … and waiting. And when the buzzer sounded for the final college basketball game of the season on March 29, in Philadelphia, they were still waiting.

Entering the season, coach Bob Knight's biggest challenge was definitely replacing Green and Laskowski, who combined to average 26.1 PPG in 1974-75. Senior Tom Abernathy, a 6'7" forward who had been IU's primary frontcourt reserve as a junior, stepped in to take Green's starting spot. Abernathy wasn't as much of a scorer as Green, but he was a stronger rebounder and a better defender, especially in the post, and he had the versatility to play all three frontcourt positions. Senior Jim Crews, a 6'5" guard, took Laskowski's role as Indiana's sixth man. Crews had been a starting guard as a freshman on the IU team that went to the Final Four in 1973, but then played more of a limited reserve role as a sophomore and junior. He became a valuable sub at guard and small forward as a senior. Although he didn't score

Senior forward Tom Abernathy stepped into the starting lineup for the 1975-76 Hoosiers and provided excellent defense and rebounding—and he also chipped in a quiet 10.0 PPG. IU Archives

1975-76 TEAM ROSTER

Head coach: Bob Knight
Assistant coaches: Harold Andreas, Bob Donewald, Bob Weltlich

No.	Player	Hometown	Class	Position	Height
33	Tom Abernathy	South Bend, IN	Sr	F	6-7
25	Bob Bender	Bloomington, IL	Fr	G	6-3
54	Kent Benson	New Castle, IN	Jr	C	6-11
21	Quinn Buckner (Capt.)	Phoenix, IL	Sr	G	6-3
45	Jim Crews	Normal, IL	Sr	G	6-5
31	Scott Eells	Hoopeston, IL	Fr	F	6-9
32	Mark Haymore	Cleveland, OH	So	F/C	6-8
42	Scott May (Capt.)	Sandusky, OH	Sr	F	6-7
22	Wayne Radford	Indianapolis, IN	So	G/F	6-3
43	Jim Roberson	Rochester, NY	Fr	F/C	6-9
34	Rich Valavicius	Hammond, IN	Fr	F	6-5
20	Bob Wilkerson	Anderson, IN	Sr	G/F	6-7
23	Jim Wisman	Quincy, IL	So	G	6-2

was much as Laskowski, he was a steady role player that rarely turned the ball over, made his free throws, played tough defense, and helped set up other players on offense. Versatile sophomore Wayne Radford, a 6'3" guard/forward, also became a valuable contributor off the bench.

To pick up the slack in the scoring department, junior center Kent Benson and senior forward Scott May took on more of the scoring load. Benson improved his hook shot and his power moves in the lane to increase his scoring average from 15.0 to 17.3. May simply became more aggressive in looking for his shot, both slashing to the basket and hitting the jumper, and improved his average from 16.1 as a junior to 23.5 as a senior. In moving into a starting role, Abernathy also increased his scoring production by going from 4.2 PPG in 1974-75 to 10.0 PPG in 1975-76. IU's starting backcourt of 6'7" Bobby Wilkerson and 6'3" Quinn Buckner didn't produce a ton of points—although both could score when needed—but they did a lot of the other things to help the Hoosiers win. They ran the floor and distributed the basketball, they rebounded, and above all else, they hounded opposing guards with an intimidating brand of ball-hawking defense.

With all of those pieces in place, the Hoosiers were clearly prepared to open the season as the Big Ten favorite and the top-ranked team in the nation.

However, there was another intangible quality about this team that would be crucial to its success. It stemmed from the fact that the year before, the Hoosiers had roared through the regular season with a 29-0 record, 18-0 in the Big Ten, and had mowed down opponents by record margins. Unfortunately, a late-season injury to Scott May—the team's leading scorer at the time—meant that IU wasn't at full strength in the NCAA tournament. That led to a 92-90 upset at the hands of the Kentucky Wildcats in the regional finals. But, that gut-wrenching loss forged an indomitable resolve in IU's returning players. As a result, they played the 1975-76 season as if something that was rightfully theirs had been unjustly taken from them, and they were out to get it back.

In a team meeting on the day before the first practice to officially begin the season, Coach Knight said that the goal of the season was not to just win the Big Ten or the NCAA tournament. "The objective of this team is to not lose a game," he said, "and you're capable of doing that. Nothing less than that should be satisfactory to you and it will not be to me. The only way we will lose is when we have ourselves to blame."

For a team that was on a mission to prove that it deserved a place among the elite teams in the history of college basketball, the IU squad couldn't have asked for a more auspicious start to the season in its

1975-76 SEASON STATISTICS

Team Statistics	G	FG%	FT%	R	A	TO	PF	PTS	PPG
Indiana	32	.517	.698	41.3	20.5	16.9	19.5	2628	82.1
Opponents	32	.436	.699	35.6	10.2	20.3	20.3	2074	64.8

Player Statistics	G-GS	FG%	FT%	R	A	TO	PF	PTS	PPG
May	32-32	.527	.782	7.7	2.1	2.6	3.0	752	23.5
Benson	32-32	.578	.684	8.8	1.6	2.3	2.9	554	17.3
Abernathy	32-31	.561	.743	5.3	2.0	2.0	2.0	321	10.0
Buckner	32-30	.441	.488	2.8	4.2	2.7	3.2	286	8.9
Wilkerson	32-29	.493	.630	4.9	5.3	3.1	2.4	251	7.8
Radford	30-2	.570	.712	2.2	1.4	1.3	1.5	140	4.7
Crews	31-1	.462	.857	0.7	1.4	0.8	0.6	100	3.2
Wisman	26-3	.367	.724	0.8	2.2	1.3	1.6	65	2.5
Valavicius	28-0	.483	.625	1.8	0.3	0.7	1.5	68	2.4
Bender	17-0	.565	.750	0.8	0.8	0.8	0.8	35	2.1
Haymore	13-0	.407	.286	2.2	0.3	0.8	1.3	24	1.8
Roberson	12-0	.583	.833	1.3	0.0	1.3	1.6	16	1.6
Eells	12-0	.308	.750	0.8	0.0	0.4	0.3	11	1.0

first two games. Indiana opened with a game that didn't count in its win-loss records, but made an emphatic statement about how good this Hoosier team could be. On November 3, in Market Square Arena in Indianapolis, the Hoosiers played an exhibition game against the Soviet National Team. This was the same Soviet team—with many of the same players—that had defeated the U.S. team for the gold medal on a controversial call in the final seconds of the 1972 Olympics in Munich, Germany. It was the first time in Olympic history that the U.S. men's team failed to capture the gold medal, after winning the basketball competition seven straight times and amassing a 71-0 record in Olympic play before the loss to the Soviets. Hence, the Soviets were considered the top amateur basketball team in the world at that time. The game was played according to international rules, and the

Forward Scott May elevates to connect on one of many jump shots he hit during the 1975-76 season. May averaged 23.5 PPG and earned Big Ten MVP and national player of the year honors.
IU Archives

physical Soviets got May, Benson, Wilkerson and Buckner in foul trouble in the first half, but IU still led 48-42, thanks to the strong play of reserves Wayne Radford, Jim Crews and Mark Haymore in the final minutes before the break. In the second half, May didn't miss a shot and finished with 34 points (on 13-15 from the field) and IU's defense put the squeeze on the Soviets to deliver a 94-78 Hoosier victory.

Almost four weeks later on Saturday, November 29, Indiana officially opened the season with a nationally televised game against defending NCAA champion UCLA on a neutral floor in St. Louis. In the 1975 NCAA Tournament, the Bruins captured the national championship that the Hoosiers thought they had been destined to claim. After that win, legendary UCLA coach John Wooden retired, but the Bruins—like the Hoosiers—returned most of their roster for the 1975-76 season. In the preseason polls, Indiana was ranked No. 1 and UCLA was No. 2. The game was televised live from coast to coast by NBC (during the 1970s that was an extremely rare occurrence for a college game in November). As they did against the Soviets, the Hoosiers used their disruptive defense to keep UCLA from running its plays. IU led by eight at the break and opened the second half with 8-0 run that put the game out of reach for the Bruins. May had another big second half and finished with 33 points, and three other Indiana starters joined him in double figures as IU rolled to an easy 84-64 win. After the game, UCLA All-American Richard Washington, who led the Bruins with 28 points, said, "I think we'll see them again, in Philadelphia [for the Final Four] or wherever. And then I'm pretty sure the outcome will be different. We'll give them a little better battle next time."

After handily defeating the defending Olympic champion and the defending NCAA champion, the Hoosiers clobbered Florida State 83-59 and then had to get ready for two battles against key rivals Notre Dame and Kentucky, which were both ranked in the top 15. IU hosted the eighth-ranked Fighting Irish in Bloomington and pulled out a grueling 63-60 victory. "It was a game that was kind of a struggle for both teams," said Knight after the game. "And I guess we just outstruggled them." Next, Indiana went down to Louisville to play the Kentucky Wildcats, the team that had ended the Hoosiers' dream season nine months earlier in the 1975 NCAA Tournament. The two teams played another back-and-forth game in which neither squad gave ground. Kentucky had a couple of opportunities to put the Hoosiers away in the final minutes, but couldn't do it, and a Kent Benson tip-in in the waning seconds tied the game at 64-64 and sent it to overtime, where Indiana took control and won 77-68. In his post-game comments, Knight didn't attach any special significance to the game as revenge for the 1975 NCAA loss. "That was last season and that ended there. We don't play last season's games this season. We lost, we made no excuses, and that is that. This is a new season, and we're trying to play it as best we can."

IU rounded out the preconference season by notching five more victories and winning the championship of both the Indiana Classic in Bloomington, and the Holiday Festival in New York City. In the Holiday Festival title game, the Hoosiers defeated previously-unbeaten No. 17 St. John's 76-69, led by 29 points and eight rebounds from Scott May, who was named tournament MVP.

During his IU career, center Kent Benson collected a lot of hardware, including All-America awards in three straight seasons and the Most Outstanding Player award for the 1976 NCAA Final Four.
IU Archives

At 9-0, Indiana headed into Big Ten play knowing that the games were about to get a lot more difficult. As the top-ranked team in the nation and the defending conference champion, Indiana was the target that every other team in the Big Ten was shooting for. The Hoosiers opened the conference with four of their first five games on the road—the most difficult stretch on the schedule. They started with a game against Ohio State on January 3, in Columbus, which had proved to be the most difficult place for Indiana to win during the three previous seasons. During the 1973 and 1974 Big Ten seasons, losses at St. John Arena nearly cost the Hoosiers the conference title during both years, and in 1975, the Hoosiers' 72-66 win in Columbus was the closest any Big Ten team came to beating IU with a healthy Scott May in the lineup. In the 1976 Big Ten opener, the Buckeyes, who had gone 4-4 in their preconference games, once again gave the Hoosiers all they could handle. IU stayed a step ahead of Ohio State for most of the game and could have iced it in the final minutes, but the

1975-76 SEASON RESULTS

Date	Court	Opponent	Result	Score
11/29/1975	N1	(#2) UCLA	W	84-64
12/8/1975	N2	Florida State	W	83-59
12/11/1975	H	(#8) Notre Dame	W	63-60
12/15/1975	N3	(#14) Kentucky	W	77-68
12/19/1975	H	Georgia	W	93-56
12/20/1975	H	Virginia Tech	W	101-74
12/26/1975	N4	Columbia	W	106-63
12/27/1975	N4	Manhattan	W	97-61
12/28/1975	N4	(#17) St. John's	W	76-69
1/3/1976	A	Ohio State	W	66-64
1/5/1976	H	Northwestern	W	78-61
1/10/1976	A	(#19) Michigan	W	80-74
1/12/1976	A	Michigan State	W	69-57
1/17/1976	A	Illinois	W	83-55
1/19/1976	H	Purdue	W	71-67
1/24/1976	A	Minnesota	W	85-76
1/26/1976	A	Iowa	W	88-73
1/31/1976	H	Wisconsin	W	114-61
2/7/1976	H	(#16) Michigan	W	72-67
2/9/1976	H	Michigan State	W	85-70
2/14/1976	H	Illinois	W	58-48
2/16/1976	A	Purdue	W	74-71
2/21/1976	H	Minnesota	W	76-64
2/23/1976	H	Iowa	W	101-81
2/26/1976	A	Wisconsin	W	96-67
3/1/1976	A	Northwestern	W	76-63
3/6/1976	H	Ohio State	W	96-67

NCAA Tournament

Date	Court	Opponent	Result	Score
3/13/1976	N5	(#17) St. John's	W	90-70
3/18/1976	N6	(#6) Alabama	W	74-69
3/20/1976	N6	(#2) Marquette	W	65-56
3/27/1976	N7	(#5) UCLA	W	65-51
3/29/1976	N7	(#9) Michigan	W	86-68

1 St. Louis, MO
2 Indianapolis, IN
3 Louisville, KY
4 New York, NY
5 South Bend, IN
6 Baton Rouge, LA
7 Philadelphia, PA

1975-76 BIG TEN STANDINGS

	W	L	PCT
Indiana	18	0	1.000
Michigan	14	4	.778
Purdue	11	7	.661
Michigan St.	10	8	.556
Iowa	9	9	.500
Minnesota	8	10	.444
Illinois	7	11	.389
Northwestern	7	11	.389
Wisconsin	4	14	.222
Ohio State	2	16	.111

Hoosiers missed the front end of three straight one-and-one opportunities in the last 1:03. Still, IU barely held on to beat the Buckeyes 66-64, led by 24 points from May and 23 points and 12 rebounds from Benson.

Back in Assembly Hall, Indiana walloped Northwestern 78-61, and then started a three-game road swing by heading north to take on 19th-ranked Michigan on January 10. IU blasted out to a 16-2 lead with 14 minutes left in the first half and then settled for a 36-33 lead going into the locker room. The Hoosiers got off to another quick start in the second half with a 10-4 run and then held off every Michigan charge on the way to an 80-74 triumph, as Benson scored a game-high 33 points. Indiana followed that up with easier road wins over Michigan State and Illinois, to improve to 5-0 in league play and 14-0 overall. With eight of its final thirteen Big Ten games being played in Bloomington, IU was in the driver's seat in the conference race.

The Hoosiers scarcely survived a 71-67 nail-biter over Purdue in Assembly Hall on January 19, but then rolled to three relatively easy wins over Minnesota, Iowa and Wisconsin. That set up a nationally televised rematch with Michigan, now ranked 16th, in Bloomington. The charged-up Wolverines stormed to the early lead as Indiana made only four of its first 20 field goal attempts. The Hoosiers trailed 39-29 at the intermission, but they slowly clawed their way back into the game throughout the second half. Michigan led 60-58 when Wolverine guard Steve Grote was fouled with 0:14 remaining. Grote missed the front end of the one-and-one, and the Hoosiers called time-out. Knight drew up a play for May or Benson, but when neither could get an open look, Buckner released a jump shot that went in and out. IU guard Jim Crews grabbed the rebound and attempted a quick putback that missed, and then Benson tipped in Crews's miss just as the buzzer sounded, sending the game in to overtime, where Indiana eventually prevailed 72-67. Scott May led all scorers with 27 points (but only shot 11-30 from the field), Benson added 21 points and 15 rebounds, and sophomore Wayne Radford provided a big spark off the bench with 16 points and five rebounds.

Over the final eight games of the conference season, the Hoosiers were only tested a couple more times, most notably in a 74-71 victory over Purdue in Mackey Arena. Thus, IU finished out a second consecutive undefeated regular season (this one at 27-0), recorded a second straight 18-0 finish in the Big Ten, and won the team's fourth straight conference title. Nevertheless, there was still one score left to settle—winning the NCAA championship.

However, when the official NCAA pairings were solidified, Indiana soon discovered that the path wasn't going to be easy. Before 1979, there was no seeding in the NCAA Tournament, and the pairings were based almost exclusively on geography. In 1976, that meant IU would potentially have to face two top-ten powerhouses before the team even reached the Final Four. But Knight and the Hoosiers didn't whine

INDIANA'S RANKING IN THE 1975-76 ASSOCIATED PRESS POLLS

PS	12/2	12/9	12/16	12/23	12/30	1/6	1/13	1/20	1/27	2/3	2/10	2/17	2/24	3/2	3/9	3/16
1	1	1	1	1	1	1	1	1	1	1	1	1	1	1	1	1

about getting a bad draw. They felt like they were the best team in the country and that they could beat anyone. They were out to make history, and they didn't want anyone saying they won the national title because they got a lucky draw in the tournament.

The first round wasn't expected to be a cakewalk, either. The Hoosiers played No. 17 St. John's, a team that they had barely defeated in the Holiday Festival tournament back in December. Playing in South Bend, the IU team had a much easier time with the Redmen the second time around, winning 90-70 on March 13. May poured in 33 points, Benson had 20 points and 13 rebounds, and Quinn Buckner chipped in 15 points.

The following week in the Mideast Regional Semifinals in Baton Rouge, Louisiana, the Hoosiers matched up against No. 6 Alabama, coached by C.M. Newton. Knight would later call the Crimson Tide the toughest team IU faced all season, and they ended up giving the Hoosiers their closest scrape of the tournament. Indiana broke to 9-0 lead and clung to a 37-

29 advantage at halftime. However, the Tide got rolling in the second half, led by All-America center Leon Douglas, and Alabama took a 69-68 lead with 3:58 remaining. A tough 17-footer from May over an Alabama defender with 2:02 left on the clock gave Indiana back the lead, and Abernathy and Wilkerson each buried two free throws to give IU a hard-fought 74-69 win. May had 25 points and 16 rebounds, while Bobby Wilkerson posted 14 points, 12 rebounds, and four assists.

Next, in the regional finals, came the game that the college basketball world had been hoping for: No. 1 Indiana (29-0) against No. 2 Marquette (27-1). Al McGuire had a quick, athletic Marquette squad, just the kind of team that analysts had predicted could beat Indiana. May got in early foul trouble to complicate matters for IU, and when he was in the game, the Golden Eagles used a box-and-one defense that denied him from getting the ball. Indiana still led 36-35 at the half. The Hoosiers extended the lead to 10 midway through the second half, weathered the Golden Eagles' inevitable run, and then closed out a 65-56 triumph to earn a ticket to the Final Four. Benson led the Hoosiers with 18 points and nine rebounds, while Buckner added nine points, 8 rebounds, and five assists.

In the 1976 Final Four in Philadelphia, there were two firsts. It was the first time two teams from the same conference—Indiana and Michigan both from the Big Ten—made it to the NCAA finals. It was also the first time that two teams—Indiana and Rutgers—entered the finals undefeated. However, most of the attention was focused on the monumental rematch between No. 5 UCLA, the defending NCAA champ, and No. 1 Indiana. The Bruins talked big before their semifinal with the Hoosiers game and acted like they fully expected to win, but once the ball was tipped, they never found an answer for the Indiana defense. The key was that after Kent Benson picked up two quick fouls trying to guard UCLA's

Guard Bobby Wilkerson breaks down the St. John's defense and dishes to his backcourt mate Quinn Buckner (21). As seniors, Wilkerson and Buckner were as hard-nosed and tough-minded as any backcourt in college basketball. IU Archives

*Quinn Buckner, Scott May, and Coach Knight celebrate a joyful end to a long journey as the Hoosiers com-
pleted their undefeated season with a resounding victory over Michigan in the 1976 NCAA title game.*
IU Archives

All-America 6'11" forward, Richard Washington, Knight switched Abernathy to guarding Washington, and Abernathy did a brilliant job of it. Washington shot only 6-15 from the floor and scored 15 points. IU held the Bruins to 34 percent shooting for the game and dealt UCLA a convincing 65-51 defeat. Four of the five Hoosier starters scored in double figures and the only one who didn't reach double figures, Bobby Wilkerson, was probably the most effective player on the court, as he contributed game highs of 19 rebounds and seven assists.

In the other national semifinal, Michigan upset undefeated Rutgers 86-70. That set up an all-Big Ten championship game to decide the 1976 NCAA title (the first time that two conference rivals met in the title game). When the game began on March 29, at The Spectrum, Michigan struck the first blow—literally—when Wolverine forward Wayman Britt inadvertently struck IU's Wilkerson with an elbow that

knocked him cold less than three minutes into the game. Wilkerson, who had played so well against UCLA two nights earlier, had to be taken to the hospital and didn't return to the game. Without Wilkerson, the Hoosiers fell back on their heels and allowed the Wolverines to shoot 62 percent from the field in the first half. Michigan led heavily favored Indiana 35-29 at the break and Indiana's dream appeared in jeopardy. Knight inserted sophomore point guard Jim Wisman in Wilkerson's place to start the second half, and the Hoosier offense started to click as May, Benson and Buckner began to find their openings. Indiana quickly tied the game at 39-39 less than five minutes into the second half. The game was tied again at 51-51 with 10:15 remaining. From that point on, it was all Indiana as the Hoosiers outscored Michigan 35-17 the rest of the way and won 86-68. After allowing the Wolverines to shoot the lights out in the first half, IU held them to 35 percent from the field in the second half. May led all scorers with 26 points and added eight rebounds. Buckner, the consummate floor leader, did a little bit of everything with 16 points, eight rebounds, four assists, and five steals. Benson had 25 points and nine rebounds and earned the Most Outstanding Player award for the Final Four.

"It's been kind of a two-year quest for us," said Knight afterwards. "These kids are very, very deserving. I know better than anybody how hard and how long they have worked for this."

With a 32-0 record, the 1976 Hoosiers tied the 1957 North Carolina Tar Heels for the most wins ever for an undefeated NCAA champion. On a national level, Bob Knight was the consensus coach of the year, and Scott May was the consensus player of the year. May, Buckner and Benson were All-Americans for the second season in a row. They started the year ranked No. 1 and never vacated that spot. They faced the toughest group of opponents that an NCAA champion ever had to face. In the end, there were still those who contended that the 1974-75 team was actually the better team. While the 1974-75 team—with a

healthy Scott May—went out and steamrolled its opponents by record margins, the 1975-76 team simply refused to lose and, in many ways, vindicated the 1974-75 team's claim to greatness by winning the NCAA championship in 1976. Combined, those two teams amassed a 63-1 record over a period of two years. In the history of NCAA basketball, no school—save UCLA—can match the two-year dominance of those two Hoosier squads. The seniors on that 1975-76 team had captured the Big Ten championship in each of their four seasons, they went to two Final Fours, won an NCAA championship, and put together a four-year record of 108-12 overall and 59-5 in Big Ten play. And of course, they achieved the last undefeated season in NCAA basketball.

On Senior Day, Knight told the Indiana crowd, which had just gotten its last glimpse of the five seniors in their final game in Assembly Hall, "Take a good look at these kids, because you're never going to see the likes of them again." That was true not only for Indiana, but for nearly three decades and counting, it has also been true for all of college basketball as well.

Coach Bob Knight shares a smile with captains Scott May and Quinn Buckner after Indiana completed its undefeated season by defeating Michigan 86-68 in the 1976 NCAA title game.
IU Archives

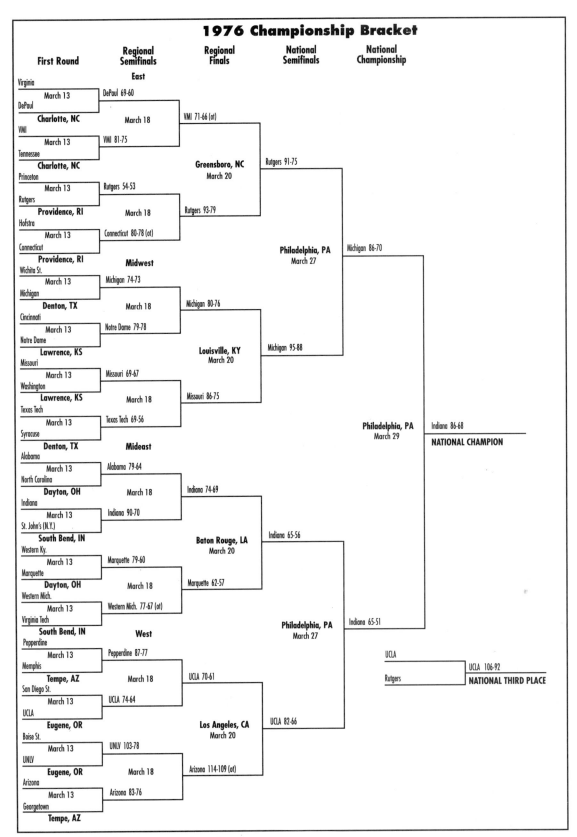

1976 Championship Bracket

First Round	Regional Semifinals	Regional Finals	National Semifinals	National Championship

East

Virginia
March 13
DePaul
— DePaul 69-60
Charlotte, NC
VMI
March 13
Tennessee
— VMI 81-75
Charlotte, NC
— VMI 71-66 (ot)
March 18

Greensboro, NC
March 20

Princeton
March 13
Rutgers
— Rutgers 54-53
Providence, RI
Hofstra
March 13
Connecticut
— Connecticut 80-78 (ot)
Providence, RI
— Rutgers 93-79
March 18

Rutgers 91-75

Midwest

Wichita St.
March 13
Michigan
— Michigan 74-73
Denton, TX
Cincinnati
March 13
Notre Dame
— Notre Dame 79-78
Lawrence, KS
— Michigan 80-76
March 18

Louisville, KY
March 20

Missouri
March 13
Washington
— Missouri 69-67
Lawrence, KS
Texas Tech
March 13
Syracuse
— Texas Tech 69-56
Denton, TX
— Missouri 86-75
March 18

Michigan 95-88

Philadelphia, PA
March 27

Michigan 86-70

Mideast

Alabama
March 13
North Carolina
— Alabama 79-64
Dayton, OH
Indiana
March 13
St. John's (N.Y.)
— Indiana 90-70
South Bend, IN
— Indiana 74-69
March 18

Baton Rouge, LA
March 20

Western Ky.
March 13
Marquette
— Marquette 79-60
Dayton, OH
Western Mich.
March 13
Virginia Tech
— Western Mich. 77-67 (ot)
South Bend, IN
— Marquette 62-57
March 18

Indiana 65-56

West

Pepperdine
March 13
Memphis
— Pepperdine 87-77
Tempe, AZ
San Diego St.
March 13
UCLA
— UCLA 74-64
Eugene, OR
— UCLA 70-61
March 18

Los Angeles, CA
March 20

Boise St.
March 13
UNLV
— UNLV 103-78
Eugene, OR
Arizona
March 13
Georgetown
— Arizona 83-76
Tempe, AZ
— Arizona 114-109 (ot)
March 18

UCLA 82-66

Philadelphia, PA
March 27

Indiana 65-51

Philadelphia, PA
March 29

Indiana 86-68

NATIONAL CHAMPION

UCLA
Rutgers
— UCLA 106-92

NATIONAL THIRD PLACE

The 1976 NCAA tournament bracket.

CHAPTER 2

McCRACKEN RUNS THE TABLE A SECOND TIME

1952-53

OVERALL RECORD: 23-3

CONFERENCE RECORD: 17-1 (FIRST PLACE)

TEAM HONORS:

BIG TEN CHAMPIONSHIP, NCAA CHAMPIONSHIP

HOLIDAY FESTIVAL CHAMPION

INDIVIDUAL HONORS:

BRANCH MCCRACKEN—NATIONAL COACH OF THE YEAR (CONSENSUS)

BOB LEONARD—ALL-AMERICA, ALL-FINAL FOUR, ALL-BIG TEN (FIRST TEAM)

DON SCHLUNDT—ALL-AMERICA, ALL-FINAL FOUR,

ALL-BIG TEN (FIRST TEAM), BIG TEN MVP

The seeds of Indiana's 1952-53 championship season were sown during 1951. That was when coach Branch McCracken recruited 6'9" center Don Schlundt from South Bend. Schlundt was one of the most highly coveted high school players in country and had originally favored Kentucky before Big Mac wooed him to Bloomington. Previously, McCracken had relied on small, quick lineups in which all five players raced up court for quick scores. McCracken's pressing, fast-breaking system had been highly successful, as Indiana used it to win a national championship in 1940 and compile a 157-53 record in Big Mac's first ten seasons at IU. However, by the late 1940s, the Hoosiers had been hurt by the lack of a big man to defend tall centers on opposing teams and to provide a reliable scoring presence inside when the Hoosiers' offense was forced to play in the half court. McCracken had nearly landed a big man in 1948 when he seemed to have locked up 6'9" Clyde Lovellette from Terre Haute. Lovellette moved to Bloomington just before the 1948-49 season began, but a few days before enrollment, he told Coach McCracken that he needed to go back to Terre Haute to get some more clothes and he never returned. A news story the following week reported that Lovellette was enrolled at Kansas. As a Jayhawk, he eventually became an All-American and led Kansas to the 1952 NCAA championship.

When Schlundt enrolled at IU for the 1951-52 season, he didn't have to follow the normal policy of sitting out of varsity competition as a freshman, since the Korean War Waiver was in effect (because of the draft for the Korean War, the number of young men on college campuses was naturally depleted, and so freshmen were allowed to compete in order to fill out the rosters of collegiate teams). Thus, Schlundt gained invaluable experience by playing on the varsity as a freshman. Defensively, he struggled at times against stronger, more mature players, but offensively Schlundt was brilliant. He broke IU's single-season record with 376 points (17.1 PPG) and set the single-game scoring record with 35 points against Purdue. He would re-break both records with even more impressive numbers in the years that followed.

As a sophomore, Schlundt perfected his greatest weapon, a deadly accurate hook shot, and became just as proficient shooting it with either hand. That made him an almost unstoppable force in the paint. However, as good as Schlundt was, the 1952-53 Hoosiers were far from a one-man team. Indiana returned seven lettermen from the 1951-52 squad that had gone 16-6 overall and finished fourth in the Big Ten. The team's only significant losses were a trio of guards—Sam Miranda, Bob Masters and Sam Esposito. With the graduation of Miranda and Masters, IU lost its starting backcourt. Plus, Esposito was a 5'9" sparkplug who had shown signs

The 1952-53 team. First row (left to right): Bob Leonard, Charley Kraak, Don Schlundt, Dick Farley, Burke Scott; Second row: manager Ron Fifer, Dick White, Jim DeaKyne, head coach Branch McCracken, Paul Poff, Phil Byers, assistant coach Ernie Andres; Third row: Ron Taylor, Jim Schooley, Goethe Chambers, Jack Wright.　IU Archives

of greatness, but decided to leave IU after his sophomore season to pursue a career in major league baseball (he ended up playing 10 seasons in the American League). With the departure of those guards, junior Bob Leonard moved to the backcourt full time after splitting his minutes between guard and forward as a sophomore. That move ended up being one of the keys to Indiana's success in 1952-53, because Leonard was a natural point guard. He was a crafty passer and was excellent at feeding the ball into Schlundt in positions where the big guy could score. He was also a phenomenal outside shooter that kept defenses from collapsing on Schlundt out of fear that Leonard

would stand outside and bury jump shots all night. Leonard's 319 points (14.5 PPG) in 1951-52 would have broken the school record, had Schlundt not bested him with 376, and Leonard increased his average to 16.3 during the 1952-53 campaign. Leonard became known as "Mr. Outside" while Schlundt was "Mr. Inside." The tandem played off of each other very well and became one of the most potent 1-2 punches in the history of college basketball.

While Schlundt and Leonard grabbed most of the accolades, they were also surrounded by some terrific role players. Schlundt was joined in the frontcourt by an excellent pair of forwards in juniors Dick

Guard Bob Leonard releases one of his sweet jump shots. Leonard rose to All-America stature during the 1952-53 campaign. IU Archives

Farley and Charley Kraak. The 6'3" Farley would have probably been a top scorer on almost any other team in the Big Ten. As a sophomore he was Indiana's third-leading scorer at 8.9 PPG and he upped that to 10.1 PPG for the 1952-53 season, when his field goal percentage of .443 led the conference. He was also a strong ball handler and passer, but above all, he served as Indiana's defensive stopper. He almost always guarded the opposing team's top scorer. McCracken considered the Hoosiers' other forward, 6'5" Charley Kraak, the best rebounder in the Big Ten. His lightning-quick instincts and jumping ability made him a beast to keep off the glass. He also ran the floor very well, which made him a perfect fit for McCracken's system. Big Mac also had the luxury of another big center to backup Schlundt. At 6'10", junior Lou Scott was just as imposing as Schlundt, but not quite as skilled. He was a strong rebounder and a solid defender, and most of all, if Schlundt got in foul trouble, the Hoosiers didn't lose any height when Scott replaced him. Unfortunately, Scott ended

1952-53 TEAM ROSTER

Head coach: Branch McCracken
Assistant coaches: Ernie Andres

No.	Player	Hometown	Class	Position	Height
14	Phil Byers	Evansville, IN	So	G	5-11
20	Goethe Chambers	Union City, IN	So	F	6-3
22	Jim DeaKyne	Fortville, IN	Jr	G	6-3
15	William Ditius	Mt. Pulaski, IL	So	F	6-1
31	Dick Farley	Winslow, IN	Jr	F	6-3
14	James Fields	Andrews, IN	So	F	6-1
33	Dick Hendricks	Huntington, IN	Jr	C	6-5
42	Don Henry	Evansville, IN	So	F	6-2
13	Charlie Kraak	Collinsville, IL	Jr	F	6-5
21	Bob Leonard (Capt.)	Terre Haute, IN	Jr	G	6-3
31	Paul Poff	New Albany, IN	So	G	6-1
34	Don Schlundt	South Bend, IN	So	C	6-9
19	Jim Schooley	Auburn, IN	Sr	C	6-5
25	Burke Scott	Tell City, IN	So	G	6-0
35	Lou Scott	Chicago, IL	Jr	C	6-10
23	Ron Taylor	Chicago, IL	Jr	F	6-3
41	Dick White	Terre Haute, IN	So	F	6-1
24	Jack Wright	New Castle, IN	Jr	F	5-10

up being ineligible for the second semester of the 1952-53 season, which left Farley and Kraak to back up Schlundt. The Hoosiers also had another Scott—Burke Scott (no relation to Lou). In his first season on the varsity in 1952-53, the 6'1" sophomore earned the other starting guard spot next to Leonard. He was an outstanding ball handler that could also feed the post and score when needed, but mostly he made his mark as a tenacious competitor and a ball-hawking defender who pestered opposing guards.

Indiana was fully expected to be one of the top contenders in the Big Ten and one of the best teams in college basketball. Those expectations seemed a little skewed during the first two weeks of the season when the Hoosiers went 1-2 in their first three games. Things looked great on opening night when the Hoosiers raced past Valparaiso 95-56. In his first varsity game, Burke Scott scored 16 points to tie his backcourt mate Leonard for team-high honors. Charlie Kraak chipped in 13 points and 12 rebounds. After that easy win, the Hoosiers, who were ranked eighth in the preseason coaches' poll, had their work cut out for them as they traveled to face Notre Dame (13th in the preseason coaches' poll) and Kansas State (second in the coaches' poll). IU ended up los-

Forward Charlie Kraak runs down a long rebound. McCracken often referred to the 6'5" Kraak as the best rebounder in the conference. IU Archives

Coach Branch McCracken barks instructions to the Hoosiers during a timeout. IU Archives

1952-53 SEASON STATISTICS

Team Statistics	G	FG/A	PCT	FT/A	PCT	R	TP	AVG
Indiana	26	737-2019	.365	638-910	.701	45.7	2112	81.2
Opponents	26	611-2041	.299	586-937	6.25	36.0	1808	69.5

Player Statistics	G	FG/A	PCT	FT/A	PCT	R	TP	AVG
Schlundt	26	206-477	.432	249-310	.803	10.0	661	25.4
Leonard	26	164-503	.326	96-144	.667	4.2	424	16.3
Farley	26	94-212	.443	75-108	.694	6.7	263	10.1
B. Scott	26	76-206	.369	55-85	.647	3.5	207	8.0
L. Scott	10	28-83	.337	18-28	.643	5.7	74	7.4
Kraak	26	63-177	.356	60-102	.588	10.7	186	7.2
White	22	40-128	.313	43-58	.741	3.5	123	5.6
Poff	13	14-45	.311	12-19	.632	1.2	40	3.1
Byers	23	25-72	.347	13-24	.542	0.9	63	2.7
Wright	3	2-11	.182	4-4	1.00	0.7	8	2.7
DeaKyne	20	20-87	.230	5-12	.417	1.5	45	2.3
Chambers	2	1-1	1.00	0-0	.000	0.0	2	1.0
Henry	2	0-1	.000	2-4	.500	0.0	2	1.0
Taylor	2	1-2	.500	0-0	.000	1.0	2	1.0
Schooley	16	3-14	.214	6-12	.500	1.9	12	0.8

ing both games in the final seconds. Against the Fighting Irish, Indiana led 70-69 with 12 seconds remaining and reserve forward Jim DeaKyne at the line for two free throws. DeaKyne missed them both, and Notre Dame guard Jack Stephens grabbed the rebound on the second miss and took the ball coast to coast to score a lay-up with two seconds left to deliver a 71-70 Irish victory in South Bend. A week later, IU led Kansas State 80-78, but the Wildcats scored twice in the final 35 seconds to beat the Hoosiers 82-80. What the Hoosiers didn't realize at the time was that it would be almost three months before the team would suffer another loss.

Because of the Big Ten's expanded conference schedule, those three games were Indiana's only pre-conference tune-ups for the 1952-53 season. The Big Ten decided to try a full round-robin schedule in which every conference team played every other team twice—once at home and once on the road. That increased the number of league games from 14 to 18, cut the number of nonconference games that Big Ten teams could play, and moved back the start of the conference season into mid-December.

IU opened league play with an 88-60 trouncing of Michigan on December 20, in Bloomington. Schlundt topped all scorers with 24 points. Two days later, the Hoosiers captured their first road win of the season with a 92-72 clobbering of Iowa in Iowa City. Leonard dropped in 27 points while Schlundt had 24 points and 13 rebounds. Next, the Hoosiers trekked north for a two-game road trip against Michigan and Michigan State, and Schlundt powered IU to two straight wins. The big guy scored 39 points against the Wolverines and 33 against the Spartans. Burke Scott was the hero in Indiana's next game against No. 19 Minnesota in the IU Fieldhouse. The Hoosiers trailed 63-62 in the final minute. The Gophers drove in for a layup, but the ball went in and out and Bob Leonard grabbed the rebound and flipped it ahead to Scott who scored at the other end. Minnesota came back down and tried a quick shot to regain the lead, but missed. The Hoosiers grabbed the rebound and hit Burke for another layup at the end of the fast break to give IU a 66-63 victory. Then Indiana improved to 6-0 in Big Ten play with an 88-68 win at Ohio State. IU was alone atop the Big Ten standings and had already notched four conference road wins.

1952-53 SEASON RESULTS

Date	Court	Opponent	Result	Score
12/1/1952	H	Valparaiso	W	95-56
12/6/1952	A	Notre Dame	L	70-71
12/13/1952	N1	Kansas State	L	80-82
12/20/1952	H	Michigan	W	88-60
12/22/1952	A	Iowa	W	91-72
1/3/1953	A	Michigan	W	91-88
1/5/1953	A	Michigan State	W	69-62
1/10/1953	H	(#19) Minnesota	W	66-63
1/12/1953	A	Ohio State	W	88-68
1/17/1953	H	(#4) Illinois	W	74-70
1/19/1953	A	Purdue	W	88-75
2/2/1953	H	Butler	W	105-70
2/7/1953	A	Northwestern	W	88-84
2/9/1953	H	Wisconsin	W	66-48
2/14/1953	H	Michigan State	W	65-50
2/16/1953	A	Wisconsin	W	72-70
2/21/1953	H	Ohio State	W	81-67
2/23/1953	H	Purdue	W	113-78
2/28/1953	A	(#10) Illinois	W	91-79
3/2/1953	H	Northwestern	W	90-88
3/7/1953	A	Minnesota	L	63-65
3/9/1953	H	Iowa	W	68-61

NCAA Tournament

Date	Court	Opponent	Result	Score
3/13/1953	N2	DePaul	W	82-80
3/14/1953	N2	(#17) Notre Dame	W	79-66
3/17/1953	N1	(#7) Louisiana State	W	80-67
3/18/1953	N1	(#5) Kansas	W	69-68

1 Kansas City, MO
2 Chicago, IL

On January 17, the sixth-ranked Hoosiers hosted No. 4 Illinois, which was in second place in the league at 5-1. The Fighting Illini were the defending Big Ten champs and were not only voted as the favorite to win the Big Ten in the preseason coaches' poll, but were also voted as the favorite to win the national championship. In this game, Indiana and Illinois locked into an epic tug of war that lasted two overtimes before the Hoosiers finally prevailed 74-70. Schlundt had 22 points and 11 rebounds before fouling out in the first overtime, while his counterpart, Illinois center Johnny "Red" Kerr, suffered through a nightmarish shooting performance of six of 30 from the field. In the final game before the semester break (which was in January back then), Indiana manhandled Purdue 88-75 in West Lafayette. In that game, IU set a new Big Ten record by making 42 free throws (in 54 attempts). At 8-0, the Hoosiers were now a full two games ahead of the field in the conference race and ranked No. 2 in the nation.

After the two-week break between semesters, Indiana got back to business with its usual non-conference game following the break. Playing Butler in the IU Fieldhouse, the Hoosiers showed no signs of

1952-53 BIG TEN STANDINGS

	W	L	PCT
Indiana	17	1	.944
Illinois	14	4	.778
Minnesota	11	7	.611
Michigan St.	11	7	.611
Wisconsin	10	8	.556
Iowa	9	9	.500
Ohio State	7	11	.389
Northwestern	5	13	.278
Michigan	3	15	.167
Purdue	3	15	.167

rust as they buried the Bulldogs in a 105-70 onslaught. It was the first time an IU team had ever broken the century mark, and the 105 points set the new school scoring record. Schlundt led the way with 33 points and 10 rebounds. After that, the Hoosiers resumed the task of mowing down Big Ten opponents as they won six straight games to up their record to 14-0. The final win of the six-game spurt was a 113-78 shellacking of Purdue.

With only four games remaining, Indiana's only realistic challenger was two-time defending champion Illinois at 11-3, but the Fighting Illini were on the ropes. They had a chance to close the gap when they hosted the Hoosiers on February 28, in Champaign. For IU, a win would clinch the Big Ten title outright. Indiana jumped out to a 14-7 lead, controlled the game for the rest of the first half, and took a 43-37 advantage into the intermission. An 8-0 run to start the second half increased the lead to 51-37 and the Hoosiers never looked back from there. The final was 91-79. IU's top three scorers all did better than their season average as Schlundt scored 33, Leonard added

23 and Farley chipped in 19. The win gave Indiana its first ever undisputed conference crown, after sharing titles in 1926, 1928, and 1936. It was also the first Big Ten championship for McCracken in his 12 seasons at IU (which included seven second-place finishes).

The Hoosiers had a predictable letdown after the emotional win over Illinois. IU needed a thrilling 40-foot shot from sophomore reserve Paul Poff in the final seconds of overtime to slip by Northwestern 90-88 in Bloomington on March 2. After that win, the Hoosiers ascended to the No. 1 spot in the national rankings. Then, the IU squad went up to Williams Arena in Minneapolis and saw their 17-game winning streak come to an end when Minnesota's sharp-shooting guard Chuck Mencel buried a running 20-footer with two seconds left in the game to give the Golden Gophers a 65-63 upset in front of the largest home crowd (18,114) in Minnesota history. The loss was a definite wake-up call for the Hoosiers, letting them know that they could, in fact, be beaten when they didn't play their best basketball. IU bounced back, though, and defeated Iowa 68-60 in the final game of the regular season to finish conference play at 17-1 (and 19-3 overall).

Indiana retained its No. 1 national ranking entering the NCAA tournament and received a first-round bye. In the regional semifinals, the Hoosiers faced the DePaul Blue Demons, who had been ranked seventh in the country in February and had edged Miami of Ohio 74-72 in the first round. IU had the misfortune of facing the Blue Demons in Chicago Stadium, just a few miles away from the DePaul campus. IU controlled the lead nearly wire to wire, but the pesky Blue Demons never gave up and kept making runs at the Hoosiers, including a 7-2 spurt to finish the game. IU outlasted them for an 82-80 win as Schlundt scored 23 points and Leonard notched 22. In the regional finals, IU collided with in-state rival Notre Dame, one of three teams that already had beaten IU that season. Schlundt decimated the

INDIANA'S RANKING IN THE 1952-53 ASSOCIATED PRESS POLLS

12/16	12/23	12/30	1/6	1/13	1/20	1/27	2/3	2/10	2/17	2/24	3/3	3/10	3/24
19	15	12	7	6	2	2	2	2	2	2	1	1	1

Forward Dick Farley was the most underrated Hoosier on the 1952-53 squad. Farley was a terrific defender who usually guarded the opponent's top scorer, plus he led the Big Ten in shooting percentage. IU Archives

Fighting Irish in the paint with 41 points, and IU cruised to a 79-66 victory to earn a berth in the Final Four in Kansas City.

Entering the Final Four, the buzz was not centered on the top-ranked Hoosiers but on the Washington Huskies and their 6'7" center Bob Houbregs, who had set the NCAA tournament record with 45 points against Seattle in the regionals. Washington was considered the favorite to come away with the trophy, and that was fine with IU coach Branch McCracken because it focused all the media attention—and pressure—on another team. In its Final Four matchup against Louisiana State, Indiana came out red hot and hit 14 of its first 16 shots in the opening ten minutes to take a 31-20 lead. Because of the damage Schlundt did against Notre Dame, the Tigers started the game with a defense that sagged around Schlundt to deny him any room in the lane. However, that left Leonard wide open on the perimeter and he hit his first six shots, which forced LSU back into its typical man-to-man defense. At that point, Leonard immediately started feeding the ball to Schlundt, who went to work inside for a flurry of baskets. After IU took its early lead, LSU—led by its All-America center Bob Pettit—continued to battle the Hoosiers, but could never catch back up. IU won 80-67 as Schlundt and Pettit tied for game-high honors with 29 points each, and Leonard added 22 for IU. In the evening game, Kansas, the defending NCAA champion,

pulled off a surprising 79-53 upset over Washington and Houbregs to set up an Indiana-Kansas final, a rematch of the 1940 title game that was played on the same court in Kansas City.

The 1953 championship game ended up being much more competitive than the 1940 game (which IU won 60-42). Like the 1940 contest, it was a partisan crowd in favor of the Jayhawks, whose campus was only 40 miles away, but this time the Hoosiers had 500 boosters (a huge number for that era) who made the trip west. The two teams battled each other from the opening tip, and neither squad could ever

Don Schlundt drops in two easy points over a helpless defender. As a sophomore, Schlundt became the first Hoosier to ever average 20 points per game for the season in 1952-53 when he averaged 25.4 PPG. By the time he left Bloomington, Schlundt owned nearly every IU scoring record in the books. IU Archives

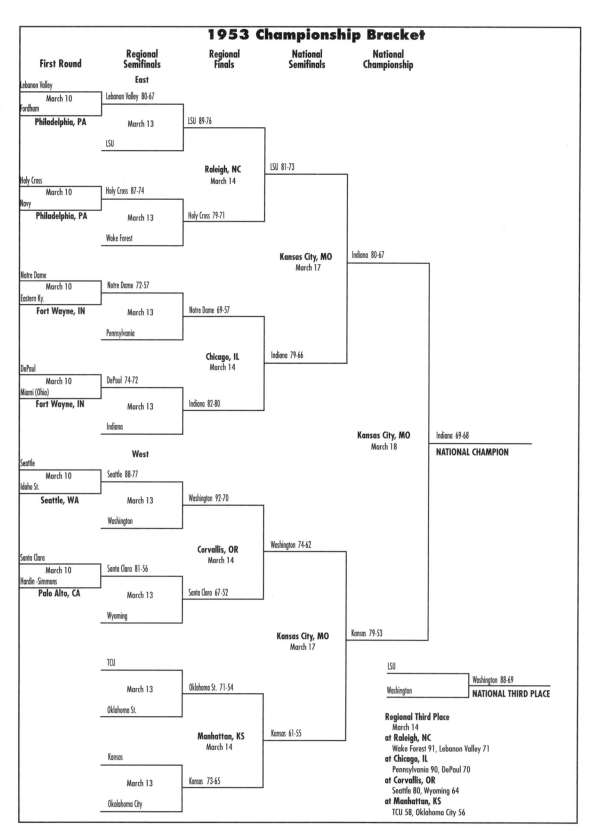

The 1953 NCAA tournament bracket.

The jubilant Hoosiers erupt in celebration after edging out Kansas 69-68 in the 1953 NCAA title game in Kansas City. In the middle of the melee is coach Branch McCracken and team captain Bob Leonard, while big Don Schlundt joins in from the left. IU Archives

gain a decided advantage. The score was tied 41-41 at the break, and the tug of war continued at the start of the second half. Controversy ensued midway through the second half when Kansas center and leading scorer B.H. Born appeared to foul out of the game when he was called for his fifth foul. Kansas coach Phog Allen angrily argued that Born only had four and was supported by some members of the press. When the officials acquiesced and let Born stay in the game, McCracken exploded. He argued that Born had five fouls in the official records and that it was against the rules to alter the books. He was overruled, and Born was allowed to play. IU clung to a slim lead, or was tied, throughout the final ten minutes. The Jayhawks' Dean Kelly buried a jump shot to tie the game at 68-68 with 58 seconds remaining, but then Kelly fouled Bob Leonard on a drive to the basket with 30 seconds remaining. Leonard, a strong foul shooter, missed the

first free throw but calmly drilled the second one. The Hoosiers defense put the clamps on the Jayhawks in the final seconds, limiting them to a long shot from the corner with only three seconds remaining. When that shot harmlessly bounced off the iron, the Hoosiers celebrated the second national championship in school history.

Three weeks earlier, after the Illinois victory that clinched the Big Ten title, McCracken told his players, "I never praise you fellows, and sometimes you must think I'm pretty hard. I criticize and tell you where you do the wrong things, and leave the praise to your mothers and sweethearts and friends. But tonight I'll have to say that you're the greatest team in the country." The IU players could have gotten complacent from McCracken's remarks, but instead they went out and proved him right.

CHAPTER 3

THE MOST DOMINANT TEAM IN IU HISTORY

1974-75

OVERALL RECORD: 31-1

CONFERENCE RECORD: 18-0 (FIRST PLACE)

TEAM HONORS:

UPI NATIONAL CHAMPION, BIG TEN CHAMPION, RAINBOW CLASSIC CHAMPION,

INDIANA CLASSIC CHAMPION

INDIVIDUAL HONORS:

BOB KNIGHT—NATIONAL COACH OF THE YEAR (CONSENSUS),

BIG TEN COACH OF THE YEAR

STEVE GREEN—ALL-AMERICA, ALL-BIG TEN (FIRST TEAM),

ACADEMIC ALL-AMERICA, ACADEMIC ALL-BIG TEN

QUINN BUCKNER—ALL-AMERICA, ALL-BIG TEN (FIRST TEAM)

SCOTT MAY—ALL-AMERICA, ALL-BIG TEN (FIRST TEAM), BIG TEN MVP

KENT BENSON—ALL-AMERICA, ALL-BIG TEN (FIRST TEAM)

It may have been, quite simply, the most eagerly anticipated season in the history of IU basketball up until that time—and for good reason. The Hoosiers returned all five starters and all of the regular reserves from the 1973-74 team that had shared the Big Ten title with Michigan and went on to win the short-lived CCA postseason tournament. Entering the 1974-75 campaign, the Hoosiers had it all: coaching, experience, leadership, inside scoring, outside scoring, defense and depth. Plus, they had ambition. After a team dominated by freshmen and sophomores made it to the 1973 Final Four and lost to eventual champion UCLA, those young players longed to make it back and show their mettle by capturing the national championship. They barely missed the 1974 NCAA Tournament by losing a playoff game to Big Ten co-champion Michigan two days after the regular season ended. For the 1974-75 campaign, those players who were freshmen and sophomores in the 1973 Final Four were now juniors and seniors, and were ready to make a run at the top prize in college basketball.

With 12 lettermen and all of the players from the regular rotation returning, Coach Knight knew exactly what he had to work with. After trying nine different starting lineups the previous season, Knight settled on a solid rotation that he stuck with throughout most of the 1974-75 campaign with sophomore Kent Benson at center, senior Steve Green and junior Scott May at the two forwards, and juniors Quinn Bucker and Bobby Wilkerson at the guard spots. Off the bench, Knight used senior John Laskowski to fill in at guard and on the wing, while junior Tom Abernathy filled in up front.

At 6'11", Benson was a space-eater on the inside. Although not a great athlete, he was a hard worker and probably the most improved player on the team. After winning the MVP award as a freshman in the CCA tournament in the spring of 1974, Benson was ready to carry more of the offensive load as a sophomore. He used a hook shot, a reliable face-up jumper, and a variety of post moves to provide the Hoosiers with a solid presence in the paint. The two forwards, Green and May, were both 6'7" players that could score inside and outside. May was the better athlete and better at taking the ball to the basket, but Green was a more effective perimeter shooter. At guard, the 6'3" Buckner was the floor leader of the Hoosier attack on both sides of the ball. He had outstanding

The 1974-75 team. First row (left to right): Scott May, Steve Green, John Laskowski, Kent Benson, Don Noort, Tom Abernathy; Second row: Steve Alfeld, Wayne Radford, Jim Crews, Quinn Buckner, Doug Allen, John Kanstra, Mark Haymore; Third row: head coach Bob Knight, trainer Bob Young, manager Larry Sherfick, Bob Wilkerson, Jim Wisman, assistant coach Dave Bliss, assistant coach Bob Donewald, assistant coach Bob Weltlich. IU Archives

court vision, quick reflexes, and the kind of basketball moxie that every coach wants his point guard to possess. His backcourt running mate, 6'7" Bobby Wilkerson, jumped center for the Hoosiers at tip-off, played guard on offense, and then usually covered the other team's best offensive player. The Hoosiers basically had another starter coming off the bench in 6'5" sharp-shooter John Laskowsi. "Laz" started a few games as a sophomore and junior but mostly relished his role coming off the bench and sparking the Hoosiers. He may not have started many games, but he was usually on the floor at the end because he was the team's best clutch performer. Early in his career he earned the nickname "Super Sub" for his excellence as a reserve, and if college basketball gave out a sixth man award, Laskowski would have probably been the top candidate to receive it. IU's other key reserve was 6'7" Tom Abernathy, who was also a former high school teammate of Laskowski's. Abernathy was a

versatile offensive and defensive player that could fill in at both forward spots and at center. He was an excellent passer, a strong defender, and a steady player that rarely made mistakes on the floor.

Other players filled in for a few minutes here and there, but the seven players mentioned above dominated the action when the game was on the line. They were so effective that they didn't leave much room for other players to make it onto the floor, except in mop-up duty, and fortunately there ended up being plenty of that available.

Coach Knight had an outstanding group of freshmen—Wayne Radford, Jim Wisman and Mark Haymore—that benefited from getting some of those mop-up minutes. Radford was a 6'3" guard/forward from Indianapolis that was strong, quick and aggressive. He was a good outside shooter that could also slash to the basket. Wisman was a 6'2" guard from Quincy, Illinois, who was a high school All-American

1974-75 TEAM ROSTER

Head coach: Bob Knight
Assistant coaches: Dave Bliss, Bob Donewald, Bob Weltlich

No.	Player	Hometown	Class	Position	Height
33	Tom Abernathy	South Bend, IN	Jr	F	6-7
24	Steve Ahlfeld	Wabash, IN	Sr	G	6-0
25	Doug Allen	Champaign, IL	Sr	F	6-6
54	Kent Benson	New Castle, IN	So	C	6-11
21	Quinn Buckner (Capt.)	Phoenix, IL	Jr	G	6-3
45	Jim Crews	Normal, IL	Jr	G	6-5
34	Steve Green (Capt.)	Sellersburg, IN	Sr	F	6-7
32	Mark Haymore	Shaker, OH	Fr	F/C	6-8
30	John Kamstra	Frankfort, IN	Sr	G	6-1
31	John Laskowski	South Bend, IN	Sr	G/F	6-5
42	Scott May	Sandusky, OH	Jr	F	6-7
43	Don Noort	Worth, IL	Jr	C	6-8
22	Wayne Radford	Indianapolis, IN	Fr	G/F	6-3
20	Bob Wilkerson	Anderson, IN	Jr	G/F	6-7
40	Jim Wisman	Quincy, IL	Fr	G	6-2

as a senior. A natural point guard, Wisman had excellent ball-handling and passing skills and was also a good perimeter shooter. Haymore was a 6'8" forward/center from Shaker, Ohio, that averaged 25 points, 20 rebounds, and seven assists as a senior in high school. He had good strength, a variety of inside moves, and a soft shooting touch. The IU coaching staff hoped that he could develop into a player similar to former IU All-American Steve Downing. However, Haymore only lasted two years at IU before transferring to Massachusetts.

The fourth member of that freshman class left Indiana before official practices even started. A 6'7" forward named Larry Bird from tiny French Lick, was a player that Knight had taken a chance on even though he had struggled academically in high school and played against mostly small-school competition. Knight liked Bird's great hands and court vision, and at the time he recruited Bird, he felt like Larry really wanted to come to IU. Unfortunately, when Bird arrived in Bloomington, he was overwhelmed by the huge campus and he was flat broke. He felt completely out of place and eventually just went back home without really letting anyone at IU know why he was leaving.

Guard Bobby Wilkerson was an imposing presence. As a 6'7" guard, Wilkerson could see over defenders to easily deliver passes to his teammates, and on defense he would hound opposing guards to the keep them from being able to start their offense. IU Archives

1974-75 SEASON STATISTICS

Team Statistics	G	FG%	FT%	R	A	TO	PF	PTS	PPG
Indiana	32	.509	.718	44.8	18.8	15.7	19.1	2817	88.0
Opponents	32	.440	.688	36.1	11.1	21.5	21.5	2109	65.9

Player Statistics	G-GS	FG%	FT%	R	A	TO	PF	PTS	PPG
Green	31-31	.582	.797	4.3	1.4	1.8	2.7	516	16.6
May	30-27	.510	.766	6.6	1.9	2.4	2.2	490	16.3
Benson	32-32	.541	.743	8.9	1.3	1.9	3.0	480	15.0
Buckner	32-32	.493	.583	3.8	5.5	3.3	3.2	379	11.8
Laskowski	28-6	.486	.829	2.8	2.4	0.9	1.2	266	9.5
Wilkerson	32-32	.452	.623	4.4	3.5	2.2	2.5	229	7.2
Abernathy	32-0	.526	.574	3.0	0.7	0.3	1.2	133	4.2
Radford	26-0	.587	.703	1.8	0.6	0.7	1.0	80	3.1
Wisman	23-0	.459	.762	0.2	1.0	0.6	1.1	50	2.2
Noort	27-0	.480	.667	1.5	0.1	0.3	0.3	54	2.0
Haymore	23-0	.370	.800	1.7	0.3	0.7	1.1	38	1.7
Crews	26-0	.455	1.00	0.5	0.8	0.5	0.3	36	1.4
Ahlfeld	28-0	.351	.667	0.1	0.3	0.5	0.5	32	1.1
Kamstra	24-0	.350	.727	0.5	0.4	0.5	0.1	22	0.9
Allen	22-0	.556	.400	0.5	0.0	0.2	0.1	12	0.6

He eventually transferred to Indiana State, grew a couple inches, and became one of the best college basketball players of all time, as well as an NBA Hall of Famer with the Boston Celtics. Knight later regretted that he let Bird leave so easily and always believed that Larry would have been a perfect fit in the IU system.

Of course, at the time, Indiana was loaded with talent and was preparing for its highly anticipated season. The loss of one recruit who was unhappy in Bloomington and felt like he made the wrong college choice seemed fairly inconsequential. The biggest concern Knight and the Hoosiers had to worry about at the time was a grueling schedule. The team was set to play a school-record 29 games, including preconference matchups with several strong opponents, and 18 conference games in a newly reinstituted round-robin schedule for Big Ten play. IU entered the season as the Big Ten favorite and the No. 3 team in the country in the preseason AP poll.

"I look upon this season as a great challenge," said Knight in the fall of 1974. "Naturally, I'm pleased that our squad is creating interest and excitement—it's good for the players, fans, and Indiana basketball

in general. But at the same time, our success of the past two seasons and our high preseason rating makes us the target for everyone on our schedule. I just hope we can play good, consistent basketball over the course of the season, and if we do, the record will take care of itself."

If there were any lingering doubts about just how potent this IU team could be, they were momentarily quelled on November 30, when the Hoosiers opened with a 113-60 annihilation of Tennessee Tech in Assembly Hall. May was the game's high scorer with 22 points, while Green added 20 and Benson and Buckner scored 17 apiece. Next, the Hoosiers got to try their mettle against three ranked teams and had to play two of them on the road. No. 7 Kansas hosted IU in Allen Fieldhouse on December 4. In a nip-and-tuck affair, Indiana led 60-58 in the final minute, but the Jayhawks' Norm Cook scored on a rebound basket to send the game into overtime. Kansas was ahead 70-69 until John Laskowski buried a 16-footer with 0:43 left on the clock to give IU a one-point lead. The Hoosiers got a defense stop and then played keep away with the ball until Green scored and was fouled with one second remaining. When he completed the

Center Kent Benson goes up to block an opponent's shot. As a sophomore, Benson showed tremendous maturity and improvement and became an All-American for the 1974-75 campaign. His inside presence anchored Indiana's potent offense and solidified the defense. IU Archives

three-point play with a free throw, the final score was 74-70 in IU's favor. Green finished with 19 points, while May led IU with 29 points and 10 rebounds. After that, the IU squad steamrolled 15th-ranked Kentucky 98-74 in Bloomington, led by 26 points and 13 rebounds from Kent Benson, and then beat No. 11 Notre Dame 94-84 in South Bend, as six different Hoosiers scored in double figures.

Following those three key wins over top 15 teams, Indiana cruised to four straight double-digit victories over Texas A&M, Toledo, Creighton and Nebraska, and in the process, moved up to No. 2 in the AP poll. The wins over Toledo and Creighton came in the first ever Indiana Classic. The Hoosiers then wrapped up the preconference season by traveling to Honolulu, Hawaii, for the Rainbow Classic. In the opening round, IU outlasted a stubborn Florida team 98-84, behind 32 points from Green and 17 from Laskowski, in his first game back since the Notre Dame win when suffered a foot injury. Then, Indiana whipped Big Ten rival Ohio State 102-71 and Hawaii 69-52 to win the tournament championship and close out the preconference schedule with a perfect 11-0 record.

Making it through that early schedule without a blemish was both a blessing and a curse. With convincing wins over a lot of quality teams, the Hoosiers knew they

If college basketball gave out a "sixth man" award, the trophy for the 1974-75 season would have probably gone to IU guard John Laskowski. Laz was a deadly outside shooter and a clutch performer. IU Archives

Coach Bob Knight offers some encouragement to his floor general, junior guard Quinn Buckner.
IU Archives

could beat anyone. However, in the previous 12 years, three other Big Ten teams—Indiana in 1965, Illinois in 1969, and Minnesota in 1973—had come into league play undefeated, and all three were rudely received by their conference compatriots, as each of three teams was unceremoniously beaten in their first Big Ten road game. More importantly, none of those three teams went on to win the conference crown. Their early-season success had put a target on their backs that none of the three could overcome. That made what the Hoosiers were about to accomplish in the 1975 Big Ten season even more remarkable.

Both history and the scheduling gods appeared to be conspiring against IU as the team opened the conference season with a two-game road trip against a pair of the Big Ten's top teams, Michigan State and Michigan. "I can't imagine a tougher way to start," said Knight at the time.

However, on the day of Indiana's league opener against Michigan State, 10 of the black players on the Spartan team walked out of a morning meeting en mass when coach Gus Ganakas announced that one of the starters against the Hoosiers was going to be 6'7" freshman Jeff Tropf (one of the team's two white players). Ganakas, who said he had been unaware of any previous internal problems, was shocked by the move and indefinitely suspended all ten of the players involved. As a result, Ganakas was forced to hastily throw together a team with his remaining players and some guys from the junior varsity to play the second-ranked Hoosiers four and a half hours later. IU predictably demolished the Spartans 107-55, as six Hoosiers scored in double figures and only one player, Scott May, logged more than 20 minutes on the floor. Two days later, Indiana blew by the 17th-ranked Michigan Wolverines 90-76 in Ann Arbor. After those two road victories, Indiana ascended to No. 1 in the rankings for the first time that season, which suddenly made the Hoosiers an even bigger target.

Knight feared a letdown as the team returned to Bloomington for two games, but IU completely obliterated Iowa 102-49 and then used a late rally to blow out No. 17 Minnesota 79-59. Next came four more blowouts over Northwestern, Wisconsin, Purdue (ranked 20th), and Illinois. That put the Hoosiers at 8-0 in the conference and 19-0 overall. Then, the IU squad was put to its first real nail-biter since the December 4 game at Kansas. This time it came against Ohio State on February 1, in St. John Arena, where the Buckeyes had never lost a game that Knight was involved in. During Knight's three seasons as a player on the varsity at Ohio State, his teams amassed a record of 34-0 there, and as a coach, Knight's teams were 0-3 against the Buckeyes. IU had already beaten OSU by 31 points in the Rainbow Classic, but the Buckeyes hung tough on their home court before bowing 72-66. Scott May led all scorers with 25 points.

At the halfway mark of the conference season, IU was 9-0 and stood a full three games ahead of the field. After the OSU cliffhanger, the Hoosiers went back to steamrolling opponents as they beat Michigan, Iowa, Minnesota, Northwestern and Wisconsin by an average of 25 points, and none of those five teams came closer than 15 points. Indiana's next game was the best and the worst of the season. The Hoosiers went into West Lafayette and escaped with a thrilling 83-82 win to clinch the Big Ten title outright (with three games still remaining). However, leading scorer Scott May fractured his left arm in the first half and had to be taken to the hospital. He returned, with his arm in a cast, to see the final sec-

onds of the game and celebrate the victory with his teammates, but he was sidelined indefinitely.

Against the Boilermakers, Steve Green scored a game-high 29 points on remarkable 13-15 shooting from the field. In the nine games leading up to the Purdue contest, Green had averaged just seven PPG while recovering from a bad bout of the flu that hit

1974-75 SEASON RESULTS

Date	Court	Opponent	Result	Score
11/30/1974	H	Tennessee Tech	W	113-60
12/4/1974	A	(#7) Kansas	W	74-70
12/7/1974	H	(#15) Kentucky	W	98-74
12/11/1974	A	(#11) Notre Dame	W	94-84
12/14/1974	N1	Texas A&M	W	90-55
12/16/1974	H	Toledo	W	92-70
12/20/1974	H	Creighton	W	71-53
12/21/1974	H	Nebraska	W	97-60
12/26/1974	N2	Florida	W	98-84
12/27/1974	N2	Ohio State	W	102-71
12/30/1974	N2	Hawaii	W	69-52
1/4/1975	A	Michigan State	W	107-55
1/6/1975	A	(#17) Michigan	W	90-76
1/11/1975	H	Iowa	W	102-49
1/13/1975	H	(#17) Minnesota	W	79-59
1/18/1975	A	Northwestern	W	82-56
1/20/1975	A	Wisconsin	W	89-69
1/25/1975	H	(#20) Purdue	W	104-71
1/27/1975	H	Illinois	W	73-57
2/1/1975	A	Ohio State	W	72-66
2/3/1975	H	Michigan	W	74-48
2/8/1975	A	Iowa	W	79-56
2/10/1975	A	Minnesota	W	69-54
2/15/1975	H	Northwestern	W	82-58
2/17/1975	H	Wisconsin	W	93-58
2/22/1975	A	Purdue	W	83-82
2/24/1975	A	Illinois	W	112-89
3/1/1975	H	Ohio State	W	86-78
3/8/1975	H	Michigan State	W	94-79

NCAA Tournament

3/15/1975	N3	(#17) UTEP	W	78-52
3/20/1975	N3	(#13) Oregon State	W	81-71
3/22/1975	N4	(#5) Kentucky	L	90-92

1 Indianapolis, IN
2 Honolulu, HI
3 Lexington, KY
4 Dayton, OH

In Steve Green's final farewell in Assembly Hall, Coach Knight addresses the Senior Day crowd to tell them how much they should appreciate the team's senior forward. IU Archives

1974-75 BIG TEN STANDINGS

	W	L	PCT
Indiana	18	0	1.000
Michigan	12	6	.667
Minnesota	11	7	.611
Purdue	11	7	.611
Michigan St.	10	8	.555
Ohio State	8	10	.444
Iowa	7	11	.389
Wisconsin	5	13	.278
Illinois	4	14	.222
Northwestern	4	14	.222

him in January. Without May in the lineup, Green scored 30 points, 29 points, and 25 points to lead the Hoosiers to three final conference wins over Illinois, Ohio State, and Michigan State. They finished the regular season with a perfect 29-0 record, the first undefeated mark in school history. In the Michigan State game, May returned for the first time. His left arm was in a heavy cast, and it was also wrapped in a protective foam rubber to cushion any blows. He played only a few minutes at the end and didn't score. It was clear that if the Hoosiers were going to keep their undefeated run alive and win the NCAA title, then they would have to do it without Scott May at full strength.

In the first round of the NCAA tournament, the Hoosiers went to Lexington, Kentucky, to face UTEP, which had a renowned defense that held opponents to 54.5 PPG for the season—the best in the nation. The Miners held IU to 31 points on 36-percent shooting in the first half. But after the intermission, the Hoosiers blew the game wide open when Green, Laskowski and Buckner began finding the seams in the defense, and IU rolled to a 78-53 win. In the Mideast Regional Semifinals, Indiana matched up with Oregon State. Against the Beavers, Benson dominated the inside while Green hit almost everything in sight from the perimeter. IU opened up a 48-27 halftime lead and coasted to an 81-71 win. Benson scored 23 while Green led all scorers with 34 points on 14-19 (74 percent) shooting. That set up a showdown in the regional finals with the Kentucky team that IU had defeated by 14 in Assembly Hall in December.

Kentucky was still seething from that early-season humiliation, which was much worse than the score indicated, and which also featured a verbal (and nearly physical) confrontation between Knight and Kentucky assistant Lynn Nance. In the regional finals, Knight thought that Kentucky would employ a zone to counter the Hoosiers' precision offense, and so he

INDIANA'S RANKING IN THE 1974-75 ASSOCIATED PRESS POLLS

PS	12/3	12/10	12/17	12/24	12/31	1/7	1/14	1/21	1/28	2/4	2/11	2/18	2/25	3/4	3/11	3/18	3/25	4/2
3	3	3	3	2	2	2	1	1	1	1	1	1	1	1	1	1	3	3

Injured forward Scott May, with a cast on his left arm, kneels on the sideline and hangs his head as the Hoosiers' undefeated season comes to an end with a 92-90 upset at the hands of Kentucky in the regional finals of the NCAA tournament. IU Archives

defensive strategy: They would body-check every IU player who tried to set a screen in the lane. In the opening minutes, Steve Green went to set a pick, and Wildcat forward Bob Guyette knocked him to floor and told him that was what was going to happen all afternoon. One journalist counted eight times that Guyette decked Green to the floor in the first half, and only three of them were called as fouls. The game was knotted at 44-44 after a first half that had seen multiple ties and lead changes. In the second half, the referees continued to let Kentucky's body blows go unchecked, and the Hoosiers began to look like they were wearing out from the pressure and the physical play as the Wildcats grabbed an 85-75 lead with under four minutes remaining, but Kent Benson rallied the Hoosiers to a mere 90-88 deficit with only 33 seconds remaining. IU couldn't get any closer, and the Wildcats prevailed 92-90. Benson finished with career highs in points (33) and rebounds (22) and was named the MVP of the regional, but he left the floor with tears streaming down his face—an outward symbol of the agony that his teammates, coaches, and IU fans felt as the Hoosiers' dream season came to a premature end.

That day a resolve was born in the group of players that would return the next season. They decided that they did not want to suffer through the emotions they felt after the Kentucky loss ever again. They almost immediately began to focus

chose to start Scott May, cast and all, because May had been shooting the ball very well in practice and Knight wanted his best shooters on the floor. However, Kentucky had gotten schooled while trying to defend all of the picks and screens in the Hoosiers' offense in the first game, so they employed a simple all of their energy and attention on the 1975-76 season and what it would take to accomplish the one paramount goal that had eluded them—the national championship. However, they would have to make that journey without Steve Green and John Laskowski, two vital cogs in the Hoosier machine.

After the season, both of them were drafted by the Chicago Bulls in the second round of the NBA draft. Laz signed with the Bulls and played two seasons before going into a business career and becoming a longtime announcer of IU basketball games. Green signed with Utah in the ABA and eventually played three seasons with the Indiana Pacers in the NBA before returning to IU to finish dental school.

In the final analysis, the 1974-75 team—particularly the seven players who made up Knight's primary rotation—played a brand of basketball that was arguably the greatest and the purest in Indiana University history. No team could beat them. In the final analysis, they were defeated only by one fateful broken arm.

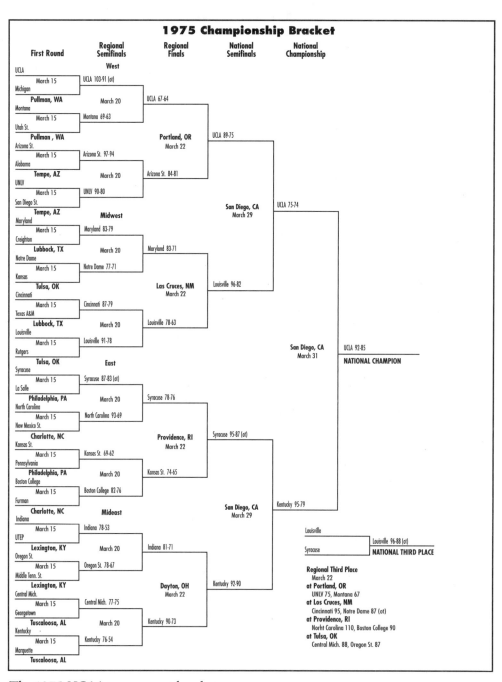

The 1975 NCAA tournament bracket.

CHAPTER 4

A TEAM THAT REFUSED TO LOSE

1986-87

OVERALL RECORD: 30-4

CONFERENCE RECORD: 15-3 (FIRST PLACE)

TEAM HONORS:

NCAA CHAMPION, BIG TEN CO-CHAMPION,

HOOSIER CLASSIC CHAMPION, INDIANA CLASSIC CHAMPION

INDIVIDUAL HONORS:

BOB KNIGHT—NAISMITH COACH OF THE YEAR, BIG TEN COACH OF THE YEAR

STEVE ALFORD—ALL-AMERICA, ALL-FINAL FOUR, ALL-BIG TEN (FIRST TEAM),

BIG TEN MVP, BIG TEN MEDAL OF HONOR

KEITH SMART—FINAL FOUR MOST OUTSTANDING PLAYER, ALL-FINAL FOUR

DEAN GARRETT—BIG TEN NEWCOMER OF THE YEAR

Seniors Steve Alford, Daryl Thomas and Todd Meier knew that they only had one chance left, and they desperately wanted to avoid becoming the first four-year players to graduate under coach Bob Knight at Indiana without winning at least one Big Ten championship. They came to Indiana as a highly touted class of recruits (which originally included 1983 Illinois Mr. Basketball Marty Simmons) and they made a big splash as freshmen, helping a very young Hoosier team to a 13-5 Big Ten record, an upset of No. 1 North Carolina in the 1984 NCAA tournament, and a trip the Elite Eight. During their sophomore year, the Hoosiers were expected to be one of the best teams in the country, but they mysteriously slid to a 7-11 conference record and missed the NCAA tournament.

The next year—their junior campaign—they overcame a lack of size in the front court and a lack of depth on the bench to restore Hoosier pride by making a serious run at the Big Ten title. However, they got demolished by Michigan on the final day of the season and had to settle for second place, and then Cleveland State upset IU in the first round of the NCAA tourney. That left Alford, Thomas and Meier with a sense of unfinished business heading into their final season in Bloomington.

IU returned 11 lettermen (with five of them coming off of redshirt seasons) from a team that had set a school record with a sizzling field goal percentage of .537 for the season, but had struggled with a lack of depth and had often gotten manhandled on the boards. The Hoosiers graduated point guard Winston Morgan, sixth man Stew Robinson, and seldom-used reserve Courtney Witte, and also lost jumping-jack Andre Harris, the team's starting power forward and leading rebounder who decided to transfer at the end of the 1985-1986 season. The Hoosiers also added four newcomers. Freshmen Tony Freeman, a 5'7" guard, and Dave Minor, a 6'5" forward, weren't expected to provide immediate help, but two junior college transfers—6'10" center Dean Garrett and 6'1" guard Keith Smart—were definitely expected to step in and become important contributors in Bob Knight's regular rotation. Garrett, a Californian with broad shoulders and long arms, definitely came to Bloomington with a lot of advanced billing. He was the inside player that the 1985-86 IU team had been sorely missing. He was a solid rebounder with a good shooting touch and some strong inside moves on offense, but his greatest value to Indiana was as a defensive intimidator in the paint. He ended up blocking a school-record 93 shots,

The 1986-87 team. Front row (left to right): Todd Jadlow, Keith Smart, Todd Meier, Steve Alford, Daryl Thomas, Dean Garrett, Kreigh Smith, Joe Hillman; Second row: Tony Freeman, Dave Minor, Jeff Oliphant, Brian Sloan, Steve Eyl, Magnus Pelkowski, Rick Calloway; Third row: trainer Tim Garl, assistant coach Ron Felling, assistant coach Joby Wright, head coach Bob Knight, assistant coach Kohn Smith, assistant coach Royce Waltman, team physician Dr. Brad Bomba; Fourth row: graduate assistant Julio Salazar, manager Mike McGlothlin, manager Bill Himebrook, graduate assistant Murray Bartow, graduate assistant Dan Dackich.
IU Archives

and he altered many more shots as well. Keith Smart was a cat-quick guard who could explode off the floor with a vertical leap that exceeded 40 inches. He had used those physical gifts to become a junior college All-American at Garden City Junior College in Kansas and he quickly earned a spot next to Alford in the Indiana backcourt. Smart's progress was accelerated by the fact that Alford took him under his wing and showed him how to be an effective college basketball player, while Thomas did the same for Garrett.

Garrett and Smart joined Alford, Thomas, and sophomore Rick Calloway to form a starting lineup that was well-balanced and extremely potent offensively. All five players ended up averaging double figures for the 1986-87 season. Thomas had come to IU as a wing player but had been forced to play center for the undersized IU squad during the 1985-86 campaign. With the arrival of Garrett, Thomas could move to power forward, but now he did it with a season of banging against Big Ten wide bodies under his belt. The final member of the frontcourt was Calloway, a 6'6" swing man who was coming back from a freshman

season in which he averaged a surprising 13.9 points and 4.9 rebounds. Calloway was a slasher who loved to get to the rim, but he also had a nice mid-range game as well.

Of course, the Hoosiers were anchored by All-American Steve Alford, who was widely regarded as the best outside shooter in college basketball. "I'll tell you a remarkable thing about Alford," said Knight. "He's not big, he's not strong, and he's not quick... It's hard for me to imagine how a kid like that can score as many points as he does. He doesn't post up, he doesn't get rebound baskets, and he doesn't really take the ball to the basket to score. He's just got to work like hell to get the jump shot." Under Knight's tutelage, Alford had become a master of moving without the ball and taking advantage of screens to get open jump shots. Any defender who drew the unlucky assignment of guarding Alford had to not only battle Steve himself, but also had to fight through dozens of body blows from the screens set by his fellow Hoosiers. Entering his senior year, Alford's career field goal percentage was 56 percent—an amazingly accurate

1986-87 TEAM ROSTER

Head coach: Bob Knight
Assistant coaches: Ron Felling, Kohn Smith, Royce Waltman, Joby Wright

No.	Player	Hometown	Class	Position	Height
12	Steve Alford (Capt.)	New Castle, IN	Sr	G	6-2
20	Rick Calloway	Cincinnati, OH	So	G/F	6-6
32	Steve Eyl	Hamilton, OH	Jr	F	6-6
10	Tony Freeman	Westchester, IL	Fr	G	5-7
22	Dean Garrett	San Clemente, CA	Jr	C	6-10
44	Joe Hillman	Glendale, CA	So	G	6-2
11	Todd Jadlow	Salina, KS	Rs	F/C	6-9
30	Todd Meier (Capt.)	Oshkosh, WI	Sr	F/C	6-8
31	Dave Minor	Cincinnati, OH	Fr	F	6-5
35	Jeff Oliphant	Lynons, IN	So	F	6-5
14	Magnus Pelkowski	Bogota, Columbia	So	F/C	6-10
45	Brian Sloan	McLeansboro, IL	Jr	F/C	6-8
23	Keith Smart	Baton Rouge, LA	Jr	G	6-1
42	Kreigh Smith	Tipton, IN	So	G/F	6-7
24	Daryl Thomas (Capt.)	Westchester, IL	Sr	F/C	6-7

number for an outside shooter. He also had an excellent chance of becoming Indiana's all-time leading scorer by passing Don Schlundt's career mark of 2,192 points, which had stood for over 30 years.

While Alford and the other starters logged most of the minutes on the court, the Hoosiers also got sparks from several key reserves. Sophomore guard Joe Hillman, who had led the state of California by averaging 41.3 PPG as a senior in high school in 1984, was IU's primary backcourt reserve. Hillman was a hard-nosed guard and an excellent floor leader with an assist-to-turnover ratio of better than two-to-one. He was a good shooter and passer who knew how to run Knight's motion offense, and he was also a tough defender. Knight's primary frontcourt reserve was junior Steve Eyl, a versatile 6'6" athlete who could score, rebound and defend. Senior Steve Meier was slowed by a set of bad knees, but the former high school All-American also came off the bench to contribute solid minutes in the frontcourt and provided excellent senior leadership.

The addition of Smart and Garrett to an already-solid Indiana team pushed expectations sky high. The Hoosiers were ranked No. 3 in the nation in the preseason. Their archrival Purdue was ranked No. 4, and those two squads were viewed as the favorites in the Big Ten, with Iowa (ranked No. 10 in the preseason) and Illinois (No. 14) expected to be right on their heels. Preseason expectations usually don't count for a whole lot in the Big Ten, but in the 1986-87 season they turned out to be quite prophetic.

In a November 16 exhibition game against the Soviet National Team, Indiana trailed 91-88 in the final minutes, but Daryl Thomas scored inside then buried six straight free throws to carry IU to a 97-95 come-from-behind victory in Assembly Hall. Indiana's late-game charge turned out to be a sign of things to come as this team would show time and time again that it knew how to win close games. Against the Soviets, Thomas ended up finishing with 24 points and eight rebounds, Alford had 23 points and six assists, and Rick Calloway had a game-high 25 points to go with eight rebounds. Garrett proved to be the inside presence that IU was hoping for, as he had 17 points and 10 rebounds against the big and physical Soviet front line. Smart ended up pulling a groin muscle during warmups and missed the game.

The new-look Hoosiers cruised through their preconference schedule with a 9-1 record. That included solid wins over Notre Dame (in South

Team captains Todd Meier (left), Daryl Thomas (middle), and Steve Alford (right) hoist the NCAA championship trophy after Indiana defeated Syracuse 74-73 in the NCAA title game. IU Archives

Steve Alford steps to the podium and addresses Hoosier fans during a reception in Assembly Hall after the IU squad returned from Baton Rouge, Louisiana, as the 1987 NCAA champion. IU Archives

1986-87 SEASON STATISTICS

Team Statistics	G	FG%	3FG%	FT%	R	A	TO	S	B	PF	PTS	PPG
Indiana	34	.513	.508	.767	35.0	16.0	13.2	6.3	4.0	18.3	2806	82.5
Opponents	34	.451	.384	.677	34.7	13.2	15.3	5.3	2.4	21.6	2412	70.9
Player Statistics	**G-GS**	**FG%**	**3FG%**	**FT%**	**R**	**A**	**TO**	**S**	**B**	**PF**	**PTS**	**PPG**
Alford	34-34	.473	.530	.889	2.6	3.6	1.9	1.1	0.1	1.5	749	22.0
Thomas	34-34	.538	.000	.786	5.7	0.8	2.1	1.3	0.4	2.9	534	15.7
Calloway	29-27	.531	.000	.742	4.4	1.9	2.3	1.1	0.2	2.7	364	12.6
Garrett	34-33	.542	.000	.635	8.5	0.6	1.2	0.5	2.7	2.7	387	11.4
Smart	34-31	.517	.364	.841	2.9	3.2	2.2	0.9	0.1	3.0	382	11.2
Pelkowski	14-1	.522	.667	.600	1.9	0.1	0.5	0.1	0.2	1.6	53	3.8
Eyl	34-1	.648	.000	.674	3.4	1.2	0.8	0.5	0.2	1.3	101	3.0
Hillman	32-5	.483	.200	.742	1.2	2.1	0.9	0.3	0.1	1.4	80	2.5
Freeman	16-0	.417	.250	.700	0.9	2.4	1.2	0.6	0.0	1.0	35	2.2
Sloan	17-1	.448	.000	.500	1.1	0.5	0.4	0.2	0.2	0.9	35	2.1
Smith	25-1	.500	.875	.857	0.8	0.6	0.2	0.2	0.0	0.5	37	1.5
Oliphant	2-0	.000	.000	.600	2.0	0.5	0.5	0.0	0.0	0.5	3	1.5
Meier	29-0	.450	.000	.591	1.5	0.2	0.5	0.2	0.0	1.2	31	1.1
Minor	18-2	.250	.000	.714	0.8	0.6	0.7	0.0	0.0	0.5	15	0.8

Bend), 13th-ranked Kentucky, and Louisville. Alford led the attack against the Fighting Irish and the Wildcats with 26 points in each of those games. Garrett was headliner against the Cardinals as he scored 12 points, grabbed 11 rebounds, and held Louisville's star center Pervis Ellison to just eight points on 3-14 from the field. Another huge performance from Garrett came against UNC-Wilmington as he tallied 17 points, 16 rebounds, and seven blocked shots in response to being benched by Coach Knight for a lackluster effort in the previous game. It ended up being the only game of the season he didn't start.

Another one of the best performances of the preconference season was Alford's 26-point game against Princeton. The Hoosier sniper took advantage of college-basketball's newly implemented three-point shot by draining eight of 11 threes in an 83-54 win against Pete Carril's Tigers. The only speed bump in IU's preconference run was a 79-75 loss to C.M. Newton's Vanderbilt Commodores in rowdy Memorial Gymnasium in Nashville, Tennessee. The biggest scare of the preconference came on opening night when Calloway went down with a knee injury. At the time, IU feared that it could be serious enough to end Calloway's season and deal a blow to the Hoosiers' championship hopes. However, it turned out to be a stretched ligament, and Calloway returned to the line-up at nearly full strength by the end of December.

When the Big Ten season tipped off with Indiana at Ohio State on January 4, it was Keith Smart's turn to shine. Buckeye coach Gary Williams had his team focus on Steve Alford, so they double-teamed him, ran a box-and-one at him, and helped out on him whenever he got the ball. As a result, they decided to leave Smart open on the outside because their scouting report told them that Smart had deadly quickness but limited shooting range. Smart blew holes in that theory by hitting open jumper after open jumper and scoring 20 points in the first half as the Hoosiers raced to a 47-33 lead. Smart hit a three-pointer at the start of the second half and IU led 50-33. Ohio State mounted a desperate comeback and cut the lead to 74-70. At that point, IU had the ball and got it to Alford, who missed a baseline jump shot. As the IU and OSU big men jostled for position and went up for the rebound, a body in a red jersey flew out of nowhere and got a hand on the ball way above the rim. It was Smart. Ohio State's 6'7" Tony White said he felt Smart's knees brush his shoulders. Smart said

he remembered looking across the rim and seeing Alford on the floor. It was one of the most dazzling leaps that anyone had ever seen on a basketball court, and sportswriter Bob Hammel calculated that it was a jump of better than 50 inches. Smart's tip-in missed, and he was called for a foul (even the refs were a little bewildered by his fantastic leap). Smart also twisted his ankle when he came down and had to leave the

Using the All-America form that made him famous, Steve Alford releases one of his deadly accurate jump shots. During his four-year career at Indiana, Alford was widely hailed as the best outside shooter in college basketball. IU Archives

game. Nevertheless, it was a play that was long remembered by those who witnessed it. After Smart exited, Alford took over the game, hitting back-to-back threes and scoring 10 straight points down the stretch to lift IU to a 92-80 win. Smart finished with a career-high 31 points on 13-18 shooting from the field, including 5-5 from three-point range. Alford

had 22 points and nine assists, and Calloway chipped in 20 points.

After the win in Columbus, IU went north and beat Michigan State 79-60 and Michigan 85-84. Against the Wolverines, the Indiana squad opened up a 17-point halftime lead, but, just as they had done against Ohio State, the Hoosiers let Michigan back in

1986-87 SEASON RESULTS

Date	Court	Opponent	Result	Score
11/29/1986	H	Montana State	W	90-55
12/2/1986	A	Notre Dame	W	67-62
12/6/1986	H	(#13) Kentucky	W	71-66
12/9/1986	A	Vanderbilt	L	75-79
12/12/1986	H	UNC-Wilmington	W	73-72
12/13/1986	H	East Carolina	W	96-68
12/20/1986	H	Morehead State	W	84-62
12/23/1986	H	Louisville	W	67-58
12/26/1986	N1	Princeton	W	83-54
12/27/1986	N1	Illinois State	W	82-58
1/4/1987	A	Ohio State	W	92-80
1/8/1987	A	Michigan State	W	79-60
1/12/1987	A	Michigan	W	85-84
1/15/1987	H	Wisconsin	W	103-65
1/17/1987	H	Northwestern	W	95-43
1/22/1987	A	(#1) Iowa	L	88-101
1/24/1987	A	Minnesota	W	77-53
1/28/1987	H	(#12) Illinois	W	69-66
1/31/1987	H	(#4) Purdue	W	88-77
2/4/1987	H	Michigan State	W	84-80
2/8/1987	H	Michigan	W	83-67
2/11/1987	A	Northwestern	W	77-75
2/16/1987	A	Wisconsin	W	86-85
2/19/1987	H	Minnesota	W	72-70
2/21/1987	H	(#7) Iowa	W	84-75
2/26/1987	A	(#6) Purdue	L	64-75
3/1/1987	A	(#14) Illinois	L	67-69
3/7/1987	H	Ohio State	W	90-81

NCAA Tournament

Date	Court	Opponent	Result	Score
3/12/1987	N1	Fairfield	W	92-58
3/14/1987	N1	Auburn	W	107-90
3/20/1987	N2	(#17) Duke	W	88-82
3/22/1987	N2	Louisiana State	W	77-76
3/28/1987	N3	(#1) UNLV	W	97-93
3/30/1987	N3	(#10) Syracuse	W	74-73

1 Indianapolis, IN
2 Cincinnati, OH
3 New Orleans, LA

the game. In fact, the game was tied with 0:08 left and Michigan guard Gary Grant on the line. Grant made the first free throw, but missed the second one. Thomas grabbed the rebound for IU and whipped the ball ahead to Alford, who drove the ball deep into the lane and pulled up for a 10-footer that rattled home for an 85-84 Indiana victory. That win gave IU a 3-0 record during a tough three-game road trip to open the Big Ten season. It was a terrific shot in the arm for a team that desperately craved the conference crown.

Next, IU returned to Bloomington and whipped Wisconsin (105-63) and Northwestern (95-43). Undefeated in league play and riding an 11-game winning streak, the red-hot Hoosiers traveled for a showdown with Iowa on Thursday, January 22. If the third-ranked Hoosiers were hot, then the Hawkeyes were a blazing inferno. They were 17-0, ranked No. 1 in the nation, and loaded with as much talent as any team in the country. All 12 members of that Iowa squad went on to play professional basketball in one form or another. Their headliners were sophomores B.J. Armstrong and Roy Marble, and they also had big center Brad Lohaus and sixth-man Jeff Moe, an Indiana native. In the Iowa City battle, the Hawkeyes jumped out to a 33-20 lead, but IU closed it to 46-44 at the half, and then snatched the lead early in the second half. However, Iowa was a deep team with a pressing, trapping defense, and they kept attacking until they had built an 83-68 lead. Then it was IU's turn to put on a run. The Hoosiers closed it to 93-88 when Alford came off a screen and drilled a three-pointer with 1:25 left on the clock. Unfortunately, a referee ruled that Alford's foot had touched the out-of-bounds line and waved off the shot. Over the final minute and a half, Iowa ran off an 8-0 run to close out a 101-88 victory. It was the first time a team had ever broken the century mark against a Knight-coached team. Six different Hawkeyes scored in double figures, led by Jeff Moe and Kevin Gamble with 17

points each. Daryl Thomas led IU with a game-high 22 points, along with five rebounds and 10 assists.

Iowa's win put the Hawkeyes in sole possession of first place in the Big Ten at 6-0, while IU dropped into third place at 5-1 (a half-game behind Purdue). Nevertheless, the Iowa game was a turning point. Up until that contest, IU was 14-1, but had only played one ranked team, Kentucky, and so there was a sense that no one knew just how good the Hoosiers really were. Iowa had proven that it fully deserved the No. 1 ranking, but, in the final minutes of the game, IU had an excellent opportunity to beat them in Iowa City, in a contest in which Iowa performed at the top of its game. Plus, the Hoosiers had gotten massacred on the boards 46-19, and still stayed in the game. As a result, Knight and the Hoosiers felt like they could beat any team in the country. However, Knight was so impressed with Iowa that he didn't expect them to lose another game, and he told his IU players that their best shot at the conference title was to win their next eight games and then beat Iowa in Bloomington on February 21—and then finish off their final three games with wins.

1986-87 BIG TEN STANDINGS

	W	L	PCT
Indiana	15	3	.833
Purdue	15	3	.833
Iowa	14	4	.778
Illinois	13	5	.722
Michigan	10	8	.556
Ohio State	9	9	.500
Michigan St.	6	12	.333
Wisconsin	4	14	.222
Minnesota	2	16	.111
Northwestern	2	16	.111

INDIANA'S RANKING IN THE 1986-87 ASSOCIATED PRESS POLLS

PS	12/2	12/9	12/16	12/23	12/30	1/6	1/13	1/20	1/27	2/3	2/10	2/17	2/24	3/3	3/10
3	3	2	8	8	6	4	4	3	4	2	2	2	3	4	3

All-American Steve Alford was brilliant during the 1987 NCAA tournament, averaging 23.0 PPG as he led IU to a fifth NCAA championship. IU Archives

The Hoosiers did just what Knight had asked of them. They pulled off eight straight victories. That included Assembly Hall wins over No. 12 Illinois and No. 4 Purdue, but it also included a couple of lackluster road victories over Big Ten bottom-feeders Northwestern and Wisconsin. In fact, IU had to go three overtimes to beat the Badgers in Madison. Still, IU was 13-1 in league play heading into its rematch with Iowa, which was 10-3 after suffering several unexpected setbacks. Instead of being a game the Hoosiers needed to catch up with the Hawkeyes, it turned into one in which IU dealt a knockout blow to Iowa's Big Ten title hopes. Indiana led 46-27 at the half, weathered a big second-half run from the Hawkeyes, and won 84-75.

With three games remaining in conference play, IU held a game-and-a-half lead over second-place Purdue in the conference standings. The Hoosiers were 23-2 overall, ranked second in the country, and were on track for a No. 1 seed in the NCAA tournament's Midwest Regional, where IU would get to play the first two rounds in the Hoosier Dome in Indianapolis. However, IU's conference title hopes and postseason positioning were thrown into uncertainty when the Hoosiers lost back-to-back road games at No. 6 Purdue and No. 14 Illinois. After the Illinois loss, IU (14-3) trailed Purdue (15-2) heading into the final weekend of the regular season, and it looked like the Boilermakers were now on track to get the No. 1 seed in the Midwest. But a change of fortune reshuffled the deck on Saturday, March 7, when IU rolled to a 90-81 win over Ohio State on Senior Day in Assembly Hall, and then Purdue got crushed 104-68 by Michigan in Ann Arbor. Thus, the Hoosiers and the Boilermakers tied for the Big Ten title.

Purdue's unimpressive showing against Michigan caused the Boilermakers to slip to a No. 3 seed in the East Regional of the NCAA tournament and opened the way for Indiana to get its coveted No. 1 seed in the Midwest. Just as Knight had hoped, IU used the Hoosier Dome as a launching pad for a deep NCAA run. In the first round, the Hoosiers manhandled Fairfield 92-58 as the IU frontcourt of Garrett, Thomas and Calloway combined for 51 points. Then, in the second round, IU fell behind Auburn early and ended up having to play at the Tigers' fast pace in order to keep up. The Hoosiers got huge performances out of several players and pulled away in the second half to post a 107-90 victory. Alford hit seven three-

pointers and led all scorers with 31 points. Smart nearly had a triple-double with 20 points, 15 assists, and nine rebounds. Thomas added 27 points and eight rebounds while Calloway chipped in 18 points and 13 rebounds.

In the Sweet Sixteen, IU matched up with 17th-ranked Duke, the NCAA runner-up from 1986. It was the first time that Knight and his former player and assistant Mike Krzyzewski—the skipper at Duke since 1980—had squared off in the coaching arena. The Blue Devils had a talented roster that included multiskilled sophomore Danny Ferry and guards Tommy Amaker and Quinn Snyder, and they jumped out to an early 29-21 lead. But then the Hoosiers started opening up things on offense for Alford and Calloway, who triggered a 28-10 run to give IU a 49-39 halftime lead. In the second half, the Blue Devils hung tough, but the Hoosiers never relinquished control of the game and won 88-82. All five Hoosier starters scored in double figures, led by 21 apiece from Smart and Calloway.

In the regional finals, IU had a surprising matchup with the 10th-seeded LSU Tigers, who had already upset No. 2 seed Temple and No. 3 seed DePaul. The year before, LSU was an 11th seed in the Southeast Regional and upset the No. 1, 2, and 3 seeds to make a run to the 1986 Final Four. They nearly repeated that improbable accomplishment. The Tigers had IU down for most of the second half and led 75-66 with 4:38 remaining. But then Dean Garrett dunked in a rebound, Daryl Thomas stole the ball, and Joe Hillman converted a fast-break layup and a foul for a three-point play. Next, Thomas sank two free throws. Suddenly IU trailed only 75-73 with 3:01 left to play. LSU stalled, and then guard Daryl Joe put them up 76-73 with 0:50 to go when he got fouled and made one of two free throws. Ten seconds later, Keith Smart hit both ends of a one-and-one to cut the lead to 76-75. When LSU freshman Fess Irvin missed the front end of one-and-one on the other end, Indiana got the rebound and had a chance to win with 0:26 remaining. As he often chose to do, Knight didn't call a timeout. IU made its move when Thomas screened for Alford, the defenders followed Alford and Thomas cut to the middle and received the ball. He faked and then released a ten-footer as he jumped into LSU's Jose Vargas. Thomas's shot came up short —an air ball—but Calloway swooped in and snatched it out of the air and then softly banked it into the basket all in one motion. IU won 77-76. Alford had 20 points and seven assists and Garrett had 17 points and 15 rebounds, but the hero was Calloway, the Cincinnati native who made the game-winning play in his hometown and also contributed 11 points, five rebounds, and five assists.

In the Final Four in New Orleans, IU played UNLV in one national semifinal while Jim Boeheim's Syracuse Orangemen faced Rick Pitino's Providence Friars in the other semifinal. All the talk was about IU-UNLV game, which pitted the No.1-ranked Runnin' Rebels with their free-wheeling, high-scoring attack, against the No. 2-ranked Hoosiers and their precision offense. UNLV was 37-1, with the only loss being a one-point defeat to Oklahoma, and they looked nearly unbeatable. Almost everyone expected IU to play a ball control game to slow down UNLV, but Coach Knight actually feared the Rebels' rugged, physical defense more than their offense. Surprisingly, he decided the best way to beat UNLV was to outrun them, and the Hoosiers did just that. Sixteen minutes into the game, IU led 41-27, but UNLV closed it to 53-47 at the break. The Rebels, who got huge per-

formances out of Armon Gilliam (32 points and 10 rebounds), Freddie Banks (38 points on 10 three-pointers), and Mark Wade (18 assists), led briefly midway through the second half, but then IU went on a 12-2 run and never trailed again on the way to a 97-93 triumph. Alford pumped in 33 points, Garrett had 18 points and 11 rebounds, and Calloway added 12 points, six rebounds, and six assists.

In the NCAA championship game, Indiana met Syracuse, who had defeated Providence 77-63. In the regional finals, Syracuse, ranked 10th in the nation, had also knocked off third-ranked North Carolina, one of the favorites to win the tournament. In the first half of the NCAA final, both teams played well, and neither could gain the upper hand. Alford carried IU throughout the first 20 minutes, and he drilled a three-pointer as time expired to give the Hoosiers a 34-33 lead going into the locker room. For the Orangemen, freshman power forward Derrick Coleman already had 13 rebounds, and he and center Rony Seikaly were dominating the inside against the Hoosiers.

Syracuse quickly grabbed the lead at the start of the second half and upped their advantage to as much

Indiana's game-winning basket swishes through the net as Keith Smart's momentum carries him past the base-line. Smart was the one who shot the basket that downed Syracuse 74-73 in one of the most thrilling NCAA championship games in the history of the tournament. IU Archives

In a ceremony at the White House, U.S. president Ronald Reagan congratulates coach Bob Knight, Steve Alford, Daryl Thomas, and Todd Meier on IU's national championship victory. IU Archives

as eight points. They led 52-46 with 12:12 left to play. That's when Keith Smart, who had been pulled out of the game early in the second half following an errant lob pass, re-entered the fray. Knight would later say that over those final 12 minutes "Keith Smart made as many big plays in critical situations as anybody I've ever seen."

Within minutes of returning, Smart broke down the Syracuse defense with a drive and fed Thomas for a dunk to tie the game at 52-52. Then Smart gave IU the lead with a flying, twisting layup around Siekaly, but the Orangemen fought back and went ahead 61-56 on several key plays by point guard Sherman Douglas. A couple of minutes later, Smart tied it again at 61-61 with a driving layup. Syracuse didn't back down and made several key plays of its own, but every time the Orangemen seemed ready to pull away, Smart almost always responded. Siekaly scored to give Syracuse a 70-68 lead with time ticking away, but Smart came back and drove the baseline, sliced between Siekaly and Coleman and sank a reverse layup. Then, Syracuse forward Howard Triche broke loose inside and scored to give the Orangemen back the lead at 72-70 with 0:52 left. Smart missed a jumper, and Triche rebounded and

was fouled. He buried the first and missed the second, which caromed off the front of the rim and was deflected out to Smart, who grabbed the ball and raced it up court. He pulled up and sank a leaning 10-footer to cut the lead to 73-72 with 30 seconds left. IU put on a full-court press and fouled Coleman at the 0:28 mark.

When Coleman missed the front end of the one-and-one, and Thomas snatched the rebound, IU went down court without a timeout to go for one last shot. Alford ran off multiple screens, but he couldn't shake loose from Douglas. The ball went to Smart, who drove to the left elbow and jumped into the air, drawing Coleman off Thomas. Smart dished back to Thomas, who tried to drive the baseline but Coleman quickly recovered and didn't bite on Thomas's head fake. Instead of forcing a tough shot, Thomas (who had been rejected by Siekaly and Coleman several times earlier in the game) dished to Smart, who curled behind him. Smart received the pass and leapt high in the air and faded toward the baseline in order to create enough space for an open shot. The ball looped precipitously through the air and then hit the bottom of the net with 0:05 left on the clock. Syracuse couldn't get a timeout called until 0:01. They tried a desperation full-court pass, but it was intercepted by Smart, and the game was over. IU won 74-73 and Coach Knight clinched his third national championship at Indiana. Smart finished with 21 points, six assists, and five rebounds and was named the Most Outstanding Player of the Final Four. Alford scored 23 points and was also named to the All-Final Four team. Thomas had 20 points and seven rebounds and Garrett finished with 10 points and 10 rebounds. For Syracuse, Siekaly and Coleman combined for 26 points and 29 rebounds.

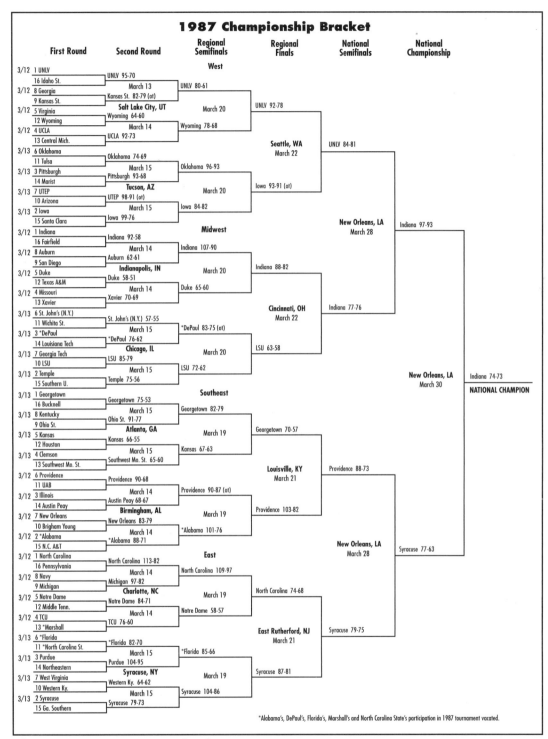

The 1987 NCAA tournament bracket.

It was only fitting that IU won the 1987 national championship in a game that went down to the wire. These Hoosiers were a perfect 4-0 in one-point games and 13-2 in games decided by five points or less. Knight said, "This team played the last five minutes of critical games as well as I've ever seen a team play." That was legacy of greatness left by the 1986-87 Hoosiers.

CHAPTER 5

THE BEST DEFENSE IN COLLEGE BASKETBALL

1980-81

OVERALL RECORD: 26-9

CONFERENCE RECORD: 14-4 (FIRST PLACE)

TEAM HONORS:

NCAA CHAMPION, BIG TEN CHAMPION, INDIANA CLASSIC CHAMPION

INDIVIDUAL HONORS:

BOB KNIGHT—BIG TEN COACH OF THE YEAR

ISIAH THOMAS—ALL-AMERICA, FINAL FOUR MOST OUTSTANDING PLAYER,
ALL-FINAL FOUR, ALL-BIG TEN (FIRST TEAM)

RAY TOLBERT—BIG TEN MVP

LANDON TURNER—ALL-FINAL FOUR

JIM THOMAS—ALL-FINAL FOUR

RANDY WITTMAN—ACADEMIC ALL-BIG TEN

After Indiana won the national championship in 1976, Coach Bob Knight lost a group of five seniors that had come to Indiana as part of the top recruiting class in school history and left as the most decorated group to ever wear the cream and crimson. However, Knight's opponents in the coaching profession must have been shaking their heads, because in the fall of 1976 he had a group of six freshmen coming to Bloomington that were being hailed as a recruiting class that surpassed even the one that the seniors in 1976 had been a part of in 1972.

When the 1979-80 season rolled around, and the 1976 recruiting class readied for their senior campaign, the team was ranked No. 1 team in the preseason polls, just like the seniors in 1975-76 had been. Although only three of the original six recruits remained, they appeared destined to follow in the footsteps of the 1976 team and lead IU to another national championship.

Unfortunately, that date with destiny was spoiled when senior Mike Woodson, IU's leading scorer and co-captain, went down with a back injury in December. Woodson returned in February, and led IU to six straight victories to close the Big Ten season and

capture the conference crown, but he didn't have enough left in the tank for the NCAA Tournament, and the Hoosiers bowed out in the Sweet Sixteen. It seemed as if the Hoosiers had missed a rare opportunity to snare another NCAA title. Surprisingly, that date with destiny simply got postponed for a year.

With the graduation of Woodson and senior co-captain Butch Carter, Indiana seemed to be losing the very heart of its team. Woodson had been the Hoosiers' go-to guy for three straight seasons, while Carter had been a steady performer that had come through in the clutch in several big games. Both of them had also shown tremendous leadership as seniors. Their departure not only left a gaping leadership void, but also took a big punch out of the Hoosiers' offense because the two of them combined to average 30.4 points per game.

The role of team captains now fell to seniors Ray Tolbert, IU's most potent inside player, and Glen Grunwald, a versatile forward who had actually been part of the 1976 recruiting class with Woodson and Carter, but had sat out a season as a medical redshirt. Tolbert was Indiana's top returning rebounder. In fact, he had led the Hoosiers in rebounding for three

The 1980-81 team. First row (left to right): manager Steve Skoronski, Eric Kirchner, Ray Tolbert, Glen Grunwald, Steve Risley, Phil Isenbarger. Second row: assistant coach Gerry Gimelstob, assistant coach Jene Davis, Chuck Franz, Randy Wittman, Isiah Thomas, Ted Kitchel, assistant coach Jim Crews, trainer Bob Young; Third row: team physician Dr. Brad Bomba, head coach Bob Knight, Landon Turner, Mike LaFave, Steve Bouchie, Tony Brown, Jim Thomas, administrative assistant Steve Downing. IU Archives

straight seasons (and he would do it again as a senior). Tolbert was strong, athletic, and always active on the court, and he often energized the IU squad and the Assembly Hall crowd with his powerful dunks. Grunwald was slowed by two knee surgeries and limited to a role as a reserve. The team's other seniors, Phil Isenbarger, Steve Risley and Eric Kirchner, also played limited reserve roles. The only other upperclassman on the roster was 6'10" junior Landon Turner, who was skilled, athletic and versatile, but his inconsistent play during this first two years had made him a near-permanent resident of Knight's doghouse. Turner would later joke that he was the one who built Coach Knight's doghouse.

While there were six upperclassmen on the IU roster, and Tolbert and Grunwald were the co-captains, the mantle of leadership was firmly grasped by sophomore guard Isiah Thomas. His grooming for that role had actually begun the previous season, when, as a freshman, he became IU's floor leader during the time when Woodson was sidelined by midseason back surgery. During his sophomore season, the Hoosiers became Isiah's team. The strong-willed point

guard was not only the team's catalyst on the floor, but he also emerged as the leader off the court, even though he was still a teenager. Thomas had come to Indiana as one of the most widely renowned recruits of that era, and he was spectacular as a freshman, averaging 14.6 points, 5.5 assists, and 4.0 rebounds per game and earning first-team All-Big Ten honors (the first freshman to ever merit that selection). He stood only 6'1" (in sneakers), but he was quick, agile and deceptively strong. He was a tremendous shooter and scorer who could put up points in bunches, but only did so when the team needed it. He had the basketball savvy that belied his baby face and enabled him to make the right pass, anticipate a steal on defense, and know when to drive and when to pull up for the jump shot. But beyond all that, he was a hard-nosed competitor that seemed to want to win just a little bit more than everyone else, and was willing to do whatever his team needed to pull out a victory. With Woodson gone, he also became the Hoosiers' primary scorer.

Four other sophomores joined Isiah in the Hoosiers' regular rotation. Ted Kitchel, a 6'8" forward,

1980-81 TEAM ROSTER

Head coach: Bob Knight
Assistant coaches: Roy Bates, Jim Crews, Jene Davis, Gerry Gimelstob

No.	Player	Hometown	Class	Position	Height
42	Craig Bardo	Carbondale, IL	Fr	G	6-5
54	Steve Bouchie	Washington, IN	So	F	6-8
31	Tony Brown	Chicago, IL	So	G	6-2
23	Chuck Franz	Clarksville, IN	So	G	6-2
40	Glen Grunwald (Capt.)	Franklin Park, IL	Sr	F	6-9
44	Phil Isenbarger	Muncie, IN	Sr	F	6-8
33	Eric Kirchner	Edelstein, IL	Sr	F	6-8
30	Ted Kitchel	Galveston, IN	So	F	6-8
43	Mike LaFave	Indianapolis, IN	Fr	F	6-9
34	Steve Risley	Indianapolis, IN	Sr	F	6-8
11	Isiah Thomas	Chicago, IL	So	G	6-1
20	Jim Thomas	Fort Lauderdale, FL	So	G	6-3
45	Ray Tolbert (Capt.)	Anderson, IN	Sr	F/C	6-9
32	Landon Turner	Indianapolis, IN	Jr	F/C	6-10
24	Randy Wittman	Indianapolis, IN	So	G/F	6-6

1980-81 SEASON STATISTICS

Team Statistics	G	FG%	FT%	R	A	TO	S	B	PF	PTS	PPG
Indiana	35	.530	.744	32.7	16.6	12.9	6.4	2.2	18.5	2451	70.0
Opponents	35	.436	.716	31.5	11.8	15.2	5.2	2.1	19.0	2048	58.5

Player Statistics	G-GS	FG%	FT%	R	A	TO	S	B	PF	PTS	PPG
I. Thomas	34-34	.554	.742	3.1	5.8	3.1	2.2	0.1	3.1	545	16.0
Tolbert	35-35	.588	.740	6.4	1.4	2.0	0.7	1.1	2.6	428	12.2
Wittman	35-32	.542	.768	2.3	2.2	1.1	0.8	0.1	1.8	363	10.4
Turner	33-18	.561	.717	3.7	0.8	2.0	0.5	0.5	2.8	314	9.5
Kitchel	34-27	.465	.854	3.3	1.4	1.3	0.5	0.1	2.6	314	9.2
J. Thomas	33-10	.495	.771	3.2	2.3	1.0	0.7	0.2	1.3	121	3.7
Brown	28-8	.458	.536	1.3	1.2	1.1	0.5	0.0	0.8	91	3.3
Risley	31-8	.452	.651	2.3	0.7	0.5	0.3	0.1	1.0	94	3.0
Grunwald	27-1	.512	.615	1.2	0.6	0.6	0.1	0.0	1.1	50	1.9
Isenbarger	26-0	.600	.650	1.2	0.6	0.5	0.2	0.0	0.8	43	1.7
Bouchie	29-0	.383	.818	1.2	0.3	0.2	0.1	0.0	1.3	45	1.6
Franz	21-0	.583	.875	0.3	0.6	0.4	0.1	0.0	0.7	28	1.3
Bardo	4-0	.333	.667	0.3	0.0	0.5	0.0	0.0	1.3	4	1.0
LaFave	15-0	.375	.625	0.9	0.1	0.1	0.1	0.1	0.3	11	0.7

Isiah Thomas, Ray Tolbert, Randy Wittman, and Ted Kitchel share a laugh on the bench during an IU blowout.
IU Archives

and Randy Wittman, a 6'6" guard, were both third-year players that had lost a season to a medical redshirt. Both were starters on the 1980-81 team. Kitchel was an excellent shooter who also possessed some crafty moves in the paint and was a strong defender. Wittman started alongside Isiah in the backcourt and served as a reliable sniper from the outside and could use his size to disrupt smaller guards on defense. Sophomore guards Tony Brown, a tough 6'2" playmaker, and Jim Thomas, a well-rounded 6'3" wing player, provided additional punch off the bench.

Clearly, the Hoosiers were still well stocked with talent, even with the departure of Woodson and Carter. The big question mark was how all of the pieces would fit together and gel into a new dynamic, since IU lost the two players that served as the heart of the team and its unifying thread. The process was anything but smooth at first, and the difficulty was compounded by an intense preconference schedule that included three tough road games, two tournaments, and three top-ten opponents.

Isiah Thomas sat out Indiana's opener because of a pulled groin muscle. IU still beat Ball State 75-69 on November 29, in Assembly Hall, but it wasn't pretty. The Hoosiers missed a lot of shots within 10 feet of the basket and struggled to stop the Cardinals' 5'9" guard Ray McCallum, who scored a game-high 25 points. Isiah returned for IU's second contest of the season, but things didn't get much better. The Hoosiers trailed Murray State 33-30 at the half in Bloomington on December 1, but IU bounced back and held the Racers to just eight second-half points on the way to a 59-41 Indiana victory.

After two shaky wins to start the season, IU certainly didn't appear well prepared to host the second-ranked Kentucky Wildcats on December 6. However, fifth-ranked Indiana stayed right with Kentucky and even took control of the game at the beginning of the second half, but faltered down the stretch and lost 68-66. The pivotal play of the game came in the final minutes with the game tied 62-62. Isiah tossed an alley-oop pass over Kentucky's Sam Bowie to Ray

Indiana's powerful center Ray Tolbert smiles as he cuts down the net in Assembly Hall following the Hoosiers' 78-46 win over St. Joseph's in the NCAA's Mideast regional final, which was held in Bloomington.
IU Archives

Tolbert, who leapt up and slammed it, but the ball went in and out. Kentucky scored on its next possession and then controlled the ball in the final minutes. The Wildcats also won the game by outrebounding the Hoosiers 37-28.

In the first road game of the season, Indiana lost to No. 9 Notre Dame 68-64 in South Bend, as John Paxson shot down the Hoosiers with a game-high 18 points. Landon Turner led all scorers with 23 points for IU. After that, Indiana rolled to wins over California and Baylor in the Indiana Classic and beat Oral Roberts in Indianapolis to improve to 5-2. However, IU would lose three of next five games.

On December 20, the Hoosiers went down to Chapel Hill, North Carolina, and grabbed a 30-24

halftime lead from Dean Smith's North Carolina Tar Heels. IU pushed the lead to 34-26, before the Tar Heels got hot and ran to a 65-56 win in front of a booming home crowd. Isiah Thomas had a game-high 20 points, but also had second-half defensive problems against UNC's Al Wood, who finished with 18 points. North Carolina manhandled IU on the glass, with a 35-21 advantage. Three days later, IU captured its first road game by winning 51-44 at Kansas State. Isiah dished out 10 assists, Randy Wittman scored 14 points, and Ted Kitchel chipped in 10 points. Finally, the Hoosiers closed out the preconference schedule in Hawaii at the Rainbow Classic. In the opening round, Indiana got off to a fast start and then barely held on to beat Rutgers 55-50. The next night, Clemson

Point guard Isiah Thomas confers with coach Bob Knight about IU's strategy during a game in Bloomington.
IU Archives

scored the final four points of the game to steal a 58-57 victory from the Hoosiers. To add insult to injury, in the consolation game IU got manhandled in the paint and on the boards by Pan American and lost 66-60. Thus, the Hoosiers finished the pre-conference slate with a disappointing 7-5 record.

"We have a lot of unanswered questions about our team that I had hoped to have answered by this time," said Knight after the Pan American game. "There's a certain way we have to play in our league, and we're certainly not there yet… I'm very, very dissatisfied with the play of our inside people. We have been getting beaten very, very badly inside. If we can't improve ourselves inside, we're going to have a long 18 games [in the Big Ten]."

Fortunately, the Hoosiers opened conference play with two home games, and they used those two contests to steady themselves. Isiah's 20 points sparked a 55-43 win over Michigan State on January 8, and two days later, Ted Kitchel exploded for 40 points (on 11-13 shooting from the field and 18-18 from the line) to catapult Indiana to a 78-61 upset of No. 12 Illinois. Ray Tolbert also added 16 points for IU, and the Hoosiers outrebounded their opponents for the second straight game.

After jumping to the head of the pack with a 2-0 start, Indiana had to play four of its next five games on the road. The Hoosiers were able to pull out three victories during that tough stretch and remain at the top of the league standings. They lost to No. 9

Michigan in Ann Arbor and fell to No. 14 Iowa in Assembly Hall, but they won road games at Ohio State, at Northwestern, and at No. 19 Minnesota. Then IU took sole possession of first place in the Big Ten by defeating archrival Purdue 69-61 in Gene Keady's first introduction to the IU-Purdue series as the Boilermaker coach. Isiah Thomas led all scorers with 26 points against Purdue, while Kitchel contributed 19 points and seven rebounds for the Hoosiers. It was an extremely physical—and sometimes combative—contest that set the tone for two decades of highly intense and competitive games between Knight and Keady teams. A week later, after IU had blown out Wisconsin 89-54, Keady got his first taste of crimson blood as Purdue upset 17th-ranked IU 68-66 in Mackey Arena where Kevin Stallings sank two free throws with only five seconds left in the game to deliver a Boilermaker triumph.

Next, Indiana beat Northwestern and Wisconsin to improve to 9-3 in the conference and set up a showdown with co-league leader Iowa in Iowa City on February 19. The Hawkeyes trailed by two at the half, but came back and pulled off a 78-65 win to take sole possession of first place. However, despite the disheartening loss that included a late-game ejection of Isiah Thomas, there was one positive note for the Hoosiers. Landon Turner came off the bench to lead IU with 18 points, and the 6'10" center showed some great defense by locking down Iowa's Jeff Boyle, a wing player. It was one of

Isiah Thomas (left) and Jim Thomas talk at center court during the Final Four. Both of the Thomases ended up being named to the All-Final Four team, with Isiah winning the Most Outstanding Player award.
IU Archives

1980-81 SEASON RESULTS

Date	Court	Opponent	Result	Score
11/29/1980	H	Ball State	W	75-69
12/1/1980	H	Murray State	W	59-41
12/6/1980	H	(#2) Kentucky	L	66-68
12/9/1980	A	(#9) Notre Dame	L	64-68
12/12/1980	H	California	W	94-58
12/13/1980	H	Baylor	W	83-47
12/15/1980	N1	Oral Roberts	W	65-56
12/20/1980	A	(#8) North Carolina	L	56-65
12/23/1980	A	Kansas State	W	51-44
12/28/1980	N2	Rutgers	W	55-50
12/29/1980	N2	Clemson	L	57-58
12/30/1980	N2	Pan American	L	60-66
1/8/1981	H	Michigan State	W	55-43
1/10/1981	H	(#12) Illinois	W	78-61
1/15/1981	A	(#9) Michigan	L	52-55
1/18/1981	A	Ohio State	W	67-60
1/22/1981	H	(#14) Iowa	L	53-56
1/24/1981	A	Northwestern	W	93-56
1/29/1981	A	(#19) Minnesota	W	56-53
1/31/1981	H	Purdue	W	69-61
2/5/1981	H	Wisconsin	W	89-64
2/7/1981	A	Purdue	L	66-68
2/12/1981	H	Northwestern	W	86-52
2/14/1981	A	Wisconsin	W	59-52
2/19/1981	A	(#12) Iowa	L	65-78
2/21/1981	H	Minnesota	W	74-63
2/26/1981	H	Ohio State	W	74-58
2/28/1981	H	Michigan	W	98-83
3/5/1981	A	(#16) Illinois	W	69-66
3/7/1981	A	Michigan State	W	69-48

NCAA Tournament

Date	Court	Opponent	Result	Score
3/14/1981	N3	(#18) Maryland	W	99-64
3/20/1981	N4	UAB	W	87-72
3/22/1981	N4	St. Joseph's	W	78-46
3/28/1981	N5	(#4) Louisiana State	W	67-49
3/30/1981	N5	(#6) North Carolina	W	63-50

1 Indianapolis, IN
2 Honolulu, HI
3 Dayton, OH
4 Bloomington, IN
5 Philadelphia, PA

Turner's best all-around performances in an Indiana uniform, and it was his third strong performance in a row. He had struggled badly with inconsistent effort early in the season, but it looked as if he was finally ready to step up and help provide the missing punch that the Hoosiers needed on the inside. His performance against Iowa earned him a starting spot in the next game. Turner never relinquished that starting spot for the rest of the reason, and the Hoosiers didn't lose another game.

After the Iowa loss, IU returned to Bloomington and mowed down Minnesota, Ohio State, and Michigan—all by double digits. Turner scored 16, 20, and 15 points in those three games, while Isiah Thomas broke loose for 39 against Michigan. Unfortunately, Iowa also won three straight to stay a game ahead of IU with only two games remaining in the regular season. Both the Hawkeyes and the Hoosiers played their final two games on the road. While Iowa played at Michigan State and Ohio State, two second-division Big Ten teams, 14th-ranked Indiana had to play at No.16 Illinois and then at Michigan State.

The Illinois team that awaited Indiana in Champaign on March 5, was like a coiled, crouching tiger waiting to pounce. The Fighting Illini were only a game behind the Hoosiers, and a win would tie them with IU for second place, with an outside shot at the Big Ten crown if Iowa lost two straight. Illinois hadn't won a conference title in 18 years, and the Illini felt like they had a score to settle with IU and Knight for robbing the state of some of its best players during the previous decade. Those players included Isiah Thomas and Quinn Buckner, the leader of IU's 1976 national championship team. The Illinois campus and the city of Champaign were bursting with anticipation for the crucial game. Predictably, the Fighting Illini broke quickly out of the starting gate, but only led 32-28 at the half. IU quickly caught

1980-81 BIG TEN STANDINGS

	W	L	PCT
Indiana	14	4	.778
Iowa	13	5	.722
Illinois	12	6	.667
Purdue	10	8	.556
Minnesota	9	9	.500
Ohio State	9	9	.500
Michigan	8	10	.444
Michigan St.	7	11	.389
Wisconsin	5	13	.278
Northwestern	3	15	.167

up at the beginning of the second half, and the two fiercely competitive teams traded baskets and the lead several times until IU spread the floor on offense and worked the ball for two straight lay-ups to take a 59-56 lead. The Hoosiers were never out of control after that and deflated the raucous Illinois crowd with a 69-66 victory. Ray Tolbert led the Hoosiers with 14 points and eight rebounds. That same night, Michigan State upset Iowa 71-70, which opened the door for IU in the Big Ten race. Two days later, Ohio State upset Iowa in the early afternoon game, which meant the Hoosiers could claim the conference title outright with a win in their season finale later that afternoon. Playing in East Lansing, the Indiana squad came out and pummeled Michigan State 69-48 to seize the undisputed Big Ten crown—IU's second straight. Tolbert had a game-high 17 points while Turner had 16 points and nine rebounds.

With five straight wins, Indiana was one of the hottest teams in the nation. Because of their less-than-stellar overall record (21-9), they were only granted a

INDIANA'S RANKING IN THE 1980-81 ASSOCIATED PRESS POLLS

PS	12/2	12/9	12/16	12/23	12/30	1/6	1/13	1/20	1/27	2/3	2/10	2/17	2/24	3/3	3/10
5	5	7	11	15	15	—	—	—	—	17	20	16	16	14	9

No. 3 seed in the NCAA Tournament, but they were given the blessing of having a first-round bye and playing in the Mideast Regional, which was hosting its regional semifinals and finals in Assembly Hall in Bloomington. If IU could get win its first matchup, then it would have an excellent shot at winning two straight games in Assembly Hall and making it to the Final Four. The Hoosiers blasted the 18th-ranked Maryland Terrapins 99-64 in Dayton, Ohio, as Turner and Tolbert combined for 46 points and 15 rebounds and Isiah Thomas had 19 points and 14 assists.

The next week, IU took advantage of the rare opportunity of playing on its home floor in the NCAA Tournament. In the regional semifinals, the Hoosiers won an 87-72 victory over a scrappy UAB team that had upset No. 2 seed Kentucky in the second round. Isiah Thomas had 27 points and eight assists and his backcourt mate Randy Wittman chipped in 20 points. In the regional finals, IU charged to a 78-46 win over St. Joseph's, which had upset No. 1 seed DePaul in the second round. Tolbert and Turner scored 14 points apiece and Jim Thomas contributed 12 points off the bench. The Hoosiers set a new NCAA record by shooting .686 (35-51) from the field against St. Joseph's. The victory gave Coach Knight a berth in his third Final Four in ten seasons at IU.

Indiana had defeated the teams seeded six, nine and seven in the Mideast Regional and had the good fortune of playing two of the three games on its home court. However, if there were any feelings that IU was only in the Final Four in Philadelphia because it had an easy road in the early rounds, then those notions were shattered when the Hoosiers soundly thumped LSU, the No. 1 seed from the Midwest Regional, 67-49 in the national semifinals. IU trailed by three points at the intermission, but opened the second half on 21-4 run in the first nine minutes to take a 48-34 lead with 10:52 remaining. The key to that run was Turner, who ended up scoring 12 of Indiana's first 25 points in the second half and went on to a 20-point, eight-rebound performance. Jim Thomas came off the bench to lead IU

During the 1981 NCAA finals at the Spectrum in Philadelphia, IU guard Randy Wittman finds a seam in the defense and pulls up for one of his classic jump shots.
IU Archives

on the glass with nine rebounds.

In the other national semifinal, North Carolina upset ACC rival Virginia, led by All-America center Ralph Sampson. That set up an NCAA championship game between two of college basketball's master coaches—Bob Knight and Dean Smith. Both were proponents of disciplined, precision offense and aggressive defense and both had already accomplished unprecedented success at their respective schools. For Smith, it was his sixth trip to the Final Four, and this time he did it with a supremely talented team led by a front court of James Worthy, and Sam Perkins. In the previous five occasions, Smith had failed to win the title, and he would have to wait one more year to have his first breakthrough.

Mobbed by reporters and Hoosier fans, Ray Tolbert lifts the NCAA symbol in triumph after Indiana's 63-50 victory over the North Carolina Tar Heels in the 1981 NCAA championship game. IU Archives

The game itself was nearly postponed or cancelled after an assassination attempt earlier in the day against president Ronald Reagan, but the game went on as scheduled. The Tar Heels led 16-8 in the opening minutes and looked capable of blowing out the Hoosiers. Indiana never led in the first half until Randy Wittman buried a jumper as the horn sounded to give IU a 26-25 lead heading into the locker room. The Hoosiers grabbed the momentum at the start of the second half when Isiah Thomas picked off a pair of Tar Heel passes and converted them into layups to give Indiana a 31-28 advantage. IU soon built the lead to 43-34 and never looked back on the way to a 63-50 victory. Thomas, who scored only four points on 1-7 shooting in the first half, was brilliant in the second half, scoring 19 points to finish with a game-high 23. He was named the Most Outstanding Player of the Final Four. Turner added 12 points, Tolbert grabbed 11 rebounds, and Jim Thomas came off the bench and dished out a game-high eight assists.

At the time, IU's nine losses were the most ever by an NCAA champion, providing a counterpoint to the 1976 IU team that recorded the most wins ever by an NCAA champion with 32 (tying the 1957 North Carolina team). However, by the end of the season, the 1981 team was playing nearly at the same level of excellence as the 1976 team had achieved.

The enduring memories of this team tend to be

Isiah Thomas slashing to the basket, Randy Wittman burying jump shots, Ray Tolbert slamming home dunks, and Landon Turner sinking short baseline jump shots, but the real key to this squad was defense. They held opponents to a miserly 58.5 points per game, the lowest since the 1950-51 Indiana team held opponents to a 53.3 scoring average in a low-scoring era in which most teams shot only 20-30 percent from the field. And no Hoosier team since the 1980-81 season has been able to match that defensive stinginess of that team. Interestingly, IU's leader, Isiah Thomas, jumped to the NBA after the 1981 season and became a member of the Detroit Pistons, a team that eventually revolutionized the NBA by relying on a record-setting defense to win back-to-back NBA championships in 1989 and 1990.

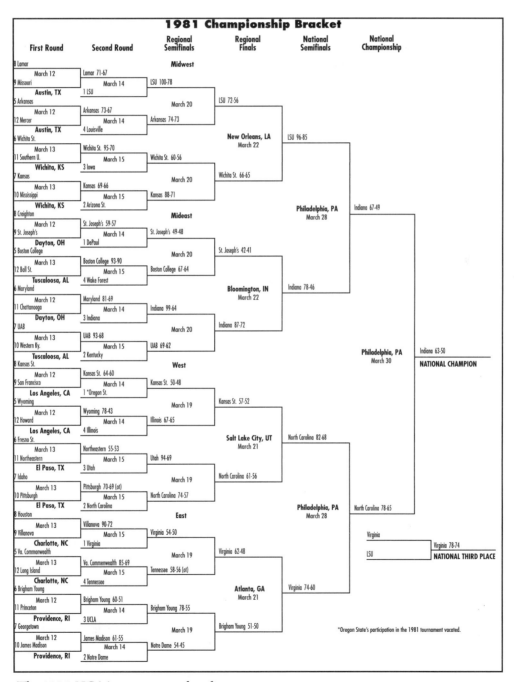

The 1981 NCAA tournament bracket.

CHAPTER 6

THE ARRIVAL OF THE HURRYIN' HOOSIERS

1939-40

OVERALL RECORD: 20-3

CONFERENCE RECORD: 9-3 (SECOND PLACE)

TEAM HONORS:

NCAA CHAMPIONSHIP

INDIVIDUAL HONORS:

BRANCH McCRACKEN—UPI NATIONAL COACH OF THE YEAR

MARV HUFFMAN—ALL-AMERICA,

FINAL FOUR MOST OUTSTANDING PLAYER, ALL-FINAL FOUR

BILL MENKE—ALL-AMERICA, ALL-FINAL FOUR

JAY McCREARY—ALL-FINAL FOUR

CURLY ARMSTRONG—ALL-BIG TEN (FIRST TEAM)

When Everett Dean turned over the reins of IU basketball to Branch McCracken and headed out to Stanford University in 1938, he left the Indiana program with a full cupboard of talent—especially young talent that Dean had recruited before his departure. The nucleus of this talented group was the recruiting class of 1937. Its players were freshmen during Dean's final season in Bloomington and joined the varsity as sophomores during McCracken's first year on the Hoosier sidelines. The headliners were Bill Menke, Paul "Curly" Armstrong, Herm Schaefer and Bob Dro, and in their three seasons on the varsity they would amass an overall record of 54-9.

They got an immediate opportunity for quality playing time as sophomores during the 1938-39 season, because the Hoosiers only had two seniors on the roster. McCracken molded that young team into a fast-breaking juggernaut that ran to a 17-1 record near the end of February and had some journalists calling them the best team in college basketball. However, the Hoosiers dropped their final two games of the season to lose the Big Ten championship and finish 17-3. Despite the disappointing ending, it was one of the most successful seasons in IU history. The team's 17 wins was the second highest total ever racked up by an Indiana team.

That powerful squad returned 12 lettermen and three of its top four scorers for the 1939-40 season. The Hoosiers lost All-America guard Ernie Andres and three-year letterman Bill Johnson to graduation, but two other seasoned players rejoined the Hoosiers. High-scoring Herm Schaefer had been ineligible during the second semester of the 1938-39 season, and he returned for a full campaign in 1939-40. Jay McCreary, a former all-state player who led Frankfort to the 1936 Indiana high school championship while being coached by the legendary Everett Case, returned to IU as a junior after taking a year off of school. He had played on Dean's 1937-38 squad as a sophomore.

Indiana's top returning scorer was junior center Bill Menke, who had averaged 9.8 PPG as a sophomore and finished fourth in the Big Ten scoring race. The 6'3", 175-pound Menke was a fast and agile pivotman who was a perfect fit for McCracken's running game. In his first two years on campus, Menke showed off his speed and endurance by winning IU's intramural cross-country run both years. On the basketball court, his younger brother, Bob, served as his backup at center. Junior forward Curly Armstrong was Indiana's other high-scoring returnee. He averaged 7.6 PPG as a sophomore, which trailed only Menke and Andres. Although he stood only 5'11", Armstrong was an

The 1939-40 team. First row (left to right): Jim Gridley, Herm Schaefer, Bob Dro, Marv Huffman, Jay McCreary, Curly Armstrong, Ralph Dorsey; Second row: head coach Branch McCracken, Chet Francis, Bill Menke, Andy Zimmer, Bob Menke, assistant coach Ralph Graham. IU Archives

excellent shooter who knew how to put the ball in the basket, and he would end up leading the Hoosiers in scoring in 1939-40. Armstrong was from Fort Wayne, where he had teamed with fellow Hoosier Herm Shaefer since the fourth grade and had played on the 1936 Fort Wayne Central team that finished as the runner-up in the Indiana state tournament.

While those five juniors—Menke, Armstrong, Schaefer, Dro, and McCreary— handled most of the scoring for the Hoosiers, the team's stalwart floor leader and captain was senior Marv Huffman. Although he wasn't a prolific scorer, Huffman was an excellent all-around player that could dribble, pass, defend, and, above all else, lead. "I'm telling you, if you were slacking off, not playing your best, you had better watch him—because he'd punch you," said Bob Dro years later. "You did your best or you had to face him."

It wasn't a big team (the starters averaged 6'0" in height), but they were fast and versatile—with an emphasis on fast. McCracken loved the running game and always preferred players that could get up and down the floor. During his first season at IU, Big Mac had begun to unveil his running attack, and by his second season (1939-40) he fully implemented it. Coach McCracken believed that the players enjoyed the running game and had fun playing that style, and thus, he could get more out of them by running. He had also seen professional basketball beginning to draw crowds using a high-scoring running attack and he was very interested in promoting the sport and increasing attendance at games. And, of course, McCracken felt that he could win with the fast break by simply overwhelming opponents in many games.

"All we care about is getting the ball in the enemy basket in the shortest possible time," said McCracken.

1939-40 TEAM ROSTER

Head coach: Branch McCracken
Assistant coach: Ralph Graham

No.	Player	Hometown	Class	Position	Height
33	Curly Armstrong	Fort Wayne, IN	Jr	F	5-11
16	James Clifton	Bentonville, IN	Jr	C	6-3
30	Ralph Dorsey	Horse Cave, KY	Sr	F	5-10
38	Bob Dro	Berne, IN	Jr	G	5-11
9	Chet Francis	Avon, IN	Jr	G	6-1
25	Bill Frey	Kokomo, IN	So	F	6-1
27	James Gridley	Vevay, IN	Jr	G	6-0
21	Max Hasler	Elnora, IN	So	G	5-10
11	Everett Hoffman	Evansville, IN	So	C	6-3
23	Don Huckleberry	Salem, IN	So	G	5-9
34	Marv Huffman (Capt.)	New Castle, IN	Sr	G	6-2
10	Jay McCreary	Frankfort, IN	Jr	G	5-10
29	Robert Menke	Huntingburg, IN	Jr	F	6-3
35	William Menke	Huntingburg, IN	Jr	C	6-3
26	Tom Motter	Fort Wayne, IN	Jr	F	6-1
19	Ed Newby	Indianapolis, IN	So	G	5-11
13	Jim Ooley	Spnecer, IN	Sr	G	6-2
32	Herm Schaefer	Fort Wayne, IN	Jr	F	6-0
20	Jack Stevenson	Indianapolis, IN	Sr	F	6-1
28	William Torphy	Bedford, IN	So	G	6-0
24	John Torphy	Bedford, In	So	F	5-11
18	Cliff Weithoff	Seymour, IN	So	G	6-0
7	Andy Zimmer	Goodland, IN	So	C	6-4
10	Harold Zimmer	Springfield, OH	Jr	F	5-8

"Our emphasis is on rolling up those points. Our defense lies primarily in our offense. 'Go! Go! Go!' is our watchword. Think of the ball as a red-hot potato that must be kept moving … and the faster the better."

McCracken's other major innovation was to begin converting his players from shooting the traditional two-handed set shot to the new one-handed shot (popularized by Stanford's Hank Luisetti in the late 1930s). Players could develop a much quicker release with the one-handed shot, and it was much more difficult to defend. Big Mac had his players regularly practice hundreds of one-handed shots in order to master the technique.

The Hoosiers jumped out of the starting gates with easy wins over Wabash (37-24) and Xavier (58-24). Herm Shaefer led IU in scoring in both games with eight points against the Little Giants and 14 against the Musketeers. In its first road game at Nebraska, Indiana kept its fast-breaking attack hitting on all cylinders by beating the Cornhuskers 49-39. IU trailed 19-15 at the break, but simply blew past Nebraska in the second half. Bob Dro led all scorers with 16 points, while Bill Menke chipped in 12 and Curly Armstrong added 10. Next, the Hoosiers continued to mow down opponents, crushing Pittsburgh 51-35 in Bloomington and coming from behind to beat Butler 40-33 in Indianapolis. That put the Hoosiers at 5-0.

Finally, Indiana closed out the preconference schedule with a two-game road trip to Pennsylvania during the holiday break. The first game was a December 27 matchup with Duquesne in Pittsburgh.

1939-40 SEASON STATISTICS

Team Statistics	G	FG/A	PCT	FT/A	PCT	TP	AVG
Indiana	23	428-1561	.274	192-359	.535	1048	45.6
Opponents	23					814	35.4

Player Statistics	G	FG/A	PCT	FT/A	PCT	TP	AVG
Armstrong	23	78-276	.283	48-85	.565	204	8.9
Schafer	23	77-247	.312	30-53	.566	184	8.0
W. Menke	23	71-269	.264	35-66	.530	177	7.7
Dro	23	65-250	.260	16-36	.444	146	6.4
McCreary	21	40-126	.317	14-30	.467	94	4.5
Huffman	23	41-180	.228	16-28	.571	98	4.3
A. Zimmer	18	13-56	.232	6-10	.600	32	1.8
Francis	13	9-30	.300	3-5	.600	21	1.6
Frey	2	1-4	.250	1-2	.500	3	1.5
R. Menke	19	10-38	.263	5-10	.500	25	1.3
J. Torphy	11	5-10	.500	4-8	.500	14	1.3
Dorsey	19	8-40	.200	7-11	.636	23	1.2
Gridley	16	7-28	.250	4-10	.400	18	1.1
Stevenson	6	1-2	.500	2-4	.500	4	0.7
Ooley	3	1-3	.333	0-0	.000	2	0.7
Motter	7	1-2	.500	1-1	1.00	3	0.4
Hasler	3	0-2	.000	0-0	.000	0	0.0
Clifton	1	0-1	.000	0-0	.000	0	0.0
Hoffman	1	0-0	.000	0-0	.000	0	0.0
Weithoff	1	0-0	.000	0-0	.000	0	0.0
H. Zimmer	1	0-1	.000	0-0	.000	0	0.0

Both teams were undefeated, and they locked horns in a terrific battle. The Dukes jumped out to a 29-17 lead with under three minutes left in the first half, but Indiana reeled off a 10-0 run over the final minutes of the first half and the opening minutes of the second half to cut the lead to 29-27. It was a see-saw battle the rest of the way. Bill Menke carried the Hoosiers by repeatedly scoring on one-handed shots that bewildered the Duquesne defense. But the Dukes kept pace. The score was tied at 45, 47 and 49, but on each of those occasions, the Hoosiers made clutch baskets to push back in front. The final was a 51-49 Indiana victory, as Menke scored a game-high 22 points. The next day, IU went down to Philadelphia and beat Villanova 45-33, as Armstrong broke loose for 18 points. The Wildcats had been riding a six-game winning streak before Indiana came to town.

Conference play began on January 6, when IU hosted Illinois. That game ran counter to the Hoosiers' normal pattern of play, which was to hold their ground in the first half and then make a big run in the second half to put the game away. Indiana led Illinois 21-12 at the break, but the Fighting Illini made a big second half surge to get back in the game. IU barely held on for a 38-36 victory, led by 17 points from Armstrong. Two days later, Indiana won its ninth straight game by clobbering Iowa 45-30 as Bill Menke scored a game-high 11 points and Dro added 11.

On January 13, in the Minnesota Fieldhouse (later renamed Williams Arena), the Hoosiers' winning streak came to an end in breathtaking fashion. Indiana trailed Minnesota 29-16 at the half, and the Hoosiers' first loss looked like a forgone conclusion. However, in the first eight minutes of the second half,

Agile center Bill Menke was the third leading scorer on Indiana's 1940 NCAA championship team. He later became a navy pilot and served in World War II. In January 1945 he was declared missing in action (and presumed dead) when he didn't return from a flight in the Caribbean. IU Archives

Team captain Marv Huffman was a demanding floor leader and a fierce competitor. He wasn't a huge scorer but was an excellent passer, defender, and rebounder. After scoring 12 points in the NCAA championship game and serving as the catalyst of the Hoosiers' revolutionary fast-break attack, Huffman was named the Most Outstanding Player of the 1940 NCAA finals. IU Archives

the IU squad outscored the Golden Gophers 20-1 to take a 36-30 lead. With a minute and a half left to play, Indiana led 44-40, but the Gophers cut the lead in half when backup center Willie Warhol scored inside. Then, Minnesota tied it with another basket with 0:25 left on the clock. Indiana hurried the ball up court to look for a winning shot, but with four seconds left to play, the ball came loose under the basket and Minnesota's John Pearson grabbed it and threw it ahead to Warhol, who took a dribble past midcourt and released a desperation heave. The final gun

sounded as the ball hung precipitously in the air, and when it swished through the net, the Minnesota Fieldhouse exploded into a frenzy. The Gophers pulled off the upset 46-44.

After the heartbreaking loss to Minnesota, IU had to stay up north and play at Wisconsin a couple days later. The Hoosiers bounced back with a 40-34 win over the Badgers that gave IU a 3-1 record heading into its two-week semester break. After the break, Indiana cruised to a 51-30 nonconference win over DePaul in Chicago. Then the Big Ten race started heating up. Indiana pulled even with Purdue at 4-1 by beating the Boilermakers 46-39 in front of a sellout crowd of 6,500 in Bloomington on February 10. Next, the Hoosiers throttled second-place Michigan 57-30 in the IU Fieldhouse, but then dropped a 40-36 contest to Northwestern in Evanston. Against the Wildcats, Indiana trailed 25-12 at the half, but the team made its usual second-half run. Herm Schaefer came off the bench to spark the Hoosiers with nine straight points to cut the Northwestern lead to 38-34 with two minutes to play, but Indiana couldn't get any closer and ended up with its second conference loss. That put the Hoosiers a game behind Purdue. Indiana won its next two games over Iowa and Chicago to improve to 7-2, but Purdue also kept winning and stayed a step ahead at 8-1.

Nearly all the air went out of Indiana's title hopes on February 28, in Columbus, Ohio. The Hoosiers fell behind Ohio State early and never caught up, as the Buckeyes easily prevailed 44-26. The Hoosiers shot an abysmal 12-77 (16 percent) from the field. The loss put Indiana a full two games behind the Boilermakers with only two games left to play. And next, IU had to go into West Lafayette to take on Purdue on Saturday, March 2.

The Hoosiers hadn't won in West Lafayette in 17 years. An overflowing, record-setting crowd of 9,150 greeted the IU squad, but the Hoosiers kept them fairly quiet by controlling the game nearly start to finish and posting a surprising 51-45 victory. Dro led IU with 13 points, while Armstrong and McCreary chipped in 11 each. The following Monday, Indiana crushed Ohio State 52-31 in Bloomington to finish with a 9-3 conference record. The Hoosiers could only hope that Illinois could knock off Purdue in Champaign that same night, which would have given

Indiana a share of the conference crown. Unfortunately, not long after IU finished off the Buckeyes, word came that Purdue defeated Illinois 34-31 to win the Big Ten title outright. One small consolation for the Hoosiers is that they broke the Big Ten scoring record with 519 points in conference play, besting the record of 512 set by Purdue in 1934.

Then, the day after the season ended, the Hoosiers received a pleasant surprise when they heard that the NCAA's selection committee had chosen them to represent the Big Ten in the new postseason tournament that was being held to crown a national champion. Even though Purdue had won the Big Ten title, the committee selected IU because it viewed the Hoosiers as the stronger team since they had a better overall record (17-3 to 16-4), and because they had defeated the Boilermakers twice that season (an alternative account claims that Purdue was actually offered the invitation but declined since Purdue coach Piggy Lambert and the Purdue administration felt that Indiana deserved to go).

The 1940 tournament was actually the first one that was organized by the NCAA. The year before, the National Association of Basketball Coaches (NABC) had held a national tournament, with the approval of the NCAA, and Oregon emerged as the winner of the 1939 title. The NCAA officially recognized the 1939 tournament, and then took over the affair in 1940. One of the prime motivators for a national tournament came from the fact that a private group of promoters had started the National Invitational Tournament (NIT) in 1938, which was played in New York City's Madison Square Garden. If money was going to be made on a postseason tournament, then the NCAA and the schools it represented wanted some of that money

returned to the schools themselves, rather than just fattening the pockets of a few private promoters.

The field for the 1940 tournament included eight teams that were divided into two regions. A group of four eastern teams (Indiana, Springfield, Duquesne, and Western Kentucky) were set to play in Indianapolis, while four western teams (USC, Colorado, Rice, and Kansas) would play in Kansas City. The winners of those two regionals would then meet in a title game in Kansas City to decide the national championship. Entering the tournament, the two favorites were probably USC, which was 19-2 and considered by many to be the best team in col-

The Indiana defense stifles a Purdue scoring opportunity during a 46-39 victory over the Boilermakers in the IU Fieldhouse. IU's sweep of Purdue was the key to the season because it ultimately earned the Hoosiers a berth in the 1940 NCAA Tournament. IU Archives

1939-40 SEASON RESULTS

Date	Court	Opponent	Result	Score
12/9/1939	H	Wabash	W	37-24
12/11/1939	H	Xavier	W	58-24
12/15/1939	A	Nebraska	W	49-39
12/18/1939	H	Pittsburgh	W	51-35
12/23/1939	A	Butler	W	40-33
12/27/1939	A	Duquesne	W	51-49
12/28/1939	A	Villanova	W	45-33
1/6/1940	H	Illinois	W	38-36
1/8/1940	H	Iowa	W	45-30
1/13/1940	A	Minnesota	L	44-46
1/15/1940	A	Wisconsin	W	40-34
2/3/1940	A	DePaul	W	51-30
2/10/1940	H	Purdue	W	46-39
2/12/1940	H	Michigan	W	57-30
2/17/1940	A	Northwestern	L	36-40
2/19/1940	A	Iowa	W	46-42
2/24/1940	H	Chicago	W	38-34
2/28/1940	A	Ohio State	L	26-44
3/2/1940	A	Purdue	W	51-45
3/4/1940	H	Ohio State	W	52-31

NCAA Tournament

Date	Court	Opponent	Result	Score
3/22/1940	N1	Springfield	W	48-24
3/23/1940	N1	Duquesne	W	39-30
3/30/1940	N2	Kansas	W	60-42

1 Indianapolis, IN
2 Kansas City, MO

lege basketball, and Colorado, which had already won the 1940 NIT. Those two powerhouses ended up facing off in the opening round of the NCAA tournament, and USC prevailed 38-32.

Indiana had to wait two and a half weeks after its season ended before playing its first-round tournament game on Friday, March 22, at the Butler Fieldhouse. The Hoosiers were pitted against Springfield College, which had racked up a 16-2 record and averaged a gaudy 49 PPG (IU had averaged a record-setting 43 PPG). Surprisingly, Indiana ran Springfield right out of the gym. IU led 30-11 at the half, and then 41-14 when McCracken removed the rest of his starters. The final was 48-24. Ten different Hoosiers scored in the

game, led by 14 points from Herm Schaefer. In the second round the next day, Indiana met Duquesne, which had only lost twice. They lost to IU in December and to Colorado in the NIT championship game. IU jumped out to another big halftime lead at 25-13, but the Dukes made a determined comeback and cut the lead to five midway through the second half. With four minutes to play, the Hoosiers went into an effective stall and pulled out a 39-30 victory to win the eastern regional.

In the western regional, Kansas upset USC 43-42. If the Trojans had won, it would have made for a title game with a heavy Indiana flavor since the USC team was made up primarily of recruits from Indiana

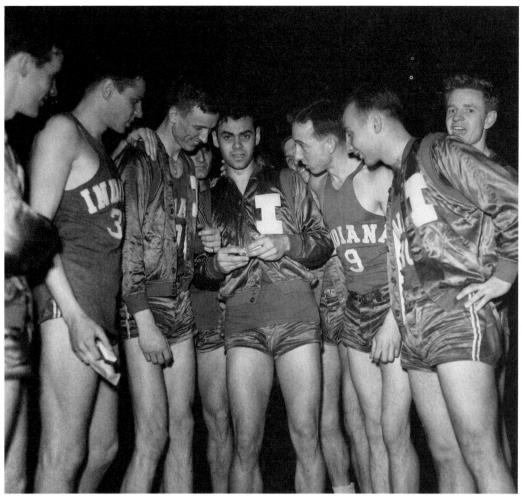

The Hoosiers gather around team captain Marv Huffman to admire one of the gold watches that all of the team members received after winning the 1940 NCAA championship game over the Kansas Jayhawks. IU Archives

high schools, including All-American Ralph Vaughn (who had been a former teammate of Jay McCreary's at Frankfort).

For the NCAA championship game, 10,000 fans crowded into the Kansas City Municipal Auditorium on Saturday, March 30. The crowd had a distinctly Jayhawk flavor since the game was being played only 40 miles away from the University of Kansas campus. Still, IU was playing some of its best basketball of the season, and the Hoosiers strode into the game with a lot of confidence. Early on, they had a little fun with the Jayhawks. IU swung the ball around to Curly Armstrong, who gave a terrific head and shoulder fake. Bob Allen, the son of Kansas coach Phog Allen, fell for the fake, and as a result, took a shot to the chin

1939-40 BIG TEN STANDINGS

	W	L	PCT
Purdue	10	2	.833
Indiana	9	3	.750
Ohio State	8	4	.667
Illinois	7	5	.583
Northwestern	7	5	.583
Michigan	6	6	.500
Minnesota	5	7	.417
Iowa	4	8	.333
Wisconsin	3	9	.250
Chicago	1	11	.083

One of Indiana basketball's most colorful characters, Paul "Curly" Armstrong was a practical joker, but he was also the leading scorer on the high-powered 1940 IU squad. Armstrong went on to a fruitful career in professional basketball. *IU Archives*

from Armstrong that knocked him down. Allen was dazed and lying on the floor when Armstrong leaned over, pointed to the Kansas bench and told Allen, "Maybe you better sit with daddy." Armstrong got called for a foul, which prompted him to playfully ruffle up the referee's hair and then get back to the contest at hand.

The Indiana squad couldn't pull away from the Jayhawks early in the game the way they had against Springfield and Duquesne. After 13 minutes of play, IU led only 17-14, but then the Hoosiers kicked their running game into overdrive and hit Kansas with a 15-5 run that put IU up 32-19 at the half. From there, the Hoosiers kept running all the way to an impressive 60-42 triumph. After the game, Sam Barry, coach of the high-powered USC team, declared, "I knew Indiana was fast, but not that fast."

Jay McCreary, Bill Menke and Marv Huffman were named to the all-tournament team, and Huffman, the Hoosiers' erstwhile leader who had scored 12 points against Kansas, was fittingly given the Most Outstanding Player award for the tournament.

At the time, Indiana was often known nationally as "the basketball state." Thus, after the NCAA triumph, IU president Herman Wells said, "It is fitting that the state of Indiana should be the home of the national basketball champions."

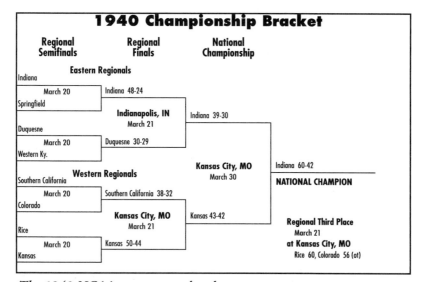

The 1940 NCAA tournament bracket.

CHAPTER 7

A RETURN TO THE INDIANA TRADITION

2001-02

OVERALL RECORD: 25-12

CONFERENCE RECORD: 11-5 (FIRST PLACE)

TEAM HONORS:

NCAA RUNNER-UP, BIG TEN CO-CHAMPION

INDIVIDUAL HONORS:

JARED JEFFRIES—ALL-AMERICA, BIG TEN MVP,

ALL-BIG TEN (FIRST TEAM)

DANE FIFE—BIG TEN DEFENSIVE PLAYER OF THE YEAR

KYLE HORNSBY—ACADEMIC ALL-BIG TEN

MIKE ROBERTS—ACADEMIC ALL-BIG TEN

When the 2001-02 college basketball season rolled around, it had been nine long years since Indiana had won a Big Ten title, eight years since the team had made it past the second round in the NCAA tournament, ten years since the Hoosiers had been to the Final Four, and 15 years since IU had won a national championship. The Indiana Basketball program was still reeling from the controversial dismissal of longtime coach Bob Knight in September 2000. That event had split the fan base between those who still supported the IU team, and those who remained disgruntled over Knight's firing and ambivalent about rooting for the Hoosiers now that Knight was no longer leading them.

Following Knight's dismissal, the IU administration named his assistant coach Mike Davis as the interim head coach for the 2000-01 season. Surprisingly, Davis led a Hoosier team with no seniors and only three juniors to 21 wins, including five victories over ranked opponents (including two top five teams), and a run to the championship game of the Big Ten conference tournament. At the end of the season, Davis's interim tag was removed. Also, as that 2000-01 season came to a close, the young Indiana Hoosiers looked like they would enter the following season (2001-02) as one of the top ranked teams in college basketball and one of the favorites for the national championship. However, junior center Kirk Haston threw an unexpected wrench

into those plans. Haston, an All-American and All-Big Ten selection and the Hoosiers' leading scorer and rebounder, chose to leave IU and enter the 2001 NBA draft.

Haston's exodus meant that Indiana had to find a new go-to guy on offense, and 6'10" sophomore forward Jared Jeffries was the heir apparent. He was IU's top returning scorer and rebounder at 13.8 PPG and 6.9 RPG and he had earned Big Ten Freshman of the Year honors in his rookie season in Bloomington. He came to IU as the 2000 Indiana Mr. Basketball, the 2000 Gatorade National Player of the Year, and a McDonald's All-American, and he had seriously considered turning pro straight out of high school. Jeffries also came to Indiana with a reputation as a highly versatile performer that could play both inside and outside and who possessed excellent ball-handing and passing skills for a player of his size. Between his freshman and sophomore seasons, Jeffries bulked up, improved his strength, and developed his low-post moves so that he could be more effective playing the power forward position. The other important—but often overlooked —aspects of Jeffries's game were his defense and his high basketball IQ. On defense, the long-armed Jeffries was a good post defender and also provided excellent help defense and shot blocking. On both ends of the floor, he was a confident player that usually made good decisions and helped his team-

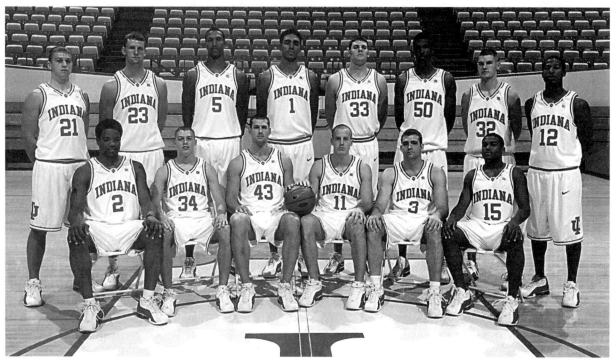

The 2001-02 team. First row (left to right): A.J. Moye, Ryan Tapak, Jarrad Odle, Dane Fife, Tom Coverdale, Scott May, Jr.; Second row: Mark Johnson, Sean Kline, George Leach, Jared Jeffries, Mike Roberts, Jeff Newton, Kyle Hornsby, Donald Perry. IU Athletics

mates stick to the game plan. He was tabbed as a preseason All-American heading into the 2001-02 campaign and he didn't disappoint.

Next to Jeffries, Indiana's top returning scorer was junior point guard Tom Coverdale, who had been one of the most improved players in America as a sophomore in 2000-01. After seeing limited minutes as a freshman, Coverdale, the 1998 Indiana Mr. Basketball, won the starting point guard job on the 2000-01 squad and averaged 10.7 PPG and 4.8 APG. He earned a reputation as a good floor leader, a hardnosed defender, and dangerous three-point shooter with deep range. Meanwhile, Coverdale's backcourt running mate, 6'4" senior Dane Fife, was a defensive specialist who always matched up against the opponent's best wing player. "Fife is one of the toughest players to play against in the country," said Coach Davis. "He works so hard on defense, and his dedication on that end of the court forces [his teammates] to play even harder." Fife had been a big-time scorer in high school, averaging over 25 PPG as a senior and earning a spot as a McDonald's All-American, but entering his senior year he had only averaged 4.4 PPG in his IU career.

Since his arrival in Bloomington, Fife had been one of the Hoosiers' best shooters in practice, but he had a hard time carrying it over to games. Davis asked him to take on more of a scoring role as a senior, and Fife would respond with the best offensive season of his career.

While returning starters Jeffries, Coverdale and Fife were expected to be the heart of the team, the two biggest wildcards for the Hoosiers were guard Kyle Hornsby and forward Jeff Newton. Both of them had flashed the potential for excellent play, but neither had been consistent—Hornsby because of a series of injuries and Newton because he had a laidback personality and was still learning the type of consistent effort required in college basketball. Hornsby was a three-point sniper who always kept the defense honest. Netwon was a lithe 6'9" athlete who could score inside with a variety of spin moves and fade away jumpers. He was also an excellent shot blocker on defense, but his skinny frame sometimes allowed him to be pushed around in the paint by bigger, stronger players.

In the battle to fill Haston's starting spot in the lineup, Newton had to compete with 6'8" senior

2001-02 TEAM ROSTER

Head coach: Mike Davis
Assistant coaches: John Treloar, Jim Thomas, Ben McDonald

No.	Player	Hometown	Class	Position	Height
3	Tom Coverdale	Noblesville, IN	Jr	G	6-2
32	Kyle Hornsby	Anacoco, LA	Jr	G	6-5
11	Dane Fife (Capt.)	Clarkston, MI	Sr	G	6-4
1	Jared Jeffries	Bloomington, IN	So	F	6-10
23	Sean Kline	Huntington, IN	Rs	F	6-8
5	George Leach	Charlotte, NC	So	C	6-11
21	Mark Johnson	Oregon, WI	Fr	G	6-2
15	Scott May Jr.	Bloomington, IN	Rs	G	6-0
2	A.J. Moye	Atlanta, GA	So	G	6-3
50	Jeff Newton	Atlanta, GA	Jr	F	6-9
43	Jarrad Odle (Capt.)	Swayzee, IN	Sr	F	6-8
12	Donald Perry	Tallulah, LA	Fr	G	6-2
33	Mike Roberts	Eugene, OR	Rs	F	6-9
34	Ryan Tapak	Indianapolis, IN	Fr	G	6-2

2001-02 SEASON STATISTICS

Team Statistics	G	FG%	3FG%	FT%	R	A	TO	S	B	PF	PTS	PPG
Indiana	37	.460	.411	.694	35.2	14.8	13.7	6.9	5.2	17.0	2607	70.5
Opponents	37	.408	.359	.662	33.5	11.1	14.0	7.1	3.7	19.0	2316	62.6

Player Statistics	G-GS	FG%	3FG%	FT%	R	A	TO	S	B	PF	PTS	PPG
Jeffries	36-36	.457	.380	.667	7.6	2.1	2.8	1.5	1.3	2.4	539	15.0
Coverdale	37-32	.417	.370	.788	3.2	4.8	2.7	1.5	0.1	2.0	439	11.9
Odle	35-23	.540	.444	.620	5.0	0.7	1.2	0.3	0.2	2.2	309	8.8
Fife	37-37	.461	.478	.702	2.6	2.5	1.8	1.4	0.2	2.7	321	8.7
Newton	37-5	.496	.500	.737	5.1	0.8	1.5	0.6	1.9	2.3	298	8.1
Hornsby	37-33	.429	.447	.552	2.6	1.9	1.0	0.7	0.2	1.9	286	7.7
Moye	37-4	.479	.400	.805	3.1	0.6	0.6	0.3	0.2	1.6	218	5.9
Leach	32-10	.500	.000	.514	2.5	0.3	0.7	0.2	1.5	1.2	90	2.8
Perry	37-5	.378	.226	.634	1.4	1.1	1.4	0.3	0.0	1.0	95	2.6
Tapak	14-0	.375	.500	.500	0.3	0.1	0.1	0.1	0.0	0.0	9	0.6
Johnson	12-0	.167	.500	.000	0.3	0.0	0.1	0.2	0.0	0.1	3	0.3

Sophomore forward Jared Jeffries uses his long reach to extend for an easy finger roll against Penn State. Jeffries was a force on both ends of the court during the 2001-02 season, and his outstanding play earned him Big Ten MVP honors. IU Athletics

Jarrad Odle and 6'11" sophomore George Leach. Odle offered strength, experience, leadership and a nice face-up jump shot, while Leach was an incredible athlete who could run and jump but was very raw in terms of basketball skills. Two younger frontcourt

players, Sean Kline and Mike Roberts, ended up redshirting. In the backcourt, sophomore A.J. Moye and freshman Donald Perry both challenged for starting spots but ended up as key reserves. Moye, who averaged over 30 PPG as a forward in high school and was the 2000 Mr. Basketball in Georgia, was a tough, athletic, high-energy player who provided a spark off the bench by hustling, getting offensive rebounds, and scoring inside and outside. Perry, the 2001 Louisiana Mr. Basketball, was quick and had decent dribbling and ball-handling skills that allowed him to become a much-needed backup for Coverdale at point guard.

At the start of the season, Coach Davis decided to go with a three-guard lineup of Coverdale, Fife and Hornsby, with Jeffries and Newton manning the frontcourt. That left Leach and Odle to back up the frontcourt, Moye to fill in for Fife and Hornsby on the wings, and Perry to sub for Coverdale. Even without Haston, Indiana started the 2001-02 campaign ranked 22nd in the country, but the Hoosiers faced a brutal preconference schedule and took some lumps in November and December.

IU opened the season in a hostile arena in Charlotte, North Carolina, where the Charlotte 49ers of Conference USA had the Hoosiers down by 12 points in the middle of the second half. That's when Charlotte native George Leach came in and sparked IU with several key baskets, blocks and rebounds. His mammoth dunk at the 6:35 mark tied the game at 51-51, and the Hoosiers went on to a 65-61 win. Tom Coverdale scored a game-high 18 points, and Leach finished with eight points, seven rebounds, and four blocks in 18 minutes of play.

Next, the Hoosiers flew north for the Great Alaska Shootout on November 21-24. IU opened with a 101-66 drubbing of tournament host, Alaska Anchorage. The Hoosiers set a new school record by hitting 16 three-pointers, led by Dane Fife, who shot 6-8 from three-point land and scored a career-high 20 points. In the second round, IU lost to Marquette (which ended up being ranked in the top 10 later in the season) 50-49 when guard Dwayne Wade scored on a rebound basket with 11 seconds remaining. In the tournament's consolation game, Davis benched Newton, Hornsby and Coverdale in favor of Leach, Moye, and Perry and the Hoosiers beat Texas 77-71. It was virtually the same Texas team that had clobbered IU 70-58 the year before in the Preseason NIT.

This time, Fife and Jeffries made all the big plays down the stretch to deliver the victory for the Hoosiers, who finished third in Alaska and improved to 3-1 on the season.

Led by 20 points and six rebounds from Moye, the Hoosiers then went into Chapel Hill and stole a 79-66 win from the North Carolina Tarheels in the ACC-Big Ten Challenge on November 28. Coverdale added 17 points off the bench. Three days later, the road-weary Hoosiers dropped a 72-60 game to a very good Southern Illinois team, to fall back to 4-2 on the season.

Then, IU finally got to play a couple of games in Assembly Hall. The Hoosiers slipped by Notre Dame 76-75, led by a game-high 28 points from Jeffries, and pounded No. 15 Ball State 74-61 as Jeffries scored 22 points and Coverdale added 19. At that point, IU was 6-2 and ranked No. 21 in the country. The team looked like it was coming together and headed toward a good season. But then, the Hoosiers dropped three of their final four games of the preconference schedule to fall to 7-5. The worst loss during that final stretch was a 66-52 defeat to Kentucky at the RCA Dome in Indianapolis on December 22. Against the Wildcats, Indiana really struggled offensively, making only 32 percent of its field goals.

Coach Mike Davis appeals to his team to calm down.
IU Athletics

Leading scorer Jared Jeffries was only 4-15 from the floor. During the game, Kentucky's athleticism just seemed to overwhelm the Hoosiers. Afterwards, a disheartened Mike Davis seemed to be stating the obvious when he admitted, "We're not going to win a national championship this year." He was right, of course, but on that night he never would have guessed just how close his team would come to capturing the national title.

In IU's Big Ten opener at Northwestern on January 2, center George Leach got his ninth start of the year. However, on the opening tip, Leach injured his ankle and had to go to the bench. He was replaced by Jarrad Odle, who hadn't started a game all season. Odle ended up having a huge game with 16 points and 15 rebounds, and IU prevailed 59-44. The 6'8" senior ended up starting all but one of the Hoosiers' final 23 games. For Indiana, the Northwestern win

was the first time since 1987 that the team had opened the conference season with a victory on the road. However, the Hoosiers followed up that win with a lackluster performance against Penn State in Assembly Hall, in which IU shot 28 percent from the field and barely scraped out a 61-54 victory.

Then, Indiana suddenly caught fire. It started with an 83-65 throttling of 25th-ranked Michigan State on January 8. In a game that was nationally televised on ESPN, Jared Jeffries did a little bit of everything for the Hoosiers with 21 points, eight rebounds, seven assists, and six blocked shots, while Tom Coverdale hit six consecutive threes in the first half and finished with 22 points. Coming into the game, Coverdale had been on a five-for-26 streak on three-pointers.

The Hoosiers followed up the Michigan State win with an impressive 77-66 triumph over No. 13

2001-02 SEASON RESULTS

Date	Court	Opponent	Result	Score
11/18/2001	A	Charlotte	W	65-61
11/21/2001	A	Alaska-Anchorage	W	101-66
11/23/2001	N1	Marquette	L	49-50
11/24/2001	N1	Texas	W	77-71
11/28/2001	A	North Carolina	W	79-66
12/1/2001	A	Southern Illinois	L	60-72
12/4/2001	H	Notre Dame	W	76-75
12/8/2001	H	(#15) Ball State	W	74-61
12/15/2001	N2	Miami	L	53-58
12/22/2001	N3	(#7) Kentucky	L	52-66
12/28/2001	N3	Eastern Washington	W	87-60
12/29/2001	N3	(#23) Butler	L	64-66
1/2/2002	A	Northwestern	W	59-44
1/5/2002	H	Penn State	W	64-54
1/8/2002	H	(#25) Michigan State	W	83-65
1/13/2002	A	(#13) Iowa	W	77-66
1/19/2002	A	Ohio State	L	67-73
1/23/2002	A	Penn State	W	85-51
1/26/2002	H	(#9) Illinois	W	88-57
1/31/2002	H	Purdue	W	66-52
2/2/2002	A	Minnesota	L	74-88
2/5/2002	H	Iowa	W	79-51
2/9/2002	H	Louisville	W	77-62
2/13/2002	H	Wisconsin	L	63-64
2/17/2002	A	Michigan	W	75-55
2/20/2002	H	(#19) Ohio State	W	63-57
2/24/2002	A	Michigan State	L	54-57
2/26/2002	A	(#15) Illinois	L	62-70
3/2/2002	H	Northwestern	W	79-67

Big Ten Tournament

Date	Court	Opponent	Result	Score
3/8/2002	N3	Michigan State	W	67-56
3/9/2002	N3	Iowa	L	60-62

NCAA Tournament

Date	Court	Opponent	Result	Score
3/14/2002	N4	Utah	W	75-56
3/16/2002	N4	UNC Wilmington	W	76-67
3/21/2002	N5	(#1) Duke	W	74-73
3/23/2002	N5	Kent State	W	81-69
3/30/2002	N6	(#3) Oklahoma	W	73-64
4/1/2002	N6	(#4) Maryland	L	52-64

1 Anchorage, AK
2 Miami, FL
   (American Airlines Arena)
3 Indianapolis, IN
4 Sacramento, CA
5 Lexington, KY
6 Atlanta, GA

Iowa in Iowa City, where IU hadn't won since 1994. Jeffries led the way with 26 points and seven rebounds and Coverdale chipped in 15 points and eight assists. The Iowa victory put Indiana at 4-0 in league play and tied for the Big Ten lead, but on January 19, the Hoosiers suffered their first loss, 73-67 to conference co-leader Ohio State in Columbus. IU bounced back and closed out its three-game road trip by stomping Penn State 85-51 as Jeffries put up 22 points and 13 rebounds, and Coverdale had 13 points and nine assists against the Nittany Lions.

Next, Indiana collided with No. 9 Illinois, the Big Ten favorite, on Saturday, January 26, in Bloomington. The Hoosiers and the Fighting Illini had developed an edgy rivalry after facing each other in the Big Ten Tournament in each of the three previous seasons. The Illini upset the Hoosiers in 1999 and then edged them out with a last-second shot in 2000, while the Hoosiers upset the top-seeded Illini in 2001. Coming into this game, Indiana was 5-1 in conference play while Illinois was 4-2 (having already lost at Wisconsin and Purdue). The Illini needed a win to pull even with the Hoosiers in the conference race, while the Hoosiers needed a victory to keep up with Ohio State. Because Jeffries had burned three straight opponents with 20-point games, the Illini started out by hawking him early in the game, but he kept passing out of double teams to find the open man, and the Hoosiers used excellent ball rotation to get open shots. The result was a three-point barrage that resembled IU's earlier attacks against Alaska Anchorage (16 threes) and Michigan State (14 threes). Against the Illini, IU got the home crowd rocking by drilling nine out of 15 threes in the first half. Plus, Jeff Newton further ignited Assembly Hall with a beautiful tip-in jam, as well as the dunk of the year—a vicious slam in which he ran the floor, got a pass from Dane Fife, elevated high above Illini forward Lukas Johnson, cocked the ball behind his head, and threw it down with authority. He also drew the foul and hit the free throw for a three-point play. IU led 46-35 at the break.

In the locker room, Coach Davis challenged the Hoosiers by telling them that a really good team would take a 10-point lead and try to turn it into 20 at the beginning of the second half. His team did even better than that. They opened the half with a 26-6 run to put Illinois into a 72-41 hole. The most exciting stretch during that run came when Kyle Hornsby

2001-02 BIG TEN STANDINGS

	W	L	PCT
Ohio State	11	5	.688
Illinois	11	5	.688
Indiana	11	5	.688
Wisconsin	11	5	.688
Michigan State	10	6	.625
Minnesota	9	7	.563
Northwestern	7	9	.438
Iowa	5	11	.313
Purdue	5	11	.313
Michigan	5	11	.313
Penn State	3	13	.188

buried a three, then Jeffries got a tip-jam on the fast break, then on the ensuing possession, Jeffries stole the ball and went the length of the court for a reverse dunk. Then Hornsby capped off the 10-0 spurt with another three. When the dust finally settled, Indiana walked away with an 88-57 victory and the Hoosiers had set a new school and Big Ten record by hitting 17 three-pointers. Fife was the head sniper, hitting 6-7 from three-point land and scoring a game-high 20 points. Coverdale added 16 points and Hornsby contributed 15. Jeffries finished with 13 points, 11 rebounds. Not to be overlooked, Indiana's defense held Illinois, one of the highest-scoring teams in the Big Ten, to 37 percent shooting for the game. Overall, it ended up being Indiana's most dominating performance of the season.

IU followed up the Illinois win by manhandling archrival Purdue 66-52 in Assembly Hall to finish the first half of the league schedule at 7-1 and tied atop the standings with Ohio State. Next, the Hoosiers traveled up to "The Barn" in Minneapolis and blew an 11-point halftime lead in a tough 88-74 loss to Minnesota. Indiana shook off that loss and completed the season sweep of Iowa with a 79-51 drubbing of the Hawkeyes in Bloomington, as all five Hoosier starters scored in double figures. Next, the Hoosiers got an early NCAA tune-up when Rick Pitino's running, pressing Louisville Cardinals came into Assembly Hall. The Cardinals needed a quality win over a marquee opponent in order to improve their

Donald Perry, Jarrad Odle, Jared Jeffries, and Tom Coverdale raise the Big Ten championship trophy. The 2002 conference title broke a nine-year drought for league championships in Bloomington. IU Athletics

a 64-63 heartbreaker to Wisconsin to fall back to 8-3 in conference play.

However, after IU whipped Michigan 75-55 in Ann Arbor later that week, the Hoosiers stood tied with Ohio State for the Big Ten lead. And the 19th-ranked Buckeyes were on their way to Assembly Hall for a February 20 matchup with the 23rd-ranked Hoosiers. Over the first 30 minutes, both teams battled like champions as the momentum swung back and forth. IU led 28-24 at the half, but with under 10 minutes remaining, the score was tied 41-41. That's when Jeffries stepped out and buried a three-pointer to trigger a 13-0 Hoosier run that put Indiana in the driver's seat. Indiana buried its free throws in the final minutes to clinch a 63-57 victory and sole possession of first place in the Big Ten with only three games remaining. Although Jeffries hit that big three against the Buckeyes, he was still hobbled by his ankle and thigh injuries and wasn't 100 percent. Jeff Newton stepped up his game to help take up the slack. He sparked IU with 16 points, four rebounds, and three blocks against OSU, and also had two spectacular dunks in the first half that ignited the home crowd. Odle, Jeffries, and Fife added 10 points apiece, and Coverdale dished out eight assists without a single turnover.

own NCAA chances, but the Hoosiers didn't accommodate them. Led by 25 points and 11 rebounds from Jarrad Odle, IU won 77-62. Jeffries, who was already hobbled with a bruised thigh, turned an ankle in the Louisville game and ended up missing IU's next contest. Without Jeffries, the Hoosiers dropped

In the final three games of the regular season, the IU squad had the difficult assignment of playing two of those three games on the road at Michigan State and at Illinois, two of the toughest road trips in the Big Ten during that period. In the Breslin Center in

East Lansing, where IU hadn't won since 1991, Indiana came out aggressive and led Michigan State nearly wire to wire. But MSU rallied and, with 0:55 remaining, tied the game at 53-53 on a three-pointer from power forward Adam Ballinger, an Indiana native. The Spartans went on to win 57-54. Two days later, Indiana went to Champaign for a rematch with No. 15 Illinois. The Hoosiers trailed by 12 at the half but staged a big second-half rally that came up just short in a 70-62 loss. After losing two straight games, the despondent IU squad figured that it had lost its chance at the Big Ten crown. However, on the flight home from the Illinois game, the team got word that Michigan State had upset Ohio State in Columbus. That meant that if the Hoosiers could win their final game of the season against Northwestern in Assembly Hall, then they could clinch a share of the title. Led by 20 points and five assists from Tom Coverdale, IU beat the Wildcats 79-67 to sew up Indiana's 20th Big Ten championship, and first since 1993. Jeffries was named Big Ten MVP and Fife was voted the conference's Defensive Player of the Year (in a tie with Travarus Bennett of Minnesota).

In the Big Ten Tournament in Indianapolis, the Hoosiers ended Michigan State's five-game winning streak by dominating the Spartans in a 67-56 Indiana victory. Jeffries began to show signs of regaining his form with 14 points, and Coverdale added 11 points and seven assists. After the game, MSU coach Tom Izzo said, "I thought Indiana played with a lot more intensity than us today… I don't think they get enough credit for how good they are defensively. Even though they're not as athletic, they're just tough." However, in the semifinals against Iowa the next day, the Hoosiers spent all of an eight-point lead late in the second half and lost 62-60 when 1997 Indiana Mr. Basketball, and former IU star, Luke Recker buried a 15-footer over Jeffries at the buzzer.

After losing three out of their last five games, and with Jeffries still not at full strength, the Hoosiers appeared to be stumbling into the NCAA tournament. The team looked ripe for another one of the early exits that had plagued Indiana during the previous seven seasons when IU suffered five first-round defeats and two second-round losses. However, just as they had done early in the Big Ten season, the Hoosiers pulled together and got on a hot streak.

Awarded the No. 5 seed in the South Regional, Indiana opened the tournament with a tough matchup against 12th-seeded Utah, which was 8-0 in first round games under Coach Rick Majerus. The Hoosiers roared to a 42-27 lead at the half, but on the final play before halftime, Tom Coverdale twisted his ankle. That made coach Mike Davis extremely nervous because the year before, Coverdale injured his hip in IU's first-round game against Kent State, and the Hoosiers ended up blowing a 12-point halftime lead and getting beat by the Golden Flashes 77-73. This time, Indiana turned up the defensive pressure and quickly extended the lead to 20 points. Utah never got within striking distance after that, and IU cruised to a 75-56 victory. Coverdale got his ankle wrapped, and although he was noticeably limping, he returned for the second half and finished with 19 points, eight rebounds, and four assists. Jeff Newton also provided a big lift off the bench with 15 points.

In the second round, IU faced 13th-seed UNC Wilmington, which had upset No. 4-seed USC 93-89 in overtime. The Hoosiers led the Seahawks 31-25 at the half and built the lead up to 17 points with 12:41 remaining in the game. Then Seahawk guard Brett Blizzard got hot and rallied his team to within 66-63 at the 2:45 mark. That's when Jared Jeffries, who had been held scoreless in the first half, stepped up and took control of the game. He was the catalyst in a 10-4 IU run to close the game. The Hoosiers won 76-67

INDIANA'S RANKING IN THE 2001-02 ASSOCIATED PRESS POLLS

PS	11/20	11/27	12/4	12/11	12/18	12/25	1/1	1/8	1/15	1/22	1/29	2/5	2/12	2/19	2/26	3/5	3/12
22	20	—	—	21	—	—	—	—	25	—	—	—	22	23	25	23	—

The Hoosiers huddle up and prepare to go to battle in the 2002 NCAA tournament. IU Athletics

and Jeffries finished with 22 points and seven rebounds. After the game, Coach Davis said, "The whole season, our guys really fought hard. ... To be able to go to the Sweet Sixteen is a great achievement for this basketball team."

Waiting for Indiana in the Sweet Sixteen was No. 1 Duke, the defending NCAA champion and the top seed in the South Regional. Playing in Rupp Arena in Lexington, Kentucky, IU came into the game fired up for a great performance. Unfortunately, The Hoosiers were a little too wound up as they launched too many quick shots, turned the ball over 16 times, and fell behind Duke 42-29 at the break. The Blue Devils' 42 points were the most that Indiana had given up in the first half all season. However, in the second half, IU turned up the defensive pressure and began disrupting Duke's offensive flow. As a result, the Blue Devils began launching a lot of three-point shots. Meanwhile, the Hoosiers, who were known for their prolific three-point shooting, pounded the ball inside, and Jeffries,

Odle, and Newton shredded Duke's interior defense. However, in the first ten minutes of the second half, every time Indiana made a run, Duke responded with a score to take away the momentum. But slowly, the Hoosiers clawed their way back into the game. Duke still led 59-45 with 12 minutes to go, but Indiana rattled off six straight points, capped by two free throws from A.J. Moye, to cut it to 59-51 with 9:46 remaining. A gorgeous spin move and score from Moye at the 7:23 mark cut the lead to 61-55. A backdoor cut and a layup by Moye—on an excellent pass from Jeff Newton—cut it to 63-59 with 6:20 left. A rebound basket from Jeffries cut it to 63-62 with 5:42 remaining.

Then, the emotional climax of that run came on Duke's next possession, when the Blue Devils got the ball to a 6'8" power forward Carlos Boozer, who was wide open underneath. He turned and took the ball up to dunk it, but Moye rotated over, leapt into the air, and stuffed Boozer back to the floor. A jump ball was called, and the possession arrow gave it to the

Hoosiers with 5:22 remaining and Rupp Arena in a frenzy as the crowd embraced the underdog Indiana team. Then, the veteran Blue Devils calmed down and made a 7-2 run to grab a 70-64 advantage. IU responded gamely with its own 6-0 run to tie the game with 1:54 left on the clock. After Duke turned it over on its next possession, the Hoosiers got the ball to Tom Coverdale in the post against Duke's Chris Duhon. Coverdale took one dribble and launched a quick little turnaround jump shot that bounced around and in at the 0:59 mark, giving the Hoosiers their first lead of the game at 72-70. Duke guard Daniel Ewing missed a three-point try with 0:44 left and IU rebounded. A.J. Moye was fouled with 11.1 seconds to go. The sophomore sank both free throws to make it a two possession game. The Blue Devils rushed the ball up court and Ewing missed another three, but this time All-America guard Jason Williams snatched the rebound, stepped back behind the three-point line at the top of the key, and launched a 19-foot jumper just as Dane Fife came flying at him to disrupt the shot. Williams's three-pointer swished through the net and a whistle blew. Fife was nailed with a foul, giving Williams a chance to tie the game with a four-point play with 4.2 seconds remaining. Williams missed the free throw, but Boozer pushed Jeffries out of the way, grabbed the rebound, and put up a potential game-winning shot. Boozer's putback missed, Newton grabbed the round, and the Hoosiers' bench poured onto the court in celebration as Indiana upset Duke 74-73. Jeffries, who was almost the goat by missing his final blockout of Boozer, ended up being one of the main heroes with 24 points and 15 rebounds. Moye's 14 points off the bench were also huge, as the 6'3" sophomore made a flurry of clutch plays in the second half.

In the postgame press conference, Duke coach Mike Krzyzewski said, "Their kids hung tough the whole ball game. They played with determination and won the game, I think, through their toughness."

Unlike 1984 when IU upset No. 1 North Carolina but then got beat by a lower-seeded Virginia team in the Elite Eight, these Hoosiers didn't suffer a letdown after the emotional win over Duke. They hit 15 of 19 three-pointers to shoot down 10th-seeded Kent State 81-69 in the regional finals. It was sweet revenge against the same Golden Flashes squad that had knocked IU out of the tournament the previous

Guard Dane Fife starts to celebrate during the Hoosiers' victory over Kent State in the Elite Eight. IU Athletics

year. Fife led the way with 17 points and Hornsby had 16 points and seven assists. Coverdale added 14 points and seven assists, but he re-injured his bad ankle in the second half and looked like he might not be able to play the following week in the Final Four in Atlanta (Coverdale's ankle became one of the biggest stories of the media-oversaturated week leading up the Final Four).

In the national semifinals in the Georgia Dome, Indiana collided with third-ranked Oklahoma, one of the hottest teams in the country and the pick of many analysts to win the national championship. The Sooners were rugged, athletic, and aggressive, and during the course of the season they had already defeated national powers such as Kansas, Maryland, Connecticut and Arizona. On the Hoosiers' best day, Oklahoma was a team they would have a lot trouble beating. With IU's two best players—Jared Jeffries

After the Hoosiers captured the South Regional of the 2002 NCAA tournament, Tom Coverdale and his teammates took turns cutting down the nets in Rupp Arena in Lexington, Kentucky. IU Athletics

the bench and Price struggling, the Sooners didn't have a go-to guy down the stretch, and IU prevailed 73-64. For Jeff Newton, the Oklahoma game was the culmination of two months of outstanding basketball. Coming into the season, Newton owned a career scoring average of 6.4 PPG, and during the first 23 games of the season, he averaged 6.1 PPG. However, after Jeffries was injured and forced to miss the Wisconsin game, Newton stepped up and averaged 10.7 points, 5.4 rebounds, and 2.3 blocks per game during the rest of the regular season and the postseason.

Following the Oklahoma game, Davis said, "Newt was great tonight. I just wish I could bottle up this performance and save it for [the championship game on] Monday." Indiana had been to the NCAA championship game five previous times and had come away with five national championships. Unfortunately, the 2001-02 team couldn't bottle up the magic that had enabled the Hoosiers to shoot a remarkable 55 percent from the field in their first five games of the NCAA tournament. In the title game against fourth-ranked Maryland, the Hoosiers shot an anemic 35 percent. The Terrapins controlled the lead for almost the entire contest. Indiana's one big rally came midway through the second half when Jeffries scored to give IU its first lead at 44-42. It looked like the Hoosiers were about to make another historic rally, but Maryland quickly quenched Indiana's momentum with an 11-2 run that was keyed by seniors Juan Dixon and Lonnie Baxter. IU never threatened again and Maryland won 64-52.

In four consecutive weeks in March, the Hoosiers faced teams led by four of the best coaches in college basketball—Tom Izzo, Rick Majerus, Mike Krzyzewski and Kelvin Sampson. Each time, those coaches had nearly a full week to prepare for the IU squad, and in each game, Indiana prevailed and was lauded by each of those coaches for their toughness and heart.

Before the Duke game, Mike Davis told his players, "To play basketball at Indiana is great honor. If you do something special, the fans of Indiana will remember you for the rest of your life." Despite coming up just short of winning Indiana's sixth NCAA championship, this team restored a lot of Hoosier pride by winning Indiana's first Big Ten title in nine years and making a Cinderella run in the NCAA tournament that will long be remembered and reminisced among the IU faithful.

and Tom Coverdale—hobbled by injuries, it looked like a foregone conclusion that Oklahoma would easily trample Indiana, and most commentators approached the game that way. In fact, Oklahoma may have even approached the game that way. However, the two factors that none of them considered were Dane Fife and Jeff Newton. Fife locked down Oklahoma's star guard Hollis Price, the MVP of the West Regional, holding him to a dismal 1-11 from the floor and only six points. Meanwhile, Atlanta native Jeff Newton burned Oklahoma's interior defense with his quickness, scored 19 points, and fouled out the Sooners' best player, forward Aaron McGee, with 4:41 left in the game. With McGee on

2002 Championship Bracket

First Round	Second Round March 16-17	Regional Semifinals	Regional Finals	National Semifinals	National Championship

South

3/14 1 Duke — Duke 84-37
16 Winthrop — Greenville, SC — Duke 84-77
3/14 8 Notre Dame — Notre Dame 82-63
9 Charlotte

March 21 — Indiana 74-73

3/14 5 Indiana — Indiana 75-56
12 Utah — Sacramento, CA — Indiana 76-67
3/14 4 Southern Cal — UNC Wil. 93-89 (ot)
13 UNC Wilmington

Lexington, KY
March 23 — Indiana 81-69

3/15 6 California — California 82-75
11 Pennsylvania — Pittsburgh, PA — Pittsburgh 63-50
3/15 3 Pittsburgh — Pittsburgh 71-54
14 Central Conn. St.

March 21 — Kent St. 78-73 (ot)

3/14 7 Oklahoma St. — Kent St. 69-61
10 Kent St. — Greenville, SC — Kent St. 71-58
3/14 2 Alabama — Alabama 86-78
15 Florida Atlantic

Atlanta, GA
March 30 — Indiana 73-64

West

3/15 1 Cincinnati — Cincinnati 90-52
16 Boston University — Pittsburgh, PA — UCLA 105-101 (ot)
8 UCLA — UCLA 80-58
9 Mississippi

March 21 — Missouri 82-73

3/15 5 Miami (Fla.) — Missouri 93-80
12 Missouri — Albuquerque, NM — Missouri 83-67
4 Ohio St. — Ohio St. 69-64
13 Davidson

San Jose, CA
March 23 — Oklahoma 81-75

3/14 6 Gonzaga — Wyoming 73-66
11 Wyoming — Albuquerque, NM — Arizona 68-60
3/14 3 Arizona — Arizona 86-81
14 UC Santa Barb.

March 21 — Oklahoma 88-67

3/15 7 Xavier — Xavier 70-58
10 Hawaii — Dallas, TX — Oklahoma 78-65
2 Oklahoma — Oklahoma 71-63
15 Illinios-Chicago

Atlanta, GA
April 1

Maryland 64-52
NATIONAL CHAMPION

East

3/15 1 Maryland — Maryland 85-70
16 %Siena — Washington, DC — Maryland 87-57
8 Wisconsin — Wisconsin 80-70
9 St. John's

March 22 — Maryland 78-68

5 Marquette — Tulsa 71-69
12 Tulsa — St. Louis, MO — Kentucky 87-82
3/14 4 Kentucky — Kentucky 83-68
13 Valparaiso

Syracuse, NY
March 24 — Maryland 90-82

6 Texas Tech — Southern Ill. 76-68
3/15 11 Southern Illinois — Chicago, IL — Southern Ill. 77-75
3 Georgia — Georgia 85-68
14 Murray St.

March 12 — Connecticut 71-59

3/15 7 North Carolina St. — North Carolina St. 69-58
10 Michigan St. — Washington, DC — Connecticut 77-74
3/15 2 Connecticut — Connecticut 78-67
15 Hampton

Atlanta, GA
March 30 — Maryland 97-88

Midwest

3/14 1 Kansas — Kansas 70-59
16 Holy Cross — St. Louis, MO — Kansas 86-63
3/14 8 Stanford — Stanford 84-68
9 Western Kentucky

March 22 — Kansas 73-69

3/15 5 Florida — Creighton 83-82 (2ot)
12 Creighton — Chicago, IL — Illinois 72-60
3/15 4 Illinois — Illinois 93-64
13 San Diego St.

Madison, WI
March 24 — Kansas 104-86

3/15 6 Texas — Texas 70-57
11 Boston College — Dallas, TX — Texas 68-64
3/15 3 Mississippi St. — Mississippi St. 70-58
14 McNeese St.

March 22 — Oregon 72-70

3/14 7 Wake Forest — Wake Forest 83-74
10 Pepperdine — Sacramento, CA — Oregon 92-87
3/14 2 Oregon — Oregon 81-62
15 Montana

% Opening Round
March 12—Dayton, OH
Alcorn St. 77
Siena 81

The 2002 NCAA tournament bracket.

CHAPTER 8

THE CULMINATION OF A THREE-YEAR RUN

1992-93

OVERALL RECORD: 31-4

CONFERENCE RECORD: 17-1 (FIRST PLACE)

TEAM HONORS:

BIG TEN CHAMPION, PRESEASON NIT CHAMPION,

HOOSIER CLASSIC CHAMPION, INDIANA CLASSIC CHAMPION

INDIVIDUAL HONORS:

BOB KNIGHT—BIG TEN COACH OF THE YEAR

CALBERT CHEANEY—NATIONAL PLAYER OF THE YEAR (CONSENSUS),

ALL-AMERICA, BIG TEN MVP, ALL-BIG TEN (FIRST TEAM)

GREG GRAHAM—ALL-BIG TEN (FIRST TEAM),

BIG TEN DEFENSIVE PLAYER OF THE YEAR

ALAN HENDERSON—ACADEMIC ALL-BIG TEN

CHRIS REYNOLDS—ACADEMIC ALL-BIG TEN

Indiana's 1989 recruiting class arrived in Bloomington amid a clamor of hype and fanfare. College basketball analysts and recruiting specialists were spouting hyperbole such as calling IU's group of seven high school standouts the greatest recruiting class ever assembled in college basketball, while Hoosier fans across the state of Indiana were blustering that this group would lead IU to multiple national championships and would rival the legendary accomplishments of the Hoosier teams in the mid-1970s. Coach Bob Knight, of course, showed a lot more equanimity when talking about his prized recruits, saying simply, "Whether this group is any good or not will not be decided in 1990. It will be decided in 1993. Then we'll know."

When the 1992-93 season dawned, the two inside players from that recruiting class—Lawrence Funderburke and Chris Lawson—had long since transferred to other schools. That left Calbert Cheaney, Greg Graham, Chris Reynolds, Pat Graham and Todd Leary to carry the burden of those high expectations. Leary and Pat Graham had each gone through a redshirt season so they were now juniors,

while 6'8" center Matt Nover had redshirted the season before the 1989 class arrived, which made him a senior for the 1992-93 campaign along with Cheaney, Greg Graham and Reynolds. Following the 1989 recruiting season, IU signed two other highly coveted prospects, guard Damon Bailey in 1990 and power forward Alan Henderson in 1991. Bailey was now a junior and Henderson a sophomore.

That core group of outstanding players made a spirited run to the 1992 NCAA Final Four in Minneapolis where they were edged out by eventual champion Duke in the national semifinals. The only players lost from that squad were starting forward Eric Anderson and reserve guard Jamal Meeks, both of whom graduated that spring. As a result, the talented Hoosier team that went into the 1992-93 season was one of the top-ranked clubs in college basketball and one of the favorites for the NCAA championship.

Swingman Calbert Cheaney was the heart of the team. The 6'7" Cheaney came in as one of the lesser-rated prospects of the 1989 group, but it quickly became apparent that he was the hardest-working and most skilled of the seven recruits. He had a smooth

The 1992-93 team. First row (left to right): Todd Leary, Calbert Cheaney, Chris Reynolds, Greg Graham, Matt Nover; Second row: Damon Bailey, Pat Knight, Brian Evans, Todd Lindeman, Alan Henderson, Pat Graham.
IU Athletics

left-handed shooting stroke in which he cocked the ball right next to his head, elevated, and followed through with a silky-soft release. He was also a lithe athlete who could put the ball on the floor and drive past defenders, as well as finish inside with a dunk. One of his signature moves was a ball and head fake on the wing to draw the defender off his feet, then Cheaney would streak down the baseline for a two-handed dunk. Cheaney was also a good three-point shooter, but he didn't take ill-advised threes, because another one of his best qualities was his shot selection. He rarely took a bad shot or one that wasn't in the flow of the offense. Like Hoosier swingmen Scott May and Mike Woodson before him, Cheaney had an excellent mid-range game, and Coach Knight's motion offense provided him with lots of opportunities for mid-range jumpers. In his rookie season he led IU in scoring at 17.1 PPG, and during his sophomore

and junior seasons he improved and earned All-Big Ten and All-America honors. However, despite Calbert's excellent play during his first three seasons at IU, he spent most of that time in the shadow of another Big Ten small forward—Ohio State's Jim Jackson. It was Jackson, and not Cheaney, who won the Big Ten Freshman of the Year award in 1990, and it was Jackson who beat out Cheaney for the Big Ten MVP in both 1991 and 1992. But in the spring of 1992, Jackson chose to forgo his final season as a Buckeye and enter the NBA draft. That left Cheaney as the Big Ten's marquee player heading into his senior season.

The other member of the 1989 recruiting class who made a big splash right away was 6'4" shooting guard Greg Graham. His game was a lot like Cheaney's. He could use his quickness and athleticism to drive and score, and he also developed into an excellent

1992-93 TEAM ROSTER

Head coach: Bob Knight
Assistant coaches: Dan Dakich, Norm Ellenberger, Ron Felling

No.	Player	Hometown	Class	Position	Height
22	Damon Bailey	Heltonville, IN	Jr	G	6-3
40	Calbert Cheaney (Capt.)	Evansville, IN	Sr	F	6-7
34	Brian Evans	Terre Haute, IN	Fr	F	6-8
20	Greg Graham (Capt.)	Indianapolis, IN	Sr	G	6-4
33	Pat Graham	Floyd Knobs, IN	Jr	G	6-5
44	Alan Henderson	Indianapolis, IN	So	F	6-9
25	Pat Knight	Bloomington, IN	So	G	6-6
30	Todd Leary	Indianapolis, IN	Jr	G	6-3
50	Todd Lindeman	Channing, MI	Rs	C	7-0
24	Matt Nover (Capt.)	Chesterton, IN	Sr	C	6-8
21	Chris Reynolds (Capt.)	Peoria, IL	Sr	G	6-1
11	Malcolm Sims	Shaker Heights, OH	Fr	G	6-4

outside shooter. Graham was shorter and skinnier than Cheaney, but his game was similar enough that when the two of them were on opposite wings they could really put a lot of pressure on opposing teams, because both of them were such dangerous scorers. Graham stepped up his play as a senior and became one of the best guards in the Big Ten, and one of the most underrated guards in the country.

Joining Graham in the backcourt for the 1992-93 season was 6'3" sparkplug Damon Bailey, the 1990 Indiana Mr. Basketball. Bailey came to IU as the all-time leading scorer in Indiana high school history, but with the offensive firepower Indiana already had, he focused his energy mostly on running the offense and doing the little things to help IU win—but he usually turned back into a scorer whenever the team needed a lift, such as the 32 points he scored at Ohio State as a freshman.

In the frontcourt, 6'9" sophomore Alan Henderson and 6'8" senior Matt Nover joined Cheaney. Henderson was coming off an extremely impressive freshman campaign in which he averaged 11.6 PPG and 7.2 RPG. Henderson was intelligent and aggressive and played with great intensity. He wasn't a great leaper, but he was a very good at getting position to rebound and to score on the blocks. He also had a nice face-up jumper that he liked to shoot along the baseline. Nover, on the other hand, was a banger, pure and simple. His job was to set screens, play defense, and rebound, and he did all three quite well. He didn't have a lot of offensive moves, but he was strong and agile, and he knew how to finish inside when he got the ball in scoring position.

Off the bench, the Hoosiers were very deep in the backcourt and very thin up front. Senior guard Chris Reynolds was a versatile athlete, a relentless defender, and an excellent leader. His only drawback was that he wasn't a big offensive threat, but he was great at getting the Hoosiers on the right track when they needed direction. Conversely, sharpshooter Todd Leary was good at coming off the bench and rekindling the Hoosier attack with a quick three-pointer.

One of IU's most valuable reserves was swingman Pat Graham (no relation to Greg), the 1989 Indiana Mr. Basketball and a McDonald's All-American. He wasn't a great athlete like Calbert Cheaney and Greg Graham, but he was a deadly outside shooter and a crafty scorer. After a productive first two seasons, he suffered a broken foot and missed the entire 1991-92 season as a medical redshirt. He would end up re-injuring that foot at the beginning of the 1992-93 season and would miss 22 games because of it. That hurt IU, because Pat Graham could fill in at both the shooting guard and small forward spots. When it was decided to redshirt seven-footer Todd Lindeman for 1992-93, that meant the only real frontcourt reserve

Senior guard Chris Reynolds often toiled in the background as his more famous teammates grabbed the headlines during the 1992-93 campaign. However, when the Hoosiers were out of sync, it was often Reynolds whom coach Bob Knight called upon to get the team back on track. IU Athletics

that the Hoosiers had was redshirt freshman Brian Evans, a 6'8" forward that was a much better outside shooter than inside scorer at that point in his career. Evans turned out to be a nice surprise off the bench, but his minutes and production were somewhat limited by a bad shoulder. As a result, when Henderson or Nover got in foul trouble or needed a break, Coach Knight often went to a three-guard lineup and moved Cheaney to the "4" spot.

Still, despite its limitations in the frontcourt, this was an outstanding team. It got great leadership from Reynolds and Cheaney and the players utilized their wealth of on-court experience after being ranked

among the top-ten teams in the country for 33 out of 35 weeks during the previous two seasons, and having sat in the top spot in the Big Ten race for much of that period as well. Entering the season, Coach Knight said, "I'm hoping that this team will be difficult to play against on our offensive end from most spots, but we've got to see about developing some kind of ability to score from in and around the basket. I think this team will score from the perimeter, but whether it will score enough from within 12 feet of the basket to get other people in foul trouble, to make other people really conscious of what we're doing, remains to be seen."

A rigorous preconference schedule quickly gave the Hoosiers an idea about what kind of team they had. They matched up against six teams ranked in the top 25 during the preconference, including four of them in the Hoosiers' first five games. IU opened in the Preseason NIT and came out firing with a pair of impressive wins over Murray State and 17th-ranked Tulane. That sent Indiana to Madison Square Garden in New York City for the final two rounds of the NIT. In the semifinals, IU faced No. 7 Florida State, a team the Hoosiers had knocked out of the NCAA tournament in each of the two previous seasons. IU was down by 12 points midway through the second half. That's when Pat Graham came off the bench and rallied the Hoosiers to a 69-67 lead with one minute remaining, but the Seminoles got a steal and a score in the final seconds to force overtime. Then Calbert Cheaney took over. He scored seven points in the final minute and a half, and IU barely survived for an 81-78 victory. Cheaney finished with a career-high 34 points, but Knight said afterward, "Cheaney scored a lot of points and didn't play basketball very well." Knight was particularly displeased with Cheaney's defense, rebounding, and screening (or lack thereof). He was also unhappy that the Hoosiers allowed Florida State to get 28 offensive rebounds and outrebounded IU 56-43 overall. The other piece of bad news from the game was that Pat Graham, who had sparked IU's second-half comeback, re-broke his foot in overtime and was expected to be out of action for at least 10-12 weeks.

In the NIT championship game, fourth-ranked Indiana faced No. 6 Seton Hall, which would go on to win the Big East. *The New York Post* said that the matchup had a "March Madness-like atmosphere" and it turned out to be a terrific college basketball

1992-93 SEASON STATISTICS

Team Statistics	G	FG%	3FG%	FT%	R	A	TO	S	B	PF	PTS	PPG
Indiana	35	.522	.425	.717	36.6	17.7	12.9	6.2	2.8	15.9	3028	86.5
Opponents	35	.437	.360	.701	33.7	13.4	15.5	5.7	2.5	22.4	2506	71.6

Player Statistics	G-GS	FG%	3FG%	FT%	R	A	TO	S	B	PF	PTS	PPG
Cheaney	35-35	.549	.427	.795	6.4	2.4	2.4	0.9	0.3	2.2	785	22.4
G. Graham	35-32	.551	.514	.825	3.2	2.9	1.9	1.3	0.2	2.0	577	16.5
Henderson	30-25	.487	.167	.637	8.1	0.9	1.5	1.2	1.4	2.5	333	11.1
Nover	35-35	.628	.000	.575	5.9	0.7	2.0	0.3	0.7	2.5	389	11.0
Bailey	35-24	.459	.418	.728	3.3	4.1	1.7	0.6	0.2	2.3	355	10.1
P. Graham	13-3	.508	.429	.722	1.3	1.4	1.2	0.5	0.0	1.2	84	6.5
Evans	35-4	.425	.354	.685	3.9	1.3	0.8	0.5	0.1	1.4	184	5.3
Leary	35-4	.467	.386	.889	1.0	1.2	0.7	0.3	0.0	0.9	168	4.8
Reynolds	35-13	.547	.000	.606	2.0	2.9	1.1	0.8	0.0	1.6	113	3.2
Sims	8-0	.000	.000	.917	0.4	0.1	0.8	0.4	0.0	1.0	11	1.4
Knight	32-0	.467	.000	.445	0.5	0.8	0.5	0.1	0.0	0.3	32	1.0

game. The first 30 minutes were a lot like the FSU game, as the Hoosiers broke out to an early lead and then fell into a hole by the midway point of the second half. Then Calbert Cheaney took over—again. He scored 16 points over the final 12 minutes as IU prevailed 78-74 over a gritty, tough-minded Seton Hall team. With 36 points, Cheaney set a new career high for the second game in a row. His performance earned him the MVP award for the tournament, and unlike the previous game, it also earned a tribute from his coach, as Knight said, "I really think tonight he played a great basketball game, and I use that word 'great' sparingly." The NIT performance rocketed Cheaney to the role of front runner for college player of the year.

After returning from New York, the second-ranked Hoosiers played third-ranked Kansas in the Bank One Classic in the Hoosier Dome in Indianapolis. Indiana blew a three-point lead in the final minutes as the Jayhawks, who would go on to win the Big Eight conference, finished the game on an 8-0 run and beat the Hoosiers 74-69. IU went on to

Guard Pat Graham spent another frustrating season struggling with foot injuries. However, he also sparked the Hoosiers with key performances in several important games. IU Archives

win its next eight games, including a tough 75-70 win at Notre Dame and a 79-64 victory over No. 19 Cincinnati in which all five Indiana starters scored in double figures. That put IU at 12-1 with one game remaining before the start of Big Ten play.

On January 3, the fourth-ranked Hoosiers trekked to Freedom Hall in Louisville for a nationally televised game with border-rival Kentucky, which was undefeated and ranked No. 3. The Wildcats used a 35-17 run in the middle of the first half (including seven of eight three-pointers during the run) to snatch a 42-36 halftime lead. However, the Hoosiers got serious in the second half and took a 72-68 lead with 3:55 to play. Then, Kentucky's scrappy little guard Travis Ford nailed two threes as part of an 8-0 run that put Kentucky ahead 74-72. After the Hoosiers tied it up on a Matt Nover basket inside, Wildcat forward Jamal Mashburn put Kentucky ahead for good with a three-pointer. UK clinched an 81-78 win when Damon Bailey missed a three-pointer at the buzzer. Four different players scored 29 points in this game—Ford and Mashburn for Kentucky, and Cheaney and Nover for Indiana. Mashburn and Cheaney were both All-Americans and expected to put up big numbers, but Ford was only averaging 7.9 PPG entering the contest and Nover's previous career-high was 19. The two keys for the Hoosiers were Ford, who hit seven of 12 three-pointers and repeatedly burned IU's best defensive player Greg Graham, and the fact the IU made only 18 of 36 free throws (50 percent).

Still reeling from the Kentucky loss, the Hoosiers opened conference play three days later. Although IU was ranked fifth in nation, the Hoosiers were not the favorite to win the Big Ten title. That honor went to Michigan, which was ranked No. 3 heading into league play and was coming off a season in which they made it to the NCAA championship game with a lineup of five freshmen (from Michigan's

Forward Calbert Cheaney slices through the Northwestern defense for a reverse layup. Cheaney capped off an excellent collegiate career in 1992-93 by earning national player of the year honors and becoming the all-time leading scorer in Big Ten conference history. IU Athletics

recruiting class of 1991, which now claimed the distinction of "the best recruiting class ever"). Furthermore, the Big Ten was anything but a two-team race. Iowa, Purdue and Michigan State were all ranked in the top 15, and Ohio State and Minnesota would break the top 25 during January.

A fixture in the starting lineup, 6'8" senior center Matt Nover developed into a solid post player on both ends of the floor. He averaged 11.0 PPG and 5.9 RPG during the 1992-93 season.
IU Athletics

IU tipped off league play by hosting ninth-ranked Iowa on January 6. The undefeated Hawkeyes were the top rebounding team in the country and had the kind of players who could hurt the Hoosiers inside with 6'10" center Acie Earl and 6'8" power forward Chris Street (who was tragically killed in an auto accident less than two weeks later). Iowa was all over the offensive glass early on and took a 19-11 lead. But then, Damon Bailey, who along with Greg Graham got benched because of poor play against Kentucky, came off the pine and sparked IU to a 22-7 run to close the first half. Bailey went on to score a game-high 21 points, and Greg Graham added 17, as the Hoosiers won 75-67 in Assembly Hall. Later that week, Bailey had 28 points, six assists, and five rebounds as the Hoosiers blistered Penn State 105-57 to improve to 2-0 in conference play and 14-2 overall.

After two home wins, IU embarked on a brutal three-game road trip. The first assignment was a showdown between No. 6 Indiana and No. 2 Michigan that was televised nationally by ESPN. In the pre-conference season, the Wolverines had defeated two top-five teams—North Carolina and Kansas—and their only loss was to No. 1 Duke at Cameron Indoor Stadium. Meanwhile, the Hoosiers were beaten the only two times they had faced top five teams—Kansas and Kentucky. Coach Knight blamed Indiana's losses in those two games to not matching their opponents' effort. "We didn't have it in the Kansas game, we didn't have it a month later in the Kentucky game, and when we don't have it again we'll get beat again," said Knight.

Fortunately, the Hoosiers played with tremendous effort against Michigan—but the Wolverines played just as hard. IU led by six at the break, and increased the lead to 43-33 with a 6-2 run to start the second half, but Michigan surged back with a 12-2 run of its own to tie the game at 45-45. From there to the finish, both teams engaged in some of the most intense and well-played basketball in the history of the Big Ten. The second half alone featured six ties and eight lead changes and a flurry of clutch plays from both teams. At one point during that fierce stretch run, the Wolverines scored on seven out of eight possessions, but the Hoosiers answered each time by converting on seven straight possessions of their own. In the final minutes, Cheaney gave IU a 74-73 lead when he twisted free and sank a jump shot, but Michigan's 6'8" point guard, Jalen Rose,

responded with a jumper to put Michigan back in front 75-74. Indiana then used almost all of the 0:45-second shot clock and got the ball to sophomore power forward Alan Henderson, who confidently stroked an 18-footer to give IU a 76-75 lead. With 14.1 seconds left, IU had a chance to increase the lead when Todd Leary stepped to the free throw line, but the Hoosiers were called for a lane violation and Michigan had one final chance to win the game. Rose brought the ball up court, drove into the heart of the defense and dished to sharpshooter James Voskuil, who uncorked a three-pointer from the corner. Voskuil's shot missed, but Michigan's Chris Webber grabbed the rebound and went straight up with it to score, but Henderson swatted his shot away and preserved the victory for IU. Henderson finished with 22 points, eight rebounds, and five blocks, out-dueling the All-American Webber, who finished with 18 points, six rebounds, and three blocks.

That was the turning point in Indiana's season. Greg Graham later said, "That's where it started. ... When we beat Michigan, I knew we were really developing as a team." After departing from Ann Arbor, Indiana completed its grueling three-game road trip by grinding out an 83-79 win at Illinois and clobbering 13th-ranked Purdue 74-65 in Mackey Arena, powered by 33 points and 10 rebounds from Calbert Cheaney. IU returned home and dispatched Ohio State, ranked No. 24, and Minnesota in Assembly Hall and then went back on the road for another three-game road trip. The Hoosiers drilled Northwestern in Evanston, survived a 73-66 win over No. 9 Iowa, and needed two overtimes to outlast a charged-up Penn State team 88-84. However, when they returned to Bloomington after the Penn State victory, the Hoosiers were a perfect 10-0 in league play, held a two-and-a-half-game lead in the Big Ten, were ranked No. 1 in country, and were set to play five of their final eight conference games in Assembly Hall.

The first game of that final stretch was a rematch with Michigan, now ranked No. 4 and standing in second place in the conference at 7-2. The Wolverines needed to pull out a win to have any chance at catching Indiana in the league race, and they played with a desperation that showed that they realized that. Michigan jumped out to a 27-14 lead, but IU closed the gap to just 46-44 at the half. The Wolverines hit

1992-93 SEASON RESULTS

Date	Court	Opponent	Result	Score
11/18/1992	H	Murray State	W	103-80
11/20/1992	H	(#17) Tulane	W	102-92
11/25/1992	N1	(#7) Florida State	W	81-78
11/27/1992	N1	(#6) Seton Hall	W	78-74
12/5/1992	N2	(#3) Kansas	L	69-74
12/8/1992	A	Notre Dame	W	75-70
12/11/1992	H	Austin Peay	W	107-61
12/12/1992	H	Western Michigan	W	97-58
12/19/1992	H	(#19) Cincinnati	W	79-64
12/23/1992	H	St. John's	W	105-80
12/27/1992	N2	Butler	W	90-48
12/28/1992	N2	Colorado	W	85-65
1/3/1993	N3	(#3) Kentucky	L	78-81
1/6/1993	H	(#8) Iowa	W	75-67
1/9/1993	H	Penn State	W	105-57
1/12/1993	A	(#2) Michigan	W	76-75
1/16/1993	A	Illinois	W	83-79
1/19/1993	A	(#13) Purdue	W	74-65
1/24/1993	H	(#24) Ohio State	W	96-69
1/27/1993	H	Minnesota	W	61-57
1/30/1993	A	Northwestern	W	93-71
2/6/1993	A	(#9) Iowa	W	73-66
2/9/1993	A	Penn State	W	88-84
2/14/1993	H	(#4) Michigan	W	93-92
2/17/1993	H	Illinois	W	93-71
2/21/1993	H	(#14) Purdue	W	93-78
2/23/1993	A	Ohio State	L	77-81
2/27/1993	A	Minnesota	W	86-75
3/4/1993	H	Northwestern	W	98-69
3/10/1993	H	Michigan State	W	99-68
3/14/1993	A	Wisconsin	W	87-80

NCAA Tournament

Date	Court	Opponent	Result	Score
3/19/1993	N2	Wright State	W	97-54
3/21/1993	N2	(#22) Xavier	W	73-70
3/25/1993	N4	(#15) Louisville	W	82-69
3/27/1993	N4	(#9) Kansas	L	77-83

1 New York, NY
2 Indianapolis, IN
3 Louisville, KY

eight of their first-time shots in the second half to open up a 71-60 lead, but then the Hoosiers hit them with a 28-8 run that sent Assembly Hall into a tizzy and gave IU an insurmountable 89-78 advantage with under two minutes left to play. Michigan hit a flurry of late three-pointers, but it wasn't enough as Indiana prevailed 93-92. Cheaney, Henderson and Nover combined for 52 points and 25 rebounds against Michigan's celebrated front line of Ray Jackson, Chris Webber, and Juwan Howard, who combined for 51 points and 18 rebounds. Afterwards, Michigan's Jalen Rose admitted, "It's going to be tough catching them.

But if they win the Big Ten title, we look at that as them getting the silver. We're still going for the gold." The gold, of course, was the NCAA title, and true to their word, Michigan ended up making a serious run at it. In fact, after losing to IU in Assembly Hall on February 14, the Wolverines didn't lose again until North Carolina beat them in the NCAA championship game on April 5.

After sweeping Michigan, the path was clear for Indiana to finish off the rest of the Big Ten. Calbert Cheaney's 29 points and nine rebounds led IU to a 93-72 blowout over Illinois and upped IU's Big Ten record to 12-0, a full three games ahead of the second place Wolverines. And then … disaster struck. In practice the day before Indiana was set to host Purdue in Assembly Hall, Alan Henderson leapt into the air to collect a long outlet pass and then crumpled to the floor when he landed awkwardly on his right knee. Henderson and the team soon got the dreaded news that he had torn an ACL. His season was essentially over, and he would need knee surgery after the school year ended. For an already-thin Hoosier front court, it was a fatal blow.

Over Indiana's final six games, IU's Greg Graham stepped up his play to help make up for the loss of Henderson's scoring. Graham, who averaged 16.5 PPG for the season, averaged 25.0 PPG during those final six contests, including 32-point performances against both Purdue and Michigan State. Freshman forward Brian Evans also came off the bench for a couple of nice performances, and Pat Graham returned from his early-season foot injury and gave the Hoosiers some additional depth and experience. IU won five of those final six games, including a 93-78 win over 14th-ranked Purdue the day after Henderson's injury. The only setback was an 81-77 overtime loss against Ohio State in Columbus. One of the biggest highlights of that final stretch came during Indiana's 98-69 win over Northwestern on March 4, when Calbert Cheaney dropped in 35 points and became the all-time leading scorer in both Indiana and Big Ten history.

With a 17-1 Big Ten record, an undisputed conference crown, and a No. 1 ranking in the final polls of the regular season, Indiana clinched the No. 1 seed in the Midwest Regional of the NCAA Tournament. That meant IU would play the first two rounds of the tournament in the Hoosier Dome in Indianapolis. In the first round, Indiana crushed Wright State 97-54, led by 29 points and eight rebounds from Cheaney, but in the second round, Indiana's lack of size up front began to show. No. 22 Xavier, led by future NBA big men Aaron Williams and Brian Grant, outrebounded IU 39-32 and pushed the Hoosiers to the limit before Indiana escaped with a 73-70 victory. Cheaney powered the Hoosiers with 23 points and eight rebounds.

Like Scott May, who was broke his arm at the end of the regular season against Purdue in 1975, Alan Henderson tried to mount a limited comeback to help the Hoosiers in the postseason. Unfortunately, like May, Henderson wasn't able to perform at anywhere near his normal level of play. With Cheaney scoring 32 points and Matt Nover adding 15 points and eight rebounds, IU didn't need Henderson in the Sweet 16 against 15th-ranked Louisville, who fell 82-69 to IU. But against No. 9 Kansas in the Elite Eight, the Hoosiers desperately missed Henderson's inside scoring and his interior defense. The Jayhawks exploited that weakness and used their superior depth to outlast IU for an 83-77 Kansas victory.

"I think we had absolutely the best team in the country," Knight later said. "Without Henderson, we

1992-93 BIG TEN STANDINGS

	W	L	PCT
Indiana	17	1	.944
Michigan[1]	15	3	.833
Iowa	11	7	.611
Illinois	11	7	.611
Minnesota	9	9	.500
Purdue	9	9	.500
Ohio State	8	10	.444
Michigan St.	7	11	.389
Wisconsin	7	11	.389
Northwestern	3	15	.167
Penn State	2	16	.111

[1] Due to NCAA sanctions, Michigan later vacated the records from the 1992-93 season.

With Michigan's Juwan Howard looking on, IU forward Alan Henderson throws down an emphatic dunk. A late-season knee injury to Henderson doomed Indiana's chances at a fourth national championship in the Bob Knight era. IU Athletics

were stuck just as we were without Scott May in 1975—we went on, we still had a very good team, but we had lost a key component… Maybe Kansas would have beaten us anyway, but I don't think so. I don't think anyone would have."

It was still a year with a lot of bright spots. Calbert Cheaney was the consensus college player of the year. Greg Graham was one of the most effective shooting guards in the country with a field goal percentage of .551, a three-point shooting percentage of .514, and a free throw percentage of .825. Meanwhile Matt Nover set a new school record with a field goal percentage of .628 for the season—the first time an Indiana player had ever shot better than .600—and Nover also set the Indiana record for career field goal percentage at .571 (Cheaney finished right behind him at .559). Although the celebrated 1989 recruits never won the national championships they were supposed to have been destined to capture, they did win two Big Ten titles, made a trip to the Final Four, and kept Indiana ranked among the top 10 teams in the nation for 51 out of 53 weeks over a period of three seasons. Amazingly, five players from that 1992-93 team—Cheaney, Greg Graham, Bailey, Henderson and Evans—are still ranked among the top 12 scorers in Indiana history.

After hitting a trio of three-pointers in the final minute of Indiana's 1992 Final Four game against Duke, Todd Leary gained instant celebrity status. He later became a color commentator on the IU Radio Network. IU Athletics

INDIANA'S RANKING IN THE 1992-93 ASSOCIATED PRESS POLLS

PS	11/23	11/30	12/7	12/14	12/21	12/28	1/4	1/11	1/18	1/25	2/1	2/8	2/15	2/22	3/1	3/8	3/15
4	4	2	4	4	4	4	5	6	2	2	1	1	1	1	2	2	1

1993 Championship Bracket

The 1993 NCAA tournament bracket.

CHAPTER 9

KNIGHT CRASHES THE FINAL FOUR

1972-73

OVERALL RECORD: 22-6

CONFERENCE RECORD: 11-3 (FIRST PLACE)

TEAM HONORS:

BIG TEN CHAMPIONSHIP, NCAA FINAL FOUR

INDIVIDUAL HONORS:

STEVE DOWNING—ALL-AMERICA,

ALL-BIG TEN (FIRST TEAM), BIG TEN MVP

JOHN RITTER—ACADEMIC ALL-AMERICA, ACADEMIC ALL-BIG TEN

JOHN LASKOWSKI—ACADEMIC ALL-BIG TEN

With all the championships, accolades, and big-game victories that coach Bob Knight would eventually amass during his legendary career at Indiana, it's often difficult to look back and remember when it was that he first stepped onto the national stage in college basketball. In general, it happened during the 1972-73 season, and more specifically during the 1973 NCAA tournament. In just his second season in Bloomington, Knight took an Indiana program that had finished last in the Big Ten in four out of the six seasons before he arrived, and returned it to the Final Four for the first time in 20 years.

Knight had spent most of his first season molding a group of players that he inherited from previous coach Lou Watson into a team that could play a ball control offense and a hawkish man-to-man defense. That 1971-72 squad ended up 15th in the country in team defense, led the Big Ten in free-throw shooting, and was second in the league in field goal percentage. The team went 17-8 overall, finished third in the Big Ten, and made the school's first appearance in the NIT. For the 1972-73 season, Indiana not only returned seven lettermen and four starters, but also got a boost from six sophomores that were part of Knight's first recruiting class and had learned his system on the freshman team the year before. Plus, that season was the first of freshman eligibility in NCAA basketball, so the Hoosiers immediately got the serv-ices of an outstanding group of freshman that was widely hailed as one of the best recruiting classes in the nation.

Despite all of the new blood, seniors Steve Downing and John Ritter remained the heart of the team. They were Indiana's top two returning scorers and they ended up being the Hoosiers' best scorers during the 1972-73 campaign as well. Downing was a versatile 6'8" center who had struggled with injuries during his sophomore and junior seasons, but had still put together some incredible performances, such as his 47 points and 25 rebounds against Kentucky as a junior and his 28-point, 17-rebound, 10-block effort against Michigan as a sophomore. Downing was an excellent scorer in the paint and could also hit short jumpers along the baseline, and he was a tenacious rebounder who had averaged 12.4 RPG over his first two seasons. After having off-season knee surgery, he was expected to return at full strength as a senior. Ritter was a 6'5" forward that had been a two-year starter for the Hoosiers. As a junior, Ritter led the Big Ten in free-throw shooting at 91 percent during conference play, and he also shot 51 percent from the field for the season. In addition to being an excellent shooter, he was also a reliable performer on the floor and often steadied his teammates. His leadership became one of the key factors on a team that relied heavily on contributions from freshmen and sophomores.

The 1972-73 team. First row (left to right): Frank Wilson, John Laskowski, John Ritter, Quinn Buckner, Steve Downing, Jim Crews, Steve Green, Jerry Memering; Second row: assistant coach Dave Bliss, assistant coach John Hulls, John Kamstra, Craig Morris, Tom Abernathy, Don Noort, Mike Miller, Doug Allen, Trent Smock, Steve Alfeld, head coach Bob Knight. IU Archives

IU's other seniors—Frank Wilson, Bootsie White, Jerry Memering and Kim Pemberton—saw their role greatly reduced as the freshmen and sophomores emerged to fill in the rest of the spots in Coach Knight's regular rotation. White and Pemberton left the team, but Wilson and Memering stuck it out. Two freshmen, Quinn Buckner and Jim Crews, ended up winning the nod as Knight's starting backcourt. The 6'3" Buckner may have been the most coveted recruit in the country in 1972. In high school, he led his team to 54 consecutive victories and a pair of state titles in Illinois. He was also an outstanding defensive back in football and was highly recruited in that sport as well. He was the starting safety on the IU football team in the fall of 1972 and reported for basketball practice on November 26, the day after the football team's season ended with a loss to Purdue in West Lafayette. To Coach Knight's surprise, Buckner learned the offense so quickly that during his first week of practice he began directing traffic for players that had been practicing together all fall. On opening night, a week after Buckner's final football game, he started at guard for the Hoosiers. It took Jim Crews a

little longer to break into the starting lineup—five games—but once he did, he held the spot for the rest of the season. Like Buckner, the 6'5" Crews was a top-rated recruit and a high school All-American that Knight plucked from Illinois. He was a heady player, an excellent ball handler and passer, and a good shooter, and Crews and Buckner played well together.

At forward, 6'7" sophomore Steve Green was the other newcomer to step into the starting lineup. Green had been the leading scorer and rebounder on the freshman team the year before, and he bulked up by putting on an additional 15 pounds so that he was ready to handle the physical play in the Big Ten as a sophomore. Another sophomore, 6'5" John Laskowski, became the Hoosiers' sixth man who could come off the bench and provide an instant scoring punch.

In the summer before the 1972-73 season began, Coach Knight studied under legendary coach Henry Iba at the 1972 Olympic trials. He learned everything he could about the passing game that Iba used and took that knowledge and integrated it with his own ball control schemes and other offensive ideas. The

1972-73 TEAM ROSTER

Head coach: Bob Knight
Assistant coaches: Dave Bliss, John Hulls, Bob Weltlich

No.	Player	Hometown	Class	Position	Height
55	Tom Abernathy	South Bend, IN	Fr	F	6-7
24	Steve Ahlfeld	Wabash, IN	So	G	6-0
25	Doug Allen	Champaign, IL	So	F	6-5
21	Quinn Buckner	Phoenix, IL	Fr	G	6-3
45	Jim Crews	Normal, IL	Fr	G	6-5
32	Steve Downing	Indianapolis, IN	Sr	C	6-8
34	Steve Green	Sellersburg, IN	So	F	6-7
23	Steve Heiniger	Fort Wayne, IN	Jr	G	5-10
43	John Hunter	Danville, IN	So	F	6-6
30	John Kamstra	Frankfort, IN	So	G	6-1
31	John Laskowski	South Bend, IN	So	G	6-5
33	Jerry Memering	Vincennes, IN	Sr	F/C	6-7
40	Mike Miller	Bloomington, IN	Fr	F	6-8
41	Craig Morris	DeGraff, OH	Fr	G	6-4
35	Don Noort	Worth, IL	Fr	F/C	6-8
42	John Ritter (Capt.)	Goshen, IN	Sr	F	6-5
22	Trent Smock	Richmond, IN	Fr	F	6-5
22	Bootsie White	Hammond, IN	Sr	G	5-8
20	Frank Wilson	Bluffton, IN	Sr	G	6-3

result was what would commonly become known as the "motion offense" that Knight devised and popularized. He first implemented it for the 1972-73 season.

On opening night against Harvard on December 2, in Bloomington, the new motion offense produced 97 points—a new high for a Knight team at IU—and the Hoosiers rolled to an easy 97-76 victory over a talented Harvard team. Downing had 31 points and 12 rebounds and Laskowski added 15 points. Three days later, the Indiana squad went on the road and dominated Kansas 72-55. Downing had a game-high 22 points and 16 rebounds, while Buckner added 15 points and Ritter scored 14. IU's biggest win of the preconference season came on December 9, when the unranked Hoosiers defeated No. 8 Kentucky 64-58 in Bloomington. Green, who led IU with 18 points, and Buckner both fouled out down the stretch, but Downing and Ritter each scored 14 points and the Hoosiers got great contributions off the bench from Laskowski, Crews, and sophomore John Kamstra. After the Kentucky win, IU beat Notre Dame and Ohio to improve to 5-0.

IU captain John Ritter looks for a teammate as he works to run Coach Knight's systematic "motion offense." IU Archives

All-America center Steve Downing pulls up for a baseline jumper during the Final Four. Downing was a dominant force in the paint during the 1972-73 season and was named the Big Ten MVP. IU Archives

1972-73 SEASON STATISTICS

Team Statistics	G	FG%	FT%	R	A	TO	PF	PTS	PPG
Indiana	28	.476	.706	42.3	13.6	18.0	18.8	2183	78.0
Opponents	28	.441	.665	41.4	8.8	19.9	20.5	1955	69.8

Player Statistics	G-GS	FG%	FT%	R	A	TO	PF	PTS	PPG
Downing	28-28	.520	.555	10.6	0.4	3.2	2.9	563	20.1
Ritter	28-27	.500	.873	4.4	2.0	2.2	2.4	411	14.7
Buckner	28-27	.409	.594	4.8	2.9	3.5	3.7	301	10.8
Laskowski	28-1	.491	.807	4.8	1.4	1.5	1.6	287	10.3
Green	28-26	.466	.769	4.6	1.8	2.1	3.4	282	10.1
Crews	28-22	.492	.680	2.1	2.8	2.4	2.1	147	5.3
Kamstra	13-0	.500	.600	1.4	1.2	1.2	1.3	51	3.9
Abernathy	18-2	.375	.571	2.6	0.5	0.6	0.8	40	2.2
Morris	11-0	.700	.556	0.4	0.0	0.5	0.4	19	1.7
Smock	16-0	.435	.500	1.2	0.3	0.9	0.6	22	1.4
Memering	14-0	.636	.667	0.3	0.2	0.6	0.2	18	1.3
Noort	12-0	.357	.625	1.5	0.2	0.5	0.6	15	1.3
Ahlfeld	14-0	.273	.700	0.4	0.9	0.6	0.5	13	0.9
Wilson	13-5	.300	.000	0.8	0.5	0.8	0.8	12	0.9
Allen	10-0	.167	.000	0.5	0.1	0.0	0.0	2	0.2
White	4-0	.000	.000	0.0	0.3	0.5	0.0	0	0.0

IU suffered its first loss on December 22, in Columbia, South Carolina. The Hoosiers went down to play Frank McGuire's South Carolina Gamecocks, a team that was loaded with talent that included future NBA players Mike Dunleavy Brian Winters and Alex English. However, it was a 6'3" guard named Kevin Joyce that shot down the Hoosiers. Joyce, who went on to play a couple seasons for the Indiana Pacers in the ABA, dropped in 41 points against IU, and the Gamecocks came from behind to pull out an 88-85 victory. Quinn Buckner had already earned a reputation as a rapacious defender, but even he couldn't do anything to stop Joyce that night.

Next, the Indiana team went down to El Paso, Texas, for the Sun Bowl Holiday Tournament on December 28-29. In the first game, the 15th-ranked Hoosiers beat No. 13 Houston 75-72, as Ritter and Downing combined for 40 points. In the championship game, Knight was appalled by the officiating, and with seven minutes left in the game, he drew three consecutive technicals and got ejected (it was the first time he was ejected from a game at Indiana). IU lost 74-65. The Hoosiers returned to

Bloomington and beat Ball State 94-71 to finish the preconference season 7-2 and ranked No. 20.

After opening Big Ten play 0-5 the season before and practically eliminating themselves from the race in the opening weeks, Bob Knight and the Indiana team wanted to get off to a better start in 1973 and give themselves a chance at the Big Ten title. The Hoosiers ended up getting off to a great start, winning their first six conference games to take the early lead in the conference race. IU opened with a 78-64 win over Wisconsin in Madison, led by a game-high 21 points from Ritter. Then, after notching an 80-68 nonconference win over Miami of Ohio, Indiana rolled by Ohio State 81-67 in Bloomington, led by a career-high 24 points from Buckner.

That set up an early showdown with No. 6 Minnesota, the defending conference champion, in Bloomington on January 20. Things looked bad for ninth-ranked IU early on. Downing and Buckner each picked up three early fouls in the first half, and Minnesota led 36-35 at the break. IU was plagued by cold shooting in the first half, so Minnesota coach Bill Musselman put his team in a zone in the second half

Coach Knight provides some instruction to sophomore forward Steve Green. IU Archives

from first place down to third when No. 4 Minnesota got revenge for its earlier loss in Assembly Hall by beating the Hoosiers 82-75 in Williams Arena in Minneapolis. It was Indiana's third loss in four games and put IU at 7-3 with only four games left in conference play.

The Hoosiers rose to the occasion and reeled off three straight wins, beating Michigan State and Wisconsin in Bloomington, and Iowa in Iowa City. At 10-3, IU was only a half-game behind Minnesota (10-2), but when the Gophers surprisingly lost to Iowa 79-77 in Williams Arena (two days after the Hoosiers beat the Hawkeyes 80-64), it deadlocked the conference race going into the final weekend of the season. On Saturday, March 10, Indiana hosted third-place Purdue, while Minnesota traveled to last-place Northwestern. If both teams won (or if both teams lost) then a playoff game would be staged the following Monday (March 12) to decide which of the two co-champions would represent the Big Ten in the NCAA Tournament. IU clinched at least a share of the title by pulling out a hard-fought 77-72 victory over the Boilermakers, led by 20 points from Downing, along with 15 from Green and 14 apiece from Laskowski and Crews.

In the final minutes of the Purdue game, the IU public address announcer, Chuck Crabb, invited the fans to stay in their seats for a special presentation following the game. After the Purdue team had retired to the locker room, Knight took the microphone and thanked the crowd for supporting the team. He also took a moment to thank former coach Lou Watson for bringing the team's four seniors to Indiana (unfortunately, Watson had already left the building to beat the traffic) and then he invited each of the seniors to take the mic for an impromptu last word to the home crowd. It was the beginning of a long-standing IU tradition that became known as "Senior Day", which soon spread to other colleges as well. Following the 1973 ceremony, the team got word that Northwestern had pulled off a 79-74 upset of Minnesota thanks to a 36-point performance from Northwestern senior Mark Sibley (after the season, Knight sent him an

in order to force the Hoosiers to shoot jump shots. The strategy backfired as Green, Ritter and Laskowski poured in jumper after jumper over the Gophers' zone. IU shot 18-25 (72 percent) from the field in the second half and coasted to an 83-71 win that gave Indiana a 3-0 conference record and dropped Minnesota to 1-2. Then the Hoosiers captured a pair of road wins over Michigan State and Michigan and clobbered Northwestern in Assembly Hall to improve to 6-0.

Ohio State finally handed Indiana its first conference loss on February 5, when OSU guard Allan Hornyak hit one of two free throws with 0:05 remaining to deliver a 70-69 upset for the Buckeyes. Next, Purdue tied IU at the top of the Big Ten standings (at 6-2) by defeating the Hoosiers 72-69 in West Lafayette. Indiana broke the short losing skid with an 87-66 pounding of Illinois, as Downing peppered the Illini with 41 points. Then, the IU squad got bumped

1972-73 SEASON RESULTS

Date	Court	Opponent	Result	Score
12/2/1972	H	Harvard	W	97-76
12/5/1972	A	Kansas	W	72-55
12/9/1972	H	(#8) Kentucky	W	64-58
12/12/1972	A	Notre Dame	W	69-67
12/16/1972	H	Ohio	W	89-68
12/22/1972	A	South Carolina	L	85-88
12/28/1972	N1	(#13) Houston	W	75-72
12/29/1972	N1	UTEP	L	65-74
1/3/1973	H	Ball State	W	94-71
1/6/1973	A	Wisconsin	W	78-64
1/9/1973	H	Miami of Ohio	W	80-68
1/13/1973	H	Ohio State	W	81-67
1/20/1973	H	(#6) Minnesota	W	83-71
1/22/1973	A	Michigan State	W	97-89
1/27/1973	A	Michigan	W	79-73
2/3/1973	H	Northwestern	W	83-65
2/5/1973	A	Ohio State	L	69-70
2/10/1973	A	Purdue	L	69-72
2/12/1973	H	Illinois	W	87-66
2/17/1973	A	(#4) Minnesota	L	75-82
2/19/1973	H	Michigan State	W	75-65
2/24/1973	H	Wisconsin	W	57-55
3/3/1973	A	Iowa	W	80-64
3/10/1973	H	Purdue	W	77-72
NCAA Tournament				
3/15/1973	N2	(#5) Marquette	W	75-69
3/17/1973	N2	(#17) Kentucky	W	72-65
3/24/1973	N3	(#1) UCLA	L	59-70
3/26/1973	N3	(#4) Providence	W	97-79

1 El Paso, TX
2 Nashville, TN
3 St. Louis, MO

Indiana blanket on behalf of the IU team as a token of gratitude). The Minnesota loss gave Indiana the outright Big Ten championship. At the time, it was only the fourth undisputed title in school history and the first since 1958. The seniors, who were all Indiana natives, had come to Bloomington to help restore the IU tradition after a string of last-place finishes in the late 1960s. "The thing we all felt when we came here was that we wanted to put Indiana back on top," said Ritter. With the 1973 conference title in hand, the seniors had accomplished that goal, but of course, their season wasn't done yet.

The sixth-ranked Hoosiers got a first round bye in the NCAA Tournament, but in the Mideast Regional Semifinals, IU ended up having to face No. 5 Marquette on the Vanderbilt campus in Nashville, Tennessee. Al McGuire's Golden Eagles were 24-2 and widely favored to beat the Hoosiers. The game featured a marquee matchup between IU's 6'8" Steve Downing and Marquette's 6'9" Maurice Lucas (who would go on to star in the ABA and NBA). Downing was dominant with 29 points on 12-of-17 shooting from field, while holding Lucas to six-of-15 shooting and 12 points. The other key to the game was that

Guard Jim Crews releases a baseline jump shot. In the first year of universal freshman eligibility, IU started two freshman guards—Crews and Quinn Bucker.   IU Archives

1972-73 BIG TEN STANDINGS

	W	L	PCT
Indiana	11	3	.786
Minnesota	10	4	.714
Purdue	8	6	.571
Ohio State	8	6	.571
Illinois	8	6	.571
Michigan St.	6	8	.429
Iowa	6	8	.429
Michigan	6	8	.429
Wisconsin	5	9	.357
Northwestern	2	12	.143

Buckner and Crews deftly handled Marquette's pressing defense. Marquette led by three at the break, but IU played a fiercely determined second half and prevailed 75-69. In the regional final, Indiana defeated Kentucky for the second time that season, but it wasn't easy. After roaring to a 45-32 halftime lead, the Hoosiers backpedaled in the second half as the Wildcats desperately clawed their way back into the game. Kentucky briefly surged ahead at 61-59, but Downing and Buckner were brilliant down the stretch as Buckner kept flashing to the high post to get the ball in the middle of Kentucky's zone and either fed Downing for easy scores inside, or scored himself. IU finished the game on 13-4 run to pull out a 72-65 victory. Downing finished with 23 points and 13 rebounds while Buckner had 16 points and 11 rebounds. Both were named to the regional's all-tournament team, and Downing earned the regional MVP award. Knight, coaching in his first NCAA Tournament, was now taking his team to the Final Four.

Awaiting the Hoosiers in St. Louis, Missouri, in the national semifinals, was the undefeated, top-ranked UCLA Bruins, who were on course to win their seventh consecutive NCAA title. The Bruins had been so dominant that people had starting calling the Final Four "The Annual UCLA Invitational." The conventional wisdom at the time was that it would take a high-scoring, fast-breaking team to beat UCLA, and since that wasn't Indiana's style, the general consensus was that the Bruins would run circles around the Hoosiers (people were more intrigued by a potential UCLA matchup against one of two run-and-gun teams, Memphis and Providence, that met in the other national final). However, what wasn't anticipated was that IU could neutralize the Bruins' most potent weapon—6'11" junior center Bill Walton, the college player of the year. The Hoosiers grabbed the lead early on, but then UCLA's Tommy Curtis got hot, and the Bruins made a big run to close the first half with a 40-22 lead. They increased the lead to 46-24 in the opening minutes of the second half before Indiana began to rally. Walton was having

Steve Green and Steve Downing celebrate with the IU faithful after the Hoosiers won the NCAA's Mideast Regional and earned a trip to the 1973 NCAA Final Four. IU Archives

trouble containing Downing and picked up his fourth foul early in the second half. Without Walton to clog the middle, IU began to score at will. The Hoosiers ran off 17 unanswered points and cut the lead to 54-51 with eight minutes remaining, which sent the capacity crowd into a frenzy as they realized they might be witnessing one of the great upsets in tournament history. UCLA coach John Wooden was

forced to put Walton back in the game, and shortly after returning, Walton got the ball on the baseline, turned to drive, and found Downing waiting for him. Walton threw an elbow and forearm into Downing's chest to push him off, and a whistle sounded. To the astonishment of nearly everyone in the arena, Walton was not called for a charging foul (which would have fouled him out of the game), but instead Downing

INDIANA'S RANKING IN THE 1972-73 ASSOCIATED PRESS POLLS

PS	12/5	12/12	12/19	12/26	1/2	1/9	1/16	1/23	1/30	2/6	2/13	2/20	2/27	3/6	3/13
—	—	15	9	15	20	16	16	6	5	4	11	10	12	9	6

was whistled for his fourth infraction. A minute later, Downing committed a legitimate foul and was gone with 7:57 still to play. The Hoosiers kept their rally going for a couple more minutes and cut the lead to 57-55 with 5:51 left. But then UCLA finished off Indiana with a 13-4 run and let out a sigh of relief with a 70-59 victory. Downing scored a game-high 26 points, while holding Walton to 14 points—although the big redhead also had 17 rebounds and nine assists. Two nights later, UCLA defeated Memphis 87-66 as Walton scored 44 points on 21-22 shooting in what is often called the greatest performance in college basketball history.

The second-half scare that Bob Knight and his Hoosiers had put into UCLA in the Final Four was akin to a little-known prize fighter who stepped into the ring and landed a left hook out of nowhere to knock down the heavyweight champion of world. Of course, on that day, the champ got up and eventually put down the upstart. However, before long, Knight's Hoosiers would become the heavyweight champion whom everyone else wanted to take a shot at.

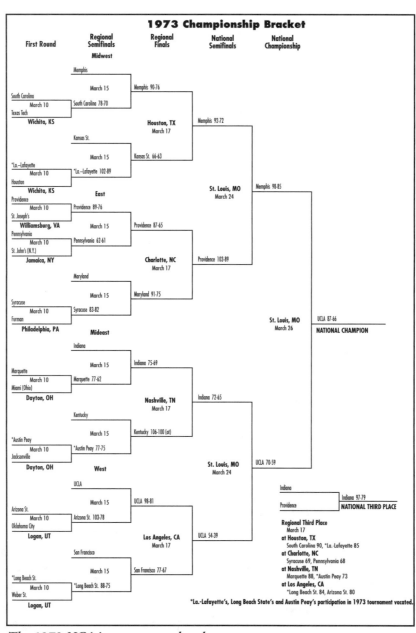

The 1973 NCAA tournament bracket.

Seniors John Ritter and Steve Downing hold up the trophy for winning the Mideast Regional in the NCAA tournament. IU went on to the Final Four and nearly upset top-ranked UCLA in the national semifinals. It was the first time Coach Knight took a team to the NCAA tournament.
IU Archives

CHAPTER 10

THE LITTLE TEAM THAT STOLE THE BIG TEN

1988-89

OVERALL RECORD: 27-8

CONFERENCE RECORD: 15-3 (FIRST PLACE)

TEAM HONORS:

BIG TEN CHAMPION, HOOSIER CLASSIC CHAMPION,

INDIANA CLASSIC CHAMPION

INDIVIDUAL HONORS:

BOB KNIGHT—NATIONAL COACH OF THE YEAR (CONSENSUS),

BIG TEN COACH OF THE YEAR

JAY EDWARDS—ALL-AMERICA, ALL-BIG TEN (FIRST TEAM),

BIG TEN PLAYER OF THE YEAR (MEDIA ONLY)

ERIC ANDERSON—BIG TEN FRESHMAN OF THE YEAR

JOE HILLMAN—ACADEMIC ALL-AMERICA, ACADEMIC ALL-BIG TEN

MAGNUS PELKOWSKI—ACADEMIC ALL-BIG TEN

When you talk about some of the greatest teams in IU basketball history, you won't often hear the 1988-89 team mentioned. That's because, quite honestly, they don't rank among the best teams in Indiana's illustrious history. They weren't very talented, nor were they were quick or athletic, and they didn't rebound the basketball very well. That's what makes their accomplishments during the 1988-89 season even more remarkable.

In a year when four different Big Ten teams were ranked in the top five, two of them went to the Final Four, and one of them (Michigan) ultimately won the national championship, an undermanned Hoosier squad bested them all by capturing the undisputed Big Ten title. What the Hoosiers lacked in talent, they made up for with teamwork and toughness—and team defense. They had a great leader in Joe Hillman, a great scorer in Jay Edwards, and a bunch of role players who embraced their duties in coach Bob Knight's system. The 19888-89 season is widely remembered in Indiana as Knight's greatest coaching job during his propitious 29 years in Bloomington,

and it was definitely one of the greatest seasons in the history of Indiana basketball, largely because its success was so unexpected.

Off the court, the summer and fall leading up to the start of the 1988-89 season could not have been much worse. Fifth-year senior Joe Hillman graduated with a degree in finance and spent the summer playing minor league baseball in the Oakland A's farm system. It looked doubtful that he would return for his final season of basketball eligibility with the Hoosiers. Sophomore Jay Edwards, the 1988 Big Ten Freshman of the Year and IU's top returning scorer, failed a drug test in September, and it looked like he would enter rehab and end up being ineligible for at least the first semester. Plus, many feared that Knight would kick Edwards off the team and end his basketball career at Indiana. During that same period, three other players got in trouble for personal indiscretions that reflected poorly on themselves, the team, and the university.

If there was one beacon of hope during the summer and fall, it was on the recruiting trail. The state of Indiana had a talented crop of high school players and

The 1988-89 team. First row (left to right): [unknown manager], Todd Jadlow, Brian Sloan, Mike D'Aloisio, Magnus Pelkowski, Kreigh Smith, Joe Hillman, [unknown manager]; Second row: Lyndon Jones, Chuckie White, Jeff Oliphant, Mark Robinson, Matt Nover, Jay Edwards, Eric Anderson, Jamal Meeks, [unknown manager]; Third row: trainer Tim Garl, head manager Julio Salazar, assistant coach Taylor Locke, assistant coach Dan Dakich, assistant coach Ron Felling, assistant coach Joby Wright, head coach Bob Knight. IU Archives

one by one nearly all of them committed to playing for IU. The native Indiana signees were Chris Lawson, Greg Graham, Pat Graham and Calbert Cheaney. The Hoosiers also beat out Duke and Michigan for the services of Chris Reynolds of Peoria, Illinois. (In the spring signing period, IU would also add highly touted Lawrence Funderburke from Columbus, Ohio, and Todd Leary from Indianapolis.) However, none of those players was going to arrive on campus for another year.

Fortunately, Knight also began to get some good news regarding his 1988-89 squad. Hillman decided to return for his senior season. Mostly, it was a matter of pride. Joe had played well, but not great, at IU, and he wanted one more shot at excellence. He also wanted one more chance to enjoy the incomparable atmosphere of college basketball. Edwards got counseling from assistant athletic director (and former IU All-American) Steve Downing and ended up entering a 10-day rehab program for his drug problem. That meant he would still be eligible, and he decided that he wanted to stay at Indiana to play. Knight let him

remain on the team, but took away his scholarship and put Edwards's class work and personal behavior under close supervision.

Hillman and Edwards were Indiana's top returning players and were really the only two players on the roster with significant experience in the starting lineup. Hillman was a gritty 6'2" sparkplug who was smart with the ball, could knock down the open shot, and played aggressive defense. The 6'4" Edwards was a smooth, fluid athlete who could shoot the lights out when he got hot and could also score off the dribble. He had a laid-back demeanor and always looked like he was in control. That composure also made him a phenomenal clutch shooter. The two other top returnees were 6'1" sophomore point guard Lyndon Jones, a former high school teammate of Edwards, and Todd Jadlow, a 6'9" senior who had started 10 games the season before and shown flashes of strong play in the post. The rest of the squad had little or no experience in Big Ten basketball. Magnus Pelkowski, Jeff Oliphant, Kreigh Smith and Brian Sloan were all upperclassmen and returning lettermen, but all of

1988-89 TEAM ROSTER

Head coach: Bob Knight
Assistant coaches: Dan Dakich, Ron Felling, Taylor Locke, Joby Wright

No.	Player	Hometown	Class	Position	Height
32	Eric Anderson	Chicago, IL	Fr	F/C	6-9
21	Mike D'Aloisio	Hillsborough, CA	Sr	G	6-4
3	Jay Edwards	Marion, IN	So	G/F	6-4
44	Joe Hillman (Capt.)	Glendale, CA	Sr	G	6-2
11	Todd Jadlow	Salina, KS	Sr	F/C	6-9
4	Lyndon Jones	Marion, IN	So	G	6-1
23	Jamal Meeks	Freeport, IL	Fr	G	6-0
24	Matt Nover	Chesterton, IN	Rs	F	6-8
35	Jeff Oliphant	Lyons, IN	Jr	G	6-5
14	Magnus Pelkowski	Bogota, Columbia	Sr	C	6-10
10	Mark Robinson	Van Nuys, CA	Jr	F	6-5
45	Brian Sloan	McLeansboro, IL	Sr	F/C	6-8
42	Kreigh Smith	Tipton, IN	Sr	G/F	6-7
5	Chuckie White	Charlotte, NC	Jr	F	6-7

The undisputed leader of the upstart 1988-89 Hoosiers was 6'2" guard Joe Hillman. Hillman returned to Bloomington for his final season and led IU to a surprising Big Ten title. IU Archives

them had been little-used reserves in the past. The newcomers included three upperclassmen: junior college transfers Mark Robinson and Chuckie White and Mike D'Aloisio, a senior who had transferred to IU from the University of San Francisco.

The other three newcomers were freshmen Matt Nover, Jamaal Meeks and Eric Anderson. Nover, a 6'8" forward from Chesterton, Indiana, ended up redshirting. Meeks was a quick, hustling 6'0" guard from Freeport, Illinois. He spent most of the season as an understudy to Jones at point guard. The most promising of the freshmen was 6'9" Chicago native Eric Anderson, a McDonald's All-American and the 1988 Illinois Mr. Basketball. Anderson was an excellent face-up shooter and a solid rebounder who had good fundamentals and an eager work ethic. He ended up becoming the first

1988-89 SEASON STATISTICS

Team Statistics	G	FG%	3FG%	FT%	R	A	TO	S	B	PF	PTS	PPG
Indiana	35	.495	.473	.734	35.3	15.1	13.7	5.7	3.3	18.4	2747	78.5
Opponents	35	.436	.381	.688	36.5	13.5	14.2	5.6	2.9	23.3	2487	71.1

Player Statistics	G-GS	FG%	3FG%	FT%	R	A	TO	S	B	PF	PTS	PPG
Edwards	34-33	.474	.448	.823	4.3	3.7	3.0	1.1	0.8	2.7	680	20.0
Hillman	34-34	.535	.581	.806	3.4	3.9	1.5	1.2	0.1	1.9	430	12.6
Anderson	34-32	.545	.000	.726	6.1	0.3	1.6	0.4	1.0	2.9	404	11.9
Jadlow	34-28	.493	.000	.723	5.1	0.4	1.7	0.5	0.5	2.8	359	10.6
Jones	34-29	.481	.500	.798	2.9	3.4	1.9	0.9	0.1	2.1	286	8.4
White	32-5	.496	.000	.595	1.9	0.3	0.8	0.3	0.3	1.3	141	4.4
Robinson	29-4	.511	.000	.366	2.6	0.5	0.6	0.3	0.3	1.0	107	3.7
Smith	15-1	.362	.500	.769	1.4	0.5	0.4	0.2	0.0	0.6	50	3.3
Meeks	35-1	.465	.333	.727	1.6	1.9	1.3	0.7	0.1	1.1	99	2.8
Sloan	34-7	.438	.000	.583	2.4	0.6	0.7	0.4	0.3	2.7	91	2.7
Pelkowski	17-1	.419	.333	.500	2.2	0.2	0.4	0.1	0.2	0.9	41	2.4
Oliphant	21-0	.524	.667	.917	0.5	0.3	0.4	0.2	0.0	0.3	39	1.9
D'Aloisio	18-0	.583	.000	.857	0.4	0.3	0.5	0.0	0.0	0.7	20	1.1

freshman since Isiah Thomas to start for IU on opening night, and he immediately became a fixture in the lineup.

One of the things that most analysts and sportswriters saw when they looked at the 1988-89 Hoosiers was the fact that they lost three double-digit scorers in center Dean Garrett, forward Rick Calloway, and guard Keith Smart. Garrett and Smart graduated and went on to play professional basketball, while Calloway decided to transfer to Kansas. IU also graduated Steve Eyl, a reliable frontcourt reserve. With those four players in 1987-88, Indiana had stumbled to a 19-10 record and a first-round exit in the NCAA tournament. Without them—and no players to provide an immediate upgrade to the lineup—the Hoosiers were expected to be even worse in 1988-89. Most Big Ten sportswriters predicted a seventh place finish in the conference for IU, and college basketball commentator Billy Packer even went so far as to say "Knight is not a story" this year.

The doomsayers appeared to have made the right call when IU struggled during the first three weeks of the season. The Hoosiers opened in the Preseason NIT and beat Illinois State and No. 20 Stanford to advance to the semifinals in New York City. The most pleasant surprise in those two games was center Todd

Jadlow, who scored 21 points against Illinois State and had 23 points and 12 rebounds against Stanford, which tried (unsuccessfully) to physically bully the Hoosiers. Indiana was also sparked by Jay Edwards, who had 14 points, six rebounds, and five assists against Illinois State and a game-high 27 points against Stanford. However, things got a lot tougher when the Hoosiers arrived in the Big Apple for the final two rounds of the NIT. Sixth-ranked Syracuse blasted IU 102-78 in the semifinals, and then No. 18 North Carolina roared to a 106-92 win over the Hoosiers in the consolation game. Edwards led all scorers with 31 points against the Tar Heels, and Jadlow chipped in 27 points and 12 rebounds, but the IU defense was ineffective for the second straight game.

After an 87-70 win against an overmatched Miami of Ohio team, the Hoosiers took a 101-79 beating from 13th-ranked Louisville at the Hoosier Dome in Indianapolis on December 3. In Bob Knight's first 16 seasons at Indiana, only one opponent had ever scored 100 points against the defensive-minded Hoosiers. Now, in less than two weeks, it had happened three times in a span of four games. Three days after the Louisville loss, IU dropped an 84-71 decision to Notre Dame in South Bend. That put

The first piece in Coach Knight's three-guard lineup that he used throughout the 1988-89 campaign was point guard Lyndon Jones. The 6'1" Jones could score when needed but mostly deferred to his teammates and focused on setting them up for easy scores. IU Archives

Indiana's record at 3-4, and it looked like it was going to be a long season in Bloomington. However, the Notre Dame game was the turning point. That was the game that Knight decided to go with a three-guard lineup of Lyndon Jones, Jay Edwards and Joe Hillman, with the 6'2" Hillman essentially playing the small forward spot on both sides of the ball. Although the Hoosiers got killed on the boards (43-27) against the Fighting Irish and lost that game, Todd Jadlow and Eric Anderson soon joined the three-guard lineup to form an effective starting five.

The Hoosiers would only lose four more games the rest of the season.

Six of IU's final seven games in the preconference season were played in the friendly confines of either Assembly Hall or Market Square Arena in Indianapolis, and the Hoosiers rolled to double-digit victories in seven straight games to improve their record to 10-4. The one road game during that stretch was a December 20 matchup against Kentucky in Rupp Arena. Entering that contest, Indiana hadn't won in Lexington since 1926 and had never defeated the Wildcats at Rupp. Twenty-nine seconds into the game, Kentucky forward Reggie Hanson broke Lyndon Jones's nose with an elbow to the face. That fired up the Hoosiers, who mounted a surprising 36-24 halftime lead. Indiana then scored the first four points of the second half to build the advantage to 16 points and controlled the rest of the game on the way to a 75-52 whipping of the Wildcats. Despite the broken nose, Jones returned to the game, played 28 minutes, and finished with six points, six assists, and no turnovers. Edwards led IU with 21 points, while Anderson had 17 points and nine rebounds. The Hoosiers held Kentucky to 35-percent shooting from the floor, held center LeRon Ellis to eight points (13.4 below his average), and outrebounded the Wildcats 38-33.

Indiana had a seven-game winning streak going into the Big Ten season, but still, most observers weren't convinced that the Hoosiers could pose a threat to Big Ten powerhouses Michigan, Illinois and Iowa. IU sent its first warning flair to the conference favorites in the Big Ten opener on January 4, when IU hammered out a tough 75-65 win over No. 14 Ohio State in Assembly Hall. Edwards paced Indiana with 24 points, six assists, and five rebounds, and Anderson had 10 points and 10 rebounds in his first conference game. Five days later, Indiana went on the road and stole a 74-73 win from Purdue in Mackey Arena. In the final minute, Edwards stepped to the line and hit five of six free throws as the Purdue crowd chanted "Just say no" in mockery of Edwards's drug problems the previous fall. Edwards finished with a game-high 22 points, but the catalyst of the win was Joe Hillman, who carried IU in the second half and finished with 18 points, seven assists, five rebounds, and zero turnovers. Ironically, the win gave Knight 214 coaching victories in Big Ten play, which allowed him to surpass Purdue's Piggy Lambert as the winningest coach in conference history.

Next, Indiana bowled down Northwestern, Wisconsin and Michigan State to improve to 5-0 in the Big Ten, a half-game ahead of Illinois for first place. IU was now ranked 19th in the country, but that ranking was put to a stern test on January 23, when the Hoosiers played No. 6 Michigan in Ann Arbor. The game went back and forth until Edwards fouled out Michigan guard Rumeal Robinson with 7:38 remaining and Indiana trailing 55-54. Edwards scored 11 points over the next four minutes as IU surged ahead, and then he pulled down the game-winning rebound to preserve a 71-70 Hoosier victory. Edwards's 28 points led all scorers and Hillman added 12 points and eight assists. The victory was Indiana's 13th-straight win, the longest winning streak for an IU team since the Hoosiers' great teams in the mid-1970s. However, Indiana didn't have long to celebrate. Later that week, Indiana had to play Illinois in Champaign.

The Fighting Illini were ranked No. 1 in the nation at the time, but IU seemed to be catching them at the right moment. The Illini had recently lost star guard Kendall Gill to a broken foot and two days earlier they lost to Minnesota, which put the first blemish on Illinois's record after 18 straight wins and basically guaranteed that they would no longer be No. 1 in the polls the following week. The Hoosiers, who were 6-0 in the conference to second-place Illinois's 4-1, smelled blood and

In a pivotal game against Michigan in Assembly Hall, sophomore guard Jay Edwards nailed this three-pointer just before the buzzer sounded to give Indiana an exhilarating 76-75 triumph over the Wolverines. Indiana went on to win the Big Ten title and Edwards was named Big Ten MVP. IU Archives

jumped out to a 35-25 lead at the half. But, with their backs against the wall, the Illini came out fighting on both ends of the floor in the second half, and stormed past the Hoosiers for a decisive 75-65 victory, led by forwards Kenny Battle and Nick Anderson, who finished with 22 points and 21 points, respectively. Afterwards Knight said, "The first nine minutes of the second half they were extremely good. If I was objective about it, that's the kind of basketball I really enjoy watching, but it's hard to be objective about it when you're getting your [butt] kicked."

Even with the Illinois loss, IU still held the conference lead by a half-game—and they didn't let up. In fact, IU started a new eight-game winning streak. Todd Jadlow's 32 points and 13 rebounds led IU past 12th-ranked Iowa, the Hoosiers overcame a six-point halftime deficit to beat Minnesota, and then they clobbered Northwestern behind 24 points each from Edwards and Anderson. At 9-1, IU was two and a half games ahead of the competition—Illinois and Michigan—in the league race.

If the Hoosiers suddenly looked like a team of destiny, then the next two games seemed to confirm that providence was smiling down on their accomplishments. Upset-minded Purdue came into Assembly Hall on Sunday, February 12, and took an 11-point lead midway through the second half before IU mounted a final charge. The game was tied with 32 seconds remaining and Indiana had possession of the ball. After running time off the clock, IU got the ball to Edwards near the top of the circle. He drove the ball to the left side, faked toward the basket, and then pulled back and buried the game-winning 16-footer for a 64-62 Indiana victory in a game that was televised throughout the Hoosier state.

A week later, No. 9 Indiana hosted 13th-ranked Michigan in Bloomington in another widely televised matchup. The capacity crowd in Assembly Hall included IU recruits Pat Graham, Chris Lawson, Lawrence Funderburke and Damon Bailey, who had already committed to the Hoosiers at the beginning of his junior season. The Wolverines came out aggres-

Freshman big man Eric Anderson was Indiana's most pleasant surprise in 1999. Anderson grabbed a starting job and gave the Hoosiers a reliable scorer in the frontcourt. His effective play earned him the Big Ten's Freshman of the Year award. IU Archives

sive, but their star forward Glen Rice got in early foul trouble. IU led 42-37 at the half and 69-65 with five minutes remaining, but Michigan ran off a 10-2 run capped by a three-pointer from Sean Higgins with a minute left to play. Suddenly Indiana was down 75-71. Jay Edwards sank two free throws with 0:54 left to cut the lead to 75-73. Michigan used all of the 45-second shot clock and got the ball to Rice, who missed a bank shot from the wing. With 0:08 left, Eric Anderson, who was playing with a dislocated thumb, grabbed the rebound and then took almost four seconds to get the ball to Lyndon Jones who grabbed the pass and quickly streaked up the court. The fans in Assembly Hall rose to their feet and the noise began to mount. Then Jones raced across the timeline, read the defence, spotted Edwards moving into scoring position at the top of the key and flipped him the ball. Edwards caught it and fluidly released a long three-pointer. Just after the ball left his hand, the buzzer went off; the ball hung high in the air and then swished through the net to give Indiana an electrifying 76-75 victory. Edwards led the Hoosiers with 23 points, including 10 of IU's final 11 points down the stretch.

The Michigan win put the Hoosiers at 11-1 in the conference, a full three games ahead of second-place Illinois with only six games remaining. IU then went on the road and won three straight games over Michigan State, Minnesota and Ohio State to clinch at least a tie for the Big Ten crown. That gave IU a chance to clinch the title outright on March 5, against eighth-ranked Illinois in Bloomington. The Hoosiers had a 12-point lead midway through the second half, but the Illini pulled in front 67-65 with 0:17 to go. Then Edwards did the impossible once again. He got the ball on the wing in front of the IU bench, faked a drive to the basket and then had to fade out of bounds to get off a shot over two Illinois players. The ball looped high in the air, floated over the corner of the backboard and dropped straight through the net to tie the game at 67-67. Illinois started asking for a timeout before the ball even went in the basket, and they were rewarded when the officials put two seconds on the clock. The Illini threw a baseball pass to Nick Anderson, who leapt high in the air to catch the ball, came down, and then released a 35-foot

1988-89 SEASON RESULTS

Date	Court	Opponent	Result	Score
11/18/1988	H	Illinois State	W	83-48
11/20/1988	H	(#20) Stanford	W	84-73
11/23/1988	N1	(#6) Syracuse	L	78-102
11/25/1988	N1	(#18) North Carolina	L	92-106
11/29/1988	A	Miami of Ohio	W	87-70
12/3/1988	N2	(#13) Louisville	L	79-101
12/6/1988	A	Notre Dame	L	71-84
12/9/1988	H	Virginia Commonwealth	W	85-68
12/10/1988	H	Santa Clara	W	64-49
12/14/1988	H	Arkansas-Little Rock	W	105-77
12/17/1988	H	UTEP	W	81-63
12/20/1988	A	Kentucky	W	75-52
12/28/1988	N2	St. Bonaventure	W	103-66
12/29/1988	N2	Utah State	W	73-61
1/4/1989	H	(#14) Ohio State	W	75-65
1/9/1989	A	Purdue	W	74-73
1/14/1989	H	Northwestern	W	92-76
1/19/1989	A	Wisconsin	W	61-58
1/21/1989	H	Michigan State	W	75-60
1/23/1989	A	(#6) Michigan	W	71-70
1/28/1989	A	(#1) Illinois	L	65-75
1/30/1989	H	(#12) Iowa	W	104-89
2/4/1989	H	Minnesota	W	66-62
2/9/1989	A	Northwestern	W	72-56
2/12/1989	H	Purdue	W	64-62
2/19/1989	H	(#13) Michigan	W	76-75
2/23/1989	A	Michigan State	W	76-65
2/25/1989	A	Minnesota	W	75-62
3/1/1989	A	Ohio State	W	73-66
3/5/1989	H	(#8) Illinois	L	67-70
3/9/1989	H	Wisconsin	W	75-64
3/11/1989	A	(#15) Iowa	L	70-87

NCAA Tournament

Date	Court	Opponent	Result	Score
3/17/1989	N3	George Mason	W	99-85
3/19/1989	N3	UTEP	W	92-69
3/23/1989	N4	(#11) Seton Hall	L	65-78

1 New York, NY
2 Indianapolis, IN
3 Tucson, AZ
4 Denver, CO

Jay Edwards shares a smile with teammate Jamal Meeks on the day the Hoosiers clinched the undisputed 1989 Big Ten championship. IU Archives

turnaround jump shot that swished through the net at the buzzer, giving Illinois a 70-67 win.

However, four days later, Indiana beat Wisconsin 75-64 on Senior Day—the final home game of the season—to clinch the undisputed Big Ten championship. With the title in hand, Knight chose to rest starters Hillman, Edwards, Jadlow and Anderson for the final game of the regular season at Iowa. All four of those players were afflicted with various ailments. Without them, Iowa easily plowed through the Hoosiers for an 87-70 victory. Unfortunately, that loss probably contributed to IU losing the No. 1 seed in the Midwest Regional in the NCAA tournament. The selection committee awarded that spot to Illinois, which had a better overall record than IU and had recently been bolstered by the return of star guard Kendall Gill. The Fighting Illini ended up going on to the Final Four. IU got the No. 2 seed in the West Regional, beat George Mason and UTEP in the first two rounds, but then fell 78-65 to Seton Hall, which eventually made it all the way to the NCAA championship game. Against the Pirates,

Edwards was limited to 23 minutes because of foul trouble and Seton Hall's stingy defense held IU to 29 percent shooting in the second half.

1988-89 BIG TEN STANDINGS

	W	L	PCT
Indiana	15	3	.833
Illinois	14	4	.778
Michigan	12	6	.667
Iowa	10	8	.556
Minnesota	9	9	.500
Wisconsin	8	10	.444
Purdue	8	10	.444
Ohio State	6	12	.333
Michigan St.	6	12	.333
Northwestern	2	16	.111

Guard Joe Hillman addresses the Hoosier crowd during the 1989 Senior Day festivities. Hillman postponed a shot at playing minor league baseball to return to IU. His toughness and leadership were key components in Indiana's surprising run to capture the undisputed conference title that season. IU Archives

Despite the disappointing defeat in the NCAA Tournament, there was no denying that Indiana put together a magical season and gave Hoosier fans a lot of terrific memories. They were one of the greatest underdogs of the Bob Knight era and had to execute their game plan with a very small margin of error because of their limitations in size, depth and athleticism. Above all, the players on this team learned to trust each other and their coach, and they learned how to pull together when things got tough.

The two players—Hillman and Edwards—who were the biggest question marks entering the season, ended up being two of the key factors in IU's successful campaign. Coach Knight called Hillman the best leader Indiana had seen since Quinn Buckner, and Knight made several public appeals for Hillman as the Big Ten MVP. Meanwhile, Edwards cleaned up his act off the court and greatly improved his play on the court. He earned All-America honors and was named the Big Ten Player of the Year by the media. However, believing that he was a hot commodity, the sophomore Edwards decided to leave IU and enter the NBA draft. That earned him a ticket to basketball oblivion when he was selected by the Los Angeles Clippers in the second round, and within a year he was no longer in the NBA.

For those who may have their doubts about the 1988-89 season being one of the best in school history, there's one more fact to consider. This IU squad won at both Rupp Arena and Mackey Arena, the home dens of Indiana's two greatest rivals. No other Hoosier team has ever accomplished that highly coveted feat.

INDIANA'S RANKING IN THE 1988-89 ASSOCIATED PRESS POLLS

PS	11/22	11/29	12/6	12/13	12/20	12/27	1/3	1/10	1/17	1/24	1/31	2/7	2/14	2/21	2/28	3/7	3/14
—	20	—	—	—	—	—	—	—	19	16	17	13	9	4	3	6	8

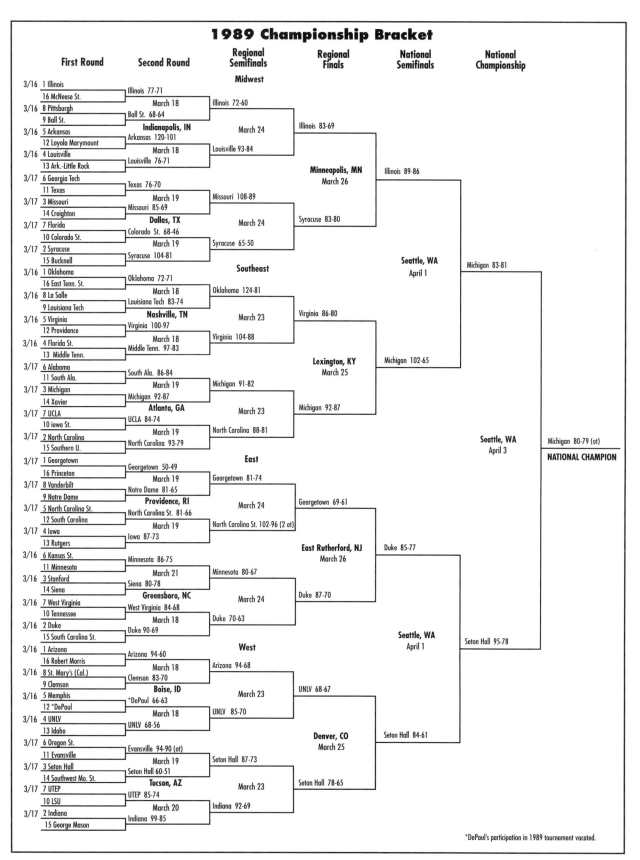

The 1989 NCAA tournament bracket.

PART II

THE TEN ERAS OF INDIANA BASKETBALL

CHAPTER 11

1900-01

OVERALL RECORD: 1-3

The 1900-01 team. First row (left to right): Phelps Darby, Ernest Strange, Jay Fitzgerald, Alvah Rucker; Second row: coach J. H. Horne, Charles Unnewehr, Earl Walker, manager Thomas Records. IU Archives

During the 1900-01 school year, the Indiana University athletic department felt confident that it had the kind of players needed to compete with rival schools in "basket ball," as it was known then. Thus, when the students returned from their holiday break at the end of 1900, Athletic Director J. H. Horne sent out the call for players to try out for the newly organized team.

Throughout the month of January 1901, the players competed in drills and daily scrimmages and learned some of the finer points of team basketball from Horne, who served as the team's coach, and Thomas Records, the team's manager. Slowly, the team whittled down to a core group of the best candidates for the varsity, and on February 1, the *Indiana Daily Student* announced, "The Basket Ball team will

1900-01 TEAM ROSTER

Head coach: J. H. Horne

Player	Hometown	Class	Position
Guy Cantwell	Spencer, IN	So	G
Phelps Darby	Evansville, IN	Fr (Law)	C
Jay Fitzgerald	Clarion, PA	Sr	F
Alvah Rucker	Evansville, IN	Jr	G
Ernest Strange (Capt.)	Arcana, IN	So	G/F
Charles Unnewehr	Batesville, IN	Jr	F/C
Earl Walker	Huntington, IN	Sr	F/G

SEASON RESULTS 1900-01

Date	Court	Opponent	Result	Score
2/8/1901	A	Butler	L	17-20
2/21/1901	H	Butler	L	20-24
3/2/1901	H	Purdue	L	15-20
3/8/1901	H	Wabash	W	26-17

play Butler, on the afternoon of February 8 at Indianapolis. A return game will be scheduled, but the dates have not yet been decided upon."

Six players were chosen to represent IU basketball in its first game—the forwards were Charles Unnewehr and Ernest Strange (team captain), the center was Phelps Darby, the guards were Earl Walker and Alvah Rucker, and Guy Cantwell was the substitute. The team, along with 100 of its fans, took the 11:00 a.m. train to Indianapolis in order to face Butler at 3:00 p.m. on Friday, February 8, 1901, at the Indianapolis YMCA gymnasium. For its first game, IU was treated to a great crowd that included not only the IU boosters and a large contingent from Butler, but also college students from across the state, who were in town for the State Oratorical Contest that night.

IU and Butler didn't disappoint the crowd. They staged a hard-fought contest that remained close for most of the game, and "the excitement approached that of an inter-collegiate football contest." The IU players definitely showed their inexperience in having never played on an opponent's floor as they got out of sync on a number of occasions; however, they kept the score close as several players made nice shots and Strange did a good job of converting at the free throw line. Nevertheless, while IU appeared to have the bet-

ter overall team, they could not stop Butler's star forward, Carl McGaughey (who was also one of the top players on the tough Indianapolis YMCA squad). McGaughey scored a game-high 10 points against the Hoosiers, including several key baskets down the stretch, as Butler prevailed 20-17. Strange led IU with nine points and seven of them came at the free throw line.

A return match-up was scheduled for Thursday, February 21, in Bloomington. In preparation for the rematch, Indiana made a few lineup changes. Jay Fitzgerald, who was injured before the first Butler game, returned to claim one of the starting forward spots and Strange and Darby switched positions, with the 5'9" Strange moving to the center position and the 5'11" Darby moving to forward to match up directly with Butler's McGaughey.

In the first half, Butler came into IU's Men's Gymnasium and hit Indiana with everything it had. McGaughey, whom the *Indiana Daily Student* described as "very tall and very active" and "the best goal thrower in the state," scored five field goals in the first half and led the Bulldogs to a 16-6 advantage at the break. Butler scored to open the second half and had Indiana down by 12 when the Hoosiers finally began to rally. Led by Strange, IU would outscore Butler 14-6 the rest of the way, but still lost 24-20. McGaughey, though scoreless in the second half, again led all scorers with 10 points. Strange and Fitzgerald led IU with six points each.

Indiana's next contest, against Purdue on Saturday, March 2, in Bloomington, was highly anticipated because of the fierce rivalry that the two state schools had already developed in football. Neither team wasted any time getting down to business after the opening tip. Purdue scored quickly in the game's first minute and IU responded as Walker buried a shot to tie the game. Then, both teams dug in on defense and turned the game into a fierce, physical battle. Purdue led 12-10 at the half, and in the second half both teams came out of the locker room with even greater intensity. IU scored first and tied the game. However, Purdue's defense eventually wore down the Hoosiers and the Boilermakers prevailed 20-15. Purdue ended up going 12-0 on the season and was probably the best team in the country (although the Helms Foundation later named Yale, who went 10-4, as the mythical 1901 national champion).

After being spurned from victory for a third time, the Hoosiers took out their frustration on the Wabash Little Giants the following week. Wabash came to Bloomington on Friday, March 8, and hung in with the Hoosiers during the first half of their game, trailing only 9-8. However, Indiana kicked into high gear in the second session and played its best basketball of the season, scoring 17 points and eventually securing their first victory by a score of 26-17.

Indiana had originally agreed to also play return games at Purdue and at Wabash during the month of March. However, after the victory over the Little Giants in Bloomington, "the games scheduled with Wabash and Purdue later in the same month were declared off, and the season ended at Indiana," according to the 1901 *Arbutus* (the IU yearbook). While some later records state that Purdue defeated Indiana 23-19 on March 15, it's likely that the game was never played. Neither the West Lafayette newspapers, nor the Bloomington or Indianapolis papers have any postgame reports from an IU-Purdue contest in West Lafayette in March.

In its postgame report after the Wabash game, the *Indiana Daily Student* was already looking to the future: "The victory of last night makes one fact more than ever evident; the future of basketball at Indiana is bright. With the experience of this year, the next season will find a team second to none in the state and one of the best in the West." Although this was clearly an optimistic assertion written by a team booster, the prediction would prove prophetic, although it would take a few decades to materialize.

1901-02

OVERALL RECORD: 4-4

Indiana University entered its second season of intercollegiate basketball with the definite expectation that its team would improve upon its record from the previous year. There was clearly some confidence that the Hoosiers had benefited from the experience of their first season, and, even though they lost three of that season's four games, they were competitive in each contest.

Several of the players who had competed on the varsity now returned to play for the 1901-02 squad, led by returning starters, guard Alvah Rucker and center Phelps Darby. In addition to being the team captain, Darby was also named the coach of the varsity, while athletic director J. H. Horne coached the second team.

Unfortunately, due to a fire in the early part of the 20th century, the original archives of the *Indiana Daily Student* (the best source of information for the early IU basketball years) were destroyed. As a result, only fragments of information and very little in the way of statistics exist for the games played during the 1901-02 and the 1902-03 seasons. Nevertheless, we do know that in 1901-02, Indiana played twice as many games (eight) as it had played in its first season and we also have the scores of those games, along with a few accounts that document the highs and lows as the Hoosiers posted a 4-4 record and entertained crowds that were growing larger and more enthusiastic for this new sport.

Just as it had the year before, IU opened the season with a game against Butler. However, the 1901-02 opener was played in Bloomington on Wednesday, January 15. The Hoosiers looked strong in the first half, charging out to a 15-9 lead, but the second half was a disaster. Butler shut out Indiana in the second half as the Hoosiers could not register a single field goal and repeatedly missed from the free throw stripe. Butler used an 8-0 second-half advantage to pull out a surprising 17-15 victory.

The following week, IU traveled to Terre Haute for a doubleheader with that town's two colleges: Indiana State Normal School (now Indiana State University) and Rose Polytechnic Institute (now Rose-Hulman Institute of Technology). On Friday, January 24, IU squared off with Indiana State. The first half went back and forth and ended with the home team up 11-8. The Hoosiers were much more aggressive in the second half and picked up the pace of the game. They outscored Indiana State 13-2 after the intermission and secured a 21-13 victory led by the scoring of Darby. Indiana's freshman guard Charles Carr and sophomore forward Willis Coval (who was also a football player and a wrestler) also played well and helped the Hoosiers grab their first ever road victory.

The 1901-02 team. First row (left to right): [unknown], Willis Coval, Alvah Rucker, Phelps Darby, [unknown], [unknown]; Second row: coach J. H. Horne, [unknown], Edmund Elfers, [unknown], [unknown]. IU Archives

The next night, Saturday, January 25, a fresh Rose Poly team awaited the Hoosiers, then pounced on them immediately after the tip, and soon opened up a big halftime lead from which IU could never recover. Despite a better team effort in the second half and strong scoring from Darby for the second straight night, the Hoosiers fell 23-16.

One week later, on Saturday, February 1, IU evened its season record at 2-2 by winning a close 26-23 victory over Wabash College. Then the Hoosiers had two weeks to prepare for a showdown with Purdue on February 15 in Bloomington. However, Purdue had another strong team, and the Boilermakers came to the IU campus and humiliated the Hoosiers 32-8, in a game the Hoosiers never had a chance to win after the opening minutes.

Ten days later, on Tuesday, February 25, IU bounced back with another road win and evened their record at .500 again. This victory came at the expense of Butler in the form of 32-29 win over the Bulldogs

at the Indianapolis YMCA. The win was especially remarkable because the Hoosiers did it without Darby —their captain, coach, and leading scorer—who remained in Bloomington with a badly sprained ankle. Edmund Elfers stepped into the starting center position and played a solid game, flanked by forwards Rucker and Coval, and guards Carr and Harry Ayers.

Three days after the Butler win, IU climbed over the .500 mark for the first time in school history by defeating Indiana State in Bloomington. That game, on Friday, February 28, was never really close. Even though IU was without Darby again, the Hoosiers dominated the first half and came away with a 16-2 advantage at the break. Butler tried to get things going in the second half, but it wasn't enough as IU ran to a 25-14 victory.

That left only a rematch with Purdue in West Lafayette standing between the Hoosiers and a winning season. Indiana needed revenge after the 24-point whipping it received from Purdue in the first

1901-02 TEAM ROSTER

Head coach: Phelps Darby

Player	Hometown	Class	Position
Harry Ayers	Hartford City, IN	Jr	G
Guy Cantwell	Spencer, IN	Jr	G
Charles Carr	Anderson, IN	Fr	F
Willis Coval	Indianapolis, IN	So	F
Phelps Darby (Capt.)	Evansville, IN	Sr (Law)	C/F
Clyde Dreisbach	Fort Wayne, IN	Jr	F
Edmund Elfers	Rising Sun, IN	Sr	G
Thomas Harrison	Evansville, IN	Sr	F
Alvah Rucker	Evansville, IN	Sr	G
Roy Shackleton	Chatterton, IN	So	G
William Stone	Spencer, IN	Jr	F
Charles Unnewehr	Batesville, IN	Sr	F/C
Marvin Wallace	Milton, IN	So	G

SEASON RESULTS 1901-02

Date	Court	Opponent	Result	Score
1/15/1902	H	Butler	L	15-17
1/24/1902	A	Indiana State	W	21-13
1/25/1902	A	Rose Poly	L	16-23
2/1/1902	W	Wabash	W	26-23
2/15/1902	H	Purdue	L	8-32
2/25/1902	A	Butler	W	32-29
2/28/1902	H	Indiana State	W	25-14
3/7/1902	A	Purdue	L	25-71

game. Fortunately, IU would end up scoring more than three times as many points as it had in the first game. Unfortunately, Purdue would more than double the high score it had registered in the first game. The result was hideous—a 71-25 Boilermaker triumph in front of a record crowd at the Purdue gymnasium.

Nevertheless, despite the disappointing season-ending loss at Purdue, IU had completed its second season with four wins and four losses. Seniors Darby and Rucker had been the team's primary scorers, but younger players such as Carr, Ayers, and Guy Cantwell had also played well, and provided some optimism for the future.

1902-03

OVERALL RECORD: 8-4

Like the 1901-02 season, scant records and game reports exist for IU's 1902-03 basketball campaign because of the lost archives of the *Indiana Daily Student*. However, we do know that Indiana recorded its first winning record with an 8-4 mark during the 1902-03 school year, and that the Hoosiers got a pleasant surprise out of freshman Leslie Maxwell, who stepped in to assume the role of starting center and became the team's leading scorer.

One thing that isn't very clear about the 1902-03 season is who served as the team's coach. A number of later sources list Willis Coval as the coach. However, Coval actually lettered as the team manager for 1902-03. Athletic director J. H. Horne was definitely still closely involved with the team. He provided at least some minimal instruction and traveled with the squad on road trips. A March 7, 1903 article in the *Lafayette Daily Courier* referred to the IU team as "Horne's five." To further confuse matters, a January 14, 1903, article in the *Bloomington Courier* refers to a "Coach Jones" working with the basketball team in preparation for its first game. However, Jones is not listed anywhere else, nor is he ever mentioned later in the season. Jones was probably a coach brought in to provide some additional instruction, or he simply may have served as a trainer and/or conditioning coach. This confusion shows how loosely organized the basketball team was during this era.

Entering the season, returning lettermen Harry Ayers and Guy Cantwell—both senior guards—were expected to play an important role on this young squad. Ayers, the team captain, would became a fixture in the starting lineup, while Cantwell badly sprained his ankle prior to the team's first game and ended up seeing only limited action throughout the season, although he came on strong at the end of the year.

For the third straight year, IU opened the season by facing off with Butler. The game was played in Bloomington on Wednesday, January 14, and the Hoosiers were dominant in posting a 28-16 victory.

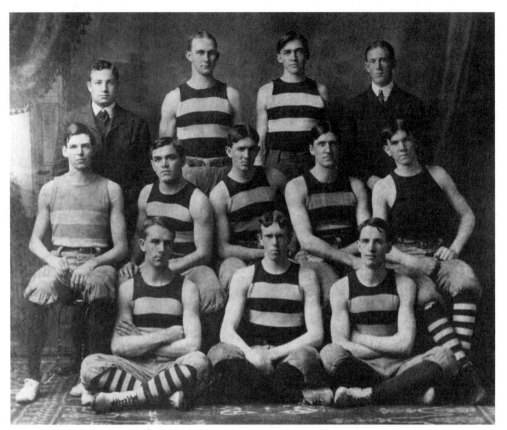

The 1902-03 team. First row (left to right): [unknown], Ralph Noel, [unknown]; Second row: [unknown], [unknown], [unknown], [unknown], [unknown]; Third row: manager Willis Coval, Guy Cantwell, Chester Harmeson, coach J. H. Horne. IU Archives

Later that week, the Hoosiers traveled up to Crawfordsville, Indiana for a doubleheader. On Friday, January 16, IU squared off with Wabash College, and the Little Giants handed them a 20-14 defeat. The following night, Indiana bounced back for a game with Crawfordsville Business College. Maxwell carried the Hoosiers to a lopsided 23-10 rout.

IU then returned to Bloomington for a January 20 matchup with DePauw. The Hoosiers raced to a 19-3 halftime lead and never looked back as they posted a 43-9 victory. Maxwell had a monster game for the Hoosiers, scoring 27 points on 13 field goals and one free throw—tripling the opponent's score by himself and shattering IU's single-game scoring record.

On Saturday, January 24, the Shortridge High School team came down from Indianapolis. They put up an excellent fight and kept the game competitive, but Maxwell and Ayers carried the home team to a 23-18 victory. Maxwell sealed the win by burying a base-line shot late in the second half to put the contest out of reach.

The Hoosiers were 4-1 and had almost a week to prepare for a meeting with their nemesis, the Purdue Boilermakers, in West Lafayette on January 30. After Purdue had beaten Indiana by a combined total of 60 points in two games the previous season, the Hoosiers should have been motivated to exact some revenge; however, they would face more of the same in this contest. Spurred on by a large crowd, the Boilermakers ran up a huge lead as their center, J. Miller overpowered Maxwell in the pivot. Miller scored 35 points and held Maxwell without a field goal as Purdue posted a 52-16 victory in a very physical game that the referees had difficulty controlling at times.

After a layoff of almost three weeks, the Hoosiers resumed their season on Thursday, February 19, with a Bloomington matchup against Wabash. That year the Little Giants had an excellent team and they

1902-03 TEAM ROSTER

Head coach: J. H. Horne

Player	Hometown	Class	Position
Harry Ayers (Capt.)	Hartford City, IN	Sr	G
Guy Cantwell	Spencer, IN	Sr	G
Zora Clevenger	Muncie, IN	Sr	G
Thomas Cookson	Anderson, IN	So	F
Chester Harmeson	Anderson, IN	Fr	F
Clarence Hocker	Beaver Dam, KY	So	F
Leslie Maxwell	Indianapolis, IN	Fr	C
Ralph Noel	Star City, IN	So	G
Albert Penn	Camden, IN	Fr	F
Roy Shackleton	Chatterton, IN	Jr	G
William Stone	Spencer, IN	Sr	F
Marvin Wallace	Milton, IN	So	G

SEASON RESULTS 1902-03

Date	Court	Opponent	Result	Score
1/14/1903	H	Butler	W	28-16
1/16/1903	A	Wabash	L	14-20
1/17/1903	A	Crawfordsville B.C.	W	23-10
1/20/1903	H	DePauw	W	43-9
1/24/1903	H	Shortridge H.S.	W	23-18
1/30/1903	A	Purdue	L	16-52
2/19/1903	H	Wabash	L	12-19
2/23/1903	A	Butler	W	35-23
2/27/1903	A	DePauw	W	54-21
2/28/1903	A	Indiana State	W	32-16
3/6/1903	H	Purdue	L	14-17
3/13/1903	H	Indiana State	W	23-22

score was tied 6-6, and the Hoosier crowd was going wild with the anticipation of a victory. The nip-and-tuck battle continued in the second session, but Purdue eventually pulled out the win by a 17-14 score. Purdue would finish its season at 8-0 overall and would once again claim the state championship of Indiana colleges.

Indiana finished its season a week later with a game against Indiana State in Bloomington on Friday, March 13. Indiana State set a quick pace and played the Hoosiers close throughout, but IU ultimately prevailed 23-22 in an exciting and well-played game. State was kept in the contest by Pelle, a forward, who buried 12 of 13 free throws.

The Hoosiers completed their first winning season and played to larger crowds than ever as basketball was becoming the focal point of winter sports. However, the Hoosiers would find that replicating the success of this winning season would prove difficult over the next decade.

1903-04

OVERALL RECORD: 5-4

Following its most successful basketball season ever, Indiana returned its top scoring threat in sophomore Leslie Maxwell, who was also named team captain of the 1903-04 squad. Once again, athletic director J. H. Horne oversaw the team, did its scheduling, and provided some remedial instruction. Some later sources list Willis Coval as the head coach for 1903-04. However, Coval, who lettered as the team manager in 1902-03, was no longer part of the team in 1903-04.

During the first part of the 1903-04 season, several *Indiana Daily Student* articles refer to "Coach Horne and Captain Maxwell" preparing the team for games and commenting on the team's performance afterwards. However, after the talented young squad got off to a rough start, Horne recognized that the team needed some more formal coaching and he wasted no time in finding his man. On February 4, he hired John Pritchard of the Indianapolis YMCA. Pritchard had been involved with basketball for

defeated the Hoosiers for the second time with a 19-12 win over the home team. Four days later, IU bounced back with a 35-23 win over Butler in Indianapolis on February 23.

Then, on Friday, February 27, the Hoosiers traveled to Greencastle to take on DePauw in the first intercollegiate basketball game ever played on their campus. The home squad played a spirited game, which pleased the large crowd, but the DePauw team did not have the conditioning to stay with Indiana, and the Hoosiers ran to a 54-21 victory, led by the strong play of senior Zora Clevenger (who was IU's first All-American in football, as well as the captain of the football and baseball teams in 1902-03). The next day, IU traveled over to Terre Haute and extended their road winning streak to three games by doubling up Indiana State 32-16.

A confident Purdue team then strolled into Assembly Hall on Friday, March 6. At the half, the

The 1903-04 team. First row (left to right): [unknown], [unknown], Leslie Maxwell,
[unknown], [unknown]; Second row: [unknown], [unknown]; Third row: Godfred
Ritterskamp, Chester Harmeson, [unknown], [unknown], Cassius Hiatt. IU Archives

1903-04 TEAM ROSTER

Head coach: John Pritchard

Player	Hometown	Class	Position
Chester Harmeson	Anderson, IN	So	F
Clarence Hocker	Beaver Dam, KY	Jr	F
Jesse Hubble	Francesville, IN	So	G
Kenneth Kizer	Poneto, IN	Fr	F
Leslie Maxwell (Capt.)	Indianapolis, IN	So	C
Ralph Noel	Star City, IN	Sr	G
Albert Penn	Camden, IN	So	F
Godred Ritterskamp	Freelandsville, IN	So	F
Earl Taber	Marion, IN	Jr	G
Marvin Wallace	Milton, IN	Sr	G
Clifford Woody	Thorntown, IN	Fr	F

SEASON RESULTS 1903-04

Date	Court	Opponent	Result	Score
1/16/1904	H	Salem H. S.	W	60-18
1/29/1904	A	DePauw	L	28-38
1/30/1904	A	Rose Poly	L	18-23
2/3/1904	H	DePauw	W	33-23
2/8/1904	A	Wabash	W	32-25
2/12/1904	H	Purdue	L	18-31
2/26/1904	H	Wabash	W	50-19
3/5/1904	H	Rose Poly	W	50-19
3/12/1904	A	Purdue	L	21-22

twelve years and was a stickler for good shot selection
and a believer in strong conditioning. "Too many
teams pay too little attention to training," he told the
Indiana Daily Student. "But a basketball player, like a
football man, must be in the best possible physical
condition … to play his swiftest and surest game."

Without Pritchard, the team had started 2-2. On
Saturday, January 16, they opened the season by defeating Salem High School 60-18, in what was essentially an
exhibition game. In that game, the Hoosiers started junior Earl Tabor at guard along with four underclassmen:
sophomore Godred Ritterskamp (forward), sophomore
Chester Harmeson (forward), sophomore Leslie
Maxwell (center), and freshman Kenneth Kizer (guard).

Next, the Hoosiers took a road trip to Greencastle
and Terre Haute to take on DePauw and Rose Poly,
respectively. On Friday, January 29, at DePauw, the
Hoosiers set a strong pace, led by Maxwell and
Harmeson, and actually outscored DePauw on field
goals, but badly lost the battle at the free throw line as
the home team prevailed 38-28. The next night, IU took
on a Rose Poly team that had nearly beaten Purdue (they
fell 19-18) the week before, and word had spread that

their team was strong and fast. They lived up to their reputation against the Hoosiers and pulled out a close win, 23-18, as free-throw shooting plagued Indiana once again.

Just a few days later, Indiana had a chance for a rematch against DePauw on Wednesday, February 3, in Bloomington. The Hoosiers leapt out of the starting gate as Harmeson had the hot hand early on, burying several shots in row. Maxwell soon joined in, as IU jumped out 19-11 at the half, and cruised to a 33-23 triumph.

With five games left in season, Coach Pritchard stepped in to coach the Hoosiers on February 5. Three days later, on Monday, February 8, IU played its first game under its new leader as the team faced Wabash in Crawfordsville. The Hoosiers got off to a terrible start, falling behind 18-9 at the half. However, IU roared back in the second half and outscored the Little Giants 23-7 to steal a 32-25 road win, stunning the home team and its crowd.

Following solid victories over DePauw and Wabash, the Hoosiers were confident that they were going to earn their first win ever over Purdue, who was coming to Bloomington on Friday, February 12. "I can't see how Purdue can win from Indiana when her showings against these two teams were not as good as Indiana's," Coach Pritchard asserted. "Indiana won from DePauw, 33-23; Purdue, 27-18. In the Wabash game, Indiana was ahead by seven points; Purdue by only four; yet I see in dispatches from the Purdue camp that they are claiming an easy victory over us; I cannot understand their methods of figuring." Pritchard's optimism looked well-founded in the first half as Indiana jumped out to an 11-10 lead at the break. But Purdue quickly grabbed the lead with two quick baskets to open the second half and used that momentum to run away with a 31-18 win.

However, for an IU-Purdue game, it was very cleanly played, according the postgame report in the *IDS*. "A commendable feature of the game was the good feeling between the teams. Purdue gave five 'rah's' for Indiana after the contest and there was no 'ragging', which makes amateur games unpleasant."

Two weeks later, Wabash paid a visit to Bloomington on Friday, February 26. The Little Giants never had a chance as Indiana set a torrid pace and came away with a 50-19 victory, led by the scoring of Maxwell and Harmeson. Amazingly, IU duplicated that score the following week, on Saturday, March 5, when Rose Poly came to town. The Hoosiers administered another 50-19

beating, as guards Hubbell and Taber led the way on defense and Maxwell took care of most of the scoring.

With the Rose Poly victory, IU moved into second place in the race for the state championship. Purdue was alone in first place, and the two rivals were set to meet for a season-ending confrontation on Saturday, March 12, in West Lafayette. If the Hoosiers could steal a victory from the Boilermakers then they would tie Purdue for first place. The Hoosiers' confidence was at an all-time high after the two blowout victories over Wabash and Rose Poly, and Purdue was hurting from injuries and illnesses to several players.

A crowd of 550 spectators—the largest of the season—greeted the teams at game time. This contest started much like the earlier one in Bloomington, as the first half finished with the score tied 12-12. The second half was even more exciting as the teams played fast and hard and the game remained close until the final buzzer. In the end, Purdue prevailed 22-21, led by Peck, their captain. The victory captured the third state championship in four seasons for the Boilermakers. However, IU's second-place finish among the Indiana colleges was its best showing ever, and with a 5-4 overall record, the Hoosiers had earned their second straight winning season.

Leslie "Doc" Maxwell was Indiana's first big-time scorer. In the fourth game of his freshman season, he demolished IU's single-game scoring record by tallying 27 points against DePauw. No other Hoosier would top that mark in a collegiate contest until 1938. As a sophomore, Maxwell captained the 1903-04 squad.
IU Archives

1904-05

OVERALL RECORD: 5-12

The 1904-05 team. First row (left to right): Godfred Ritterskamp, [unknown]; Second row: Cassius Hiatt, Earl Taber, Chester Harmeson. Third row (left to right): [unknown], coach Zora Clevenger. IU Archives

Before the promising 1904-05 season began, the Indiana basketball team suffered a huge loss when junior center Leslie Maxwell, the team's top returning scorer, sustained a football injury that would cause him to miss the entire basketball season. Senior guard Earl Taber stepped into the role of captain and ended up being the team's primary leader for most of the season. The nominal head coach for the season was former IU basketball player Zora Clevenger. However, Clevenger mostly served as a chaperone and organizer for the team rather than a tactician and motivator. There was hope that John Pritchard, of Indianapolis YMCA fame, would return to coach the team for another season, but a deal was never worked out. In February, a "Coach Conners" was brought in to help instruct the team and was credited as the catalyst of the team's improvement.

Despite the coaching uncertainty, the growing popularity of basketball at IU by 1904-05 is evidenced by the fact that some of the players began their own informal workouts and scrimmages during the first semester. IU even played its first December game as the Hoosiers traveled north to take on the Indianapolis YMCA, one of oldest and most polished teams in the region. IU was defeated 32-19 on December 13, as Taber led the team with nine points.

On January 7, IU hosted a speedy Rose Poly team and suffered a 30-14 defeat. The Hoosiers bounced back four days later and recorded their first win of the season, a 52-16 thrashing of Indiana State in the Men's Gymnasium (later called Assembly Hall) in Bloomington. Junior forward Godfred Ritterskamp led all scorers with 20 points. IU followed up that big win with two big losses. They fell 38-20 to Purdue on January 14, in West Lafayette, and then lost 39-17 to Wabash in Crawfordsville on January 20. The Purdue loss was particularly challenging. It was punctuated by numerous delays due to injured players and to fix the netting on one of the goals. After the game, Taber complained that Purdue players intentionally fouled Indiana players on many shots, but the referees kept calling jump balls instead of fouls.

Indiana returned home for a game with Butler on Thursday, January 26, and came away with an easy 41-23 victory, led by junior forward Chester Harmeson's 19 points. Ritterskamp, IU's other forward, also chipped in 14. The game was tied 12-12 at the half, but the hot shooting of Harmeson and Ritterskamp doomed Butler in the second session.

Next, IU traveled to Terre Haute to take on Indiana State and Rose Poly on February 3 and 4, respectively. First, Indiana State repaid IU for the thrashing it had received in Bloomington by squeaking out a 26-23 victory over the Hoosiers. Then, Rose Poly administered its second defeat of IU with a 39-29 win. A week later, IU returned home to host Wabash and suffered a 31-24 loss at the hands of the Little Giants. That left the Hoosiers at 2-7 overall with no hope of challenging for the state championship.

However, IU still had something to play for because their final home game of the season was against archrival Purdue on February 18. The Boilermakers were also struggling through a losing

1904-05 TEAM ROSTER

Head coach: Zora Clevenger

Player	Hometown	Class	Position
Charles Carr	Anderson, IN	Sr	F
Thomas Cookson	Anderson, IN	Sr	F
Chester Harmeson	Anderson, IN	Jr	F
Cassius Hiatt	Kirklin, IN	Jr	G
Ralph Noel	Star City, IN	Sr	G
Godfred Ritterskamp	Freelandsville, IN	Jr	F
Bernard Robinson	Marshall, IL		F
James Sanders	Jasonville, IN	So	G
Earl Tabor (Capt.)	Marion, IN	Sr	G
George Teter	Sheridan, IN	Sr	C
George Trimble	Evansville, IN	Fr	G
Clifford Woody	Thorntown, IN	So	F

SEASON RESULTS 1904-05

Date	Court	Opponent	Result	Score
12/13/1904	A	Indianapolis YMCA	L	19-32
1/7/1905	H	Rose Poly	L	14-30
1/11/1905	H	Indiana State	W	52-16
1/14/1905	A	Purdue	L	20-38
1/20/1905	A	Wabash	L	17-39
1/26/1905	H	Butler	W	41-23
2/3/1905	A	Indiana State	L	23-26
2/4/1905	A	Rose Poly	L	29-39
2/11/1905	H	Wabash	L	24-31
2/18/1905	H	Purdue	W	29-14
2/25/1905	A	Butler	L	29-44
2/27/1905	A	Allegheny	L	17-39
2/28/1905	A	Hiram (Ohio)	L	18-49
3/1/1905	A	Rayen AC	W	34-20
3/2/1905	A	Buhl AC	W	34-21
3/3/1905	A	Buchtel	L	48-24
3/4/1905	A	Ohio State	L	66-12

season, so even though Purdue had handily defeated IU in West Lafayette in January, there was hope that IU could finally win its first victory over its cross-state rival, after eight straight defeats. The first half was a struggle, and it ended with Indiana ahead, 11-10—the same halftime score for the IU-Purdue contest the previous year in Bloomington. Purdue buried Indiana 21-7 in the second half of that contest, but in this game, IU turned the tide and drowned the Boilermakers with an 18-4 second-half surge that clinched a 29-14 victory for the Hoosiers, in what the Indiana *Daily Student* called "the most exciting game ever seen here." Harmeson led IU with 21 points, including several creative shots such as a tip-in and a twisting shot in the lane.

While the Purdue victory had put an exclamation mark on an otherwise dismal season, the IU squad still had a season-ending road trip in which they were scheduled to take on a variety of basketball teams in Ohio and Pennsylvania. They started the road trip on February 25 with a visit to Butler, who defeated IU 44-29, despite 20 points from Harmeson. Then IU made its eastern trip to face Allegheny College, Hiram College, Rayen Athletic Club, Buhl Athletic Club, Buchtel College, and Ohio State. The Hoosiers played these six teams on six consecutive days between February 27 and March 4. They only managed victories over Rayen AC and Buhl AC, but the team gained valuable experience, and the Hoosiers' performance was better than Minnesota and Wisconsin had done during their eastern road trips against many of the same teams.

1905-06

OVERALL RECORD: 7-9

CONFERENCE RECORD: 2-2 (THIRD PLACE)

INDIVIDUAL HONORS:

GODFRED RITTERSKAMP—

ALL-STATE (FIRST TEAM)

The best news for the basketball team going into the 1905-06 season was that center Leslie "Doc" Maxwell had recovered to full strength and would be back on the court for the varsity after missing his junior season because of an injury. That gave the Hoosiers four seniors who were returning lettermen and who had been starters in the past. Guard Cassius Hiatt returned to the backcourt as one of the Hoosiers' most outstanding defensive players. Forwards Godfred Ritterskamp and Chester Harmeson (the team captain) were outstanding scorers and two of IU's best forwards ever. Now those two combined with Maxwell to form the most forbidding frontcourt in the state.

Even though the team was once again without the services of an experienced basketball coach (Zora Clevenger remained the nominal head coach, but was still mostly a chaperone and team manager), the savvy and experience of the seniors was expected to provide enough leadership to make this team a championship

The 1905-06 team. First row (left to right): Cassius Hiatt, Claudius Quinn, Chester Harmeson, Leslie Maxwell, Godfred Ritterskamp. Second row: [unknown]; Third row: [unkown], [unkown], coach Zora Clevenger, James Sanders. IU Archives

contender, both in the competition among state colleges and in Western Conference (Big Ten) play, which was getting its first start in the 1905-06 season. Indiana's first two games definitely helped feed the notion that this team could be a winner.

In the season opener on January 9, against Butler in Bloomington, most of the pregame anticipation surrounded Butler's big center, Louis Bohnstadt, who was one of the tallest players of that era and a prolific scorer. However, Maxwell badly outplayed Bohnstadt in the game, outscoring him 16-7. The much smaller Maxwell also outjumped Bohnstadt on nine out of 10 jump balls. Maxwell's frontcourt partners also scored in double figures as Harmeson netted 14 and Ritterskamp got 10. The result was a lopsided 42-11 Indiana victory, and after the game Bohnstadt remarked, "Indiana will win the state championship

in a walk." For the Butler game, the Hoosiers also unveiled their brand new uniforms, which sported "INDIANA" across the chest for the first time.

All three of Indiana's frontcourt stars scored in double figures again the next week as Indiana downed Rose Poly 45-23 in Bloomington on January 16. The Hoosiers won big even though the team struggled with its passing game and its shot selection. Then, just as the IU team was looking like it might become an unstoppable force, disaster struck. Maxwell re-injured his knee and it was uncertain if and when he might be able to play again.

The Hoosiers forged ahead with a 20-13 road victory over the Wabash Athletic Club (a semi-pro team from the city of Wabash). Then IU traveled to the University of Illinois and dropped a close game, 27-24. Back in Bloomington on January 27, Indiana

1905-06 TEAM ROSTER

Head coach: Zora Clevenger

Player	Hometown	Class	Position
Chester Harmeson (Capt.)	Anderson, IN	Sr	F
Cassius Hiatt	Kirklin, IN	Sr	G
Edgar Kempf	Jasper, IN	?	F
Harlan McCoy	Chrisney, IN	So	F
Robert Martin	Dana, IN	?	C
Leslie Maxwell	Indianapolis, IN	Sr	C
Claudius Quinn	Cutler, IN	Jr	G
Godfred Ritterskamp	Freelandsville, IN	Sr	F
James Sanders	Jasonville, IN	Jr	G
George Trimble	Evansville, IN	So	G
Clifford Woody	Thorntown, IN	Jr	F

SEASON RESULTS 1905-06

Date	Court	Opponent	Result	Score
1/9/1906	H	Butler	W	42-11
1/16/1906	H	Rose Poly	W	45-23
1/19/1906	A	Wabash AC	W	20-13
1/20/1906	A	Illinois	L	24-27
1/27/1906	H	New Albany YMCA	W	46-21
2/2/1906	A	Indiana State	W	27-12
2/3/1906	A	Rose Poly	L	21-30
2/5/1906	H	Wabash	L	21-29
2/10/1906	A	Purdue	L	25-27
2/16/1906	H	Illinois	W	37-8
2/20/1906	A	Wabash	L	9-29
2/27/1906	A	New Albany YMCA	L	17-18
3/1/1906	A	Cincinnati	L	23-26
3/2/1906	A	Earlham	L	23-26
3/3/1906	A	Hartford City AC	L	13-25
3/10/1906	H	Purdue	W	30-27

1905-06 BIG TEN STANDINGS

	W	L	PCT
Minnesota	6	1	.857
Wisconsin	6	2	.750
Indiana	2	2	.500
Chicago	3	5	.375
Purdue	3	6	.333
Illinois	3	7	.300
Iowa	—	—	—

Forward Chester Harmeson was a reliable and consistent scorer. He averaged double figures in scoring as both a junior and senior and was the captain of the 1905-06 Hoosier squad. IU Archives

bounced back with a 46-21 thrashing of a highly touted New Albany YMCA team in "the roughest game ever seen on the local floor." In that game, Harmeson hit for 28 points, breaking Maxwell's school record from 1903 by a single point (although Maxwell's mark remained the record for an intercollegiate game since Harmeson's total came against a YMCA club). Neither total would be eclipsed again until 1938.

Next, the Hoosiers set off for a road trip to Terre Haute. Maxwell accompanied the team, but it was still

unclear if he would be able to play. He wasn't needed in the Saturday, February 3 game against Indiana State, as the Hoosiers won 27-12. He started against Rose Poly on February 5, but was ineffective, scoring only two points as IU lost 30-21. Maxwell doggedly tried to play again in the next two games against Wabash and Purdue, but he continued to struggle, and IU lost both contests to fall to 5-4 on the season. At that point, Maxwell succumbed to the injury and retired for the season.

On Friday, February 16, in Bloomington, the Hoosiers whipped Illinois 37-8 as Harmeson and

Ritterskamp scored 12 points each in a brutal game marred by unsportsmanlike conduct from the Illinois players. Next, on February 20, the Hoosiers traveled to Crawfordsville where they were defeated by the Wabash Little Giants for the second time. The following week, IU embarked on its final road trip of the season, a four-game swing in five days. Ritterskamp was unable to make the trip, and Harmeson went even though he was ill.

In the opening game against the New Albany YMCA on Tuesday, February 27, the Hoosiers were limited by a hometown referee who made a habit of calling fouls just before IU scored on multiple occasions. IU kept the game close throughout but fell 18-17. On Thursday, March 1, the Hoosiers took on the University of Cincinnati in a very competitive game. The game ended 24-23, but then the official scorers realized there had been a mistake. The game was actually tied 23-23, so they called the players (who were washing up and getting changed) back on to the court. The crowd had already left the building, but overtime was played and Cincinnati prevailed 26-23.

The next night, Friday, March 2, Coach Clevenger and starting guard Claudius Quinn joined the team in Richmond where the Hoosiers were taking on the Earlham Quakers. Despite 12 points from forward Clifford Woody (filling in for the sickly Harmeson), IU lost the game 26-23. The final stop on the road trip was a game against the Hartford City Athletic Club, which was led by former IU captain Harry Ayers. The road-weary Hoosiers dropped their fourth straight game with a 25-13 defeat. The Hoosiers had started the road trip with a winning record at 6-5, but returned with a 6-9 mark and no hope of a winning season.

However, IU still had one chance to put a positive spin on their season. Their final game was a matchup with Purdue in Bloomington on Saturday, March 10. The rivalry game rejuvenated the Hoosiers who played with renewed tenacity. In his final collegiate game, Harmeson played center and scored 17 points (he was 13-16 from the line) in leading the Hoosiers to a 30-27 upset. With the win, IU finished the season 7-9. The Purdue win also put IU at 2-2 in the Western Conference. That was good for third place in the first official season of Big Ten play (although the Big Ten did not have its own conference schedule yet, as individual schools still scheduled their

own games). For the Boilermakers, the loss dropped them to 3-6 in the conference and a fifth-place finish.

1906-07

OVERALL RECORD: 9-5

CONFERENCE RECORD: 0-0

After losing four senior starters to graduation, including nearly all of its scorers, the IU basketball team and its fans were not expecting much success from the 1906-07 team. The athletic department seemed to acknowledge this sentiment by not scheduling a difficult slate of games for the team. In fact, IU did not schedule any games against Western Conference (Big Ten) opponents. IU didn't even play Purdue, but that was due to a "strained relationship resulting from football."

However, after having very little in the way of coaching and instruction for two seasons, the 1906-07 squad benefited from the services of several different coaches. During the fall, coach Leroy Samse (who won an Olympic silver medal in the pole vault in 1904) worked with the team to get them in shape and hone their skills. Coach James Sheldon took over the team once his duties as football coach were completed, and he served as a spirited motivator. Also, before the season started, Coach McGee, an experienced basketball man from Indianapolis, came down to Bloomington to help the IU squad shore up their fundamentals.

Senior guard James Sanders served as the team's captain. He had emerged as a starter during the second half of the 1905-06 season, and before transferring to IU he had been the captain of the Indiana State team. Senior guard Claudius Quinn, the team's top defense player from the previous season, also returned for the Hoosiers, as did center Robert Martin, who filled in admirably after Doc Maxwell's injury during the previous season.

The Hoosiers took advantage of their solid preseason preparations and got off to a hot start. They opened by beating DePauw 28-25 in Greencastle on

The 1906-07 team. First row (left to right): Edmund Cook, Harlan McCoy, James Sanders, [unknown], Claudius Quinn; Second row: coach James Sheldon, [unknown], Frank Thompson, trainer Frank Mann. IU Archives

Monday, January 7. Sanders led the way with 10 points and Martin scored the winning basket in overtime. On Saturday, January 19, IU traveled north to take on the Hartford City YMCA in their home gym. The YMCA team included many of the same players (including IU alum Harry Ayers) from the Hartford City Athletic Club team that had beaten IU by 12 points a year earlier. This time, the Hoosiers were the aggressors, with junior forward Harlan McCoy leading the way with 16 points. IU led 28-27 until the final seconds when Hartford City hit a high, looping shot just as time expired to steal the victory.

On Tuesday, January 22, IU played its home opener against DePauw. The home team prevailed 26-16 in front of a sparse crowd of 200 at the Men's Gymnasium. Next, Indiana State came to Bloomington on January 26 and was soundly beaten 29-16, even though Sanders and Hoosier forward Edmund Cook were both suffering from illnesses. McCoy helped ease their pain by carrying IU to victory with 15 points.

After a 3-1 start, Indiana's luck ran out when a veteran Wabash team charged into Bloomington on

February 2 and administered a 37-24 whipping of the Hoosiers. Rose Poly then came to Bloomington on February 6, but they didn't fare nearly as well, falling to the Hoosiers 30-20. A rejuvenated Cook led IU with 12 points, even though he didn't play the whole game.

On February 8 and 9, IU traveled to the southeastern corner of the state to take on two non-collegiate squads. First up was the New Albany YMCA, who earned a 20-17 win in a well-played game. The next night in Jeffersonville, IU bounced back and trounced the Apollo Athletic Club 49-12. A few days later, IU left for another road trip. This time they headed to Indianapolis. Indiana beat Butler 30-17 in a foul-plagued game on Monday, February 11. The frontcourt took care of most of the scoring, as McCoy hit for 14 and Cook registered eight. The next night, the Indianapolis Athletic Club used a high-scoring second half to run away from the Hoosiers and secure a 30-18 win. Cook, an Indianapolis native, scored 16 of IU's 18 points in the loss.

The Hoosiers stood at 5-3 on the season and had a week to prepare for a rematch with the Wabash

Little Giants, who had emerged as the most powerful team in the state. Traveling to Crawfordsville on February 22, Indiana played an aggressive game and kept it competitive in the first half, but ultimately could not match the "clockwork precision" of the Little Giants, who came away with a 43-20 win. Cook was terrific for the Hoosiers again, scoring 18 of their 20 points.

IU played its final home game on Saturday, February 23, and used a speedy attack to overwhelm Butler 42-7. The Hoosiers finally discovered the balanced scoring that had been missing in recent games. Cook again led the way with 12, but his frontcourt teammates Martin and McCoy chipped in 10 and

eight points, respectively. Sanders and Quinn also added six points each from the backcourt.

The following week, IU set off for Terre Haute on its last road trip of the season. On February 2, the Hoosiers fell behind early in the first half against Indiana State but recovered to claim a 21-19 win. The next day the Hoosiers finished the season just as they had started it—with an overtime game. IU and Rose Poly battled to a 27-27 tie at the end of regulation. However, Cook was fouled with no time remaining and went to the line for a free throw and a chance to win the game. In a bizarre turn of events, the Rose Poly crowd spilled onto the floor to distract Cook during his attempt. It worked. He missed, and the game went into overtime where McCoy hit the winning basket to give Indiana a 29-27 win.

The Rose Poly win gave the Hoosiers a second-place finish for the state championship and capped off their season with a surprising 9-5 overall record.

1906-07 TEAM ROSTER

Head coach: James Sheldon

Player	Hometown	Class	Position
Walt Bossert	Brookville, IN		G
Cecil Boyle	Shoals, IN		F
Edmund Cook	Indianapolis, IN		F
Louis Guedel	Evansville, IN		G
Robert Martin	Dana, IN		C
Harlan McCoy	Chrisney, IN	Jr	F
Claudius Quinn	Cutler, IN	Sr	G
James Sanders (Capt.)	Jasonville, IN	Sr	G
Frank Thompson	Winchester, IN	So	G

SEASON RESULTS 1906-07

Date	Court	Opponent	Result	Score
1/7/1907	A	DePauw	W	28-25
1/19/1907	A	Hartford City YMCA	L	28-29
1/22/1907	H	DePauw	W	26-16
1/26/1907	H	Indiana State	W	29-16
2/2/1907	H	Wabash	L	24-37
2/8/1907	A	New Albany YMCA	L	17-20
2/9/1907	A	Apollo AC	W	49-12
2/11/1907	A	Butler	W	30-17
2/12/1907	A	Indianapolis AC	L	18-30
2/22/1907	A	Wabash	L	20-43
2/23/1907	H	Butler	W	42-7
3/1/1907	H	Indiana State	W	21-19
3/2/1907	A	Rose Poly	W	29-27

1906-07 BIG TEN STANDINGS

	W	L	PCT
Chicago	6	2	.750
Minnesota	6	2	.750
Wisconsin	6	2	.750
Purdue	2	6	.250
Illinois	0	8	.000
Indiana	—	—	—
Iowa	—	—	—

1907-08

OVERALL RECORD: 9-6

CONFERENCE RECORD: 1-3 (FOURTH PLACE)

In the 1907-08 school year, the possibility of a first championship basketball season seemed palpable as IU returned its top two scorers in Edmund Cook and Harlan McCoy, along with an excellent guard in Frank Thompson. Cook, who was elected team captain at the end of the previous season, was considered a strong leader and one of the top forwards in the state.

Led by Cook and McCoy, the team started strong with a 31-30 victory over the Marion Athletic Club in Indianapolis at the end of IU's first semester. Cook was already in midseason form, but he soon got the bad news that he was ineligible to play on the varsity because of his grades. At that point, Cook took the reins of the team as its coach instead. In his coaching duties, Cook was assisted by a freshman from Indianapolis named Arthur "Cotton" Berndt, who had a lot of basketball experience. McCoy replaced Cook as team captain.

The 1907-08 team. First row (left to right): [unknown], [unknown]. Second row: [unknown], Frank Thompson, George Trimble. Third row: trainer Frank Mann, [unknown], Harlan McCoy, [unknown]. IU Archives

On January 10-11, Indiana headed north to Chicago for a double-header with two Western Conference foes: the University of Chicago and Northwestern University. Without Cook in the line-up, the Hoosiers got slaughtered 49-18 by Chicago on Friday, January 10. However, senior Clark Woody filled in for Cook at forward and led IU with a promising 12 points. The next day, IU lost a close game to Northwestern, 21-18. McCoy topped all scorers with 10 points.

On Saturday, January 18, the Hoosiers used a strong passing game to whip Indiana State 37-13 in their home opener at the Men's Gymnasium. McCoy scored 15, Woody dropped in 12, and sophomore center Clyde Chattin added eight. The next weekend IU traveled to Champaign, Illinois, to take on the University of Illinois, another Western Conference opponent. Unfortunately, they met the same fate as they had with the first two conference foes. Illinois prevailed 39-12 in a game with few positives for the Hoosiers.

After four of five games away from home, IU returned to Bloomington for a three-game homestand in a week's time—and the team would make the most of it. First up, on January 28, IU took on a DePauw team that was also crippled by the loss of its captain, as well as another one of its key players. IU took advantage of their undermanned opponent and posted a 25-4 victory in a physical game that witnessed "both teams resorting to rough and tumble football tactics." Next, Northwestern came to Bloomington for a return matchup. IU registered its first conference win of the season with a convincing 36-10 defeat of the Wildcats that came as a result of good passing and teamwork. IU even earned the victory without McCoy, who injured his knee before the game and would end up sitting out the rest of the season. With the loss of McCoy, the mantle of team captain was then passed to Thompson for the rest of the season. IU closed out its homestand on February 3 by annihilating Rose Poly 30-11, led by 20 points from Woody.

Indiana and Purdue finally settled the differences that had kept them from competing against each other in athletics since the fall of 1906, and the February 7 basketball game in West Lafayette marked the first contest in the renewed rivalry. As a result, tickets were a hot item, even for Purdue's 1,500-seat Coliseum (a large gym for that era). Tickets went on sale at 4:00 p.m. on the Wednesday before the Friday game. However, the ticket line formed at 7:00 a.m. that day—nine hours before the seats were being sold

(a nearly unprecedented occurrence at the time). In what was expected to be a very competitive game against well-matched teams, Indiana dominated the action and kept the Purdue crowd out of the game. The Hoosiers lead 14-6 at the break, opened up a 20-10 lead in the second half, and cruised to a 26-21 victory. Woody and Chattin scored 12 apiece to pace the IU attack.

Next, the varsity traveled to DePauw on Tuesday, February 11, and easily dispatched their opponents 33-11, notching their fifth straight victory and improving their season record to 7-3. The winning streak ended four days later on Saturday, February 15, as IU lost 28-17 to the Marion Athletic Club in Indianapolis. Cook, who was allowed to play since this was a non-collegiate game, led all scorers with 15.

IU returned home for its first ever basketball matchup with Notre Dame on Wednesday, February 19. A commendable crowd turned out at the Men's Gymnasium despite a heavy snowfall. However, the snow made travel slow for the Notre Dame team and they didn't arrive until 10:00 p.m. Not long after they arrived, the IU team pounced on them and took an early lead in the game. The Hoosiers held the lead through most of the second half, but the Fighting Irish made three straight field goals in the final minutes to tie the game. On the final play of the game, a Notre Dame player was fouled. With no time remaining, Dubac, a Notre Dame guard, stepped to the line and hit the winning free throw to give the Irish a 21-20 victory.

Next, IU made its annual road trip to Terre Haute for a doubleheader with Indiana State and Rose Poly. The Hoosiers easily swept both games, setting up a final showdown with Purdue in Bloomington on February 26. In a game in which the Hoosiers were handicapped by injuries to several key players, they led 10-9 at the half. Both teams played with such a furious intensity that it hindered the efficiency of their scoring in the second half. IU led 14-12 with a few minutes to go, but Purdue captured the lead with four straight points. IU could not convert in their effort to tie the score and lost the game 16-14.

For the season, this IU team tied the school record (from 1906-07) with nine wins. However, this team played a much tougher schedule and they also lost three of their games by three points or less.

1907-08 TEAM ROSTER

Head coach: Edmund Cook

Player	Hometown	Class	Position
Arthur Berndt	Indianapolis, IN	Fr	G
Cecil Boyle	Shoals, IN		F
Clarence Cartwright	New Harmony, IN		G
Clyde Chattin	Shoals, IN	So	F
Edmund Cook (Capt.)	Indianapolis, IN		F
James Kessler	Portland, IN	Sr	F
Robert Martin	Dana, IN		C
Harlan McCoy (Capt.)	Chrisney, IN	Sr	F
Arthur Rogers	Washington, IN	So	C
Frank Thompson (Capt.)	Winchester, IN	Jr	G
George Trimble	Evansville, IN	Jr	G
Clark Woody	Thorntown, IN	Sr	F

SEASON RESULTS 1907-08

Date	Court	Opponent	Result	Score
unknown	A	Marion AC	W	31-30
1/10/1908	A	Chicago	L	18-49
1/11/1908	A	Northwestern	L	18-21
1/18/1908	H	Indiana State	W	37-13
1/25/1908	A	Illinois	L	12-39
1/28/1908	H	DePauw	W	25-4
1/31/1908	H	Northwestern	W	36-10
2/3/1908	H	Rose Poly	W	30-11
2/7/1908	A	Purdue	W	26-21
2/11/1908	A	DePauw	W	33-11
2/15/1908	A	Marion AC	L	17-28
2/19/1908	H	Notre Dame	L	20-21
2/21/1908	A	Indiana State	W	28-10
2/23/1908	A	Rose Poly	W	33-19
2/26/1908	H	Purdue	L	14-16

1907-08 BIG TEN STANDINGS

	W	L	PCT
Chicago	7	1	.875
Wisconsin	7	1	.875
Illinois	5	4	.556
Minnesota	2	6	.250
Indiana	1	3	.250
Purdue	1	8	.111
Iowa	—	—	—
Northwestern	—	—	—

1908-09

OVERALL RECORD: 5-9

CONFERENCE RECORD: 2-6 (SIXTH PLACE)

INDIVIDUAL RECORDS:

COTTON BERNDT—ALL-STATE (FIRST TEAM)

The 1908-09 team. First row (left to right): [unknown], [unknown], Arthur Berndt, William Hipskind, George Trimble; Second row: trainer Frank Mann, [unknown], Dean Barnhart, coach Robert Harris. IU Archives

Although the 1908-09 team had lost most of its scoring punch from the previous season, the team did return several experienced players in forward Clyde Chattin, center Arthur Rogers, guards Frank Thompson and George Trimble, and Arthur "Cotton" Berndt (who had played very well for the freshman team and had helped coach the varsity). Forwards Dean Barnhart and William Hipskind were also two players who had excelled on the freshman team and were now ready to contribute to the varsity as sophomores. Berndt, a sophomore, was named team captain.

The IU athletic department felt confident enough about the team's prospects to hire Robert Harris to coach the squad. Harris had been a member

of the University of Chicago squad that won back-to-back Big Ten titles in 1907 and 1908. Harris arrived in Bloomington during the first week of December to begin whipping the team into shape. Harris also put together a basketball squad made up of the school's coaches, including football coach James Sheldon and trainer Frank Mann. The team was dubbed the "Crimson Coaches", and they challenged any fraternity team that was willing to take them on.

On December 9, Harris gave the varsity basketball team a live demonstration of his teachings as the Crimson Coaches scrimmaged the varsity. The IU varsity led most of the game, but the coaches came from behind and snatched a 14-12 win. The next night, the freshman team beat the varsity 13-10 as Coach Harris played a different varsity lineup in each half. On Saturday, December 12, the varsity opened its season with a game against the Marion Athletic Club in Bloomington. The Hoosiers showed some good teamwork and played well but still lost 27-23.

Right after winter break, the varsity played another game against an Indianapolis squad. This time they played Battery A on Tuesday, January 5, in Bloomington. A little rusty after no practice during the vacation, the Hoosiers fell behind early, but rallied in the second half. Despite their efforts, they still lost

1908-09 TEAM ROSTER

Head coach: Robert Harris

Player	Hometown	Class	Position
Dean Barnhart	Rochester, IN	So	F
Arthur Berndt (Capt.)	Indianapolis, IN	So	G
Clyde Chattin	Shoals, IN	Jr	F
William Hipskind	Wabash, IN	So	F
Arthur Rogers	Washington, IN	Jr	C
Frank Thompson	Winchester, IN	Sr	G
George Thompson			C
George Trimble	Evansville, IN	Sr	G
William Wellman	Indianapolis, IN		G

SEASON RESULTS 1908-09

Date	Court	Opponent	Result	Score
12/12/1908	H	Marion AC	L	23-27
1/5/1909	H	Battery A	L	21-24
1/9/1909	A	Illinois	L	30-2
1/15/1909	A	Chicago	L	18-12
1/16/1909	A	Northwestern	L	12-16
1/23/1909	H	Rose Poly	W	27-12
1/29/1909	H	Iowa	W	18-12
2/6/1909	H	Purdue	L	14-28
2/9/1909	H	DePauw	W	31-20
2/13/1909	A	Marion AC	L	31-34
2/19/1909	H	Chicago	L	10-17
2/26/1909	A	DePauw	W	31-20
3/6/1909	H	Illinois	W	23-13
3/13/1909	A	Purdue	L	13-30

1908-09 BIG TEN STANDINGS

	W	L	PCT
Chicago	12	0	1.000
Purdue	6	4	.600
Wisconsin	5	4	.556
Illinois	5	6	.455
Minnesota	3	6	.333
Indiana	2	6	.250
Northwestern	1	4	.200
Iowa	1	5	.167

24-21. That weekend IU traveled to Champaign, Illinois, to take on a University of Illinois team that had practiced daily during the holiday break. IU was annihilated 30-2, the only basket being a field goal from Barnhart at the end of the first half. The Hoosiers demonstrated a strong passing game but couldn't put the ball in the basket (even on point-blank shots).

On January 15 the Hoosiers traveled north to take on the University of Chicago, which had another strong team. IU surprised them with solid play and tough defense, and the Hoosiers and the Maroons were tied in the waning minutes of the game. That's when Chicago's star center, John Schommer, came to the rescue with several key baskets to pull out an 18-12 Chicago win. The next night, IU played strong defense again but had trouble scoring, and ultimately lost a 16-12 game to Northwestern.

After a 0-5 start, the Hoosiers righted the ship on January 23 with a 27-12 victory over Rose Poly in Bloomington. Barnhart led the way with 12 points, and Hipskind added six. On January 29, IU got its first conference win of the season with an 18-12 victory over Iowa in Bloomington. IU continued its homestand on February 6, with a contest against Purdue. Led by its tall center, Dave Charters, who repeatedly beat IU's Arthur Rogers on jump balls, the Purdue squad ran up an easy 28-14 win over IU, with Barnhart scoring 10 of the 14. The Hoosiers completed the homestand on February 9, with a 31-20 win over DePauw, as Barnhart registered a season-high 21 points.

After winning three of four games and improving their overall record to 3-6, the Hoosiers went to Indianapolis for a game with the Marion Athletic Club. Led by former Hoosier Ed Cook and former Butler star Louis Bohnstadt, Marion beat IU 34-31. Once again, Barnhart led the Hoosiers in scoring with 17.

On February 13, Chicago came to Bloomington for the first time. To open the game, the Maroons sent out their second team to face the Hoosiers. After they fell behind 7-2, the Maroons' starters were forced into the contest. Just as in the first Indiana-Chicago matchup, center John Schommer led Chicago's second-half rally, and the Maroons prevailed 17-10.

Led by Captain Berndt, the Hoosiers dominated DePauw for a second time on February 26, registering

Although short in stature, Arthur "Cotton" Berndt was a big man on campus at IU. During his four-year career he served as captain of the football, basketball, and baseball teams. As a sophomore during the 1908-09 school year, he was the captain of the basketball team and earned all-state honors as a guard for his leadership and his excellent all-round play.
IU Archives

1909-10

OVERALL RECORD: 5-8

CONFERENCE RECORD: 3-7

(SEVENTH PLACE)

Heading into the 1909-10 season, the IU basketball team faced its toughest schedule ever, with 10 of its 13 games being played against Western Conference (Big Ten) opponents. The IU squad returned its leading scorer, Dean Barnhart, a junior forward who was also the team captain. William Hipskind, another junior forward, was also a returning starter. The third returning letterman was Arthur "Cotton" Berndt, a junior guard who had been named to the All-State team in 1908-09 because of his passing and defense. Unfortunately, Berndt wasn't able to play on the basketball squad in 1909-10 because of a ruling that only allowed an athlete to play in two sports (and Berndt had already played baseball and football during the calendar year of 1909).

For the second straight season, the Hoosiers nabbed a former University of Chicago basketball player to coach the IU varsity. John Georgen, a former Maroon forward and captain, was hired for the season and arrived in Bloomington on January 4, to take over the team. Less than a week later, the Hoosiers played their first game against DePauw in Greencastle on January 10. IU coasted into the lead early on, but DePauw rallied and cut the score to 15-13 in the second half. Then the Hoosiers kicked their passing game into high gear, and got some easy baskets that resulted in a 23-17 win. Hipskind led all scorers with 13.

Next, IU prepared to take on Rose Poly in their home opener on Saturday, January 15. Not only did they have to prepare for a Rose Poly team that had already annihilated DePauw by a huge margin, but they also had to deal with the newly installed floor and backboards in the Men's Gymnasium. "With the slipperiness [of the floor] and the speed with which the ball rebounds from the banks or from the floor, the men are almost having to learn a new game. They hope to turn this speediness of the floor into an asset when playing on the home floor as the other teams are even more unused to it," reported the *Indiana Daily*

a 27-12 win in Greencastle. On March 6, the Illinois squad that had defeated IU by 28 points in Champaign, came to Bloomington for a return matchup. In their final home game of the season, the Hoosiers played their best basketball and defeated a shell-shocked Illinois team 23-13.

That left a trip to West Lafayette on March 13, and a Purdue showdown for the season finale. Injuries had slowed Barnhart and Hipskind prior to the Purdue game and had the Hoosiers worried about the Boilermaker matchup. However, IU played a strong first half, especially on defense, and was only down 9-6 at the break. In the second half, Purdue used a balanced scoring attack and better conditioning to overwhelm the Hoosiers 21-7, sealing a 30-13 win.

For the season, Barnhart had led the Hoosiers in scoring and showed a strong overall floor game in his first season on the varsity. After the Purdue game, Barnhart was unanimously elected to be the team captain for the 1909-10 team.

The 1909-10 team. First row (left to right): Merrill Davis, William Hipskind; Second row: [unknown], Phil Graves, Dean Barnhart, [unknown], [unknown]; Third row: coach John Georgen, [unknown], [unknown], trainer Frank Mann. IU Archives

Student. The floor didn't seem to bother Rose Poly as they jumped into the lead and held it for the first 15 minutes. However, IU eventually got Georgen's new offense running to perfection and ran away with a 37-21 victory, which was much appreciated by a raucous home crowd. Barnhart scored 17 and Hipskind added eight.

IU began conference play the following week with its annual Chicago swing. On Friday, January 21, the Hoosiers were ripped 50-12 by the University of Chicago in Bartlett Gymnasium. IU bounced back the next day and beat Northwestern 29-20 to split the road trip. Then IU returned home to take on the Wisconsin Badgers on Saturday, January 29, in a game that turned into a classic. Both teams played well and competed hard as the contest see-sawed back and forth. With the game tied at 11 apiece, Barnhart

made a difficult shot that sealed a 13-11 Hoosier victory. The 1910 Arbutus commented, "Both teams played championship ball on this occasion, and the game proved to be the finest exhibition of the indoor sport seen here for some time." The crowd was also the biggest to ever attend a basketball game at IU, and it resulted in an unexpected profit of $2.00 (most games lost money back then, because the gym only held about 600 people).

On February 5, the Hoosiers were defeated 30-20 at Illinois. IU had closed the margin to two points in the second half before Illinois rallied to win. Barnhart, who was slowed by an injured hand, was held to one field goal. On February 8, Purdue invaded Bloomington and came away with a 23-18 victory in front of a standing-room-only crowd that broke the record for tickets sold (which had been set less than

1909-10 TEAM ROSTER

Head coach: John Georgen

Player	Hometown	Class	Position
Jasper Abel	Tampico, IN		F
Dean Barnhart (Capt.)	Rochester, IN	Jr	F
Merrill Davis	Marion, IN	So	G
Phil Graves	Orleans, IN	So	C
William Hipskind	Wabash, IN	Jr	F
Emil Mangel	Huntingburg, IN	Sr.	C
Roscoe Stotter	Forest, IN		G
Claude Whitney	Muncie, IN		F

SEASON RESULTS 1909-10

Date	Court	Opponent	Result	Score
1/10/1910	A	DePauw	W	23-17
1/15/1910	H	Rose Poly	W	37-21
1/21/1910	A	Chicago	L	12-50
1/22/1910	A	Northwestern	W	29-20
1/29/1910	H	Wisconsin	W	13-11
2/5/1910	A	Illinois	L	20-30
2/8/1910	H	Purdue	L	18-23
2/12/1910	H	Northwestern	W	18-10
2/19/1910	H	Chicago	L	8-33
2/26/1910	A	Rose Poly	L	21-23
3/1/1910	A	Purdue	L	15-62
3/5/1910	H	Illinois	L	12-26
3/7/1910	A	Wisconsin	L	8-33

1909-10 BIG TEN STANDINGS

	W	L	PCT
Chicago	9	3	.750
Minnesota	7	3	.700
Wisconsin	7	5	.583
Illinois	5	4	.556
Iowa	2	2	.500
Purdue	5	5	.500
Indiana	3	7	.300
Northwestern	0	9	.000

two weeks earlier against Wisconsin). Dave Charters, Purdue's big center, was too much for the Hoosiers to handle as he scored 17 to lead the Boilermakers.

Northwestern was the next guest at the Men's Gymnasium, and they were handily defeated 18-10 on February 12, even though IU was without Barnhart and guard Merrill Graves, who were benched because of "alleged training infractions." Both players returned to the lineup a week later as IU tried to upset the heavily favored Chicago Maroons in the Men's Gymnasium on February 19. However, Chicago cruised to an easy 33-8 win as IU played hard, but was simply overmatched. Several IU players

suffered minor injuries in the game, which hurt the Hoosiers in their next contest against Rose Poly in Terre Haute. The Hoosiers suffered a 23-21 defeat in that game.

On March 1, IU went to West Lafayette to try to split the season series with Purdue by stealing a win from the Boilermakers, but IU had a hard time dealing with the height of Purdue once again and lost in a landslide, 62-15. Barnhart scored all the points for the Hoosiers. IU followed that game with a 26-12 loss to Illinois in the Hoosiers' home finale, and then a season-ending 33-8 defeat to Wisconsin in Madison.

Injuries plagued the IU squad down the stretch. After starting the season 5-3, the team lost its final five games to finish with a 5-8 overall record and a 3-7 conference mark.

1910-11

OVERALL RECORD: 11-5

CONFERENCE RECORD: 5-5 (FIFTH PLACE)

INDIVIDUAL HONORS:

COTTON BERNDT—ALL-STATE (FIRST TEAM)

DEAN BARNHART—ALL-STATE (FIRST TEAM)

Entering the 1910-11 season, IU had never had a more experienced basketball squad. Forwards Dean Barnhart and William Hipskind were going into their third season as starters on the varsity. Barnhart had led the Hoosiers in scoring as both a sophomore and junior. Hipskind had also been one of the team's top scorers during both seasons and now assumed the role of team captain for 1910-11. At guard, Merrill Davis was a returning starter, and former captain Arthur Berndt returned to the squad after a one-year hiatus.

Once again, the team had a new coach. Oscar Rackle, a former captain and forward for the Brown University basketball team, was hired for the season and arrived in Bloomington during the last week of December. He had only 10 days to work with the team before their season opener against Illinois. However, Hipskind had gathered the team together

The 1910-11 team. First row (left to right): Merrill Davis, Dean Barnhart, William Hipskind, Arthur Berndt, Phil Graves; Second row: coach Oscar Rackle, [unknown], Haynes Freeland, trainer Frank Mann. IU Archives

after the Thanksgiving weekend and had them practicing three times a week until Rackle arrived.

On January 8, the Hoosiers traveled west to take on a veteran Illinois team in Champaign. IU jumped out to a 15-14 halftime lead, and the game remained close until the 4:00 mark when Illinois used its superior conditioning to surge past the Hoosiers with several successive baskets and claimed a 32-22 triumph. The Hoosiers returned to Bloomington for their home opener three days later, on Wednesday, January 11, against Butler. From the outset, IU jumped all over the visitors and held a 28-10 lead at the half. With its second team playing much of the second half, Indiana cruised to a 41-16 win, as Barnhart scored 18 and junior center Phil Graves added 10.

On Saturday, January 14, Indiana traveled to Greencastle for a contest with the DePauw Tigers. Just as in the Butler game, the Hoosiers' swift passing offense was too much for their opponent as IU overwhelmed DePauw 45-20. Barnhart dropped in a career-high 25 points for the Hoosiers, and Graves added 10. Next, a tall, skilled Chicago team came to Bloomington on January 21, and was met by a capacity crowd and a fired-up Hoosier squad. IU led 10-7

at the half and rolled to a surprising 22-14 victory—Indiana's first ever win over Chicago in basketball. Once again, Barnhart led all scorers with 16. Indiana then notched its fourth straight victory a week later when Rose Poly came to town and was given a 45-6 beating by the Hoosiers. For the second time that season, and the final time in his career, Barnhart broke the 20-point barrier. His 21 points led all scorers, and no Hoosier would break 20 again for another decade.

The 4-1 Hoosiers (who were also 1-1 in conference play) then took on the undefeated Purdue Boilermakers (who were 4-0 in conference play) in Bloomington on Tuesday, January 31. IU drew its biggest crowd of the season and the game turned into a closely fought struggle as both teams made tough shots from all over the court. IU seemingly tied the game when the Hoosiers scored with a minute left to play. However, the goal was waved off because of a foul call and Indiana missed the free throw. Purdue then scored at the buzzer to make the final count 37-33 in favor of the Boilermakers.

That weekend, IU made a northern road swing and came home without a victory. The Hoosiers lost to Wisconsin 51-9 on Friday, February 3, and then succumbed to Chicago 33-17 the next day. Those losses dropped the Hoosiers to 4-4 on the season, and 1-4 in conference play. The veteran squad responded by winning their next five games in a short span of 15 days.

The first win was a 22-15 victory over Earlham in Richmond on Friday, February 10. Then Illinois came to Bloomington and was beaten back by a 19-14 count on Sunday, February 12. DePauw was the next victim, falling to the Hoosiers 41-9 on Tuesday,

February 14, as IU led the Tigers 22-1 at the half. Barnhart scored 15 and Hipskind had 10. The Hoosiers notched a conference victory on Friday, February 24, when they defeated Northwestern 33-19 in Evanston, led by Barnhart's 13 points. On the way back from the Chicago area, the Hoosiers stopped by Terre Haute on Saturday, February 25, and won a 37-24 contest from Rose Poly as Barnhart and Graves combined for 25 points.

IU traveled to West Lafayette on Saturday, March 4, for a rivalry game with Purdue, who was battling Chicago, Wisconsin and Minnesota for the conference title. The Hoosiers jumped into the lead early and stayed with the much taller Boilermakers in a first half that ended in a 6-6 tie. IU continued to come at the Boilermakers in the second half and the score was 17-16 with time running out, before Purdue made two quick field goals to secure the victory at 21-16.

The next weekend, IU closed its season with home victories over Wisconsin, 21-18, and Northwestern, 41-12. IU won eight out of its final nine games to finish 11-5 overall during a very competitive conference season. Indiana's 11 overall victories set a school record that would stand through the next five seasons.

1910-11 TEAM ROSTER

Head coach: Oscar Rackle

Player	Hometown	Class	Position
Dean Barnhart	Rochester, IN	Sr	F
Arthur Berndt	Indianapolis, IN	Sr	G
Merrill Davis	Marion, IN	Jr	G
Haynes Freeland	Indianapolis, IN	So	F
Phil Graves	Orleans, IN	Jr	C
William Hipskind (Capt.)	Wabash, IN	Sr	F
Glen Munkelt	Salem, IN	So	F
Chester Stayton	Mooresville, IN		G
Roscoe Stotter	Forest, IN		G
Claude Whitney	Muncie, IN		F

SEASON RESULTS 1910-11

Date	Court	Opponent	Result	Score
1/8/1911	A	Illinois	L	22-33
1/11/1911	H	Butler	W	41-16
1/14/1911	A	DePauw	W	45-20
1/21/1911	H	Chicago	W	22-14
1/28/1911	H	Rose Poly	W	45-6
1/31/1911	H	Purdue	L	33-37
2/3/1911	A	Wisconsin	L	9-51
2/4/1911	A	Chicago	L	17-33
2/10/1911	A	Earlham	W	22-15
2/12/1911	H	Illinois	W	19-14
2/14/1911	H	DePauw	W	41-9
2/24/1911	A	Northwestern	W	33-19
2/25/1911	A	Rose Poly	W	37-24
3/4/1911	A	Purdue	L	16-21
3/10/1911	H	Wisconsin	W	21-18
3/11/1911	H	Northwestern	W	41-12

1910-11 BIG TEN STANDINGS

	W	L	PCT
Purdue	8	4	.667
Minnesota	8	4	.667
Chicago	7	5	.583
Illinois	6	5	.545
Wisconsin	6	6	.500
Indiana	5	5	.500
Iowa	2	2	.500
Northwestern	1	12	.083

Forward Dean Barnhart led the Hoosiers in scoring for three straight seasons. As a senior, he averaged 13.5 PPG and earned all-state honors. IU Archives

1911-12

OVERALL RECORD: 6-11

CONFERENCE RECORD: 2-9 (SIXTH PLACE)

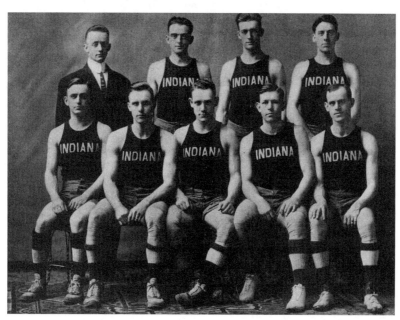

The 1911-12 team. First row (left to right): Glen Munkelt, Phil Graves, Merrill Davis, Floyd Fleming, Clyde Chattin; Second row: coach James Kase, Everett McCullough, Haynes Freeland, Chester Stayton. IU Archives

Dismal were the prospects for the IU basketball team entering the 1911-12 season. Only two experienced players—guard Merrill Davis and center Phil Graves—returned from the squad that went 11-5 the previous year. Davis was elected team captain, and Jimmy Kase, coach of the freshman team the year before, was chosen to coach the varsity. Kase, who was also an assistant athletic director, was a native of the East Coast and had a strong basketball pedigree, but he didn't have much talent to work with when he took over the IU varsity at the beginning of January. Nevertheless, Kase, the team, and the IU faithful held out hope that one or two players might step up and help the team to a respectable showing.

The squad got mixed reviews in its opener against Butler on January 16 in Bloomington. Captain Davis was kicked out of the game for rough play at the end of the first half, but the Hoosiers won 15-12.

However, the fact that they struggled to beat a mediocre Butler team was not a good sign. Things looked even worse for the Hoosiers a few days later on Friday, January 19, when DePauw came to Bloomington and ran to a 9-7 lead at the end of the first half. The DePauw squad was coached by former Hoosier captain, Cotton Berndt. Indiana finally got its attack moving in the second half, led by the scoring of Graves and guard Everett McCullough, and the disruptive defense of Davis. The Hoosiers eventually cruised to a 23-15 win.

Next, Purdue came to Bloomington on January 24. The undefeated Boilermakers had an excellent team and had already defeated Butler 51-12. As a result, there wasn't much optimism about IU's chances, and rightfully so. Purdue put on a clinic, leading 23-12 at the half, and winning by a margin of 54-18. Indiana then took to the road for the first time on January 27, traveling to Terre Haute to take on

Rose Poly. The two teams locked into a high-scoring battle, with Rose Poly leading 24-19 at the half. However, the Hoosiers faded in the second half and lost 45-24. Graves and forward Haynes Freeland each scored 10 points. Two nights later, on January 29, in Bloomington, IU came away with a 34-19 win over Ohio State (which joined the Western Conference the following season). Graves led all scorers with 18 points against OSU.

1911-12 TEAM ROSTER

Head coach: James Kase

Player	Hometown	Class	Position
Clyde Chattin	Shoals, IN	Sr	F
Cline Clouse	Hope, IN		G
Merrill Davis (Capt.)	Marion, IN	Sr	G
Scott Edwards	Greenfield, IN		G
Floyd Fleming	New Albany, IN		G
Haynes Freeland	Indianapolis, IN	Jr	F
Phil Graves	Orleans, IN	Sr	C
Everett McCullough	Brazil, IN		G
Glen Munkelt	Salem, IN	Jr	F
Chester Stayton	Mooresville, IN		G

SEASON RESULTS 1910-11

Date	Court	Opponent	Result	Score
1/16/1912	H	Butler	W	15-12
1/19/1912	H	DePauw	W	23-15
1/24/1912	H	Purdue	L	18-54
1/27/1912	A	Rose Poly	L	24-45
1/29/1912	H	Ohio State	W	34-20
2/3/1912	H	Chicago	L	16-20
2/7/1912	H	Illinois	W	24-23
2/9/1912	A	Earlham	W	25-13
2/10/1912	A	Butler	L	17-23
2/16/1912	A	Wisconsin	L	10-49
2/17/1912	A	Minnesota	L	7-34
2/23/1912	A	Illinois	L	18-41
2/24/1912	A	Chicago	L	22-36
3/3/1912	A	Purdue	L	11-45
3/9/1912	H	Rose Poly	W	29-16
3/13/1912	H	Minnesota	L	17-26
3/16/1912	H	Wisconsin	L	21-34

1911-12 BIG TEN STANDINGS

	W	L	PCT
Wisconsin	12	0	1.000
Purdue	10	0	1.000
Chicago	7	5	.583
Minnesota	6	6	.500
Illinois	4	8	.333
Indiana	1	9	.100
Iowa	0	4	.000
Northwestern	0	8	.000

On February 3, Chicago squeaked out a 20-16 victory over Indiana in a scrappy game in Bloomington. IU followed up that contest with its most exciting game of the season, a 24-23 overtime win against Illinois on February 7. The Hoosiers rallied from behind to tie the game in the second half, and then forward Glen Munkelt hit the winning basket in overtime. That win improved the Hoosiers to 4-3 for the season, but they would play their next seven games on the road.

The weekend after the Illinois game, the Hoosiers traveled to Earlham on Friday, February 9, and Butler on Saturday, February 10. The Hoosiers defeated Earlham 25-13, but fell to Butler 23-17, despite 15 points from Graves. In the Butler game, Captain Davis sustained an injury that would eventually sideline him for the rest of the season.

The Hoosiers made the grueling northern road trip to Wisconsin and Minnesota the following weekend, and came back home with two more losses. The Wisconsin score was 49-10 on February 16, and the Minnesota loss was by a count of 34-7 on February 17.

IU also came home winless the next weekend, when Illinois beat the Hoosiers 34-7 in Champaign on February 23, and then IU lost 41-18 at Chicago on February 24. The loss to the Maroons was Indiana's fifth in a row, and for the final game of their road trip, they had to play in West Lafayette on March 1, against a Purdue team that was still undefeated and was mowing down opponents at will. Indiana played hard, but Purdue blanketed Graves and held him to five points as the Boilermakers ran away with a decisive 45-11 victory.

Indiana finally played another home game on March 9, and registered a much needed win over Rose Poly, 29-16. Graves and Freeland combined for 22 points. Next, Minnesota came to Bloomington, but the Hoosiers didn't fare as well; the visitors dealt IU a 26-17 defeat. The final game of the season was a showdown with the undefeated Wisconsin Badgers. The Hoosier faithful held out hope that Indiana could pull out a win and spoil the perfect record of the Badgers. IU stayed right with Wisconsin in the first half, but the Badgers pulled away in the second session and ultimately recorded a 34-21 victory.

IU's disastrous 1-6 road trip doomed the team to a 6-11 record for the season. While the Hoosiers played hard and played pretty well at times, they couldn't get over the hump and win games against conference opponents, even when they kept the score close. That left IU with a 1-9 conference record, their worst showing since conference play began. Of course, the Western Conference was tougher than ever—both Wisconsin and Purdue finished undefeated in conference play and overall—and IU simply didn't have the basketball talent needed to keep up. Unfortunately for the Hoosiers, things would get worse before they got better.

1912-13

OVERALL RECORD: 5-11

CONFERENCE RECORD: 0-10 (NINTH PLACE)

While the rest of the Indiana University campus stood docile and quiet on Thursday, December 26, the Men's Gymnasium echoed to the sound of bouncing basketballs as 20 young men gave up the better part of their holiday vacation to participate in the first formal practice for the men's varsity basketball team. Within a couple days, the team had been cut down to 13 players by the squad's new coach, Arthur Powell, a former Syracuse University star who was wooed from the east coast and brought to Bloomington to try his hand at producing a winning basketball team.

IU returned seniors Glen Munkelt and Haynes Freeland (team captain), two of the top three scorers from the previous season, along with experienced players in guards Floyd Fleming and Cline Clouse and guard/forward Everett McCullough. Although the team had a lowly record the previous season, they had shown enough good play to provide IU students and Hoosier fans with optimism that the team could challenge for the Western Conference championship. Interest in basketball itself was also increasing in Bloomington as more and more IU games were selling out all of the available tickets. Plus, in 1911, the IU campus had begun hosting the Indiana high

school basketball tournament, which was also generating considerable interest in the sport.

The Hoosiers opened their season in a whirlwind by jumping out to a 17-2 first half lead against DePauw in Bloomington on Saturday, January 11. The visitors charged back in the second half before falling 30-14. Freeland led all scorers with 12, and forward Hugh Barnhart (the younger brother of former IU star Dean Barnhart) chipped in eight. Coach Powell was glad to get a win but wasn't happy about some of the things he witnessed from the squad and prepared to put them through some more rigorous practices before the next contest.

Powell was much happier with the team's play against Earlham the following Saturday. The Hoosiers used fast and effective ball movement to get point-blank shots as they easily defeated a good Earlham team 30-14 in Bloomington. Freeland again led all scorers with 12.

IU's 2-0 start heightened expectations in Bloomington, but Indiana next faced the daunting prospect of a five-game road trip, including three games against conference opponents. The first game was on Friday, January 24, in West Lafayette, where the Hoosiers fell behind Purdue by 13 points in the first half and never recovered in a 34-19 loss. The next

The 1912-13 team. First row (left to right): Haynes Freeland, Wade Nichols; Second row: Glen Munkelt, Cline Clouse, Hugh Barnhart. Third row: trainer Jesse Ferguson, coach Arthur Powell, Floyd Fleming.
IU Archives

1912-13 TEAM ROSTER

Head coach: Arthur Powell

Player	Hometown	Class	Position
Hugh Barnhart	Rochester, IN		C/F
Cline Clouse	Hope, IN		G
Scott Edwards	Greenfield, IN		G
Floyd Fleming	New Albany, IN		G
Haynes Freeland (Capt.)	Indianapolis, IN	Sr	F
Everett McCullough	Brazil, IN		G/F
Glen Munkelt	Salem, IN	Sr	F
Wade Nichols	Danville, IN		C

SEASON RESULTS 1912-13

Date	Court	Opponent	Result	Score
1/11/1913	H	DePauw	W	30-14
1/18/1913	H	Earlham	W	32-14
1/24/1913	A	Purdue	L	19-34
1/25/1913	A	Ohio State	L	22-34
1/31/1913	A	Earlham	W	31-11
2/1/1913	A	Northwestern	L	21-26
2/4/1913	A	Wabash	L	17-37
2/8/1913	H	Indiana State	W	24-6
2/13/1913	H	Wisconsin	L	19-30
2/15/1913	H	Northwestern	L	18-27
2/18/1913	H	Wabash	W	30-17
2/27/1913	A	Wisconsin	L	10-48
3/1/1913	A	Illinois	L	12-29
3/7/1913	H	Ohio State	L	17-19
3/8/1913	H	Illinois	L	17-23
3/15/1913	H	Purdue	L	21-32

1912-13 BIG TEN STANDINGS

	W	L	PCT
Wisconsin	11	1	.917
Northwestern	7	2	.778
Chicago	8	4	.667
Purdue	6	5	.545
Illinois	7	6	.538
Ohio State	4	5	.444
Minnesota	2	8	.200
Iowa	1	5	.167
Indiana	0	10	.000

Forward Haynes "Crook" Freeland was a big forward who often used his imposing presence on defense to disrupt IU opponents. As a senior during the 1912-13 season, Freeland was the team captain and the Hoosiers' second leading scorer. IU Archives

day, IU headed to Columbus, Ohio, to take on Ohio State (a new entry into the conference). This was the first conference game ever played in Columbus, and a record home crowd turned out to see their Buckeyes use a big second-half surge to down the Hoosiers 34-22. Talk of a conference championship for the Hoosiers was reduced to a scant whisper at that point.

On Friday, January 31, IU vented some of its frustration from the previous week's losses by defeating Earlham 31-11 in Richmond. Then the Hoosiers traveled up to Evanston, Illinois, to take on

Northwestern on Saturday, February 1. IU played a strong game against a Northwestern team that would finish as the conference runner-up, but the Hoosiers fell short 26-21. On Tuesday, February 4, Indiana made the short trip to Crawfordsville to take on the Wabash Little Giants, who always played a spirited game on their home floor. Wabash used a fast and physical attack to overwhelm the Hoosiers and ran away with a 37-17 win. The Hoosiers finished their major road swing with a 1-4 record, dropping the squad to 3-4 overall.

Next, in a lackluster game in front of the smallest home crowd of the season, IU pulled out a 24-6 win over an overmatched Indiana State team on Saturday, February 8. IU wasn't as lucky against conference leader Wisconsin five days later in Bloomington. The Badgers pulled out a 30-19 win after being tied with the Hoosiers 10-10 at the half. Two days later, on Saturday, February 15, Indiana suffered a similar fate against Northwestern, falling 27-18, which kept IU winless in conference play.

In its next contest, IU earned some revenge against Wabash in Bloomington in front of a large Hoosier crowd on Tuesday, February 18. Indiana defeated the Little Giants 30-17, in a rough game that was probably Indiana's best showing of the season on both offense and defense. Barnhart was the game's top scorer with 13.

Indiana stood at 5-6 (0-5 in conference play). Five games remained—the first two on the road—and all of them were against conference opponents. Indiana would lose all five. The first two losses came to Wisconsin (48-10) and Illinois (29-12) on their respective home floors. The following weekend, February 7-8, IU lost two heartbreakers at home to Ohio State (19-17) and Illinois (23-17).

Despite the Hoosiers' dim record, a huge crowd turned out for IU's season finale against Purdue on Saturday, March 15, in Bloomington. The crowd was bolstered by members of the Indiana high school teams who had just completed their state tournament in the Men's Gymnasium and who "were eager to see the Crimson [defeat] the Boilermakers." They looked as if they would get their wish as IU led by eight points until 10:00 left in the second half, but then the Boilermakers roared from behind and shocked the crowd by pulling out a 31-21 victory. The loss left Indiana with its first (and only) winless season in conference play.

1913-14

OVERALL RECORD: 2-12

CONFERENCE RECORD: 1-11 (NINTH PLACE)

Cotton Berndt, a two-time all-state selection for IU as a basketball player, had taken over the coaching reins of the DePauw basketball squad after graduating from IU in 1911. The next season, he returned to his alma mater to direct the freshman team, and then he was promoted to varsity coach for the 1913-14 season. He took over a squad whose prospects were severely limited. The team's captain-elect, Everett McCullough, didn't return to school in the fall, and Hugh Barnhart, the team's top scorer from 1912-13, was injured in football and ended up being out for the season. That left Coach Berndt with no experienced players to build a team around, and so he had to rely on sophomores such as Frank Whitaker, a defensive-minded guard who became the team captain, and James Frenzel, a top-scoring forward, to carry the team. Predictably, the Hoosiers struggled all season, although there was one bright spot.

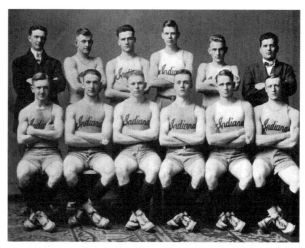

The 1913-14 team. First row (left to right): Russell Kirkpatrick, James Frenzel, Clinton Prather, Allen Maxwell, Byron Lingeman, Frank Whitaker; Second row: Trainer Jesse Ferguson, Frank Pruitt, Ward Gilbert, Morris [first name unknown], William Ferguson, coach Arthur Berndt. IU Archives

The season tipped on January 6, as the inexperienced Hoosiers traveled to Champaign, Illinois, and got whipped 35-6 by Illinois. Things didn't get any better for IU in its home opener when the Hoosiers took on Wisconsin and got trounced 59-15 on Monday, January 12. Northwestern took its turn roughing up the young Hoosiers next, as the IU squad went up to Evanston on Saturday, January 17, and was beaten 48-33. Against the Wildcats, IU got 12 points from sophomore forward Clinton Prather, and Frenzel added nine.

Back in Bloomington on January 24, IU fans "were given a severe shock" when little Earlham came to town and dealt the Hoosiers their fourth straight loss in the form of a 19-11 defeat. However, IU avenged the loss six days later in Richmond by defeating Earlham 28-25, led by 14 points from Frenzel. The next day, January 31, the Hoosiers traveled to Columbus, Ohio, and lost 31-18 to Ohio State. Prather had a team-high eight points.

Illinois arrived in Bloomington on Saturday, February 7, and used a balanced scoring attack to register a 31-15 win. Next, Indiana traveled to Purdue to take on a Boilermaker team that was also winless in conference play. After a closely fought first half, Purdue pulled away in the second session and won 35-13. Northwestern then came to town and won its second game of the season from IU by ripping the Hoosiers 40-16 on Friday, February 13.

IU stood at 1-8 overall and 0-7 in the conference, and the toughest road trip in the Western Conference was directly in front of them. The Hoosiers traveled to Minneapolis on Monday, February 23, and nearly rallied past the Minnesota Golden Gophers but fell 26-23. The next night in Madison, Wisconsin, IU showed some spunk against the conference-leading Wisconsin Badgers, but still lost 46-24.

Still looking for its first conference win, Indiana would play its final three games in Bloomington. The first contest was against Ohio State on Saturday, February 28. IU showed continued improvement in its passing game and defense, but it wasn't enough against the veteran Buckeye team, which left town with a 28-19 win.

Indiana used that momentum from a well-played OSU game and channeled it into a fast start on Tuesday, March 3, when the Purdue Boilermakers came to town. IU put the visitors back on their heels

1913-14 TEAM ROSTER

Head coach: Arthur Berndt

Player	Hometown	Class	Position
William Ferguson	Gaston, IN		G
James Frenzel	Indianapolis, IN	So	F
Ward Gilbert	Russiaville, IN		C
Russell Kirkpatrick	Rushville, IN	So	G
Byron Lingeman	Brownsburg, IN		G
Allen Maxwell	Indianapolis, IN	So	F
Clinton Prather	Wheatland, IN	So	F
Frank Pruitt	Coatesville, IN		G
Frank Whitaker (Capt.)	South Bend, IN	So	G

SEASON RESULTS 1913-14

Date	Court	Opponent	Result	Score
1/6/1914	A	Illinois	L	6-35
1/12/1914	H	Wisconsin	L	15-59
1/17/1914	A	Northwestern	L	33-48
1/24/1914	H	Earlham	L	11-19
1/30/1914	A	Earlham	W	28-25
1/31/1914	A	Ohio State	L	17-43
2/7/1914	H	Illinois	L	15-31
2/9/1914	A	Purdue	L	13-35
2/13/1914	H	Northwestern	L	16-40
2/23/1914	A	Minnesota	L	23-26
2/24/1914	A	Wisconsin	L	24-46
2/28/1914	H	Ohio State	L	19-28
3/3/1914	H	Purdue	W	30-28
3/7/1914	H	Minnesota	L	8-28

1913-14 BIG TEN STANDINGS

	W	L	PCT
Wisconsin	12	0	1.000
Ohio State	5	1	.833
Chicago	8	4	.667
Illinois	7	4	.636
Northwestern	6	5	.545
Minnesota	4	8	.333
Purdue	3	9	.250
Iowa	1	5	.167
Indiana	1	11	.083

in the opening minutes with three quick baskets, but the Boilers wrestled their way back into the game and tied it 7-7 at the half. The battle continued in the second half as both teams started heating up their offense. During the last minute and a half of regulation, the lead changed hands three times and Purdue was ahead 26-25 with 10 seconds remaining when a Boilermaker accidentally fouled IU guard Frank Whitaker. Frenzel stepped to the line for IU and buried the free throw to tie the game (during this era any player could shoot the free throw when a player was fouled). The IU crowd exploded when Frenzel hit the mark. Time soon expired and pushed the game into overtime where IU prevailed 30-28, led by forward Allen Maxwell. When the pistol was fired to mark the end of the game, the IU crowd rushed the floor and then paraded across campus to celebrate.

The victory over Purdue was Indiana's first conference win—after 27 straight losses—since February 7, 1912, when the Hoosiers defeated Illinois 24-23 in Bloomington. It was also IU's first victory over Purdue since February 7, 1908, when IU won 26-21 in West Lafayette. The Hoosiers finally managed to break their 12-game losing streak against the Boilermakers.

Predictably, Indiana had a letdown when Minnesota came to Bloomington on Saturday, March 7. The Golden Gophers, who had lost to Purdue the night before, easily defeated an overconfident IU team 28-8 to close the season.

Unlike the previous season, Indiana did manage to win a conference game during the 1913-14 season (and winning it against archrival Purdue made it even sweeter), but the Hoosiers still finished 2-12 overall, the worst season in IU history, in terms of winning percentage. Fortunately, the 1913-14 season was the low point, as IU steadily improved over the next three seasons.

1914-15

OVERALL RECORD: 4-9

CONFERENCE RECORD: 1-9 (NINTH PLACE)

The 1914-15 campaign marked the first time in school history that IU would return the same basketball coach who had led the team from beginning to end during the previous season, as Cotton Berndt came back for his second year coaching the varsity. Another first for that season was that Frank Whitaker was elected captain for the second straight year, becoming the first two-time captain in IU history. Thus, with its experienced leadership in place, and all the members of the previous year's squad returning (along with some promising sophomores), Indiana looked to improve on the disastrous 1913-14 season.

The 1914-15 team. First row (left to right): Rex Dale, Russell Kirkpatrick, Frank Whitaker, Allen Maxwell, Severin Buschmann; Second row: Cleon Nafe, John Porter, William Nash, James Frenzel, Frank Allen; Third row: coach Arthur Berndt. IU Archives

Coach Berndt began some early work with the team around Thanksgiving, and serious work began when the 11 members of the varsity returned to Bloomington right after the Christmas holiday (a week before the rest of the students). In early January, IU's first stroke of bad luck hit when Gard, a promising young player, suffered a shoulder injury that would put him out for the season.

The Hoosiers opened with a contest against Wisconsin, the three-time defending conference champs, in Bloomington on January 9. IU led 6-5 early on, but fell behind 19-11 at the half, and eventually lost 39-18. Junior forward John Porter, playing his first intercollegiate game, led IU with eight points.

Next, IU embarked on an arduous five-game road swing, with all five contests coming against conference opponents. Illinois was up first, and they defeated Indiana 34-14 in Champaign on Monday, January 11. Porter again led Hoosier scorers with nine points. On Saturday, January 16, Northwestern escaped with a 30-22 victory, after the Hoosiers led 11-9 at the half. Prior to the game, Indiana lost one of its starters and most consistent scorers, when junior forward Allen Maxwell left the team to return to his hometown, Indianapolis, upon getting the news of the death of this father.

After the Northwestern game, IU traveled farther north to take on Wisconsin in Madison on January

18. The Hoosiers received a clinic on well-executed offense and stringent defense from the Badgers, who prevailed 47-15. The next day, the Hoosiers completed their fruitless road swing in Iowa City with a disappointing 29-20 defeat at the hands of the Hawkeyes. Porter and sophomore guard Severin Buschmann each had eight points for IU.

IU's fortunes didn't improve when they returned to Bloomington for a January 26 matchup with unde-feated conference front-runner Illinois. The visitors held the Hoosiers without a field goal and waltzed to a 20-4 win. The loss left Indiana with a record of 0-6 with seven games remaining on the schedule. Fortunately, of those seven games, five of them would be in Bloomington, and three of the teams were non-conference opponents.

IU snared its first victory of the season on Friday, January 29, in Richmond, Indiana. There the Hoosiers sped past Earlham College for a 35-14 win. IU overwhelmed the Quakers from the start, jumping out to a 22-7 lead at the half. Junior James Frenzel led IU with 11 points, and Buschmann added 10. Indiana followed up that victory with a 31-25 win over Northwestern, led by 10 points from Maxwell and nine from Frenzel. The Hoosiers kept their winning streak going a week later in a game against Rose Poly in Bloomington. IU completely dominated the

1914-15 TEAM ROSTER

Head coach: Arthur Berndt

Player	Hometown	Class	Position
Frank Allen	Logansport, IN		
Severin Buschmann	Indianapolis, IN	So	F/G
Rex Dale	Lebanon, IN		F
James Frenzel	Indianapolis, IN	Jr	F
Russell Kirkpatrick	Rushville, IN	Jr	G
Cleon Nafe	Rochester, IN	So	F
Allen Maxwell	Indianapolis, IN	Jr	F
DeWitt Mullett	Columbia City	So	G
Cleon Nafe	Rochester, IN	So	F
William Nash	Brazil, IN	So	C
John Porter	Lebanon, IN	Jr	F
Clinton Prather	Wheatland, IN	Jr	F
Frank Whitaker (Capt.)	South Bend, IN	Jr	G

SEASON RESULTS 1914-15

Date	Court	Opponent	Result	Score
1/9/1915	H	Wisconsin	L	18-39
1/11/1915	A	Illinois	L	14-34
1/16/1915	A	Northwestern	L	22-30
1/18/1915	A	Wisconsin	L	15-47
1/19/1915	A	Iowa	L	20-29
1/26/1915	H	Illinois	L	4-20
1/29/1915	A	Earlham	W	35-14
2/6/1915	H	Northwestern	W	31-25
2/13/1915	H	Rose Poly	W	64-15
2/16/1915	H	Purdue	L	12-15
2/20/1915	H	Earlham	W	35-14
2/23/1915	H	Iowa	L	19-20
3/2/1915	A	Purdue	L	15-26

1914-15 BIG TEN STANDINGS

	Conference			All Games		
	W	L	Pct.	W	L	Pct.
Illinois	12	0	1.000	16	0	1.000
Chicago	9	3	.750	15	5	.737
Wisconsin	8	4	.667	13	4	.765
Minnesota	6	6	.500	12	6	.667
Northwestern	5	5	.500	5	5	.500
Purdue	4	8	.333	5	8	.385
Iowa	2	6	.250	9	8	.529
Ohio State	3	9	.250	6	10	.375
Indiana	1	9	.100	4	9	.308

Guard Frank Whitaker was Indiana's first two-time captain as he led the Hoosiers during both the 1913-14 and 1914-15 seasons. IU *Archives*

visitors and set the school record for most points scored in a 64-15 win (the record would last until December 17, 1938). Three Hoosiers scored in double figures, led by Maxwell with 20, Porter with 13, and Whitaker with 10.

IU looked like it was going to further the winning streak when the Hoosiers led Purdue 8-7 at the half in their Bloomington matchup on February 16. However, the Boilermakers surged ahead in the second half and won the game 15-12, mostly as a result of Indiana repeatedly missing free throws in the second half.38.

The Hoosiers then had a rematch with Earlham on Saturday, February 20, in Bloomington, and IU returned to its winning ways with a convincing 35-14 defeat of the Quakers. Maxwell topped all scorers with 14. Next the Hoosiers played their final home game against Iowa on February 23. In a closely fought battle, Indiana led nearly the entire game (including a 12-11 halftime advantage), but Nevins, an Iowa forward, buried a field goal just as time expired. The shot gave a 20-19 win to Iowa, who had previously lost four games by a single point earlier in the season.

Indiana closed the season by putting up a good fight against Purdue on March 2, in West Lafayette. Nevertheless, the Boilermakers swept the season series for the sixth time in seven years by pulling out a 26-15 win.

After losing their first six games (most of them by a wide margin), the Hoosiers were much more competitive in the final seven games, going 4-3, including close losses to Purdue and Iowa. The Hoosiers' 1-9 conference record placed them in last place in the conference for the third straight year. However, the young squad continued to gain valuable game experience and would begin its move out of the conference cellar the next season.

1915-16

OVERALL RECORD: 6-7

CONFERENCE RECORD: 3-5 (FIFTH PLACE)

After a dreary string of losing campaigns, the IU athletic department hired E. Allen Williford to take over the basketball squad from Cotton Berndt, who resigned as the coach of both the baseball and basketball teams the previous year in order to take a job in the private sector. Williford had just graduated from Illinois, where he had captained the basketball team to an undefeated season and a conference championship during his senior year. The new coach inherited an experienced team with a number of seniors who had seen significant playing time over the past two seasons. However, those players had also been part of teams that had posted a combined record of 2-20 in conference play, so it wasn't exactly a squad bursting with basketball talent. Nevertheless, Coach Williford turned the Hoosiers into a tough team to beat and nearly pulled off a winning campaign in the 1915-16 season.

IU opened the schedule on Saturday, January 8, with a home game against Franklin College, the first ever meeting between the two teams. The Hoosiers played inconsistently but came away with a 33-17 victory. Senior forward Clinton Prather was the game's high scorer with 13. Junior center William Nash also contributed 12 points for the Hoosiers. Three days later, Wabash College came to Bloomington and turned the tables on the Hoosiers, winning 33-18 with tough defense and superior ball movement on offense.

The Hoosiers went on the road for the first time on Saturday, January 15, when they traveled north to take on Purdue in West Lafayette. IU limped into the contest without the services of two starters: Team captain Allen Maxwell and Frank Whitaker, one of the team's top defenders. After leading 12-10 at the half, Indiana dropped a 26-17 contest to the Boilermakers in Memorial Gymnasium.

On January 25, Indiana traveled to Greencastle and decimated DePauw 37-5, lead by 13 points from junior guard Severin Buschmann, and 10 from Maxwell. The Hoosiers captured their second straight road

The 1915-16 team. First row (left to right): Allen Maxwell, Frank Whitaker, Clinton Prather, William Nash, Henry Miller, John Porter; Second row: Russell Kirkpatrick, James Frenzel, Phillip Bowser, Severin Buschmann, Ward Gilbert; Third row: coach Allen Williford, DeWitt Mullet, Gard [first name unknown], Cleon Nafe, trainer Jesse Ferguson. IU Archives

game on February 9, when they upended the Earlham Quakers 30-18 by using a balanced scoring attack.

Next, IU captured its first conference win of the season against Ohio State with a 26-17 victory on February 12, in Bloomington. Buschmann and Whitaker had eight points apiece to lead the Hoosier attack. Minnesota came to Bloomington two days later and stole a 29-20 win from IU, despite 12 points from Buschmann.

Northwestern was the next conference foe and they came to town on Saturday, February 19, and bolted out to a 14-1 lead before the Hoosiers knew what had hit them. Despite a valiant attempt at a comeback, IU fell 40-26 in a fast-paced game. Three nights later, Indiana won its second conference game of the year, 29-26, over the Ohio State Buckeyes in Columbus. Buschmann spearheaded the attack with 11 points; Whitaker added eight.

IU went north to Evanston, Illinois, on February 28, for a rematch with Northwestern, but the Wildcats jumped out to another fast start. This time, the count was 14-3 about midway through the first half, and they eventually prevailed 38-20. The next night, IU journeyed up to Minneapolis to take on the Minnesota Golden Gophers. Again the Hoosiers fell

behind early and then battled back in the second half. They ran out of time as the Gophers pulled out a 27-20 win.

Next, the Hoosiers played Wabash in Indianapolis on Saturday, March 4, and hoped to avenge the embarrassing early-season loss that they had suffered to the Little Giants in Bloomington. The Hoosiers jumped out to an 18-12 halftime lead and held Stonebreaker, Wabash's big center, scoreless in the first session. However, Stonebreaker and the Little Giants broke out in the second half, outscoring Indiana 18-7 to pull out a 30-25 win. IU's center William Nash matched Stonebreaker with 10 points, although the Wabash center scored all of his down the stretch with the game on the line.

The Wabash loss left Indiana at 5-7 and no chance for a winning season. The final game on the schedule was a March 11 matchup against Purdue in Bloomington. The Hoosiers played their best offensive game of the season, moving the ball well and shooting a good percentage. At the half they led 19-16, but the game remained close until the Hoosiers pulled away in the final minutes for a 39-29 triumph. Buschmann had 15 points (including seven of eight free throws) and Nash chipped in 10.

The victory against Purdue gave Indiana a 3-5 conference record and clinched fifth place, four spots ahead of the Boilermakers, who fell into the conference cellar. Overall, the Hoosiers went 6-7 in their last full season in the Men's Gymnasium (later known as Assembly Hall). It was the team's best showing in five years, and the next season the Hoosiers would break through and begin a streak of winning seasons.

1915-16 TEAM ROSTER

Head coach: Allen Williford

Player	Hometown	Class	Position
Phillip Bowser	Syracuse, IN	So	C
Severin Buschmann	Indianapolis, IN	Jr	G
James Frenzel	Indianapolis, IN	Sr	F
Russell Kirkpatrick	Rushville, IN	Sr	G
Allen Maxwell (Capt.)	Indianapolis, IN	Sr	F
DeWitt Mullet	Columbia City, IN	Jr	G
Cleon Nafe	Rochester, IN	Jr	F
William Nash	Brazil, IN	Jr	C
John Porter	Lebanon, IN	Sr	F
Clinton Prather	Wheatland, IN	Sr	F
Frank Whitaker	South Bend, IN	Sr	G

SEASON RESULTS 1915-16

Date	Court	Opponent	Result	Score
1/8/1916	H	Franklin	W	33-17
1/11/1916	H	Wabash	L	18-33
1/15/1916	A	Purdue	L	17-26
1/25/1915	A	DePauw	W	37-5
2/9/1916	A	Earlham	W	30-18
2/12/1916	H	Ohio State	W	26-17
2/14/1916	H	Minnesota	L	20-29
2/19/1906	H	Northwestern	L	26-40
2/22/1906	A	Ohio State	W	29-26
2/28/1906	A	Northwestern	L	20-38
2/29/1906	A	Minnesota	L	20-27
3/4/1906	N	Wabash	L	25-30
3/11/1906	H	Purdue	W	39-29

1915-16 BIG TEN STANDINGS

	Conference			All Games		
	W	L	Pct.	W	L	Pct.
Wisconsin	11	1	.917	20	1	.952
Illinois	9	3	.750	13	3	.813
Northwestern	9	3	.750	9	3	.750
Minnesota	6	6	.500	8	6	.571
Indiana	3	5	.375	4	6	.400
Iowa	2	4	.333	12	4	.750
Chicago	4	8	.333	9	9	.500
Ohio State	2	8	.200	10	12	.455
Purdue	2	10	.167	4	10	.286

SEASON STATISTICS
1900-01 TO 1915-16

1900-01

Team Statistics	G	FG	FT	TP	AVG
Indiana	4	27	24	78	19.50
Opponents	4	28	27	83	20.75
Player Statistics	G	FG	FT	TP	AVG
E. Strange	4	2	18	22	5.50
E. Walker	4	10	0	20	5.00
C. Unnewehr	2	4	0	8	4.00
P. Darby	4	5	3	13	3.25
J. Fitzgerald	3	5	3	13	3.25
A. Rucker	4	1	0	2	0.50

1901-02

Team Statistics	G	TP	AVG
Indiana	8	168	21.0
Opponents	8	222	27.8

1902-03

Team Statistics	G	TP	AVG
Indiana	12	317	26.4
Opponents	12	243	20.3

1903-04

Team Statistics	G	TP	AVG
Indiana	9	310	34.4
Opponents	9	218	24.2

1904-05

Team Statistics	G	TP	AVG
Indiana	17	436	25.6
Opponents	17	575	33.8
Player Statistics	G	TP	AVG
Harmeson	13	137	10.5
Ritterskamp	12	76	6.3
Taber	12	56	4.7
Carr	10	42	4.2
Teter	11	30	2.7
Trimble	4	6	1.5
Hiatt	7	6	0.9
Robinson	3	0	0.0
Cookson	1	0	0.0
Sanders	1	0	0.0
Woody	1	0	0.0

[Only includes the 13 games with box scores]

1905-06

Team Statistics	G	TP	AVG
Indiana	16	423	26.4
Opponents	16	352	22
Player Statistics	G	TP	AVG
Harmeson	13	144	12.1
Maxwell	5	42	8.4
Ritterskamp	12	86	7.2
McCoy	3	18	6.0
Woody	5	25	5.0
Martin	7	28	4.0
Trimble	1	2	2.0
Quinn	11	10	0.9
Sanders	6	4	0.7
Hiatt	11	6	0.5
Kempf	2	0	0.0
Daniel	1	0	0.0

[Only includes the 15 games with box scores]

1906-07

Team Statistics	G	TP	AVG
Indiana	14	391	27.9
Opponents	14	318	22.7
Player Statistics	G	TP	AVG
Cook	9	87	9.7
McCoy	11	81	7.4
Guedel	1	6	6.0
Martin	11	64	5.8
Thompson	8	26	3.3
Sanders	11	24	2.2
Quinn	9	10	1.1
Boyle	2	2	1.0
Bossert	5	0	0.0

[Only includes the 11 games with box scores]

1907-08

Team Statistics	G	TP	AVG
Indiana	15	378	25.2
Opponents	15	303	20.2
Player Statistics	G	TP	AVG
Cook	1	15	15.0
Woody	12	129	10.8
McCoy	5	50	10.0
Chattin	12	59	4.9
Rogers	11	34	3.1
Thompson	13	23	1.8
Trimble	9	2	0.2
Boyle	2	0	0.0
Cartwright	2	0	0.0
Berndt	1	0	0.0
Kessler	1	0	0.0
Martin	1	0	0.0

[Only includes the 14 games with box scores]

1908-09

Team Statistics	G	TP	AVG
Indiana	14	264	18.9
Opponents	14	293	20.9
Player Statistics	**G**	**TP**	**AVG**
Barnhardt	8	88	11.0
Wellman	1	4	4.0
Hipskind	8	27	3.4
Berndt	8	24	3.0
Chattin	2	6	3.0
Rogers	6	10	1.7
Thompson	7	6	0.9
Trimble	6	2	0.3

[Only includes the 9 games with box scores]

1909-10

Team Statistics	G	TP	AVG
Indiana	13	234	18.0
Opponents	13	359	27.6
Player Statistics	**G**	**TP**	**AVG**
Barnhart	10	89	8.9
Hipskind	11	45	4.1
Graves	9	18	2.0
Mangel	11	20	1.8
Whitney	4	4	1.0
Davis	11	8	0.7
Stotter	6	0	0.0
Abel	1	0	0.0

[Only includes the 11 games with box scores]

1910-11

Team Statistics	G	TP	AVG
Indiana	16	464	29.0
Opponents	16	342	21.4
Player Statistics	**G**	**TP**	**AVG**
Barnhart	15	202	13.5
Graves	14	104	7.4
Hipskind	15	58	3.9
Freeland	5	18	3.6
Berndt	15	30	2.0
Munkelt	1	2	2.0
Davis	14	10	0.7
Whitney	2	1	0.5
Stotter	3	0	0.0
Stayton	1	0	0.0

[Only includes the 15 games with box scores]

1911-12

Team Statistics	G	TP	AVG
Indiana	17	331	19.5
Opponents	17	506	29.8
Player Statistics	**G**	**TP**	**AVG**
Graves	16	164	10.3
Freeland	16	54	3.4
Munkelt	16	42	2.6
Clouse	2	4	2.0
Fleming	6	10	1.7
McCullough	11	14	1.3
Chattin	3	4	1.3
Davis	8	7	0.9
Edwards	5	4	0.8
Stayton	14	2	0.1
Jones	1	0	0.0
Reis	1	0	0.0

[Only includes the 16 games with box scores]

1912-13

Team Statistics	G	TP	AVG
Indiana	16	340	21.3
Opponents	16	401	25.1
Player Statistics	**G**	**TP**	**AVG**
Barnhart	13	98	7.5
Freeland	13	75	5.8
Munkelt	12	42	3.5
Nichols	8	26	3.3
McCullough	13	18	1.4
Clouse	13	6	0.5
Fleming	9	2	0.2
Edwards	1	0	0.0
Stout	1	0	0.0

[Only includes the 13 games with box scores]

1913-14

Team Statistics	G	TP	AVG
Indiana	14	258	18.4
Opponents	14	491	35.1
Player Statistics	**G**	**TP**	**AVG**
Frenzel	14	115	8.2
Prather	13	42	3.2
Gilbert	14	34	2.4
Maxwell	7	18	2.6
Whitaker	13	32	2.5
Pruitt	5	7	1.4
Ferguson	2	2	1.0
Kirkpatrick	14	10	0.7
Morris	4	0	0.0
Fleming	2	0	0.0
Lingeman	2	0	0.0
Decker	1	0	0.0

1915-16

Team Statistics	G	TP	AVG
Indiana	13	340	26.2
Opponents	13	335	25.8
Player Statistics	**G**	**TP**	**AVG**
Buschmann	13	107	8.2
Nash	13	76	5.8
Maxwell	11	52	4.7
Whitaker	11	28	2.5
Prather	8	27	3.4
Porter	9	26	2.9
Bowser	4	10	2.5
Kirkpatrick	3	6	2.0
Frenzel	2	2	1.0
Mullett	13	6	0.5
Miller	1	0	0.0

1914-15

Team Statistics	G	TP	AVG
Indiana	13	304	23.4
Opponents	13	328	25.2
Player Statistics	**G**	**TP**	**AVG**
Maxwell	10	66	6.6
Porter	13	76	5.8
Frenzel	13	56	4.3
Nafe	2	6	3.0
Whitaker	13	36	2.8
Buschmann	13	34	2.6
Kirkpatrick	8	13	1.6
Prather	4	5	1.3
Dale	4	4	1.0
Nash	12	8	0.7
Mullett	1	0	0.0

CHAPTER 12

A WINNING TRADITION BEGINS: 1916-17 TO 1923-24

1916-17

OVERALL RECORD: 13-6

CONFERENCE RECORD: 3-5 (FIFTH PLACE)

INDIVIDUAL HONORS:

DEWITT MULLETT—BIG TEN MEDAL OF HONOR

In many ways, the 1916-17 season marked the turning of the tide of the Indiana University basketball program from being a perennial also-ran to a regular champion contender. For the first time, the 1916-17 squad was loaded with enough talent to adequately fill every position with a capable starter and a solid backup, which heightened the competition in practice and improved the team's performance and intensity in games. The team set school records in both victories and winning percentage and christened the opening of the school's first full-fledged basketball stadium. The confluence of all these factors ignited the interest of both Indiana students and IU basketball fans.

On thing that didn't change for the 1916-17 season was the coaching carousel. Once again, the Hoosiers had a new leader. The man in charge was Guy Lowman, the coach of the freshman football team and an employee of the Department of Physical Education. Lowman had competed in football, basketball and track in college and had previously coached at the Kansas Agricultural College. While football was more of his specialty, Lowman turned out to be an organized and experienced coach who was able to mold a talented group of IU players into a successful basketball squad.

Indiana returned three senior starters in center Penn Nash and guards DeWitt Mullet and Severin Buschmann, the team captain. The forward spots were up for grabs, with a lot of different players jostling for a place in the rotation. When IU opened with a convincing 40-10 victory over Indiana Dental College on December 8, in Bloomington, Buschmann was still injured from football season, so sophomore

Arlo Byrum took over his guard spot and ended up becoming a regular fixture in the backcourt. As a result, Buschmann moved to forward when he returned to the lineup for Indiana's second game of the year, a December 15 contest against Earlham. Buschmann led all scorers with 14 in a 44-23 IU win in Bloomington. Indiana closed out its December schedule by defeating the Vincennes YMCA 28-18 in a December 18 home game. Nash was the top scorer with 10.

The Hoosiers kept the winning streak alive with a 24-14 victory over DePauw on Wednesday, January 3, in a game punctuated by stiff defense and cold shooting. Indiana held the visitors without a field goal for the first 15 minutes of the game. IU's defense shined again two days later in a 35-9 win over Rose Poly in the last game ever played in the Hoosiers' first basketball arena, the original Assembly Hall.

Indiana went on the road for the first time for its conference opener on Friday, January 12, against the Iowa Hawkeyes. After leading 9-7 at the half, the Hoosiers pulled away in the second session after Iowa's captain and star forward, Bannick, left the game with an injury. The next day, Indiana played the Iowa State Teachers College in Cedar Falls, and the Hoosiers came away with a 29-13 win, as Buschmann scored 10, and sophomore forward Heber Williams added nine.

Riding a school-record seven-game winning streak, the Hoosiers returned home to play their first contest in the school's new gym, a $250,000 arena with a regular seating capacity of 2,400 (over 4,000 could cram in with extra seats and standing room), along with athletics offices, locker rooms, and a trophy display. At the time, the gym was simply known

The 1916-17 team. First row (left to right): Arlo Byrum, Heber Williams, DeWitt Mullett, Severin Buschmann, William Nash, Phillip Bowser; Second row: coach Guy Lowman, Herm Schuler, William Zellar, George Reed, trainer Jesse Ferguson. IU Archives

as the New Gymnasium or the Men's Gymnasium. Regardless of what it was called, it was a huge step up from the makeshift arena that the Hoosiers were used to. However, it took a while for the team to get used to the new floor and the new baskets. The opening game on Friday, January 19, was a rematch with Iowa. After the first half, Indiana's lead was 5-4, as both squads had difficulty scoring the ball. The Hoosiers prevailed 12-7, in what remains the lowest-scoring victory in IU history.

Purdue came to town on Sunday, January 28, and didn't have much trouble in the new area. The Boilermakers snatched away a 22-15 win and ended the Hoosiers' unbeaten streak. On February 2, IU rebounded with an 18-9 win over Butler in the new

gym. Then the Hoosiers traveled to West Lafayette on February 6, for a rematch with Purdue, but came up short again with a 24-18 loss. IU squeaked out a 14-13 road win over DePauw two nights later on Thursday, February 8. The team returned to Bloomington the next night and whipped Central Normal College (now called the University of Indianapolis) 61-9, with sophomore forward Herm Schuler leading the way with 19 points. Sophomore forward Bill Zellar also contributed 12 points.

The Wabash "Wonder Five" (as they were known that season) were the next visitors to IU's new gym on February 16, and they engaged in a spirited battle with the Hoosiers, who eventually lost 20-17. Next, Indiana grabbed a 24-19 conference win over Ohio

State on February 24, in Columbus, Ohio. Unfortunately, IU followed that up by losing to OSU 30-14 in Bloomington on March 2.

Indiana traveled to Wisconsin on Tuesday, March 6, and dropped another conference game to the

1916-17 TEAM ROSTER

Head coach: Guy Lowman

Player	Hometown	Class	Position
Phillip Bowser	Syracuse, IN	Jr	C
Severin Buschmann (Capt.)	Indianapolis, IN	Sr	F
Arlo Byrum	Anderson, IN	So	G
Henry Miller	Bloomington, IN		G
DeWitt Mullett	Columbia City, IN	Sr	G
Cleon Nafe	Rochester, IN	Sr	F
W. Penn Nash	Brazil, IN	Sr	C
George Reed	Bloomington, IN		G
Bob Rogers	Bloomington, IN		F
Herm Schuler	Elkhart, IN	So	F
Heber Williams	Kokomo, IN	So	F
William Zellar	Brazil, IN	Fr	F

SEASON RESULTS 1916-17

Date	Court	Opponent	Result	Score
12/8/1916	H	Indiana Dental College	W	40-10
12/15/1916	H	Earlham	W	44-23
12/18/1916	H	Vincennes YMCA	W	28-18
1/3/1917	H	DePauw	W	24-14
1/5/1917	H	Rose Poly	W	35-9
1/12/1917	A	Iowa	W	21-12
1/13/1917	A	Iowa State Teachers College	W	29-13
1/19/1917	H	Iowa	W	12-7
1/28/1917	H	Purdue	L	15-22
2/2/1917	H	Butler	W	18-9
2/6/1917	A	Purdue	L	18-24
2/8/1917	A	DePauw	W	14-13
2/9/1917	H	Central Normal College	W	61-9
2/16/1917	H	Wabash	L	17-20
2/24/1917	A	Ohio State	W	24-19
3/2/1917	H	Ohio State	L	14-30
3/6/1917	A	Wisconsin	L	13-29
3/7/1917	A	Milwaukee Normal College	W	39-12
3/15/1917	H	Wisconsin	L	16-18

1916-17 BIG TEN STANDINGS

	W	L	PCT
Minnesota	10	2	.833
Illinois	10	2	.833
Purdue	7	2	.778
Wisconsin	9	3	.750
Indiana	3	5	.375
Chicago	4	8	.333
Ohio State	3	9	.250
Northwestern	2	10	.167
Iowa	1	8	.111

Badgers. On the way home, IU stopped in Milwaukee and hammered Milwaukee Normal Central 39-12 on March 7. On Thursday, March 15, Indiana had a chance to even its conference record with a season-ending victory over Wisconsin in Bloomington. Things looked good for the Hoosiers, who led 14-12 at the break, but the Badgers squeezed IU with their patented defense in the second half and came away with an 18-16 win.

Although the Wisconsin loss dropped the Hoosiers' conference record to 3-5 (for a fifth-place finish), it had been an exciting season with plenty for the Hoosier faithful to cheer about, which was sorely needed because, at the time, the United States stood on the brink of entering World War I.

1917-18

OVERALL RECORD: 10-4

CONFERENCE RECORD: 3-3 (FOURTH PLACE)

With the First World War raging in Europe, the IU athletic department scaled back its sports activities. There had even been some debate about discontinuing athletic events altogether during the war, as a number of athletes had already gone off to serve in the military and many others were awaiting their call. However, the IU board of trustees and Indiana president William Lowe Bryan decided to keep the athletic program active, albeit on the back burner. For the basketball season, the slate of games was reduced to 14 (the team had played 19 the previous year) and road trips were limited. The Hoosiers played only six conference games, the fewest of any team in the league. Amidst this subdued atmosphere, 1917 was also the year in which the Big Ten became the Big Ten, as Michigan rejoined the conference, giving the conference 10 member schools for the first time.

For the IU squad, the tradition of changing coaches on an annual basis continued as Dana Evans

The 1917-18 team. First row (left to right): William Easton, Ardith Phillips, Phillip Bowser, Edward Von Tress, Willard Stahr, McFarland [first name unknown]; Second row: coach Dana Evans, William Zellar, Huxford [first name unknown], James Ingles, Urban Jeffries, trainer Jesse Ferguson. IU Archives

took the reins of the team. Evans, who was also the varsity track coach and an assistant football coach, had previously coached at Beloit College in Wisconsin. He inherited a Hoosier team that was depleted by the loss of three senior starters and a sophomore starter, Arlo Byrum, who was on active duty in the army. Only two players—junior forward Bill Zellar and senior center Phillip Bowser (the team captain)—had any college basketball experience. Thus, expectations were low heading into the season, but those expectations soon lifted when the Hoosiers raced out of the starting gates and won their first six games.

The season opened on Friday, December 7, when Indiana wiped out Manchester College 45-18. On December 14, the Hoosiers played a sloppy first half, but still led 17-4 against a badly overmatched Indiana Central Normal team. IU played with better effectiveness in the second half and cruised to a 49-6 win. DePauw was the next victim on Thursday, December 20. They put up a fight, but the Hoosiers prevailed 26-20. After the winter break, Indiana played Wabash in a defensive grudge match on Friday, January 11.

The Hoosiers led 16-6 at the half and prevailed 21-9 for their fourth straight win.

Before the Big Ten schedule began, it was announced that the two Indiana-Purdue contests for the season would be cancelled. For the second time in the history of the rivalry, athletic relations between the two schools had been suspended because of disputes and ill feelings between the two institutions.

On Friday, January 18, Indiana traveled to Ann Arbor, Michigan, to take on the Michigan Wolverines in the conference opener for both teams. IU opened a six-point lead early on and never trailed after that, although the Wolverines put up a fierce fight and cut the lead to one in the final minutes, until IU forwards Urban Jeffries and William Easton each scored a basket to push the lead to five. Michigan managed a final free throw, but the Hoosiers won 21-17. "The game is said to have been the most furious ever fought on the Michigan floor," the *Indiana Daily Student* reported the next day.

On Thursday, January 24, Detroit University traveled down to Bloomington and became the final victim of Indiana's six-game unbeaten streak, losing

24-15 to the Hoosiers. Zellar and sophomore guard Ardith Phillips tied for game-high honors with seven points. The streak came to an end on Friday, February 1, when Ohio State defeated IU 28-22 in Columbus. Zellar led IU with 10 points in the losing cause. But IU jumped back into the winning circle on February 11, by outclassing DePauw 34-22 in Greencastle. After falling behind 4-0, Indiana turned things around by leading 16-9 at the intermission, and then cruising to victory in the second half. The next day, the Hoosiers returned home for a rematch with the Ohio State Buckeyes. Bowser was out to illness, and Phillips, though slowed by illness, was still able to play. Indiana fought hard, but showed little stamina, trailing 14-12 at the half and losing by the same margin as OSU came away with a 23-21 victory.

Still without Bowser, the Hoosiers defeated Iowa 29-25 on Saturday, February 16, in Iowa City, led by a game-high 15 points from Zellar. Two nights later, Indiana dropped a 28-18 contest to Wabash in Crawfordsville. Zellar once again led all scorers with 12. Indiana won its second game of the season over Michigan (who was winless in conference play) on Friday, February 22, in Bloomington. The Hoosiers triumphed 21-20 on the strength of 10 points from Phillips. Next, Rose Poly came to Bloomington on Friday, March 1, and was annihilated 43-7. Zellar was the top scorer with 15.

IU closed its season a week later on March 8, with a home game against Iowa. At the end of the first half, the Hoosiers led 4-3 and it looked as though the two teams might not eclipse the combined score from their 12-7 match a year earlier. The teams continued to miss easy shots in the second half, but Indiana pulled ahead 11-10 in the waning minutes before Iowa scored the game's final three points and won 13-11. Indiana lost the game at the free throw line where the Hoosiers made only one of six attempts.

Despite the season-ending defeat, Indiana had recorded its second straight winning season, and for the 1917-18 campaign it did it without a stockpile of talented and experienced players. The Hoosiers played well in all of their Big Ten games and dominated nearly all of their non-conference contests. Since most of its regular players were sophomores and juniors, and a bumper crop of strong players from the freshmen team was ready to join next season's varsity, the IU squad looked like they could be even better over the next few seasons.

1917-18 TEAM ROSTER

Head coach: Dana Evans

Player	Hometown	Class	Position
Phillip Bowser (Capt.)	Syracuse, IN	Sr	C
William Easton	Bloomington, IN	So	F
James Ingles	Indianapolis, IN	Sr	G
Urban Jeffries	Rockville, IN	So	F
Ardith Phillips	Amo, IN	So	G
Elliott Risley	Bloomington, IN		F
Willard Stahr	Hagerstown, IN		G
Edward Von Tress	Vincennes, IN	So	G
William Zellar	Brazil, IN	Jr	F

SEASON RESULTS 1917-18

Date	Court	Opponent	Result	Score
12/7/1917	H	Manchester College	W	45-18
12/14/1917	H	Indiana Central	W	49-6
12/20/1917	H	DePauw	W	26-20
1/11/1918	H	Wabash	W	21-9
1/18/1918	A	Michigan	W	21-17
1/24/1918	H	Detroit University	W	24-15
2/1/1918	A	Ohio State	L	22-28
2/11/1918	A	DePauw	W	34-22
2/12/1918	H	Ohio State	L	21-23
2/16/1918	A	Iowa	W	29-25
2/18/1918	A	Wabash	L	18-28
2/22/1918	H	Michigan	W	21-20
3/1/1918	H	Rose Poly	W	43-7
3/8/1918	H	Iowa	L	11-13

1917-18 BIG TEN STANDINGS

	W	L	PCT
Wisconsin	9	3	.750
Minnesota	7	3	.700
Northwestern	5	3	.625
Indiana	3	3	.500
Purdue	5	5	.500
Ohio State	5	5	.500
Illinois	6	6	.500
Chicago	6	6	.500
Iowa	4	6	.400
Michigan	0	10	.000

1918-19

OVERALL RECORD: 10-7

CONFERENCE RECORD: 4-6 (SIXTH PLACE)

INDIVIDUAL HONORS:

WILLIAM ZELLAR—BIG TEN MEDAL OF HONOR

The 1918-19 team. First row (left to right): Joseph Lorei, Urban Jeffries, William Zellar, Ardith Phillips, Everett Dean, Arlo Byrum, trainer Jesse Ferguson; Second row: coach Dana Evans, Byard Smith, Joy Buckner, Lawrence Busby, William Dobbins, Markham Wakefield. IU Archives

Coach Dana Evans returned to lead the IU basketball team for the 1918-19 season, and along with Evans returned the team's top two scorers, forward Bill Zellar and guard Ardith Phillips (team captain). Prior to the basketball season, both players had been involved in military training—Zellar for the navy and Phillips for the army—and so they were in top condition when they returned to campus. Another player, junior guard Arlo Bynum, returned to IU and rejoined the team after a one-year stint with the army. The Hoosiers also owned two good post players in junior Urban Jeffries, a retuning starter, and Everett Dean, a skilled and consistent sophomore who would emerge as the team's top scorer.

With all of these factors pointing toward a big season for the IU basketball team, a couple other factors would slow the progress of the team. First, the team was unable to begin their workouts during the first semester because a local naval unit was using the gym for training. As a result, the basketball team stayed on campus during IU's winter break in order to make up for lost time and get in some practice before the start of the season. In order to pay for the team's room and board during the break, the student body started a fund raising campaign in December and raised the money needed within 48 hours.

The other factor that hindered the training of the team was an outbreak of influenza on the

Bloomington campus. The rampant flu bug kept the Hoosiers from being able to use the gym at times and forced the team to play their opening games on the road. It also resulted in the cancellation of the January 18 game with Wabash.

After playing a total of only five road games during the previous season, IU started the 1918-19 campaign with five straight road contests. The first was a 47-16 victory over the Vincennes YMCA on Thursday, January 2. Then the Hoosiers went up to Minnesota on Saturday, January 11, and got whipped 35-13 by a Golden Gophers team that played like it was in midseason form. Two days later, the Hoosiers traveled to Iowa City and grabbed a 20-14 win over the Iowa Hawkeyes, led by eight points from Dean and six from Jeffries.

The next week, Indiana journeyed north to Michigan on January 20, and fell behind big in the first half. The Wolverines led 13-1 at the break, but the Hoosiers battled back in the second half and tied the game at 19 before running out of gas and losing 28-22. IU ended its road swing against Toledo the next day with a 32-25 win, improving the Hoosiers to 3-2 overall.

IU's long awaited home opener finally took place on Friday, January 24, against Iowa. Unfortunately, the large home crowd saw Iowa thoroughly outplay the Hoosiers and walk away with a 21-10 victory. Indiana continued to have trouble on their home floor on Monday, January 27, when DePauw came to town and dealt the Hoosiers a surprising 21-17 defeat. Things finally turned around on Friday, January 31, when IU trampled Franklin 35-19. Dean netted a game-high 15 points and Zellar added 10 for IU, which improved its record to 4-4 overall.

The home floor blues returned on Friday, February 7, as the Ohio State Buckeyes stole a 22-21 victory from the Hoosiers. IU led 20-17 in the final minutes, but OSU rallied and the Indiana defense was unable to stop them. Dean led all scorers with 13. The following weekend, Indiana returned the favor by going to Columbus and upending Ohio State in their home gym by the score of 37-31. IU trailed 16-12 at the half, but peppered OSU with baskets from multiple angles in the second half. Dean starred once again with 17 points, and Jeffries chipped in 12 for the Hoosiers. IU remained in Ohio for a February 17 contest with Cincinnati. Dean scored 16 points to bolster the Hoosiers to a 38-24 win.

Next, the undefeated Minnesota Golden Gophers came to Bloomington on Saturday, February 22, and were put to one of their toughest games of the year. The Gophers led 8-6 at the half and slowly pulled away for a 20-14 win, but the scrappiness of the Hoosiers pleased the home crowd. Two days later,

1918-19 TEAM ROSTER

Head coach: Dana Evans

Player	Hometown	Class	Position
Joy Buckner	Bluffton, IN	So	G
Lawrence Busby	Lapel, IN	So	C
Arlo Byrum	Anderson, IN	Jr	G
Everett Dean	Salem, IN	So	F/C
William Dobbins	Bloomington, IN	So	G
William Easton	Bloomington, IN	Jr	F
Urban Jeffries	Rockville, IN	Jr	F/C
Joseph Lohrei	Goshen, IN	So	C
Ardith Phillips (Capt.)	Amo, IN	Jr	G
Byard Smith	Decatur, IN	Sr	G
Markham Wakefield	Worthington, IN	Jr	F
William Zellar	Brazil, IN	Jr	F

SEASON RESULTS 1918-19

Date	Court	Opponent	Result	Score
1/2/1919	A	Vincennes YMCA	W	47-16
1/11/1919	A	Minnesota	L	13-35
1/13/1919	A	Iowa	W	23-14
1/20/1919	A	Michigan	L	22-28
1/21/1919	A	Toledo	W	32-25
1/24/1919	H	Iowa	L	10-21
1/27/1919	H	DePauw	L	17-21
1/31/1919	H	Franklin	W	35-19
2/7/1919	H	Ohio State	L	21-22
2/15/1919	A	Ohio State	W	37-31
2/17/1919	A	Cincinnati	W	38-24
2/22/1919	H	Minnesota	L	14-20
2/24/1919	H	Wisconsin	L	16-29
3/3/1919	H	Notre Dame	W	29-11
3/6/1919	A	DePauw	W	17-16
3/11/1919	H	Michigan	W	24-16
3/15/1919	A	Wisconsin	W	22-12

1918-19 BIG TEN STANDINGS

	W	L	PCT
Minnesota	10	0	1.000
Chicago	10	2	.833
Northwestern	6	4	.600
Michigan	5	5	.500
Illinois	5	7	.417
Indiana	4	6	.400
Iowa	4	7	.364
Purdue	4	7	.364
Ohio State	2	6	.250
Wisconsin	3	9	.250

Wisconsin came to town. Led by former IU coach Guy Lowman, the Badgers dismantled the Hoosiers 29-16, the loss dropping IU to 6-7 on the year.

Indiana pulled back to .500 on Monday, March 3, by walloping Notre Dame 29-11 on the strength of 15 points from Dean. On Thursday, March 6, the Hoosiers edged DePauw 17-16 in a cliffhanger in Greencastle. Dean buried the winning free throw shortly before time expired. Next, Dean's 10 points powered IU to a 24-16 win over Michigan on February 11. Byrum added six points for the Hoosiers and played his usual brand of tough defense. IU closed the season on Saturday, March 15, at Wisconsin. IU led 8-7 at the half, and then stormed out of the locker room in the second session and steamrolled the Badgers for a 22-12 victory. Once again, Byrum locked down the opposing scorers, while Zellar, Phillips and Dean each scored six points.

Indiana's four-game winning streak to finish out the season improved the team's record to 10-7 overall and 4-6 in the Big Ten. Interestingly, after the Hoosiers were forced to play their early games on the road, it hardened the squad and made them an excellent road team. They went 7-2 in road games for the season. Of course, playing away from home so much apparently made them rusty or overconfident on their home floor as they struggled to a 3-5 record in Bloomington. Adding to the bizarre nature of the season was the fact that IU had four opponents (Iowa, Ohio State, DePauw, and Wisconsin) that it defeated on the road, while losing to those same four teams at home.

Junior guard Ardith "Pete" Phillips, who was the captain of the 1918-19 Hoosiers, was known for his hustle and grit on both ends of the floor, and he was admired as one of the best all-around players in the Western Conference (the precursor to the Big Ten). IU Archives

1919-20

OVERALL RECORD: 13-8

CONFERENCE RECORD: 6-4 (FOURTH PLACE)

The 1919-20 team. First row (left to right): Heber Williams, Ardith Phillips, Arlo Byrum, Everett Dean, Urban Jeffries; Second row: Herm Schuler, William Zellar, Ralph Esarey, Markham Wakefield, Russell Hauss; Third row: John Kyle, William Dobbins, Harry Donovan, Gilbert Rhea. IU Archives

For one of the first times in its history, the IU basketball squad had a core group of skilled and experienced seniors to lead it into the 1919-20 season. Plus, the Hoosiers had all of their players back except one (substitute guard Byard Smith) from a 10-7 team that had been very competitive the previous year. Athletic director Ewald "Jumbo" Stiehm (who was also the football coach) had difficulty finding a new leader for the basketball team, so he took over the coaching duties himself. Stiehm had been a basketball and football standout at Wisconsin and had coached both basketball and football at Nebraska before coming to Indiana in 1916.

The Hoosiers dominated the North American Gymnastic Union (a team from Indianapolis) in the season opener on December 12. After a slow start and a mere 10-6 lead at the half, the Hoosiers kicked into high gear in the second half and pulled away for a 32-10 win in Bloomington. Junior center Everett Dean picked up right where he left off the previous season, leading all scorers with 16 points. Over the next week, IU racked up two more easy wins, 45-6 over Hanover and 24-15 over Valparaiso. Dean was the high scorer in both games, with 10 points against Hanover and 18 against Valpo.

During their winter vacation, the Hoosiers made a slight northern swing to test their skills against a couple of independent teams made up of older players. IU traveled to Huntington on December 29, and lost to the Huntington Athletics 22-15, in a bitterly fought game in which an overwhelming number of fouls were called against the Hoosiers. The next night, IU lost a 33-28 barnburner in overtime to the Merchants Heat and Light Company in Indianapolis.

On Friday, January 9, IU traveled to Delaware, Ohio, and romped over Ohio Wesleyan 38-21. Junior forward Herm Schuler and senior guard Ardith Phillips shared high scoring honors with 10. The next night, Indiana opened its Big Ten season at Ohio State and claimed a surprisingly easy 22-11 victory, as Dean himself outscored the Buckeyes with 12 points.

The next week, Indiana trekked up to East Lansing, Michigan, on Friday, January 16, and snatched away a victory from Michigan State (not yet a Big Ten member) when forward Urban Jeffries buried a field goal from the top of the key with five seconds remaining, to give the Hoosiers a thrilling 20-19 win. The Hoosiers kept that momentum alive when they defeated Michigan 22-9 in Ann Arbor the next day.

The Hoosiers suffered their first Big Ten loss on Friday, January 23, when the Purdue Boilermakers came to Bloomington and used a second-half surge to defeat Indiana 17-9. The highly anticipated game marked the resumption of athletic relations between the two schools after a two-year lay-off because of a dispute. Indiana bounced back on Saturday, January 31, and defeated Northwestern 32-11 in the Men's Gymnasium. Once again, Dean himself outscored the opponent by ringing up 14 points.

During the first week of February, IU made a road trip to Nebraska for a three-game swing. They opened by falling to Creighton 29-20 on Wednesday, February 4, and then turned around and won a see-saw battle with Nebraska 24-20 on February 5. Coach Stiehm mostly used his reserves against the

Cornhuskers the next night in a rematch game, which the Hoosiers lost 38-18. On the way home from that trip, Indiana stopped in Iowa City for a conference match with Iowa on Saturday, February 7. Playing their fourth game in as many days, the Hoosiers fell 28-20 after trailing by only one at the half.

Iowa, riding a five-game conference win streak, came to Bloomington on Friday, February 13, for a return matchup. Because the Bloomington campus was infected with influenza, the university had banned a crowd from assembling for the game. However, about 100 students snuck into the gym to watch IU upset the Hawkeyes 25-19 in overtime. The Hoosier crowds were allowed to return for a 36-12 home victory over Cincinnati on Thursday, February 19.

IU went to West Lafayette on Wednesday, February 25, for a rematch with Purdue, but fell 31-20 to the Boilermakers in their Memorial Gymnasium, which overflowed with eager spectators. On Saturday, February 28, Indiana returned to its winning ways by shaving a 17-16 victory from the Ohio State Buckeyes. Next, Indiana lost a chance to move up in the Big Ten standings by losing 36-34 to lowly Northwestern (1-6 in the conference before the IU game) on Saturday, March 6. IU closed its season on March 15, with a 19-18 victory over Michigan. After trailing by one at the intermission, the Hoosiers quickly built a six-point lead in the second half. The Wolverines made a comeback run, but ran out of time.

Indiana's six conference wins in the 1919-20 season set a school record, and their 13 overall wins tied the school mark. The Northwestern loss was the one nagging disappointment that kept the Hoosiers from an even better record and a higher finish in the conference. Nevertheless, a season of high expectations concluded with a team that turned out to be the best and most balanced squad that the Hoosiers had ever put on the floor in the first two decades of IU basketball.

1919-20 TEAM ROSTER

Head coach: Ewald Stiehm

Player	Hometown	Class	Position
Arlo Byrum (Capt.)	Anderson, IN	Sr	G
Everett Dean	Salem, IN	Jr	C
William Dobbins	Bloomington, IN	Jr	G
Harry Donovan	South Bend, IN	Jr	C
Ralph Esarey	Bloomington, IN		G
Urban Jeffries	Rockville, IN	Sr	F
John Kyle	Gary, IN	Jr	F
Ardith Phillips	Amo, IN	Sr	G
Gilbert Rhea	Clayton, IN		F
Russell Hauss	Sellersburg, IN	So	G
Herm Schuler	Elkhart, IN	Jr	F
Markham Wakefield	Worthington, IN	Sr	F
Heber Williams	Kokomo, IN	Sr	F
William Zellar	Brazil, IN	Sr	G

SEASON RESULTS 1919-20

Date	Court	Opponent	Result	Score
12/12/1919	H	N. Amer. Gymnastic Union	W	32-10
12/13/1919	H	Hanover	W	46-5
12/18/1919	H	Valparaiso	W	24-15
12/29/1919	A	Huntington Athletics	L	15-22
12/30/1919	A	Merchants Heat and Light	L	28-33
1/9/1920	A	Ohio Wesleyan	W	38-21
1/10/1920	A	Ohio State	W	22-11
1/16/1920	A	Michigan State	W	20-19
1/17/1920	A	Michigan	W	22-9
1/23/1920	H	Purdue	L	9-17
1/31/1920	H	Northwestern	W	32-11
2/4/1920	A	Creighton	L	20-29
2/5/1920	A	Nebraska	W	24-20
2/6/1920	A	Nebraska	L	18-38
2/7/1920	A	Iowa	L	20-28
2/13/1920	H	Iowa	W	25-19
2/19/1920	H	Cincinnati	W	36-12
2/25/1920	A	Purdue	L	20-31
2/28/1920	W	Ohio State	W	17-16
3/6/1920	L	Northwestern	L	34-36
3/15/1920	W	Michigan	W	19-18

1919-20 BIG TEN STANDINGS

	W	L	PCT
Chicago	10	2	.833
Purdue	8	2	.800
Illinois	8	4	.667
Indiana	6	4	.600
Wisconsin	7	5	.583
Iowa	6	6	.500
Ohio State	3	9	.250
Minnesota	3	9	.250
Michigan	3	9	.250
Northwestern	2	6	.250

1920-21

OVERALL RECORD: 15-6

CONFERENCE RECORD: 6-5 (SIXTH PLACE)

INDIVIDUAL HONORS:

EVERETT DEAN—ALL-AMERICA, ALL-BIG TEN

(FIRST TEAM), BIG TEN MEDAL OF HONOR

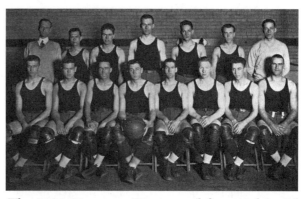

The 1920-21 team. First row (left to right): Ed DeHority, Edward Von Tress, Herm Schuler, Everett Dean, William Dobbins, Frank Cox, Relle Aldridge, Kermit Maynard; Second row: trainer Colpitts [first name unknown], Robert Marxson, Eugene Thomas, Lawrence Busby, Russell Hauss, Glen Johnson, coach George Levis. IU Archives

Following the most successful basketball season in IU history in 1919-20, the Hoosiers graduated four starters. Even though the one returning player was Everett Dean, who had led the Hoosiers in scoring for two straight seasons, the Hoosier faithful braced themselves for a tough season, because they knew that a group of inexperienced players would now be surrounding Dean. They were quite surprised when this team won its first six preconference games and then zoomed to the top of the Big Ten in January.

To complement Dean, this squad had several talented players who would step up and contribute, despite a lack of experience. Plus the athletic department pulled off a coup by discovering and hiring George Levis to coach the Hoosiers. Levis had been a two-time all-conference forward for Wisconsin and then took a coaching job at tiny Carleton College in Minnesota, where he coached two undefeated championship teams. Levis was known for his fast-paced offensive attack, and he fully implemented it upon arriving in Bloomington.

IU opened the season by steamrolling the Chicago-based Armour Institute 46-16 on December 4, in Bloomington. The Indiana Dental School was the next victim to come to Bloomington, and its squad was dominated 37-13. In both games, Dean did his usual damage scoring from the pivot, but he was also aided on the offensive end by forwards Robert Maxson and Ed DeHority. Meanwhile, the Hoosiers' defense was bolstered by the play of guards William Dobbins, Eugene Thomas, and Kermit Maynard. IU continued its dominating play during the month of December by defeating the Evansville YMCA, Manchester College, Indiana State and Kokomo American Legion. All four opponents were defeated by at least 16 points.

Indiana's preconference winning streak came to an end on January 3, when the Hoosiers suffered a 34-21 setback at the hands of Merchants Heat and Light from Indianapolis. Johnson, a forward for the Merchants squad, got hot and buried a series of long field goals in the first half that put the Hoosiers in a deficit from which they never recovered.

Big Ten play opened for IU on Saturday, January 8, in Columbus, Ohio. The Hoosiers used a 9-4 run in the game's final five minutes to capture a 29-24 victory. Two days later, Indiana went up to Michigan and soundly defeated the Wolverines 30-21. Marxson was the game's leading scorer with 12. After those two unexpected road wins, the IU campus was in a frenzy of anticipation for the Hoosiers' first Big Ten home game against Northwestern on Monday, January 17, and IU didn't disappoint the home crowd. Leading only 10-6 at the break and 17-9 with six minutes remaining, the Hoosiers broke loose and closed the contest with a 14-1 run that clinched a 31-10 win and sent an elated crowd of supporters into several boisterous rounds of cheers.

The conference winning streak continued on Friday, January 21, when IU went to Minneapolis and snared a 25-23 win from the Minnesota Golden Gophers. Marxson buried several clutch shots down the stretch to lift the Hoosiers to another unlikely win. While they were in Minnesota, they also played Levis's old team, Carleton College, on January 23, and barely escaped with a 24-23 win. The Minnesota trip was successful from a won-loss standpoint, but during the trip, Dean twisted his knee and DeHority contracted a bad virus. It was the beginning of health problems that would haunt the Hoosiers during the home stretch of the season.

Sitting atop the conference standings at 4-0, IU next traveled to West Lafayette for a Big Ten matchup with Purdue. Forward Bobby Marxson, who had the hot hand in the first four Big Ten games and was a big factor in the Hoosiers' success, had suffered an arm injury in practice and could barely shoot the ball. Coach Levis decided to let him play against Purdue, but he was severely limited, and without his scoring and playmaking (on top of the limitations to Dean

IU's first All-American came in the form of 6'0" center Everett Dean, an excellent athlete who possessed speed, agility, and a great mind for the game. The Salem, Indiana native led the Hoosiers in scoring during each of his three seasons on the varsity.
IU Archives

1920-21 TEAM ROSTER

Head coach: George Levis

Player	Hometown	Class	Position
Relle Aldridge	Lyons, IN	So	F
Joy Buckner	Bluffton, IN	Jr	G
Lawrence Busby	Lapel, IN	Jr	C
Frank Cox	Indianapolis, IN	So	F
Everett Dean (Capt.)	Salem, IN	Sr	C
Ed DeHority	Elwood, IN		F
William Dobbins	Bloomington, IN	Sr	G
Harry Donovan	South Bend, IN	Sr	C
Russell Hauss	Sellersburg, IN	Jr	G
Glen Johnson	Huntington, IN	Jr	F
Robert Marxson	Bloomington, IN	So	F
Kermit Maynard	Columbus, IN	Jr	G
Herm Schuler	Elkhart, IN	Sr	F
Eugene Thomas	Fortville, IN	So	G
Edward Von Tress	Vincennes, IN	Sr	G

SEASON RESULTS 1920-21

Date	Court	Opponent	Result	Score
12/4/1920	H	Armour Institute	W	46-16
12/10/1920	H	Indiana Dental College	W	37-13
12/15/1920	H	Evansville YMCA	W	44-15
12/18/1920	H	Manchester	W	44-12
12/22/1920	H	Indiana State	W	44-11
12/29/1920	A	Kokomo American Legion	W	34-18
1/3/1921	H	Merchants Heat and Light	L	21-34
1/8/1921	A	Ohio State	W	29-24
1/10/1921	A	Michigan	W	30-21
1/17/1921	H	Northwestern	W	31-10
1/21/1921	A	Minnesota	W	25-23
1/23/1921	A	Carleton College	W	24-23
1/28/1921	A	Purdue	L	18-27
2/4/1921	H	Louisville	W	34-17
2/9/1921	H	DePauw	W	24-18
2/14/1921	H	Ohio State	W	33-11
2/19/1921	A	Northwestern	W	23-21
2/21/1921	A	Iowa	L	15-22
2/26/1921	H	Iowa	L	17-26
3/3/1921	H	Purdue	L	20-28
3/7/1921	H	Minnesota	L	25-29

1920-21 BIG TEN STANDINGS

	W	L	PCT
Michigan	8	4	.667
Wisconsin	8	4	.667
Purdue	8	4	.667
Minnesota	7	5	.583
Illinois	7	5	.583
Indiana	6	5	.545
Iowa	6	5	.545
Chicago	6	6	.500
Ohio State	2	10	.167
Northwestern	1	11	.083

and DeHority) the Hoosiers fell to the Boilermakers 27-18 on Friday, January 28.

The Hoosiers moved on after the Purdue loss by racking up two more nonconference wins in Bloomington over Louisville, 34-17 on February 4, and DePauw, 24-18 on February 9. Ohio State was the next conference opponent, and they came to Bloomington on Monday, February 14, and were soundly beaten by the Hoosiers 33-11. Dean led all scorers with a career-high 21 points (nearly doubling OSU's score by himself). On Saturday, February 19, DeHority starred for the Hoosiers as they went to Evanston, Illinois, and snared a conference win away from the Northwestern Wildcats in the final minutes. As time ticked away, DeHority, who scored 10 points in the contest, drained a long field goal to lift IU to a 23-21 win.

The Northwestern win put the Hoosiers at 15-2 overall and 6-1 in Big Ten play (tied for first), and their success had the Bloomington campus buzzing with excitement. The Hoosiers had never led the Big Ten this late in the season. Unfortunately, injuries caught up to IU, and the team would not win another game. The first loss was at Iowa on February 21; the Hoosiers fell 22-15. DeHority was the only IU player to make a field goal (he made four and finished with eight points). Dean went ice cold, missing on repeated attempts, but managed seven points on free throws. Next, IU returned to Bloomington for a three-game homestand to complete the season, with hopes for a conference championship still hanging in the balance. However, the Hoosiers suffered three straight losses to Iowa, 26-17, Purdue, 28-20, and Minnesota, 29-25. In the Minnesota loss, Dean scored 17 points in final collegiate game.

Despite a tough finish, this IU squad, which set the school record for victories with 15 and tied the record for conference wins with six, had heightened interest in the IU basketball team to record levels. Tickets that cost 50 cents at the beginning of the season, cost 75 by the end. There was now real optimism that IU could contend for a conference championship in the sport.

1921-22

OVERALL RECORD: 10-10

CONFERENCE RECORD: 3-7 (NINTH PLACE)

The 1921-22 team. First row (left to right): trainer Colpitts [first name unknown], Sam Houston, Eugene Thomas, Russell Hauss, coach George Levis; Second row: Gilbert [first name unknown], Stanley Crowe, Wyatt May, Lawrence Michener, Wilfred Bahr, Relle Aldridge. Third row: Elder Eberhardt, George Coffey, Lawrence Busby, Wayne Swango, Harold Sanford. IU Archives

After two exciting and successful seasons, the Hoosiers slipped a bit in the 1921-22 campaign. The graduation of all-conference center Everett Dean and reliable forward Ed DeHority were tough blows. The top returning scorer, Bobby Marxson, was a quick, sharp-shooting forward, but he was out of shape because of a long recovery from an injury the previous season. He was never able to round into condition to play for the 1921-22 squad, and that was another hefty blow. The graduation of starting guard and defensive stopper William Dobbins and top reserve Herm Schuler also hurt the Hoosiers.

Thus, the loss of Dean, DeHority, Marxson, Dobbins and Schuler meant that coach George Levis lost four starters and his sixth man. Only junior guard Eugene Thomas, who was elected team captain, remained from the core group of players that had led the Big Ten race for most of the previous season. IU's varsity roster was dominated by 10 sophomores, and their inexperience would show throughout the season.

1921-22 TEAM ROSTER

Head coach: George Levis

Player	Hometown	Class	Position
Relle Aldridge	Lyons, IN	Jr	F
Wilfred Bahr	Evansville, IN	So	F
Lawrence Busby	Lapel, IN	Sr	C
Joy Buckner	Bluffton, IN	Sr	G
George Coffey	Lebanon, IN	So	C
W. Stanley Crowe	Bedford, IN	So	G
Elder Eberhardt	Evansville, IN	So	G
Russell Hauss	Sellersburg, IN	Jr	G
Samuel Houston	Salem, IN	So	F
Wyatt May	Bloomington, IN	So	G
Harold Sanford	Lebanon, IN	So	F
Joseph Sloate	Akron, OH	So	F
Wayne Swango	Oolitic, IN	So	F
Eugene Thomas (Capt.)	Fortville, IN	Jr	G

SEASON RESULTS 1921-22

Date	Court	Opponent	Result	Score
12/2/1921	H	Manchester College	W	25-15
12/7/1921	H	Hanover College	W	18-11
12/10/1921	H	Indiana Dental College	L	24-31
12/15/1921	A	Habichs	L	29-33
12/17/1921	H	Rose Poly	W	31-19
12/19/1921	A	DePauw	L	23-41
1/6/1922	H	Huntington College	W	25-14
1/7/1922	H	Camp Benning	W	46-20
1/14/1922	H	Northwestern	W	21-18
1/20/1922	A	Ohio State	L	17-23
1/23/1922	H	Minnesota	L	16-19
1/26/1922	H	DePauw	W	36-32
2/2/1922	A	Marquette	W	20-17
2/4/1922	A	Minnesota	W	23-19
2/11/1922	H	Purdue	L	19-24
2/13/1922	H	Michigan	W	15-14
2/18/1922	A	Northwestern	L	16-25
2/20/1922	A	Michigan	L	16-24
2/25/1922	A	Purdue	L	9-20
2/27/1922	H	Ohio State	L	18-20

1921-22 BIG TEN STANDINGS

	W	L	PCT
Purdue	8	1	.889
Michigan	8	4	.667
Wisconsin	8	4	.667
Illinois	7	5	.583
Iowa	5	6	.455
Ohio State	5	7	.417
Chicago	5	7	.417
Minnesota	4	7	.364
Indiana	3	7	.300
Northwestern	3	9	.250

IU played six games in December, and with so many new faces, the team predictably got off to a slow start. The Hoosiers struggled to beat overmatched opponents Manchester College (25-15 on December 2) and Hanover College (18-11 on December 7). Both games were played in Bloomington, and IU led Manchester by only one point at the half and was only ahead of Hanover by two points at the break. Then IU lost two straight games. The first loss came at the hands of lightweight Indiana Dental College 31-24 on December 10, in Bloomington. Next, IU fell to Habichs (an independent team from Indianapolis) by the score of 33-29 on December 15. The Hoosiers had led 16-12 at the break, but couldn't hold off the Habichs squad in the second half. Two nights later in Bloomington, IU got back on track with a 31-19 win over Rose Poly. One positive from the first five games was that sophomore forward Harold Sanford emerged as a reliable free throw shooter and scorer, averaging 9.8 points per game in these first five contests.

Indiana suffered a setback on December 19, when the team got trounced 41-23 by DePauw in Greencastle. After the winter break, IU breezed to an easy victory over Huntington College, 25-14 on Friday, January 6, and then hammered Camp Benning, 46-20 on Saturday, January 7. Against Camp Benning, all three of IU's frontcourt players scored in double figures. Sanford led all scorers with 15, center Lawrence Busby added 13, and forward Wilfred Bahr chipped in 12.

On Saturday, January 14, in Bloomington, the Hoosiers opened Big Ten play by defeating Northwestern 21-18, powered by a big second-half run. IU got 11 points from Sanford and eight from Bahr. Indiana put up a stiff fight on Friday, January 20, in Columbus, Ohio, but fell 23-17 to the Ohio State Buckeyes. Back in Bloomington on January 23, the Hoosiers jumped out to a 10-7 lead on the Minnesota Golden Gophers before faltering in the second half and losing 19-16.

Next, the Hoosiers repaid DePauw with a 36-32 win over the Tigers in Bloomington on Thursday, January 26. Sanford scored 10 and so did Eugene Thomas, while Bahr led all scorers with 12. On February 2, IU went up to Wisconsin and defeated Marquette 20-17 in front of a spirited crowd of 3,000 spectators. The Hoosiers continued their northern trek on February 4, by going up to Minneapolis, where they surprised Minnesota (the undefeated Big Ten leader at the time) with a 23-19 victory in a game that IU led from start to finish. Sophomore center George Coffey led the IU scoring attack with 10 points.

The new league leader, Purdue, came to the IU campus on Saturday, February 11, and steamrolled the Hoosiers in the first half, jumping out to an 18-5 lead. IU clawed back into the game in the second half, but lost 24-19. Another one of the conference contenders, Michigan, came to Bloomington two days later. This time Indiana pulled off the upset when guard Stanley Crowe buried a long field goal in the final minutes to give IU a one-point lead. Then Michigan missed a chance to tie the game with a free throw, giving Indiana a 15-14 victory.

The Hoosiers ran out of luck the following week at Northwestern, who would eventually finish last in the conference. The Wildcats secured one of only three conference victories by beating IU 25-16 on Saturday, February 18. Then, IU journeyed to Ann Arbor for a rematch with Michigan on February 20. The Wolverines exacted their revenge with a convincing 24-16 win.

Frustrated after the two losses, Coach Levis called for a series of private practices for the team and threatened to shake up the lineup before the team's showdown with Purdue the following Saturday. "I'm going to whip a good team together by Saturday or know the reason why. I'm tired of high school basketball from a [Big Ten] team," Levis told the *Indiana Daily Student*.

Unfortunately, Levis's tactic didn't work as Purdue rolled through the Hoosiers 20-9 on February 25. On Monday, February 27, Ohio State came to town for the season finale and stole away a closely fought 20-18 win.

Just as they had done the season before, the Hoosiers closed the 1921-22 campaign with four straight defeats. In this case, it turned a fairly successful season into a marginal one as the Hoosiers finished the year at 10-10 overall and 3-7 in the Big Ten, which landed them in ninth place in the conference. The lack of veterans showed in close games as the Hoosiers posted a record of 2-5 in games decided by five points or less.

1922-23

OVERALL RECORD: 8-7

CONFERENCE RECORD: 5-7 (SEVENTH PLACE)

INDIVIDUAL HONORS:

MIKE NYIKOS—ALL-BIG TEN (FIRST TEAM)

The IU basketball team got one of its earliest starts ever in the 1922-23 season when Coach George Levis had the six returning members of the squad and 10 members of the previous freshman team report for the first practice of the year on October 11. Throughout the fall semester, Levis and team captain Wilfred Bahr ran regular practices to get the team into shape and work on fundamentals. However, Levis decided to take a job as a manager for the Shower Brothers Furniture Company in Bloomington, and he tendered his resignation as basketball coach before the season actually started.

As a result, the IU athletic department had to scramble to find a coach. The man they chose was Leslie Mann. Les had previously coached at Rice University, but coaching was an off-season activity for Mann, who played professional baseball during the summer. The 30-year-old outfielder had played for the St. Louis Cardinals in 1923, but he had also been a member of the Chicago Cubs' 1918 World Series team.

As a coach, Mann was a strict disciplinarian who subjected the Hoosiers to strenuous training rules including no smoking, no eating candy, no eating between meals, no drinking coffee, alcohol or soft drinks, and a requirement that players go to bed at 10:30 p.m. in order to get their rest. Mann had these regulations printed up and distributed around campus so that students would not tempt the players and would report any observed violations. The document said, "The player that cheats, sneaks around and breaks training, is a traitor, is a man without honor or respect."

After having a minimal amount of practice to whip his team into shape, Mann sent the Hoosiers into their first game of the year against the Indiana Dental College on Thursday, December 7, in

The 1922-23 team. First row (left to right): Relle Aldridge, Harold Sanford, Wilfred Bahr, George Coffey, Adolph Seidensticker; Second row: Stephen Harvey, Michael Nyikos, Weiss [first name unknown], Ken Alward, Harry Yoars, Moomaw [first name unknown], Harry Champ, Lawrence Crane, Paul Parker, manager Isaacs [first name unknown]; Third row: coach George Levis [replaced by Leslie Mann], Richard Woodward, Kilty [first name unknown], Shelton [first name unknown], Kight [first name unknown], Hayworth [first name unknown], Elder Eberhardt, Joseph Sloate, Jones [first name unknown], Hardin [first name unknown]. IU Archives

Bloomington, and IU easily secured a 28-12 win, led by a game-high 15 points from Bahr, who played center that night. On Friday, December 15, IU doubled-up Franklin College 36-18 in Bloomington. Once again, Bahr had game-high honors with 14 points. Forward Harold Sanford, the team's top returning scorer, added 10.

That was it for the preconference season, and IU prepared to begin Big Ten play after winter break. The newly agreed upon Big Ten scheduling stipulated that each team would play 12 conference games and could only add a maximum of three games against nonconference teams to its schedule. IU would play its third nonconference game against Notre Dame in February.

Wisconsin came down to Indiana on Monday, January 8, and the Badgers showed off their early season form by defeating the Hoosiers 17-10. On Saturday, January 13, IU trekked over to Champaign, Illinois, and dropped another conference game when Illinois rebuffed the Hoosiers 31-22. It was a rough

game, but Indiana had its chances to win if its players could have converted more point-blank field goal attempts.

A hopeful note was sounded at the end of January when sophomore forward Mike Nyikos and 6'7" sophomore center Paul Parker both became eligible with the start of the second semester. Their return to the lineup gave IU a formidable frontcourt of Bahr, Nyikos, and Parker, which immediately powered the Hoosiers to four straight victories. The first came in West Lafayette on January 31, when IU recovered from a one-point halftime deficit to nab a 31-26 win from the Purdue Boilermakers. Parker and guard Eugene Thomas led IU with 10 points each, and Nyikos added seven. On February 7, the Hoosiers downed another cross-state opponent when Notre Dame came to Bloomington and was defeated 33-18, as Nyikos scored 16 to lead the Hoosiers.

Another conference victory was sealed on February 12, when Indiana used a swift passing attack and clutch shooting in the second half to upend

1922-23 TEAM ROSTER

Head coach: Leslie Mann

Player	Hometown	Class	Position
Relle Aldridge	Lyons, IN	Sr	F
Ken Alward	South Bend, IN	So	G
Wilfred Bahr (Capt.)	Evansville, IN	Jr	F
Harry Champ	Rochester, IN	Jr	F
George Coffey	Bloomington, IN	So	F
Lawrence Crane	Indianapolis, IN		F
William Crowe	Bedford, IN	Jr	G
Elder Eberhardt	Evansville, IN	Jr	G
Stephen Harvey	Zionsville, IN	So	C
Earl Knoy	Martinsville, IN	So	G
Michael Nyikos	South Bend, IN	So	F
Paul Parker	Kokomo, IN	So	C
Harold Sanford	Lebanon, IN	Jr	F
Eugene Thomas	Fortville, IN	Sr	G
Richard Woodward	Lapel, IN	Jr	F
Harry Yoars	Amboy, IN		G

SEASON RESULTS 1922-23

Date	Court	Opponent	Result	Score
12/7/1922	H	Indiana Dental College	W	28-12
12/15/1922	H	Franklin College	W	36-18
1/8/1923	H	Wisconsin	L	10-17
1/13/1923	A	Illinois	L	22-31
1/31/1923	A	Purdue	W	31-26
2/7/1923	H	Notre Dame	W	33-18
2/12/1923	H	Illinois	W	31-12
2/17/1923	H	Minnesota	W	33-20
2/20/1923	A	Northwestern	L	26-30
2/22/1923	A	Iowa	L	13-19
3/3/1923	H	Northwestern	W	31-25
3/5/1923	H	Iowa	W	23-21
3/10/1923	A	Minnesota	L	25-29
3/12/1923	A	Wisconsin	L	17-35
3/15/1923	H	Purdue	L	29-31

1922-23 BIG TEN STANDINGS

	W	L	PCT
Iowa	11	1	.917
Wisconsin	11	1	.917
Michigan	8	4	.667
Illinois	7	5	.583
Purdue	7	5	.583
Chicago	6	6	.500
Indiana	5	7	.417
Northwestern	3	9	.250
Ohio State	1	11	.083
Minnesota	1	11	.083

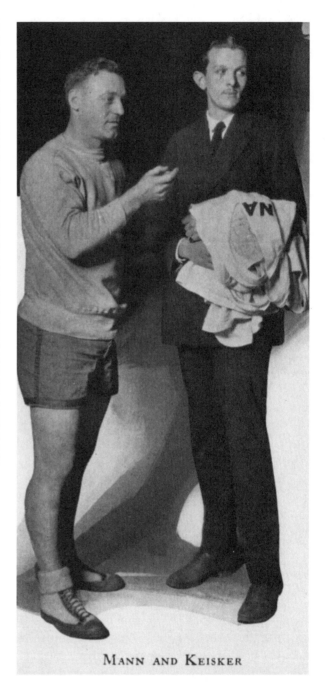

MANN AND KEISKER

Coach Leslie Mann instructs manager Earl Keisker during a team practice. Mann, a strict disciplinarian with high standards, was Indiana's last-minute replacement for George Levis before the 1922-23 season. During the summers Mann played major league baseball, including the 1914 World Series with the Boston Braves and the 1918 World Series with the Chicago Cubs. IU Archives

Illinois 31-24 in the Men's Gymnasium. The Hoosiers were even more relentless with their next guest, the Minnesota Golden Gophers, who fell behind 20-5 at the end of the first half and eventually lost to the Hoosiers by the score of 33-20 on Saturday, February 17.

After improving their conference record to 3-2, IU went on the road and dropped two straight. Northwestern defeated Indiana 30-26 on February 20, despite 17 points from Nyikos. Iowa, which was undefeated in the Big Ten, downed the Hoosiers 19-13 on February 22. A week later, those same two teams journeyed to Bloomington for a pair of rematches. The Hoosiers repaid Northwestern in front of a small home crowd on Saturday, March 3, with a 31-25 victory, on the strength of 19 points from Nyikos. Iowa, now 11-0 in the conference play and 12-1 overall, came to town on March 5. A howling crowd of 3,500 Hoosier fans met the Hawkeyes, and an emboldened IU team upset the league leaders 23-21 and eventually cost them the outright Big Ten title. Nyikos monopolized the scoring with 21 points for IU.

IU had a bit of a letdown after the team's huge upset over Iowa. The Hoosiers lost both games in their northern swing to Minnesota, 29-25 on March 10, and Wisconsin, 35-17 on March 12. That left the Hoosiers with only a Bloomington matchup with Purdue on March 15, to finish out the season. As usual, the game featured a large crowd in the stands and intense, physical play on the court. IU led at the half and had a one-point lead in the final minute, but Purdue used one final spurt to pull out a 31-29 victory.

Losing streaks to end the season were becoming a common refrain. IU's three straight losses to close the schedule in 1922-23 dropped the squad to 8-7 overall and 5-7 in the Big Ten (after improving to 8-4 and 5-4 after the Iowa win). Nevertheless, the IU team competed well and showed that it had a talented squad that could beat the league's top contenders. Opponents had begun to dread the trip to Bloomington.

1923-24

OVERALL RECORD: 11-6

CONFERENCE RECORD: 7-5 (FOURTH PLACE)

The 1923-24 team. First row (left to right): Paul Parker, Max Lorber, Ken Alward, Harlan Logan, Palmer Sponsler, Lindley Ricketts; Second row: Daniel Bernoski, John Rosenberry, Robert Sinks, Carl Bordner, John Cox, Elton Harrison, Emery Druckamiller; Third row: coach Leslie Mann, manager Earl Keisker, athletic director Zora Clevenger. IU Archives

In his second season at the helm of the Hoosiers' basketball program, coach Les Mann began practice on Tuesday, October 23, with a core group of four returning lettermen: captain Ken Alward, high-scoring forward Mike Nyikos, big center Paul Parker, and guard Earl Knoy (who wouldn't join the team full time until after football season), as well as a number of other experienced returning players. At the first team meeting, Mann emphasized the importance of his training rules, which would immediately go into effect for all players. "The basketball season is the longest of any sport and requires the most energy," said Mann (as reported in the *Indiana Daily Student*). "To give the proper stuff in a game, a man must have gone through a comprehensive season of training."

The Hoosiers' successes on the court in recent seasons and the growing popularity of basketball in the state of Indiana swelled the number of players who tried out for the team to 50, and over 20 players made the final cut. The squad was divided between the varsity and a second team they called the "hustlers." Throughout the season, a number of players would move between the varsity and the hustlers, depending on the needs of the varsity and how well players were performing.

After seven weeks of practice, the Hoosiers opened their season on Friday, December 7, against Indiana State in the Men's Gymnasium. IU showed spurts of excellent play, but also looked rusty and out of sync at times, but still prevailed 27-24. On Saturday, December 15, the Hoosiers played much better when Rose Poly came to town. IU hammered the visitors 51-15 as Nyikos scored 18, and junior forward Harlan Logan exploded for a game-high 23. IU kept its high-scoring attack in gear on December 20, with a 53-30 win over Drake in Des Moines, Iowa. Logan and Nyikos were a potent one-two punch again as the latter scored 19 points and the former netted 18. The Hoosiers stumbled for the first time the following night when the Creighton Bluejays beat them 39-29 in Omaha, Nebraska, in front of one of the largest crowds in Creighton history at that time.

Back in Bloomington, 3,500 fans greeted the Hoosiers as they opened Big Ten play on Saturday, January 5, against Wisconsin. IU fell behind 10-6 at the intermission and 16-6 several minutes into the second half, before rattling off a 13-3 run and tying the game at 19. However, the Badgers came back and rallied for a 23-21 triumph. A week later, IU evened its conference record when Minnesota came to town. IU used a balanced scoring attack to upend the Gophers 29-23. Then, on January 14, IU lost another one-point game to Wisconsin when the Hoosiers traveled to Madison. IU led by six points with six minutes remaining before the Badgers rallied, but the Hoosiers still held a one-point lead in the final minute before Wisconsin buried a field goal and stole away a 28-27 win. IU followed up the Wisconsin loss with a 29-24 defeat at Chicago on Saturday, January 19.

Sitting at 1-3 in conference play, Indiana began turning the ship around on Monday, January 21, at Northwestern, beating the Wildcats 39-24 as Nyikos scored 16 and Logan dropped in 13. The Hoosiers grabbed another victory on Friday, January 25, when Parker scored just before time expired to give IU a 31-29 victory. Minnesota was the next victim when

1923-24 TEAM ROSTER

Head coach: Leslie Mann

No.	Player	Hometown	Class	Position	Height
1	Ken Alward (Capt.)	South Bend, IN	Jr	G	5-8
	Daniel Bernoski	Michigan City, IN	So		5-10
6	Karl Bordner	Brookston, IN	So	C	6-0
	Harry Champ	Rochester, IN	Sr	F	5-10
12	George Coffey	Bloomington, IN	Sr	F	6-1
	John Cox	Richmond, IN	So	G	5-11
	Emery Druckamiller	Syracuse, IN	So	F	5-8
8	Elton Harrison	Lebanon, IN	So	F	5-10
10	Earl Knoy	Martinsville, IN	Jr	G	5-10
2	Harlan Logan	Bloomington, IN	Jr	F	6-2
7	Max Lorber	Columbia City, IN	Jr	G	5-3
5	Michael Nyikos	South Bend, IN	Jr	F	6-0
3	Paul Parker	Kokomo, IN	Jr	C	6-7
	Lindley Ricketts	Lynville, IN		G	5-7
	John Rosenberry	Anderson, IN	So		6-0
11	Harold Sanford	Lebanon, IN	Sr	F	6-0
	Adolph Seidensticke	Indianapolis, IN		G	5-10
9	Robert Sinks	Lafayette, IN		C	6-1
	Palmer Sponsler	Bloomington, IN	So	G	6-0

SEASON RESULTS 1923-24

Date	Court	Opponent	Result	Score
12/7/1923	H	Indiana State	W	27-24
12/15/1923	H	Rose Poly	W	51-15
12/20/1923	A	Drake	W	53-30
12/21/1923	A	Creighton	L	29-39
1/5/1924	H	Wisconsin	L	21-23
1/12/1924	A	Minnesota	W	29-23
1/14/1924	A	Wisconsin	L	27-28
1/19/1924	A	Chicago	L	24-29
1/24/1924	A	Northwestern	W	39-24
1/25/1924	H	Ohio State	W	31-29
2/2/1924	H	Minnesota	W	39-25
2/8/1924	H	Northwestern	W	30-13
2/12/1924	H	Notre Dame	W	21-20
2/16/1924	A	Ohio State	L	27-31
2/18/1924	A	Michigan	W	23-22
2/23/1924	H	Chicago	L	25-26
3/3/1924	H	Michigan	W	31-20

1923-24 BIG TEN STANDINGS

	W	L	PCT
Wisconsin	8	4	.667
Illinois	8	4	.667
Chicago	8	4	.667
Ohio State	7	5	.583
Purdue	7	5	.583
Indiana	7	5	.583
Michigan	6	6	.500
Minnesota	5	7	.417
Iowa	4	8	.333
Northwestern	0	12	.000

the Gophers came to Bloomington on February 2, and fell 38-25. IU sophomore Palmer Sponsler led all scorers with 14 points. Nyikos added 11 points in what turned out to be his final game as a Hoosier because his first semester grades came back sub-par, and he was declared ineligible (he transferred to Notre Dame but never became eligible there).

Even without Nyikos, the Hoosiers kept their winning streak alive on February 8 by whipping Northwestern 30-13 in front of a crowd of 4,000 in Bloomington. Logan topped all scorers with 16 in the easy win. IU extended its winning streak to five games by topping Notre Dame 21-20 on February 12, in the Men's Gymnasium. The win gave IU a 9-4 overall record and a 5-3 conference mark. Parity reigned in the Big Ten as virtually every team except Northwestern still had a chance at the conference title with only a few weeks left in the season. With four conference games remaining, IU would have to win three out of four of them in order to have a chance at the crown.

The Hoosiers' chances for a title took a hit on February 16, at Ohio State, where the Buckeyes came back from a four-point deficit in the final five minutes and secured a 31-27 win. Two nights later in Ann Arbor, Michigan, the Hoosiers' luck turned around as they stole a 23-22 victory from the Michigan Wolverines. In the final minutes, IU's 5'3" sophomore guard Max Lorber stole the ball at midcourt and then scored the winning basket.

The Hoosiers returned to Bloomington to play their final two games on their home court. In order to have a chance at the conference title, IU had to defeat Chicago on February 23. What was probably the largest crowd in IU basketball history up until that point—approaching nearly 5,000 spectators—somehow squeezed into the Men's Gymnasium. Both teams played a terrific game, but IU fell behind in the second half until the final minutes when the Hoosiers made a furious rally and grabbed the lead with under a minute to play. However, Chicago buried a shot at the very end to break the Hoosiers' hearts and claim a 26-25 triumph. IU gained a small consolation prize on March 3, by defeating Michigan 31-20 in Bloomington, led by 14 points from Logan.

The Michigan win put IU at 7-5 in conference play and tied for fourth place, only one game out of first. IU's seven Big Ten wins set a school record, and

once again, the Hoosiers had finished within striking distance of their first conference title. They would only have to wait a couple more seasons before their first breakthrough.

SEASON STATISTICS
1916-17 TO 1923-24

1916-17

Team Statistics	G	TP	AVG
Indiana	19	482	25.4
Opponents	19	311	16.4
Player Statistics	**G**	**TP**	**AVG**
Williams	17	136	8.0
Buschmann	16	96	6.0
Rogers	2	12	6.0
Zellar	5	28	5.6
Nash	16	80	5.0
Schuler	11	52	4.7
Nafe	5	12	2.4
Bowser	13	28	2.2
Byrum	11	22	2.0
Reed	9	19	1.1
Mullett	16	6	0.4
Miller	2	0	0.0
Harlos	1	0	0.0

1917-18

Team Statistics	G	TP	AVG
Indiana	14	385	27.5
Opponents	14	251	17.9
Player Statistics	**G**	**TP**	**AVG**
Zellar	14	134	9.6
Phillips	14	73	5.2
Von Tress	13	50	3.8
Bowser	12	38	3.2
Easton	12	38	3.2
Risley	1	2	2.0
Stahr	12	22	1.8
Jeffries	14	24	1.7
Ingles	11	4	0.4
McFarland	4	0	0.0
Huxford	3	0	0.0
Richey	2	0	0.0
English	1	0	0.0

1918-19

Team Statistics	G	TP	AVG
Indiana	17	417	24.5
Opponents	17	360	21.2
Player Statistics	**G**	**TP**	**AVG**
Dean	17	158	9.3
Phillips	17	73	4.3
Jeffries	16	64	4.0
Zellar	15	50	3.3
Busby	3	8	2.7
Wakefield	5	10	2.0
Lohrei	4	6	1.5
Smith	11	16	1.5
Buckner	5	6	1.2
Byrum	11	20	1.2
Dobbins	6	2	0.3
Easton	1	10	10.0

1920-21

Team Statistics	G	TP	AVG
Indiana	21	618	29.4
Opponents	21	419	19.9
Player Statistics	**G**	**TP**	**AVG**
Dean	21	234	11.1
Dehority	21	137	6.5
Marxson	21	118	5.6
Schuler	16	43	2.7
Thomas	18	48	2.7
Maynard	8	8	1.0
Buckner	7	6	0.9
Donovan	7	6	0.9
Dobbins	21	16	0.8
Johnson	7	0	0.0
Von Tress	4	0	0.0
Cox	1	0	0.0

1919-20

Team Statistics	G	TP	AVG
Indiana	21	521	24.8
Opponents	21	420	20.0
Player Statistics	**G**	**TP**	**AVG**
Dean	21	201	9.6
Phillips	18	64	3.6
Rhea	3	10	3.3
Schuler	17	55	3.2
Williams	18	44	2.4
Jeffries	19	44	2.3
Donovan	13	30	2.3
Byrum	20	42	2.1
Esarey	4	8	2.0
Rucklehaus	1	2	2.0
Wakefield	8	10	1.3
Kyle	4	5	1.3
Dobbins	14	6	0.4
Zellar	2	0	0.0

1921-22

Team Statistics	G	TP	AVG
Indiana	20	447	22.4
Opponents	20	439	21.9
Player Statistics	**G**	**TP**	**AVG**
Sanford	20	153	7.7
Busby	9	52	5.8
Coffey	17	73	4.3
Bahr	12	56	4.7
Houston	4	10	2.5
Aldridge	12	24	2.0
Thomas	20	30	1.5
Crowe	17	24	1.4
Swango	3	4	1.3
May	2	2	1.0
Buckner	7	5	0.7
Sloate	7	4	0.6
Hauss	16	8	0.5
Eberhardt	3	0	0.0
Gilbert	1	0	0.0

1922-23

Team Statistics	G	TP	AVG
Indiana	15	388	25.9
Opponents	15	356	23.7
Player Statistics	**G**	**TP**	**AVG**
Nyikos	11	141	12.8
Bahr	15	79	5.3
Parker	10	44	4.4
Coffey	8	26	3.3
Sanford	4	12	3.0
Knoy	14	33	2.4
Thomas	14	30	2.1
Aldridge	3	4	1.3
Champ	2	2	1.0
Harvey	4	3	0.8
Alward	15	10	0.7
Woodward	4	2	0.5
Crowe	6	2	0.3
Yoars	2	0	0.0
Crane	1	0	0.0
Eberhardt	1	0	0.0

1923-24

Team Statistics	G	TP	AVG
Indiana	17	527	31.0
Opponents	17	421	24.8
Player Statistics	**G**	**TP**	**AVG**
Nyikos	11	120	10.9
Logan	17	167	9.8
Sponsler	16	83	5.2
Lorber	15	67	4.5
Bordner	4	11	2.8
Parker	17	45	2.7
Sinks	6	14	2.3
Knoy	9	7	0.8
Alward	15	10	0.7
Coffey	4	2	0.5
Sanford	2	1	0.5
Harrison	4	0	0.0
Champ	2	0	0.0
Ricketts	1	0	0.0
Seidensticke	1	0	0.0
Druckmiller	1	0	0.0

1924-25

OVERALL RECORD: 12-5

CONFERENCE RECORD: 8-4 (SECOND PLACE)

INDIVIDUAL HONORS:

HARLAN LOGAN—ALL-BIG TEN (FIRST TEAM), BIG TEN MEDAL OF HONOR

The 1924-25 team. First row (right to left): Art Beckner, Harlan Logan, Frank Sibley, Paul Parker, Jack Winston, Palmer Sponsler, Julius Krueger, Ken Alward; Second row: athletic director Zora Clevenger, coach Everett Dean, Millard Easton, Elton Harrison, Emery Druckamiller, Lindley Ricketts, H. N. Replogle, trainer Jesse Ferguson. IU Archives

IU fans were getting used to having competitive basketball teams. The Hoosiers hadn't had a losing season in nine years. However, over those nine seasons, five different basketball coaches had graced the sidelines for Indiana. When athletic director Zora Clevenger took the reins of the athletic department in 1923, he sought to create some stability for IU's sports teams by hiring coaches who would stick around for more than a year or two and would take the time to build a successful program. For the basketball team, Clevenger selected former IU All-American Everett Dean as the man to run the program. Since graduating in 1921, the 26-year-old Dean had led the Carleton College basketball squad to a 48-4 record. It didn't take long for Dean's brand of precision basketball to win over Hoosier fans, who quickly

1924-25 TEAM ROSTER

Head coach: Everett Dean

No.	Player	Hometown	Class	Position	Height
1	Ken Alward	South Bend, IN	Sr	G	5-8
	Art Beckner	Muncie, IN	So	G	6-0
18	Charles Benzel	Bedford, IN	So	G	5-8
6	Karl Bordner	Brookston, IN	Jr	C	6-0
	Emery Druckamiller	Syracuse, IN	So	F	5-8
	Millard Easton	Sanborn, IN	Jr	G	6-0
8	Elton Harrison	Lebanon, IN	Jr	F	5-11
	Julius Krueger	Bloomington, IN	So	F	6-0
2	Harlan Logan	Bloomington, IN	Sr	F	6-2
7	Max Lorber	Columbia City, IN	Sr	G	5-3
	Robert Nicholson	Bloomington, IN	So	F	
3	Paul Parker (Capt.)	Kokomo, IN	Sr	C	6-7
	H. N. Replogle	Muncie, IN	So	F	5-8
	Lindley Ricketts	Lynville, IN		G	5-7
	Frank Sibley	Gary, IN	So	C	6-2
	Palmer Sponsler	Bloomington, IN	Jr	G	6-0
	Jack Winston	Washington, IN	Jr	C	6-6

SEASON RESULTS 1924-25

Date	Court	Opponent	Result	Score
12/11/1924	H	Indiana State	L	24-28
12/15/1924	H	Washington Univ. (MO)	W	35-18
12/18/1924	A	Kentucky	W	20-18
1/3/1925	H	Cincinnati	W	51-7
1/6/1925	H	Mercer University	W	31-19
1/10/1925	A	Ohio State	L	22-30
1/17/1925	A	Illinois	L	24-34
1/24/1925	H	Chicago	W	40-11
1/31/1925	A	Iowa	W	30-28
2/4/1925	H	Purdue	W	39-36
2/9/1925	H	Iowa	W	28-21
2/14/1925	A	Michigan	W	29-28
2/21/1925	A	Chicago	W	33-22
2/23/1925	H	Illinois	W	30-24
2/27/1925	A	Purdue	L	29-38
3/2/1925	H	Michigan	W	51-33
3/7/1925	H	Ohio State	L	26-28

1924-25 BIG TEN STANDINGS

	W	L	PCT
Ohio State	11	1	.917
Indiana	8	4	.667
Illinois	8	4	.667
Purdue	7	4	.636
Michigan	6	5	.545
Minnesota	6	6	.500
Iowa	5	7	.417
Northwestern	4	8	.333
Wisconsin	3	9	.250
Chicago	1	11	.083

realized that their team was now being led by one of the best basketball minds in the country.

When Dean called the first practice on October 15, optimism ran high for the team's prospects, and not only because of its new coach. The squad returned several veteran starters and added an excellent sophomore forward in Julius Krueger. For the first two weeks of practice, Dean drilled the team heavily on fundamentals, and then set about implementing his offensive and defensive schemes. But it took a while for the talented squad to click with Dean's new team concepts. The Hoosiers dropped their opener 28-24 to Indiana State in overtime on Thursday, December 11, in Bloomington, as Dean substituted often to get a look at various players. The Hoosiers were down 21-9 a few minutes into the second half, but they used a 14-2 run to tie the game at 23 at the end of regulation. Krueger led IU with eight points in his first varsity game.

Indiana's attack kicked into gear four days later when Washington University came to Bloomington and fell 35-18 to the methodical Hoosiers; Krueger led all scorers with 12. Next, IU went to Lexington, Kentucky, and defeated the Wildcats 20-18 in a sloppy game on December 18—the first ever meeting between the two teams. The Hoosiers turned in a much better performance on Saturday, January 3, when they blistered the Cincinnati Bearcats 51-7 in Bloomington, led by 15 points from Krueger and 13 from senior forward Harlan Logan. Indiana closed out their preconference schedule on Tuesday, January 6, with a 31-19 win over Mercer College.

IU had the difficult task of opening the Big Ten season against a very talented Ohio State team in Columbus on Saturday, January 10. The Buckeyes were only up by two at the half but pulled away for a 30-22 win. Things didn't get any easier for the Hoosiers on January 17, when they had to travel to take on another one of the Big Ten's top teams, Illinois. Again, the Hoosiers hung on in the game in the first half (they were only down one at the break), but Illinois ran away with the game in the second half and claimed a 34-24 victory.

The Hoosiers' roster changed with the start of the second semester as Max Lorber graduated, and Karl Bordner left school, while two sophomores became eligible to play for the varsity. Art Beckner, a former all-state player from Muncie, and Jack Winston, a

After amassing a 48-4 record in four years of coaching at Carleton College, Everett Dean returned to his alma mater to take over the Hoosier basketball program. The 26-year-old Dean brought an approach to the game that was marked by an almost scientific precision, and his dedication to excellence soon produced championship-level basketball in Bloomington.
IU Archives

6'6" center who played on the Purdue freshmen team during 1922-23 season, became immediate contributors for Indiana. On January 24, Beckner and Winston came off the bench to help IU annihilate Chicago 40-11 in the Men's Gymnasium; Logan led all scorers with 12 points. Indiana got its first road win a week later when the Hoosiers came from behind in the final minutes to defeat Iowa 30-28 in Iowa City.

The most exciting game of season was played on February 4, when the Purdue Boilermakers came to Bloomington to take on the Hoosiers in front of 5,000 raucous fans that squeezed into the Men's Gymnasium. In a game that featured five ties and numerous lead changes, IU pulled out a 39-36 win as Winston held down Purdue's Carl Cramer, who was leading the conference in scoring prior to the game. Meanwhile, IU's Logan dropped in 19 points to surpass Cramer for the top spot in conference scoring.

The Purdue victory was IU's third straight conference win, and the Hoosiers would rattle off four more conference victories before their rematch with Purdue in West Lafayette. On February 9, IU easily dispatched the visiting Iowa Hawkeyes 28-21. On February 14, Indiana stole a 29-28 win away from Michigan in Ann Arbor when guard Palmer Sponsler scored the winning basket in the final minute. Chicago fell to IU for the second time with a 33-22 verdict in the Windy City on February 21. The Hoosiers' seventh straight Big Ten win came against Illinois in Bloomington on Monday, February 23. IU was down 18-8 with 16 minutes left in the game before the Hoosiers went on a 14-2 run to take their first lead at 22-20, and then cruised to a 30-24 victory.

The streak came to an end on Friday, February 27, when IU fell to Purdue 38-29 in West Lafayette. The loss put IU two games behind Ohio State in the conference race, and all but shattered IU's hopes of winning its first Big Ten title. IU took out its frustration on Michigan on March 2, by whipping the Wolverines 51-33 in Bloomington. The Hoosiers then closed their season on Saturday, March 7, by losing a hard-fought contest to first place Ohio State 28-26.

Indiana's 8-4 record in Big Ten play and second-place finish was its best showing ever in the conference. While Logan, IU's leading scorer, and Paul Parker, the team's center and captain, were graduating, the Hoosiers also had a core group of experienced players that would return to challenge for the Big Ten championship again the next season.

1925-26

OVERALL RECORD: 12-5

CONFERENCE RECORD: 8-4 (FIRST PLACE)

TEAM HONORS:

BIG TEN CO-CHAMPIONS

INDIVIDUAL HONORS:

JULIUS KRUEGER—ALL-BIG TEN (FIRST TEAM)

The Hoosier basketball team entered the 1925-26 season in the unfamiliar role of favorite in the Big Ten. While this showed how far the IU basketball program had come since the beginning of the previous decade (when the Hoosiers were perennial bottom dwellers in the conference), it also put them in a position that they weren't accustomed to. IU was no longer going to sneak up on other teams as a talented but underrated squad. Instead, other teams would now be squarely focused on taking out the Hoosiers, who were viewed as the top dog. Veterans Julius Krueger, Palmer Sponser, Art Beckner and Jack Winston were expected to deliver the school's first conference championship, and—although they took an unconventional route—they would eventually accomplish that goal, to the delight of the growing horde of Hoosier fans.

The IU veterans looked like they were in midseason form in Indiana's 47-26 victory over Miami of Ohio on Thursday, December 10. Krueger led all scorers with 14, and Beckner chipped in 10. However, Indiana's well-oiled offensive attack sputtered against the defense of the DePauw Tigers in Greencastle on Tuesday, December 15. The Hoosiers led 12-10 at the half, but got blasted 23-8 in the second half and lost 33-20.

Wabash came to Bloomington on Saturday, December 19, and the Hoosiers got back on track with a convincing 35-27 win over the scrappy Little Giants. Sponsler was the game's top scorer with 11. IU found its starting center on January 5, when Kentucky came to Bloomington and got rebuffed 34-23. Indiana's junior pivotman Frank Sibley stepped up and scored a game-high 13 points against the Wildcats and gave the Hoosiers the consistent inside presence they needed at both ends of the court. Meanwhile, 6'6" Jack Winston, who played center for the Hoosiers much of the previous season, was not much of a scoring threat, so he was now being used to jump center and then play the "back" guard spot as a menacing defensive presence. After recording a 3-1 preconference record, the Hoosiers prepared for a Big Ten schedule in which three of their first four games would be played on the road. They opened by grinding out a 33-28 win over Minnesota in the Men's Gymnasium on the strength of 11 points from Sibley and 10 from Beckner. IU then traveled up to Wisconsin on January 11, and lost a 33-31 heartbreaker to the Badgers despite getting a game-high 14 points from Krueger. IU fell to 1-2 in conference play on Saturday, January 16, when the Iowa Hawkeyes used their stingy defense to upend the Hoosiers 29-

The 1925-26 team. Front row (left to right): Julius Krueger, Frank Sibley, Ed Farmer, Jack Winston, Palmer Sponsler, Art Beckner, Robert Correll; Second row: coach Everett Dean, Hall [first name unknown], Herman Byers, Millard Easton, Harold Derr, trainer Jesse Ferguson; Third row: manager George Talbot, assistant coach Harlan Logan. IU Archives

22. The Hoosier offense kicked back into high gear on January 18, with a 39-31 win at Northwestern. Sibley had the hot hand with 15 points.

On Saturday, January 23, Purdue invaded Bloomington, and the Boilermakers and Hoosiers engaged in an epic battle in front of an overflowing crowd of about 5,000 spectators. Purdue grabbed the early advantage, but Indiana led 18-15 at the break. The Boilermakers again forged ahead at the beginning of the second half, but the Hoosiers quickly responded, and the game went back and forth until the final whistle sounded, and IU came away with a 37-34 win. Krueger scored 12, Beckner chipped in 10, and Sibley added nine for IU.

Indiana got revenge on Iowa when the Hawkeyes came to town on February 1. The Hoosiers ran away with a 30-20 win in front of another capacity home crowd. At 4-2 in conference play, IU was tied for second place. However, their conference title hopes began to fade when the Hoosiers dropped a 31-29 cliffhanger to Purdue in West Lafayette on February 13. Beckner, who led all scorers with 19 points, missed an attempted tip-in that would have tied the game just as time expired. The Hoosiers' title hopes looked all but extinguished when they next dropped a 21-20 game against Illinois, who repeatedly stalled and held the ball, on February 19, in Bloomington.

One week after the Illinois loss, the Hoosiers turned their disappointment into fury as they crushed Minnesota 41-23 in Minneapolis, behind 14 points from Beckner and 12 from Krueger. The next day, the Hoosiers used a late rally to net a 38-36 nonconference win over Carleton College, the school where Dean got his coaching start.

On March 2, the Hoosiers swept away the Northwestern Wildcats 34-28 as Sponsler had a game-high 12 points. On March 6, IU traveled to Illinois and won a 28-25 rematch as Beckner led all scorers with 12.

Indiana's three straight conference victories, coupled with losses by other conference leaders, gave the Hoosiers a chance to tie for the Big Ten crown if they could win their final game of the season against Wisconsin in Bloomington. IU's veterans rose to the occasion, and after the opening minutes, the game was never in doubt as the Hoosiers overwhelmed the Badgers 35-20 to claim a share of the conference title. With 13 points, Beckner was the game's high man,

1925-26 TEAM ROSTER

Head coach: Everett Dean
Assistant coach: Harlan Logan

No.	Player	Hometown	Class	Position	Height
3	Art Beckner	Muncie, IN	Jr	F	6-0
18	Charles Benzel	Bedford, IN	Jr	G	5-8
	Herman Byers		So	F	
4	Robert Correll	Bloomington, IN	So	G	6-0
	Harold Derr	Huntington, IN	So	F	5-8
	Millard Easton	Sanborn, IN	Sr	G	6-0
10	Ed Farmer	Bloomington, IN	So	C	6-4
	Edward Jones	Oolitic, IN	So	C	
	Julius Krueger	Bloomington, IN	Jr	F	6-0
	Ralph McClintock	Bloomington, IN		F	
	Gale Robinson	Connersville, IN		C	
	Frank Sibley	Gary, IN	Jr	C	6-2
	Palmer Sponsler (Capt.)	Bloomington, IN	Sr	G	6-0
	Jack Winston	Washington, IN	Sr	G/F	6-6

SEASON RESULTS 1925-26

Date	Court	Opponent	Result	Score
12/10/1925	H	Miami of Ohio	W	47-26
12/15/1925	H	DePauw	L	20-33
12/19/1925	H	Wabash	W	35-27
1/5/1926	H	Kentucky	W	34-23
1/9/1926	H	Minnesota	W	33-28
1/11/1926	A	Wisconsin	L	31-33
1/16/1926	A	Iowa	L	22-29
1/18/1926	A	Northwestern	W	39-31
1/23/1926	H	Purdue	W	37-34
2/1/1926	H	Iowa	W	30-20
2/13/1926	A	Purdue	L	29-31
2/19/1926	H	Illinois	L	20-21
2/26/1926	A	Minnesota	W	41-23
2/27/1926	A	Carleton College	W	38-36
3/2/1926	H	Northwestern	W	34-28
3/6/1926	A	Illinois	W	28-25
3/9/1926	H	Wisconsin	W	35-20

1925-26 BIG TEN STANDINGS

	W	L	PCT
Purdue	8	4	.667
Indiana	8	4	.667
Michigan	8	4	.667
Iowa	8	4	.667
Ohio State	6	6	.500
Illinois	6	6	.500
Minnesota	5	7	.417
Wisconsin	4	8	.333
Chicago	4	8	.333
Northwestern	3	9	.250

1926-27

OVERALL RECORD: 13-4

CONFERENCE RECORD: 9-3 (SECOND PLACE)

INDIVIDUAL HONORS:

CHARLES BENZEL—BIG TEN MEDAL OF HONOR

Big Jack Winston stood 6'6" and used his height and long arms to clean the backboards and make life miserable for opposing scorers. He wasn't a prolific scorer, but Winston was one of the first dominant defenders in IU history, and he was one of the key components of Indiana's 1926 Big Ten championship team.
IU Archives

With experienced returning players like forwards Julius Krueger and Art Beckner, center Frank Sibley, and oversized guard Jack Winston (who would graduate at the end of the first semester), Indiana was once again the favorite to win the Big Ten in 1926-27. Now that they were more familiar with the role of marked men, the Hoosiers posted an even better conference record than the year before, but in the end it wasn't enough to secure a second straight Big Ten title.

Coach Everett Dean opened practice during the week of October 25, with lectures on sportsmanship and training. Then he drilled the players on shooting and passing fundamentals. As had been his tradition in the past during the early part of the preseason, Dean also had the young men play volleyball at the end of practice to help their conditioning and coordination.

The season tipped off on Friday, December 10, in Bloomington, when the Hoosiers buried DePauw 44-30 and gained a measure of revenge from the loss they suffered in Greencastle the year before. IU's junior forward Harold Derr led all scorers with 10 points, and the normally defensive-minded Jack Winston added a career-high eight points off the bench for IU. Franklin College was the Hoosiers' next pre-conference victim on December 16, in Bloomington. The Hoosiers rolled to an easy 37-17 win, powered by 17 points from Beckner. On December 21, IU went down and walloped Kentucky 38-19 in Lexington, as Krueger topped all scorers with 11.

Carleton College, which was on a tour playing several Big Ten teams, came to Bloomington on January 4, and gave the Hoosiers their first competitive game of the season. The visitors, who were coached by one of Dean's former protégés, led 15-11

and his total of 108 points made him the top scorer in Big Ten play.

All season, the Hoosiers had used a balanced scoring attack and a methodical offense to overmatch its opponents. Despite all of the basketball talent that Indiana had, the IU faithful gave much of the credit for the success of the team to Everett Dean. The *Arbutus* yearbook wrote, "Too much credit can not be given Coach Dean, who, in his first two years, has tutored one second-place team and one winner. It speaks well for Indiana's future in the great winter sport."

The 1926-27 team. First row (left to right): Harold Derr, Art Beckner, Julius Krueger, Frank Sibley, Jack Winston, Maurice Starr, Dale Wells, Robert Correll; Second row: coach Everett Dean, manager Lee Streaker, Charles Benzel, Harold Anderson, Ed Farmer, Carl Scheid, James Gill, Starr [first name unknown], trainer Jesse Ferguson. IU Archives

early in the second half, before IU went on a 14-2 run and never looked back in a 31-29 win.

The undefeated Hoosiers then began their Big Ten schedule with the toughest road swing in the conference—the northern trek to Wisconsin and Minnesota. IU slipped past the Badgers 28-23 in Madison on Saturday, January 8, and then accosted the Minnesota Golden Gophers 37-24 on January 10. Against the Gophers, Beckner and Krueger combined for 24 points. The next weekend, IU went on the road again. This time they traveled to Evanston, Illinois, where they used a big second-half surge to roll past Northwestern 36-24, behind 10 points from Krueger and nine from Beckner.

The fact that IU had started 3-0 in the conference after opening with three road games sent a powerful message to the other Big Ten teams that the Hoosiers were going to be a powerful force. However, on Saturday, January 22, a big, experienced Michigan team came to Bloomington and showed that it was up to the challenge. In the opening minutes of the game it looked as if the Hoosiers were going to run the Wolverines out of town, as IU blazed out to an 8-0 advantage, but the Hoosiers then settled into a 13-10 halftime lead. Michigan's defense took over in the second half and held Indiana without a field goal for a stretch of 13 minutes. Indiana made a run at the end, but Michigan prevailed 31-27.

Chicago came to town the following Saturday and grabbed an 11-9 halftime lead before falling 28-

23 to the Hoosiers. The two teams staged a rematch a week later in the Windy City. And although Indiana led 15-11 at the half, the Hoosiers never found their rhythm and eventually lost 25-21 to the Maroons, who effectively instituted a stalling offense to disrupt the Hoosiers' attack.

On February 7, IU completed its season sweep of Minnesota with a 42-16 victory in Bloomington. Beckner led all scorers with 10, Krueger added nine, and Sibley chipped in eight. The Hoosiers followed up that dominating performance with a lackluster effort on Saturday, February 12, against the Wabash Little Giants, who came to Bloomington for a non-conference matchup. Wabash led 34-20 early in the second half before the IU squad awoke to realize that a basketball game was in progress. The Hoosiers made a furious rally, but fell short for a 35-33 defeat.

After the improbable Wabash upset, Indiana traveled north to Ann Arbor, Michigan, on February 19, to take on the league-leading Michigan squad. An inspired Hoosier team outplayed the Wolverines in front of 9,000 Michigan fans and claimed a 37-34 victory that put IU back into a tie for first place in the Big Ten. Three days after the Michigan win, the Hoosiers turned in a subpar effort and fell to the mediocre Ohio State Buckeyes 27-18 in Bloomington.

Their Big Ten title hopes in doubt, the Hoosiers bounced back on February 26, and grabbed a key win over Wisconsin, another title contender, by the score

1926-27 TEAM ROSTER

Head coach: Everett Dean

No.	Player	Hometown	Class	Position	Height
15	Harold Anderson	Lapel, IN	So	F	
3	Art Beckner	Muncie, IN	Sr	F	6-0
18	Charles Benzel	Bedford, IN	Sr	G	5-8
4	Robert Correll	Bloomington, IN	Jr	G	6-0
	Harold Derr	Huntington, IN	Jr	F	5-8
10	Ed Farmer	Bloomington, IN	Jr	C	6-4
13	James Gill	Washington, IN	So	G	6-2
	Julius Krueger (Capt.)	Bloomington, IN	Sr	F	6-0
15	John Leonard	Rochester, IN	So	C	
9	Carl Scheid	Vincennes, IN	So	G	6-1
	Frank Sibley	Gary, IN	Sr	C	6-2
8	Maurice Starr	Anderson, IN	Jr	F	6-0
5	Dale Wells	LaPorte, IN	So	F	6-0
	Jack Winston	Washington, IN	Sr (5th)	G	6-6

SEASON RESULTS 1926-27

Date	Court	Opponent	Result	Score
12/10/1926	H	DePauw	W	44-30
12/16/1926	H	Franklin	W	37-17
12/21/1926	A	Kentucky	W	38-19
1/4/1927	H	Carleton	W	31-29
1/8/1927	A	Wisconsin	W	28-23
1/10/1927	A	Minnesota	W	37-24
1/17/1927	A	Northwestern	W	36-24
1/22/1927	H	Michigan	L	27-31
1/29/1927	H	Chicago	W	28-23
2/5/1927	A	Chicago	L	21-25
2/7/1927	H	Minnesota	W	42-16
2/12/1927	H	Wabash	L	33-35
2/19/1927	A	Michigan	W	37-34
2/22/1927	H	Ohio State	L	18-27
2/26/1927	H	Wisconsin	W	31-23
3/5/1927	H	Northwestern	W	44-25
3/9/1927	A	Ohio State	W	36-31

1926-27 BIG TEN STANDINGS

	W	L	PCT
Michigan	10	2	.833
Indiana	9	3	.750
Purdue	9	3	.750
Wisconsin	7	5	.583
Illinois	7	5	.583
Iowa	7	5	.583
Ohio State	6	6	.500
Chicago	3	9	.250
Minnesota	1	11	.083
Northwestern	1	11	.083

of 31-23. IU then annihilated lowly Northwestern 44-25 on March 5, in Bloomington, as four Hoosiers scored eight points or more. IU closed its season with a 36-31 win over Ohio State in Columbus, but Michigan had already claimed the Big Ten crown with a 10-2 record, one game better than IU's 9-3 mark.

The biggest disappointment for IU was that the team had lost its focus in suffering a home loss to Ohio State and a road loss at Chicago. Both of those squads were second-division Big Ten teams, and IU had both teams easily overmatched. If the Hoosiers had taken care of business and beaten both teams, then they could have earned the school's first outright conference championship. That was a bitter pill to swallow for such a talented squad. Nevertheless, they celebrated the fact that, at 9-3, they had earned the best conference record in school history.

1927-28

OVERALL RECORD: 15-2

CONFERENCE RECORD: 10-2 (FIRST PLACE)

TEAM HONORS:

BIG TEN CO-CHAMPIONS

INDIVIDUAL HONORS:

BOB CORRELL—ALL-BIG TEN (FIRST TEAM)

DALE WELLS—ALL-BIG TEN (FIRST TEAM)

ART BECKNER—BIG TEN MEDAL OF HONOR

After reigning as the perennial Big Ten favorite for two seasons, the Hoosier basketball squad entered the 1927-28 campaign with a lot of doubts about its potential to compete in the conference. High-scoring forward Art Beckner was the top returning player, but he would graduate at the end of the first semester in January. Robert Correll, the team captain, was another top returnee, but he had only played in a reserve role in the past. Sophomores James Strickland and Branch McCracken were expected to be strong players, but they had yet to compete in a varsity game. Fortunately for Coach Everett Dean, he ended up with the best possible scenario from all of these players, and he also had others, such as returning lettermen Dale Wells and Maurice Starr, step up

The 1927-28 team. First row (left to right): Robert Correll, Maurice Starr, James Strickland, Branch McCracken, Carl Scheid, James Gill, Dale Wells; Second row: manager Jim Johnson, Charles Benzel, Donald Cooper, John Leonard, coach Everett Dean, James Hickey, Noble Sprunger, trainer Jesse Ferguson. IU Archives

and play an important role on the team, which would go on to break several school records.

Franklin College served as Indiana's first opponent on Tuesday, December 13, in Bloomington. The Hoosiers fell behind by a point at halftime but easily outpaced the visitors in the second half and cruised to a 34-25 win. Correll was the game's leading scorer with 11 points, and McCracken netted eight in his first collegiate game. Next, the Hoosiers walloped Wabash 39-26 in the Men's Gymnasium on December 18, as McCracken scored 16 and Wells added nine. IU closed the preconference schedule on New Year's Eve in Bloomington with a balanced scoring attack that overwhelmed Cincinnati 56-41. McCracken and Wells each scored 14, and Correll registered 13 points.

The balanced scoring attack went out the window when Chicago came to Bloomington on Saturday, January 7, to open conference play. The Hoosiers rode McCracken's hot hand to an easy 32-13 win, as Big Mac dropped 24 on the Maroons. A week later, IU went on the road for the first time to face Michigan in Ann Arbor, and the Hoosiers came up just short in a 42-41 loss. Michigan forward Bennie Oosterbaan was difficult to stop and scored a game-

high 14 points in leading the Wolverines to the win. Beckner led the Hoosiers with 13.

On January 16, the Hoosiers went to Chicago and slaughtered the Maroons 35-12. The score was 13-2 at the half. Eight different players scored for IU in the contest, led by nine points from Correll. Back in Bloomington on January 21, Indiana ran to another big victory. This time, Illinois was the victim, as the Hoosiers used a 28-13 second-half advantage to snatch away a 44-29 win. McCracken led the way with 14 points, and Wells and Correll added 10 apiece.

The Hoosiers dropped back to 3-2 in the conference on January 25, when they were defeated 28-25 by Purdue in West Lafayette. McCracken fouled out of the game early in the second half. Nevertheless, IU rallied before ultimately falling short down the stretch. The Purdue loss, though bitter, would be IU's final setback of the season.

Kentucky, which had only one loss on the season, came to Bloomington on Saturday, February 4, and suffered the same fate they had in the previous three meetings. IU won 48-29 as forward James Strickland exploded for 19 points. Indiana returned to conference play on February 11, when Iowa came to

1927-28 TEAM ROSTER

Head coach: Everett Dean

No.	Player	Hometown	Class	Position	Height
3	Art Beckner	Muncie, IN	Sr (5th)	F	6-0
18	Charles Benzel	Bedford, IN	Sr (5th)	G	5-8
10	Donald Cooper	North Vernon, IN	So	F	6-0
4	Robert Correll (Capt.)	Bloomington, IN	Sr	G	6-0
13	James Gill	Washington, IN	Jr	G	6-2
15	John Leonard	Rochester, IN	So	C	6-4
7	Branch McCracken	Monrovia, IN	So	C	6-5
9	Carl Scheid	Vincennes, IN	Jr	G	6-1
8	Maurice Starr	Anderson, IN	Sr	F	6-0
6	James Strickland	Owensville, IN	So	F	6-2
5	Dale Wells	LaPorte, IN	Jr	F	6-0

SEASON RESULTS 1927-28

Date	Court	Opponent	Result	Score
12/13/1927	H	Franklin	W	34-25
12/18/1927	H	Wabash	W	39-26
12/31/1927	H	Cincinnati	W	56-41
1/7/1928	H	Chicago	W	32-13
1/14/1928	A	Michigan	L	41-42
1/16/1928	A	Chicago	W	35-12
1/21/1928	H	Illinois	W	44-29
1/25/1928	A	Purdue	L	25-28
2/4/1928	H	Kentucky	W	48-29
2/11/1928	H	Iowa	W	50-33
2/13/1928	H	Ohio State	W	43-26
2/18/1928	H	Purdue	W	40-37
2/20/1928	H	Coe College	W	35-14
2/22/1928	A	Ohio State	W	52-17
2/27/1928	A	Iowa	W	49-39
3/3/1928	H	Michigan	W	36-34
3/6/1928	A	Illinois	W	27-23

1927-28 BIG TEN STANDINGS

	W	L	PCT
Indiana	10	2	.833
Purdue	10	2	.833
Wisconsin	9	3	.750
Northwestern	9	3	.750
Michigan	7	5	.583
Chicago	5	7	.417
Iowa	3	9	.250
Ohio State	3	9	.250
Illinois	2	10	.167
Minnesota	2	10	.167

Bloomington and got whipped by the Hoosiers 50-33. The Ohio State Buckeyes suffered a similar fate two days later when they came to Bloomington and were dispatched by a 43-26 count. IU had three players in double figures against Iowa, with Strickland and Correll each scoring 12, while McCracken led the way against OSU with 11.

Saturday, February 18, marked IU's rematch with Purdue in Bloomington. Entering the game, coach Piggy Lambert's Boilermakers were undefeated and were leading the Big Ten, while Indiana was 5-2 in conference play and in danger of being eliminated from the race. The Hoosiers came out of the gates fast and played with precision and urgency, but could never keep a sizable lead against the Boilermakers, who kept fighting back. McCracken fouled out down the stretch when he retaliated against Purdue's Babe Wheeler, who had tried to undercut him. Still, the Hoosiers were able to close the deal on a 40-37 win that sent the players and the home crowd into a frenzy. Strickland stepped up again and led the Hoosiers with 16 points.

Next IU notched an easy 35-14 nonconference win over Coe College on February 20. Then the Hoosiers downed Ohio State for the second time with a 52-17 win in Columbus on February 22. IU was led by 16 points from Correll. Iowa City was the Hoosiers' next destination on Monday, February 27. The Hoosiers defeated the Iowa Hawkeyes 49-39 on the strength of 16 points from McCracken, 11 from Correll and nine each from Strickland and Wells.

In Bloomington on March 3, Strickland and McCracken took care of most of the scoring as they combined for 31 points in a grueling 36-34 win against Michigan. With that victory, Indiana prepared for its season-ending game at Illinois with the knowledge that a victory could clinch at least a share of the Big Ten championship. The Hoosiers went to Champaign on Tuesday, March 6, and fell behind 11-9 at the half. However, Indiana gamely fought back and tied the game at 22 as the gun sounded, and then outscored the home team 5-1 in overtime to claim a 27-23 triumph.

On March 10, Purdue defeated Minnesota 32-24 to tie the Hoosiers for the conference title, as the two teams posted identical 10-2 records. For the Hoosiers, after starting the conference season 3-2, they had to win seven straight games to earn a share of the second

1928-29

OVERALL RECORD: 7-10

CONFERENCE RECORD: 4-8 (EIGHTH PLACE)

INDIVIDUAL HONORS:

JAMES STRICKLAND—ALL-AMERICA

Senior guard Bob Correll was the captain of Indiana's 1928 Big Ten championship team. Correll was a heady guard and an excellent outside shooter.
IU Archives

In coach Everett Dean's first four seasons at the helm of the Indiana basketball program, his squads registered two second-place finishes in the Big Ten and two co-championships. The team's success created a fever of interest in the Hoosier team and made their games a hot ticket. As a result, in the spring of 1928, the IU trustees decided to build a new 8,000-seat fieldhouse adjacent to the Men's Gymnasium so that the Hoosiers could seat more fans for their home games. The fieldhouse was ready for the basketball team at the beginning of the 1928-29 season in which the Hoosiers were once again expected to challenge for the conference crown.

IU returned nearly all of its regulars from a 15-2 season that witnessed the Hoosiers rip through the competition. Indiana put together what was arguably the toughest preconference schedule in the nation for the 1928-29 season. The idea was that the Hoosiers wanted to make their preconference games just as challenging as their Big Ten contests, so that they would be better prepared than other conference teams once Big Ten play began. Any type of edge would have been helpful, since the Big Ten was stacked with many powerful teams that season. However, while everything went their way during the previous season, the breaks went against the Hoosiers in 1928-29, at least that's how Coach Dean expressed it. The result was that Indiana slid into the second division of the Big Ten for the first time in six seasons.

The team's opening game was a portent of things to come, as the Hoosiers christened their new arena by dropping a 31-30 contest to Washington University (St. Louis) on Saturday, December 8. IU fell behind in the first half and tried to mount a furious rally in the final minutes but came up just short. Indiana fared better in the official dedication game for the new fieldhouse on Thursday, December 13,

conference crown in school history. Including the two nonconference victories, IU had closed the season on a nine-game winning streak, which improved their overall record to 15-2 to set a new school record for the best single-season winning percentage. The 10-2 conference mark set an IU record as well.

The 1928-29 team. First row (left to right): Jay Campbell, Claron Veller, Lucian Ashby, Donald Cooper, James Strickland, Bernard Miller; Second row: coach Everett Dean, James Gill, Branch McCracken, Paul Jasper, Leonard Miller, Carl Scheid. IU Archives

when they defeated Pennsylvania 34-26 in front of a packed house of excited Hoosier fans.

Indiana went up to South Bend on December 21, and beat Notre Dame 29-17, powered by 10 points from center Branch McCracken, nine from forward Dale Wells, and eight from forward James Strickland. Next, the Hoosiers traveled for a New Year's Day game at Pittsburgh, where the Panthers put on a show with their quick-hitting passing attack. Led by 25 points from its agile forward, Charley Hyatt, Pittsburgh outclassed the Hoosiers 52-31. Three days later, IU finished its preconference slate with a 3-2 record by running over Missouri 41-29. McCracken was the game's high scorer with 14.

Conference play opened on the road on Tuesday, January 8, at Illinois. The Fighting Illini used stall tactics to the slow down the game and frustrate the Hoosiers. Neither team scored until eight minutes had elapsed in the first half, and the halftime count was a mere 6-4 in favor of Illinois. Eventually, the Illini prevailed 20-16.

Next, IU made the northern swing to Minnesota and Wisconsin. On Saturday, January 12, Indiana won a 37-36 overtime thriller against the Golden Gophers in Minneapolis. In overtime, IU's Robert

Correll tipped in a follow-up shot to give the Hoosiers the winning basket. However, with no time left on the clock, the Gophers had a chance to tie with two free throws, but their captain only made one of two foul shots and the Hoosiers escaped with the win. Strickland scored a game-high 20 points for IU. Two nights later, Indiana fell behind 13-6 to Wisconsin at the half, but stormed back to tie the game at 20-20 before running out of gas in the final minutes and losing 24-20.

The Hoosiers, now 1-2 in conference play, returned to Bloomington and faced off with Purdue on Saturday, January 19. IU got off to a strong start, but Purdue center Stretch Murphy carried the Boilermakers to a 29-23 victory with a game-high 15 points. Murphy outdueled IU's center, McCracken, who finished with 11 points. Two nights later, McCracken and Strickland combined for 23 points to lead IU over Minnesota in a 41-22 victory. The Minnesota contest was the final game for Indiana guard Robert Correll, who graduated at the end of the first semester. The Hoosiers, who were already struggling in conference play, would miss Correll's veteran presence on the floor. As if that wasn't tough enough, Dean also found out that forward Dale Wells was

In 1928-29, high-scoring forward James Strickland became Indiana's first All-American since Everett Dean in 1921. IU Archives

1928-29 TEAM ROSTER

Head coach: Everett Dean

No.	Player	Hometown	Class	Position	Height
2	Lucian Ashby	Evansville, IN	Jr	F	5-11
12	Jay Campbell	Shelbyville, IN	So	F	5-7
10	Donald Cooper	North Vernon, IN	Jr	F	6-0
4	Robert Correll	Bloomington, IN	Sr (5th)	G	6-0
13	James Gill	Washington, IN	Sr	G	6-2
3	Paul Jasper	Fort Wayne, IN	So	C	6-2
7	Branch McCracken	Monrovia, IN	Jr	C	6-5
11	Bernard Miller	Waldron, IN	So	F	6-1
18	Leonard Miller	Waldron, IN	Jr	F	6-0
9	Carl Scheid	Vincennes, IN	Sr	G	6-1
6	James Strickland	Owensville, IN	Jr	F	6-2
8	Claron Veller	Linton, IN	So	G	5-9
5	Dale Wells (Capt.)	LaPorte, IN	Sr	F	6-0

SEASON RESULTS 1928-29

Date	Court	Opponent	Result	Score
12/8/1928	H	Washington Univ. (MO)	L	30-31
12/13/1928	H	Pennsylvania	W	34-26
12/21/1928	A	Notre Dame	W	29-17
1/1/1929	A	Pittsburgh	L	31-52
1/4/1929	H	Missouri	W	41-29
1/8/1929	A	Illinois	L	16-20
1/12/1929	A	Minnesota	W	37-36
1/14/1929	A	Wisconsin	L	20-24
1/19/1929	H	Purdue	L	23-29
1/21/1929	H	Minnesota	W	41-22
2/5/1929	H	Northwestern	L	30-31
2/11/1929	A	Iowa	L	27-29
2/16/1929	H	Wisconsin	L	25-27
2/18/1929	A	Purdue	L	16-30
2/25/1929	A	Northwestern	L	26-28
2/26/1929	H	Illinois	W	32-22
3/4/1929	H	Iowa	W	35-30

1928-29 BIG TEN STANDINGS

	W	L	PCT
Wisconsin	10	2	.833
Michigan	10	2	.833
Purdue	9	3	.750
Northwestern	7	5	.583
Illinois	6	6	.500
Ohio State	6	6	.500
Iowa	5	7	.417
Indiana	4	8	.333
Chicago	2	10	.167
Minnesota	1	11	.083

ineligible for the second semester because of poor grades. Wells and Correll were the team's third and fourth leading scorers.

The Hoosiers, now 2-3, would lose their next three games by a combined total of five points. Northwestern dealt the first loss by the score of 31-30 on February 5, in Bloomington. Next, the Hoosiers traveled to Iowa and lost 29-27 in overtime. Back in Bloomington on February 16, IU lost another heartbreaker, this time to Wisconsin in a 27-25 game that the Hoosiers had two chances to tie in the final minutes. Then the Hoosiers lost to Purdue for the second time, with a 30-16 shellacking in West Lafayette on February 18. A week later, IU went to Northwestern and lost another overtime game, 28-26, which sent Indiana's conference record spiraling down to 2-8.

The five-game losing skid finally came to an end in Bloomington on February 26, when IU beat Illinois 32-22 on the strength of 12 points from McCracken and eight from junior forward Donald Cooper. IU was down one at the half, but used a delay game in the second half to draw the Illini defenders toward halfcourt, and then the Hoosiers attacked the basket for easy scores. Indiana salvaged one more win on March 4 when Iowa came to town. McCracken punished the Hawkeye interior players with 20 points, and IU pulled away down the stretch for a 35-30 win.

A puzzling season ended with the Hoosiers posting a 4-8 record in Big Ten play and a 7-10 record overall. Eight of the losses came by a total of 22 points, or an average of less than three points per game. The team simply didn't find a way to win close games and was never able to turn the season around once they suffered some tough losses in Big Ten play.

1929-30

OVERALL RECORD: 8-9

CONFERENCE RECORD: 7-5 (FOURTH PLACE)

INDIVIDUAL HONORS:

BRANCH MCCRACKEN—ALL-AMERICA,

ALL-BIG TEN (FIRST TEAM)

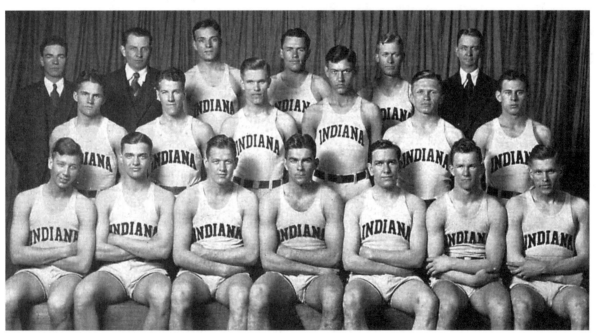

The 1929-30 team. First row (left to right): Donald Cooper, James Strickland, Paul Jasper, Branch McCracken, James Gill, Joseph Zeller, Bernard Miller; Second row: Claron Veller, Lucian Ashby, Leonard Miller, Bill Blagrave, Victor Dauer, Maurice Massy; Third row: manager Joe Smith, coach Everett Dean, Clark [first name unknown], Henry [first name unknown], Jacob Bretz, trainer Jesse Ferguson. IU Archives

While the previous season had turned into a nightmare for the Indiana basketball squad, there was optimism in the IU camp that a similar performance would not be repeated in 1929-30. After all, the Hoosiers returned their top two scorers in center Branch McCracken and forward James Strickland, both of whom were now seniors and veterans of Big Ten play. Plus, coach Everett Dean had a long bench of capable players to call on. Indiana would again play a very challenging preconference schedule. As a result, memories of the previous season flooded back after the first several games. However,

the Hoosiers got their act together during conference play and made a respectable showing.

The opening tip of the season came on Saturday, December 7, when DePauw came to the Fieldhouse and stole away a 26-24 win from the Hoosiers. The game was tied at 24 when Copeland, a backup center for the Tigers, buried a shot in the final minute (his only points of the game) and was carried off the floor by his teammates and a small band of DePauw followers. McCracken netted 19 points to lead all scorers, and Strickland scored the Hoosiers' other five points.

1929-30 TEAM ROSTER

Head coach: Everett Dean

No.	Player	Hometown	Class	Position	Height
2	Lucian Ashby	Evansville, IN	Sr	F	5-11
	Bill Blagrave	Washington, IN	So	G	6-2
19	Jacob Bretz	Huntingburg, IN	Jr	F	6-0
10	Donald Cooper	North Vernon, IN	Sr	F	6-0
12	Victor Dauer	Gary, IN	So	F	5-11
18	Carl Eber	Plymouth, IN		G	
13	James Gill	Washington, IN	Sr (5th)	G	6-2
3	Paul Jasper	Fort Wayne, IN	Jr	C	6-2
21	Maurice Massy	Indianapolis, IN		G	6-0
7	Branch McCracken (Capt.)	Monrovia, IN	Sr	C	6-5
11	Bernard Miller	Waldron, IN	Jr	F	6-1
17	Leonard Miller	Waldron, IN	Sr	F	6-0
6	James Strickland	Owensville, IN	Sr	F	6-2
8	Claron Veller	Linton, IN	Jr	G	5-9
22	Joseph Zeller	East Chicago, IN	So	G	6-1

SEASON RESULTS 1929-30

Date	Court	Opponent	Result	Score
12/7/1929	H	DePauw	L	24-26
12/13/1929	H	Pittsburgh	L	31-35
12/21/1929	A	Pennsylvania	L	21-26
1/7/1930	H	Notre Dame	L	29-30
1/11/1930	A	Chicago	W	36-24
1/18/1930	H	Northwestern	W	36-22
1/20/1930	A	Michigan	L	26-45
1/23/1930	H	Wisconsin	L	21-23
2/3/1930	A	Washington Univ. (MO)	W	33-21
2/8/1930	A	Ohio State	W	26-22
2/12/1930	A	Northwestern	W	39-31
2/15/1930	H	Chicago	W	28-16
2/22/1930	H	Michigan	L	18-21
3/1/1930	H	Ohio State	W	27-15
3/3/1930	H	Minnesota	W	31-25
3/8/1930	A	Wisconsin	L	23-34
3/10/1930	A	Minnesota	L	29-34

1929-30 BIG TEN STANDINGS

	W	L	PCT
Wisconsin	10	2	.833
Michigan	10	2	.833
Purdue	9	3	.750
Northwestern	7	5	.583
Illinois	6	6	.500
Ohio State	6	6	.500
Iowa	5	7	.417
Indiana	4	8	.333
Chicago	2	10	.167
Minnesota	1	11	.083

Next, a tough Pittsburgh team came to Bloomington on December 13 and won a nip-and-tuck 35-31 victory. McCracken scored 15 points to tie the Panthers' Hyatt for game-high honors. The Hoosiers then journeyed to Philadelphia on December 21 to take on Penn in front of 6,000 fans in the now-legendary Palestra. IU lost another close game down the stretch when Penn pulled out a 26-21 win in the final minutes. Unfortunately, the Hoosiers' misery continued two weeks later when Notre Dame came to Bloomington. In a game that featured strong play from both teams, the Fighting Irish pulled out a 30-29 win when Crowe, a reserve forward, sank a mid-range field goal in the waning seconds to deliver the victory.

The 0-4 Hoosiers had a chance to win each of those four games, but were now winless and had less than a week to prepare for Big Ten play. As the Arbutus mildly stated, "With but four days to reorganize the team, Coach Dean outlined a strenuous practice program."

Dean succeeded in whipping the team into shape. The Hoosiers went to Chicago on Saturday, January 11, and easily took a 36-24 win from the Maroons, as McCracken scored 16. A week later, IU claimed its second victory with a 36-22 romp over Northwestern in Bloomington. Indiana's diminutive guard, Claron Veller, led the team with 11 points. The Hoosiers couldn't celebrate for long since they had a quick turnaround in which they had to travel up to Michigan two days later. The Wolverines had much more energy than the Hoosiers, and they used it to cruise to a 45-26 win.

Wisconsin came to Bloomington on January 23, and along with them came the close-game demons that had been haunting Indiana. The Badgers and the Hoosiers locked horns in a superb defensive battle, and the score was tied 19-19 at the end of regulation. In overtime, the Badgers scored first, but then McCracken, who had hit the shot that sent the game to OT, scored to tie the contest at 21. In the end, Wisconsin's Carl Matthusen drained the game-winner from the top of the key to give the Badgers a 23-21 victory.

Indiana followed up that devastatingly familiar loss with its first nonconference win of the season, a

IU's 6'4" senior center Branch McCracken capped off a stellar three-year career by setting the Big Ten single-season scoring record and earning all-conference and All-America honors during the 1929-30 season.
IU Archives

points. The Hoosiers completed a season sweep of Chicago when the Maroons came to Bloomington three days later and got trounced 28-16. McCracken once again led all scorers with 12.

The Michigan Wolverines ended the Hoosiers' brief four-game winning streak when they used their stingy defense to grab a 21-18 win in front of 7,000 fans in Bloomington on Saturday, February 22. Despite another close loss, the Hoosiers kept fighting. On Saturday, March 1, they came back and walloped the Ohio State Buckeyes 27-15 behind McCracken's game-high 14 points. Two days later, the Minnesota Golden Gophers came to town and tried to rough-house the Hoosiers. The Gophers "fouled [McCracken] nearly every time he attempted to take a shot." In a game that featured seven ties, Indiana fought through the Gophers' rough tactics and pulled away for a 31-25 win in the Hoosiers' final home game of the season.

With a record of 7-3 in the conference, IU still had a shot at a second-place finish. However, their final two games would be played over a span of three days on a road swing up to Wisconsin and Minnesota. The Badgers easily won the first game, 34-23, on March 8. Then, the Gophers got their revenge on the Hoosiers by winning a 34-29 overtime game on March 10.

After a tough start to the season, Indiana had regrouped and put together a decent run in the Big Ten. Like the season before, the team continued to have trouble winning close games. The Hoosiers were 1-7 in games decided by five points or less. If the Hoosiers could have reversed those numbers, or even won 50 percent of those games, then they would have had a very successful season.

33-21 win against Washington (Missouri) in St. Louis. Next, the Hoosiers won their first close game of the season by defeating Ohio State 26-22 in front of a smaller than normal crowd in the Fieldhouse. Then IU traveled to Northwestern and completed a season sweep of the Wildcats with a 39-31 win. McCracken was practically unstoppable with 18

1930-31

OVERALL RECORD: 9-8

CONFERENCE RECORD: 5-7 (SIXTH PLACE)

The 1930-31 season played out almost exactly the opposite of the season before. The Hoosiers looked like world-beaters in winning their four preconference games against stiff competition. The Hoosiers also looked pretty good in winning three of their first four Big Ten games. But then the IU machine sputtered down the stretch, and Indiana ended up finishing in the second division of the Big Ten.

With the graduation of James Strickland and Branch McCracken, who finished his career as the leading scorer in IU history, the Hoosiers now looked for their scoring punch from the combination of guards Joe Zeller and Claron "Lefty" Vellar, forward Bernard Miller, and center Bernard Dickey. In the beginning, Veller took the lead by shooting down DePauw with four long field goals that captivated the Bloomington crowd on December 10, in a 26-18 victory to open the season. On December 18, IU rushed out to an early lead and then stalled down the stretch

to rebuff a rally from the Washington (Missouri) Bears. The Hoosiers prevailed 17-15.

Next, IU journeyed to Pennsylvania for a two-game road trip. On New Year's Eve, IU fell behind 11-8 in the first half against Penn, and then the Hoosiers stunned the crowd at The Palestra when they came back from a 17-11 deficit early in the second half to pull out a 24-20 win over the Quakers. Miller was the game's high scorer with nine. The next day, Indiana got out of the gates quickly and used its depth to overwhelm the Pittsburgh Panthers 27-19, as Zeller and Miller scored six points apiece. Two nights earlier, Pitt had defeated the visiting Purdue Boilermakers 24-22.

Chicago came to Bloomington on Saturday, January 10, to open the Big Ten season and the old close-game jinx bit the Hoosiers again as the Maroons triumphed 31-30 in overtime. During regulation, Chicago made nine out of 22 field goal attempts, for 41 percent—an excellent percentage for that era. By contrast, the Hoosiers made only 10-48 attempts for 21 percent.

IU overcame its recent history of close-game woes on January 12, when Ohio State came to town. The game was knotted at 11 at the half, and OSU pulled ahead by three late in the game, but the Hoosiers fought back and scratched out a 23-21 win. The

The 1930-31 team. First row (left to right): Clark [first name unknown], Henry [first name unknown], Victor Dauer, Maurice Massy, Lucian Ashby, Bernard Miller, Joseph Zeller, Claron Veller, Jacob Bretz; Second row: trainer Jesse Ferguson, Costas [first name unknown], Bernard Dickey, Bill Blagrave, Taylor Hoffar, Glendon Hodson, Henley [first name unknown], coach Everett Dean; Third row: Jay Campbell, George Reed, Edmonds [first name unknown], Tiernam [first name unknown], Oren [first name unknown], Rainbolt [first name unknown]. IU Archives

Hoosiers claimed another close victory on January 17, when they traveled to Illinois and made all the right plays down the stretch to steal a 35-34 triumph over the Fighting Illini. IU's Miller was the top scorer in the contest with 12 points. Two nights later, IU went to Iowa City and used a 15-7 advantage in the second half to down the Iowa Hawkeyes 28-20. That improved the Hoosiers' conference record to 3-1.

Notre Dame came to Bloomington on February 3 for a nonconference rivalry game. With Miller, IU's leading scorer, sidelined because of an illness, the Hoosiers couldn't keep their three-game winning streak alive against the Fighting Irish, who prevailed 25-20, led by a game-high 12 points from their forward Bob Newbold. Dickey led IU with eight. The Hoosiers lost another rivalry game on Saturday, February 7, when the Purdue Boilermakers came to Bloomington and laid claim to a 30-23 victory, which dropped IU to 3-2 in the conference and all but dashed the team's hopes of a conference crown.

On February 9, Indiana got back in the win column with a 31-18 trouncing of Iowa, as IU abandoned the slow-down offense it had used in recent games and went back to using swift passes to get quick shots. The win put IU into a tie for second place and rejuvenated their hopes of a possible conference championship, even though Veller had suffered an eye injury in the Iowa game and Miller was still recovering from an illness.

Indiana's title hopes received a near-death blow on Saturday, February 14, when the Hoosiers were dominated by Purdue 28-15 in West Lafayette. Indiana, which was without coach Everett Dean for the game, may have grown prematurely optimistic about its chances when Purdue's star guard, John Wooden, fouled out in the first half. The Hoosiers were only down 13-11 at the break, but the Boilermakers got on a roll in the second session and turned the game into a blowout.

A week later in Ann Arbor, the Hoosiers were only down by one to the Michigan Wolverines at the half, but lost 33-24. On Monday, February 23, Indiana dropped its third straight conference game when Illinois came to Bloomington and whipped the Hoosiers 39-25. IU was able to briefly stop the bleeding on February 28, by defeating the Chicago Maroons 33-22 in Chicago, behind a game-high 12

1930-31 TEAM ROSTER

Head coach: Everett Dean

No.	Player	Hometown	Class	Position	Height
2	Lucian Ashby	Evansville, IN	Sr (5th)	F	5-11
10	Bill Blagrave	Washington, IN	Jr	G	6-2
19	Jacob Bretz	Huntingburg, IN	Sr	F	6-0
12	Jay Campbell	Shelbyville, IN	Jr	F	5-7
15	Victor Dauer	Gary, IN	Jr	F	5-11
5	Bernard Dickey	Fort Wayne, IN	So	F/C	6-1
13	Glendon Hodson	Amo, IN	So	F	6-0
	Taylor Hoffar	Seymour, IN	So	C	6-1
3	Paul Jasper	Fort Wayne, IN	Sr	C	6-2
21	Maurice Massy	Indianapolis, IN		G	6-0
11	Bernard Miller (Capt.)	Waldron, IN	Sr	F	6-1
	Franklin Rainbolt	Salem, IN		F	6-3
22	George Reed	Kokomo, IN		C	6-3
8	Claron Veller	Linton, IN	Sr	G	5-9
9	Joseph Zeller	East Chicago, IN	Jr	G	6-1

SEASON RESULTS 1930-31

Date	Court	Opponent	Result	Score
12/10/1930	H	DePauw	W	26-18
12/18/1930	H	Washington Univ. (MO)	W	17-15
12/31/1930	A	Pennsylvania	W	24-20
1/1/1931	A	Pittsburgh	W	27-19
1/10/1931	H	Chicago	L	27-28
1/12/1931	H	Ohio State	W	23-21
1/17/1931	A	Illinois	W	35-34
1/19/1931	A	Iowa	W	28-20
2/3/1931	H	Notre Dame	L	20-25
2/7/1931	H	Purdue	L	23-30
2/9/1931	H	Iowa	W	31-18
2/14/1931	A	Purdue	L	15-28
2/21/1931	A	Michigan	L	24-33
2/23/1931	H	Illinois	L	25-39
2/28/1931	A	Chicago	W	33-22
3/2/1931	A	Ohio State	L	15-31
3/7/1931	H	Michigan	L	20-21

1930-31 BIG TEN STANDINGS

	W	L	PCT
Northwestern	11	1	.917
Michigan	8	4	.667
Minnesota	8	4	.667
Purdue	8	4	.667
Illinois	7	5	.583
Indiana	5	7	.417
Wisconsin	4	8	.333
Chicago	4	8	.333
Ohio State	3	9	.250
Iowa	2	10	.167

points from Miller. Unfortunately, it was the last win of the season for IU.

Ohio State crushed the Hoosiers 31-15 in Columbus on March 2, despite a game-high 12 points from IU's Zeller. The Hoosiers closed out the season with a well-played, closely fought game against second-place Michigan on Saturday, March 7, in Bloomington. However, the Wolverines prevailed 21-20.

A season that started out so promising finished with Indiana losing seven of its final nine games to close the year at 9-8 overall and 5-7 in the Big Ten. Of course, injuries and illnesses conspired to cripple the Hoosier squad at several points in the season as Indiana fell back into the second division of the Big Ten for the second time in three years.

1931-32

OVERALL RECORD: 8-10

CONFERENCE RECORD: 4-8 (SEVENTH PLACE)

INDIVIDUAL HONORS:

JOSEPH ZELLER—ALL-BIG TEN (FIRST TEAM)

While the Indiana basketball team of 1931-32 returned several lettermen such as Bernard Dickey, Joe Zeller, Jay Campbell, and Vic Dauer, uncertainty surrounded the team because no one knew who would step up to provide better performances than what the Hoosiers got from last season's team, which slid down to the second tier of the Big Ten. Unfortunately, this team wasn't able to meet the record from the previous season, let alone exceed it. However, several younger players did step forward and earned valuable playing time and experience that would benefit the team in future seasons.

Miami of Ohio came to Bloomington on Tuesday, December 8, and the Hoosiers beat the Redhawks 24-18 to open the season. IU sophomore Arnold Suddith, a former all-state guard at Martinsville, buried his very first collegiate shot from the top of the key in the opening minutes of the game, and went on to score eight points to lead all scorers. IU went up to South Bend on Saturday, December 12, and faced off with Notre Dame. After

1931-32 TEAM ROSTER

Head coach: Everett Dean

No.	Player	Hometown	Class	Position	Height
10	Bill Blagrave	Washington, IN	Sr	G	6-2
3	Jay Campbell (Capt.)	Shelbyville, IN	Sr	F	5-7
17	William Cordell	Bloomington, IN	Jr	G	5-9
16	Ray Dauer	Gary, IN	So	F	6-1
15	Victor Dauer	Gary, IN	Sr	F	5-11
5	Bernard Dickey	Fort Wayne, IN	Jr	F/C	6-1
13	Glendon Hodson	Amo, IN	Jr	F	6-0
21	Taylor Hoffar	Seymour, IN	Jr	C	6-1
22	George Reed	Kokomo, IN		C	6-3
14	Halary Sawicki	Georgetown, IL	Jr	C	6-3
8	Arnold Suddith	Martinsville, IN	So	G	6-0
4	Warren Tucker	Salem, IN		F	6-0
18	Woodrow Weir	Scottsburg, IN	So	F	5-10
12	Ernest Youngblood	Veedersburg, IN	So	F	5-11
9	Joseph Zeller	East Chicago, IN	Sr	G	6-1

SEASON RESULTS 1931-32

Date	Court	Opponent	Result	Score
12/8/1931	H	Miami University (OH)	W	24-18
12/12/1931	A	Notre Dame	W	23-18
12/16/1931	H	Pittsburgh	W	27-19
12/30/1931	A	DePauw	L	19-26
1/4/1932	A	Purdue	L	30-49
1/9/1932	A	Northwestern	L	23-29
1/11/1932	H	Illinois	L	22-30
1/16/1932	A	Minnesota	L	35-37
1/18/1932	H	Iowa	W	35-27
2/2/1932	A	Xavier	W	18-16
2/4/1932	H	Marquette	W	30-18
2/8/1932	H	Northwestern	L	25-29
2/13/1932	H	Minnesota	W	27-22
2/15/1932	H	Wisconsin	W	33-21
2/20/1932	A	Iowa	W	34-33
2/22/1932	H	Purdue	L	29-42
3/5/1932	A	Wisconsin	L	26-34
3/7/1932	A	Illinois	L	32-33

1931-32 BIG TEN STANDINGS

	W	L	PCT
Purdue	11	1	.917
Minnesota	9	3	.750
Northwestern	9	3	.750
Michigan	8	4	.667
Illinois	7	5	.583
Ohio State	5	7	.417
Indiana	4	8	.333
Wisconsin	3	9	.250
Iowa	3	9	.250
Chicago	1	11	.083

The 1931-32 team. First row (left to right): George Reed, Glendon Hodson, Bernard Dickey, Joseph Zeller, Bill Blagrave, Rainbolt [first name unknown], Victor Dauer, Jay Campbell; Second row: Ray Dauer, Halary Sawicki, Arnold Suddith, Taylor Hoffar, Warren Tucker, Everitt [first name unknown], Woodrow Weir, Tucker [first name unknown], Opasik [first name unknown]. IU Archives

the Fighting Irish led for most of the game, the Hoosiers mounted a charge in the final 10 minutes and stole away a 23-18 victory. Zeller and Suddith scored seven points each for IU.

What IU did to Notre Dame, Pittsburgh did to IU on December 16. The Panthers came to Bloomington and trailed the Hoosiers for most of the way before tying the game at 21 in the final minutes. Suddith hit what appeared to be the game-winning shot with only a few seconds remaining, but the Panthers raced the ball down the court, and forward Tim Lawry hit an improbable field goal to send the game into overtime, where Pitt outscored IU 6-1 to earn a 29-24 victory. Two weeks later, on December 30, the Hoosiers dropped their final preconference game to a tough DePauw squad in Greencastle. The Tigers dominated the game and won 26-19. IU junior Glendon Hodson tied a couple Tigers for game-high honors with seven points.

Indiana then opened the conference season against Purdue in West Lafayette on Monday, January 4. The Boilermakers, who would go on to win the conference title in a walk, opened up a 28-9 halftime lead and easily sewed up a 49-30 win over the

Hoosiers. Indiana played better at Northwestern on Saturday, January 9, but still lost 29-23.

The Hoosiers came back to Bloomington and played their first conference home game on January 11, against Illinois, but didn't fare any better. The Fighting Illini controlled the game and dealt the Hoosiers a 30-22 defeat. IU traveled to Minnesota to play the Golden Gophers in the Minnesota Fieldhouse (now known as Williams Arena) on January 16, and looked very good in the first half as they charged out to a 20-17 lead at the break. However, the Gophers, who were contending for the conference crown, opened the second half with an 11-0 run and then weathered a Hoosier comeback to nail down a 37-35 victory.

The Hoosiers' five-game losing streak (including the first four conference contests) was finally broken on January 18, when IU soundly defeated Iowa 35-27 in Bloomington. Suddith led the Hoosiers with nine points, and junior center Taylor Hoffar added eight. Next IU rattled off two nonconference victories. The first was an 18-16 come-from-behind win over Xavier in Cincinnati on February 2. The second was a 30-18 ambush of the Marquette Golden Eagles in

Bloomington on February 4. In that game, Suddith led all scorers with 11 points. IU's overall record was improved to 6-5.

In their next contest against Northwestern on February 8, in Bloomington, the Hoosiers continued their strong play for most of the game, but faltered in the final minutes and let the victory slip away to the Wildcats by the count of 29-25. On Saturday, February 13, in Bloomington, the Hoosiers dampened Minnesota's title hopes by upending the Golden Gophers 27-22, led by 10 points from sophomore forward Woodrow Weir. Two nights later, Weir scored 10 points again and led the Hoosiers to another win, this time at the expense of Wisconsin. The Hoosiers prevailed 33-21 over the Badgers in Bloomington. Indiana's conference winning streak was extended to four games on Saturday, February 20, in Iowa City, where the Hoosiers outlasted the Hawkeyes for a 34-33 win. Weir topped all scorers with 14 points.

League-leading Purdue brought the Hoosiers back to earth on February 22, by using a 19-4 second-half run to win 42-29. Purdue guard John Wooden scored a game-high 17 points to lead the Boilermakers to victory in IU's last home game of the season. On their final road trip of the year, IU fell to Wisconsin 34-26 in Madison on March 5, and then dropped a 33-32 nail-biter at Illinois on March 7. Suddith was the top scorer in the Illinois game with 12 points.

While the Hoosiers had played well at times, the team suffered its second straight finish in the lower tier of the Big Ten by closing the season in seventh place. However, the strong play of sophomores Suddith and Weir and juniors Hoffar and Hodson provided Indiana fans with hopeful prospects for the future.

1932-33

OVERALL RECORD: 10-8
CONFERENCE RECORD: 6-6 (FIFTH PLACE)

Not only did the Hoosiers lose graduating seniors Joe Zeller, Jay Campbell, and Victor Dauer from the previous team, but IU's leading scorer, Arnold Suddith, didn't return to IU for his junior year in 1932-33. Nevertheless, Indiana returned three lettermen in center Taylor Hoffar and forwards Woodrow Weir and Glendon Hodson. That trio anchored the IU squad and led the Hoosiers back into the upper division of the Big Ten. Sophomores Willard Kehrt and Jack Heavenridge also emerged as important contributors, and senior Bernhard Dickey re-emerged as the valuable player he had been during his sophomore year. Also after several years of waning attendance (as the Great Depression began to take hold across the U.S.), IU cut its ticket prices from $1.00 to $0.40, and the result was much larger crowds (as well as higher returns at the box office).

The IU squad opened its season on Tuesday, December 6, with a barn-burner against Wabash in Bloomington. The Hoosiers led the Little Giants 11-10 at the intermission, and the game continued to seesaw back and forth in the second half before IU prevailed 22-21. Hodson, who scored a game-high 13 points, led the Hoosiers to the win with a pair of key baskets down the stretch. On Friday, December 9, Indiana notched its second victory with a 41-12 slaughter of the Cincinnati Bearcats in the IU Fieldhouse. Hodson was the game's leading scorer with 10, and Weir added eight.

DePauw served as the Hoosiers' next opponent on December 14, in Bloomington, and IU rocked the Tigers 34-19, behind 14 points from Hoffar and a strong defensive effort from the Indiana squad. The Hoosiers went on the road for the first time on December 20, when the team trekked north to Milwaukee to face a big, strong Marquette team. The Golden Eagles led by one at the half, and that proved to be the final margin in a 21-20 loss for IU. The pre-conference season wrapped up on January 3, when IU

The 1932-33 team. First row (left to right): William Coulter, Robert Porter, Halary Sawicki, Ray Dauer, Taylor Hoffar, Glendon Hodson, Woodrow Weir, Bernard Dickey; Second row: coach Everett Dean, Manager Charles Harrell, Joe Dugan, Keith Campbell, Willard Kehrt, Charlie Hollers, Carl Gerber, Jack Heavenridge, Peters [first name unknown], Joe Gansinger, Floyd Henry, Morris Himmelstein, Gilbert Carter, trainer Jesse Ferguson. IU Archives

traveled to Miami of Ohio and got beat 33-29, despite mounting a big second half comeback. IU played the game without Weir, who had suffered a knee injury in practice and did not make the trip.

With a 3-2 preconference mark, IU opened the Big Ten season on Saturday, January 7, at Ohio State with a 35-28 defeat at the hands of the Buckeyes. Indiana had tied the game at 24-24 in the second half, but ran out of gas as OSU closed with an 11-4 run. Two days later, the Hoosiers evened their conference record with a convincing 34-21 rout of Chicago, as Heavenridge netted 14 points to lead all scorers.

Weir returned to the team on January 14, against Wisconsin in Bloomington; however, Hodson came down with an illness and was only able to play a few minutes. Weir wasn't expected to return for a couple more weeks, so Dean unveiled a surprise when he inserted him into the starting lineup. The 5'10" forward led IU to an early 11-2 lead, but the Badgers grabbed a 19-16 halftime advantage. A hard-fought second half ended in a 33-33 tie, and then the Badgers rallied in the final minute of overtime to come away with 38-37 victory. Weir and Heavenridge tied for the game's top scoring honors with 11.

IU hosted a game against the Falcon Athletic Club of Mexico City on February 1, and the Hoosiers

cruised to a 56-27 win. IU got back to Big Ten action on February 6, when conference contender Northwestern paid the Hoosiers a visit and slipped away from Bloomington with a 32-28 victory that dropped IU to 1-3 in the Big Ten. On February 11, IU bounced back with a relatively easy 31-22 victory over Minnesota in Bloomington. But two days later, the Hoosiers dropped another conference game when Michigan came to town and beat IU 32-25.

Hodson was finally back to full strength and in the starting lineup when Indiana faced Wisconsin in Madison on February 18. Hodson scored 10 and Kehrt scored eight to power the Hoosiers to a 29-28 victory, avenging the Badgers' one-point win in Bloomington a month earlier. Two days later, IU went up to Minnesota and completed a season sweep of the Golden Gophers by defeating them 36-25, as Hodson and Kehrt combined for 24 points.

A week after sweeping the two northern schools, the Hoosiers went on the road again for another doubleheader. This time it was against the Big Ten's two Chicago-area teams, and IU's fortunes were reversed as they dropped both games. On February 25, IU played the Chicago Maroons, who were winless in conference play. The Hoosiers led 30-26 in the final minutes before Chicago used an 8-2 run to claim a

1932-33 TEAM ROSTER

Head coach: Everett Dean

No.	Player	Hometown	Class	Position	Height
	Keith Campbell	Logansport, IN	So	G	5-10
	Gilbert Carter	Indianapolis, IN		G	5-8
17	William Cordell	Bloomington, IN	Sr	G	5-9
	William Coulter	Paoli, IN	So	C	6-3
16	Ray Dauer	Gary, IN	Jr	F	6-1
5	Bernard Dickey	Fort Wayne, IN	Sr	F/C	6-1
	Joe Gansinger	East Chicago, IN		F	6-0
	Carl Gerber	Decatur, IN		G	6-1
	Jack Heavenridge	Washington, IN	So	G	6-1
14	Floyd Henry	Kendalville, IN	So	F	5-10
	Morris Himmelstein	Fort Wayne, IN		G	5-7
13	Glendon Hodson (Capt.)	Amo, IN	Sr	F	6-0
21	Taylor Hoffar	Seymour, IN	Sr	C	6-1
	Charlie Hollers	Switz City, IN		G	5-11
	Willard Kehrt	Shelbyville, IN	So	F	5-11
	Robert Porter	Logansport, IN	So	G	6-1
14	Halary Sawicki	Georgetown, IL	Sr	C	6-3
20	Warren Tucker	Salem, IN		F	6-0
18	Woodrow Weir	Scottsburg, IN	Jr	G/F	5-10

SEASON RESULTS 1932-33

Date	Court	Opponent	Result	Score
12/6/1932	H	Wabash	W	22-21
12/9/1932	H	Cincinnati	W	41-12
12/14/1932	H	DePauw	W	34-19
12/20/1932	A	Marquette	L	20-21
1/3/1933	A	Miami (OH)	L	29-33
1/7/1933	A	Ohio State	L	28-33
1/9/1933	H	Chicago	W	34-21
12/15/1933	H	Wisconsin	L	37-38
2/1/1933	H	Falcons of Mexico	W	56-27
2/6/1933	H	Northwestern	L	28-32
2/11/1933	H	Minnesota	W	31-22
2/13/1933	H	Michigan	L	25-32
2/18/1933	A	Wisconsin	W	29-28
2/20/1933	A	Minnesota	W	36-25
2/25/1933	A	Chicago	L	32-34
2/27/1933	A	Northwestern	L	32-45
3/2/1933	A	Michigan	W	31-30
3/6/1933	H	Ohio State	W	40-28

1932-33 BIG TEN STANDINGS

	W	L	PCT
Ohio State	10	2	.833
Northwestern	10	2	.833
Iowa	8	4	.667
Michigan	8	4	.667
Illinois	6	6	.500
Purdue	6	6	.500
Indiana	6	6	.500
Wisconsin	4	8	.333
Minnesota	1	11	.083
Chicago	1	11	.083

34-32 win. Hodson netted 16 to lead all scorers. Two nights later in Evanston, Kehrt exploded for 12 points in the first half and IU led Northwestern, the conference leader, 24-17 at the break. However, the Wildcats held the Hoosiers without a field goal for the first 17 minutes of the second half and ran to a 45-32 comeback win.

Indiana went on the road for its fifth straight game on March 2, in Ann Arbor and won a cliffhanger over Michigan 31-30 when Kehrt buried a 25-foot field goal in the game's final seconds. Hodson was the game's high scorer with 16. On March 6, in Bloomington, the Hoosiers closed out their season by drilling Ohio State 40-28, which cost the Buckeyes the outright Big Ten title (they had to share it with Northwestern). Hodson scored 17 for the Hoosiers and Kehrt added 10.

IU's two wins to close the season gave the Hoosiers a 10-8 overall record, the first time the team had won 10 or more games since the 1927-28 campaign. More importantly, the Hoosiers were competitive against the Big Ten's best teams and found a way to win several close games. Indiana's 6-6 record in conference play placed them fifth in the league.

1933-34

OVERALL RECORD: 13-7

CONFERENCE RECORD: 6-6 (FIFTH PLACE)

After a half-decade of struggles with mediocrity, the Indiana basketball squad rebounded into the role of title contender in 1933-34. The Hoosiers entered the season as one of the favorites to claim the Big Ten crown. While this IU team wasn't quite ready to recapture a conference title, the team consistently played a high level of basketball—with the exception of two disappointing blowouts at the hands of the eventual conference champion.

The season tipped off when Franklin College came to the IU Fieldhouse on Tuesday, December 5, and jumped on the Hoosiers in the first half, grabbing a 10-5 lead. In the second half, the Hoosiers got a big boost from sophomore Vern Huffman, a former all-

The 1933-34 team. First row (left to right): Gilbert Carter, Gorrell [first name unknown], Lester Stout, Wendel Walker, Fred Fechtman, Vern Huffman, Robert Porter, Woodrow Weir; Second row: manager Marshall Hubbard, Keith Campbell, Willard Kehrt, Halary Sawicki, coach Everett Dean, William Coulter, Charles Scott, Joe Gansinger, Floyd Henry, trainer Jesse Ferguson. IU Archives

state guard who led Newcastle to the 1932 state championship. Huffman, playing center, scored eight points early in the second session to get IU back in the game, and the Hoosiers went on to a 20-16 victory. On Saturday, December 9, the Hoosiers again fell behind in the first half. This time the opponent was DePauw, who led 15-10 at the break. However, the Hoosier defense stifled the Tigers in the second half, holding them without a field goal, as IU ran to a 24-16 victory.

IU's first-half woes continued when the Hoosiers played at Wabash on Saturday, December 16, and fell behind 11-2 at the intermission. Despite a second-half push that put IU into the lead at 15-14, the Little Giants were able to win 26-22. Next, Indiana traveled to play the St. Louis Billikens. The Hoosiers used a big second-half run to crush the Billikens 47-32. Woodrow Weir had a game-high 12 points for the Hoosiers, and William Coulter chipped in 11.

At the end of their holiday break, the Hoosiers made an east coast swing and swept three games from quality opponents. The first was against Marshall on December 28, in Huntington, West Virginia, where IU won 36-20, behind 12 points from Coulter. On December 30, IU trekked over to College Park,

Maryland, and steamrolled the Maryland Terrapins 30-17. IU forward Williard Kehrt was the game's top scorer with 11. Weir added 10. Indiana closed the trip with a dominating 43-29 win over Temple in Philadelphia on New Year's Day. Weir was sensational with 15 points, and Huffman nearly matched him with 13.

At 6-1, the Hoosiers were hitting on all cylinders and looked prepared to make a serious run in the Big Ten. Those expectations were only heightened when IU blasted its first two opponents, Michigan and Ohio State. The Wolverines came to Bloomington on Saturday, January 6, and got run out of the building by the score of 29-18, as Kehrt scored a game-high 13. Ohio State came to town on January 8, and was accorded similar treatment in a 38-22 vanquishment. Eight different Hoosiers scored in that game, led by eight apiece from Kehrt and Huffman.

That set up a showdown with Coach Piggy Lambert's Purdue Boilermakers on Saturday, January 13, in Bloomington. Both the Hoosiers and the Boilers were riding six-game winning streaks. Both were 8-1 on the season and 2-0 in Big Ten play. Both were contenders for the conference crown. The game

1933-34 TEAM ROSTER

Head coach: Everett Dean
Assistant coach: Paul Harrell

No.	Player	Hometown	Class	Position	Height
	Keith Campbell	Logansport, IN	Jr	G	5-10
	Gilbert Carter	Indianapolis, IN		G	5-8
	William Coulter	Paoli, IN	Jr	C	6-3
14	Fred Fechtman	Indianapolis, IN	So	C	6-8
	Joe Gansinger	East Chicago, IN		F	6-0
	Floyd Henry	Kendalville, IN	Jr	F	5-10
5	Vern Huffman	New Castle, IN	So	C	6-2
	Willard Kehrt	Shelbyville, IN	Jr	F	5-11
	Robert Porter	Logansport, IN	Jr	G	6-1
	Halary Sawicki	Georgetown, IL	Sr (5th)	C	6-3
11	Charles Scott	Jeffersonville, IN	So	G	6-2
7	Lester Stout	Winimac, IN	So	F	5-9
4	Wendel Walker	Vincennes, IN	So	G	5-11
18	Woodrow Weir (Capt.)	Scottsburg, IN	Sr	F	5-10

SEASON RESULTS 1933-34

Date	Court	Opponent	Result	Score
12/5/1933	H	Franklin	W	20-16
12/9/1933	H	DePauw	W	24-16
12/16/1933	A	Wabash	L	22-26
12/19/1933	A	St. Louis	W	47-32
12/28/1933	A	Marshall	W	36-20
12/30/1933	A	Maryland	W	30-17
1/1/1934	A	Temple	W	43-29
1/6/1934	H	Michigan	W	29-18
1/8/1934	H	Ohio State	W	38-22
1/13/1934	H	Purdue	L	13-47
1/15/1934	A	Ohio State	L	23-27
1/31/1934	H	Wabash	W	32-28
2/5/1934	H	Iowa	W	34-25
2/10/1934	A	Illinois	L	25-28
2/17/1934	A	Chicago	W	30-28
2/19/1934	A	Iowa	L	26-29
2/24/1934	H	Illinois	W	36-24
2/26/1934	H	Chicago	W	39-30
3/3/1934	A	Purdue	L	28-55
3/5/1934	A	Michigan	L	32-35

1931-32 BIG TEN STANDINGS

	W	L	PCT
Purdue	10	2	.833
Wisconsin	8	4	.667
Northwestern	8	4	.667
Illinois	7	5	.583
Iowa	6	6	.500
Indiana	6	6	.500
Minnesota	5	7	.417
Ohio State	4	8	.333
Michigan	4	8	.333
Chicago	2	10	.167

was expected to be another classic grudge match between these two archrivals. The slight edge was given to the Hoosiers on their home court, which was being outfitted with extra seats for all the enthusiastic spectators. No one predicted the massacre that would ensue. Purdue blind-sided Indiana in the first half with its clockwork offense and rang up a 22-5 lead at the break. The game was all but over, although Purdue kept the freight train rolling in the second half, and the final score was a jaw-dropping 47-13.

Two nights later, the Hoosiers—still reeling from the demoralizing Purdue defeat—dropped a 27-23 verdict to an Ohio State team that it had thoroughly dominated just a week earlier. Fortunately, with the end of the first semester, the Hoosiers had a couple weeks off to regroup. They responded on Wednesday, January 31, with a 32-28 win over Wabash in the Fieldhouse. On February 5, IU got back in the win column in Big Ten play with a 34-25 win over Iowa in which the Hoosiers led nearly wire to wire. Huffman was the game's high scorer with 13 points. The win renewed IU's hopes of a strong finish in the Big Ten, but those hopes were deflated on February 10, when IU lost a nail-biter at Illinois, 28-25, dropping Indiana to 4-3 in conference play.

On Saturday, February 17, the Hoosiers traveled to Chicago and stalled down the stretch to nab a 30-28 win over the Maroons. Next, the Hoosiers went to Iowa City on February 19 and came up just short against the Hawkeyes who pulled out a 29-26 victory.

The Hoosiers returned to Bloomington for their final two-game homestand of the season. They easily defeated Illinois 36-24 on February 24, and breezed by Chicago 39-30 on February 26. Huffman was the top scorer against the Fighting Illini with 12 points, and Weir had a game-high 14 against the Maroons in the final home game of the season.

On March 3, Indiana went to West Lafayette with thoughts of avenging the Boilermakers' earlier win in Bloomington. However, the Hoosiers ended up in another blowout. Purdue led by 11 after a slow first half, but the Boilermakers scored 34 second-half points to trounce the Hoosiers 55-28. Two days later, IU closed out its season by letting a close win slip away down the stretch to the Michigan Wolverines in Ann Arbor. IU's 5'9" forward Lester Stout was the top scorer with 15 points in the 35-32 loss.

At 13-7 overall, the Hoosiers had put up a good mark for the season. Their 6-6 record in the Big Ten was a bit disappointing because it could have been much better if they hadn't let several close games out of their grasp in the final minutes. However, the team played the kind of basketball that Coach Dean was looking for, and with a lineup dominated by sophomores and juniors, the prospects of continuing that level of play were very good.

1934-35

OVERALL RECORD: 14-6

CONFERENCE RECORD: 8-4 (FOURTH PLACE)

With seven returning letterman from a team that had competed well the previous season, the 1934-35 Hoosiers were once again talking about the prospects of a Big Ten championship. The one setback the team had to deal with before the season began, was the loss of Vern Huffman, who suffered a serious injury in football and ended up missing the entire year (he would return the next season with two years of eligibility remaining). As a sophomore, Huffman had been the starting center all season and had anchored the IU offense. Huffman's replacement ended up being 6'8" junior Fred Fechtman, who had never played organized basketball before coming to Indiana. Surprisingly, the lengthy Fechtman (the tallest player in IU history up until that time) turned in a solid performance in the middle, and the Hoosiers, who were solid at all of the other positions, put together their best conference run in seven years.

To open the season, Fechtman scored a game-high 11 points on Friday, December 7, in IU's 35-19 home win over Ball State, which was coached by former IU All-American Branch McCracken. The Hoosiers had a tougher time with Hamline University on December 12. IU forward and team captain Willard Kehrt buried a long field goal just before the final gun sounded to deliver a 31-29 victory over the determined Pipers. IU was led by 10 points from

1934-35 TEAM ROSTER

Head coach: Everett Dean

No.	Player	Hometown	Class	Position	Height
	William Baise	Seymour, IN		G	5-10
	Louis Boink	Evansville, IN	So	F	6-0
	George Braman	South Bend, IN	So	G	6-0
	William Coulter	Paoli, IN	Sr	C	6-3
9	Bob Etnire	Logansport, IN	So	G	5-11
14	Fred Fechtman	Indianapolis, IN	Jr	C	6-8
	Russell Grieger	Wanatah, IN		F	6-0
3	Ken Gunning	Shelbyville, IN	So	G/F	5-11
	Floyd Henry	Kendalville, IN	Sr	F	5-10
10	Willis Hosler	Huntington, IN	So	C	6-3
	Willard Kehrt (Capt.)	Shelbyville, IN	Sr	F	5-11
	Robert Porter (Capt.)	Logansport, IN	Sr	G	6-1
11	Charles Scott	Jeffersonville, IN	Jr	G	6-2
7	Lester Stout	Winimac, IN	Jr	F	5-9
	William Stout	Bloomington, IN		F	6-1
4	Wendel Walker	Vincennes, IN	Jr	G	5-11

SEASON RESULTS 1934-35

Date	Court	Opponent	Result	Score
12/7/1934	H	Ball State	W	35-19
12/12/1934	H	Hamline	W	31-29
12/15/1934	H	DePauw	L	24-31
12/20/1934	A	Maryland	W	30-25
12/21/1934	A	George Washington	W	45-41
12/22/1934	A	Temple	L	30-50
1/1/1935	A	Miami (OH)	W	32-15
1/5/1935	A	Illinois	W	32-28
1/12/1935	H	Wisconsin	L	23-30
1/14/1935	H	Illinois	W	42-29
1/19/1935	A	Iowa	W	40-35
2/4/1935	A	Vanderbilt	W	39-30
2/9/1935	H	Minnesota	W	48-23
2/11/1935	H	Iowa	W	34-30
2/16/1935	A	Wisconsin	L	27-37
2/18/1935	A	Purdue	L	38-44
2/23/1935	H	Northwestern	L	36-32
2/25/1935	H	Purdue	W	41-35
3/2/1935	A	Northwestern	L	22-40
3/9/1935	A	Minnesota	W	38-29

1934-35 BIG TEN STANDINGS

	W	L	PCT
Purdue	9	3	.750
Illinois	9	3	.750
Wisconsin	9	3	.750
Indiana	8	4	.667
Ohio State	8	4	.667
Iowa	6	6	.500
Minnesota	5	7	.417
Northwestern	3	9	.250
Michigan	2	10	.167
Chicago	1	11	.083

The 1934-35 team. First row (left to right): Robert Porter, Lester Stout, Willard Kehrt, Fred Fechtman, Wendel Walker, Ken Gunning, Charles Scott, Bob Etnire; Second row: coach Everett Dean, Russell Grieger, George Braman, Willis Hosler, manager Charles Schaab, William Stout, Louis Boink, William Baise, trainer Jesse Ferguson. IU Archives

Lester Stout. The Hoosiers suffered their first setback on Saturday, December 15, when DePauw came to town and used a balanced scoring attack to hand IU a 31-24 defeat. Fechtman scored 11 points to lead all scorers.

The Hoosiers once again made an east coast road trip during their winter vacation. On December 20, IU beat Maryland 30-25, after falling behind by two points at the half. Kehrt scored a game-high 11 points and Stout added 10. The next night, Indiana used another second-half surge to defeat the George Washington Colonials 45-41 with a team-high 13 points from Fechtman. The Hoosiers' third stop was on Saturday, December 23, in Philadelphia, where the Temple Owls outscored IU 31-15 in the second half to garner a 50-30 victory. Sophomore guard Ken Gunning scored 18 points for Indiana to lead all scorers. The IU squad returned to Bloomington and finished out its preconference schedule on Tuesday, January 1, by pummeling Miami of Ohio 32-15. Gunning scored 10 and Fechtman added nine.

On Saturday, January 5, Indiana opened the Big Ten season on the road against Illinois and brought

home a 32-28 win. Fechtman led the Hoosiers with 10 points, although he was outscored and often out-maneuvered by Illinois's crafty 6'4" center Bob Riegel. On Saturday, January 12, Indiana played Wisconsin in Bloomington, and the Badgers surprised the Hoosiers by dominating most of the game and walking away with a 30-23 win. On January 14, the Fighting Illini came to Bloomington for a rematch, but forwards Kehrt and Stout combined for 27 points as IU routed Illinois 42-29.

Kehrt and Stout were on target again on January 19, in Iowa City. The duo rang up 20 points (10 apiece) as Indiana came back from a nine-point halftime deficit to beat Iowa 40-35. Prior to the loss, the Hawkeyes were the only undefeated team left in the Big Ten, and the game was played in front of a crowd of 12,000 (which was huge for that era).

After the semester break, Indiana went to Nashville, Tennessee, on February 4, and used a second-half comeback to beat Vanderbilt 39-30, as Gunning scored 13. Next, Minnesota came to Bloomington on Saturday, February 9, and got annihilated 48-23, as Gunning scored 14 and Stout added

10. Iowa was the next Bloomington visitor on Monday, February 11. The Hawkeyes jumped out to a 15-14 halftime lead, but IU prevailed 34-30, improving its Big Ten record to 5-1. The Hoosiers were tied with Purdue for first place at the halfway mark of the Big Ten schedule, but IU would play four of its final six conference games on the road.

The first was on Saturday, February 16, when the Wisconsin Badgers beat the Hoosiers for the second time with a 37-27 overtime win in Madison. IU scored nine straight points at the end of regulation to tie the game at 27 but ran out of gas in OT. Indiana dropped another game on Monday, February 18, in West Lafayette as Purdue's Robert Kessler shot down the Hoosiers with 23 points in a 44-38 Purdue win. Stout led Indiana with 14 points.

IU got back in the win column on Saturday, February 23, with a 36-32 win over Northwestern in Bloomington. Then the Hoosiers took revenge on Purdue on Monday, February 25, in Bloomington, with a 41-35 triumph in a game that the Hoosiers controlled from beginning to end. Kehrt and Fechtman topped IU with 12 points each, while Gunning added 11.

Indiana still had an outside shot at the conference title, but those hopes were dashed on Saturday, March 2, in Evanston, Illinois, when the hot-shooting Northwestern Wildcats downed the Hoosiers 40-22. A week later, IU was able to finish its season on an upswing by defeating the Minnesota Golden Gophers 38-29 in the Minnesota Fieldhouse. Kehrt had a game-high 11 points and Gunning added 10.

At 8-4, IU finished the season only one game behind the conference co-leaders Purdue, Illinois and Wisconsin, and the Hoosiers' 14-6 overall record was only one game away from tying the school record for wins in a season. However, with Huffman returning the following season, the Hoosiers' success in the 1934-35 campaign was merely an appetizer for a much more successful season the next year.

1935-36

OVERALL RECORD: 18-2

CONFERENCE RECORD: 11-1 (FIRST PLACE)

TEAM HONORS:

BIG TEN CO-CHAMPION

INDIVIDUAL HONORS:

VERN HUFFMAN—ALL-AMERICA,

ALL-BIG TEN (FIRST TEAM)

Entering the 1935-36 season, just about everyone around the Big Ten knew that the IU basketball squad was going to be good. IU returned four starters and seven lettermen. Plus, Vern Huffman, who lettered in 1933-34 and was the team's third leading scorer that season as a sophomore, returned to the team after missing a year because of a football injury. However, even coach Everett Dean and his Hoosiers didn't realize just how good they were going to be until the season really got rolling.

Leading the returnees was 5'11" junior Ken Gunning, who topped the Hoosiers in scoring at 8.4 PPG as a sophomore. In addition to his scoring prowess, Gunning was IU's fastest player and was an excellent ball handler and passer. After playing mostly guard as a sophomore, Coach Dean moved Gunning to forward to give him even more scoring opportunities for the 1935-36 season. Another big asset for the Hoosiers was the return of 6'8" center Fred Fechtman, who was affectionately known as "Reach" to his teammates. Fechtman had shown great improvement during his career and had become a valuable scorer inside, as well as an intimidator on defense. Co-captains Lester Stout and Wendel Walker were also expected to be important contributors. Stout was a scrappy, aggressive little guy who could shoot the ball and was a pest on defense. Walker, who was also a football player, was rugged and aggressive. He was best on defense, but his strength also enabled him to shoot the long ball.

For the second year in a row, IU kicked off its campaign with a game against Ball State in Bloomington. The Hoosiers routed the Cardinals 44-28 on Friday, December 6, in a sloppy game that showed both teams still needed a lot of work. IU cen-

The 1935-36 team. First row (left to right): coach Everett Dean, Bob Etnire, Willis Hosler, Charles Scott, Wendel Walker, Fred Fechtman, Lester Stout, Ken Gunning, Vern Huffman, athletic director Zora Clevenger; Second row: Charles Campbell, Willie Silberstein, John Hobson, Joseph Platt, George Ditrich, Roger Ratliff, Charles Mendel, McNaughton [last name unknown], James Birr, Phil Liehr, Carlos Brooks, William Anderson, manager DeGrey Bishop, trainer Jesse Ferguson. IU Archives

ter Fred Fechtman was the game's high scorer with 17. Indiana went on the road for the first time on Saturday, December 14, and defeated Loyola Chicago 32-25 on the strength of 14 points from Ken Gunning, who also held Loyola's leading scorer to four points. Two nights later, Indiana clobbered Miami of Ohio 41-15 in Bloomington as seven different Hoosiers scored.

After coming off the bench for the first three games, Vern Huffman regained a spot in the starting lineup against Vanderbilt on Saturday, December 21. The 6'2" Huffman, who played center during the 1933-34 season, now moved to guard where his team-first attitude, defensive skills, ball handling and passing proved to be huge assets for IU. The Hoosiers dominated the Commodores in Nashville en route to a 56-18 blowout win. On their way back to Bloomington, the Hoosiers stopped in southern Indiana to play Evansville on Monday, December 23, and defeated the Purple Aces 39-32. Fechtman had a game-high 10 points. IU completed the preconference schedule by dropping its first game of the season in Chicago against DePaul. The Blue Demons pre-

vailed 35-31 in a nip-and-tuck contest that wasn't decided until the final minute.

Indiana opened Big Ten play at Michigan on Monday, January 6, by outscoring the Wolverines 33-27 behind a game-high 10 points from Huffman. Then Northwestern came to Bloomington on Saturday, January 11. The Wildcats opened up a 15-13 lead at the half, but IU came back to edge the visitors 27-24 with the help of a six-minute stall down the stretch. Next, IU took out Chicago 33-30 at the IU Fieldhouse on January 13, as Gunning dropped in 19 points on the Maroons.

On January 18-20, Indiana made the tough northern trek for a pair of road games against Minnesota and Wisconsin over the short span of 72 hours and came back with a pair of two-point victories. The first was against the Golden Gophers on January 18, where Indiana used its stingy defense and stalling tactics in the final four minutes to earn a 33-31 win. On January 20, IU led the Wisconsin Badgers 15-9 at the half and then came back to win 26-24 after the Badgers had pulled ahead 23-22 late in the second half. The clutch free throw shooting of Joe

1935-36 TEAM ROSTER

Head coach: Everett Dean
Assistant coach: Ralph Graham

No.	Player	Hometown	Class	Position	Height
	William Anderson	Marion, IN	So	G	5-10
	James Birr	Indianapolis, IN	So	C/G	6-3
16	Carlos Brooks	Mays, IN	So	G	6-0
	Charles Campbell	Shelbyville, IN	So	G	5-3
	George Ditrich	Bloomington, IN	So	C	6-2
9	Bob Etnire	Logansport, IN	Jr	G	5-11
14	Fred Fechtman	Indianapolis, IN	Jr	C	6-8
3	Ken Gunning	Shelbyville, IN	Jr	F	5-11
15	John Hobson	Indianapolis, IN	So	F	5-10
10	Willis Hosler	Huntington, IN	Jr	C	6-3
5	Vern Huffman	New Castle, IN	Jr	G	6-2
12	Phil Liehr	Indianapolis, IN	So	C	6-3
15	Charles Mendel	Bourbon, IN	So	G/F	6-3
8	Joseph Platt	Young American, IN	So	G	5-11
17	Roger Ratliff	Mooresville, IN	So	G	6-3
11	Charles Scott	Jeffersonville, IN	Sr	G	6-2
13	Willie Silberstein	Brooklyn, NY	So	F	5-8
7	Lester Stout (Capt.)	Winimac, IN	Sr	F	5-9
4	Wendel Walker (Capt.)	Vincennes, IN	Sr	G	5-11

SEASON RESULTS 1935-36

Date	Court	Opponent	Result	Score
12/6/1935	H	Ball State	W	44-28
12/14/1935	A	Loyola Chicago	W	32-25
12/16/1935	H	Miami (OH)	W	41-15
12/21/1935	A	Vanderbilt	W	56-18
12/23/1935	A	Evansville	W	39-32
1/3/1936	A	DePaul	L	31-35
1/6/1936	A	Michigan	W	33-27
1/11/1936	H	Northwestern	W	27-24
1/13/1936	H	Chicago	W	33-30
1/18/1936	A	Minnesota	W	33-31
1/20/1936	A	Wisconsin	W	26-24
1/31/1936	A	Louisville	W	48-26
2/3/1936	H	Minnesota	W	26-23
2/8/1936	A	Chicago	W	42-24
2/10/1936	H	Franklin	W	39-29
2/15/1936	A	Ohio State	L	34-43
2/22/1936	H	Wisconsin	W	54-21
2/29/1936	A	Northwestern	W	41-34
3/2/1936	H	Ohio State	W	40-34

1935-36 BIG TEN STANDINGS

	W	L	PCT
Indiana	11	1	.917
Purdue	11	1	.917
Michigan	7	5	.583
Illinois	7	5	.583
Northwestern	7	5	.583
Ohio State	5	7	.417
Iowa	5	7	.417
Wisconsin	4	8	.333
Minnesota	3	9	.250
Chicago	0	12	.000

Platt sealed the game for IU down the stretch and improved the Hoosiers to 5-0 in Big Ten play.

IU played a nonconference game against Louisville in Kentucky on January 31 and trounced the Cardinals 48-26. Nine different players scored for Indiana. The Hoosiers got back to Big Ten action on February 3, when Minnesota came to Bloomington and suffered a 26-23 loss to the Hoosiers. On Saturday, February 8, IU went to the Windy City and blasted the Chicago Maroons 42-24, as Gunning scored 15 and Huffman hit for 12. The Hoosiers played one final nonconference game on Monday, February 10, against Franklin College in Bloomington. IU fell behind 15-13 at the half, but kicked into high gear in the second half and easily won a 39-29 victory.

Ohio State finally handed Indiana its first conference loss on Saturday, February 15, in Columbus, Ohio. OSU jumped ahead early and the Hoosiers could never catch up in a 43-34 loss. IU brushed off the loss by using a big second-half run to smite Michigan 37-23 in Bloomington on Monday,

One of the toughest competitors and best athletes to ever wear the cream and crimson, Vern Huffman was the epitome of a team player and a floor leader. After missing the 1934-35 season because of a football injury, Huffman was an All-Big Ten and All-America performer in 1935-36 while leading IU to a stellar 18-2 record and a conference title. IU Archives

February 17, as Gunning and Huffman each scored 11 points. Next, the Hoosiers leveled the Wisconsin Badgers 54-22 on Saturday, February 22. Gunning had a game-high 17 points and Fechtman scored 13.

A week later, Indiana cruised to another easy win. This time, the victim was Northwestern, who was conquered 41-34 in Evanston on February 29. Gunning continued to have the hot hand with a game-high 19 points. Indiana closed out its season on Monday, March 2, with a 40-34 triumph over the Ohio State Buckeyes in Bloomington. Huffman led IU with 10 points.

The OSU win, which avenged IU's only conference defeat, put the Hoosiers' record at 11-1 in the Big Ten and clinched a tie with Purdue for the conference championship. Because of the Big Ten's round-robin scheduling, Indiana and Purdue never met on the court that season. Overall, Purdue went 16-4, while the Hoosiers were 18-2, the best mark in school history. For his leadership and outstanding team play, Vern Huffman earned All-America honors.

These Hoosiers set the school record for overall wins, conference wins, and winning percentage—both overall and in the conference. While those records would eventually be broken, the 1935-36 season remains the greatest season of coach Everett Dean's championship-building tenure.

1936-37

OVERALL RECORD: 13-7

CONFERENCE RECORD: 6-6 (SIXTH PLACE)

INDIVIDUAL HONORS:

KEN GUNNING—ALL-AMERICA

VERN HUFFMAN—BIG TEN MEDAL OF HONOR

Co-captains Ken Gunning and Vern Huffman headlined a group of seven returning letterman from a 1935-36 team that had lifted Indiana basketball to new heights. After losing only two seniors from that 18-2 squad, the Hoosiers' 1936-37 team was expected to be just as potent. However, while IU remained one of the favorites in the Big Ten race, the Hoosiers drew one of the tough-est conference schedules and were forced to match up almost exclusively with other title contenders in a year when the Big Ten was stacked with excellent teams. As a result, Indiana played very well in its preconference schedule but suffered through an up-and-down conference season and slipped back to the middle of the pack in the Big Ten.

When IU opened the season on Friday, December 4, against Cincinnati in Bloomington, the Hoosiers looked very similar to the team that had steamrolled opponents the year before. Indiana jumped to a 28-3 halftime lead and held the Bearcats without a field goal in the first half, eventually cruising to a 46-13 win. Huffman was the star of the game, even though he scored only three points. The tenacious guard played the role of stopper on defense and used his deft passing to repeatedly set up teammates on offense.

On Saturday, December 12, Miami of Ohio came to Bloomington, and the Hoosiers led the Redhawks 20-5 at the half and eventually triumphed 43-13. Senior Bob Etnire led the Hoosiers with 13 points, and sophomore Ernie Andres chipped in 10. IU kept rolling on December 14 against Kansas State at the IU Fieldhouse. After leading the Wildcats by only two points at the intermission, Indiana went wild in the second half and walked away with a 60-33 win. Sophomore William Johnson had a game-high 19 points and Huffman added 12.

Indiana made its annual eastern swing over the holiday break and snagged two more wins. The Hoosiers went to New York City on Saturday, December 19, and beat Manhattan College 42-34 in front of 11,000 New York basketball fans. After leading 27-11 at the half, IU had to rebuff a determined second-half rally from the Jaspers. Gunning led IU with 12 points. Two days later, Indiana went down to Philadelphia and pulled out a 43-28 win from Villanova on the strength of a 25-12 advantage in the second half. Back in Indianapolis on Friday, January 1, IU closed out the preconference slate with a 61-27 trouncing of Butler, as Gunning led all scorers with 15 points and Huffman and Andres added 10 each. The Butler win put Indiana at 6-0 and looking dominant as the team prepared to begin Big Ten play.

Gunning shot down the Iowa Hawkeyes with 14 points on Monday, January 4, in Bloomington as the Hoosiers opened the conference schedule with a 28-

The 1936-37 team. First row (left to right): trainer Jesse Ferguson, Bob Etnire, Willis Hosler, Fred Fechtman, Vern Huffman, Ken Gunning, Joseph Platt, Willie Silberstein, coach Everett Dean; Second row: Lymann Abbot, William Squier, Raymond Guard, William Johnson, Charles Mendel, Roger Ratliff, James Birr, James Menefee, Ernie Andres, Ralph Dorsey, manager Henry Decker. IU Archives

24 victory. IU stalled down the stretch to stymie an Iowa comeback, and Gunning buried a shot in the final seconds to secure the win. On Saturday, January 9, the Hoosiers notched their eighth consecutive win by blasting the Chicago Maroons 46-26 in Chicago. Gunning once again was the top scorer with 13 points.

IU stumbled for the first time on January 11, when Illinois used its fast-paced attack to surprise and overwhelm the Hoosiers 40-31 in Champaign. Next, an undefeated Purdue squad came to Bloomington on Saturday, January 16, and outplayed the Hoosiers from beginning to end in front of a capacity crowd in the Fieldhouse, which had been sold out for weeks in anticipation of a classic battle. The Boilermakers prevailed 41-30.

On Monday, January 18, the Hoosiers bounced back and dealt Ohio State its first Big Ten loss in a 43-36 IU win in Bloomington. Johnson led Indiana with 13 points and Fred Fechtman chipped in 10. The IU win, coupled with a Purdue loss against Illinois, gave the Hoosiers renewed hopes of competing for the conference crown. Before continuing Big Ten play, the Hoosiers faced another undefeated team on January 30, when they traveled to the Windy City to take on Loyola Chicago, which blitzed Indiana 18-2

to start the game. The Hoosiers showed some heart by fighting back, but still fell 36-30. Two days later, IU defeated Ball State 31-22 in Muncie as five different Hoosiers scored five points or more.

Big Ten play resumed for the Hoosiers on Saturday, February 6, when they went to Iowa City and snatched a four-point win from the Iowa Hawkeyes by the count of 38-34. Johnson led all scorers with 13 points as the Hoosiers played for the first time without center Fred Fechtman, who graduated at the end of the first semester. On Monday, February 8, IU grabbed another victory when Chicago came to the Fieldhouse and got outclassed 47-36, as Huffman scored 13 and Gunning added 11.

At 5-2 in conference play, Indiana was still in the thick of the Big Ten race. However, the Hoosiers had to play three of their next four games on the road. As it turned out, all four of the games would prove disastrous as Indiana lost in succession to Ohio State in Columbus (48-44), Michigan in Ann Arbor (55-31), Illinois at the IU Fieldhouse (42-25), and Purdue in West Lafayette (69-45).

In the final game of the season, the Hoosiers brought their conference record back to .500 with a 31-27 win over Michigan in Bloomington, as Etnire and Johnson scored 10 points apiece. Nevertheless,

Shooting ace Ken Gunning led the Hoosiers in scoring during each of his three seasons in Bloomington and closed out his career by taking home All-America honors as a senior. IU Archives

1936-37 TEAM ROSTER

Head coach: Everett Dean
Assistant coach: Ralph Graham

No.	Player	Hometown	Class	Position	Height
20	Lymann Abbot	Martinsville, IN	So	G	5-9
16	Ernie Andres	Jeffersonville, IN	So	G	6-1
12	James Birr	Indianapolis, IN	Jr	C	6-3
11	Ralph Dorsey	Horse Cave, KY	So	F	6-0
9	Bob Etnire	Logansport, IN	Sr	G/F	5-11
14	Fred Fechtman	Indianapolis, IN	Sr (5th)	C	6-8
8	Raymond Guard	Chalmers, IN	So	G	6-1
3	Ken Gunning (Capt.)	Shelbyville, IN	Sr	F	5-11
10	Willis Hosler	Huntington, IN	Sr	C	6-3
5	Vern Huffman (Capt.)	New Castle, IN	Sr	G	6-2
4	William Johnson	Jeffersonville, IN	So	F	6-0
15	Charles Mendel	Bourbon, IN	Jr	G	6-3
	James Menefee	Fort Wayne, IN	So	C	6-3
8	Joseph Platt	Young American, IN	Jr	G	5-11
6	Roger Ratliff	Mooresville, IN	Jr	C/G	6-3
17	Willie Silberstein	Brooklyn, NY	Jr	F	5-8
13	William Squier	Richmond, IN	So	F	6-0
	Richard White	Lebanon, IN	So	F	6-0

SEASON RESULTS 1936-37

Date	Court	Opponent	Result	Score
12/4/1936	H	Cincinnati	W	46-13
12/12/1936	H	Miami (OH)	W	43-13
12/14/1936	H	Kansas State	W	60-33
12/19/1936	A	Manhattan	W	42-34
12/21/1936	A	Villanova	W	43-28
1/1/1937	A	Butler	W	61-27
1/4/1937	H	Iowa	W	28-24
1/9/1937	A	Chicago	W	46-26
1/11/1937	A	Illinois	L	31-40
1/16/1937	H	Purdue	L	30-41
1/18/1937	H	Ohio State	W	43-36
1/30/1937	A	Loyola Chicago	L	30-36
2/1/1937	A	Ball State	W	31-22
2/6/1937	A	Iowa	W	38-34
2/8/1937	H	Chicago	W	47-36
2/13/1937	A	Ohio State	L	44-48
2/15/1937	A	Michigan	L	31-55
2/20/1937	H	Illinois	L	25-42
2/27/1937	A	Purdue	L	45-69
3/1/1937	H	Michigan	W	31-27

1936-37 BIG TEN STANDINGS

	W	L	PCT
Minnesota	10	2	.833
Illinois	10	2	.833
Michigan	9	3	.750
Purdue	8	4	.667
Ohio State	7	5	.583
Indiana	6	6	.500
Northwestern	4	8	.333
Iowa	3	9	.250
Wisconsin	3	9	.250
Chicago	0	12	.000

the four-game losing streak down the stretch of the Big Ten season had devastated the Hoosiers' prospects for a championship season. Dropping to a sixth-place finish in the Big Ten with such a talented team was disappointing for the Hoosiers and their fans. Plus, Indiana was looking at a rebuilding year the following season since many of its key veterans would not be returning.

For the 1936-37 season, Ken Gunning ended up earning All-America honors for his outstanding play, while Vern Huffman was awarded a Big Ten Medal of Honor given to outstanding athletes who also excel in the classroom. Huffman, who was also an All-American football player at IU, went on to complete a law degree and played a couple seasons for the Detroit Lions in the NFL.

1937-38

OVERALL RECORD: 10-10
CONFERENCE RECORD: 4-8 (EIGHTH PLACE)
INDIVIDUAL HONORS:
ERNIE ANDRES—ALL-BIG TEN (FIRST TEAM);
ALL-AMERICA

Without the return of its top scorer (Ken Gunning), its top playmaker and best defensive player (Vern Huffman), and its top pivotman (Fred Fechtman), IU embarked on the 1937-38 campaign with a lot of question marks and little optimism about the team's prospects. The young squad definitely struggled at times, and its inexperience became especially evident in close games in the Big Ten. However, junior guard Ernie Andres blossomed into one of the conference's biggest stars, and the Hoosiers developed several other talented young players such as Marv Huffman and Jay McCreary, who would lead the team to new heights in the ensuing years.

DePauw came to Bloomington on Monday, December 6, and the Tigers played the role of easy prey as the Hoosiers devoured them for an easy 45-25 victory to open the season, Andres leading IU with 10 points. On Saturday, December 11, coach Everett Dean's Hoosiers traveled to Muncie to take on coach Branch McCracken's Ball State Cardinals. The student surpassed the mentor for the first time in four tries as the Cardinals made all the right moves down the stretch to defeat the Hoosiers 42-38 (which remains the only time Ball State has ever defeated Indiana in the 17-game history of the series).

A formidable Bradley team served up another nonconference defeat to the Hoosiers on Thursday, December 21, in Peoria, Illinois. The Braves used a 26-14 run in the second half to nab a 50-39 win. On Thursday, December 23, Indiana traveled to Nebraska and won a 43-42 contest from the Cornhuskers on a free throw from Andres in the final seconds. Andres and senior guard Joe Platt scored 10 points each to lead IU.

Next, instead of making their annual east coast swing during their holiday break, the Hoosiers trav-

1937-38 TEAM ROSTER

Head coach: Everett Dean
Assistant coach: Ralph Graham

No.	Player	Hometown	Class	Position	Height
20	Lyman Abbot	Martinsville, IN	Jr	G	5-9
5	Ernie Andres	Jeffersonville, IN	Jr	G	6-1
6	James Birr	Indianapolis, IN	Sr	C	6-3
10	David Bowman	Veedersburg, IN	So	G	6-1
3	Ralph Dorsey	Horse Cave, KY	Jr	F	5-9
11	James Fausch	Michigan City, IN	So	F	6-2
19	Dale Gentil	Mount Vernon, IN	So	F	6-2
15	Peter Grant	Indianapolis, IN	So	F	6-2
8	Marv Huffman	New Castle, IN	So	G	6-2
4	William Johnson	Jeffersonville, IN	Jr	G	6-0
12	Jay McCreary	Frankfort, IN	So	G	5-10
13	Jim Ooley	Spencer, IN	So	G	6-2
18	Ed Page	Shelbyville, IN	So	G	6-0
7	Joseph Platt	Young American, IN	Sr	G	5-11
17	Roger Ratliff	Mooresville, IN	Sr	C/G	6-3
16	Greg Ricke	Shelbyville, IN	So	G	5-11
9	Jack Stevenson	Indianapolis, IN	So	F	6-1

SEASON RESULTS 1937-38

Date	Court	Opponent	Result	Score
12/6/1937	H	DePauw	W	45-25
12/11/1937	A	Ball State	L	38-42
12/21/1937	A	Bradley	L	39-50
12/23/1937	A	Nebraska	W	43-42
12/28/1937	A	UCLA	W	42-33
12/29/1937	A	USC	W	42-39
1/4/1938	H	Illinois	W	51-46
1/8/1938	A	Iowa	L	38-48
1/10/1938	A	Minnesota	W	39-38
1/15/1938	H	Northwestern	L	29-32
1/17/1938	H	Iowa	L	32-36
2/1/1938	A	Butler	W	42-23
2/5/1938	A	Purdue	L	36-28
2/7/1938	H	Wisconsin	W	47-44
2/12/1938	N1	Louisville	W	59-40
2/19/1938	A	Northwestern	L	41-52
2/21/1938	H	Minnesota	L	36-37
2/26/1938	H	Purdue	L	36-50
2/28/1938	A	Wisconsin	L	32-34
3/4/1938	A	Illinois	W	45-35

1 Jeffersonville, IN

1937-38 BIG TEN STANDINGS

	W	L	PCT
Purdue	10	2	.883
Minnesota	9	3	.750
Ohio State	7	5	.583
Northwestern	7	5	.583
Michigan	6	6	.500
Iowa	6	6	.500
Wisconsin	5	7	.417
Indiana	4	8	.333
Illinois	4	8	.333
Chicago	2	10	.167

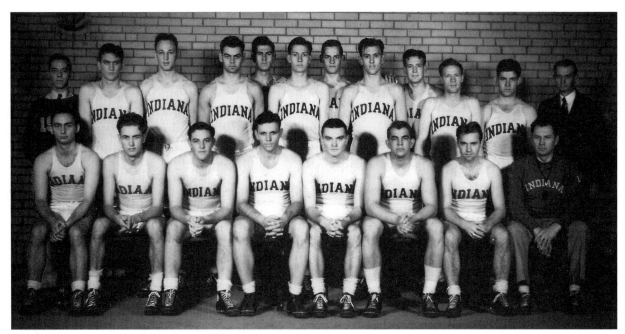

The 1937-38 team. Front row (left to right): Ralph Dorsey, Jack Stevenson, Ernie Andres, Roger Ratliff, Joseph Platt, James Birr, Lyman Abbot, coach Everett Dean; Second row: manager Sam Mitchell, Ed Page, James Fausch, Marv Huffman, Han [first name unknown], Dale Gentil, Peter Grant, Jim Ooley, David Bowman, Jay McCreary, Greg Ricke, trainer Jesse Ferguson. IU Archives

eled west to take on a couple California opponents in Los Angeles. On December 28, Indiana pounced on UCLA and won a 42-33 tussle behind a game-high 14 points from junior William Johnson and 13 points from Platt. The next night, IU faced a Southern California team that was made up almost entirely of Indiana high school basketball players. Andres, who scored a game-high 12 points, was too much for the Trojans in the final minutes as IU prevailed 42-39.

The Big Ten season tipped off for the Hoosiers with a high-scoring affair against Illinois on Tuesday, January 4, in Bloomington. Indiana got the best of the Fighting Illini in a 51-46 triumph in which Johnson and Andres tied for game-high honors with 18. On Saturday, January 8, IU went on the road and suffered a 48-39 loss to the Iowa Hawkeyes, who got 23 points from forward Benny Stephens. Sophomore guard Marv Huffman (the younger brother of Vern Huffman) led the Hoosiers with 13 points, while Andres added 12. The following Monday, Indiana journeyed north to Minnesota and jumped out to a five-point halftime lead, and then held on down the stretch for a 39-38 win. Andres scored a game-high 14 points and Huffman added 13.

Northwestern came to Bloomington on Saturday, January 15, and swiped a 32-29 win, even though Platt scored a game-high 13 points for the Hoosiers. Two days later, Iowa came to town and edged the Hoosiers 36-32. It was only Iowa's second conference win (both of them coming at IU's expense), and the loss dropped IU to 2-3 in the Big Ten. The Hoosiers tried to right the ship with the help of a 42-23 blowout win over Butler on February 1, in Bloomington.

IU used the momentum from the Butler game to go into West Lafayette on Saturday, February 5, and surprise the Purdue Boilermakers (the eventual conference champs). The Hoosiers jumped out to a 21-16 halftime advantage and continued to lead for much of the second half before Purdue mounted a furious rally in the final ten minutes of the game and tied the score at 36. Purdue's Pat Malaska then hit the game-winning field goal in the final seconds to deliver a two-point Boilermaker victory. After the Purdue game, the usually mild-mannered Dean let his frustration boil over. He went into the officials' locker room and upbraided referee John Getchell and umpire George Levis (who, coincidentally, had formerly coached Dean at IU) for their loose officiating that allowed Purdue to play their aggressive defense against the Hoosiers and get whistled for only six fouls in the entire game.

The following Monday, the Hoosiers went back to Bloomington and edged out the Wisconsin Badgers 47-44 on the strength of 14 points from Andres. Next, the Hoosiers played Louisville in Jeffersonville, Indiana, on Saturday, February 12, and ran up an easy 59-40 win. Johnson led all scorers with 16 points, and Andres scored 15. Both Johnson and Andres prepped at Jeffersonville High School, where the game was played.

Indiana resumed Big Ten play on February 19, when the team went to Northwestern and dropped a 52-41 contest despite 20 points from Andres. Things didn't get much better when IU returned to Bloomington and played Minnesota two nights later. The Golden Gophers triumphed 37-36, and the Hoosiers fell to 3-6 in conference play. Purdue came to town on Saturday, February 26, and pounded the Hoosiers 50-36 behind 19 points from their star forward, Jewell Young. The following Monday, Indiana traveled up to Wisconsin and gave the Badgers a serious battle, but lost 34-32 when Wisconsin guard Ernie Davis scored in the final minute. Andres scored 18 points for game-high honors.

Indiana closed out its season at Champaign, Illinois, on Friday, March 4. Andres scored a career-high 30 points to lead the Hoosiers to a convincing 45-35 win. His scoring explosion set the single-game scoring record at Indiana and in the Big Ten. What made Andres's performance even more remarkable was the fact that he was sick with a virus and stomach cramps that night. Andres may have had a cold, but he was undoubtedly hot when he was shooting the ball. According to team records, he hit 13 of 30 (43 percent) from the field—a good percentage for that era.

At 4-8 in conference play, the Hoosiers' eighth-place finish put them in the second division of the Big Ten for the second straight season. Little did the players know that it would be their final season under Dean at IU. He would resign in June to coach basketball and baseball at Stanford. However, the talent that Dean had assembled in his final years in Bloomington, combined with the enthusiasm and fast-paced game plan of a talented new coach, would lead to excellent results in the coming seasons.

SEASON STATISTICS
1924-25 TO 1937-38

1924-25

Team Statistics	G			TP	AVG
Indiana	17			542	31.9
Opponents	17			423	24.9
Player Statistics	G	FG	FT	TP	AVG
Logan	17	58	38	154	9.1
Krueger	17	53	31	137	8.1
Beckner	10	24	18	66	6.6
Sponsler	17	36	13	85	5.0
Bordner	5	8	1	17	3.4
Parker	10	10	10	30	3.0
Lorber	6	4	4	12	2.0
Replogle	5	3	4	10	2.0
Druckamiller	7	2	5	9	1.3
Winston	9	3	3	9	1.0
Harrison	5	1	2	4	0.8
Easton	3	1	0	2	0.7
Sibley	4	0	2	2	0.5
Alward	11	1	3	5	0.5
Nicholson	2	0	0	0	0.0
Benzel	1	0	0	0	0.0

1925-26

Team Statistics	G			TP	AVG
Indiana	17			553	32.5
Opponents	17			468	27.5
Player Statistics	G	FG	FT	TP	AVG
Beckner	17	58	33	149	8.8
Krueger	17	63	14	140	8.2
Sibley	17	37	26	100	5.9
Sponsler	17	37	19	93	5.5
Robinson	3	3	1	7	2.3
Farmer	2	2	0	4	2.0
Correll	7	4	3	11	1.6
Jones	9	6	2	14	1.6
Winston	17	5	14	24	1.4
Derr	6	2	4	8	1.3
McClintock	1	0	1	1	1.0
Easton	4	1	0	2	0.5
Druckamiller	1	0	0	0	0.0

1926-27

Team Statistics	G			TP	AVG
Indiana	17			568	33.4
Opponents	17			436	25.6
Player Statistics	G	FG	FT	TP	AVG
Beckner	16	51	28	130	8.1
Krueger	17	51	18	119	7.0
Correll	17	36	21	93	5.5
Sibley	17	32	21	87	5.1
Wells	17	19	14	52	3.3
Winston	8	8	10	26	2.8
Farmer	2	2	0	4	2.0
Derr	15	12	3	27	1.8
Anderson	5	3	2	8	1.6
Leonard	9	6	2	14	1.6
Starr	9	4	2	10	1.1
Scheid	2	0	0	0	0.0
Benzel	1	0	0	0	0.0

1927-28

Team Statistics	G	FG/A	PCT	FT/A	PCT	TP	AVG
Indiana	17	265-987	.268	157-251	.625	687	40.4
Opponents	17					467	27.5
Player Statistics	G	FG/A	PCT	FT/A	PCT	TP	AVG
McCracken	17	64-211	.303	44-71	.620	172	10.1
Wells	17	56-193	.290	20-31	.645	132	7.8
Strickland	16	46-132	.348	22-28	.786	114	7.1
Correll	17	46-238	.193	25-48	.521	117	6.9
Beckner	8	18-70	.257	13-23	.565	49	6.1
Starr	16	10-34	.294	16-23	.696	36	2.3
Scheid	15	9-45	.200	12-19	.632	30	2.0
Gill	10	8-40	.200	2-3	.667	18	1.8
Cooper	10	5-18	.278	3-5	.600	13	1.3
Benzel	2	1-2	.500	0-0	.000	2	1.0
Leonard	6	2-4	.500	0-0	.000	4	0.7

1928-29

Team Statistics	G	FG/A	PCT	FT/A	PCT	TP	AVG
Indiana	17	189-825	.229	115-198	.581	493	29.0
Opponents	17					483	28.4
Player Statistics	G	FG/A	PCT	FT/A	PCT	TP	AVG
McCracken	17	54-216	.250	40-66	.606	148	8.7
Strickland	17	54-241	.224	11-21	.524	119	7.0
Wells	12	22-113	.195	11-19	.579	55	4.6
Correll	10	13-78	.167	16-29	.552	42	4.2
Cooper	9	15-32	.469	2-10	.200	32	3.6
Scheid	15	10-48	.208	14-22	.636	34	2.3
Vellar	11	6-42	.143	12-14	.857	24	2.2
Ashby	10	6-12	.500	3-6	.500	15	1.5
Gill	10	4-28	.143	4-8	.500	12	1.2
Jasper	10	4-10	.400	1-2	.500	9	0.9
B. Miller	5	1-5	.200	1-1	1.00	3	0.6

1929-30

Team Statistics	G	FG/A	PCT	FT/A	PCT	TP	AVG
Indiana	17	173-937	.185	132-224	.589	478	28.1
Opponents	17					450	26.5
Player Statistics	G	FG/A	PCT	FT/A	PCT	TP	AVG
McCracken	17	76-326	.233	54-92	.587	206	12.1
Zellar	16	26-179	.145	21-37	.568	73	4.6
Strickland	17	23-163	.141	10-15	.667	56	3.3
Vellar	17	17-105	.162	21-36	.583	50	3.2
Cooper	7	8-41	.195	2-3	.667	18	2.6
Blagrave	8	5-15	.333	7-9	.778	17	2.1
B. Miller	17	11-60	.183	9-17	.529	31	1.8
Gill	15	5-43	.116	4-10	.400	13	0.9
Ashby	3	0-0	.000	2-2	1.00	2	0.7
Massy	2	0-0	.000	1-1	1.00	1	0.5
Eber	8	1-1	1.00	1-2	.500	3	0.4
Jasper	9	1-4	.250	0-0	.000	2	0.2
Bretz	2	0-0	.000	0-0	.000	0	0.0

1930-31

Team Statistics	G	FG/A	PCT	FT/A	PCT	TP	AVG
Indiana	17	151-852	.177	111-213	.521	413	24.3
Opponents	17	155-816	.190	112-192	.586	422	24.8
Player Statistics	G	FG/A	PCT	FT/A	PCT	TP	AVG
Miller	15	32-129	.248	25-36	.694	89	5.9
Zeller	17	22-160	.138	32-46	.696	76	4.5
Dickey	16	29-142	.204	12-28	.429	70	4.4
Campbell	17	22-128	.172	9-21	.429	53	3.1
Rainbolt	1	1-5	.200	1-1	1.00	3	3.0
Veller	17	16-116	.138	15-36	.417	47	2.8
Blagrave	5	4-20	.200	4-10	.400	12	2.4
Jasper	12	9-70	.129	4-11	.364	22	1.8
Dauer	16	11-57	.193	7-12	.583	29	1.8
Massy	12	3-12	.250	1-7	.142	8	0.7
Bretz	6	1-4	.250	2-3	.667	4	0.7
Ashby	4	1-3	.333	0-1	.000	2	0.5

1931-32

Team Statistics	G	FG/A	PCT	FT/A	PCT	TP	AVG
Indiana	18	171-903	.189	147-240	.613	439	24.4
Opponents	18	186-876	.216	139-243	.572	511	28.4
Player Statistics	G	FG/A	PCT	FT/A	PCT	TP	AVG
Suddith	18	43-216	.199	35-49	.714	121	6.7
Hoffar	12	17-73	.233	18-29	.621	52	4.3
Hodson	18	28-135	.207	19-33	.576	75	4.2
Zeller	18	19-122	.156	29-40	.725	67	3.7
Weir	17	23-103	.223	10-20	.500	56	3.3
V. Dauer	11	14-42	.333	4-8	.500	32	2.9
Campbell	18	16-111	.144	19-34	.559	39	2.8
Dickey	7	7-54	.130	5-10	.500	19	2.7
Tucker	7	4-20	.200	5-8	.625	13	1.9
Sawicki	2	0-4	.000	2-4	.500	2	1.0
Blagrave	5	0-1	.000	1-1	1.00	1	0.2
Reed	8	0-3	.000	0-1	.000	0	0.0
Smith	1	0-0	.000	0-0	.000	0	0.0
Youngblood	1	0-0	.000	0-0	.000	0	0.0
Cordell	1	0-0	.000	0-0	.000	0	0.0
R. Dauer	1	0-0	.000	0-0	.000	0	0.0

1932-33

Team Statistics	G	FG/A	PCT	FT/A	PCT	TP	AVG
Indiana	18	234-979	.239	117-212	.552	585	32.5
Opponents	18	189-816	.231	125-201	.622	503	27.9
Player Statistics	G	FG/A	PCT	FT/A	PCT	TP	AVG
Hodson	17	49-197	.249	35-45	.778	133	7.8
Weir	15	37-152	.243	16-27	.593	93	6.2
Kehrt	15	43-148	.291	7-14	.500	90	6.0
Heavenridge	14	25-100	.250	11-21	.524	61	4.4
Dickey	17	28-146	.192	14-32	.438	70	4.1
Hoffar	18	20-78	.256	11-22	.500	51	2.8
Campbell	9	10-45	.222	4-7	.571	24	2.7
Cordell	1	1-2	.500	0-0	.000	2	2.0
Henry	11	7-25	.280	7-11	.636	21	1.9
Porter	17	10-59	.169	11-21	.524	31	1.8
Coulter	2	1-5	.200	0-0	.000	2	1.0
Gannsinger	2	1-1	1.00	0-0	.000	2	1.0
Hollers	2	1-2	.500	0-0	.000	2	1.0
Sawicki	1	0-1	.000	1-2	.500	1	1.0
Gerber	2	0-0	.000	0-0	.000	0	0.0
Carter	1	0-1	.000	0-1	.000	0	0.0
Himmelstein	1	0-3	.000	0-0	.000	0	0.0
Tucker	1	0-1	.000	0-1	.000	0	0.0

1933-34

Team Statistics	G	FG/A	PCT	FT/A	PCT	TP	AVG
Indiana	20	237-974	.243	133-228	.583	607	30.4
Opponents	20					552	27.6
Player Statistics	G	FG/A	PCT	FT/A	PCT	TP	AVG
Weir	20	64-254	.252	29-48	.604	157	7.9
Stout	20	50-185	.270	34-58	.586	134	6.7
Huffman	20	44-189	.233	14-30	.467	102	5.1
Kehrt	19	31-164	.189	18-26	.692	80	4.2
Coulter	11	12-50	.240	9-11	.818	33	3.0
Fechtman	4	4-7	.571	3-8	.375	11	2.8
Walker	14	14-81	.173	8-13	.615	36	2.6
Porter	17	9-23	.391	11-24	.458	29	1.7
Scott	8	5-15	.333	3-5	.600	13	1.6
Henry	5	2-3	.667	0-0	.000	4	0.8
Carter	6	1-1	1.00	2-3	.667	4	0.7
Gansinger	6	1-2	.500	2-2	1.00	4	0.7

1934-35

Team Statistics	G	FG/A	PCT	FT/A	PCT	TP	AVG
Indiana	20	279-1040	.268	150-241	.622	687	34.4
Opponents	20	246-995	.247	140-258	.534	632	31.6
Player Statistics	G	FG/A	PCT	FT/A	PCT	TP	AVG
Gunning	20	63-255	.247	42-56	.750	168	8.4
Kehrt	20	58-209	.278	23-36	.639	139	7.0
L. Stout	20	50-195	.256	25-40	.625	125	6.3
Fechtman	20	48-191	.251	24-54	.444	120	6.0
Walker	19	23-81	.284	20-22	.909	66	3.5
Etnire	15	12-51	.235	8-14	.571	32	2.1
Porter	13	8-36	.222	3-10	.300	19	1.5
Greiger	1	0-1	.000	1-1	1.00	1	1.0
Hosler	13	5-10	.500	2-3	.667	12	0.9
Scott	9	2-4	.500	1-2	.500	5	0.6
Baise	5	0-1	.000	0-0	.000	0	0.0
Henry	3	0-0	.000	0-0	.000	0	0.0
W. Stout	2	0-1	.000	0-0	.000	0	0.0
Boink	1	0-0	.000	0-0	.000	0	0.0
Coulter	1	0-0	.000	0-0	.000	0	0.0

1935-36

Team Statistics	G	FG/A	PCT	FT/A	PCT	TP	AVG
Indiana	20	290-1029	.281	176-269	.654	756	37.8
Opponents	20	199-873	.228	148-262	.565	546	27.3
Player Statistics	G	FG/A	PCT	FT/A	PCT	TP	AVG
Gunning	20	70-220	.318	43-61	.705	183	9.2
Fechtman	18	46-154	.299	32-49	.653	124	6.9
Walker	19	35-142	.246	25-40	.625	95	5.0
Huffman	20	34-128	.266	27-42	.643	95	4.8
Platt	17	27-59	.458	11-19	.579	65	3.8
Etnire	16	16-57	.281	16-18	.889	48	3.0
Hosler	19	16-32	.500	7-10	.700	39	2.1
Silberstein	8	8-17	.471	0-0	.000	16	2.0
Scott	8	4-8	.500	2-2	1.00	10	1.3
Birr	2	1-3	.333	0-0	.000	2	1.0
Hobson	2	0-0	.000	0-0	.000	0	0.0
Brooks	1	0-0	.000	0-0	.000	0	0.0
Liehr	1	0-1	.000	0-0	.000	0	0.0
Ratliff	1	0-0	.000	0-0	.000	0	0.0

1937-38

Team Statistics	G	FG/A	PCT	FT/A	PCT	TP	AVG
Indiana	20	342-1279	.267	129-206	.626	813	40.7
Opponents	20	317-1227	.258	150-273	.549	784	39.2
Player Statistics	G	FG/A	PCT	FT/A	PCT	TP	AVG
Andres	20	104-367	.283	42-63	.667	250	12.5
Johnson	20	73-292	.250	29-41	.707	175	8.8
Platt	17	60-201	.299	12-16	.750	132	7.8
Birr	12	32-110	.291	5-20	.250	69	5.8
Huffman	20	38-175	.217	18-28	.643	94	4.7
McCreary	15	18-79	.228	7-15	.467	43	2.9
Dorsey	14	9-18	.500	7-10	.700	25	1.8
Ratliff	7	3-14	.214	2-4	.500	8	1.1
Ooley	15	4-20	.200	5-7	.714	13	0.9
Stevenson	5	1-3	.333	2-2	1.00	4	0.8
Gentil	1	0-2	.000	0-1	.000	0	0.0
Grant	1	0-0	.000	0-0	.000	0	0.0

1936-37

Team Statistics	G	FG/A	PCT	FT/A	PCT	TP	AVG
Indiana	20	325-1164	.279	145-248	.585	795	39.8
Opponents	20	258-1176	.219	165-272	.607	684	34.2
Player Statistics	G	FG/A	PCT	FT/A	PCT	TP	AVG
Gunning	18	66-227	.291	31-49	.633	163	9.1
Johnson	20	58-208	.279	26-45	.578	142	7.1
Etnire	20	48-140	.343	31-45	.689	127	6.4
Huffman	19	41-178	.230	18-38	.474	100	5.3
Andres	20	43-155	.277	15-24	.625	101	5.1
Fechtman	13	20-71	.282	14-30	.467	54	4.2
Platt	19	21-81	.259	7-8	.875	49	2.6
Hosler	20	18-27	.667	3-5	.600	39	1.9
Birr	10	8-28	.286	0-3	.000	16	1.6
Silberstein	7	2-4	.500	0-0	.000	4	0.6
Mendel	7	0-1	.000	0-1	.000	0	0.0
Ratliff	2	0-2	.000	0-0	.000	0	0.0
Abbot	1	0-2	.000	0-0	.000	0	0.0

1938-39

OVERALL RECORD: 17-3

CONFERENCE RECORD: 9-3 (SECOND PLACE)

INDIVIDUAL HONORS:

BRANCH McCRACKEN—BIG TEN COACH OF THE YEAR

ERNIE ANDRES—ALL-BIG TEN (FIRST TEAM)

The 1938-39 team. First row (left to right): Jack Stevenson, Ralph Dorsey, Marv Huffman, head coach Branch McCracken, Ernie Andres, William Johnson, Jim Ooley, Dale Gentil; Second row: assistant coach Joe Platt, Curly Armstrong, Herm Schaefer, Tom Motter, Edgar Mansfield, Jim Gridley, Chet Francis, Robert Hansen, Russell Clifton, trainer Jesse Ferguson; Third row: manager Richard Schannen, Richard McGaughey, Gordon McLaughlin, William Menke, Robert Menke, Bill Tipmore, Bob Dro, Jim Lettellier. IU Archives

With the return of standouts such as Ernie Andres, William Johnson, and Marv Huffman, the addition of several excellent sophomores from a highly successful freshmen squad, and the arrival of a new coach in Branch McCracken, the Hoosiers entered the 1938-39 season with a mix of excitement and uncertainty. Indiana appeared to have the talent needed to challenge for the conference championship, but it was going to have to rely on several newcomers and a coach who was embarking on his first season at the helm of a Big Ten squad. As it turned out, the sophomores played terrifically, and McCracken began to unveil a new style of play that excited the crowds and intimidated many opponents.

On Monday, December 5, in Bloomington, the McCracken era officially began when the Hoosiers annihilated the Ball State Cardinals (where McCracken had coached the previous eight seasons) 54-28, led by 14 points from Andres. IU led by only three points at the half but broke the game open in the second half, holding the visitors scoreless for the first 13 minutes. On Saturday, December 10, Miami of Ohio came to town and suffered a similar fate, losing 49-23. Sophomore center Bill Menke (whose brother Bob was also on the Hoosier squad) was the game's high scorer with 12 points. Sophomore forward Paul "Curly" Armstrong chipped in 10 points.

The Indiana steamroller continued to accelerate on December 12 when Wabash came to Bloomington and got wiped out by the score of 47-23. The next victim to come to town was Connecticut State, who got pummeled 71-38 as the Hoosiers broke the team's single-game scoring record. Armstrong had a game-high 15 points.

After a 4-0 start at home, the Hoosiers went on the road for three more preconference games. On Friday, December 23, in Indianapolis, the Hoosiers wrested a 46-29 win from Butler, which had been undefeated and had already beaten Wisconsin and Iowa from the Big Ten. Next the Hoosiers went to Cleveland, Ohio, on December 30 and came back from a one-point halftime deficit to defeat Western Reserve 45-33. Andres had a game-high 11 points, and Bill Menke and sophomore Herm Schaefer each added 10. The next day Indiana went to Michigan State (which was not yet a member of the Big Ten) and grinded out a tough 37-33 win led by 11 points from sophomore guard Bob Dro.

The undefeated Hoosiers opened Big Ten play on Saturday, January 7, when they traveled to Ohio State. The Buckeyes had an excellent team, and they put the Hoosiers back on their heels in the first half. IU was down 30-15 at the break but made a big push in the second half to make it a game again before falling 45-38. Two days later, Indiana traveled to Illinois and nabbed a 29-28 win with another furious second-half comeback.

On Saturday, January 14, Indiana hosted its first Big Ten game in Bloomington against Wisconsin, and the Hoosiers ran the Badgers out of the building in a 43-19 victory. Armstrong led all scorers with 11 points. On Monday, January 16, Coach McCracken

1938-39 TEAM ROSTER

Head coach: Branch McCracken
Assistant coaches: Ralph Graham, Joe Platt

No.	Player	Hometown	Class	Position	Height
25	Ernie Andres (Capt.)	Jeffersonville, IN	Sr	G	6-1
22	Curly Armstrong	Fort Wayne, IN	So	F	5-11
16	Russell Clifton	Bentonville, IN	So	C	6-3
30	Ralph Dorsey	Horse Cave, KY	Jr	F	5-9
21	Bob Dro	Berne, IN	So	G	5-11
9	Chet Francis	Avon, IN	So	G	6-1
19	Dale Gentil	Mount Vernon, IN	Jr	F	6-2
12	Jim Gridley	Vevay, IN	So	G	6-0
11	Robert Hansen	Chicago, IL	So	C	6-3
28	Marv Huffman	New Castle, IN	Jr	G	6-2
24	William Johnson	Jeffersonville, IN	Sr	F/G	6-0
18	Jim Lettellier	Bloomington, IN	So	F	5-10
7	Edgar Mansfield	LaPorte, IN	So	G	5-11
8	Richard McGaughey	Crawfordsville, IN	So	G	5-11
4	Gordon McLaughlin	Terre Haute, IN	So	F	6-1
29	Robert Menke	Huntingburg, IN	So	F	6-3
23	William Menke	Huntingburg, IN	So	C	6-3
26	Tom Motter	Fort Wayne, IN	So	F	6-1
13	Jim Ooley	Spencer, IN	Jr	G	6-2
24	Herm Schaefer	Fort Wayne, IN	So	F	6-0
20	Jack Stevenson	Indianapolis, IN	So	F	6-1
10	Bill Tipmore	Elkhart, IN	So	C	6-2

SEASON RESULTS 1938-39

Date	Court	Opponent	Result	Score
12/5/1938	H	Ball State	W	54-28
12/10/1938	H	Miami (OH)	W	49-23
12/12/1938	H	Wabash	W	47-23
12/17/1938	H	Connecticut State	W	71-38
12/23/1938	A	Butler	W	46-29
12/30/1938	A	Western Reserve	W	45-33
12/31/1938	A	Michigan State	W	37-33
1/7/1939	A	Ohio State	L	38-45
1/9/1939	A	Illinois	W	29-28
1/14/1939	H	Wisconsin	W	43-19
1/16/1939	H	Purdue	W	39-36
2/3/1939	A	Xavier	W	48-39
2/6/1939	H	Ohio State	W	46-34
2/11/1939	A	Iowa	W	50-39
2/13/1939	A	Chicago	W	46-33
2/18/1939	H	Northwestern	W	44-37
2/20/1939	H	Iowa	W	45-40
2/25/1939	H	Minnesota	W	49-37
2/27/1939	A	Purdue	L	34-45
3/4/1939	A	Michigan	L	45-53

1938-39 BIG TEN STANDINGS

	W	L	PCT
Ohio State	10	2	.833
Indiana	9	3	.750
Illinois	8	4	.667
Minnesota	7	5	.583
Purdue	6	6	.500
Northwestern	5	7	.417
Michigan	4	8	.333
Wisconsin	4	8	.333
Chicago	4	8	.333
Iowa	3	9	.250

Ernie Andres was a solidly built guard who made his presence felt on both ends of the floor. As a senior, he was Indiana's captain and floor general under the tutelage of first-year coach Branch McCracken. IU Archives

endeared himself to the IU faithful by leading his squad to a 39-36 win over cross-state rival Purdue, in McCracken's first game against the Boilermakers as Indiana coach. Andres scored a game-high 15 points and Armstrong added 11.

IU played a nonconference game against Xavier in Cincinnati on Friday, February 3, and rolled to a relatively easy 48-39 win, as Dro and Bill Menke each scored 12 points. Indiana resumed Big Ten play on Monday, February 6, when Ohio State came to Bloomington. The Hoosiers avenged their earlier loss in Columbus with a 46-34 triumph behind 13 points from Andres. IU logged another win on Saturday, February 11, when the Hoosiers traveled to Iowa City

and handed the Iowa Hawkeyes a 50-39 defeat. Andres broke loose for 18 points and Bill Menke added 15. The following Monday, Indiana went to Chicago and ran over the Maroons 46-33. Bill Menke took top scoring honors with 12 points, and Huffman and Andres added 11 points each.

The Hoosiers returned to Bloomington and faced Northwestern on February 18. After the Wildcats wrestled the Hoosiers to a 14-14 tie at the half, Indiana pulled away for a 44-37 win. Armstrong scored a game-high 16 points. Next, last-place Iowa came to Bloomington on February 20. However, the Hoosiers had to play the Hawkeyes without starters Andres and Dro, who were both hospitalized because they were sick with the flu. Iowa jumped to a 21-20 halftime lead, but Bill Menke and Bill Johnson ignited a 15-6 IU run to start the second half, and the Hoosiers ultimately prevailed 45-40.

Minnesota then came to Bloomington on Saturday, February 25 and jumped ahead of IU at the half by the score of 24-22. But the Hoosiers once again worked their second-half magic and ran to a 49-37 victory over the Golden Gophers. Bill Menke carried IU with 28 points—two points off the IU and Big Ten record set by Andres a year earlier. The win was the Hoosiers' tenth straight, including nine in conference play. It put IU at 17-1 overall and 9-1 in the Big Ten, one game ahead of second-place Ohio State. Some were calling the Hoosiers the best team in the country.

With only two games remaining, the Hoosiers could clinch the Big Ten title outright by winning both games or could guarantee themselves a portion of the title by winning one of two. Unfortunately, both games were on the road, and the Hoosiers lost them both. The first came on Monday, February 27, against Purdue in West Lafayette. IU was down by four at the half and was never able to mount one of its patented second-half rallies. The Boilermakers prevailed 45-34. The final game was against Michigan (which was 3-8 in conference play before the game) in Ann Arbor on Saturday, March 4. The Wolverines put an exclamation point on a dismal season by upsetting the Hoosiers 53-45. Michigan's Jim Rae, who returned for the game after missing most of the season with a back injury, scored a game-high 19 points to lead the Wolverines to victory.

Indiana's loss to Michigan, coupled with Ohio State's season-ending win against Purdue, gave the Buckeyes the Big Ten title (and a berth in the first ever NCAA tournament), while the Hoosiers had to settle for an outright second-place finish. Despite the disappointing two-game skid to finish out the schedule, the Hoosiers had put together a highly successful season. Sophomores Bob Dro, Bill Menke, Curly Armstrong and Herm Schaefer had stepped up and shown that they were going to make the Hoosiers a force to be reckoned with in the coming years. And Coach McCracken had amply demonstrated that he had the expertise needed to mold a powerful Big Ten team.

1939-40

For the commentary and statistics for the 1939-40 season, please see Chapter 6, "1939-40: The Arrival of the Hurryin' Hoosiers."

1940-41

OVERALL RECORD: 17-3
CONFERENCE RECORD: 10-2 (SECOND PLACE)
TEAM HONORS:
SUGAR BOWL CARNIVAL CHAMPION
INDIVIDUAL HONORS:
BOB DRO—ALL-BIG TEN (FIRST TEAM)

The marquee players from the class of 1941—Bill Menke, Curly Armstrong, Herm Schaefer and Jay McCreary—who had been the heart of the two highly successful IU teams that graced the court during coach Branch McCracken's first two seasons at Indiana, were now seniors determined to make the 1940-41 season their best ever. And in some ways they succeeded. The team's 10-2 conference record was the best the Hoosiers had recorded during their magnificent three-year run. However, it was one game shy of what they needed to secure first place in the Big Ten and earn a chance to defend their NCAA title.

During McCracken's first two seasons, the Hoosiers had never lost a preconference game. However, repeating those undefeated starts was going to be much more difficult in 1940-41, because only two of IU's eight preconference games would be played in Bloomington. The Hoosiers opened against Georgia on Saturday, December 7, and handily dismissed the southerners 44-31 in front of a crowd of 4,100 in the IU Fieldhouse. The Hoosiers followed up that win with a 39-36 squeaker against Butler on

The 1940-41 team. Front row (left to right): Bob Dro, Jay McCreary, William Menke, Herm Schaefer, Jim Gridley, Tom Motter, Robert Menke; Second row: trainer Jesse Ferguson, Chet Francis, Ed Denton, Hal Driver, Andy Zimmer, Everett Hoffman, Cliff Forsyth, head coach Branch McCracken; Third row: Anthony Scheidler, William Torphy, John Logan, Irv Swanson, Guy Wellman, Ordine Heine. IU Archives

Thursday, December 12. The Bulldogs led 31-28 with seven minutes remaining, but Indiana rattled off an 11-5 run over the next three minutes and then stalled down the stretch to clinch the victory. IU center Bill Menke led all scorers with 12 points. Next, Marshall came to Bloomington on Saturday, December 14, and got hammered 53-22. Bill Menke again led IU with 11 points.

During the holiday break, the Hoosiers made a grueling west coast trip to take on four of the top teams in the west. The first showdown was on Saturday, December 21, against Stanford, which was now coached by former IU skipper Everett Dean. An enthusiastic crowd of 3,000 got to see one of the great games in college basketball that season. Stanford led 22-21 at the half, but the Hoosiers grabbed their first lead at 27-25 early in the second half. The game seesawed back and forth, and Indiana took a 54-52 lead in the final minute, when Stanford's Bill Cowden

dribbled nearly the length of the court and scored to tie the game in the final seconds, sending it to overtime. Indiana outlasted the westerners 60-59 in OT. Bill Menke scored 16 points and Curly Armstrong added 15 for IU.

The Hoosiers won their next two games relatively easily—a 42-39 win over California on December 23 and a 51-26 triumph against UCLA on December 27—and that set up a showdown with a powerful USC team on December 28. The Trojans took a 19-15 lead into the intermission, but as usual, the Hoosiers surged back in the second half. However, IU came up just short in this contest, as USC sneaked out with a 41-39 win when IU's Armstrong missed a shot from the corner in the final seconds. On their way back to Bloomington, Indiana stopped in New Orleans on December 30 and played Kentucky in the fifth annual Sugar Bowl Carnival game. Both teams played well, but the Hoosiers led for most of the contest and came away with a 48-45 win, as Bill Menke scored a game-high 15 points and Armstrong hit for 13.

A convincing 48-38 win over Illinois in Champaign was how the Hoosiers opened the Big Ten season on Saturday, January 11. Indiana opened an eight-point halftime lead and was never really threatened in the second half. Bill Menke broke out for a season-high 24 points. Next, Northwestern came to Bloomington on Monday, January 13, and was rebuffed 52-32, as Armstrong led IU with 11 points. Two weeks later, after IU's semester break, the Hoosiers traveled to Ann Arbor and seized a 41-37 victory from Michigan. After the Wolverines pulled ahead 26-25 early in the second half, IU put together a 14-5 run and then coasted to victory.

Senior Curly Armstrong, IU's second leading scorer, was held out of the Michigan game because of his grades and was eventually declared ineligible for the second semester. So in February he joined the Indianapolis Kautskys of the National Basketball League. Still it was a tough way for Armstrong's college career to come to an end. Armstrong was one of the most colorful characters in IU history. During one team practice, Armstrong arrived a little bit late, prompting Coach McCracken to mockingly declare, "Well, I guess we can go ahead and have practice now, by God, the great Armstrong is here!" A few weeks later, McCracken had to leave to a take a phone call during the middle of a practice. Armstrong told all his teammates to stop what they were doing and sit on a basketball. When McCracken re-entered the gym, Armstrong bellowed out, "Well, I guess we can start practicing, the great McCracken is here!"

Without Armstrong, the Hoosiers still had a good team, but they missed Curly during several big games. Purdue dealt Indiana its first conference loss on Saturday, February 1, in West Lafayette. The Boilermakers led by five at the break, but the Hoosiers tied the game at 34 in the final minutes, before Purdue pulled away for a 40-36 win. IU got back on track a couple days later when the Hoosiers mauled Ohio State 45-25 in Bloomington. Sophomore forward John Logan led IU with 12 points. The Hoosiers ran to another easy win on February 11, against Iowa in Bloomington. IU led 23-9 at the half and went on to beat the Hawkeyes 50-40. Forward Bob Menke was IU's high scorer with

1940-41 TEAM ROSTER

Head coach: Branch McCracken
Assistant coach: Ralph Graham

No.	Player	Hometown	Class	Position	Height
40	Curly Armstrong	Fort Wayne, IN	Sr	F	5-11
18	Ed Denton	Jeffersonville, IN	So	C	6-2
27	Hal Driver	Aurora, IN	So	C	6-3
43	Bob Dro	Berne, IN	Sr	G	5-11
24	Cliff Forsyth	Terre Haute, IN	So	G	6-2
9	Chet Francis	Avon, IN	Sr	G	6-1
8	Bill Frey	Kokomo, IN	Jr	F	6-1
12	Jim Gridley	Vevay, IN	Sr	G	6-0
21	Max Hasler	Elnora, IN	Jr	G	5-10
	Ordine Heine	New Haven, IN	So	C	6-2
42	Everett Hoffman	Evansville, IN	Jr	C	6-3
7	John Logan	Richmond, IN	So	F	6-0
22	Jay McCreary	Frankfort, IN	Sr	G	5-10
29	Robert Menke	Huntingburg, IN	Sr	F	6-3
35	William Menke	Huntingburg, IN	Sr	C	6-3
26	Tom Motter	Fort Wayne, IN	Sr	F	6-1
30	Herm Schaefer	Fort Wayne, IN	Sr	F	6-0
36	Anthony Scheidler	Muncie, IN	So	F	6-0
14	Irv Swanson	LaPorte, IN	So	G	5-10
11	William Torphy	Bedford, IN	Jr	G	6-0
	Guy Wellman	Valparaiso, IN	So	G	5-10
	Cliff Wiethoff	Seymour, IN	Jr	F	6-0
	Robert White	Joliet, IL	So	G	6-0
41	Andy Zimmer	Goodland, IN	Jr	C	6-4

SEASON RESULTS 1940-41

Date	Court	Opponent	Result	Score
12/7/1940	H	Georgia	W	44-31
12/12/1940	A	Butler	W	39-36
12/14/1940	H	Marshall	W	53-22
12/21/1940	A	Stanford	W	60-59
12/23/1940	A	California	W	42-39
12/27/1940	A	UCLA	W	51-26
12/28/1940	A	USC	L	39-41
12/30/1940	N1	Kentucky	W	48-45
1/11/1941	A	Illinois	W	48-38
1/13/1941	H	Northwestern	W	52-32
1/27/1941	A	Michigan	W	41-37
2/1/1941	A	Purdue	L	36-40
2/3/1941	H	Ohio State	W	45-25
2/11/1941	H	Iowa	W	50-40
2/15/1941	H	Minnesota	W	44-34
2/17/1941	A	Ohio State	W	40-33
2/22/1941	A	Iowa	W	47-36
2/24/1941	H	Wisconsin	L	30-38
3/1/1941	H	Purdue	W	47-29
3/3/1941	A	Chicago	W	49-33

1 Sugar Bowl Carnival Game in New Orleans, LA

1940-41 BIG TEN STANDINGS

	W	L	PCT
Wisconsin	11	1	.917
Indiana	10	2	.833
Illinois	7	5	.583
Minnesota	7	5	.583
Ohio State	7	5	.583
Purdue	6	6	.500
Michigan	5	7	.417
Iowa	4	8	.333
Northwestern	3	9	.250
Chicago	0	12	.000

10 points. Minnesota came to Bloomington on Saturday, February 15, and fell to the fast-paced Hoosier attack by the score of 44-34. Bill Menke had a game-high 13 points.

The Hoosiers went on the road to face Ohio State in Columbus on Monday, February 17. OSU grabbed a 21-18 halftime lead, but Indiana outclassed the Buckeyes in the second half to win 40-33, as eight different Hoosiers scored. On Saturday, February 22, the Hoosiers traveled to Iowa City and blasted the Iowa Hawkeyes in the first half. IU led by 13 at the break and cruised to a 47-36 triumph. Forward Herm Schaefer was the game's leading scorer with 17.

The Iowa victory put Indiana at 8-1 in Big Ten play, a half-game behind the 9-1 Wisconsin Badgers. IU's next game was against Wisconsin on February 24, in Bloomington, where the Hoosiers had won 27 consecutive home games, including 16 in a row in conference play. To have a chance at an outright Big Ten title, the Hoosiers had to defeat the first-place Badgers. Indiana opened the game in an offensive funk and fell behind by as many as 10 points in the opening half, before going to the break with a 20-12 deficit. A torrid pace ensued in the second half as both teams battled for control of the game. The Badgers bent, but never broke, and maintained a lead throughout the game on the way to a 38-30 victory.

Indiana easily won its final two games—47-29 over Purdue on March 1 and 49-33 over Chicago on March 3—but Wisconsin won the Big Ten title by defeating Minnesota 42-32 in the Badgers' season finale in Madison. As a result, Wisconsin also won a berth in the NCAA Tournament, which the Badgers went on to win. It was the second straight national championship by a Big Ten team.

1941-42

OVERALL RECORD: 15-6

CONFERENCE RECORD: 10-5 (SECOND PLACE)

INDIVIDUAL HONORS:

ANDY ZIMMER—ALL-AMERICA,

ALL-BIG TEN (FIRST TEAM)

Although Indiana returned nine lettermen for the 1941-42 campaign, it lost five of its top seven scorers and all of the valuable experience of a senior class that had gone 54-9 in three varsity seasons. As a result, coach Branch McCracken's team was a bit of an unknown entity, and few prognosticators expected the Hoosiers to challenge for the Big Ten championship or even finish in the upper division of the conference. The team's only experienced returnee was Andy Zimmer, a lanky 6'4" senior who had improved tremendously during his time at IU. Nevertheless, McCracken's Hurryin' Hoosiers used their running game and a balanced attack to surprise a lot of opponents. Ultimately, the Hoosiers went on to earn a second-place finish in the Big Ten for the fourth straight season.

The Hoosiers opened the schedule against a very good Wabash team on Wednesday, December 10, in Bloomington. IU grabbed control early and led most of the way en route to a 36-27 victory. IU center Andy Zimmer led the Hoosiers with 10 points. The next day, IU hosted the Great Lakes Naval Training Station basketball squad, which contained two former Hoosiers—Ernie Andres and Bill Menke. Indiana led the Navy men 19-18 at the break, but couldn't keep up in the second half and lost 41-36. IU sophomore Ralph Hamilton led the Hoosiers with 10 points, while Menke was one of two Navy players with a game-high 11 points.

Nebraska came to Bloomington on Monday, December 15. The Cornhuskers never found a way to slow down the Hoosiers' rapid-fire attack, as IU opened the game with a 15-0 run, led 38-10 at the half, and went on to a 56-29 win. Zimmer led all scorers with 17. The next squad to come to Bloomington was UCLA on Thursday, December 18,

The 1941-42 team. First row (left to right): Everett Hoffman, Ed Denton, Andy Zimmer, head coach Branch McCracken, William Torphy, Bill Frey, Irv Swanson; Second row: Ralph Hamilton, Robert Gwin, Hal Driver, manager Dick Morris, John Logan, Swift Wunker, Roy Kilby; Third row: Warren Lewis, Lawrence Alleyne, Dick Wittenbraker, Neil Funk, William Royer, Al Wise, James Partheimer. IU Archives

and they had the same luck in trying to stymie the IU offense. The Hoosiers won 47-33, led by 13 points from Zimmer. Then the Hoosiers went east for a pair of winter vacation games against Pittsburgh and George Washington. In a game that featured seven ties and multiple lead changes, Indiana used a 10-1 run in the final three minutes to defeat Pitt 50-41 on December 26. Hamilton topped all scorers with 16. The next night, Indiana fell behind by a point at the half, but outdistanced George Washington 52-43. Junior forward John Logan led IU with 13 points and sophomore guard Dick Wittenbraker added 12.

On Saturday, January 3, Indiana opened the Big Ten season with a 50-40 setback at Northwestern. The Hoosiers were only down by one with ten minutes remaining before Northwestern closed the game on a 14-5 run. IU bounced back on Monday, January 5, and edged out a veteran Wisconsin team 38-34, as

eight different players scored for Indiana. Next, the Hoosiers went up to Minnesota on Saturday, January 10. The Gophers ran with the Hoosiers, and the game remained close until the final five minutes, when Minnesota started pouring in baskets from every angle to close out a 63-43 blowout. Logan led IU with 11 points, while Zimmer and junior Irv Swanson chipped in 10 apiece.

Purdue came to Bloomington on Monday, January 12, for the only game between the two rivals that season. The Boilermakers, who were undefeated in conference play, went into the locker room at the half trailing 22-18. Purdue scrapped back into the game and tied it at 28. Each team struggled to gain an advantage until the score was tied again at 37 with time running out. Swanson hit a free throw to give the Hoosiers a one-point lead, and then Purdue appeared to take back the lead when Boilermaker forward

1941-42 TEAM ROSTER

Head coach: Branch McCracken
Assistant coach: Ralph Graham

No.	Player	Hometown	Class	Position	Height
	Lawrence Alleyne	Bloomington, IN	So	F	6-1
18	Ed Denton	Jeffersonville, IN	Jr	C	6-2
27	Hal Driver	Aurora, IN	Jr	C	6-3
8	Bill Frey	Kokomo, IN	Sr	F	6-1
39	Neil Funk	LaPorte, IN	So	F	6-3
17	Robert Gwin	Shoals, IN	So	G	6-1
10	Ralph Hamilton	Fort Wayne, IN	So	F	6-1
35	Bob Hines	Fort Wayne, IN	So	C	6-2
42	Everett Hoffman	Evansville, IN	Sr	C	6-3
15	Roy Kilby	Muncie, IN	So	G	5-10
16	Warren Lewis	New Castle, IN	So	F	6-0
7	John Logan	Richmond, IN	Jr	F	6-0
14	Irv Swanson	LaPorte, IN	Jr	F/G	5-10
11	William Torphy	Bedford, IN	Sr	G	6-0
25	Al Wise	Brookville, IN	So	F	6-3
21	Dick Wittenbraker	New Castle, IN	So	G	6-2
38	Swift Wunker	Lawrenceburg, IN	So	F	
41	Andy Zimmer (Capt.)	Goodland, IN	Sr	C/G	6-4

SEASON RESULTS 1941-42

Date	Court	Opponent	Result	Score
12/10/1941	H	Wabash	W	36-27
12/11/1941	H	Great Lakes Naval Station	L	36-41
12/15/1941	H	Nebraska	W	56-29
12/18/1941	H	UCLA	W	47-33
12/26/1941	A	Pittsburgh	W	50-41
12/27/1941	A	George Washington	W	52-43
1/3/1942	A	Northwestern	L	40-50
1/5/1942	H	Wisconsin	W	38-34
1/10/1942	A	Minnesota	L	43-63
1/12/1942	H	Purdue	W	40-39
1/24/1942	A	Wisconsin	L	36-42
1/26/1942	H	Michigan	W	64-36
1/31/1942	A	Chicago	W	63-34
2/2/1942	A	Ohio State	W	46-43
2/9/1942	H	Illinois	W	41-36
2/14/1942	H	Chicago	W	52-20
2/16/1942	A	Michigan	W	47-42
2/23/1942	A	Iowa	L	52-55
2/28/1942	H	Minnesota	W	54-45
3/2/1942	H	Northwestern	L	45-49
3/7/1942	H	Ohio State	W	48-23

1941-42 BIG TEN STANDINGS

	W	L	PCT
Illinois	13	2	.867
Indiana	10	5	.667
Wisconsin	10	5	.667
Iowa	10	5	.667
Minnesota	9	6	.600
Purdue	9	6	.600
Northwestern	5	10	.333
Michigan	5	10	.333
Ohio State	4	11	.267
Chicago	0	15	.000

Forrest Sprowl buried a field goal. However, he was called for traveling, and the basket was waived off. Then IU center Ed Denton scored on an out-of-bounds play to give the Hoosiers an insurmountable lead. Purdue scored just before time expired to make the final score 40-39. Swanson led IU with a career-high 14 points, while Denton added 13. The win evened the Hoosiers' conference record at 2-2.

Wisconsin avenged their earlier loss against the Hoosiers on Saturday, January 24, when IU went to Madison and dropped a 42-36 contest to the Badgers. Swanson again led Indiana with 12 points. The Hoosiers got back to the running game by blowing out their next two opponents—Michigan went down 64-36 on January 26, in Bloomington, and Chicago was clobbered 63-34 on January 31, in the Windy City. On February 2, at Ohio State, Indiana used a 19-5 run in the middle of the second half to defeat the Buckeyes 46-43. Hamilton and Everett Hoffman scored 11 points each to pace the Hoosiers.

Big Ten front-runner Illinois, which was 7-0 in conference play, came to the IU Fieldhouse on Monday, February 9. The Fighting Illini looked in control after holding a 22-19 halftime advantage. However, IU grabbed the momentum in the second half and kept coming after Illinois until the Hoosiers grabbed the lead in the final minutes and prevailed 41-36. Logan and Zimmer tied for game-high honors with 10 points each. IU followed up the Illinois upset by crushing the Chicago Maroons 52-20 in Bloomington on Saturday, February 14. Eleven different Hoosiers scored in the game, led by sophomore Warren Lewis with 15. Then Indiana went up to Ann Arbor and snatched a 47-42 win from the Michigan Wolverines on Monday, February 16. Denton was IU's top scorer with 15. The triumph over the Wolverines was Indiana's sixth consecutive victory and improved the Hoosiers to 8-2 in conference play.

Next, the Hoosiers suffered their first setback in six games when they lost 55-52 at Iowa on February 23. In the second half, the Hoosiers erased the Hawkeyes' 13-point halftime advantage and briefly took a 41-40 lead with eight minutes remaining before fading down the stretch. The Hoosiers bounced back on Saturday, February 28, when they easily conquered Minnesota 54-45 on the strength of 16 points from Logan and 11 from Zimmer. Then the Hoosiers hosted Northwestern (4-9 in conference

Senior captain Andy Zimmer was the Hoosiers' only experienced performer heading into the 1941-42 campaign. The 6'4" Zimmer anchored the squad and helped lead Indiana to a surprising second-place finish in the Big Ten. IU Archives

play) on Monday, March 2. The Wildcats surprised IU by roaring to a 25-13 lead at the break, then holding on for a 49-45 upset of the Hoosiers. Otto Graham, who would later become a hall of fame football player in the NFL, led Northwestern to victory with 14 points. Indiana finished the season on Saturday, March 7, by annihilating Ohio State 48-23. OSU actually led by a point at the half, but Indiana outscored the Buckeyes 30-4 in the second session.

The Hoosiers' loss to Northwestern, a team IU should definitely have beaten at home, cost them a chance to claim an outright second-place finish in the conference. Nevertheless, at 10-5, the Hoosiers tied Wisconsin and Iowa for second, while Illinois's "Whiz Kids" ran away with the title. For a team that was not expected to finish in the upper division of the conference, the Hoosiers had played some excellent basketball, highlighted by their wins over Purdue and

Illinois. In fact, IU's play was good enough to draw attention to their senior captain and floor leader, Andy Zimmer, who was named an All-American. Meanwhile, juniors Irv Swanson and Ed Denton emerged as Hoosier stars. Swanson was a heady guard and an excellent team player, while Denton was a talented, high-scoring pivot man. Sophomore Ralph Hamilton also flashed good speed and a nice little hook shot.

1942-43

OVERALL RECORD: 18-2
CONFERENCE RECORD: 11-2 (SECOND PLACE)

With Indiana's surprise performance during the 1941-42 season, many IU fans were optimistic that coach Branch McCracken would find a way to coax another excellent season out of the Hoosiers in 1942-43. The Hoosiers lost All-American Andy Zimmer and reserve center Everett Hoffman to graduation but returned all of their other starters and six of their top seven scorers. Entering the season, the Hoosiers were without their leading scorer from the previous year, Ed Denton, who suffered from a bad case of pneumonia throughout the fall.

"Naturally, we do not know how much we can depend upon our sophomores, and so, with Ed Denton out indefinitely, Indiana doesn't know what to expect from its basketball team," stated McCracken. "But we do think we have a good nucleus for a team that will win some important games. We lack sufficient qualities for a championship contender; we'll let Illinois, Wisconsin and Ohio State settle that matter."

Once again, the Hoosiers surprised everyone with their outstanding play, and after the first 16 games of the season, it even looked as though they might just prove Coach McCracken wrong about not being a championship team. Junior Ralph Hamilton and sophomore Ward Williams stepped up to become

Indiana's top two scorers and led the upstart IU squad to an excellent season.

With the outbreak of World War II, wartime travel restrictions led to some unorthodox scheduling of Big Ten games. In many cases, teams would travel to another school and play two conference games over a period of three days and then return home.

Indiana opened its schedule against DePauw on Saturday, December 5, in Bloomington, and IU easily defeated the Tigers 57-40, after leading by only two at the half. Four Hoosiers scored in double figures, led by guard Dick Wittenbraker and forward Ralph Hamilton with 11 points each. On Monday, December 7, the Hoosiers had an even easier time with Wabash, winning 58-40, as Hamilton scored 17. On December 14, IU rang up another easy victory when the Hoosiers pummeled Fort Knox 64-19 in Bloomington.

Adolph Rupp's Kentucky squad (which entered the game undefeated) gave IU its first challenge of the season on December 23, on a neutral court in Louisville. The Hoosiers led for most of the second half, but the Wildcats kept clawing back into the game before losing 58-52 in the final minutes. Hamilton led all scorers with 18 points. Indiana got another challenge when the team went to the Windy City on December 28 and had to repulse a second-half comeback from Loyola Chicago to secure a 51-43 victory.

Next, IU traveled to Nebraska and won a 40-39 victory over the Cornhuskers when Dick Wittenbraker blocked a layup attempt from Nebraska's Ralph Heinzelman, who stole the ball in the final seconds and was streaking down court to score the winning basket. Then the Hoosiers closed out their preconference season with a perfect 7-0 record by defeating Butler 42-27 in Indianapolis on January 4. However, the Hoosiers got a scare in the final minutes when Ralph Hamilton, the team's leading scorer, injured his back by ramming into the supports behind the basket and had to be taken to Methodist Hospital in Indianapolis for X-rays. He ended up being okay.

Ohio State was Indiana's first opponent in Big Ten play. OSU came to Bloomington for a pair of games on Saturday, January 9, and Monday, January 11. The Hoosiers easily swept both contests, winning the Saturday game 45-37 and the Monday game 61-

The 1942-43 team. Front row (left to right): Roy Kilby, Ralph Hamilton, John Logan, Irv Swanson, Ed Denton, Neil Funk, Dick Wittenbraker; Second row: Warren Lewis, Ed Schienbein, Bob Hines, head coach Branch McCracken, James Smith, Maurice Stohler, Maurice Hooper; Third row: Billy McGinnis, Don Blemker, Sterling Scott, Ward Williams, Leroy Mangin. IU Archives

31. IU center Ward Williams was the top scorer in the first game with 13 points, and Hamilton scored 13 to lead all scorers in the second contest. The Hoosiers went up to Chicago for a single game with the Chicago Maroons on Saturday, January 16, and breezed to a 55-27 win.

IU made its first doubleheader road trip against Iowa on Saturday, January 23, and Monday, January 25, and the Hoosiers cruised to two more easy victories. Indiana defeated the Hawkeyes 71-55 in the first game, as Hamilton poured in 31 points (on 13-25 from the field and 5-7 from the line) to break IU's single-game scoring record. The Hoosiers won the second game 64-43, powered by 21 points from Hamilton. Purdue came to Bloomington on January 30 and surprisingly didn't provide much more of an

obstacle than any of the other conference teams that IU had faced so far. Indiana overwhelmed the Boilermakers 53-35, led by 12 points from guard Irv Swanson and 11 points each from Williams and Hamilton.

Next, Michigan came down to Bloomington for a doubleheader on February 6-8. In the first game, Michigan led early on, but IU came back to tie the game at 14 at the half, then ran to a 32-24 win. In the second game, IU jumped out to a 14-point halftime lead and never looked back in a 48-33 whipping of the Wolverines. With 12 points, Swanson led three Hoosiers in double figures in the second game.

It was the Hoosiers' turn to go on the road again for a Saturday-Monday doubleheader on February 13 and 15, in Madison, Wisconsin. In the opener, IU

1942-43 TEAM ROSTER

Head coach: Branch McCracken
Assistant coach: Bill Johnson

No.	Player	Hometown	Class	Position	Height
9	Bob Cowan	Fort Wayne, IN	Fr	G	5-10
18	Ed Denton	Jeffersonville, IN	Sr	C	6-2
39	Neil Funk	LaPorte, IN	Jr	F	6-3
17	Ralph Hamilton	Fort Wayne, IN	Jr	F	6-1
35	Bob Hines	Fort Wayne, IN	Jr	C	6-2
	Maurice Hooper	Anderson, IN	So	G	5-10
15	Roy Kilby	Muncie, IN	Jr	G	5-10
16	Warren Lewis	New Castle, IN	Jr	F	6-0
7	John Logan	Richmond, IN	Sr	F	6-0
5	Leroy Mangin	Washington, IN	So	F	5-10
4	Billy McGinnis	Eminence, IN	So	G	5-9
	George Poolitson	Bloomington, IN	So	F	6-0
	Ed Schienbein	Southport, IN	Jr	G	5-9
	Sterling Scott	Hammond, IN	So	C	6-6
11	James Smith	Shelbyville, IN	Jr	F	6-2
32	Maurice Stohler	Anderson, IN	So	F	6-0
14	Irv Swanson (Capt.)	LaPorte, IN	Sr	G	5-10
21	Dick Wittenbraker	New Castle, IN	Jr	G	6-2
20	Ward Williams	Colfax, IN	So	C	6-3
19	Sam Young	Rushville, IN	Fr	G	6-2

SEASON RESULTS 1942-43

Date	Court	Opponent	Result	Score
12/5/1942	H	DePauw	W	57-40
12/7/1942	H	Wabash	W	58-40
12/14/1942	H	Fort Knox	W	64-19
12/23/1942	N1	Kentucky	W	58-52
12/28/1942	A	Loyola Chicago	W	51-43
12/30/1942	A	Nebraska	W	40-39
1/4/1943	A	Butler	W	42-27
1/9/1943	H	Ohio State	W	45-37
1/11/1943	H	Ohio State	W	61-31
1/16/1943	A	Chicago	W	55-27
1/23/1943	A	Iowa	W	71-55
1/25/1943	A	Iowa	W	64-43
1/30/1943	H	Purdue	W	53-35
2/6/1943	H	Michigan	W	32-24
2/8/1943	H	Michigan	W	48-33
2/13/1943	A	Wisconsin	W	51-44
2/15/1943	A	Wisconsin	L	53-57
2/20/1943	H	Minnesota	W	51-39
2/22/1943	H	Minnesota	W	40-28
3/1/1943	A	Purdue	L	38-41

1 Louisville, KY

1942-43 BIG TEN STANDINGS

	W	L	PCT
Illinois	12	0	1.000
Indiana	11	2	.846
Northwestern	7	5	.583
Wisconsin	6	6	.500
Purdue	6	6	.500
Minnesota	5	7	.417
Ohio State	5	7	.417
Michigan	4	8	.333
Iowa	3	9	.250
Chicago	0	9	.000

streaked to a 15-3 lead to open the game and led 23-13 at the half. The Hoosiers went on to a 51-44 win, as Williams scored 17 and Hamilton hit for 16, to deliver Indiana's ninth straight Big Ten win and improve the Hoosiers' season record to 16-0. However, the Badgers ended the streak in their second game against the Hoosiers by pulling a 57-53 upset. Wisconsin led 33-27 at the break and fended off every IU challenge in the second half.

The Hoosiers played the final doubleheader of the season against Minnesota on Saturday, February 20, and Monday, February 22. In the first game, Indiana started slowly and fell behind 28-16 at the break, but caught fire in the second half and outscored the Gophers 35-11 on the way to a 51-39 victory. Williams led all scorers with 16. In the second game, Williams went to the bench in the opening minutes of the first half because of foul trouble, but Indiana still led 20-14 at the half and eventually coasted to a 40-28 win. However, in the second half, Hamilton, IU's leading scorer, suffered a knee injury and Swanson was hobbled by a boil on his knee.

All that remained for the Hoosiers was a season-ending showdown with Purdue in West Lafayette on Monday, March 1. If winless Chicago could upset undefeated Illinois in Champaign and the Hoosiers could beat the Boilermakers, then IU would win the Big Ten title by half a game. Unfortunately, that unlikely scenario didn't happen as the Illinois "Whiz Kids" crushed the Maroons 92-25 and the Boilermakers upset the Hoosiers 41-38.

With a perfect 12-0 record, Illinois won their second consecutive Big Ten title. However, the Hoosiers were one of the hottest teams in America during the 16-0 streak to start the season and had risen to No. 2 in the polls. With an 18-2 overall record, the Hoosiers had tied the best mark in school history, and their 11-2 conference record secured an outright second-place finish, three and a half games ahead of the third-place team.

SEASON STATISTICS
1938-39 TO 1942-43

1938-39

Team Statistics	G	FG/A	PCT	FT/A	PCT	TP	AVG
Indiana	20	356-1470	.242	193-320	.603	905	45.3
Opponents	20	257-1281	.201	180-340	.529	692	34.6
Player Statistics	G	FG/A	PCT	FT/A	PCT	TP	AVG
W. Menke	20	80-262	.305	36-64	.563	196	9.8
Andres	19	68-305	.223	24-36	.667	160	8.4
Armstrong	17	46-203	.227	37-59	.627	129	7.6
Dro	19	44-167	.263	16-38	.421	104	5.5
Johnson	16	32-126	.254	24-33	.727	88	5.5
Huffman	20	33-162	.204	23-35	.657	89	4.5
Schafer	11	19-71	.263	9-16	.563	47	4.3
Motter	15	8-41	.195	9-14	.643	25	1.7
R. Menke	17	9-47	.191	10-15	.667	28	1.7
Dorsey	15	7-37	.189	1-2	.500	15	1.0
Stevenson	11	5-23	.217	1-2	.500	11	1.0
Francis	9	2-10	.200	2-4	.500	6	0.7
Tipmore	6	1-4	.250	1-1	1.00	3	0.5
Gridley	4	1-3	.333	0-0	.000	2	0.5
Lettellier	4	1-4	.250	0-1	.000	2	0.5
Ooley	7	0-4	.000	0-0	.000	0	0.0
McLaughlin	1	0-1	.000	0-0	.000	0	0.0

1939-40

PLEASE SEE CHAPTER 6

1940-41

Team Statistics	G	FG/A	PCT	FT/A	PCT	TP	AVG
Indiana	20	361-1097	.329	183-293	.625	905	45.3
Opponents	20	252-907	.278	210-375	.560	714	35.7
Player Statistics	G	FG/A	PCT	FT/A	PCT	TP	AVG
W. Menke	20	36-189	.365	38-63	.603	176	8.8
Armstrong	9	27-90	.300	13-19	.684	67	7.4
Schafer	20	42-133	.316	27-40	.675	111	5.6
Zimmer	20	41-102	.402	19-28	.679	101	5.1
Logan	19	37-88	.420	18-28	.643	92	4.8
Dro	20	37-146	.253	11-25	.440	85	4.3
McCreary	18	30-108	.278	16-22	.727	76	4.2
Swanson	16	20-55	.364	10-16	.625	50	3.1
R. Menke	17	20-66	.303	11-16	.688	51	3.0
Francis	16	15-47	.319	8-12	.667	38	2.4
Denton	14	14-56	.250	5-8	.625	33	2.4
Motter	4	1-2	.500	3-5	.600	5	1.3
Hoffman	4	1-1	1.00	2-5	.400	4	1.0
Gridley	9	3-6	.500	0-1	.000	6	0.7
Driver	11	3-7	.429	1-2	.500	7	0.6
Heine	2	0-0	.000	1-2	.500	1	0.5
Torphy	7	1-1	1.00	0-1	.000	2	0.3
Forsyth	1	0-0	.000	0-0	.000	0	0.0
Hasler	1	0-0	.000	0-0	.000	0	0.0
Scheidler	1	0-0	.000	0-0	.000	0	0.0
Wellman	1	0-0	.000	0-0	.000	0	0.0

1941-42

Team Statistics	G	FG/A	PCT	FT/A	PCT	TP	AVG
Indiana	21	398-1174	.339	192-304	.632	986	47.0
Opponents	21					825	39.3
Player Statistics	G	FG/A	PCT	FT/A	PCT	TP	AVG
Denton	20	70-184	.380	35-50	.700	175	8.8
Zimmer	21	64-165	.388	38-54	.704	166	7.9
Swanson	21	72-194	.371	23-37	.622	165	7.9
Logan	20	47-161	.292	38-51	.745	132	6.6
Hamilton	20	57-175	.326	14-33	.424	128	6.4
Wittenbraker	21	23-100	.230	17-40	.425	63	3.0
Lewis	18	23-70	.329	6-10	.600	52	2.9
Hoffman	15	19-55	.345	4-5	.800	42	2.8
Funk	9	5-15	.333	5-7	.714	15	1.7
Kilby	11	5-20	.250	6-8	.750	16	1.5
Driver	9	5-10	.500	2-4	.500	12	1.3
Frey	7	3-11	.273	2-3	.667	8	1.1
Bunker	4	1-4	.250	2-2	1.00	4	1.0
Torphy	9	4-10	.400	0-0	.000	8	0.9
Gwin	2	0-0	.000	0-0	.000	0	0.0
Wise	2	0-0	.000	0-0	.000	0	0.0
Alleyne	1	0-0	.000	0-0	.000	0	0.0

1942-43

Team Statistics	G	FG/A	PCT	FT/A	PCT	TP	AVG
Indiana	20	412-1268	.325	208-311	.669	1032	51.6
Opponents	20					754	37.7
Player Statistics	G	FG/A	PCT	FT/A	PCT	TP	AVG
Hamilton	20	97-281	.345	53-68	.779	247	12.4
Williams	20	81-251	.324	47-69	.681	209	10.5
Logan	16	16-61	.339	22-35	.629	144	9.0
Swanson	20	58-192	.302	18-35	.514	134	6.7
Wittenbraker	20	33-132	.250	31-50	.620	97	4.9
Denton	18	25-106	.236	17-26	.654	67	3.7
McGinnis	16	21-65	.323	8-10	.800	50	3.1
Mangin	3	2-4	.500	2-2	1.00	6	2.0
Stohler	1	1-1	1.00	0-0	.000	2	2.0
Lewis	16	13-20	.650	3-5	.600	29	1.8
Cowan	17	13-27	.481	4-7	.571	30	1.8
Smith	9	4-6	.667	3-4	.750	11	1.2
Hines	7	2-11	.182	0-0	.000	4	0.6
Funk	4	1-2	.500	0-0	.000	2	0.5
Kilby	3	0-1	.000	0-0	.000	0	0.0
Hooper	1	0-0	.000	0-0	.000	0	0.0
Schienbein	1	0-2	.000	0-0	.000	0	0.0
Scott	1	0-1	.000	0-0	.000	0	0.0
Young	1	0-1	.000	0-0	.000	0	0.0

1943-44

OVERALL RECORD: 7-15

CONFERENCE RECORD: 2-10 (EIGHTH PLACE)

The 1943-44 team. First row (left to right): Art Lehman, Richard Peed, Bob Rowland, Sam Young, George Tipton, Paul Shields, Les Ray; Second row: Ed Sidwell, Richard Doyle, Charles Traux, Claude Retherford, Jr., Jack Mercer, Richard Stozek, Irvin Leary, head coach Harry Good; Third row: Max Williams, Roy Bradenburg, Eugene Latham, Tom Thompson, Bob Ravensburg, Herod Toon, Bob Taylor, Jim Jensen, Art Marshall, manager Leon Kaminski. IU Archives

With the acceleration of World War II, which called for nearly every able-bodied man in the U.S. to serve in the armed forces, the Hoosiers' 1943-44 team lost all of its returning lettermen (and all of its "numeral winners" from the freshman team). That left a rag-tag roster of players—mostly freshmen—who had a little basketball experience from high school to compete for a lot of open spots on the IU roster. With Branch McCracken on a leave of absence to serve in the navy, Indiana hired Harry Good, a highly successful basketball coach at Indiana Central College (now the University of Indianapolis), to lead the Hoosiers during the war years.

"We know we will be outclassed in almost every game, and the boys have a lot to learn," admitted Good. "It will be well into the season before we know just what kind of team we will have."

The other challenge for Good was that additional young men were being called to military service at all times. "We won't know from game to game who will be able to play," said Good.

In that uncertain atmosphere, Indiana started the season against Camp Atterbury on Wednesday, December 1, in Bloomington. The Hoosiers started five freshmen and used a slow, deliberate attack (they didn't have the players to run the fast break) to slog through a 40-28 win. Center George Tipton led IU with 11 points. The next day, four of the Hoosiers who had played in the Atterbury game (including Ed Scheinbein, the 1940 Indiana Mr. Basketball) left the team for the U.S. Navy.

On Saturday, December 4, IU traveled to DePauw and was beaten 47-36, as the Tigers' Charley Radcliffe (who had played on the IU freshman team in 1942-43) dropped in 27 points against his former school. Tipton led IU with 16. On Tuesday, December 7, the Hoosiers dug themselves out of an eight-point hole in the second half to win a 38-35 game over Wabash in Crawfordsville. IU forward Paul Shields had a game-high 16 points. On Saturday, December 11, Indiana suffered its first blowout of the season in a 66-41 loss to Kentucky in Louisville.

Wabash came to Bloomington for a rematch on December 14, and the Hoosiers easily dispatched the Little Giants 44-27 after opening a 24-10 lead at the half. Shields led all scorers with 13 points. IU traveled to Chicago on Saturday, December 18, and got crushed 81-43 by future NBA star George Mikan and his DePaul Blue Devils. Mikan scored a game-high 27 points, while Richard Peed (who hadn't scored all season) led Indiana with 15 points. The Hoosiers avenged their earlier loss at DePauw when the Tigers came to Bloomington on December 21, and got edged out by the Hoosiers 38-34. IU closed out the preconference slate with an easy 42-32 win at Camp Atterbury on Tuesday, January 4. That gave Indiana a 5-3 record heading into conference play.

After blowing away most Big Ten opponents the year before, the Hoosiers were on the other end of the blowouts in 1943-44. The first one came in the conference opener against Purdue in West Lafayette. The Boilermakers overran the Hoosiers 63-43 in front of 8,000 rowdy Purdue fans.

Once again, the Big Ten schedule called for some doubleheaders when teams went on the road, in order

1943-44 TEAM ROSTER

Head coach: Harry Good (interim)
Assistant coach: Bill Johnson

No.	Player	Hometown	Class	Position	Height
	Philip Bowser	Goshen, IN	Fr	F	6-2
37	Roy Bradenburg	Corydon, IN	Fr	G	5-10
16	John Crouch	Evansville, IN	So	C	6-3
8	Don Earnhart	Marion, IN	Fr	C	6-2
4	Gene Farris	Campbellsburg, IN	Fr	F	6-1
9	Jack Herron	Logansport, IN	So	G	5-8
30	Irvin Leary	Greenfield, IN	Fr	F	5-11
43	Art Lehman	Cedar Lake, IN	Fr	F	6-1
11	Jack Mercer	Brazil, IN	Fr	G	6-1
25	Richard Peed	Richmond, IN		C	6-3
	Pete Pithos	Fort Wayne, IN	Jr	F	6-1
32	Bob Ravensburg	Bellevue, KY	So	F	6-1
38	Les Ray	Sullivan, IN	Fr	F	6-1
22	Claude Retherford, Jr.	French Lick, IN	Fr	F	6-0
14	Bob Rowland	Martinsville, IN	Fr	G	6-0
5	Ed Schienbein	Southport, IN	Sr	G	5-9
33	Paul Shields (Capt.)	Monrovia, IN	Fr	F	6-2
42	Ed Sidwell	New Castle, IN	Fr	G	6-2
7	George Tipton	Terre Haute, IN	Fr	C	6-3
24	Herod Toon	Indianapolis, IN	Fr	G	5-10
6	Charles Traux	Spring Lake, NJ		G	5-11
19	Sam Young	Rushville, IN	So	G	6-2

SEASON RESULTS 1943-44

Date	Court	Opponent	Result	Score
12/1/1943	H	Camp Atterbury	W	40-28
12/4/1943	A	DePauw	L	36-43
12/7/1943	A	Wabash	W	38-35
12/11/1943	N1	Kentucky	L	41-66
12/14/1943	H	Wabash	W	44-27
12/18/1943	A	DePaul	L	43-81
12/21/1943	H	DePauw	W	38-34
1/4/1944	A	Camp Atterbury	W	42-32
1/8/1944	A	Purdue	L	43-63
1/14/1944	A	Ohio State	L	46-72
1/15/1944	A	Ohio State	L	38-74
1/22/1944	H	Miami (OH)	L	50-52
1/28/1944	H	Iowa	L	42-43
1/29/1944	H	Iowa	L	40-52
2/4/1944	A	Michigan	L	49-65
2/5/1944	A	Michigan	L	44-46
2/11/1944	H	Wisconsin	L	43-62
2/12/1944	H	Wisconsin	L	31-52
2/18/1944	A	Minnesota	L	47-78
2/19/1944	A	Minnesota	W	48-47
2/25/1944	H	Bunker Hill	L	36-41
3/4/1944	H	Purdue	W	51-45

1 Louisville, KY

1943-44 BIG TEN STANDINGS

	W	L	PCT
Ohio State	10	2	.833
Iowa	9	3	.750
Wisconsin	9	3	.750
Northwestern	8	4	.667
Purdue	8	4	.667
Illinois	5	7	.417
Michigan	5	7	.417
Minnesota	2	10	.167
Indiana	2	10	.167
Chicago	0	8	.000

In 1943, Branch McCracken took a leave of absence from Indiana University to become a lieutenant in the U.S. Navy as the U.S. involvement in World War II was building to a crescendo.   McCracken would spend almost three years in the service before returning to his coaching post in Bloomington.   IU Archives

to accommodate wartime travel restrictions. The Hoosiers' first doubleheader was against Ohio State in Columbus on Friday, January 14, and Saturday, January 15, and OSU crushed the Hoosiers in both contests. The first was 72-46 and the second was 74-38. Indiana came back to Bloomington and faced a different Ohio team on Saturday, January 22. Unfortunately, the Hoosiers also lost to Miami of Ohio, 52-50. IU's Claude Retherford had tied the game with two clutch free throws in the final minute, but Miami's Glenn Bruning scored just before time expired to clinch the win for the Redhawks. The

Hoosiers' Paul Shields and Sam Young tied for game-high honors with 15 points each.

Iowa, the undefeated Big Ten co-leader, came to Bloomington for a pair of games on Friday, January 28, and Saturday, January 29. The first game was a nip-and-tuck affair that the Hoosiers appeared to have in the bag when Roy Bradenburg hit a baseline shot to give IU a 42-41 lead in the final minute. Then, the Hoosier defense stopped the Hawkeyes, but Iowa's Dave Danner collected an errant Indiana pass and scored in the final seconds to allow the Hawkeyes to steal a 43-42 win. The next night, Iowa had an easier time in downing the Hoosiers 52-40.

Indiana went to Ann Arbor and dropped two games to Michigan on February 4 and 5. The first was a 65-49 cakewalk for the Wolverines, but IU led for most of the second game before faltering down the stretch and losing 46-44. The next weekend, IU hosted Wisconsin, and the Badgers whipped the Hoosiers in both games. The first game ended 62-43, while the score of the second game was 52-31. Next, the Hoosiers went to Minnesota for a two-game battle between teams that had yet to win a conference game. The Gophers won the first contest 48-47 on a free throw in the final seconds. However, the Hoosiers turned the tables and beat their host by the same score, 48-47, in the second game—an over-time contest that was decided when IU's Bob Rowland buried a free throw at the end of OT.

After leading 26-19 at the half, Indiana dropped another nonconference game by losing to the Bunker Hill Flying Patriots 41-36 on Friday, February 25. However, after a dismal 1-10 run in the Big Ten, the Hoosiers gained a measure of redemption on Saturday, March 4, when they upset archrival Purdue 51-45 in Bloomington. Peed was Indiana's top scorer with 11, while Jack Mercer added 10 and Shields chipped in nine.

The Purdue win was IU's best-played game of the season as the Hoosiers fought off every Boilermaker charge in the second half. It provided one of the few bright spots in a season that was one of the worst in Indiana basketball history.

1944-45

OVERALL RECORD: 10-11

CONFERENCE RECORD: 3-9 (NINTH PLACE)

The 1944-45 team. First row (left to right): Dean Daniels, Norbert Hermann, Dick Schnieder, Jack Mercer, Al Kravolansky, Ted Kluszewski, Gene Johnson, Gene Farris; Second row: Louis Teats, Charles Leedke, Freeland Armstrong, Charles Radcliffe, John Roper, Ed Murray, George Cherry, Zygmund Belsowski, Del Russell; Third row: Robert Goodman, Jack Herron, Gene Turner, Mihajlovich [first name unknown], Dave Etchison, George Milan, Bruenoehler [first name unknown], George Laughery. IU Archives

Entering the 1944-45 campaign, Indiana once again lost several of its top returnees to the military. However, unlike the previous season, the Hoosiers returned four lettermen and several other experienced players. Coach Harry Good knew that his team would be more competitive than the previous season, but he also knew that he still didn't have the material to be a Big Ten contender. Unfortunately for Good and the Hoosiers, Gene Faris, who was Indiana's leading scorer at 13.5 PPG through the first 14 games of the season, got called to military service during the Big Ten season. After Faris left, the Hoosiers dropped six of the final seven contests.

On Thursday, November 30, the Hoosiers kicked off the schedule by edging out Wabash 43-39 in Crawfordsville. Junior forward Charley Radcliffe (who was back in a Hoosier uniform after a year at DePauw) led all scorers with 14 points. On Saturday, December 2, the Hoosiers doubled up Camp Atterbury 44-22 in Bloomington. Three days later, IU suffered its first setback when DePauw came to Bloomington and beat the Hoosiers 51-50 on a field

1944-45 TEAM ROSTER

Head coach: Harry Good (interim)
Assistant coach: Bill Johnson

No.	Player	Hometown	Class	Position	Height
23	Freeland Armstrong	Paoli, IN	Fr	G	5-11
24	Zygmund Belsowski	LaPorte, IN	Fr	G	5-11
15	Ray Brandenburg	Corydon, IN	So	G	5-10
6	George Cherry	Greensburg, IN	Fr	G	5-11
22	James Copeland	Elwood, IN	Fr	F	6-2
21	Dean Daniels	South Bend, IN	Fr	F	5-11
8	Dave Etchison	Alexandria, IN	Fr	F	6-0
4	Gene Farris	Campbellsburg, IN	So	F	6-3
14	Marion Fine	Indianapolis, IN	So	G	5-6
10	Robert Goodman	Patterson, NJ	Fr	F	6-0
12	Norbert Hermann	Brownstown, IN	Fr	G	6-2
9	Jack Herron	Logansport, IN	Jr	G	5-8
7	Gene Johnson	Hartford City, IN	Fr	C	6-3
41	Ted Kluszewski	Argos, IL	Fr	F	6-2
35	Al Kravolansky (capt.)	East Chicago, IN	So	F/C	6-3
17	George Laughery	Robinson, IL	Fr	F	6-1
18	Charles Leedke	Connersville, IN	Fr	G	5-10
11	Jack Mercer	Brazil, IN	So	G	6-1
25	George Milan	East Chicago, IN	Fr	G	5-11
40	Milton Mink	Rochester, IN	Fr	C	6-5
29	Ed Murray	Cincinnati, OH	Fr	F	5-10
5	Charles Radcliffe	Paoli, IN	Jr	F	5-10
45	John Roper	Campbell, OH	Fr	C	6-5
39	Del Russell	Park Ridge, IL	So	F	6-0
5	Ed Schienbein	Indianapolis, IN	Sr	G	5-9
22	Dick Schnieder	LaPorte, IN	Fr	G	5-11
16	Louis Teats	Aurora, IN	Fr	G	5-6
27	Gene Turner	Kokomo, IN	Fr	G	5-11

SEASON RESULTS 1944-45

Date	Court	Opponent	Result	Score
11/30/1944	A	Wabash	W	43-39
12/2/1944	H	Camp Atterbury	W	44-22
12/5/1944	H	DePauw	L	50-51
12/8/1944	A	Camp Atterbury	W	63-48
12/14/1944	H	Wabash	W	55-39
12/16/1944	N1	Kentucky	L	43-61
12/30/1944	H	Nebraska	W	65-42
1/2/1945	H	Pentathlon of Mexico	W	53-33
1/5/1945	A	Michigan	L	53-54
1/9/1945	A	DePauw	W	58-38
1/17/1945	H	Purdue	W	51-50
1/20/1945	A	Minnesota	W	48-46
1/22/1945	A	Iowa	L	51-56
1/27/1945	H	Michigan	L	43-47
2/3/1945	H	Minnesota	L	48-56
2/7/1945	A	Purdue	L	48-62
2/10/1945	H	Iowa	L	40-45
2/12/1945	A	Illinois	L	48-71
2/17/1945	H	Ohio State	L	45-63
2/24/1945	A	Ohio State	L	52-85
2/28/1945	H	Illinois	W	65-55

1 Louisville, KY

1944-45 BIG TEN STANDINGS

	W	L	PCT
Iowa	11	1	.917
Ohio State	10	2	.833
Illinois	7	5	.583
Purdue	6	6	.500
Michigan	5	7	.417
Wisconsin	4	8	.333
Minnesota	4	8	.333
Northwestern	4	8	.333
Indiana	3	9	.250
Chicago	-	-	-

goal from the Tigers' reserve center, Joe Gerich, in the final 30 seconds.

Indiana traveled over to Camp Atterbury on December 8 and won its second game from the servicemen, 63-48. Radcliffe was the high scorer with 17 points, while sophomore Gene Farris added 14. Radcliffe's 22 points on Thursday, December 14, sunk the Wabash Little Giants 55-39 in the IU Fieldhouse. Kentucky dealt Indiana its second loss of the season in a 61-43 blowout on Saturday, December 16, in Louisville. Radcliffe had the hot hand again with 15 points.

Two weeks later, on Saturday, December 30, Nebraska came to Bloomington and the Hoosiers raced by the Cornhuskers for a 65-42 win. Farris was the game's top scorer with 15, while Radcliffe dropped in 12. The Pentathlon of Mexico team was the next visitor to Bloomington on Tuesday, January 2, as part of the team's goodwill tour across the United States. Indiana handily won a 53-33 game against the Mexicans, who were outsized but very scrappy.

The Hoosiers opened Big Ten play by losing a see-saw battle to Michigan 54-53 on Friday, January 5, in Ann Arbor. Michigan freshman Ted Berce sank his only field goal attempt of the game in the final minute to give the Wolverines the victory. IU then played its final nonconference game of the season against DePauw and clobbered the Tigers 58-38 in Greencastle on January 9, which served as revenge for DePauw's one-point win over the Hoosiers in Bloomington a month earlier. Farris led all scorers with 22 points, and Al Kravolansky chipped in 10 for IU.

On Wednesday, January 17, Purdue came to Bloomington for a showdown with its cross-state rival. The Hoosiers built a 13-point advantage at the break and turned it into a 47-33 lead by the middle of the second half. The Boilermakers fought back, but the Hoosiers stalled the game and eventually prevailed 51-50. Forward James Copeland paced IU with 16 points. The Hoosiers won another close game on January 20 at Minnesota. Ray Brandenburg buried a field goal in the final seconds as Indiana triumphed 48-46. Farris led the Hoosiers with 13 points, while Copeland added 11, and Brandenburg scored 10. The Minnesota victory improved IU to 2-1 in conference play.

IU played another good game on Monday, January 22, at Iowa City, but the Iowa Hawkeyes prevailed 56-51. Farris led IU with 18 points. The Hoosiers then dropped another nail-biter on Saturday, January 27, when Michigan came to Bloomington and slipped away with a 47-43 victory. Charley Radcliffe returned to the lineup (after missing the previous six games) and scored 13 points to lead the Hoosiers. Farris added 11 but it was his last game of this season, as he was inducted into the army soon thereafter.

Indiana hosted Minnesota on Saturday, February 3, and the Golden Gophers avenged their earlier loss to the Hoosiers by winning 56-48 in Bloomington. Four days later, Purdue also avenged its earlier loss to the Hoosiers with a convincing 62-48 win in West Lafayette. IU had led by seven points at one time in the first half. Freshman forward Norbert Hermann led the Hoosiers with 14 points, while sophomore Al Kravolansky scored 12.

League leader Iowa came to Bloomington on Saturday, February 10, and completed its season sweep of the Hoosiers with a 45-40 win in a game that was tied seven times before the Hawkeyes pulled away at the end. The following Monday, Indiana traveled to Illinois and got crushed by the Fighting Illini 71-48. Copeland scored 16 points for the Hoosiers in the losing effort.

Next, Indiana played a home-and-home series on consecutive Saturdays with title contender Ohio State and got blown out in both games. On February 17, OSU won 63-45 in Bloomington. On February 24, the Buckeyes blasted the Hoosiers 85-52 in Columbus. In the second game, 5'8" guard Jack Herron was the only bright spot for the Hoosiers with 19 points. Including the two defeats to OSU, the Hoosiers had lost eight straight games.

However, just as they done the previous season, the Hoosiers closed out a dismal conference campaign with an impressive home win. On Wednesday, February 28, the Illinois squad that had beaten Indiana by 23 points a couple weeks earlier came to Bloomington and got outplayed by a determined IU team. The Hoosiers led 33-28 at the break and never gave up the lead in the second half on the way to a 65-55 victory. Center Al Kravolansky shined for Indiana with 23 points.

With a 3-9 conference record, the Hoosiers improved on their Big Ten mark from the previous season by one game. However, in many contests, IU competed much better than they had the year before, and their 10-11 overall record was certainly a better showing, although definitely not up to the standard that Indiana had established during the previous two decades.

1945-46

OVERALL RECORD: 18-3

CONFERENCE RECORD: 9-3 (SECOND PLACE)

INDIVIDUAL HONORS:

JOHN WALLACE—ALL-AMERICA

By the time the 1945-46 basketball season started, World War II was all but over, and many U.S. servicemen were returning home. This included a number of former IU basketball players, as well as navy lieutenant commander Branch McCracken, who came back to Bloomington in December for a reception at the university, and soon began negotiating his return as basketball coach. Thus, the interim coach, Harry Good, knew that this would be his last season on the sidelines for Indiana, and he made it count by leading the Hoosiers to an outstanding record. Good's squad was led by a pair of high-scoring forwards, John Wallace and Al Kralovansky. Those two would combine to average 23.1 PPG, and with 302 points for the year, Wallace shattered Ernie Andres's single-season scoring record (250) and earned All-America honors. IU's other high scorer was senior guard Dick Wittenbraker. Unfortunately, after a great start to the season, Wittenbraker came down with an illness that cut his season short midway through the campaign.

The schedule opened on Saturday, December 1, against Camp Atterbury in Bloomington. With guard Dick Wittenbraker, a discharged military veteran and a member of the 1942-43 IU squad leading the running attack, the Hoosiers handed Atterbury a 59-49 defeat. Forward John Wallace led IU with 14

The 1945-46 team. First row (left to right): Dean Daniels, Norbert Hermann, Dick Schnieder, Jack Mercer, Al Kravolansky, Ted Kluszewski, Gene Johnson, Gene Farris; Second row: Louis Teats, Charles Leedke, Freeland Armstrong, Charles Radcliffe, John Roper, Ed Murray, George Cherry, Zygmund Belsowski, Del Russell; Third row: Robert Goodman, Jack Herron, Gene Turner, Mihajlovich [first name unknown], Dave Etchison, George Milan, Bruenoehler [first name unknown], George Laughery. IU Archives

points, and Wittenbraker added 12. A week later, Washington University, St. Louis, came to Bloomington and was soundly beaten 53-39 after trailing the Hoosiers by only a point at the half. A return game against Camp Atterbury was next on the schedule on Tuesday, December 11. The Hoosiers went to the Atterbury base and scored a 56-53 victory in front of an audience of 3,000 soldiers.

On Saturday, December 15, the Hoosiers played at Louisville and stole a 62-59 victory led by 21 points from Wallace. That was followed by a Bloomington showdown with Cincinnati on Tuesday, December 18. The Bearcats forged ahead 27-26 at the half, but Indiana put on a big surge in the second session and claimed a 54-44 win. Wittenbraker led IU with 13, including 11 in the second half.

Indiana went to Ann Arbor for its first Big Ten game against Michigan on Saturday, December 22.

The two teams engaged in a classic Big Ten struggle, and the game was up for grabs in the final minutes. The score was knotted at 58-58 when IU guard Jack Herron seemed to hit the game-winning field goal as time expired and deliver a two-point victory for Indiana. However, the referee ruled that the shot went in after the final gun sounded, but he had to call the players back on the floor because they had already run into the locker rooms and the crowd had started filing out of the arena. The Hoosiers were enraged by the call and turned their anger into a 9-0 run in overtime to claim a 67-58 victory.

On New Year's Day, IU went to Indianapolis and took on the Butler Bulldogs. Wallace broke loose for 27 points to lead the Hoosiers to a 58-47 triumph. On Saturday, January 5, Indiana got back to conference play with a 59-34 pounding of the Chicago Maroons in the Windy City. Ten different IU players scored in the victory, which improved the Hoosiers to 8-0 on the season. The streak stopped abruptly on Monday, January 7, when the Golden Gophers outran the Hurryin' Hoosiers for a 58-47 win in the IU Fieldhouse. IU returned to their winning ways on Saturday, January 12, with a 45-39 win over the visiting Iowa Hawkeyes, as Wittenbraker led all scorers with 16.

Purdue hosted Indiana on January 16 in West Lafayette, and the Boilermakers led nearly the entire way en route to a 49-38 win. Purdue's 6'6" center Bob Miller sank the Hoosiers with 19 points. After falling to 3-2 in conference play with the Purdue loss, IU took advantage of three consecutive home games against conference opponents by notching victories in all three contests: 44-39 against Ohio State on January 19; 46-43 against Michigan on January 21; and 61-32 against Chicago on January 26. The Hoosiers were now 6-2 and within striking distance of the Big Ten leaders.

IU opened the month of February with a nonconference game against Washington University in St. Louis on Tuesday, February 5. The Hoosiers had their offense working like clockwork as they defeated the Bears 56-46. Wallace scored 16 points to lead IU, and freshman Dave Walker added 13. Four days later, Indiana's conference title hopes dimmed when the Hoosiers went to Ohio State and lost a 53-52 cliffhanger in overtime.

On the way back from Columbus, IU stopped in Cincinnati on Monday, February 11, and thrashed the Cincinnati Bearcats 60-22 on the strength of 22 points from Wallace. On Saturday, February 16, Purdue came to Bloomington for a rematch and led the Hoosiers for most of the first half before IU grabbed a 25-23 lead at the break. The Hoosiers pushed the lead to nine points at the beginning of the second half and rode that momentum to a 57-47 victory. A different in-state rival, Ball State, came to Bloomington on Tuesday, February 19, and the Hoosiers crushed the Cardinals 84-41 (IU's 84 points set the school's single-game scoring mark).

The Hoosiers closed out their schedule with two road games and won them both. The first was a surprisingly easy 75-52 win at Minnesota on Saturday, February 23. Five different Hoosiers scored in double figures, led by Wallace with 21, while the Golden Gophers had only one player in double digits. Two

1945-46 TEAM ROSTER

Head coach: Harry Good (interim)

No. Height	Player	Hometown	Class	Position
16 Louis Amaya	Pueblo, CO	Fr	G	6-1
23 Freeland Armstrong	Paoli, IN	So	G	5-11
38 Dee Baker	Indianapolis, IN	Fr	F	5-11
37 Stephen Chaleff	Indianapolis, IN	Fr	G	6-1
32 James Copeland	Elwood, IN	So	F	6-2
25 Don Dewer	Aurora, IN	Fr	G	6-2
6 Louis Edmonds	Frankfort, IN	Fr	F	6-2
12 Norbert Hermann	Brownstown, IN	So	G	6-2
9 Jack Herron	Logansport, IN	Sr	G	5-8
15 Roy Kilby	Muncie, IN	Sr	G	5-10
35 Al Kravolansky	East Chicago, IN	Jr	F	6-3
40 Robert Mehl	Indianapolis, IN	Fr	F	6-1
4 Joseph Normington	Greenwood, IN	Fr	F	5-10
17 Jim Powers	South Bend, IN	Fr	G	6-0
29 Charles Radcliffe	Paoli, IN	Sr	F	5-10
11 Tom Schwartz	Kokomo, IN	Fr	C	6-6
8 Bill Shephard	Hope, IN	Fr	F	6-0
14 Jim Stepler	Greentown, IN	Fr	C	6-4
27 Gene Turner	Kokomo, IN	So	G	5-11
7 Dave Walker	Loogootee, IN	Fr	F	6-3
10 John Wallace	Richmond, IN	So	F	6-3
26 Richard Westlake	New Palestine, IN	Fr	G	6-0
21 Dick Wittenbraker (Capt.)	New Castle, IN	Sr	G	6-2

SEASON RESULTS 1945-46

Date	Court	Opponent	Result	Score
12/1/1945	H	Camp Atterbury	W	59-49
12/8/1945	H	Washington (MO)	W	53-39
12/11/1945	A	Camp Atterbury	W	56-53
12/15/1945	A	Louisville	W	62-59
12/18/1945	H	Cincinnati	W	54-44
12/22/1945	A	Michigan	W	67-58
1/1/1946	A	Butler	W	58-47
1/5/1946	A	Chicago	W	59-34
1/7/1946	H	Minnesota	L	47-58
1/12/1946	H	Iowa	W	45-39
1/16/1946	A	Purdue	L	38-49
1/19/1946	H	Ohio State	W	44-39
1/21/1946	H	Michigan	W	46-43
1/26/1946	H	Chicago	W	61-32
2/5/1946	A	Washington (MO)	W	56-46
2/19/1946	A	Ohio State	L	52-53
2/11/1946	A	Cincinnati	W	60-22
2/16/1946	H	Purdue	W	57-47
2/19/1946	H	Ball State	W	84-41
2/23/1946	A	Minnesota	W	75-52
2/25/1946	A	Iowa	W	49-46

1945-46 BIG TEN STANDINGS

	W	L	PCT
Ohio State	10	2	.833
Indiana	9	3	.750
Iowa	8	4	.667
Northwestern	8	4	.667
Illinois	7	5	.583
Minnesota	7	5	.583
Michigan	6	6	.500
Purdue	4	8	.333
Wisconsin	1	11	.083
Chicago	0	12	.000

nights later, the Hoosiers went to Iowa City and ended Iowa's 22-game home winning streak by beating the Hawkeyes 49-46. The defeat also cost Iowa a chance to share the conference title with Ohio State.

The season-ending road wins over Minnesota and Iowa allowed the 9-3 Hoosiers to claim sole possession of second place in the Big Ten, one game behind Ohio State. Since the Hoosiers went 18-3 overall, while the Buckeyes were 15-4, the NCAA selection committee awarded Indiana the NCAA tournament bid. However, the Hoosiers turned it down because their starting center, 6'6" Tom Schwartz, was being inducted into the army and would have been unable to play. OSU got the bid and lost in the second round to North Carolina.

Good had originally inherited a second-place team from McCracken, and now he turned a second-place team back over to him.

SEASON STATISTICS
1943-44 TO 1945-46

1943-44

Team Statistics	G	FG/A	PCT	FT/A	PCT	TP	AVG
Indiana	22	369-1345	.274	192-333	.577	930	42.3
Opponents	22					1112	50.5
Player Statistics	G	FG/A	PCT	FT/A	PCT	TP	AVG
Tipton	11	42-186	.226	13-27	.481	97	8.8
Shields	22	71-219	.324	36-64	.563	178	8.1
Peed	18	48-147	.327	25-47	.532	121	6.7
Earnhart	4	10-20	.500	5-8	.625	25	6.3
Young	21	52-249	.209	22-34	.647	126	6.0
Retherford	19	42-194	.216	26-37	.703	110	5.8
Farris	9	22-66	.333	8-16	.500	52	5.8
Brandenburg	18	20-112	.179	28-51	.549	68	3.8
Rowland	17	23-69	.333	16-25	.640	62	3.7
Herron	6	7-15	.467	2-4	.500	16	2.7
Mercer	19	20-45	.444	5-10	.500	45	2.4
Toon	3	2-9	.222	2-3	.667	6	2.0
Schienbein	2	2-9	.222	0-1	.000	4	2.0
Sidwell	6	2-4	.500	2-4	.500	6	1.0
Ray	7	2-4	.500	1-1	1.00	5	0.7
Lehman	12	3-10	.300	1-2	.500	7	0.6
Torak	3	0-0	.000	0-0	.000	0	0.0
Pithos	2	0-4	.000	0-3	.000	0	0.0
Crouch	1	0-0	.000	0-0	.000	0	0.0
Traux	1	0-0	.000	0-0	.000	0	0.0
Young	1	0-1	.000	0-0	.000	0	0.0

1944-45

Team Statistics	G	FG/A	PCT	FT/A	PCT	TP	AVG
Indiana	21	422-1421	.297	222-370	.600	1066	50.8
Opponents	21					1063	50.6
Player Statistics	G	FG/A	PCT	FT/A	PCT	TP	AVG
Farris	14	82-195	.421	25-34	.735	189	13.5
Radcliffe	11	54-176	.315	13-26	.500	121	11.0
Kravolansky	21	70-219	.320	55-83	.663	195	9.3
Copeland	15	52-165	.315	32-48	.667	136	9.1
Herron	16	33-125	.264	16-34	.471	82	5.1
Hermann	18	34-114	.298	20-38	.526	88	4.9
Brandenburg	18	25-152	.164	27-46	.587	77	4.3
Johnson	9	12-47	.255	4-12	.333	28	3.1
Mercer	17	21-70	.300	7-11	.636	49	2.9
Russell	8	6-29	.207	7-12	.583	19	2.4
Fine	7	7-27	.259	2-4	.500	16	2.3
Teats	4	3-12	.250	2-2	1.00	8	2.0
Leedke	1	1-5	.200	0-0	.000	2	2.0
Armstrong	14	10-38	.263	4-6	.667	24	1.7
Schneider	15	9-38	.237	4-10	.400	22	1.5
Murray	2	1-1	1.00	0-0	.000	2	1.0
Schienbein	1	0-4	.000	2-2	1.00	2	1.0
Turner	4	1-4	.250	1-1	1.00	3	0.8
Cherry	3	1-3	.333	0-0	.000	2	0.7
Roper	5	0-0	.000	1-1	1.00	1	0.2
Goodman	3	0-3	.000	0-0	.000	0	0.0
Belsowski	2	0-1	.000	0-0	.000	0	0.0
Kluszewski	2	0-0	.000	0-0	.000	0	0.0
Daniels	2	0-1	.000	0-0	.000	0	0.0
Laughery	1	0-1	.000	0-0	.000	0	0.0
Milan	1	0-0	.000	0-0	.000	0	0.0
Mink	1	0-2	.000	0-0	.000	0	0.0

1945-46

Team Statistics	G	FG/A	PCT	FT/A	PCT	TP	AVG
Indiana	21	467-1485	.314	248-422	.588	1182	56.3
Opponents	21					950	45.2
Player Statistics	G	FG/A	PCT	FT/A	PCT	TP	AVG
Wallace	21	133-390	.341	36-56	.643	302	14.4
Wittenbraker	12	44-157	.280	26-40	.650	114	9.5
Kravolansky	21	69-210	.329	45-84	.536	183	8.7
Schwartz	21	69-225	.307	32-65	.492	170	8.1
Hermann	21	50-183	.273	38-62	.613	138	6.6
Walker	18	33-87	.379	30-48	.625	96	5.3
Herron	21	28-75	.373	23-35	.657	79	3.8
Mehl	15	22-68	.324	7-15	.467	51	3.4
Powers	2	1-5	.200	2-2	1.00	4	2.0
Copeland	8	5-20	.250	4-5	.800	14	1.8
Westlake	8	6-28	.214	1-2	.500	13	1.6
Kilby	3	1-7	.143	2-2	1.00	4	1.3
Radcliffe	2	1-4	.250	0-1	.000	2	1.0
Shephard	2	1-2	.500	0-0	.000	2	1.0
Armstrong	7	2-10	.200	0-0	.000	4	0.6
Edmonds	3	0-0	.000	1-1	1.00	1	0.3
Baker	4	0-0	.000	0-0	.000	0	0.0
Amaya	2	0-0	.000	0-0	.000	0	0.0
Chaleff	2	0-0	.000	0-0	.000	0	0.0
Dewer	2	0-0	.000	0-1	.000	0	0.0
Normington	1	0-0	.000	0-0	.000	0	0.0
Turner	1	0-0	.000	0-0	.000	0	0.0

1946-47

OVERALL RECORD: 12-8

CONFERENCE RECORD: 8-4 (SECOND PLACE)

INDIVIDUAL HONORS:

RALPH HAMILTON—ALL-AMERICA, ALL-BIG TEN (FIRST TEAM),

BIG TEN MEDAL OF HONOR

From left to right: Kenneth Brown, Don Ritter, head coach Branch McCracken, Ralph Hamilton, Ward Williams. IU Archives

Al Kravolansky, Dave Walker, Robert Mehl, Norbert Hermann, John Wallace. IU Archives

I n his first season back at the helm of the basketball squad, coach Branch McCracken had a conglomeration of different players that he had to forge into a single team. Five lettermen returned from the previous year (including All-American John Wallace), and several former players returned from military service to rejoin the team, including Ralph Hamilton, Ward Williams and Don Ritter (an outstanding player from the 1942-43 freshman squad). Plus, McCracken would have the services of some older freshmen who were now coming to IU after

serving in the military right out of high school. These players, such as 22-year-old freshman Lou Watson, were eligible to compete on the varsity right away. It took a while for the team's chemistry to jell, but the squad eventually put together a solid season in which McCracken's fast-break offense was re-instituted in full force.

IU had a deep roster with a lot of players who could score, but the big gun was 6'1" senior forward Ralph Hamilton. Four years earlier, Hamilton set Indiana's single-game scoring record with 31 points

1946-47 TEAM ROSTER

Head coach: Branch McCracken

No.	Player	Hometown	Class	Position	Height
15	Bob Armstrong	Fort Wayne, IN	Fr	C	6-4
22	Kenneth Brown	Muncie, IN	So	F	6-4
4	Bob Cowan	Fort Wayne, IN	Sr	G	5-10
5	Ralph Hamilton (Capt.)	Fort Wayne, IN	Sr	F	6-1
8	Al Herman	Bloomington, IN	Fr	F	6-3
12	Norbert Hermann	Brownstown, IN	Jr	G	6-2
11	Lou Jensen	New Albany, IN	Fr	G	5-11
13	Al Kravolansky	East Chicago, IN	Sr	F	6-3
	Ray Krupa	East Chicago, IN	So	F	6-2
4	Bob Lollar	Indianapolis, IN	So	F	6-2
40	Robert Mehl	Indianapolis, IN	So	F	6-1
5	Murray Mendenhall	Fort Wayne, IN	Fr	G	5-9
19	Charlie Meyers	Jeffersonville, IN	Fr	C	6-5
37	Don Ritter	Aurora, IN	So	G	5-10
3	Jerry Stuteville	Attica, IN	Fr	F	6-3
7	Dave Walker	Loogootee, IN	So	F	6-3
17	John Wallace	Richmond, IN	Jr	F	6-3
6	Lou Watson	Jeffersonville, IN	Fr	G/F	6-5
14	Ward Williams	Colfax, IN	Jr	C	6-3

SEASON RESULTS 1946-47

Date	Court	Opponent	Result	Score
12/2/1946	H	Wabash	W	69-46
12/7/1946	H	Miami (OH)	W	69-36
12/9/1946	H	Notre Dame	L	60-70
12/14/1946	A	Louisville	L	46-53
12/21/1946	A	Loyola Chicago	L	53-60
12/23/1946	A	Marquette	W	74-50
1/2/1947	A	Butler	L	41-52
1/6/1947	A	Ohio State	W	62-39
1/11/1947	A	Wisconsin	L	49-70
1/13/1947	H	Purdue	W	62-46
1/18/1947	H	Iowa	W	50-48
1/25/1947	A	Minnesota	L	56-59
2/3/1947	H	Michigan	W	55-42
2/8/1947	A	Earlham	W	93-41
2/15/1947	A	Illinois	L	50-59
2/17/1947	A	Northwestern	W	69-43
2/22/1947	A	Iowa	L	46-68
2/24/1947	H	Ohio State	W	46-43
3/1/1947	H	Illinois	W	48-41
3/3/1947	A	Purdue	W	54-38

1946-47 BIG TEN STANDINGS

	W	L	PCT
Wisconsin	9	3	.750
Illinois	8	4	.667
Indiana	8	4	.667
Minnesota	7	5	.583
Michigan	6	6	.500
Iowa	5	7	.417
Ohio State	5	7	.417
Purdue	4	8	.333
Northwestern	2	10	.167

against Iowa during his junior season in 1942-43. During his service in the U.S. Army, the 6'1" Hamilton played three years of basketball for his unit. The year before he returned to Bloomington, he played center and scored nearly 1,000 points for the Army Service Depot team in Atlanta, Georgia. When he returned to the Hoosiers for his senior year in 1946-47, Hamilton picked up right where he left off —as Indiana's leading scorer.

A huge crowd turned out for Indiana's season opener against Wabash on Monday, December 2. In fact, the Fieldhouse, which typically seated 6,500 for a normal game, was equipped with extra bleachers to seat 9,300 because of the frenzied demand for tickets. And the Hoosiers didn't disappoint their fans. They ran to a 30-17 halftime lead and kept running in the second half until they had defeated the Little Giants 69-46. Wallace topped IU with 12 points, while Ritter and Hamilton added 11 apiece. Another big crowd turned out at the Fieldhouse on Saturday, December 7, to see IU trounce Miami of Ohio 69-36, as Wallace scored a game-high 19 points and Ritter added 15.

On Monday, December 9, Notre Dame came to Bloomington and handed the Hoosiers their first loss, 70-60. The Fighting Irish closed the game on an 11-3 run to clinch the win. Hamilton led IU with 15 points. A strong Louisville team came to Bloomington on Saturday, December 14, and handed IU another loss, 53-46. The Cardinals held a 10-point halftime lead and were able to fight off a late change from Indiana, which was now 2-2. Next, the Hoosiers went on the road for the first time and dropped their third straight game in a 60-53 loss to Loyola Chicago, despite a game-high 24 points from Wallace.

Indiana evened its record at 3-3 by pounding Marquette 74-50 in Milwaukee on Monday, December 23. Wallace scored 24 points for the second game in row. IU's record dipped below .500 again on January 2, when Butler convincingly defeated the Hoosiers 52-41 in Indianapolis. The Bulldogs jumped to an 8-1 advantage to start the game, and IU was never able to get the lead below six points the rest of the way.

Despite a tough run in the preconference schedule, the Hoosiers started conference play on the right foot by pummeling Ohio State 62-39 in Columbus on Monday, January 6. With 14 points, Hamilton led

After leading the Hoosiers in scoring during the 1942-43 campaign, 6'1" forward Ralph Hamilton spent three years in the U.S. Army during World War II, before returning to Bloomington for his senior year in 1946-47. As a senior, he served as IU's team captain and earned All-America honors. IU Archives

four Hoosiers in double figures. IU didn't have the same luck with Wisconsin on Saturday, January 11. The Badgers grabbed the lead six minutes into the game and never relinquished it again in a 70-49 Wisconsin win.

On January 13, 9,330 fans crowded into the Fieldhouse when the Purdue Boilermakers came to Bloomington. The rowdy Indiana fans were thrilled to watch their Hoosiers run by the Boilermakers for a 62-46 win. Watson led IU with 16 points while Hamilton scored 15. Next, the Hoosiers played host to Iowa on January 18. The Hawkeyes opened up a nine-point lead at the half, but the Hoosiers stormed back in the second half and prevailed 50-48 when the Iowa player who appeared to score the tying basket in the final second was called for an offensive foul. Hamilton led Indiana with 21 points. A week later, IU went up to Minnesota and suffered a 59-56 setback in front of 16,388 fans in the Minnesota Fieldhouse (now Williams Arena).

Back in Bloomington, the Hoosiers improved their conference record to 4-2 with a 55-42 defeat of the Michigan Wolverines on Monday, February 3. IU then evened its nonconference record for the season at 4-4 by bashing Earlham 93-41 (breaking the IU single-game scoring record in the process).

Next, Indiana had a three-game road swing, and the Hoosiers would drop two of the three games to put their conference title hopes in jeopardy. The first contest was a 59-50 loss to Illinois in Champaign on Saturday, February 15. Two days later, Indiana sprinted to a 69-43 win over last-place Northwestern, as the Hoosiers got 21 points from Hamilton. Then, on Saturday, February 22, Iowa ran the Hoosiers out of Iowa City with a 68-46 Hawkeye victory that dropped IU to 5-4 in conference play.

Looking to make the best of a season that seemed to be slipping away, the Hoosiers used a strong second-half surge to defeat Ohio State 46-43 on Monday, February 24, in Bloomington. Then, on Saturday, March 1, Indiana repaid Illinois for its earlier triumph with a 48-41 Hoosier victory in Bloomington. Finally, the Hoosiers added the proper exclamation point to the season by walloping Purdue for a second time on Monday, March 3. The game was supposed to take place in West Lafayette but had to be played at Butler's Fieldhouse because of the collapse of some of the bleachers in the Purdue stadium.

Thus, 15,000 fans in Indianapolis got to watch the Hoosiers open a 31-17 halftime lead and then secure a 54-38 win. Four Hoosiers scored in double figures, led by 14 from Ritter.

An extremely talented Indiana team salvaged an 8-4 conference record with three straight wins to close the season. That gave coach Branch McCracken his sixth second-place finish in six seasons as the IU skipper.

1947-48

OVERALL RECORD: 8-12

CONFERENCE RECORD: 3-9 (EIGHTH PLACE)

The Indiana squad that prepared for the 1947-48 campaign had a lot of firepower, even though it lost its leading scorer, All-American Ralph Hamilton, to graduation. The Hoosiers returned Ward Williams, Lou Watson, Don Ritter, John Wallace and Norbert Hermann (all of whom averaged five points or more the previous season). Plus, the Hoosiers also regained the services of 6'6" center Tom Schwartz, after a one-year absence serving in the army. As a result, Indiana was one of the Big Ten favorites, along with Michigan and Minnesota. Unfortunately for the Hoosiers, a variety of setbacks would conspire against them and lead to an underachieving season.

The Hoosiers captain and leader was senior Ward Williams. As a sophomore in 1942-43, Williams had averaged 10.7 PPG during conference play. Then he returned to IU for his last two years of eligibility after serving in the U.S. Air Force for three years during World War II. Fast, strong, and an excellent rebounder, the 6'3" Williams was an ideal "big man" for McCracken's run-and-run offense. While Williams was the heart of the team, Indiana's best scorer was junior guard Don Ritter, who also served three years in the Air Force in World War II. A deadly sharpshooter from the outside on the basketball court, Ritter was also a relentless ball hawk on defense. In addition to Williams and Ritter, IU was bolstered by a pair of former teammates from Jeffersonville High

The 1947-48 team. First row (left to right): Don Ritter, Norbert Hermann, coach Branch McCracken, Charlie Meyer, Bob Armstrong; Second row: Jerry Stuteville, John Wallace, Tom Schwartz, Murray Mendenhall, Ward Williams, Lou Watson. IU Archives

School in 6'5" sophomores Charley Meyer and Lou Watson.

Things looked promising on opening day, Saturday, December 6, when IU held DePauw without a field goal for the first 11 minutes of the game and rushed to a large lead in front of an enthused home crowd in Bloomington. Indiana eventually prevailed 59-43 as Watson lit up the Tigers for 22 points. A week later IU blasted Carleton College 76-42, as Ritter scored a game-high 20 points.

On Monday, December 15, Indiana played Kansas State on a neutral floor in Kansas City and fell 61-53 in the game that the Wildcats led nearly wire to wire. On Friday, December 19, Loyola Chicago came to Bloomington and couldn't keep up with the Hoosiers in a 59-40 IU win. Ritter scored a game-high 15 points and forward Bob Armstrong added 13. It was also the final game in an IU uniform for John Wallace (an All-American in 1946). Wallace was on

schedule to graduate at the end of the first semester and decided to accept a job that started immediately. Four days after the Loyola win, Indiana went to East Lansing and lost a 64-60 contest to Michigan State, which was not yet part of the Big Ten. The Hoosiers led 60-56 with less than four minutes remaining, before the Spartans closed the game on an 8-0 run.

Indiana closed the preconference schedule with the first annual Hoosier Classic at Butler Fieldhouse in Indianapolis. The Classic involved four teams: Indiana, Purdue, Notre Dame and Butler. In their first game, the Hoosiers annihilated the Fighting Irish 72-46 on Thursday, January 1. Ritter poured in 27 points to lead IU. The next day, Indiana lost to Butler for the second straight year as the Bulldogs pulled out a 64-51 win.

With a 4-3 preconference record, Indiana's Big Ten fortunes didn't look quite as bright as they had before the season started. Nevertheless, no one would

1947-48 TEAM ROSTER

Head coach: Branch McCracken
Assistant coach: Jay McCreary

No.	Player	Hometown	Class	Position	Height
15	Bob Armstrong	Fort Wayne, IN	So	F/C	6-4
	Joe Blumenthal	Rochester, IN	So	C	6-4
22	Jack Brown	Bloomington, IN	So	F	6-3
8	Stuart Chestnut	Terre Haute, IN	So	F	6-2
4	Gene Farris	Campbellsburg, IN	So	F	6-1
	Joe Gerich	Francesville, IN	So	F	6-1
12	Norbert Hermann	Brownstown, IN	Sr	G	6-2
	Pyard Hey	Fort Wayne, IN	So	G	6-0
11	Lou Jensen	New Albany, IN	So	G	5-11
34	Bob Lollar	Indianapolis, IN	Jr	F	6-2
	Robert McKinnis	Evansville, IN	So	G	6-0
5	Murray Mendenhall	Fort Wayne, IN	So	G	5-9
19	Charlie Meyer	Jeffersonville, IN	So	C	6-5
	Joe Pitake	Hammond, IN	So	C	6-3
7	Don Ritter	Aurora, IN	Jr	G	5-10
	Robert Ritter	Anderson, IN	So	F	5-10
18	Tom Schwartz	Kokomo, IN	So	C	6-6
3	Jerry Stuteville	Attica, IN	So	G	6-3
	Ed Stuteville	Attica, IN	So	C	6-4
	Lloyd Vogel	Fort Wayne, IN	So	G	6-1
10	John Wallace	Richmond, IN	Sr	F	6-3
6	Lou Watson	Jeffersonville, IN	So	G	6-5
14	Ward Williams (Capt.)	Colfax, IN	Sr	C	6-3

SEASON RESULTS 1947-48

Date	Court	Opponent	Result	Score
12/6/1947	H	DePauw	W	59-43
12/13/1947	H	Carleton	W	76-42
12/15/1947	N1	Kansas State	L	53-61
12/19/1947	H	Loyola Chicago	W	59-40
12/23/1947	A	Michigan State	L	60-64
1/1/1948	N2	Notre Dame	W	72-46
1/2/1948	A	Butler	L	51-64
1/5/1948	A	Purdue	L	49-58
1/10/1948	A	Wisconsin	L	54-58
1/12/1948	H	Ohio State	W	71-45
1/17/1948	A	Iowa	L	52-61
1/19/1948	A	Illinois	L	45-46
1/24/1948	H	Minnesota	W	65-43
2/7/1948	A	Miami (OH)	W	57-48
2/14/1948	H	Iowa	W	49-47
2/16/1948	A	Michigan	L	54-66
2/21/1948	A	Northwestern	L	42-47
2/23/1948	A	Ohio State	L	45-60
2/28/1948	H	Purdue	L	49-51
3/1/1948	H	Illinois	L	51-52

1 Kansas City, MO
2 Indianapolis, IN

1947-48 BIG TEN STANDINGS

	W	L	PCT
Michigan	10	2	.833
Iowa	8	4	.667
Illinois	7	5	.583
Wisconsin	7	5	.583
Purdue	6	6	.500
Ohio State	5	7	.417
Minnesota	5	7	.417
Indiana	3	9	.250
Northwestern	3	9	.250

have predicted the futility that the Hoosiers would experience in conference play. It began on Monday, January 5, at West Lafayette, where Purdue handed Indiana a 58-49 defeat. Things didn't get any better when the Hoosiers went back to Bloomington and hosted defending conference champion Wisconsin on Saturday, January 10. The Badgers raced out of the starting gate for a 9-0 lead and repulsed the Hoosiers down the stretch to secure a 58-54 Wisconsin victory. Two days later, IU finally put a notch in the win column with a 71-54 conference win over the Ohio State Buckeyes in Bloomington. Ritter led IU with 14 points and center Charlie Meyer added 13.

Next, Indiana went on the road and lost two more conference games, which all but dashed any remaining hopes that the Hoosiers could compete for the conference crown. The first loss came against the Iowa Hawkeyes on Saturday, January 17. Indiana was down five at the half and lost 61-52. Two nights later in Champaign, the Hoosiers had Illinois down 18-16 at the half but lost 46-45. Indiana recovered some pride on Saturday, January 24, by using a great second-half performance to beat Minnesota 65-43. Watson and Ritter scored 19 points apiece for Indiana, which was now 2-4 in conference play.

On Saturday, February 7, IU traveled to Oxford, Ohio, and trailed the Miami of Ohio Redhawks 26-17 at the break. However, the Hoosiers grabbed the nonconference victory by using a 13-2 run in the final minutes to tie the game and send it to overtime, and then ran off nine unanswered points in OT for a 57-48 triumph. Ritter led IU with a season-high 26 points. Next, Indiana upset Iowa 49-47 on Saturday, February 14, in Bloomington. The Hoosiers were down 31-20 at the half, but they kept chipping away at the lead in the second half until the score was tied 47-47. Ritter then buried two free throws to clinch the game for Indiana. Although it was the third straight win, it was also the last victory of the season for IU.

After the Iowa triumph, Indiana dropped three straight road games: 66-54 to Michigan on February 16; 47-42 to Northwestern on February 21; and 60-45 to Ohio State on February 23. The Hoosiers lost all three games in the second half. Against Michigan, Indiana was only down by a point at the break. The Hoosiers led Northwestern 25-22 at intermission. Ohio State held a small, three-point lead at halftime of their contest with IU. Watson led IU with 19 points against both Michigan and Northwestern.

Indiana came back to Bloomington for two home games, and the Hoosiers were looking to simply finish the season on a positive note. Unfortunately, the nightmare continued as IU lost two heartbreakers. The first one hurt the most because it was to archrival Purdue on Saturday, February 28. The Boilermakers led 34-26 at the half, but Indiana made a spirited charge in the second session and tied the game at 49-49 in the final minute. With 10 seconds remaining, Boilermaker guard Howard Williams drove into the lane and released a shot that missed the mark. Williams crashed to the floor, but the rebound fell right into his hands and he quickly released a shot while still sitting on the court. The ball went in, and Purdue won 51-49. Two nights later, IU lost another cliffhanger to Illinois, 52-51.

Indiana's 3-9 record left the Hoosiers tied with Northwestern for the worst finish in the conference, and their 8-12 overall record represented coach Branch McCracken's first losing season as the IU leader. McCracken couldn't help but shake his head in trying to figure out why this team finished so poorly. "I thought we had what it takes [to win] in this league … and look what happened," he said.

1948-49

OVERALL RECORD: 14-8
CONFERENCE RECORD: 6-6 (FOURTH PLACE)

After a dismal 1947-48 season in which a talented IU team finished in the cellar of the Big Ten, the Hoosiers' prospects for the 1948-49 campaign were as uncertain as they had been at any time during the previous seven seasons under Branch McCracken. IU returned two excellent guards in Don Ritter and Lou Watson, but McCracken knew that he would have to get some excellent performances out of several sophomores if the Hoosiers were going to improve their position in the conference. Of course, relying on newcomers to handle key positions always makes a coach nervous, but McCracken was fortunate to get major contributions from sophomores Bill Tosheff, Gene Ring and Bill Garrett. The latter was Indiana's 1947 Mr. Basketball, and he had led Shelbyville High School to the 1947 Indiana state title. At IU, he became the first African-American player to ever play on the IU varsity. Garrett's arrival and success at IU also broke the color barrier in Big Ten basketball, and led to other Big Ten schools also recruiting black players—even though McCracken and athletic director Zora Clevenger were originally concerned that playing Garrett might lead to other Big Ten schools boycotting games with IU. The even-mannered Garrett handled himself with the same kind of grace and poise exhibited by baseball's barrier-breaker, Jackie Robinson.

Garrett and the Hoosiers kicked off the season on Saturday, December 4, against DePauw in front of a capacity crowd in the Fieldhouse. The Hoosiers had little trouble dispatching the Tigers 61-48. Watson led all scorers with 19, while Tosheff added 10, and Garrett scored eight while dominating the boards. Two nights later, the Hoosiers grabbed another victory when Michigan State came to town. The Hoosiers dominated the Spartans and won the game 48-36, as Watson scored a game-high 12 points. IU won another game on Saturday, December 11 as the Hoosiers used a determined second-half push against Xavier to a grab a 63-55 victory. Watson led all scorers with 16, while Garrett chipped in 12. Indiana was 3-0.

Drake was the next Hoosier victim on Monday, December 13, and IU used a balanced attack to pound the Bulldogs 57-35, as 10 different Hoosiers scored. Kansas State suffered a similar loss on Thursday, December 16, when the Wildcats were overwhelmed 56-36 by the Hurryin' Hoosiers attack. Watson was the game's top scorer with 14 and Garrett chipped in 13. IU improved to 6-0 on the season on December 21, by beating Washington (MO) in its own gym by the count of 51-44. Garrett led IU with 13 points and Tosheff contributed 11.

On Monday, December 27, Indiana lost to Butler for the third consecutive year. The Hoosiers' first loss of the season came by the score of 64-55 in the second annual Hoosier Classic at Butler Fieldhouse in Indianapolis. The next night, IU bounced back and won a 50-47 contest against Notre Dame (which had defeated Purdue the previous night). Garrett and center Tom Schwartz each scored

The 1948-49 team. First row (left to right): Bob Armstrong, Charlie Meyer, Bill Garrett, Tom Schwartz, Lou Watson; Second row: assistant coach Jay McCreary, Gene Ring, Bob Lollar, Jerry Stuteville, Ted Kaufman, Tyrie Robbins, head coach Branch McCracken; Third row: Don Ritter, Bob Lukemeyer, Bill Tosheff, Phil Buck, Gordon Neff. IU Archives

11 points for Indiana. The Hoosiers closed out the preconference season with a come-from-behind 56-47 win over Marquette in Bloomington, to put IU at 8-1.

Indiana opened Big Ten play by losing to Illinois on a last-second shot on Saturday, January 8, in Bloomington. The 44-42 loss was the Hoosiers' third straight defeat to the Fighting Illini on last-second heroics (Illinois claimed two one-point victories over IU the previous season). In this game, Illinois center Fred Green hit an improbable 20-foot hook shot in the final seconds of double overtime. The following Monday, Indiana notched its first conference win with a 50-39 victory over Iowa in Bloomington, as Tosheff led all scorers with 12 points.

Wisconsin hosted IU on Saturday, January 15, and the Hoosiers fell 58-48, despite leading by one at

the half. Badger center Don Rehfeldt blistered IU with 27 points. Two days later, the Hoosiers turned in one their best performances of the season in a 56-42 romp over Purdue in Bloomington. Indiana leapt out to a 34-15 halftime lead and never looked back. Tosheff dropped in a game-high 18 points, as Indiana improved to 2-2 in the conference. The Hoosiers then traveled to league-leading Minnesota for a Saturday, January 17, showdown with the Golden Gophers. Minnesota controlled the tempo with its deliberate attack and easily secured a 35-28 victory, the Gophers' fifth straight win to start the conference season and thirteenth consecutive win overall.

DePaul then hosted a nonconference game with the Hoosiers on Saturday, February 5. In a nip-and-tuck battle that saw 10 ties and 11 lead changes, the Blue Demons prevailed 47-46 in overtime at Chicago

Stadium. The Hoosiers got back to Big Ten play at Ohio State on Monday, February 7, and after deadlocking the game at 36-36 at the half, the Hoosiers got manhandled in the second session and lost 72-59. Sophomore guard Gene Ring provided the one bright spot for IU by scoring 20 points.

Indiana dropped its third straight Big Ten contest (and fourth straight game overall) on Saturday, February 12, when Michigan came to Bloomington and took a 54-47 win from the Hoosiers in front of over 10,000 fans who crowded into every nook and cranny of the Fieldhouse. IU finally stopped the bleeding two nights later with a 56-41 blowout over cellar-dweller Northwestern in Bloomington. That put the Hoosiers at 3-5 in the Big Ten.

The season became a success in one aspect on Saturday, February 19, when the Hoosiers completed a season sweep of Purdue with a 56-50 win over the Boilermakers in West Lafayette. Tosheff, who scored a game-high 18 points, ignited the final rally that put Purdue away. On Monday, February 21, Indiana pummeled Ohio State 65-45, as Garrett and Watson tied for game-high honors with 18 points, and the Hoosiers evened their conference record at 5-5. On Saturday, February 26, the Hoosiers won their fourth straight game by trouncing Iowa with a late run that led to a 76-60 Indiana victory. Forward Jerry Stuteville notched a game-high 21 points for IU, while Garrett contributed 17.

The schedule came to end for the Hoosiers with a Monday, February 28 contest at Illinois, and once again the Fighting Illini put the Hoosiers away. After winning three straight close games against IU, Illinois crushed Indiana 91-68 in this game. The win delivered a conference title to the Illini.

For the Hoosiers, their 6-6 conference mark resulted in a tie for fourth place, and their 14 wins overall was IU's highest mark in the three seasons since McCracken had returned from military service. However, the most promising note for the season was the rapid development of sophomores Garrett, Tosheff and Ring, who looked prepared to help Indiana contend for the conference crown once again.

1948-49 TEAM ROSTER

Head coach: Branch McCracken
Assistant coaches: Jay McCreary, Ernie Andres

No.	Player	Hometown	Class	Position	Height
15	Bob Armstrong	Fort Wayne, IN	Sr	C	6-4
	Jack Brown	Bloomington, IN	Jr	C	6-3
12	Phil Buck	Rossville, IN	So	F	5-10
16	Stuart Chestnut	Terre Haute, IN	Jr	F	6-2
8	Bill Garrett	Shelbyville, IN	So	C/F	6-3
24	Pyard Hey	Fort Wayne, IN	Jr	G	6-0
24	Ted Kaufman	Brownsville, IN	So	C	6-3
34	Bob Lollar	Indianapolis, IN	Sr	F	6-2
5	Bob Lukemeyer	Jasper, IN	So	F	5-10
19	Charlie Meyer	Jeffersonville, IN	Jr	C	6-5
25	Gordon Neff	Terre Haute, IN	So	G	6-0
11	Gene Ring	South Bend, IN	So	G	6-1
7	Don Ritter (Capt.)	Aurora, IN	Sr	G	5-10
21	Tyrie Robbins	Gary, IN	So	F	6-3
18	Tom Schwartz	Kokomo, IN	Jr	C	6-6
14	Harlan Sturgeon	Indianapolis, IN	So	G	5-10
3	Jerry Stuteville	Attica, IN	Jr	F	6-3
9	Bill Tosheff	Gary, IN	So	F	6-0
6	Lou Watson	Jeffersonville, IN	Jr	G	6-5

SEASON RESULTS 1948-49

Date	Court	Opponent	Result	Score
12/4/1948	H	DePauw	W	61-48
12/6/1948	H	Michigan State	W	48-36
12/11/1948	H	Xavier	W	63-55
12/13/1948	H	Drake	W	57-35
12/16/1948	H	Kansas State	W	56-36
12/21/1948	A	Washington (MO)	W	51-44
12/27/1948	A	Butler	L	55-64
12/28/1948	N1	Notre Dame	W	50-47
1/3/1949	H	Marquette	W	56-47
1/8/1949	H	Illinois	L	42-44
1/10/1949	H	Iowa	W	50-39
1/15/1949	A	Wisconsin	L	48-58
1/17/1949	H	Purdue	W	56-42
1/22/1949	A	Minnesota	L	28-35
2/5/1949	A	DePaul	L	46-47
2/7/1949	A	Ohio State	L	59-72
2/12/1949	H	Michigan	L	47-54
2/14/1949	H	Northwestern	W	56-41
2/19/1949	A	Purdue	W	56-50
2/21/1949	H	Ohio State	W	65-45
2/26/1949	A	Iowa	W	76-60
2/28/1949	A	Illinois	L	68-91

1 Indianapolis, IN

1948-49 BIG TEN STANDINGS

	W	L	PCT
Illinois	10	2	.833
Minnesota	9	3	.750
Michigan	7	5	.583
Ohio State	6	6	.500
Indiana	6	6	.500
Purdue	6	6	.500
Wisconsin	5	7	.417
Iowa	3	9	.250
Northwestern	2	10	.167

1949-50

OVERALL RECORD: 17-5

CONFERENCE RECORD: 7-5 (THIRD PLACE)

TEAM HONORS:

HOOSIER CLASSIC CHAMPION

INDIVIDUAL HONORS:

LOU WATSON—ALL-AMERICA, ALL-BIG TEN (FIRST TEAM)

The 1949-50 team. First row (left to right): Charlie Meyer, Don Luft, Jerry Stuteville, Bill Garrett, Lou Watson, Tyrie Robbins; Second row: assistant coach Ernie Andres, Sheldon Turner, John Scott, Bill Tosheff, Tony Hill, Gene Ring, head coach Branch McCracken; Third row: Frank O'Bannon, Sam Miranda, Phil Buck, Dale Vieau, Charles Vaughn, Marvin Christie, Hal Summers. IU Archives

In winning four of their final five games in the 1948-49 season, the Hoosiers relied heavily on a lineup of sophomores and juniors who now returned to make up the core of the 1949-50 team. Even though this rotation was a bit undersized, with 6'3" Bill Garrett logging most of the minutes at the center position, coach Branch McCracken liked his chances with this group.

"We will have to depend upon our speed and versatility to balance the superior height we are certain to meet," stated McCracken. "But we should be a first division factor in the conference race."

Garrett, who led IU in scoring as a sophomore in 1948-49, could run the court like a gazelle and beat opponents down the floor for easy scores. But he was also an excellent shooter and a deceptively adept rebounder. He was IU's go-to guy, but right behind him were two other potent scorers in guard Lou Watson, a floor leader who could score and drive, and forward Jerry Stuteville, an energetic competitor who knew how to put the ball in the basket.

The preconference schedule opened in Bloomington on Monday, December 5, when the Hoosiers hosted Wabash at the Fieldhouse and crushed the Little Giants 64-33 in front of 10,000 fans. IU then played Michigan State (which was still one year away from joining the Big Ten) in East Lansing on Saturday, December 10. MSU jumped out to a slim halftime lead, but the Hoosiers got their fast break going in the second half and ran to a 73-58 victory. Indiana forward Bill Tosheff led all scorers with 16 points, and Garrett added 15.

DePaul came to Bloomington on Tuesday, December 13. Like Michigan State, the Blue Demons grabbed a halftime lead, 32-31, but Indiana owned the second half and won 61-55. Watson scored 14 and Garrett notched 13. Two nights later, Garrett dropped 20 points on Arkansas, which got overwhelmed by the speedy Hoosier attack in a 75-50 Indiana victory in Bloomington. Next the Hoosiers traveled to Oregon State to play a doubleheader against the Beavers on December 19-20. Both games were very competitive, but Indiana won the first game 65-60 and prevailed 58-53 in the second game. IU was 6-0.

The third annual Hoosier Classic at Butler Fieldhouse in Indianapolis was next on Indiana's schedule. In the first game, IU outran Notre Dame for a 79-69 victory, led by 24 points from Jerry Stuteville and 17 from Garrett. In their second game, the Hoosiers were able to do something that they hadn't been able to accomplish in four years—beat the Butler Bulldogs. IU jumped to a nine-point halftime lead and then rolled to a 68-57 win, powered by 21 points from Garrett. Butler's Ralph O'Brian burned the Hoosiers for 33 points in a losing effort.

Indiana got its final preconference tune-up in a rematch against Michigan State on Monday, January 2, in Bloomington. The Spartans nabbed a 28-26 halftime lead, but Indiana controlled the second half and won 60-50. Watson led all scorers with 19 points. The MSU win made the Hoosiers a perfect 9-0 entering league play.

IU started the Big Ten schedule in style by winning a grudge match against one of the conference favorites, Wisconsin, on Saturday, January 7, in Bloomington. Garrett, who scored a team-high 15 points, used a magnificent fake to clear enough space to drop in a point-blank basket with eight seconds remaining to give Indiana a 61-59 victory. The win was the Hoosiers' first against the Badgers in seven years. The following Monday, Michigan handed IU

1949-50 TEAM ROSTER

Head coach: Branch McCracken
Assistant coach: Ernie Andres

No.	Player	Hometown	Class	Position	Height
12	Phil Buck	Rossville, IN	Jr	F	5-10
17	Marvin Christie	Indianapolis, IN	So	F	6-0
8	Bill Garrett	Shelbyville, IN	Jr	C	6-3
25	Tony Hill	Seymour, IN	So	F	6-1
16	Don Luft	Sheboygan, WI	So	C	6-5
9	Bob Masters	Lafayette, IN	So	G	6-3
19	Charlie Meyers	Jeffersonville, IN	Sr	C	6-5
5	Sam Miranda	Collinsville, IL	So	G	5-10
15	Frank O'Bannon	Corydon, IN	So	G	5-10
7	Gene Ring	South Bend, IN	Jr	G	6-1
24	Tyrie Robbins	Gary, IN	Jr	F	6-3
18	Tom Schwartz	Kokomo, IN	Sr	C	6-6
22	John Scott	Madison, IN	So	F	6-1
3	Jerry Stuteville	Attica, IN	Sr	F	6-3
14	Hal Summers	Lawrenceville, IL	So	F	6-1
11	Bill Tosheff	Gary, IN	Jr	F	6-0
21	Sheldon Turner	Albany, IN	So	F	6-0
10	Charles Vaughn	Lafayette, IN	So	F	5-11
4	Dale Vieau	Hammond, IN	So	G	5-10
6	Lou Watson (Capt.)	Jeffersonville, IN	Sr	G	6-5

SEASON RESULTS 1949-50

Date	Court	Opponent	Result	Score
12/5/1949	H	Wabash	W	64-33
12/10/1949	A	Michigan State	W	73-58
12/13/1949	H	DePaul	W	61-55
12/15/1949	H	Arkansas	W	75-50
12/19/1949	A	Oregon State	W	65-60
12/20/1949	A	Oregon State	W	58-53
12/29/1949	N1	Notre Dame	W	79-69
12/30/1949	A	Butler	W	57-49
1/2/1950	H	Michigan State	W	60-50
1/7/1950	H	Wisconsin	W	61-59
1/9/1950	A	Michigan	L	67-69
1/14/1950	A	Iowa	L	64-65
1/16/1950	H	Butler	W	57-49
1/21/1950	A	Purdue	W	49-39
2/4/1950	A	Northwestern	W	64-59
2/6/1950	H	Ohio State	L	55-56
2/11/1950	H	Minnesota	W	59-39
2/15/1950	A	Illinois	W	83-72
2/18/1950	H	Purdue	W	60-50
2/20/1950	A	Ohio State	L	65-75
2/25/1950	H	Iowa	L	53-59
2/27/1950	H	Illinois	W	80-66

1 Indianapolis, IN

1949-50 BIG TEN STANDINGS

	W	L	PCT
Ohio State	11	1	.917
Wisconsin	9	3	.750
Indiana	7	5	.583
Illinois	7	5	.583
Iowa	6	6	.500
Minnesota	4	8	.333
Michigan	4	8	.333
Northwestern	3	9	.250
Purdue	3	9	.250

Floor general Lou Watson was a 6'5" point guard who served as McCracken's coach on the floor. As a senior he was an All-American, and he finished his career as the all-time leading scorer in school history. IU Archives

its first loss of the season when Wolverine guard Charley Murray buried a field goal right as time expired to give Michigan a 69-67 win in Ann Arbor. Watson's 26 points topped all scorers.

Iowa handed the Hoosiers another setback on Saturday, January 14, when the Hawkeyes defeated IU 65-64 in Iowa City. Iowa nearly let the game slip away after leading by 12 points with only nine minutes remaining, but the Hawkeyes fought off the Hoosiers' late charge. On Monday, January 16, Indiana played a nonconference rematch against Butler in Bloomington and beat the Bulldogs 57-49. Then Indiana traveled to West Lafayette for a rivalry matchup with Purdue on Saturday, January 21. The Boilermakers fought hard, but Indiana outclassed them in a 49-39 Hoosier win that evened IU's Big Ten record at 2-2.

After the semester break, IU traveled to Northwestern on Saturday, February 4, and squeezed by the Wildcats 64-59, as five different Hoosiers scored in double digits, led by Tosheff with 12. On Monday, February 6, Indiana played host to conference leader Ohio State in the Fieldhouse. IU led 35-26 at the half, but the Buckeyes made their push in the second session and stole a 56-55 win, which dimmed IU's chances in the conference race. Ohio State forward Dick Schnittker poured in a game-high 27 points, including 13 of 13 from the free throw line. IU took out its frustration on Minnesota, the next visitor to the Fieldhouse on Saturday, February 11. The Hoosiers trailed by two points at the half, but ambushed the Golden Gophers in the second half and sped to a 59-39 win, as Watson scored 20. The win improved IU to 5-3 in conference play.

Next, Indiana grabbed its first victory over Illinois in three years with a satisfying 83-72 triumph over the Fighting Illini in Champaign on Wednesday, February 15. The Hoosiers' fast break simply overwhelmed the home team in the second half. Garrett

INDIANA'S RANKING IN THE 1949-50 ASSOCIATED PRESS POLLS

1/5	1/10	1/17	1/24	1/30	2/7	2/14	2/21	2/28	3/7
5	4	8	9	12	16	—	17	—	20

led IU with 20 points. On Saturday, February 18, in Bloomington, the Hoosiers fell behind Purdue 31-23 at the half but completed their second consecutive season sweep of the Boilermakers with a 60-50 win. Garrett and Stuteville each scored 13 for IU. Two nights later, IU went to Ohio State and didn't have any luck in trying to derail the league-leading Buckeyes, who prevailed 75-65, despite a frantic push from the Hoosiers in the second half.

IU's hopes for a runner-up finish in the Big Ten were dashed on Saturday, February 25, when the big Iowa Hawkeyes came into the Fieldhouse and dominated the boards in a 59-53 win over the Hoosiers. However, on Monday, February 27, Indiana moved into third place in the conference by closing the season with a flourish in the form of a dominating 80-66 win over Illinois. Garrett scored a season-high 23 points and Stuteville dropped in 20 for the Hoosiers.

Just as McCracken had hoped, these Hoosiers brought IU back to a position where Indiana was challenging for the Big Ten championship again. A two-game stumble early in the schedule and another two-game stumble at the end cost the Hoosiers a better finish. Nevertheless, this team competed at a strong level in every game and helped renew the high standard of IU basketball.

1950-51

OVERALL RECORD: 19-3

CONFERENCE RECORD: 12-2 (SECOND PLACE)

TEAM HONORS:

HOOSIER CLASSIC CHAMPION

INDIVIDUAL HONORS:

BILL GARRETT—ALL-AMERICA,

ALL-BIG TEN (FIRST TEAM)

The biggest question entering the 1950-51 season was how would the Hoosiers replace Lou Watson at guard. The 6'5" Watson was one of the great big guards in college basketball. He could score, defend, pass and rebound. But, above all, Watson was the Hoosiers' undisputed floor leader. "It was like having a coach on the floor to have Lou in the lineup," said coach Branch McCracken.

Fortunately, a trio of guards—Gene Ring, Bob Masters and Sam Miranda—ended up taking care of the backcourt duties quite effectively. The other big issue was the size of the frontcourt. Indiana would once again rely on Bill Garrett, a phenomenally versatile basketball player—but only 6'3"—to handle the center position, and 6'0" Bill Tosheff to man one of the forward slots. Meanwhile, the other forward position was rotated among several other regulars, who were all 6'3" or under.

"The main thing we lack this year is size. We aren't big enough," said McCracken. "We have a chance in the Big Ten, but I don't think we are big enough." McCracken was right. The Hoosiers' lack of height was the team's ultimate downfall, but the undersized IU squad didn't go down without making a serious challenge.

The Indiana faithful got their first look at the 1950-51 Hoosiers on Saturday, December 2, when the DePauw Tigers came to town. IU broke into the lead early and captured a 59-45 victory to open the season. Masters was the high scorer for Indiana with 10 points, and McCracken used 17 different players in the game. Oregon State was the next visitor on Saturday, December 9, and the Indiana offense started to round into form in the 72-45 blowout. Ring led all scorers with 18 points and Garrett scored 13. Texas Christian became the next Fieldhouse victim on Tuesday, December 12. The Horned Frogs ran with the Hoosiers for a while, but couldn't keep up in the end as IU took an 87-68 victory, led by 23 points from Ring.

The Hoosiers went to Kansas City on Saturday, December 16, to face off with Kansas State. The Hoosiers led big early on, but had to fight off the Wildcats down the stretch for a 58-52 win. Garrett led all scorers with 15 points, even though he sat out much of the game with foul trouble. Next, Indiana played its annual doubleheader in the Hoosier Classic at Butler Fieldhouse. In the first game on Friday, December 22, IU defeated Butler 61-46 in a sloppy game marred by 38 turnovers (21 by Butler and 17 by Indiana). Garrett's 17 points were a game high, but he was again limited to less than 25 minutes by foul trouble. The next night, Indiana blew an eight-point halftime lead against Notre Dame, who tied the game at 48-48, and then again at 56-56, before Indiana ran off the final eight points for a 64-56 win. Garrett

The 1950-51 team. First row (left to right): Tony Hill, Tyrie Robbins, Bill Garrett, Gene Ring, Bill Tosheff, Bob Masters; Second row: assistant coach Lou Watson, Phil Buck, Dick Baumgartner, Tom Satter, head coach Branch McCracken, Otto Case, Hal Summers, Sam Miranda, assistant coach Ernie Andres; Third row: Bob Dobson, Don Luft, Jack McDermond, Jack Brown, Jim Schooley, Dale Vieau.
IU Archives

scored 17 points for the second straight night for game-high honors. The Hoosiers were 6-0.

On Wednesday, December 27, two of the country's top-ranked teams squared off when Indiana dropped a 64-62 thriller to Bradley in Peoria, Illinois. The Braves' Charley Grover knocked down the winning field goal with 0:14 remaining. Two nights later in Des Moines, Iowa, the fifth-ranked Hoosiers finished their preconference schedule by taking out Drake 59-49, powered by a game-high 17 points from Ring.

Big Ten play opened for IU on a snowy Saturday night in Columbus, Ohio, on January 6. The Hoosiers grabbed the lead over Ohio State in the opening minutes and never relinquished it on the way to a 77-62 win. Garrett peppered the Buckeyes for 23

points (on 9-14 from the field and 5-5 from the line). On Saturday, December 13, the Hoosiers went up to East Lansing to take on Michigan State, who was playing its first season in the Big Ten. The Hoosiers easily put down the Spartans 47-37. Indiana returned home for a Monday, January 15 contest against Illinois, which was already 4-0 in conference play. The game was nip and tuck in the first half, but IU raced ahead in the second session and defeated the Illini 64-53, led by 21 points from Garrett and 19 from Sam Miranda. For the Illini, the loss ended up being their only setback of the conference season. For the Hoosiers, it improved their record to 3-0.

Next, the Indiana squad sorely disappointed a large crowd in West Lafayette on Saturday, January 20, when the Hoosiers crushed the Purdue

Boilermakers 77-56 with a huge run in the game's final ten minutes. With 13 points, Masters led five Hoosiers in double figures. The following Monday, Indiana won a rematch with Ohio State 69-59 in Bloomington, as Garrett scored 17. The Hoosiers extended their conference winning streak to six games on Saturday, January 27, in Bloomington, by defeating the stalling Minnesota Golden Gophers 32-26. The Golden Gophers changed tactics two weeks later on Saturday, February 10, in a rematch with the Hoosiers in Williams Arena in Minneapolis. The Gophers used a bigger lineup and played the Hoosiers straight up, and it worked. The Minnesota front line scored 39 points, and the Gophers derailed the Hoosiers 61-54.

Two nights after the Minnesota defeat, Indiana went to Iowa City and captured a 63-54 win over the Iowa Hawkeyes, led by 19 points from Tosheff. On Saturday, February 17, in Bloomington, IU scorched a good Northwestern team 94-63, as Garrett dropped in 22 points and Ring added 18. That set up a big showdown with Illinois on Monday, February 19, in Bloomington. The Hoosiers and the Illini had distanced themselves from the rest of the pack in the conference, and this game had the feel of a playoff tilt. The first half went back and forth before Indiana took a 35-34 lead into the locker room. The struggle continued until the Hoosiers built a 58-53 lead with under ten minutes remaining. Then, at the 6:10 mark, Garrett fouled out and the Illini hit both free throws to tie the game at 60-60. Without Garrett to defend the post, Illinois pounded the ball inside for five point-blank field goals down the stretch and snatched away a 71-65 victory.

The Hoosiers gained a little redemption by whipping Purdue 68-53 on Saturday, February 24, at the Fieldhouse. It was Indiana's sixth consecutive win against their archrival. Two nights later, IU handily dispatched Iowa 63-53 in Bloomington. Next, Indiana went up to Ann Arbor on Saturday, March 3, and pounded the Michigan Wolverines 57-42, as Garrett and Tosheff scored 14 points apiece. The Hoosiers then closed out their season back in Bloomington on March 5, against Wisconsin. IU had its attack in top form—especially in the second half—as the Hoosiers ran past the Badgers 68-58. Garrett scored a game-high 21 points in his final contest in a Hoosier uniform.

1950-51 TEAM ROSTER

Head coach: Branch McCracken
Assistant coaches: Ernie Andres, Lou Watson

No.	Player	Hometown	Class	Position	Height
10	Dick Baumgartner	LaPorte, IN	So	G	6-0
22	Jack Brown	Bloomington, IN	Sr	F	6-3
12	Phil Buck	Rossville, IN	Sr	F	5-10
21	Otto Case	Jeffersonville, IN	So	G	5-8
16	Bob Dobson	Bloomington, IN	So	F	6-1
8	Bill Garrett	Shelbyville, IN	Sr	C	6-3
25	Tony Hill	Seymour, IN	Jr	F	6-1
16	Don Luft	Sheboygan, WI	Jr	C	6-5
9	Bob Masters	Lafayette, IN	Jr	G	6-3
18	Jack McDermond	Attica, IN	So	F	6-2
5	Sam Miranda	Collinsville, IL	Jr	G	5-10
7	Gene Ring	South Bend, IN	Sr	G	6-1
21	Tyrie Robbins	Gary, IN	Sr	F	6-3
6	Tom Satter	Franklin, IN	So	F	5-10
19	Jim Schooley	Auburn, IN	So	C	6-5
14	Hal Summers	Lawrenceville, IL	Jr	F	6-1
11	Bill Tosheff (Capt.)	Gary, IN	Sr	F	6-0
4	Dale Vieau	Hammond, IN	Jr	G	5-10

SEASON RESULTS 1950-51

Date	Court	Opponent	Result	Score
12/2/1950	H	DePauw	W	59-45
12/9/1950	H	Oregon State	W	72-45
12/12/1950	H	Texas Christian	W	87-68
12/16/1950	N1	Kansas State	W	58-52
12/22/1950	A	Butler	W	61-46
12/23/1950	N2	Notre Dame	W	64-56
12/27/1950	A	Bradley	L	62-64
12/29/1950	A	Drake	W	59-49
1/6/1951	A	Ohio State	W	77-62
1/13/1951	A	Michigan State	W	47-37
1/15/1951	H	Illinois	W	64-53
1/20/1951	A	Purdue	W	77-56
1/22/1951	H	Ohio State	W	69-59
1/27/1951	H	Minnesota	W	32-26
2/10/1951	A	Minnesota	L	54-61
2/12/1951	A	Iowa	W	63-54
2/17/1951	H	Northwestern	W	94-63
2/19/1951	A	Illinois	L	65-71
2/24/1951	H	Purdue	W	68-53
2/26/1951	H	Iowa	W	63-53
3/3/1951	A	Michigan	W	57-42
3/5/1951	H	Wisconsin	W	68-58

1 Kansas City, MO
2 Indianapolis, IN

1950-51 BIG TEN STANDINGS

	W	L	PCT
Illinois	13	1	.929
Indiana	12	2	.857
Iowa	9	5	.643
Minnesota	7	7	.500
Northwestern	7	7	.500
Wisconsin	7	7	.500
Michigan St.	5	9	.357
Purdue	4	10	.286
Michigan	3	11	.214
Ohio State	3	11	.214

While IU was upending Wisconsin, Illinois beat Michigan State 49-43 to close the season with a 13-1 conference record, one game better than the Hoosiers at 12-2. Thus, McCracken had his seventh second-place team in his ten seasons as Indiana coach. Illinois closed the season ranked fifth in the country. IU was ranked seventh.

For the third straight season, Bill Garrett led the Hoosiers in scoring, and he finished his career as Indiana's all-time leading scorer with 792 points, breaking the record of 757 set by Lou Watson just a year earlier. However, the All-American Garrett's successor at center would end up scoring more points than Garrett and Watson combined.

Because Indiana lacked a true center, 6'3" Bill Garrett used his quickness and craftiness to hold down the pivot position. He was so effective that he was named an All-American for the 1950-51 season. The Big Ten's first African-American basketball recruit, Garrett also passed his former teammate Lou Watson to become the all-time leading scorer in IU history.   *IU Archives*

INDIANA'S RANKING IN THE 1950-51 ASSOCIATED PRESS POLLS

12/19	12/26	1/3	1/9	1/16	1/23	1/30	2/6	2/13	2/20	2/27	3/7
4	5	6	6	6	5	3	3	6	4	7	7

1951-52

OVERALL RECORD: 16-6

CONFERENCE RECORD: 9-5 (FOURTH PLACE)

TEAM HONORS:

HOOSIER CLASSIC CHAMPION

INDIVIDUAL HONORS:

BOB MASTERS—BIG TEN MEDAL OF HONOR

The 1951-52 team. First row (left to right): John Wood, Tony Hill, Bob Masters, Sam Miranda, Dale Vieau, Sam Esposito; Second row: assistant coach Lou Watson, Dick Swan, Jim Schooley, Don Schlundt, head coach Branch McCracken, Lou Scott, Charlie Kraak, Dick Farley, assistant coach Ernie Andres; Third row: Bob Dobson, Dick Baumgartner, Bob Leonard, Jim DeaKyne, Ron Taylor. IU Archives

With the graduation of Bill Garrett, Bill Tosheff and Gene Ring, the 1951-52 season represented a changing of the guard as Coach Branch McCracken's marquee recruiting class of 1950 now emerged as a group of sophomores ready to make their mark in an Indiana uniform. Plus, McCracken also had the services of highly touted 6'9" freshman Don Schlundt, who was eligible to play right away because of the Korean War waiver (which allowed freshmen to compete in varsity athletics because the U.S. draft drained the number of young men on college campuses). After relying on the under-sized—though very effective—Bill Garrett at center for most of the previous three seasons, McCracken now had Schlundt and 6'10" sophomore Lou Scott battling for the pivot position. Schlundt prevailed and would go on to become one of the most prolific scorers in college basketball history. For the 1951-52 season, Schlundt and the IU sophomores experienced a trial by fire, which prepared them well for the championship battles of the years to come.

Indiana opened the season by victimizing Valparaiso 68-59 on Thursday, December 6, in Bloomington. The Hoosiers fell behind by 2 at the

1951-52 TEAM ROSTER

Head coach: Branch McCracken
Assistant coaches: Ernie Andres, Lou Watson

No.	Player	Hometown	Class	Position	Height
13	Dick Baumgartner	LaPorte, IN	Jr	G	6-0
22	Jim DeaKyne	Fortville, IN	So	G	6-3
17	Bob Dobson	Bloomington, IN	Jr	G	6-1
13	Sam Esposito	Chicago, IL	So	G	5-9
31	Dick Farley	Winslow, IN	So	F	6-3
25	Tony Hill	Seymour, IN	Sr	F	6-1
30	Charlie Kraak	Collinsville, IN	So	F	6-5
21	Bob Leonard	Terre Haute, IN	So	G/F	6-3
20	Bob Masters	Lafayette, IN	Sr	G	6-3
5	Sam Miranda	Collinsville, IN	Sr	G	5-10
34	Don Schlundt	South Bend, IN	Fr	C	6-9
32	Jim Schooley	Auburn, IN	Jr	C	6-5
35	Lou Scott	Chicago, IL	So	C	6-10
11	Ron Taylor	Chicago, IL	So	F	6-3
14	Dick Swan	Gary, IN	So	F	6-4
4	Dale Vieau	Hammond, IN	Sr	G	5-10
24	John Wood	Morristown, IN	So	G	5-7

SEASON RESULTS 1951-52

Date	Court	Opponent	Result	Score
12/6/1951	H	Valparaiso	W	68-59
12/8/1951	H	Xavier	W	92-69
12/14/1951	A	Colorado A&M	W	80-48
12/15/1951	A	Wyoming	W	57-55
12/22/1951	H	Kansas State	W	80-75
12/28/1951	N1	Notre Dame	W	67-54
12/29/1951	A	Butler	W	87-71
1/5/1952	H	Michigan	W	58-46
1/7/1952	A	Ohio State	L	72-73
1/12/1952	A	Iowa	L	59-78
1/14/1952	A	Illinois	L	66-78
1/19/1952	A	Purdue	W	82-77
1/21/1952	H	Iowa	W	82-69
2/2/1952	H	St. Johns	L	55-65
2/9/1952	H	Purdue	W	93-70
2/11/1952	A	Minnesota	L	61-74
2/16/1952	A	Northwestern	W	96-85
2/18/1952	H	Illinois	L	70-77
2/23/1952	A	Wisconsin	W	63-48
2/25/1952	H	Ohio State	W	95-80
3/1/1952	H	Minnesota	W	68-52
3/3/1952	H	Michigan State	W	70-67

1 Indianapolis, IN

1951-52 BIG TEN STANDINGS

	W	L	PCT
Illinois	12	2	.857
Iowa	11	3	.786
Minnesota	10	4	.714
Indiana	9	5	.643
Michigan St.	6	8	.429
Ohio State	6	8	.429
Wisconsin	5	9	.357
Michigan	4	10	.286
Northwestern	4	10	.286
Purdue	3	11	.214

half, but built a 13-point lead midway through the second half and then cruised to victory. IU sophomore forward Dick Farley topped all scorers with 19 points, while Schlundt showed some first-game jitters by going 1-5 from the field. Schlundt and the Hoosiers looked better on Saturday, December 8, when Xavier came to Bloomington. Schlundt led IU with 16 points, and the Hoosiers used a 47-26 second-half advantage to defeat the Musketeers 92-69. Lou Scott also played well off the bench, scoring 11 points and grabbing nine rebounds.

A doubleheader in Laramie, Wyoming, to dedicate the new Wyoming Fieldhouse on December 14-15, served as the Hoosiers' first road trip. IU blasted Colorado A&M 80-48 on Friday night and then slipped by a veteran (and previously undefeated) Wyoming team 57-55 on Saturday night. The Hoosiers trailed the Cowboys 54-50 with four minutes remaining, until IU reeled off a final 7-1 run with Schlundt hitting the game-winning basket. Leonard led the Hoosiers with 24 points, while Schlundt added 18 for the Hoosiers, who improved to 4-0.

On Saturday, December 22, in Bloomington, Leonard and Schlundt again teamed up to deliver a victory, but this time Kansas State was the victim. The Hoosiers used a furious comeback in the final five minutes of regulation to tie the game and send it to overtime, and then grabbed an 80-75 victory in OT, as Schlundt scored 28 and Leonard dropped in 18. In the Hoosier Classic on December 28-29, Indiana defeated Notre Dame 67-54 in the first game, and then pummeled Butler 87-71 in the second contest. Schlundt was IU's high scorer in both games, as he dropped 17 points on the Fighting Irish and scored 19 against the Bulldogs.

After a 7-0 romp through the preconference season, the Hoosiers began Big Ten play by hosting Michigan on Saturday, January 5. The Wolverines took advantage of the Hoosiers' inexperienced front line by repeatedly scoring inside, while IU guards Sam Miranda and Bob Leonard gave Michigan fits. The Wolverines hung tough, but Indiana led most of the game and prevailed 58-46, led by 18 points from Leonard.

Next, the young Indiana squad learned just how tough it is to go on the road in the Big Ten, as the previously 8-0 Hoosiers dropped three straight road games to conference opponents. The first came on Monday, December 7, in Columbus, Ohio, where Ohio State came back from a seven-point deficit in the final six minutes to upset the fourth-ranked Hoosiers 73-72, when OSU's 5'10" guard Dick Dawe swished a desperation shot just as time expired. The next road setback came on Saturday, December 12, at the hands of the Iowa Hawkeyes, who broke loose from the Hoosiers in the final ten minutes and recorded a 78-59 victory. Schlundt scored 20 points and grabbed eight rebounds, but Iowa center Chuck Darling out-dueled him with 27 points and 16 rebounds. The third straight road defeat came at Illinois on Monday, January 14, when the Fighting Illini clobbered IU 78-66.

The Hoosiers finally got their first road win on Saturday, January 19, against lowly Purdue. Indiana opened up an eight-point halftime lead and then outlasted the Boilermakers for an 82-77 win. Schlundt hit 12 of 18 field goals and scored 29 points, while holding Purdue's senior center Carl McNulty to 8-31 from the field. The Hoosiers finally returned home to the Fieldhouse for a Monday, January 21 game against Iowa, who was leading the conference with a 5-0 record. The Hoosiers found themselves in a see-saw battle, but broke the game open with a 19-6 run to close the game, which secured an 82-69 IU win.

After the semester break, Indiana looked rusty in losing a 65-55 nonconference game to St. Johns in Bloomington on Saturday, February 2. The Johnnies' Bob Zawoluk, an All-America center, dominated the inside, scoring 25 points and pulling down 10 rebounds. The loss broke Indiana's 17-game home winning streak. A week later, Indiana got back to Big Ten play when Purdue came to town. The Hoosiers crushed the Boilermakers 93-70, as Schlundt set the IU single-game scoring record with 35 points. Next, Indiana went on the road again and suffered another setback on February 11 at Minnesota. The Golden

Gophers led from start to finish in beating IU 74-61. The Hoosiers bounced back and nabbed their second road victory of the season on February 16 by winning a 96-85 triumph at Northwestern. IU's 5'9" sophomore, Sammy Esposito, topped all scorers with a career-high 25 points.

Big Ten co-leader Illinois came to Bloomington on Monday, February 18, and finished the game on a 12-5 run to steal a 77-70 win from the Hoosiers in front of over 10,000 fans in the Fieldhouse and an estimated television audience of 230,000. The Illinois loss dropped Indiana to 5-5 in conference play, but the Hoosiers finished the season with four consecutive conference victories. The first win came on the road against Wisconsin on February 23, when IU rolled to a 63-48 win. Then the Hoosiers swept their final three games at home. They bested Ohio State 95-80 on February 25, as Schlundt scored 24 points and grabbed 13 rebounds. Minnesota was rebuffed 68-52 on Saturday, March 1, as Farley scored 23 points, collected 12 rebounds, and helped lock down Minnesota center Ed Kalafat. Indiana then closed out the schedule with a come-from-behind 70-67 win over Michigan State in Bloomington on Monday, March 3.

Indiana's four-game winning streak to close the season gave the Hoosiers a fourth-place finish in the conference. However, the once highly ranked Hoosiers learned a lot about what it takes to win in the Big Ten. While Schlundt set several new scoring records for Indiana and was sensational for a freshman, he also got overpowered at times by older, stronger, and craftier centers. However, starting the next season, it was Schlundt and the Hoosiers who began to overpower their opponents.

INDIANA'S RANKING IN THE 1951-52 ASSOCIATED PRESS POLLS

12/11	12/18	12/26	1/2	1/8	1/15	1/22	1/29	2/5	2/12	2/19	2/26	3/4
11	6	5	5	4	14	20	13	18	20	—	—	—

1952-53

For the commentary and statistics for the 1952-53 season, please see Chapter 2, "1952-53: McCracken Runs the Table a Second Time."

1953-54

OVERALL RECORD: 20-4

CONFERENCE RECORD: 12-2 (FIRST PLACE)

TEAM HONORS: BIG TEN CHAMPION

INDIVIDUAL HONORS:

BOB LEONARD—ALL-AMERICA,

ALL-BIG TEN (FIRST TEAM)

DON SCHLUNDT—ALL-AMERICA,

ALL-BIG TEN (FIRST TEAM)

The scariest thing for opponents of Indiana's 1952-53 team, which went 23-3 and won the national championship, may have been the fact that the Hoosiers' entire rotation of regular players was made up of sophomores and juniors, who returned in 1953-54 to steamroll other teams once again. The challenge for the 1953-54 Hoosiers was that their 1953 NCAA title had also put a target on their backs, so that every opponent was now looking to see if they could knock off the best team in the land.

"We're really on the spot this year," said coach Branch McCracken. "People figure that with the same bunch we had last year we should breeze through. It's not that simple, and a lot of things can happen. … The [Big Ten] is much tougher from top to bottom this year than last. Add to that the fact that everyone is going to be pointing at us and that the pressure is going to be on us from start to finish." The Hoosiers

would answer the call, but they couldn't quite make it to the summit that they had reached during 1952-53.

Indiana's two All-Americans, "Mr. Outside" Bobby Leonard and "Mr. Inside" Don Schlundt, picked up right where they left off the previous season when the Hoosiers opened against Cincinnati on Saturday, December 5, in Bloomington. Schlundt and Leonard scored 20 points apiece as IU used the full-court press to shake the Bearcats and earn a 78-65 victory. Two nights later, Indiana blasted Kansas State 92-66, as Schlundt rang up 25 points. Next, the Hoosiers went up to Indianapolis on Saturday, December 12, and easily tamed the Butler Bulldogs 76-57. Thirteen different IU players scored in the game, led by 17 points from Schlundt.

Notre Dame came to Bloomington Monday, December 14, and the Fighting Irish used three players to blanket Schlundt (who poured in 41 points against them in the NCAA tournament the year before). The strategy led to open shots for other Hoosiers, especially Leonard, who scored 21 in a 66-55 Indiana win. The Hoosiers then went on the road for a three-game swing before Big Ten play. Montana hosted IU on Friday, December 18, and the Hoosiers buried the Grizzlies 74-54, even though Leonard sat out the game with an injured shoulder. Forward Dick Farley paced IU with 18 points. On Monday, December 21, the Hoosiers, ranked No.1 in the country, defeated No. 11 Oregon State 76-72 in Corvallis, Oregon. Schlundt led all scorers with 34 points. The next night Oregon State got its revenge in a rematch on the same court. The Beavers ran to an early lead and controlled the rest of the game by double- and triple-teaming Schlundt to keep the ball out of his hands. Meanwhile, Oregon State's 7'3" center Wade Halbrook scored 21 points to lead the Beavers to a 67-51 upset.

Indiana, which went 6-1 in the preconference season, opened the Big Ten schedule on the road at Michigan on Saturday, January 2. The Hoosiers stole away a 62-60 win when Leonard buried a 25-footer just as the buzzer sounded. Schlundt dropped in 30 points to lead all scorers, and Leonard finished with 16 for IU. The following Monday, the Wisconsin Badgers came to Bloomington, and the Hoosiers barely held them off for a 70-67 victory, as Schlundt scored a game-high 29 points. Next, IU went on the road to Minnesota, where the Hoosiers had dropped

The 1953-54 team. First row (left to right): Burke Scott, Charlie Kraak, Lou Scott, Don Schlundt, Dick Farley, Bob Leonard; Second row: Dick White, Wally Choice, head coach Branch McCracken, Paul Poff, Jim DeaKyne; Third row: Sherrill Marginet, Neal Skeeters, Cliff Williamson, Phil Byers, Warren Fisher; Fourth row: Frank Stemle, Bill Maetschke, Charles Mead, Jim Barley, Jim Phipps. IU Archives

their only conference game the year before, and where IU hadn't won since 1946. The Indiana squad showed its championship mettle by completely controlling the game and winning 71-63. Four Hoosiers scored in double figures, led by 20 points from Leonard.

The last-place team in the Big Ten took on the first-place team when Purdue came to Bloomington on Monday, January 11. The Boilermakers did their best to slow down the Hoosiers' fast break, but Schlundt took advantage of the Purdue squad in the half court and scored 30 points to lead IU to a 73-67 win. Farley added 22 points for Indiana. On Saturday, January 16, Indiana went up to Madison for a rematch with Wisconsin and used the one-two punch of Leonard-Schlundt to knock out the Badgers 90-74. Schlundt blistered the nets for 33 points, while Leonard poured in 23.

The Hoosiers, now 5-0 in conference play, headed into a four-game homestand (which included a nonconference game). Ohio State came to town on Monday, January 18, and became the unfortunate victim of a 47-point explosion from Don Schlundt

INDIANA'S RANKING IN THE 1953-54 ASSOCIATED PRESS POLLS

12/8	12/15	12/22	12/29	1/5	1/12	1/19	1/26	2/2	2/9	2/16	2/23	3/2	3/9	3/23
1	1	1	3	3	3	3	3	3	3	3	3	2	2	4

1953-54 TEAM ROSTER

Head coach: Branch McCracken
Assistant coach: Ernie Andres, Phil Buck

No.	Player	Hometown	Class	Position	Height
20	Jim Barley	Marion, IN	So	G	6-2
14	Phil Byers	Evansville, IN	Jr	G	5-11
44	Wally Choice	Montclair, NJ	So	F	6-4
22	Jim DeaKyne	Fortville, IN	Sr	G	6-3
31	Dick Farley	Winslow, IN	Sr	F	6-3
32	Warren Fisher	Kokomo, IN	So	F	6-3
13	Charlie Kraak	Collinsville, IL	Sr	F	6-5
21	Bob Leonard (Capt.)	Terre Haute, IN	Sr	G	6-3
33	Bill Maetschke	New Albany, IN	So	F	6-3
24	Sherrill Marginet	Fort Branch, IN	So	G	6-0
42	Charles Mead	Oak Park, IL	So	G	6-3
23	Jim Phipps	Kokomo, IN	So	G	5-11
30	Paul Poff	New Albnay, IN	Jr	G	6-1
34	Don Schlundt	South Bend, IN	Jr	C	6-10
25	Burke Scott	Tell City, IN	Jr	G	6-0
35	Lou Scott	Chicago, IL	Sr	C	6-10
15	Neal Skeeters	Louisville, KY	So	G	5-10
45	Frank Stemle	New Albany, IN	So	F	6-3
41	Dick White	Terre Haute, IN	Jr	F	6-1
43	Cliff Williamson	Kokomo, IN	So	F	6-3

SEASON RESULTS 1953-54

Date	Court	Opponent	Result	Score
12/5/1953	H	Cincinnati	W	78-65
12/7/1953	H	Kansas State	W	92-66
12/12/1953	A	Butler	W	76-57
12/14/1953	H	Notre Dame	W	66-55
12/18/1953	A	Montana	W	74-54
12/21/1953	A	Oregon State	W	76-72
12/22/1953	A	Oregon State	L	51-67
1/2/1954	A	Michigan	W	62-60
1/4/1954	H	Wisconsin	W	70-67
1/9/1954	A	Minnesota	W	71-63
1/11/1954	H	Purdue	W	73-67
1/16/1954	A	Wisconsin	W	90-74
1/18/1954	H	Ohio State	W	94-72
2/1/1954	H	Louisville	W	80-71
2/6/1954	H	Michigan State	W	79-74
2/8/1954	H	Minnesota	W	90-77
2/13/1954	A	Northwestern	L	90-100
2/15/1954	A	Purdue	W	86-50
2/20/1954	A	Michigan State	W	63-61
2/22/1954	H	Iowa	L	64-82
2/27/1954	A	Ohio State	W	84-68
3/6/1954	H	Illinois	W	67-64
NCAA Tournament				
3/12/1954	N1	Notre Dame	L	65-64
3/13/1954	N1	Louisiana State	W	73-62

1 Iowa City, IA

1953-54 BIG TEN STANDINGS

	W	L	PCT
Indiana	12	2	.857
Iowa	11	3	.786
Illinois	10	4	.714
Minnesota	10	4	.714
Wisconsin	6	8	.429
Northwestern	6	8	.429
Ohio State	5	9	.357
Michigan St.	4	10	.286
Michigan	3	11	.214
Purdue	3	11	.214

that led Indiana to a 94-72 win. Schlundt's outburst set the new Big Ten single-game scoring record. Two weeks later, Schlundt continued his torrid scoring pace with 29 points in an 80-71 nonconference win over Louisville on Monday, February 1. Then, successive home wins over Michigan State (79-74 on February 6) and Minnesota (90-77 on February 8) put Indiana at 8-0 in conference play and they looked as dominant as ever. That's when Northwestern, who was fighting just to stay in the middle of the pack in the Big Ten, sprung a surprise. The Wildcats beat the Hoosiers 100-90 in overtime on Saturday, February 13, in Evanston.

The Northwestern loss dropped IU into a tie with Iowa for first place in the Big Ten. However, the Hoosiers regained the top spot on Monday, February 15, when they dismantled Purdue 86-50 in West Lafayette. IU had improved its conference record to 9-1, while Ohio State upset Iowa the same night to drop the Hawkeyes to 8-2. On Saturday, February 20, the Hoosiers journeyed up to East Lansing and squeezed out a 63-61 victory when guard Burke Scott sank a shot from the top of the key in the final seconds. An Iowa loss to Illinois in Iowa City gave Indiana a two-game cushion over those two foes in the conference race, and gave the Hoosiers a chance to clinch at least a tie for the Big Ten title if they could beat Iowa in Bloomington on Monday, February 22. However, the Hawkeyes came to the Fieldhouse and played with a desperation and aggressiveness that enabled them to walk out of the gym with a surprising 82-64 win.

"This team is tired," said McCracken. "Not as much physically as mentally. Every team we've met has pointed for us and gone all out against us. The constant strain of meeting that challenge every night and getting ourselves up for it is showing its effects."

Indiana came back and took care of business on Saturday, February 27, in Columbus, Ohio, where the Hoosiers blew through Ohio State 84-68, as Schlundt scored 27 points and sophomore Wally Choice chipped in 20. That set up a season-ending battle with Illinois in Bloomington on Saturday, March 6. If IU won, the Hoosiers claimed the title outright, but if they lost, then they would have to share the title with Illinois. In the latter scenario, Illinois would likely be awarded the berth in the NCAA tournament, and the Hoosiers would not have a chance to defend their national championship. The game was everything it was expected to be as it came down to the final minutes, when Leonard buried a series of clutch free throws to deliver a 67-64 Hoosier victory, and a celebration ensued in Bloomington as IU won its second consecutive undisputed Big Ten title.

In the first round of the NCAA tournament in Iowa City, Iowa, the No. 1-ranked Hoosiers met a familiar foe in No. 5 Notre Dame. The Hoosiers had knocked the Fighting Irish out of the tournament the year before and soundly beaten them in Bloomington earlier in the season. Just as they had done in December, the Irish crowded Schlundt and forced the rest of the Hoosiers to do the scoring. Leonard tried to step up, but he was mired in a cold-shooting night. Thus, the game became a struggle to the finish. IU was down 63-60 when Leonard drove into the lane and scored just as a whistle blew. Indiana excitedly thought Leonard was going to the line with a chance to tie the game, but instead he was called for a charging foul after he released the ball. The basket was good, but Notre Dame made both free throws. Leonard quickly came down and scored again just before time expired, but Notre Dame ran off the last few ticks on the clock and won 65-64.

"We weren't at our best, and it cost us," said McCracken. "Notre Dame played a great game and deserved to win. But I wish it could have been the other way around because of our fans. I don't think any basketball team in history has had a more loyal following, and I wanted to win for them more than anyone else." Indiana had nearly 1,000 boosters that followed the team to Iowa City. Meanwhile, Notre Dame had about 50 fans, and the other two teams in the regional, Penn State and Louisiana state, each had about 25.

The day after the Notre Dame loss, Indiana won a consolation game against Louisiana State 73-62, while Penn State upset Notre Dame 71-63. The Hoosiers finished the season at 20-4 overall. It was the second straight 20-win season, and only the third in school history, and it would be two decades until IU saw the next one.

After graduation, Leonard went on to a long-time playing and coaching career in professional basketball. He coached the Indiana Pacers to three straight ABA championships in the 1970s.

1954-55

OVERALL RECORD: 8-14

CONFERENCE RECORD: 5-9 (SIXTH PLACE)

INDIVIDUAL HONORS:

DON SCHLUNDT—ALL-AMERICA,

ALL-BIG TEN (FIRST TEAM)

After two dominating seasons in which IU racked up a 43-7 overall record and claimed two outright Big Ten titles, seniors Don Schlundt and Burke Scott returned to lead the Hoosiers, who were ranked fourth in the nation going into the 1954-55 season, and were the favorite to win the Big Ten for a third straight season. However, Coach Branch McCracken wasn't confident that the Hoosiers would be that good. "We don't figure to be any more than respectable," he said. "You don't lose such outstanding players as Bob Leonard, Dick Farley and Charley Kraak, who were vitally important to us over the last three seasons, without feeling it."

In addition to the three starters that McCracken mentioned, the Hoosiers were also losing a key reserve in 6'10" backup center Lou Scott. That left 6'4" junior forward Wally Choice and 6'5" sophomore forward Dick Neal to fill in at center when Schlundt was on the bench. The other big question facing these Hoosiers would be which players could provide the outside shooting that Leonard did, which helped keep defenses from sagging in on Schlundt. There was hope that sophomore Hallie "The Bomber" Bryant could fill that role. Bryant, the 1953 Indiana Mr. Basketball from Indianapolis Crispus Attucks, had been a high-scoring prep player who was known for his outside shooting and playmaking.

Unfortunately, everyone was adjusting to a new role, except for Schlundt and Scott, and the transition didn't go very smoothly. While many expected these Hoosiers to continue the high standards of the preceding years, McCracken merely wanted them to be respectable. However, respectability didn't come easy.

Indiana opened the season by struggling to defeat Valparaiso 77-66 on Saturday, December 4, in Bloomington. Choice broke out for a game-high 29

The 1954-55 team. First row (left to right): John Wood, Charlie Hodson, Burke Scott, Don Schlundt, Dick White, Phil Byers, Wally Choice; Second row: Jim Barley, Dick Baumgartner, Paul Poff, Jim Phipps; Third row: Hallie Bryant, Cliff Williamson, Charles Mead, Neal Skeeters, Bill Maetschke; Fourth row: Dick Neal, Clarence Doninger, Frank Stemle, Dick Kirkpatrick. IU Archives

points and was extremely active on the boards and on defense before fouling out with 4:42 left in the game. Two nights later, Missouri came to town and promptly handed the Hoosiers their first defeat of the season. Indiana led by three at the half, but scored only five field goals and 26 points in the second half and fell 64-61.

On December 11, in South Bend, the Hoosiers did manage to repay Notre Dame for its upset of IU in the NCAA tournament the year before. Indiana never led until Hallie Bryant buried a shot from the right corner with 0:44 remaining to give the Hoosiers a 69-68 lead. IU went on to win 73-70 and broke the Fighting Irish's 22-game winning streak at home.

After starting 2-1, IU would lose its next four preconference games to SMU (83-78), Cincinnati (97-65), Kansas State (91-74), and St. Louis (80-78). The 32-point defeat to the Bearcats was the Hoosiers' worst loss in 10 seasons. IU's defense and rebounding were

especially bad during this stretch in which three of the four games were played on the road. At 2-5, Indiana had already lost more games in the preconference season than it had during entire season the year before. That was a bad omen heading into Big Ten play.

Michigan came to Bloomington for the Big Ten opener on Monday, January 3, and the Hoosiers reinvigorated their fast break for a 95-77 win. Schlundt led all scorers with 30 points, and he also led the Hoosiers to a much better showing on boards. Next, Indiana went on the road for three straight conference games and was handily defeated in all three. Illinois won 99-75 on Saturday, January 8, Minnesota downed IU 88-74 on January 10, and Wisconsin prevailed 77-66 on January 15. Schlundt scored 34, 30, and 22 points, respectively, in the three games, but he didn't get enough help from his teammates for IU to have a chance to win any of three contests. The Hoosiers were 1-3 in the conference and sitting in last place.

Things looked like they were getting worse on Monday, January 17, when Michigan State came to Bloomington and ran to a 19-point lead late in the first half. However, the Hoosiers opened the second half with a 20-3 run and eventually overran the Spartans for an 88-79 win, led by 36 points from Schlundt, 16 from Wally Choice, and 14 from Burke Scott. Two weeks later, after the semester break, Indiana posted its most dominant win of the season with an 87-56 whipping of Butler in Bloomington. Schlundt had a game-high 23 points and Choice added 20.

On February 5, IU blew a 12-point second-half lead at Ohio State and lost 90-87 to the lowly Buckeyes, who were battling the Hoosiers for the Big Ten cellar. Indiana bounced back and scratched out a 65-58 win over Wisconsin in Bloomington on February 7, behind 20 points from Schlundt and 19 from guard Jim Barley. That put Indiana at 3-4 in conference play and sparked some hope that the Hoosiers could still put together a solid finish in the Big Ten. Unfortunately, IU would lose its next three games.

IU put up a good fight in Iowa City on February 12, before falling 90-75 to the Iowa Hawkeyes, the eventual Big Ten champs. Choice matched his season high with 29 points in the loss. Next, IU dropped two straight home games. The first was an 80-70 defeat to Minnesota on February 14, and the second was an 85-78 loss to Northwestern on February 19. The Hoosiers finally notched another victory on Monday, February 21, when arch-rival Purdue came to Bloomington. IU handed the Boilermakers a 75-62 defeat, as Choice topped all scorers with 29 points. It was his fourth straight 20-point game, and the third time in four games that he was the Hoosiers' top scorer. The win was also Indiana's 13th consecutive victory against Purdue. However, that streak came to end five days later when the Boilermakers torched the Hoosiers 92-67 in West Lafayette, to drop IU to 4-8 in the Big Ten.

On Monday, February 28, Indiana went up to Michigan State and suffered a big loss, 93-77, to the Spartans, as MSU had two players score in the 30s—forward Al Ferrari had 35 points and center Duane Patterson had 30. Schlundt led IU with 26 points. The season wrapped up in Bloomington on Saturday, March 5, when IU defeated Ohio State 84-66 to

1954-55 TEAM ROSTER

Head coach: Branch McCracken
Assistant coach: Ernie Andres, Phil Buck

No.	Player	Hometown	Class	Position	Height
20	Jim Barley	Marion, IN	Jr	G	6-2
13	Dick Baumgartner	LaPorte, IN	Sr	G	6-0
21	Hallie Bryant	Indianapolis, IN	So	G	6-3
14	Phil Byers	Evansville, IN	Sr	G	5-11
44	Wally Choice	Montclair, NJ	Jr	F	6-4
22	Warren Fisher	Kokomo, IN	Jr	F	6-3
23	Charlie Hodson	Muncie, IN	So	G	5-9
32	Dick Kirkpatrick	Terre Haute, IN	So	F	6-3
33	Bill Maetschke	New Albany, IN	Jr	F	6-4
42	Charles Mead	Oak Park, IL	Jr	G	6-3
35	Dick Neal	Reelsville, IN	So	F	6-5
23	Jim Phipps	Kokomo, IN	Jr	G	5-11
31	Paul Poff	New Albany, IN	Sr	G	6-1
34	Don Schlundt (Capt.)	South Bend, IN	Sr	C	6-10
25	Burke Scott	Tell City, IN	Sr	G	6-0
15	Neal Skeeters	Louisville, KY	Jr	G	5-11
45	Frank Stemle	New Albany, IN	Jr	F	6-3
41	Dick White	Terre Haute, IN	Sr	F	6-1
43	Cliff Williamson	Kokomo, IN	Jr	F	6-3
24	John Wood	Morristown, IN	Sr	G	5-7

SEASON RESULTS 1954-55

Date	Court	Opponent	Result	Score
12/4/1954	H	Valparaiso	W	77-66
12/6/1954	H	Missouri	L	61-64
12/11/1954	A	Notre Dame	W	73-70
12/13/1954	H	SMU	L	78-83
12/18/1954	A	Cincinnati	L	65-97
12/21/1954	A	Kansas State	L	74-91
12/27/1954	A	St. Louis	L	78-80
1/3/1954	H	Michigan	W	95-77
1/8/1954	A	Illinois	L	75-99
1/10/1954	A	Minnesota	L	74-88
1/15/1954	A	Wisconsin	L	66-77
1/17/1954	H	Michigan State	W	88-79
1/31/1954	H	Butler	W	87-56
2/5/1954	A	Ohio State	L	87-90
2/7/1954	H	Wisconsin	W	65-58
2/12/1954	A	Iowa	L	75-90
2/14/1954	H	Minnesota	L	70-80
2/19/1954	H	Northwestern	L	78-85
2/21/1954	H	Purdue	W	75-62
2/26/1954	A	Purdue	L	67-92
2/28/1954	A	Michigan State	L	77-93
3/5/1954	H	Ohio State	W	84-66

1954-55 BIG TEN STANDINGS

	W	L	PCT
Iowa	11	3	.786
Illinois	10	4	.714
Minnesota	10	4	.714
Michigan St.	8	6	.571
Northwestern	7	7	.500
Purdue	5	9	.357
Michigan	5	9	.357
Wisconsin	5	9	.357
Indiana	5	9	.357
Ohio State	4	10	.286

Burke Scott was a three-year starter for IU. This scrappy little guard was known for his hustle, ball handling, and passing skills, but most of all, he was a ball-hawking defender who made a pest of himself against opposing backcourt players. IU Archives

avoid a last-place finish in the conference. The Buckeyes led for the first 30 minutes of the game, but IU outscored Ohio State 24-5 in the final 10 minutes. Schlundt scored 17 points during that run and finished with 47 points to tie the Big Ten record that he had set against OSU in Bloomington the year before. Schlundt's offensive explosion also moved him from third place in conference scoring to first place, which made him the first player in Big Ten history to lead the conference in scoring for three consecutive seasons. That was a fitting end to a great career for Schlundt, who also finished as the all-time leading scorer in Big Ten history.

While Schlundt continued his pattern of excellence, as a team, the Hoosiers faltered to a 8-14 record and a sixth-place finish in the Big Ten (at 5-9, the Hoosiers were only one game ahead of last-place Ohio State). McCracken was puzzled and frustrated by just how far the Hoosiers had fallen, and some worried that he might walk away from the game. As a result, 5,000 students held a rally and paraded to McCracken's home on the east side of Bloomington on March 5, to show their support. McCracken told them, "We'll be back at the top with a winning ball club."

INDIANA'S RANKING IN THE 1954-55 ASSOCIATED PRESS POLLS

12/7	12/14	12/21	12/28	1/4	1/11	1/18	1/25	2/1	2/8	2/15	2/22	3/1	3/8
6	7	—	—	—	—	—	—	—	—	—	—	—	—

1955-56

The 1955-56 team. First row (left to right): Charlie Hodson, Sam Gee, Cliff Williamson, Paxton Lumpkin, Jim Phipps; Second row: head coach Branch McCracken, Hallie Bryant, Dick Neal, Pete Obremskey, Jim Barley, assistant coach Ernie Andres; Third row: trainer Dwayne Dixon, Ray Ball, Charlie Brown, Warren Fisher, manager Roland Cutter; Fourth row: Wally Choice, Archie Dees, Dick Custer, Jerry Thompson. IU Archives

Three-time All-American Don Schlundt, who had scored a third of the Hoosiers' points during the 1954-55 season, graduated and left a gaping hole in the middle of the IU offense as the Hoosiers prepared for the 1955-56 season. The previous Indiana squad had suffered from a lack of offensive balance, poor outside shooting, and deficiencies in rebounding and defense that led to an 8-14 finish. With the loss of Schlundt and guard Burke Scott, the team's two steadiest performers, the Hoosiers needed some younger players to step up and embrace new roles if IU was going to avoid another abysmal season.

Indiana had a phenomenal group of eight sophomores that had been a part of an outstanding recruiting class in 1954. As part of the freshman team, this group had nearly upset the varsity in a preseason scrimmage the year before (the varsity came from behind to win 76-73). Coach Branch McCracken was forced to rely on several of these sophomores to play key roles on the team, and in many ways, they held the fate of the Hoosiers' season in their hands. Luckily, they came through, and the team posted a better overall record, although they didn't climb back into the upper division of the Big Ten quite yet.

1955-56 TEAM ROSTER

Head coach: Branch McCracken
Assistant coaches: Ernie Andres, Lou Watson

No.	Player	Hometown	Class	Position	Height
24	Ray Ball	Elkhart, IN	So	F	6-3
20	Jim Barley	Marion, IN	Sr	G	6-2
13	Charlie Brown	Chicago, IL	So	F	6-2
21	Hallie Bryant	Indianapolis, IN	Jr	G	6-3
44	Wally Choice (Capt.)	Montclair, NJ	Sr	F	6-4
32	Dick Custer	Parkersburg, WV	So	C	6-6
33	Archie Dees	Mount Carmel, IL	So	C	6-8
22	Warren Fisher	Kokomo, IN	Sr	F	6-3
15	Sam Gee	Washington, IN	So	G	6-1
30	Charlie Hodson	Muncie, IN	Jr	G	5-9
14	Paxton Lumpkin	Chicago, IL	So	G	6-0
35	Dick Neal	Reelsville, IN	Jr	F	6-5
31	Pete Obremskey	Jeffersonville, IN	So	F	6-3
23	Jim Phipps	Kokomo, IN	Sr	G	5-11
45	Jerry Thompson	South Bend, IN	So	F	6-5
43	Cliff Williamson	Kokomo, IN	Sr	F	6-3

SEASON RESULTS 1955-56

Date	Court	Opponent	Result	Score
12/3/1955	H	Ohio	W	93-74
12/10/1955	H	Kansas State	W	96-72
12/12/1955	H	St. Louis	L	75-86
12/17/1955	A	Missouri	W	81-78
12/19/1955	H	Cincinnati	W	80-61
12/22/1955	A	Drake	W	82-79
12/27/1955	A	Butler	W	94-70
1/2/1956	H	Northwestern	W	94-81
1/7/1956	A	Wisconsin	W	75-71
1/9/1956	A	Minnesota	L	71-77
1/14/1956	H	Illinois	L	72-96
1/16/1956	H	Michigan State	W	79-70
1/30/1956	H	Notre Dame	W	81-76
2/4/1956	A	Ohio State	L	82-100
2/6/1956	A	Illinois	L	89-92
2/11/1956	H	Michigan	W	97-73
2/13/1956	H	Wisconsin	L	67-69
2/18/1956	A	Michigan	W	80-75
2/20/1956	H	Iowa	L	83-87
2/25/1956	A	Northwestern	W	84-82
3/3/1956	H	Purdue	L	71-73
3/5/1956	A	Iowa	L	73-84

1955-56 BIG TEN STANDINGS

	W	L	PCT
Iowa	13	1	.929
Illinois	11	3	.786
Ohio State	9	5	.643
Purdue	9	5	.643
Michigan St.	7	7	.500
Indiana	6	8	.429
Minnesota	6	8	.429
Michigan	4	10	.286
Wisconsin	4	10	.286
Northwestern	1	13	.071

IU's top returning scorer was senior captain Wally Choice, a powerful and highly athletic forward. Choice, who was the first African-American player to follow Bill Garrett and come to IU, was a terrific rebounder and possessed an excellent touch around the basket. He also used his athleticism to get a lot of tip-ins. He was also known for his unguardable jump shot, in which he would use his athleticism to leap high in the air and release an accurate one-handed shot. The other returnee who was expected to play a critical role on the team was 6'3" junior guard Hallie Bryant, who was renowned as one of the greatest high school basketball players in Indiana history. Bryant had struggled a bit as a sophomore but was expected to return to his customary form as a deadly outside shooter.

Sophomore Archie Dees was the headliner of the 1954 recruiting class. The widely coveted 6'8" center from Mount Carmel, Illinois, was expected to be Schlundt's replacement in the pivot. Dees was a little more agile and athletic than Schlundt and was an excellent face-up shooter, but he still needed to develop his hook shot in order to be fully effective in the half court. Dees's classmates included former Indiana All-Stars Jerry Thompson, Ray Ball and Pete Obremsky, as well as a pair of high school stars from Chicago named Paxton Lumpkin and "Sweet" Charlie Brown. Lumpkin had marvelous dribbling and passing skills, while Brown had a sweet jump shot along with long arms and huge hands that enabled him to be an excellent rebounder and defender.

On opening night, Dees scored 21 points to the lead the Hoosiers to a 93-74 victory over Ohio University on December 3, in Bloomington. The fact that Dees started well and looked like he was going to be effective in the pivot was a shot in the arm for the team. Plus, four other Hoosiers scored in double figures, including two sophomores: forward Charlie Brown scored 15 and Jerry Thompson notched 14 off the bench. On December 10, the Hurryin' Hoosiers ran to a victory over Kansas State, 96-72, as Hallie Bryant warmed up from the outside and dropped in a game-high 23 points. His hot shooting also loosened up the Wildcat defense, which had been sagging in on Dees, who ended up with 21 points and 22 rebounds.

Two nights after the Kansas State win, St. Louis came to Bloomington and dealt the Hoosiers their first setback, 86-75. The Billikens led for most of the game as Indiana never got its fast break in gear, mostly because of poor ball handling. However, that ended up being the Hoosiers' only preconference defeat. The IU squad rattled off four straight wins, two of them on the road. The first was an 81-78 come-from-behind win at Missouri on December 17. Next was an easy 80-61 victory over No. 14 Cincinnati, and then a slim 82-79 win at Drake. The Hoosiers closed the preconference schedule with a 94-70 whipping of Butler on December 27. Bryant was the hero of the Cincinnati and Drake games. Against the Bearcats he poured in 31 points, and he single-handedly stole the game from Drake with a "spectacular" field goal and two free throws down the stretch. Wally Choice was the high scorer against Butler with 26 points, while guard Bobby Plump led the Bulldogs with 19. The Hoosiers finished the preconference schedule with a 6-1 record.

Big Ten play opened for the Hoosiers on Monday, January 2, against Northwestern in Bloomington. IU led the entire second half and finished off the Wildcats 94-81. Choice led Indiana with 26 points for the second straight game. Next, the Hoosiers took a road trip to Wisconsin and Minnesota on Saturday, January 7, and Monday, January 9, respectively, and split the two games. After trailing the Badgers by seven points at the half, Indiana came back and won 75-71, as Archie Dees and Charlie Brown scored 19 points apiece. Brown scored 15 of his points in the second half, including four straight baskets at one point. The Hoosiers went cold two nights later in Minnesota and lost 77-71. Indiana then fell to 2-2 in conference play on January 14, when Illinois, the only undefeated team left in the Big Ten, came to Bloomington and administered a 96-72 beating to the Hoosiers, who went cold from the outside for a second straight game.

On January 16, Indiana climbed back above the .500 mark in Big Ten play with a 79-70 win over

Powerful 6'4" forward Wally Choice was IU's second African-American recruit. As a senior, Choice captained the Hoosiers and led the team in scoring with 21.0 PPG.
IU Archives

Michigan State in Bloomington, as five different IU players scored in double figures. However, when the Hoosiers played their next game against Notre Dame two weeks later (after the semester break), they had to do it without sophomores Charlie Brown and Paxton Lumpkin. Both of the Chicago duo, who had come to Indiana from DuSable High School, were declared academically ineligible for the second semester and both of them left the team. The Hoosiers rolled on,

INDIANA'S RANKING IN THE 1955-56 ASSOCIATED PRESS POLLS

12/6	12/13	12/20	12/27	1/3	1/10	1/17	1/24	1/31	2/7	2/14	2/21	2/28	3/6
—	19	18	—	13	12	—	—	—	—	—	—	—	—

defeating the Fighting Irish 81-76 on January 30, in Bloomington. Choice and Dees scored 24 points each.

When they resumed Big Ten play, the Hoosiers dropped two straight road games to fall back to 3-4 and all but end their hopes of challenging for the conference title. The first loss came at Ohio State by the score of 100-82 on February 4. The second one was dealt on February 6, by No. 6 Illinois, 92-89, as a result of a controversial foul call against Bryant in the final minute. Indiana pulled back to 4-4 with a convincing 97-73 home win over Michigan on February 11. But two nights later Indiana lost an 11-point second-half lead in a 69-67 defeat to Wisconsin in Bloomington. Again, the Hoosiers bounced back with a win over Michigan. This time it came in Ann Arbor on February 18, in the form of an 80-75 victory, which evened the Hoosiers' conference record at 5-5.

However, Indiana closed the season by losing three of their final four games to slide down to 6-8 in the Big Ten. The only win was an 84-82 squeaker over Northwestern in Evanston on February 25. The Hoosiers were defeated twice by eventual Big Ten champion Iowa during this stretch—87-83 in Bloomington on February 20, and 84-73 in Iowa City on March 5. In the first Iowa contest, Choice led all scorers with 24 points. It was his seventh consecutive 20-point game. The Hoosiers' other loss came in Bloomington on March 3, to archrival Purdue by the score of 73-71. In the Purdue game, the Hoosiers mounted a furious rally, led by 18 second-half points from Bryant, before falling short at the end.

Indiana struggled in the second half of the season and ended up matching their sixth-place finish in the Big Ten from the season before but still finished with a 13-9 overall record. The midseason loss of Charlie Brown and Paxton Lumpkin definitely hurt. The Hoosiers were 4-6 without them (3-6 in conference play). "With Brown and Lumpkin we had the potential to be a dangerous team," Dees later said. Nevertheless, in addition to Dees's fine play, sophomores Jerry Thompson, and Pete Obremsky, and juniors Hallie Bryant and Charlie Hodson stepped up their play and provided a new core of players for McCracken to build around the next season.

1956-57

OVERALL RECORD: 14-8

CONFERENCE RECORD: 10-4 (FIRST PLACE)

TEAM HONORS:

BIG TEN CO-CHAMPION

INDIVIDUAL HONORS:

ARCHIE DEES—ALL-AMERICA, BIG TEN MVP,

ALL-BIG TEN (FIRST TEAM)

DICK NEAL—BIG TEN MEDAL OF HONOR

With eight lettermen and four starters returning from a 13-9 squad, Indiana was well prepared to return to title contention in the Big Ten after a two-year hiatus in the second division. While IU lost its top scorer, forward Wally Choice, to graduation, and lost two promising performers in Charlie Brown and Paxton Lumpkin, because of academic problems the previous year, the Hoosiers still returned plenty of firepower with center Archie Dees, guards Hallie Bryant and Charlie Hodson, and forwards Jerry Thompson and Pete Obremskey.

Coach Branch McCracken stated, "I'm not predicting where we'll finish, but we plan to have a lot of say concerning the outcome of the race." McCracken was also thrilled to have the kind of players who could run the fast break. "This is going to be one of our better running ball clubs," he said. "I think it will be the fastest since our 1951 club and with considerably more size."

Indiana, ranked No. 7 in the country, wasn't very impressive in its opener against Valparaiso on Friday, December 4, in Bloomington. However, Archie Dees was phenomenal at both ends of the court and carried IU to a 64-57 win. Dees scored 28 points, collected 25 rebounds, and rejected six of the Crusaders' shots. Dees continued his strong play in leading IU to two more victories in Bloomington the following week—an 80-57 blowout of Southern Illinois and a 73-68 cliffhanger over Butler. The Hoosiers went on the road for the first time on December 15, and suffered their first loss, 84-77 in overtime, to No. 14 Kansas

The 1956-57 team. First row (left to right): Charlie Hodson, Hallie Bryant, Archie Dees, Dick Neal, Pete Obremskey; Second row: Clarence Doninger, Gene Flowers, Jerry Thompson, Sam Gee; Third row: head coach Branch McCracken, Bill Balch, manager Jerome Daniel, Lee Aldridge, assistant coach Ernie Andres.
IU Archives

1956-57 TEAM ROSTER

Head coach: Branch McCracken
Assistant coaches: Ernie Andres, Lou Watson

No.	Player	Hometown	Class	Position	Height
30	Lee Aldridge	Switz City, IN	So	C	6-6
42	Bill Balch	Crawfordsville, IN	So	F	6-5
24	Ray Ball	Elkhart, IN	Jr	F	6-3
21	Hallie Bryant	Indianapolis, IN	Sr	G	6-3
22	Archie Dees	Mount Carmel, IL	Jr	C	6-8
25	Clarence Doninger	Evansville, IN	Sr	F	6-3
32	Gene Flowers	Muncie, IN	So	F	6-2
15	Sam Gee	Washington, IN	Jr	G	6-1
40	Thomas Hayes	Chicago, IL	So	G	6-1
31	Jim Hinds	Muncie, IN	So	F	6-5
23	Charlie Hodson (Capt.)	Muncie, IN	Sr	G	5-9
35	Dick Neal	Reelsville, IN	Sr	F	6-5
43	Pete Obremskey	Jeffersonville, IN	Jr	F	6-3
20	Jerry Schofield	Columbus, IN	So	F	6-3
45	Jerry Thompson	South Bend, IN	Jr	F	6-5

SEASON RESULTS 1956-57

Date	Court	Opponent	Result	Score
12/4/1956	H	Valparaiso	W	64-57
12/8/1956	H	Southern Illinois	W	80-57
12/10/1956	H	Butler	W	73-68
12/15/1956	A	Kansas State	L	77-84
12/18/1956	A	LaSalle	W	93-80
12/20/1956	A	Villanova	L	69-79
12/29/1956	H	UCLA	L	48-52
1/5/1957	H	Michigan	W	73-68
1/7/1957	H	Wisconsin	W	79-68
1/12/1957	A	Purdue	L	64-70
1/14/1957	A	Illinois	L	91-112
1/29/1957	A	Notre Dame	L	82-94
2/2/1957	A	Iowa	W	82-66
2/4/1957	H	Northwestern	W	74-56
2/9/1957	H	Ohio State	W	69-59
2/11/1957	H	Minnesota	W	91-72
2/16/1957	A	Northwestern	W	87-74
2/18/1957	H	Iowa	W	90-76
2/23/1957	A	Wisconsin	W	85-74
2/25/1957	A	Michigan	L	86-87
3/2/1957	A	Michigan State	L	61-76
3/4/1957	H	Illinois	W	84-76

1956-57 BIG TEN STANDINGS

	W	L	PCT
Indiana	10	4	.714
Michigan St.	10	4	.714
Minnesota	9	5	.643
Ohio State	9	5	.643
Purdue	8	6	.571
Michigan	8	6	.571
Illinois	7	7	.500
Iowa	4	10	.286
Wisconsin	3	11	.214
Northwestern	2	12	.143

State. IU let an 11-point lead slip away with 10 minutes remaining in the game.

Next, Indiana traveled to Philadelphia for a double-header against LaSalle and Villanova at The Palestra on December 18-20. IU beat LaSalle 93-80 as Dees scored 31 points and pulled down 18 rebounds. Two nights later, Villanova used a 1-2-2 zone to stymie the Hoosiers' attack and claim a 79-69 victory. Dees was held to a career-low eight points against Villanova. Indiana lost another game back in Bloomington on December 29, when UCLA came to town and escaped with a 52-48 victory, in an ugly game plagued by poor shooting from both teams. The loss to the Bruins put Indiana at 4-3 heading into the Big Ten season.

IU hosted Michigan to open the Big Ten schedule on Saturday, January 5, and the Hoosiers victimized the Wolverines for a 73-68 victory, as Dees scored a game-high 26 points and IU forward Dick Neal chipped in 22. Two nights later, Wisconsin came to town and received a similar treatment as IU beat the Badgers 79-68. That was the last game the Hoosiers would play in Bloomington in January, as the team prepared for a four-game road swing.

On Saturday, January 12, Purdue downed IU 70-64 in West Lafayette as Boilermaker center Lamar Lundy neutralized Dees. The following Monday, Indiana got back to its running game in Champaign, Illinois. Unfortunately, No. 10 Illinois outran the Hoosiers and handed them a 112-91 loss. Following a two-week layoff for the semester break, Indiana went up to Notre Dame on January 29, and suffered its third straight setback, 94-82 to the Fighting Irish. The defeat put Indiana's record at 6-6 overall. With the start of the second semester, IU also lost several players to academic ineligibility for the second straight year, and that thinned out the team's bench. The Hoosiers, who were once ranked among the top ten teams in the nation, found themselves in danger of seeing their promising season unravel; however, the team responded by winning its next seven games.

The first win came on February 2, at Iowa, where the Hoosiers rolled past the Hawkeyes for an 82-66 victory. Hodson and Neal led IU with 21 points each, while Dees added 18 and Bryant scored 17. Back in Bloomington, the Hoosiers crushed Northwestern 74-56 on February 4, and then outplayed conference leader Ohio State for a 69-59 win on February 9. All of a sudden, IU was now 5-2 in conference play and back in sole possession of first place in the Big Ten.

The Hoosiers kept their winning streak alive by trouncing Minnesota 91-72 on February 11, and then went up to Northwestern and tamed the Wildcats 87-74 on February 16. Against Northwestern, Bryant burned the Wildcats' zone defense for 24 points, while Neal and Dees each scored 22. On Monday, February 18, Dees had the hot hand with 37 points to help Indiana clobber Iowa 90-76 in Bloomington. Then Wisconsin became the final victim of the winning streak on February 23, when the Hoosiers went up to Madison and snatched an 85-74 win.

It was Michigan that brought Indiana's winning streak to an end on Monday, February 25, in Ann Arbor. The Wolverines led by as many as 17 points in the second half, but Dees, who scored a game-high 39 points, led the Hoosiers back to a two-point deficit in the final minute. However, Michigan prevailed 87-86. Now 9-3 in conference play, Indiana fell into a first place tie with Michigan State, the Hoosiers' next opponent. On March 2, in East Lansing, the Spartans led nearly wire to wire in an impressive 76-61 defeat of the Hoosiers. It was the tenth straight win for the Spartans, who earned at least a tie for the conference crown and an automatic berth in the NCAA tournament (since Indiana had more recently competed in the NCAA tourney in 1954).

For their part, the Hoosiers came back to Bloomington and defeated Illinois 84-76 on March 4 to claim a piece of the Big Ten championship (since Michigan State lost to Michigan the same night). Seniors Neal, Hodson and Bryant all scored in double figures in their final collegiate game. All three seniors had played a key role in helping Indiana return to the top of the Big Ten, and with a solid group of sophomores and juniors on the IU roster, the Hoosiers were well-positioned to remain there.

INDIANA'S RANKING IN THE 1956-57 ASSOCIATED PRESS POLLS

12/11	12/18	12/26	1/2	1/8	1/15	1/22	1/29	2/5	2/12	2/19	2/26	3/5	3/12
—	—	—	—	—	—	—	—	—	18	11	10	—	—

1957-58

OVERALL RECORD: 13-11

CONFERENCE RECORD: 10-4 (FIRST PLACE)

TEAM HONORS:

BIG TEN CHAMPION

INDIVIDUAL HONORS:

ARCHIE DEES—ALL-AMERICA, BIG TEN MVP,

ALL-BIG TEN (FIRST TEAM)

The 1957-58 team. First row (left to right): Bill Balch, Jerry Thompson, Archie Dees, Frank Radovich, Norbert Witte, Lee Aldridge; Second row: Stan Hill, Sam Gee, Gene Flowers, Ray Ball, Bob Wilkinson; Third row: head coach Branch McCracken, Jim Hinds, Glen Butte, manger Bill Stewart, Pete Obremskey, Al Schlegelmilch, assistant coach Ernie Andres. IU Archives

Indiana coach Branch McCracken, who was ever the pragmatist, downplayed his team's chances entering the 1957-58 season. "How anyone can figure that we'll be as good or better than we were last year beats me. We lost three starters. One, Dick Neal at forward, was the sparkplug who got us going. . . the other two, Hallie Bryant and Charley Hodson, were our regular guards and contributed just as heavily to

our success," said McCracken. "If everything works out as we would like it, it could be a real good team. But we have to prove it, and it's not fair to the squad to expect too much of it without justification."

The Hoosiers' top returnee was Archie Dees, the reigning Big Ten MVP and league scoring champ. Dees was one of the most complete basketball players in America. He was tough, agile and savvy on the

1957-58 TEAM ROSTER

Head coach: Branch McCracken
Assistant coaches: Ernie Andres, Lou Watson

No.	Player	Hometown	Class	Position	Height
30	Lee Aldridge	Switz City, IN	Jr	C	6-6
42	Bill Balch	Crawfordsville, IN	Jr	F	6-5
24	Ray Ball	Elkhart, IN	Sr	F	6-3
22	Archie Dees	Mount Carmel, IL	Sr	C	6-8
32	Gene Flowers	Muncie, IN	Jr	F	6-2
15	Sam Gee	Washington, IN	Sr	G	6-1
23	Stan Hill	Seymour, IN	So	G	5-11
31	Jim Hinds	Muncie, IN	Jr	F	6-5
43	Pete Obremskey (Capt.)	Jeffersonville, IN	Sr	F	6-3
33	Frank Radovich	Hammond, IN	So	F	6-7
13	Bob Reinhart	Dale, IN	So	G	5-10
20	Al Schlegelmilch	Monticello, IN	So	G	6-1
45	Jerry Thompson	South Bend, IN	Sr	F	6-5
44	Bob Wilkinson	LaPorte, IN	So	G	6-1
31	Norbert Witte	Decatur, IN	So	C	6-7

SEASON RESULTS 1957-58

Date	Court	Opponent	Result	Score
12/2/1957	H	Ohio	L	68-76
12/7/1957	H	Kansas State	L	61-66
12/14/1957	A	Missouri	L	73-78
12/19/1957	H	St. Mary's	W	79-66
12/23/1957	H	Oregon State	L	51-62
12/27/1957	A	Butler	L	78-84
12/28/1957	N1	Notre Dame	L	74-89
1/4/1958	H	Northwestern	W	68-65
1/6/1958	A	Purdue	L	66-68
1/11/1958	H	Illinois	W	89-82
1/13/1958	H	Minnesota	W	85-64
1/18/1958	A	Iowa	L	75-79
2/1/1958	A	DePaul	W	76-66
2/3/1958	A	Minnesota	L	66-69
2/8/1958	H	Michigan State	W	82-79
2/10/1958	A	Wisconsin	W	93-87
2/17/1958	H	Ohio State	L	83-93
2/22/1958	A	Ohio State	W	88-83
2/24/1958	H	Michigan	W	95-88
3/1/1958	H	Purdue	W	109-95
3/3/1958	A	Illinois	W	96-86
3/8/1958	A	Michigan State	W	75-72
NCAA Tournament				
3/14/1958	N2	Notre Dame	L	87-94
3/15/1958	N2	Miami (OH)	W	98-91

1 Indianapolis
2 Lexington, KY

1957-58 BIG TEN STANDINGS

	W	L	PCT
Indiana	10	4	.714
Michigan St.	9	5	.643
Purdue	9	5	.643
Northwestern	8	6	.571
Ohio State	8	6	.571
Iowa	7	7	.500
Michigan	6	8	.429
Illinois	5	9	.357
Minnesota	5	9	.357
Wisconsin	3	11	.214

court. He possessed an excellent shooting touch (out to 20 feet) and was a terrific rebounder. On defense, he was aggressive but knew how to avoid drawing unnecessary fouls. Fellow seniors Pete Obremsky and Jerry Thompson joined Dees to make up an experienced frontcourt. It was the backcourt that was the big question mark.

To those who still felt that Indiana was going to be pretty good despite the backcourt issue, McCracken's comments in which he downplayed Indiana's chances may have simply sounded like a coach trying to lower expectations. However, after the Hoosiers limped through the preconference season, McCracken's assertion actually sounded like an understatement.

Indiana's season began in Bloomington on December 2, when Ohio University unceremoniously thumped the Hoosiers 76-68. McCracken shuffled his lineup for the next game against Kansas State on Saturday, December 7, in Bloomington, and the Hoosiers led for most of the contest before losing 66-61. The Indiana squad dropped its third straight game on December 14, at Missouri, where the Tigers rebuffed the Hoosiers 78-73, despite 30 points from Archie Dees. It was the first time in 28 years that IU started the season 0-3.

St. Mary's College came to Bloomington on December 19, and Indiana used a balanced scoring attack to conquer the Gaels 79-66 and end the losing streak. Next No. 17 Oregon State came to town and walked away with a 62-51 win that dropped Indiana to 1-4 on the season. Then, on December 27-28, Indiana went to the Butler Fieldhouse in Indianapolis to play in the Hoosier Classic, which was being renewed for the first time since 1951. In their first game, the Hoosiers fell to Butler 84-78. Dees led all scorers with 30 points, but Butler had five players in double figures. In the second game, Notre Dame beat IU 89-74, even though Dees scored 32 points.

Thus, the Hoosiers limped into conference play with a 1-6 record and didn't look like much of a threat to defend their Big Ten title. Senior Archie Dees had continued to his impressive play from the past seasons, but Coach McCracken struggled to find a floor leader who could consistently run the team. In the Big Ten opener on January 4, against Northwestern, McCracken gave little-used senior Sam Gee a shot at the guard position early in the first half. Gee, who had only scored five points in two previous seasons on the varsity, played the rest of the game and did a solid job of handling the ball and keeping the offense moving as the Hoosiers defeated the Wildcats 68-65 in Bloomington. Gee quickly earned the starting spot and never relinquished it. On Monday, January 6, Indiana lost a heartbreaker at Purdue. The Boilermakers scored the final four points of the game to clinch a 68-66 win, which put both teams at 1-1 in conference play. Dees scored 38 points in the loss.

Against No. 17 Illinois on January 11, in Bloomington, Sam Gee made 11 of 12 free throws and scored 15 points to help the Hoosiers upset the Fighting Illini 89-82. Dees scored 26 points to lead IU and forward Pete Obremskey added 23. On January 13, IU hosted Minnesota and whipped the Golden Gophers 85-64, as Dees and IU forward Jerry Thompson scored 22 points apiece to lead all scorers, and Gee chipped in 14. At 3-1 in conference play, the Hoosiers found themselves tied for first place with Michigan. However, it didn't last long, because IU went to Iowa City on January 18, and lost a close battle to Iowa 79-75.

Indiana then got a confidence booster by grabbing only its second nonconference win of the season on Saturday, February 1, when the Hoosiers went up to Chicago and claimed a 76-66 victory over DePaul. Five different Indiana players scored in double figures, led by 25 from Dees. The following Monday up in Minnesota, IU blew several late-game opportunities and lost to the Golden Gophers 69-66 to fall back to 3-3 in conference play. However, Indiana captured two more Big Ten wins the next week: 82-79 over Michigan State in Bloomington and 93-87 over Wisconsin in Madison. With a 5-3 mark, Indiana was back in a tie for first place in the conference with Michigan State. However, the Hoosiers returned to Bloomington to host Ohio State on February 17, and dropped a 93-83 game to the Buckeyes.

IU had only five games remaining in the Big Ten season, and the Hoosiers knew that they needed to win at least three or four of them to have a shot at the title. They would win all five. The first was a rematch with Ohio State on February 22. IU swept in and captured an 88-83 victory in Columbus, led by 33 points and 19 rebounds from Dees. Two days later, Indiana played Michigan back at the IU Fieldhouse, and the Wolverines jumped out to a 50-36 lead at the half,

One of the most agile and versatile players to ever wear a Hoosier uniform, 6'8"Archie Dees could do it all—shoot, rebound, run, and defend. He was both the Big Ten MVP and an All-American during his junior and senior seasons. IU Archives

which prompted a tongue-lashing from McCracken in the Hoosier locker room. Indiana outscored Michigan 59-38 in the second half to win 95-88, as six different Hoosiers scored in double figures. Next, IU defeated the Purdue Boilermakers 109-95 on March 1, in Bloomington and then traveled to Illinois and beat the Fighting Illini 96-86 on March 3.

That set up a final contest on March 8, between Indiana and Michigan State in a winner-take-all game in which the victor would claim both the outright Big Ten championship and a berth in the NCAA tournament. The game was played in East Lansing where, just a year before, the Spartans had handily defeated the Hoosiers in a pivotal contest at the end of the season. This time, the Hoosiers sprinted out to a six-point halftime advantage and then stood their ground as MSU made several runs down the stretch. IU won 75-72. One of the heroes for Indiana was reserve guard Bob Wilkinson, who scored 18, including the Hoosiers' final five points—all on free throws. Gee added 17.

Just like the last time they received an NCAA bid in 1954, the Hoosiers (12-10) opened the NCAA tournament with a game against cross-state rival Notre Dame (23-4). The Fighting Irish had defeated Tennessee 94-61 in the first round, while Indiana had a first-round bye. The two teams met in the Mideast Regional Semifinals on Friday, March 14, and the final result was the same as in 1954, as the Irish sailed away with a 94-87 win. The next night, Indiana closed out its season by defeating Miami of Ohio 98-91 in the consolation game, while Notre Dame got blown out by Kentucky, the eventual national champion.

Despite coming up short in the NCAA tournament, the Hoosiers' season represented the most remarkable turnaround in IU history. After losing six out of seven preconference games, IU looked destined to challenge for a spot in the Big Ten cellar. Instead, they turned the ship around and became a solid basketball team that rattled off several surprising wins to become a conference contender by the time February rolled around. Then, the Hoosiers went into East Lansing on the last day of the conference season and defeated No. 12 Michigan State to win the Big Ten title outright. It was the Hoosiers' fourth conference championship in six seasons.

It ended up being the final Big Ten title of McCracken's career, and over the next 14 seasons, the Hoosiers would only win one more.

1958-59

OVERALL RECORD: 11-11
CONFERENCE RECORD: 7-7 (FIFTH PLACE)

After seven consecutive seasons of dealing with dominating Hoosier centers (four years of Don Schlundt and three years of Archie Dees), Indiana opponents may have been hoping that the middle of the Hoosiers' attack was finally going to soften in 1958-59. If so, they were sorely disappointed when they discovered that 6'11" sophomore Walt Bellamy now roamed the middle for IU. While Bellamy wasn't quite as skilled as Schlundt or Dees at the same point in their careers, he was faster and more athletic, and he ended up posting slightly better numbers than either at his two predecessors had during their first season on the varsity.

Bellamy was also joined by other talented sophomores such as Herbie Lee, Gary Long, Ron Horn and LeRoy Johnson. All of them were forced into the fire of competition in 1958-59 because the Hoosiers lost six seniors (four starters and two key reserves). As a result, this team only had one senior—guard Gene Flowers—who was part of coach Branch McCracken's regular rotation.

"We're green and we'll make mistakes," said McCracken. "I can't consider this squad a championship contender. In fact, I'd feel they'd be doing a great job if they'd finish in the upper half of the Big Ten. But we shouldn't be a pushover, and by the end of the season we could be a right respectable team."

The young Hoosiers showed a combination of speed, balanced scoring, wildness and inconsistency

INDIANA'S RANKING IN THE 1957-58 ASSOCIATED PRESS POLLS

12/10	12/17	12/24	12/31	1/7	1/14	1/21	1/28	2/4	2/11	2/18	2/25	3/4	3/11
–	–	–	–	–	–	–	–	–	–	–	–	–	12

The 1958-59 team. First row (left to right): manager Paul Pack, Leroy Gamble, Al Schlegelmilch, Gary Long, Bob Wilkinson, head coach Branch McCracken; Second row: assistant coach Lou Watson, Leroy Johnson, Herbie Lee, Gene Flowers, Stan Hill; Third row: Frank Radovich, Bill Balch, Ron Horn, Glen Butte; Fourth row: Norbert Witte, Walt Bellamy, Lee Aldridge. IU Archives

in their seven preconference games in which they posted a record of 3-4. They opened with a 68-59 win over Drake in Bloomington on December 1, as junior forward Frank Radovich led IU with 16 points and 15 rebounds, while Bellamy chipped in 12 points and 15 rebounds in his debut. Kansas State beat the Hoosiers 82-79 in overtime on December 6, in Manhattan, Kansas. Bellamy picked up four fouls in the first half and fouled out with eight minutes left in the game but still tied Herbie Lee with a team-high 16 points. A week later, Bellamy broke loose for 32 points in an 87-72 win over Missouri.

Next, Indiana went to Oregon State for a doubleheader with the Beavers on December 19-20. IU won the first game 57-53, but in the second game they blew a 10-point second-half lead and lost 73-69. The Hoosiers returned to Indiana to play in the Hoosier Classic on December 26-27, and suffered two disappointing defeats. The first came against Notre Dame,

73-67, and second came at the hands of Butler, 81-76. Missed scoring opportunities and turnovers haunted IU in both games.

After three consecutive losses to close out the preconference season, the Hoosiers began Big Ten play right where they had finished it the season before: in East Lansing, Michigan. For most of the game on January 3, they looked pretty similar to the team that had stolen a road victory over Michigan State the previous March to win the 1958 Big Ten title. However, MSU forward Horace Walker hit a jumper with 0:08 remaining to hand Indiana a gut-wrenching 79-77 defeat. IU brushed off that loss on January 7, when Purdue came to Bloomington. Frank Radovich scored a career-high 27 points (on 13-16 from field) to lift the Hoosiers to a 77-69 win.

The next week, the Hoosiers improved their Big Ten record to 3-1 and earned a share of the conference lead with consecutive wins over Northwestern

1958-59 TEAM ROSTER

Head coach: Branch McCracken
Assistant coaches: Lou Watson, Gene Ring

No.	Player	Hometown	Class	Position	Height
30	Lee Aldridge	Switz City, IN	Sr	C	6-6
42	Bill Balch	Crawfordsville, IN	Sr	F	6-5
35	Walt Bellamy	New Bern, NC	So	C	6-11
25	Glen Butte	Milan, IN	Jr	F	6-4
32	Gene Flowers (Capt.)	Muncie, IN	Sr	F	6-2
41	Leroy Gamble	Gary, IN	So	G	5-10
23	Stan Hill	Seymour, IN	Jr	G	5-10
45	Ron Horn	Gas City, IN	So	F	6-6
21	Leroy Johnson	Mishawaka, IN	So	F	6-4
24	Herbie Lee	South Bend, IN	So	G	5-11
15	Gary Long	Shelbyville, IN	So	G	6-0
33	Frank Radovich	Hammond, IN	Jr	F	6-7
13	Bob Reinhart	Dale, IN	Jr	G	5-10
20	Al Schlegelmilch	Monticello, IN	Jr	G	6-1
44	Bob Wilkinson	LaPorte, IN	Jr	G	6-1
43	Randy Williams	Gary, IN	So	F	6-3
31	Norbert Witte	Decatur, IN	Jr	C	6-7

SEASON RESULTS 1958-59

Date	Court	Opponent	Result	Score
12/1/1958	H	Drake	W	68-59
12/6/1958	A	Kansas State	L	79-82
12/13/1958	H	Missouri	W	87-72
12/19/1958	A	Oregon State	W	57-53
12/20/1958	A	Oregon State	L	69-73
12/26/1958	N1	Notre Dame	L	67-73
12/27/1958	A	Butler	L	76-81
1/3/1959	A	Michigan State	L	77-79
1/5/1959	H	Purdue	W	77-69
1/10/1959	A	Northwestern	W	76-69
1/12/1959	H	Minnesota	W	63-59
1/17/1959	H	Iowa	L	78-88
1/31/1959	H	DePaul	W	75-69
2/2/1959	A	Ohio State	W	122-92
2/7/1959	A	Michigan	W	84-79
2/9/1959	H	Illinois	L	83-89
2/14/1959	A	Minnesota	W	62-57
2/16/1959	A	Purdue	L	89-94
2/21/1959	A	Illinois	L	98-100
2/23/1959	H	Ohio State	L	83-92
2/28/1959	H	Michigan State	L	82-86
3/7/1959	H	Wisconsin	W	97-71

1 Indianapolis, IN

1958-59 BIG TEN STANDINGS

	W	L	PCT
Michigan St.	12	2	.857
Michigan	8	6	.571
Northwestern	8	6	.571
Purdue	8	6	.571
Illinois	7	7	.500
Indiana	7	7	.500
Ohio State	7	7	.500
Iowa	7	7	.500
Minnesota	5	9	.357
Wisconsin	1	13	.071

(76-69 on January 10, in Evanston) and Minnesota (63-59 on January 12, in Bloomington). However, Iowa came to Bloomington on January 17, and out-hustled the Hoosiers in an 88-78 upset win for the Hawkeyes. Two weeks later, Indiana came out rusty but still beat DePaul 75-69 in Bloomington. Bellamy scored 20 and guard Gary Long added 17. Long, a sophomore, started in place of junior Bob Wilkinson, who was lost to academic ineligibility with the end of the first semester.

On Monday, February 2, in Columbus, Ohio, the young Hoosiers erupted for a record-setting 122-92 win over Ohio State. Six Hoosiers scored in double figures, led by a surprising 29 points from Long. The outburst set a host of Big Ten scoring records at the time, and the Hoosiers' 122 points still remains as the Indiana record for a Big Ten game. After the game, McCracken simply stated, "We were just due for a good shooting game. Our last two had been pretty poor."

IU followed up its record-setting performance by going to Ann Arbor on February 7, and nabbing an 84-79 win from Michigan. Five Indiana players scored in double digits against the Wolverines, led by 22 from Bellamy. When Illinois came to Bloomington on February 9, the Hoosiers had a chance to move into a first place tie with Michigan State at 6-2, if they could defeat the Illini. After ten minutes of play, Indiana led Illinois 27-9 and it looked like the Hoosiers were on their way to an easy blowout. But IU went cold in the second half, and the Fighting Illini, who trailed by 13 points at the break, came back and won 89-83. In meeting to the press afterwards, McCracken could only shake his head in disbelief.

On February 14, the Hoosiers bounced back and won a tough 62-57 victory at Minnesota, powered by 18 points from Bellamy. That kept Indiana one game behind Michigan State in the race for the Big Ten title. However, the Spartans didn't lose another game, while the Hoosiers dropped their next four. Purdue beat IU 94-89 in overtime in West Lafayette on February 16. Illinois then dashed Indiana's title hopes on February 21, when the Illini edged the Hoosiers 100-98 in Champaign. On February 23, Indiana returned to Bloomington and played a sloppy game that resulted in a 92-83 loss to Ohio State, which it had beaten by 30 points in Columbus only three

As a 6'11" freshman, Walt Bellamy (center) towered over his classmates. For the 1958-59 season, Bellamy joined the varsity as a sophomore and followed in the footsteps of Don Schlundt and Archie Dees to give the Hoosiers a dominant presence in the paint. IU Archives

weeks earlier. No. 8 Michigan State added salt to the wound by coming to Bloomington on February 28, and beating IU 86-82 to clinch the Big Ten title outright. The loss dropped one-time conference contender Indiana to 6-7 in Big Ten play.

The Hoosiers restored a little pride by clobbering Wisconsin 97-71 on March 7, to avoid a losing season. The win put Indiana at 11-11 overall and 7-7 in conference play—only one game out of second place in the Big Ten, but five games out of first. This sophomore-heavy Hoosier team had started the Big Ten season playing well and looked like a formidable opponent in early February, before fading down the stretch. However, with all five starters coming back, this team's prospects for the future were almost staggering.

INDIANA'S RANKING IN THE 1958-59 ASSOCIATED PRESS POLLS

12/9	12/16	12/23	12/30	1/6	1/13	1/20	1/27	2/3	2/10	2/17	2/24	3/2	3/9
19	—	—	—	—	19	—	—	—	15	19	—	—	—

1959-60

OVERALL RECORD: 20-4

CONFERENCE RECORD: 11-3 (SECOND PLACE)

TEAM HONORS:

HOOSIER CLASSIC CHAMPION,

BLUE GRASS FESTIVAL TOURNAMENT CHAMPION

INDIVIDUAL HONORS:

WALT BELLAMY—ALL-AMERICA,

ALL-BIG TEN (FIRST TEAM)

The 1959-60 team. First row (left to right): Ernie Wilhoit, Leroy Johnson, Frank Radovich, Norbert Witte, Gordon Mickey, Charley Hall; Second row: manager Phil Lehman, Gary Long, Bob Wilkinson, Walt Bellamy, Art Schlegelmilch, Herbie Lee; Third row: assistant coach Lou Watson, Jerry Bass, Bill Altman, Glen Butte, Bob Reinhart, head coach Branch McCracken. IU Archives

For the 1959-60 season, the Hoosiers returned nearly their entire roster from a sophomore-dominated 1958-59 squad that had looked brilliant in several games and largely unimpressive in others. "Last year on a given night, this team could have beaten any ball club in the country," said coach Branch McCracken. "Other nights they would have had trouble with almost anyone. You have to be tough every night in this league to get anywhere, and consistency is one of the virtues we're seeking."

The rest of the Big Ten probably shuddered to think what this team could accomplish if it found some consistency. Undoubtedly, the Hoosiers' primary strength was its large and potent frontcourt.

Forwards Charley Hall (6'6") and Frank Radovich (6'7") joined 6'11" center Walt Bellamy in a formidable frontline that would dominate the boards and pour in points at will against overmatched opponents. Meanwhile, senior Bob Wilkinson, a fiery competitor and leader, and junior Herbie Lee, a swift playmaker, teamed up to provide McCracken with an excellent backcourt.

"This could be a pretty good ball club if the boys have the proper desire and make up their minds to play together as a unit, disregarding individual glory," said McCracken. The Hoosiers answered the call and put together a fantastic season. However, a few small stumbles along the way kept them from reaching the loftiest heights.

IU roared out of the starting gates on Saturday, December 5, with a 103-63 whipping of Ball State in Bloomington. Fourteen different Hoosiers scored in the game, led by Bellamy with 19 points, and Hall with 14. On December 7, the Indiana team traveled to Columbus, Missouri. The Hoosiers fell behind the Missouri Tigers by 15 points at the half, but rallied to pull within a point in the final minutes, before falling 79-76. Radovich led IU with 22 points. After the Missouri loss, Indiana swept through three straight opponents in Bloomington: Ohio (80-68 on December 12), Kansas State (67-58 on December 14), and previously undefeated Detroit (89-85 on December 19). Bellamy led the Hoosiers in scoring in all three contests. Against Detroit, he outscored Titans center Dave DeBusschere 35-28.

The 4-1 Hoosiers then triumphed in two pre-conference tournaments: the Hoosier Classic and the Bluegrass Festival Tournament. Indiana beat Butler 91-85 and Notre Dame 71-60 to claim the Hoosier Classic crown at Butler Fieldhouse in Indianapolis, on December 22-23. Then, in Louisville, on December 28-29, the Hoosiers easily defeated Maryland (72-63) and Louisville (90-71) to claim the Bluegrass title.

After the preconference season, the Hoosiers were flying high at 8-1 and looked ready to plow through the competition in the Big Ten. Other than the 9-0 Ohio State Buckeyes, it didn't look like many teams could compete with IU. However, a confident Purdue squad showed up in Bloomington on Saturday, January 2, and sprang a surprise on the Hoosiers by grabbing a 36-32 halftime lead. Led by Terry Dischinger, who scored 21 of his game-high 30

1959-60 TEAM ROSTER

Head coach: Branch McCracken
Assistant coaches: Lou Watson, Gene Ring

No.	Player	Hometown	Class	Position	Height
41	Bill Altman	Mooresville, IN	So	F	6-2
23	Jerry Bass	Morristown, IN	So	G	5-9
35	Walt Bellamy	New Bern, NC	Jr	C	6-11
25	Glen Butte	Milan, IN	Sr	F	6-4
42	Charley Hall	Terre Haute, IN	So	F	6-6
21	Leroy Johnson	Mishawaka, IN	Jr	F	6-4
24	Herbie Lee	South Bend, IN	Jr	G	5-11
15	Gary Long	Shelbyville, IN	Jr	G	6-0
30	Gordon Mickey	Chillicothe, OH	So	F	6-7
33	Frank Radovich (Capt.)	Hammond, IN	Sr	F	6-7
13	Bob Reinhart	Dale, IN	Sr	G	5-10
20	Al Schlegelmilch	Monticello, IN	Sr	G	6-1
44	Bob Wilkinson	LaPorte, IN	Sr	G	6-1
32	Ernie Wilhoit	Collinsville, IL	So	G	6-3
31	Norbert Witte	Decatur, IN	Sr	C	6-7

SEASON RESULTS 1959-60

Date	Court	Opponent	Result	Score
12/5/1959	H	Ball State	W	103-63
12/7/1959	A	Missouri	L	76-79
12/12/1959	H	Ohio	W	80-68
12/14/1959	H	Kansas State	W	67-58
12/19/1959	H	Detroit	W	89-85
12/22/1959	A	Butler	W	91-85
12/23/1959	N1	Notre Dame	W	71-60
12/28/1959	N2	Maryland	W	73-62
12/29/1959	A	Louisville	W	90-71
1/2/1960	H	Purdue	L	76-79
1/4/1960	A	Northwestern	L	57-61
1/9/1960	A	Ohio State	L	95-96
1/11/1960	A	Michigan	W	77-72
1/30/1960	A	DePaul	W	82-78
2/1/1960	H	Northwestern	W	76-58
2/6/1960	A	Wisconsin	W	97-85
2/8/1960	H	Iowa	W	87-74
2/13/1960	H	Wisconsin	W	91-71
2/15/1960	H	Michigan	W	86-69
2/20/1960	A	Iowa	W	79-64
2/22/1960	A	Illinois	W	92-78
2/27/1960	H	Minnesota	W	78-74
2/29/1960	H	Ohio State	W	99-83
3/5/1960	A	Michigan State	W	86-80

1 Indianapolis, IN
2 Louisville, KY

1959-60 BIG TEN STANDINGS

	W	L	PCT
Ohio State	13	1	.929
Indiana	11	3	.786
Illinois	8	6	.571
Minnesota	8	6	.571
Northwestern	8	6	.571
Iowa	6	8	.429
Purdue	6	8	.429
Michigan St.	5	9	.357
Wisconsin	4	10	.286
Michigan	1	13	.071

points in the second half, the Boilermakers went on to upset the Hoosiers 79-76. Purdue held Bellamy to a season-low eight points. Dischinger had a bad case of the flu and didn't travel with the Boilermakers. He wasn't even expected to play until he showed up in Bloomington on Saturday to rejoin the Purdue team. Two nights after the Purdue loss, Indiana went to Evanston, Illinois and got hit with another unprecedented scoring performance. Northwestern's 5'11" sophomore Bill Cacciatore burned Indiana for 27 points on 13-21 shooting (mostly from beyond 20-feet) as the 3-9 Wildcats handed the Hoosiers an unfathomable 61-57 defeat.

The Hoosiers, who were still winless in conference play, then faced the unenviable task of going to Columbus, Ohio, to play Ohio State, which was 11-0 overall and 2-0 in conference play. Indiana played with desperation and led for much of the game. However, in the final 1:44 Indiana turned the ball over twice, and a 95-91 Indiana lead quickly turned into a 96-95 Buckeye win. That heartbreaking loss put Indiana at 0-3 in conference play and dealt a crushing blow to the Hoosiers' championship aspirations. To their credit, the Indiana team didn't give up on the season. In fact, the Hoosiers regrouped and ran the table on the rest of their schedule.

On January 11, IU went to Michigan and notched the first win of the conference season, 77-72 over the Wolverines. Bob Wilkinson led Indiana with 23 points. In Chicago on January 30, the Hoosiers grabbed a nonconference victory, 82-78 over DePaul, led by 34 points from Bellamy. IU got back to Big Ten play on February 1, by annihilating Northwestern 76-58. Indiana went up to Wisconsin on February 13, and Walt Bellamy's 32 points and 16 rebounds powered the Hoosiers to a 97-85 win. Next, IU had a three-game home stretch and the Hoosiers cruised to easy victories in all three contests—87-74 over Iowa on February 8, 91-71 over Wisconsin on February 13,

and 86-69 over Michigan on February 15. The Michigan win was Indiana's seventh consecutive overall win and put the Hoosiers at 6-3 in the conference and in sole possession of second place. However, Ohio State was 10-0 in the Big Ten and was simply running away with the title.

Indiana went on the road and captured two more easy victories on Saturday, February 20, and Monday, February 22. First, the Hoosiers downed Iowa 79-64, and then they whipped Illinois 92-78. Bellamy pulled out a 42-point effort against the Fighting Illini. Next, Indiana returned to Bloomington for a February 27 matchup with Minnesota. The Hoosiers outlasted the Golden Gophers for a 78-74 victory. That set up a grudge match between Indiana (9-3) and Ohio State (12-0) on February 29, in Bloomington. The Buckeyes had already clinched the undisputed conference championship. However, the IU squad felt like it had given away the game in Columbus. The Hoosiers also believed they had the better team, and they made a convincing argument by crushing Ohio State 99-83, as Bellamy scored 24 points and all five Indiana starters scored in double figures (even though the Hoosiers were without starting guard Herbie Lee, who was expelled from school the morning before the game). For OSU, Jerry Lucas scored 27 points and John Havilcek dropped in 25. The OSU victory was also the last game ever played in IU's original Fieldhouse, which has since been renamed the Wildermuth Intramural Center.

On March 5, Indiana finished its season by winning 86-80 at Michigan State, while Ohio State completed its almost-perfect conference season with a 75-66 win at Minnesota. With an 11-3 conference record, the Hoosiers had to settle for second place in the Big Ten, while conference champion Ohio State went to the NCAA tournament and blew out four straight opponents by an average of 19.5 points and easily captured the national championship.

INDIANA'S RANKING IN THE 1959-60 ASSOCIATED PRESS POLLS

12/22	12/29	1/5	1/12	1/19	1/26	2/2	2/9	2/16	2/23	3/1	3/8
9	7	11	—	—	—	—	—	—	20	12	7

NCAA ISSUES FOUR-YEAR PENALTY TO IU ATHLETICS

In April 1960, the NCAA announced that it had discovered six major rules violations perpetrated by the Indiana University football team. Five of the violations occurred during 1958, when the football coach and his program were already on probation. As a result, the NCAA threw the book at the Hoosiers in order to make an example out of them. All IU sports were banned from competing in any NCAA postseason championships (and bowl games) for four years. The harshness of the penalty was unprecedented, and the Big Ten joined Indiana in appealing the punishment so that it would not affect Indiana sports other than football. However, the NCAA didn't back down. Thus, even if it won the Big Ten championship, the basketball team would be unable to compete in the NCAA tournament from the 1960-61 season to the 1963-64 season. That fact, along with the negative stigma placed on the program, made recruiting very difficult for coach Branch McCracken.

1960-61

OVERALL RECORD: 15-9

CONFERENCE RECORD: 8-6 (FOURTH PLACE)

INDIVIDUAL HONORS:

WALT BELLAMY—ALL-AMERICA,

ALL-BIG TEN (FIRST TEAM)

GARY LONG—BIG TEN MEDAL OF HONOR

Indiana returned several key players from its 1959-60 team that many around the Big Ten considered the best in the league at the end of the season—even better than Ohio State, which had won the league championship and swept through the NCAA tournament to capture the national title. For 1960-61, the leading returnees were center Walt Bellamy, forward Charley Hall, and guards Gary Long and Jerry Bass. The Hoosiers lost starters Frank Radovich and Bob Wilkinson to graduation. The 6'7" Radovich was the perfect complement to Bellamy as a rebounder and a scorer, while Wilkinson was the team's most intense competitor and a reliable shooter in the backcourt. IU also lost the services of two juniors from the 1959-60 team: guard Herbie Lee, an outstanding playmaker, and forward LeRoy Johnson, one of the team's top reserves. Both players were no longer enrolled at IU. To make up for those losses, Coach Branch McCracken was hoping for help from an outstanding sophomore class that was headed by Indiana high school superstars Jimmy Rayl, Tom Bolyard and Ray Pavy.

When IU opened the 1960-61 season against Indiana State on Saturday, December 3, the Hoosiers did it in a new arena. Known simply as the "New Fieldhouse," the arena was designed as an indoor practice facility and served as the temporary home for basketball games. It was built on the corner of 17th and Fee Lane, where the new football stadium was erected, and where an 18,000-seat basketball arena was supposed to be built a few seasons later (it ended up being 11 years before the new arena came to fruition). The Hoosiers defeated ISU 80-53 in the first game in the new fieldhouse. Bellamy led all scor-

The 1960-61 team. First row (left to right): Charley Hall, Gordon Mickey, Walt Bellamy, Winston Fairfield, Dave Granger, Tom Bolyard; Second row: assistant coach Lou Watson, Bill Altman, Dave Porter, Ernie Wilhoit, Jimmy Rayl, head coach Branch McCracken; Third row: manager Dick Anderson, Dan Prickett, Charley Roush, Ray Pavy, Gary Long, Jerry Bass, assistant coach Gene Ring. IU Archives

ers with 20 points, while Bolyard and Rayl were impressive in their first game, scoring 14 and 12 points, respectively.

After the opening win, Indiana went on the road and split two games. The Hoosiers came back from a five-point halftime deficit to crush Kansas State 98-80 on December 5, and then lost 81-79 to Detroit on a last-second shot in double overtime on December 10. IU then notched two relatively easy home victories over Missouri (66-55) and Nevada (80-52). Next, the Hoosiers played Notre Dame on the neutral floor of the Fort Wayne Coliseum on December 20, and pulled out a 74-69 win, behind 29 points and 19 rebounds from Bellamy and 18 points from Fort Wayne native Tom Bolyard. The win was the 300th victory for McCracken at Indiana (and it came on the night of his 29th wedding anniversary).

The Hoosiers closed out the preconference season by playing in the Los Angeles Classic on December 28-30, in the Memorial Sports Arena on the USC campus. IU opened with a 58-50 win over Stanford. However, the second night, the Hoosiers got whipped 94-72 by UCLA, which was coached by Indiana native John Wooden. In the third game, Indiana uncharacteristically blew an 11-point halftime lead and lost to USC 90-71.

After dropping two games in Los Angeles, the Hoosiers returned to Bloomington with a 6-3 record and prepared to begin Big Ten play. The first assignment for McCracken's students was to steal a win at Michigan on January 7, and the IU squad did just that. The Hoosiers overwhelmed the Wolverines and came home with an 81-70 win. Bellamy scored a game-high 23 points and IU forward Gordon Mickey came off the bench and grabbed 12 rebounds. On January 9, Michigan State came down to Bloomington and got steamrolled by the Hoosier attack 79-55. After nearly three weeks off because of the semester break, IU came from behind and beat DePaul 81-78 on January 28. Bellamy had a game-high 25 points, while 5'9" Jerry Bass poured in 23 (19 in the second half). Bolyard and Rayl chipped in 12 apiece. Minnesota hosted IU on January 30, and handed the Hoosiers their first conference setback in the form of a 66-58 Gopher victory. IU returned home and improved its Big Ten record to 3-1 with a 90-78 defeat of Northwestern on February 4. Bellamy made 15 of 19 field goals and scored 34 points.

Next was a showdown with No. 1 Ohio State in Columbus on Monday, February 6. For almost a year, the Buckeyes had been hearing that the Hoosiers were better than them, even though Ohio State had won the Big Ten and NCAA titles the season before. Plus, two years earlier, IU had come to St. John's Arena in Columbus and broke the conference scoring record in a 122-92 win over the Buckeyes. Thus, OSU had something to prove and was out to make a statement. The Buckeyes burst out of the gates and ran to a 46-23 halftime lead. Then, they continued to build on the lead in the second half, as OSU coach Fred Taylor kept his starters in the game until there was only 1:33 left. Buckeye forward John Havlicek even injured his thumb, but got it taped and was put back in the game in the final minutes. When Havlicek hit a basket to give Ohio State 100 points, Taylor finally pulled his starters. The final was 100-65. McCracken stormed off the court without shaking Taylor's hand, in an obvious showing of disapproval over Taylor running up the score.

After the Ohio State loss, the Hoosiers went into a short tailspin, losing to No. 9 Iowa 74-67 in Bloomington on February 11, and then falling to Purdue 64-55 in West Lafayette on February 13. Indiana evened its conference record at 4-4 by blistering Wisconsin 98-84 in Madison on February 18, as Bellamy scored 28 points and Bolyard scored 24. Then came a February 20 rematch with Ohio State in Bloomington. Both Bellamy and Ohio State center Jerry Lucas were neutralized in this game, which the Buckeyes led 41-29 at the half. The Hoosiers made a furious rally down the stretch as the home crowd exploded with excitement, but the experienced

1960-61 TEAM ROSTER

Head coach: Branch McCracken
Assistant coaches: Lou Watson, Gene Ring

No.	Player	Hometown	Class	Position	Height
41	Bill Altman	Mooresville, IN	Jr	F	6-2
23	Jerry Bass	Morristown, IN	Jr	F	5-9
35	Walt Bellamy	New Bern, NC	Sr	C	6-11
45	Tom Bolyard	Fort Wayne, IN	So	F	6-4
33	Winston Fairfield	N. Wilmington, MA	So	C	6-9
20	Dave Granger	Hillsdale, MI	So	F	6-7
42	Charley Hall	Terre Haute, IN	Jr	F	6-6
15	Gary Long (Capt.)	Shelbyville, IN	Sr	G	6-0
30	Gordon Mickey	Chillicothe, OH	Jr	F	6-7
24	Ray Pavy	New Castle, IN	So	G	6-1
43	Dave Porter	Noblesville, IN	So	F	6-4
13	Dan Prickett	Wolf Lake, IN	So	G	5-11
22	Jimmy Rayl	Kokomo, IN	So	G	6-2
25	Charley Roush	Columbus, IN	So	F	6-0
31	Dick Sparks	Bloomington, IN	So	F	6-5
32	Ernie Wilhoit	Collinsville, IL	Jr	G	6-3

SEASON RESULTS 1960-61

Date	Court	Opponent	Result	Score
12/3/1960	H	Indiana State	W	80-53
12/5/1960	A	Kansas State	W	98-80
12/10/1960	A	Detroit	L	79-81
12/12/1960	H	Missouri	W	66-55
12/17/1960	H	Nevada	W	80-52
12/20/1960	N1	Notre Dame	W	74-69
12/28/1960	N2	Stanford	W	58-50
12/29/1960	N2	UCLA	L	72-94
12/30/1960	A	USC	L	71-90
1/7/1961	A	Michigan	W	81-70
1/9/1961	H	Michigan State	W	79-55
1/28/1961	H	DePaul	W	81-78
1/30/1961	A	Minnesota	L	58-66
2/4/1961	H	Northwestern	W	90-78
2/6/1961	A	Ohio State	L	65-100
2/11/1961	H	Iowa	L	67-74
2/13/1961	A	Purdue	L	55-64
2/18/1961	A	Wisconsin	W	98-84
2/20/1961	H	Ohio State	L	69-73
2/25/1961	H	Illinois	W	93-82
2/27/1961	A	Northwestern	L	58-60
3/4/1961	A	Iowa	W	78-69
3/6/1961	H	Wisconsin	W	80-69
3/11/1961	H	Michigan	W	82-67

1 Fort Wayne, IN
2 Los Angeles, CA (Memorial Sports Arena)

1960-61 BIG TEN STANDINGS

	W	L	PCT
Ohio State	14	0	1.000
Iowa	10	4	.714
Purdue	10	4	.714
Indiana	8	6	.571
Minnesota	8	6	.571
Northwestern	6	8	.429
Illinois	5	9	.357
Wisconsin	4	10	.286
Michigan St.	3	11	.214
Michigan	2	12	.143

Buckeyes kept their composure and made their free throws to win 73-69.

The loss dropped the Hoosiers to 4-5 in conference play, but the team rallied to win four of its final five contests. Bellamy and Bolyard scored 22 apiece as Indiana beat Illinois 93-82 on February 25, in Bloomington. The Hoosiers lost to Northwestern 60-58 in overtime on February 27, in Evanston, but went to Iowa and stole a 78-69 victory over the No. 6 Hawkeyes on March 4. Indiana then finished out its schedule with two home wins over Wisconsin (80-69 on March 6) and Michigan (82-67 on March 11). Against the Badgers, Bellamy scored 27 points and pulled down a school-record 28 rebounds. Against Michigan, Bellamy scored 28 points and collected 33 rebounds, a Big Ten record. The dominating center also ended his career as Indiana's all-time leader in rebounds with 1,087 (in 1995, Alan Henderson broke the record with 1,091 rebounds, but he needed four seasons and 124 games to do it, while Bellamy only had three seasons and 70 games). "Bells" also finished third on Indiana's all-time scoring list, behind only Don Schlundt and Archie Dees.

With Bellamy, a two-time All-American, graduating, the Hoosiers ended a 10-year string of great centers. Thus, the sophomore trio of Tom Bolyard, Jimmy Rayl and Ray Pavy was expected to take over the reins of the Hoosier attack. Bolyard had an excellent sophomore campaign, earning a starting position at forward and averaging 15.5 points and 9.0 rebounds. However, Pavy struggled and Rayl, who was known as one of the greatest marksmen ever in Indiana high school basketball, shot a disappointing 30 percent from the field and averaged a mere 2.5 points per game. However, the following year, Rayl would orchestrate one of the greatest individual turnarounds in college basketball history.

1961-62

OVERALL RECORD: 13-11

CONFERENCE RECORD: 7-7 (FOURTH PLACE)

INDIVIDUAL HONORS:

JIMMY RAYL—ALL-AMERICA,

ALL-BIG TEN (FIRST TEAM)

The graduation of Walt Bellamy in 1961 brought an end to a 10-year reign of dominant centers in Bloomington. Like Don Schlundt and Archie Dees before him, Bellamy had been an All-American and served as the focal point of the Hoosier attack. For the 1961-62 season, Indiana returned nine lettermen, led by returning starters Tom Bolyard, Jerry Bass and Charley Hall. Juniors Jimmy Rayl and Ray Pavy, who had come to IU accompanied by high expectations, had both struggled as sophomores, but were fully expected to step up their play for the 1961-62 campaign. Unfortunately, Pavy was in a tragic auto accident two weeks before classes started and was paralyzed from the waist down (he eventually returned to Indiana and graduated in 1964). However, the sharp-shooting Rayl compensated for the loss of Bellamy's scoring, as the Hoosiers embraced the type of run-and-gun attack that had characterized Coach Branch McCracken's earlier teams. While his teammates did the running, Rayl did most of the gunning.

"We'll be an interesting ball club to watch," said McCracken prior to the season. "We've got some speed and a good bunch of shooters and ballhandlers. And, we're going to run. We sort of drifted away from the fire-wagon game with the succession of good big

INDIANA'S RANKING IN THE 1960-61 ASSOCIATED PRESS POLLS

12/13	12/20	12/27	1/3	1/10	1/17	1/24	1/31	2/7	2/14	2/21	2/28	3/7
4	4	4	—	—	—	—	—	—	—	—	—	—

The 1961-62 team. Front row (left to right): Dick Sparks, Gordon Mickey, Winston Fairfield, Dave Granger, Charley Hall; Second row: assistant coach Lou Watson, Tom White, Ernie Wilhoit, Bill Altman, Tom Bolyard, Dave Porter, head coach Branch McCracken; Third row: Jim Sutton, Charley Roush, Manager Marshall Goldsmith, Jimmy Rayl, Jerry Bass. IU Archives

men. ... Now we intend to go back to it and be a running club. We've played the other fellow's game long enough. We'd like to try and make him play our game."

For the first time in 17 years, IU opened its season on the road. Playing Drake on December 2, in Des Moines, Iowa, the Hoosiers nearly got run out of the gym in the first half, as the Bulldogs led by 17 at the break. IU surged back into the game in the second half with the help of the full-court press, but Drake still prevailed 90-81. Bulldogs' forward Jerry Foster and 6'10" center Larry Prins combined for 40 points and 22 rebounds against the smaller Hoosiers. Back in Bloomington on December 7, Indiana continued to struggle, falling behind New Mexico State by five points at the half. However, Rayl broke loose for 34 points, including 21 in the second half, and carried IU

to a 74-68 win. Rayl benefited from a variety of screens from his teammates (the year before, Indiana fans had grumpily complained that Rayl desperately needed some screens in order to break out of his shooting slump).

No. 4 Kansas State came to Bloomington on December 9, and Coach Tex Winter's Wildcats outlasted the Hoosiers 88-78. However, Indiana evened its record at 2-2 on December 11, with a 76-70 win over coach Dean Smith's North Carolina Tar Heels in Greensboro, North Carolina. Tom Bolyard sparked that IU win with two big field goals in the final minutes. Bolyard's 22 points tied him for game-high honors with North Carolina's Larry Brown, who went on to become a legendary coach in college and the pros.

The Hoosiers split their next four games, with home wins over Detroit (92-84) and Arizona State

1961-62 TEAM ROSTER

Head coach: Branch McCracken
Assistant coaches: Lou Watson, Don Luft

No.	Player	Hometown	Class	Position	Height
41	Bill Altman	Mooresville, IN	Sr	F	6-2
23	Jerry Bass	Morristown, IN	Sr	G	5-9
45	Tom Bolyard	Fort Wayne, IN	Jr	F	6-4
33	Winston Fairfield	N. Wilmington, MA	Jr	C	6-9
20	Dave Granger	Hillsdale, MI	Jr	F	6-7
42	Charley Hall (Capt.)	Terre Haute, IN	Sr	F	6-6
21	Dave Holland	Toledo, IN	So	F	6-5
30	Gordon Mickey	Chillicothe, OH	Sr	F	6-7
43	Dave Porter	Noblesville, IN	Jr	F	6-4
22	Jimmy Rayl	Kokomo, IN	Jr	G	6-2
25	Charley Roush	Columbus, IN	Jr	F	6-0
31	Dick Sparks	Bloomington, IN	So	C	6-5
31	Jim Sutton	Anderson, IN	So	G	5-11
32	Ernie Wilhoit	Collinsville, IL	Sr	G	6-3

SEASON RESULTS 1961-62

Date	Court	Opponent	Result	Score
12/2/1961	A	Drake	L	81-90
12/7/1961	H	New Mexico State	W	74-68
12/9/1961	H	Kansas State	L	78-88
12/11/1961	N1	North Carolina	W	76-70
12/16/1961	H	Detroit	W	92-84
12/18/1961	H	Arizona State	W	94-88
12/23/1961	A	Iowa State	L	70-83
12/30/1961	A	Loyola Chicago	L	90-95
1/2/1962	N2	Notre Dame	W	122-95
1/6/1962	H	Michigan State	W	76-71
1/8/1962	A	Minnesota	L	100-104
1/13/1962	A	DePaul	W	98-89
1/27/1962	H	Minnesota	W	105-104
1/29/1962	A	Northwestern	W	72-71
2/3/1962	A	Illinois	L	85-96
2/10/1962	A	Purdue	L	93-105
2/12/1962	H	Wisconsin	L	94-105
2/17/1962	H	Iowa	W	72-69
2/19/1962	H	Michigan	W	86-77
2/24/1962	A	Michigan State	L	85-97
2/26/1962	A	Michigan	L	89-110
3/3/1962	H	Purdue	W	88-71
3/5/1962	H	Illinois	W	104-92
3/10/1962	A	Ohio State	L	65-90

1 Greensboro, NC
2 Fort Wayne, IN

1961-62 BIG TEN STANDINGS

	W	L	PCT
Ohio State	13	1	.929
Wisconsin	10	4	.714
Purdue	9	5	.643
Illinois	7	7	.500
Indiana	7	7	.500
Iowa	7	7	.500
Minnesota	6	8	.429
Michigan	5	9	.357
Michigan St.	3	11	.214
Northwestern	3	11	.214

(94-88), and road losses to Iowa State (83-70) and Loyola Chicago (95-90). In their final preconference tune up against Notre Dame on January 2, at the Fort Wayne Coliseum, the Hoosiers erupted for a 122-95 win. IU's 122 points tied the school record set against Ohio State in 1959. Rayl led Indiana with 28 points, while 6'6" Dick Sparks, who was inserted into IU's lineup at center, scored 16 and collected 15 rebounds. Afterwards, McCracken said, "If we can play like that against the Big Ten teams, we can give 'em fits in the league."

After the excellent performance against Notre Dame, the IU squad came out and laid an egg in the first half of the team's Big Ten opener on January 6, against Michigan State in Bloomington. IU fell behind 41-29 at the break and got harangued in the locker room by McCracken for lack of effort and poor rebounding. The Hoosiers crashed the glass in the second half, and Rayl scored 21 of his 28 points in the second session as IU came back and won 76-71. In their next game, at Minnesota on January 8, the Hoosiers lit up the scoreboard for 100 points. Unfortunately, they also surrendered 104 to Minnesota and lost. The Hoosiers continued to score big in a 98-89 nonconference win at DePaul on January 13. Rayl, who had scored 32 against Minnesota, dropped in 41 against DePaul. Bolyard added 22 and 25, respectively, in those two games.

Indiana avenged the Minnesota loss when the Golden Gophers came to Bloomington on January 27. Rayl drained a 20-footer in the final seconds of overtime to lift the Hoosiers to a 105-104 victory. The hot-shooting guard blistered Minnesota for 56 points to set a new Big Ten record. Rayl made 20-39 field goals and 16-20 free throws in what is arguably the greatest individual performance in IU basketball history. McCracken called it "one of the greatest exhibitions of outside shooting that I have ever seen."

Two nights later, Indiana went up to Evanston and slipped by Northwestern 72-71 on two late free throws by IU guard Jerry Bass. The Hoosiers were 3-1 and alone in third place in the Big Ten. The IU faithful hoped that McCracken, whose teams had placed first or second in 12 of his 20 seasons at IU, would find a way to rally the Hoosiers for a title challenge. However, the Indiana squad dropped its next three games, 96-85 at Illinois, 105-93 at Purdue, and 105-94 against Wisconsin in Bloomington. IU brought its record back to .500 (4-4) with a 72-69 win over Iowa, in rough game marred by 47 fouls on February 17, in Bloomington. Rayl led IU with 35 points, but he was outscored by Hawkeyes center Don Nelson, a future NBA coach, who scored 37. Rayl scored 34 against Michigan on February 19, in Bloomington as the Hoosiers won 86-77 to improve their record to 5-4.

On February 24-26, Indiana traveled north for a doubleheader at Michigan and Michigan State. In the first game, the Spartans beat the Hoosiers 97-85, and in the second tilt, the Wolverines pummeled IU 110-89. After falling to 5-6, the Hoosiers' record bobbed back over .500 with two home wins the next week. On March 3, Indiana defeated Purdue 88-71, in a game stained by a fist fight that centered on Purdue's Darrell McQuitty and IU's Gordon Mickey. Then, on March 5, Indiana downed Illinois 104-92 in the Hoosiers' final home game of the season. IU closed out the schedule with a disappointing 90-65 loss to first-place Ohio State on March 10 in Columbus.

The OSU loss gave the Hoosiers a 7-7 conference record and a fourth-place finish in the Big Ten. The 1961-62 squad was a "running club," just as McCracken had predicted. Rayl averaged a school-record 29.8 points per game and was a consensus All-American. The Hoosiers scored 100 or more points in four games, including 122 against Notre Dame, but they also gave up 100 on six occasions. IU averaged a school-record 87.0 points per game, but also gave up an average of 88.0 points per game. The Hoosiers' struggles, and the fact that the team hadn't won a Big Ten crown in four seasons despite having some excellent talent, began to elicit some cries of "McCracken's too old" among IU fans. However, McCracken still had a pair of aces up his sleeve in the form of twins Tom and Dick VanArsdale, who were set to make their sophomore debut for the 1962-63 season.

A terrific all-around forward who could play both inside and outside, 6'4" Tom Bolyard was the Hoosiers' second leading scorer during the 1961-62 season with 18.6 PPG. IU Archives

INDIANA'S RANKING IN THE 1961-62 ASSOCIATED PRESS POLLS

PS	12/19	12/26	1/2	1/9	1/16	1/23	1/30	2/6	2/13	2/20	2/27	3/6	3/13
—	—	—	—	—	—	—	—	—	—	—	—	—	—

1962-63

Overall Record: 13-11

Conference Record: 9-5 (third place)

Individual Honors:

Jimmy Rayl—All-America,

All-Big Ten (first team)

Tom Bolyard—All-Big Ten (first team)

The 1962-63 team. First row (left to right): Dick Van Arsdale, Dave Granger, Ron Peyser, Winston Fairfield, Jon McGlocklin, Tom Van Arsdale; Second row: assistant coach Lou Watson, Ron Pease, Dave Porter, Tom Bolyard, Jimmy Rayl, head coach Branch McCracken; Third row: Gene Demaree, Al Harden, Manager Bob Stohler, Jim Sutton, Steve Redenbaugh. IU Archives

During Indiana's NCAA probation (due to the sins of the football program) from 1961 to 1964, Coach Branch McCracken had a very difficult time recruiting top players to come to IU. It was especially difficult to recruit out-of-state talent— the kind that had given him Archie Dees and Walt Bellamy in previous years. As a result, McCracken couldn't land a high-caliber big man to succeed Bellamy. However, in 1961 he landed two of the most highly recruited basketball players in the country when 6'5" twins Tom and Dick Van Arsdale chose to join the Hoosiers. "Convincing them to come to

Indiana was my greatest recruiting achievement," McCracken later said.

For the 1962-63 season, the Van Arsdales, who were both fierce competitors that could score and rebound, joined the varsity as sophomores and immediately teamed with IU stars Jimmy Rayl, a sharpshooter, and Tom Bolyard, a versatile forward, in the starting lineup. The Hoosiers' biggest weakness would once again be at the center position. Often, the Hoosiers simply played three forwards, usually rotating among four players—the Van Arsdales, the 6'4" Bolyard, and the 6'5" Jon McGlocklin, a sophomore who could play all five positions on the floor. The Hoosiers had to rely on their speed and versatility in order to compete.

Entering the season, there was a lot of hype surrounding the Van Arsdales, as various newspapers and national magazines did feature articles on the twins. That hype combined with the return of All-American Jimmy Rayl provided a lot of enthusiasm and high expectations for IU fans, who were getting antsy for another Big Ten title. The Van Arsdales turned out to be solid and consistent, although not necessarily spectacular. However, even with strong play from the twins, the Hoosiers struggled through the preconference season with a 3-6 record.

In the season opener, Indiana blasted Virginia 90-59 on December 1, in Bloomington, as Rayl scored 35 points. The Van Arsdales combined for 20 points in their collegiate debut (Dick scored 11 and Tom had nine). The Hoosiers then uncharacteristically dropped two straight home games: 87-76 to Drake and 63-55 to Iowa State. Drake used its size to muscle IU and dominate the boards, while the Hoosiers went ice cold shooting the ball against Iowa State. Indiana then went on the road and lost a 52-51 cliffhanger to Missouri to fall to 1-3 on the season.

North Carolina, which was 3-0, came to Bloomington on December 15. The Hoosiers upended Dean Smith's squad 90-76, as McGlocklin scored 20 points in his first start for IU. Billy Cunningham led the Tar Heels with a game-high 28. Two days later, Indiana improved its record to 3-3 when the Hoosiers beat Detroit 92-84 in the Motor City, led by 32 points from Rayl and 22 from Tom Van Arsdale. Indiana returned to Bloomington on December 19, and lost a 106-94 barnburner to undefeated Loyola Chicago (which would go on to win the NCAA

1962-63 TEAM ROSTER

Head coach: Branch McCracken
Assistant coaches: Lou Watson, Don Luft

No.	Player	Hometown	Class	Position	Height
45	Tom Bolyard (Capt.)	Fort Wayne, IN	Sr	F	6-4
14	Gene Demaree	New Marion, IN	So	G	5-11
33	Winston Fairfield	N. Wilmington, MA	Sr	C	6-9
20	Dave Granger	Hillsdale, MI	Sr	F	6-7
23	Al Harden	Covington, KY	So	G	5-10
54	Jon McGlocklin	Franklin, IN	So	F/C	6-5
42	Ron Pease	Muncie, IN	So	F	6-3
32	Ron Peyser	Chicago, IL	So	C	6-8
43	Dave Porter	Noblesville, IN	Sr	F	6-4
22	Jimmy Rayl	Kokomo, IN	Sr	G	6-2
44	Steve Redenbaugh	Paoli, IN	So	G	6-2
31	Jim Sutton	Anderson, IN	Jr	G	5-11
30	Dick Van Arsdale	Indianapolis, IN	So	F	6-5
25	Tom Van Arsdale	Indianapolis, IN	So	F	6-5

SEASON RESULTS 1962-63

Date	Court	Opponent	Result	Score
12/1/1962	H	Virginia	W	90-59
12/3/1962	H	Drake	L	76-87
12/8/1962	H	Iowa State	L	55-63
12/10/1962	A	Missouri	L	51-52
12/15/1962	H	North Carolina	W	90-76
12/17/1962	A	Detroit	W	92-84
12/19/1962	A	Loyola Chicago	L	94-106
12/21/1962	A	Kansas State	L	72-88
1/2/1963	N1	Notre Dame	L	70-73
1/5/1963	A	Michigan State	W	96-84
1/7/1963	H	Purdue	W	85-71
1/26/1963	H	DePaul	W	76-75
1/28/1963	A	Purdue	W	74-73
2/2/1963	H	Northwestern	L	87-100
2/4/1963	A	Illinois	L	101-104
2/9/1963	A	Michigan	L	86-90
2/11/1963	H	Minnesota	W	89-77
2/16/1963	H	Illinois	W	103-100
2/18/1963	A	Iowa	W	72-71
2/23/1963	H	Michigan State	W	113-94
2/25/1963	A	Wisconsin	L	96-102
3/2/1963	A	Minnesota	L	73-105
3/4/1963	H	Michigan	W	104-96
3/9/1963	H	Ohio State	W	87-85

1 Fort Wayne, IN

1962-63 BIG TEN STANDINGS

	W	L	PCT
Ohio State	11	3	.786
Illinois	11	3	.786
Indiana	9	5	.643
Michigan	8	6	.571
Minnesota	8	6	.571
Wisconsin	7	7	.500
Northwestern	6	8	.429
Iowa	5	9	.357
Michigan St.	3	11	.214
Purdue	2	12	.143

Dick Van Arsdale (front) and Tom Van Arsdale had opponents seeing double. The 6'5" twins arrived in Bloomington accompanied by a lot of hype and monumental expectations. Both of them quickly earned spots in the IU starting lineup as sophomores during the 1962-63 season. IU Archives

championship that season). The Hoosiers followed up that loss with defeats against Kansas State (88-72) and Notre Dame (73-70).

The 3-6 Hoosiers didn't look like much of a threat to win the Big Ten title, but the team got off to a good start in conference play and made some noise at the end. On January 5, IU went up to Michigan State and promptly stole a 96-84 victory. Rayl poured in 44 points for the Hoosiers. Back in Bloomington on January 7, Indiana easily defeated Purdue 85-71. Rayl scored 25 points and Tom Van Arsdale had 12 points along with a game-high 10 rebounds.

Indiana returned from its semester break on January 26, and beat DePaul 76-75 in Bloomington

on a tip-in from sophomore Steve Redenbaugh. The Hoosiers resumed Big Ten play on January 28, when they traveled to West Lafayette and came from behind to win 74-73. Dick Van Arsdale scored 10 points and ripped down 20 rebounds, and Tom Van Arsdale scored 12 points and collected 10 boards, while Rayl scored a game-high 25 points. Northwestern dealt the Hoosiers their first conference loss on February 2, in Bloomington. The Wildcats posted a surprising 100-87 win. Rayl struggled to a 9-30 shooting night. On February 4, No. 4 Illinois hosted Indiana and dealt the Hoosiers a tough 104-101 setback, despite 35 points from Bolyard and 31 from Rayl. The Hoosiers then dropped to 3-3 in Big Ten play on February 9,

INDIANA'S RANKING IN THE 1962-63 ASSOCIATED PRESS POLLS

PS	12/4	12/11	12/18	12/25	1/1	1/8	1/15	1/22	1/29	2/5	2/12	2/19	2/26	3/5	3/12
—	8	—	—	—	—	—	—	—	—	—	—	—	—	—	—

when they lost a 90-86 contest against Michigan in Ann Arbor.

On February 11, Indiana returned to form with a solid 89-77 win over Minnesota in Bloomington. Rayl led the way with 32 points, while Dick Van Arsdale had 20 points and 11 rebounds, and Tom Van Arsdale had 14 points and 10 rebounds. Next, the Hoosiers gained revenge on league-leading Illinois by defeating the Fighting Illini 103-100 on February 16, in Bloomington. IU trailed by nine points at the half, but blistered the visitors with 62 points in the second half. Bolyard had a team-high 34 points. In Iowa City two nights later, Indiana edged Iowa 72-71. The Hawkeyes held Rayl to a season-low two points, but Bolyard stepped up and scored 29, and the Van Arsdale twins scored 14 apiece.

Rayl came back with a vengeance against Michigan State on February 23, in Bloomington. The little guard poured in 56 points, to tie the Big Ten record he set the year before, and Indiana prevailed 113-94. Rayl's 23 field goals on 48 attempts also set new conference records. The win over MSU improved the Hoosiers to 7-3 in the Big Ten and put them only a game behind conference co-leaders Illinois and Ohio State. However, the Hoosiers dropped out of the race by losing their next two games on the road—102-96 at Wisconsin on February 25, and 105-73 at Minnesota on March 2.

Indiana did clinch an outright third-place finish in the Big Ten by winning its final two games in Bloomington. The Hoosiers rolled past Michigan 104-96 on March 4, and knocked off Ohio State 87-85 in overtime on March 9. The win over OSU cost the Buckeyes the outright Big Ten title and an NCAA berth. The game nearly got out of hand in the final seconds of overtime when two Ohio State players flattened Rayl as he received an inbounds pass with 0:09 remaining and IU leading 86-85. Both benches cleared, and a bunch of Indiana fans poured onto the court to defend their star player. Once the officials had sorted the mess out and got the fans back in their seats, Rayl made one out of two free throws, and Ohio State missed a 20-footer in the final seconds to give IU the victory, and the home crowd stormed the floor to celebrate.

For the season, the Hoosiers had finished with an identical 13-11 overall record from the previous year. Nevertheless, after a rough start in preconference games, Indiana pulled it together and showed they could play with any squad in the Big Ten. The Hoosiers defeated both of the conference co-champions, Illinois and Ohio State, and grabbed a solid third-place finish with a 9-5 record, two games behind the leaders. Rayl and Bolyard finished their careers as the fourth and fifth leading scorers in Indiana history. The only three players ahead of them were Don Schlundt, Archie Dees and Walt Bellamy.

1963-64

OVERALL RECORD: 9-15

CONFERENCE RECORD: 5-9 (EIGHTH PLACE)

INDIVIDUAL HONORS:

DICK VAN ARSDALE—ALL-BIG TEN (FIRST TEAM), ACADEMIC ALL-AMERICA, ACADEMIC ALL-BIG TEN

Coach Branch McCracken knew that losing Jimmy Rayl and Tom Bolyard, the No. 2 and No. 3 scorers in the Big Ten in 1963, was going to make it tough on the Hoosiers for the 1963-64 season. However, Indiana still had plenty of scoring power with juniors Tom and Dick Van Arsdale, Jon McGlocklin and Steve Redenbaugh. What the Hoosiers missed the most from Rayl and Bolyard was their leadership. The 1963-64 team did not have a single senior on scholarship, and it showed, as the team struggled for consistency and lost a lot of close games.

Once again, the biggest void in the lineup was at center, and the most pressing question for the Hoosiers going into the 1963-64 season was whether 6'8" junior Ron Peyser or 6'7" junior college transfer Larry Cooper could step up and fill that gaping hole.

"We're in fairly good shape, but the question, of course, is the big man," said McCracken. "You can't be tops in this tough league without the big man—a good big man. Our greatest strength should be speed and shooting ability. And if we come up with the good big man, we're going to have a pretty good ball club."

The 1963-64 team. First row (left to right): Jon McGlocklin, Tom Van Arsdale, Max Walker, Dick Van Arsdale, Ron Pease; Second row: assistant coach Lou Watson, Gary Grieger, Jack Campbell, Steve Redenbaugh, Ron Peyser, Larry Cooper, head coach Branch McCracken; Third row: Al Harden, Jim Sutton, Manager Benny Goldstein, Larry Turpen, Vern Pfaff. IU Archives

Unfortunately, Indiana didn't come up with a good big man, nor did the team turn out to be very good. Peyser and Cooper showed only sporadic effectiveness, and the Hoosiers often played three forwards, with the 6'5" McGlocklin usually holding down the pivot position. The Van Arsdales, who were both intense competitors, put up big numbers and tried to carry the team, but they couldn't prevent Indiana from sliding into the second division of the Big Ten.

Things looked promising during the season opener on November 30, in Bloomington as Larry Cooper started at center and scored 24 points and pulled down 17 rebounds to lead Indiana to an 80-65 win over Southern Illinois. On December 4, at the Fort Wayne Coliseum, the Hoosiers fell behind Notre Dame 47-40 at the half, but the Van Arsdales led a furious second-half surge and IU prevailed 108-102. Dick Van Arsdale scored 42 points (25 in the second half) and Tom Van Arsdale scored 34 (20 in the second half). North Carolina handed the Hoosiers their first loss, 77-70, on a neutral floor in Charlotte, North Carolina, on December 7.

Kansas State came to Bloomington on December 9, and overpowered Indiana 93-84, to drop the Hoosiers to 2-2. The Wildcats' seven-foot center Roger Suttner had 28 points and 17 rebounds, as neither Cooper nor Peyser could do much to stop him. The Hoosiers bounced back by rolling to two big home wins over Missouri (100-76) and Detroit (110-92). Against the Tigers, Dick Van Arsdale had 25 points and 26 rebounds, while Tom scored 26 and grabbed 17. Against Detroit, the twins teamed up for 53 points and 30 boards. Next, the Hoosiers went up to Oregon State and dropped both games in a two-day doubleheader with the Beavers. The score of the first game was 70-57, while the second contest was a 56-52 defeat. The preconference schedule ended on December 31, in Chicago, where defending national champion Loyola, ranked No. 3 in the nation, downed the Hoosiers 105-92. Ramblers center Leslie Hunter scored 37 points and grabbed 20 rebounds against the Hoosiers, even though he fouled out with 11:20 remaining in the second half.

With a record of 4-5, the Hoosiers entered Big Ten play knowing that previous IU teams had struggled in the preconference season and then came on strong to contend for the Big Ten title. In fact, Indiana had done it the previous year, and the great comeback of 1958 was also still a fresh memory. However, if the preconference was disappointing for the 1963-64 Hoosiers, then the Big Ten season was nothing less than demoralizing.

In the conference opener against Iowa on January 4, in Bloomington, IU blew a 10-point led in the final seven and a half minutes to lose 72-71. In the final seconds, Indiana led by one and had the ball, but Iowa's full-court press forced a turnover, and the Hawkeyes quickly scored to win the game. Next the Hoosiers went on the road and dropped games at Northwestern (79-65) and Michigan State (107-103). The MSU loss was Indiana's sixth in a row and put the team's overall record at 4-11, with a 0-3 mark in conference play.

Mercifully, the team had two weeks to regroup during IU's semester break. As a result, the Hoosiers came out and played much better basketball, but they still dropped their first two games after the break. On January 27, IU went up to Chicago for a nonconference showdown with No. 9 DePaul. The Hoosiers led by one at the half, but the Blue Demons pulled out an 85-78 win, as DePaul's 6'10" sophomore center Dave Mills had 25 points (he only averaged 11), 18 rebounds, and six assists. Tom Van Arsdale led IU with 21 points and 15 rebounds. Next, the Hoosiers got back to conference play on February 1, in West Lafayette, where Purdue barely escaped with an 87-84 win. Both of the Van Arsdale twins missed the front end of a one-and-one free throw opportunity in final minute to seal Indiana's fate.

The Purdue defeat was IU's eighth straight loss and it put the Hoosiers at 0-4 in conference play. At that point, the Indiana faithful had turned against McCracken in greater numbers, with many of them calling for his head. They said that he was too old (even though he was only 55), that he had lost his touch, and that his system could no longer bring IU the kind of success that it had in the past. At the low point of the losing streak, McCracken said, "The kind of job I want would be coach of an orphanage, where there are no parents to come around, or at a state penitentiary, where the alumni never come back."

The Hoosiers finally brought the streak to an end and notched their first conference win on February 3, with a 104-96 triumph over Illinois. Tom Van Arsdale

1963-64 TEAM ROSTER

Head coach: Branch McCracken
Assistant coaches: Lou Watson, Don Luft

No.	Player	Hometown	Class	Position	Height
20	Jack Campbell	East Gary, IN	So	F	6-5
45	Larry Cooper	Osborne, KS	Jr	C	6-7
43	Gary Grieger	Evansville, IN	So	F	6-4
23	Al Harden	Covington, KY	Jr	G	5-10
54	Jon McGlocklin (Capt.)	Franklin, IN	Jr	G/C	6-5
42	Ron Pease	Muncie, IN	Jr	F	6-3
32	Ron Peyser	Chicago, IL	Jr	C	6-8
24	Vern Pfaff	Ellettsville, IN	So	G	5-8
44	Steve Redenbaugh	Paoli, IN	Jr	G	6-2
31	Jim Sutton	Anderson, IN	Sr	G	5-11
40	Larry Turpen	Shawswick, IN	So	G	6-1
30	Dick Van Arsdale	Indianapolis, IN	Jr	F	6-5
25	Tom Van Arsdale	Indianapolis, IN	Jr	F	6-5
41	Max Walker	Milwaukee, WI	So	G	6-1

SEASON RESULTS 1963-64

Date	Court	Opponent	Result	Score
11/30/1963	H	Southern Illinois	W	80-65
12/4/1963	N1	Notre Dame	W	108-102
12/7/1963	N2	North Carolina	L	70-77
12/9/1963	H	Kansas State	L	84-93
12/14/1963	H	Missouri	W	100-76
12/16/1963	H	Detroit	W	110-92
12/20/1963	A	Oregon State	L	57-70
12/21/1963	N3	Oregon State	L	52-56
12/31/1963	A	Loyola Chicago	L	92-105
1/4/1964	H	Iowa	L	71-72
1/6/1964	A	Northwestern	L	65-79
1/11/1964	A	Michigan State	L	103-107
1/27/1964	A	DePaul	L	78-85
2/1/1964	A	Purdue	L	84-87
2/3/1964	H	Illinois	W	104-96
2/8/1964	H	Ohio State	L	96-98
2/10/1964	A	Iowa	L	75-82
2/15/1964	A	Michigan	L	87-99
2/17/1964	A	Wisconsin	W	82-80
2/22/1964	H	Purdue	W	92-79
2/24/1964	H	Wisconsin	W	108-82
2/29/1964	A	Ohio State	L	69-73
3/7/1964	H	Minnesota	L	89-90
3/9/1964	H	Northwestern	W	76-68

1 Fort Wayne, IN
2 Charlotte, NC
3 Portland, OR

1963-64 BIG TEN STANDINGS

	W	L	PCT
Michigan	11	3	.786
Ohio State	11	3	.786
Minnesota	10	4	.714
Michigan St.	8	6	.571
Purdue	8	6	.571
Illinois	6	8	.429
Northwestern	6	8	.429
Indiana	5	9	.357
Iowa	3	11	.214
Wisconsin	2	12	.143

had 27 points and 13 rebounds, Jon McGlocklin had 27 points and 11 rebounds, and Dick Van Arsdale had 25 points and 15 rebounds. The win diffused a rumored student protest against McCracken in which a demonstration was going to take place in the arena if the Hoosiers were behind with 10 minutes to play. Thus, members of the Hoosier football team formed a wall along the entrance to the court to show their support for the coach and to block any protestors. When the Hoosiers won, the planned protest turned into a victory celebration.

However, after the Illinois win, the Hoosiers dropped three straight games—98-96 against Ohio State in overtime, 82-75 at Iowa, and 99-87 at No. 2 Michigan—and the tide of criticism began to rise once again. However, the Indiana squad responded with three straight wins. The Hoosiers pulled out an 82-80 double overtime win at Wisconsin on February 17. Then, they came home and thumped Purdue 92-79 on February 22. (That may have been the most important game of the season when you realize that few things please the Indiana faithful more than a win over the Boilermakers.) Next, on February 24, Wisconsin came to Bloomington and got crushed 108-82 as Indiana looked like the Hurryin' Hoosiers of old.

After the three-game winning streak, IU lost a couple of close games to two of the conference's top teams, Ohio State (73-69) and Minnesota (90-89), and then closed the season with a 76-68 victory over Northwestern on March 9, in Bloomington.

Although Indiana finished with a 9-15 overall record and had slid into eighth place in the Big Ten, the team had played much better basketball after the semester break and proved that it could hold its own against the Big Ten's top teams. With all of its starters returning, IU provided a glimmer of hope to its fans that the next season would provide much more to cheer about.

1964-65

OVERALL RECORD: 19-5

CONFERENCE RECORD: 9-5 (FOURTH PLACE)

TEAM HONORS:

MEMPHIS STATE INVITATIONAL CHAMPION

INDIVIDUAL HONORS:

DICK VAN ARSDALE—ALL-AMERICA, ACADEMIC ALL-AMERICA,

ACADEMIC ALL-BIG TEN

TOM VAN ARSDALE—ALL-AMERICA,

ACADEMIC ALL-AMERICA,

ACADEMIC ALL-BIG TEN

The inexperience and lack of leadership that plagued the virtually seniorless 1963-64 IU squad, and doomed it to a 9-15 record, resulted in a battled-tested team that prepared to make Indiana a contender again during the 1964-65 campaign. The juniors, led by Dick and Tom Van Arsdale and Jon McGlocklin, who took their lumps in 1963-64, were now seniors ready to dish out some lumps to their adversaries. They were also ready to provide a steadying influence that could lead IU to victories in the close games where the team had fallen apart during the previous season.

"To do well this year we're going to have to win those close ones we were dropping last year," said coach Branch McCracken. "Those losses made us an also-ran instead of a contender. We've always been a second-half club, coming on stronger near the end. In fact, in the past I've always felt pretty good when we stayed close during the first three-fourths of the game. But last season, we led at halftime of most games and then faded off in the second. This is something we'll have to change."

INDIANA'S RANKING IN THE 1963-64 ASSOCIATED PRESS POLLS

PS	12/10	12/17	12/24	12/31	1/7	1/14	1/21	1/28	2/4	2/11	2/18	2/25	3/3	3/10
—	—	—	—	—	—	—	—	—	—	—	—	—	—	—

The 1964-65 team. First row (left to right): Al Harden, Dick Van Arsdale, Jon McGlocklin, Steve Redenbaugh, Tom Van Arsdale, Ron Peyser; Second row: assistant coach Lou Watson, Ron McMains, Gary Grieger, Jack Johnson, Erv Inniger, Dave Dickerson, head coach Branch McCracken; Third row: Butch Joyner, Bill Russell, Larry Turpen, Vern Pfaff, Max Walker, Manager Tom McGlasson. IU Archives

In addition to having senior leadership that helped guide the Hoosiers confidently in the final stretches of most games, McCracken also got a boost from 6'8" Ron Peyser and 6'7" Larry Cooper, who both stepped up to provide some adequate play at the center position after they had both struggled with inconsistency the previous season. That allowed McCracken to regularly put the 6'5" McGlocklin at guard, rather than having a three-forward front line with McGlocklin and the Van Arsdales. The Hoosiers frequently relied on that lineup the year before and were often exploited by teams with big effective post players. To help offset that problem, McCracken implemented a new 2-2-1 full-court zone press that the Hoosiers used after every made basket. McCracken borrowed the idea from his old friend, UCLA's John Wooden, who had led an undersized team to the national championship in 1964 by using the zone press. The way it worked for the Hoosiers was that the Van Arsdales trapped the first person to receive the ball; the IU guards (usually McGlocklin and Steve Redenbaugh) roamed the passing lanes inside the 10-second line, while the IU center (Peyser or Cooper) stayed back and protected the basket.

With its lineup, its strategy, and its leadership solidified, Indiana roared through the preconference season and became an unexpected force in the Big Ten. On opening night, December 1, IU's 5'10" senior sparkplug Al Harden came off the bench and triggered the Hoosier attack in both halves, leading Indiana to an 81-70 victory over Ohio University in Bloomington. Next, Indiana went to Manhattan, Kansas, and stole a 74-70 win from a No. 8 Kansas State. IU got 26 points and 14 rebounds from Tom Van Arsdale in that game.

Then, Indiana returned to Bloomington and brought out the whips, which were used to issue lashings to three straight opponents: 87-69 over Oklahoma on December 7, 107-81 over North Carolina on December 12, and 97-78 over DePaul on December 14. IU had at least four players in double figures in all three games (six players scored in double figures against the Tar Heels).

The Hoosiers stayed undefeated on December 19, with a huge second half against Detroit that led to a 108-89 win in the Motor City. On December 21, IU's zone press forced Notre Dame into 23 turnovers

1964-65 TEAM ROSTER

Head coach: Branch McCracken
Assistant coaches: Lou Watson, Don Luft

No.	Player	Hometown	Class	Position	Height
34	Dave Dickerson	Paris, IL	So	F	6-4
45	Larry Cooper	Osborne, KS	Sr	C	6-7
43	Gary Grieger	Evansville, IN	Jr	F	6-4
23	Al Harden (Capt.)	Covington, KY	Sr	G	5-10
41	Erv Inniger	Berne, IN	So	G	6-3
32	Jack Johnson	Greenfield, IN	So	F	6-6
54	Jon McGlocklin (Capt.)	Franklin, IN	Sr	F/C	6-5
35	Ron McMains	Frankfort, IN	So	F	6-5
32	Ron Peyser	Chicago, IL	Sr	C	6-8
24	Vern Pfaff	Ellettsville, IN	Jr	G	5-8
44	Steve Redenbaugh	Paoli, IN	Sr	G	6-2
22	Bill Russell	Columbus, IN	So	G	6-0
20	Gary Tofil	Indianapolis, IN	So	G	6-2
40	Larry Turpen	Shawswick, IN	Jr	G	6-1
30	Dick Van Arsdale	Indianapolis, IN	Sr	F	6-5
25	Tom Van Arsdale	Indianapolis, IN	Sr	F	6-5
41	Max Walker	Milwaukee, WI	Jr	G	6-1
	Butch Joyner	New Castle, IN	Fr	F	6-4

SEASON RESULTS 1964-65

Date	Court	Opponent	Result	Score
12/1/1964	H	Ohio	W	80-71
12/5/1964	A	Kansas State	W	74-70
12/7/1964	H	Oklahoma	W	87-69
12/12/1964	H	North Carolina	W	107-81
12/14/1964	H	DePaul	W	91-78
12/19/1964	A	Detroit	W	108-89
12/21/1964	N1	Notre Dame	W	107-81
12/28/1964	N2	St. Louis	W	98-68
12/29/1964	N2	Memphis State	W	91-68
1/4/1965	A	Illinois	L	81-86
1/9/1965	H	Northwestern	W	86-73
1/11/1965	A	Iowa	W	85-76
1/16/1965	A	Ohio State	W	84-72
1/18/1965	H	Iowa	L	68-74
2/4/1965	H	Loyola Chicago	W	109-82
2/8/1965	H	Michigan State	W	112-94
2/13/1965	A	Northwestern	W	86-76
2/15/1965	H	Michigan	L	95-96
2/20/1965	H	Wisconsin	W	100-87
2/22/1965	A	Purdue	L	70-82
2/27/1965	A	Minnesota	L	88-100
3/1/1965	H	Ohio State	W	110-90
3/6/1965	H	Purdue	W	90-79
3/8/1965	A	Wisconsin	W	92-73

1 Fort Wayne, IN
2 Memphis, TN

1964-65 BIG TEN STANDINGS

	W	L	PCT
Michigan	13	1	.929
Minnesota	11	3	.786
Illinois	10	4	.714
Indiana	9	5	.643
Iowa	8	6	.571
Ohio State	6	8	.429
Purdue	5	9	.357
Wisconsin	4	10	.286
Northwestern	3	11	.214
Michigan St.	1	13	.071

and resulted in a 107-81 Hoosier victory on the neutral court of the Fort Wayne Coliseum. To finish out the preconference season, Indiana went down to Memphis, Tennessee, for the Memphis State Invitational and easily won the tournament by crushing No. 9 St. Louis 98-68 on December 28, and burying host Memphis State 91-68 on December 29.

Entering Big Ten play, the Hoosiers were 9-0 and ranked No. 2 in the nation. However, the Big Ten was loaded with highly ranked teams, including Michigan, Minnesota and Illinois, and the college basketball world prepared for one of the most intense and competitive Big Ten seasons ever. The Hoosiers opened against No. 6 Illinois in Champaign on January 4. The Fighting Illini jumped out to a 10-point halftime lead, handled the Hoosier press with confidence, and escaped with an 86-81 lead. "Indiana's press was tougher than UCLA's," said Illinois coach Harry Combes. "They're as tough as anyone we've played this year, and I'm glad we don't have to play them at Bloomington."

With all the powerhouse teams in the Big Ten, the Hoosiers knew they couldn't afford to lose many games if they were going to win the conference title, so they were bitterly disappointed after the Illinois loss. They used that disappointment to fuel easy wins over their next three opponents: Northwestern (86-73), Iowa (85-76), and Ohio State (84-72). The wins over the Hawkeyes and the Buckeyes were both road victories. Then, in their final game before the semester break, the IU squad was set to play Iowa on January 18, in Bloomington. However, the Hoosiers faced two big setbacks before the game even started: Jon McGlocklin injured his ankle against OSU and would miss the Iowa contest, and the state fire marshal ruled that the IU Fieldhouse didn't have enough exits, so it was limited to 3,300 fans for the Iowa game (while the issue was being resolved). The Hawkeyes came to town and jumped out to a 34-20 halftime lead and then desperately held on for a 74-68 upset.

After the devastating home loss to Iowa, Indiana had a layoff of over two weeks with the end of the semester. The squad came back from that break and played with the desperation of a team that knows it cannot afford to lose any more games if it wants to meet its goals. The Hoosiers returned to action on February 4, when they mauled Loyola Chicago 109-82 in Bloomington. McGlocklin returned to the lineup and scored 25 points in 22 minutes of action. The Hoosiers looked even more impressive on February 8, when they pummeled Michigan State 112-94, as five Hoosiers scored in double figures. Next, Indiana grinded out an 86-76 road win at Northwestern on February 13.

That set up a fantastic show-down between the Hoosiers and the No. 1 Michigan Wolverines on Friday, February 15, in Bloomington. Both teams were 15-2 overall, but Michigan was seven-0 in conference play and Indiana was 5-2. The Hoosiers had to win to keep their conference titles hopes alive. A large crowd and a huge throng of reporters turned out for the game, and it looked like a classic from the open-ing tip. There were six ties and 14 lead changes in the first half, but Indiana led 50-44 at the intermis-sion. The see-saw battle resumed in the second half, but Indiana pulled ahead 81-74 with 1:09 remaining, and looked ready to close out the game. But then Michigan's Cazzie Russell, who had struggled most of the game,

During his three seasons on the varsity, 6'5" John McGlocklin played all five positions on the floor and served as the Hoosiers' captain as both a junior and a senior. He aver-aged 17.2 PPG during his sen-ior year. IU Archives

scored 7 straight points to tie the score and send it to overtime. Indiana led 92-88 in the final minute of OT, but Michigan hit two free throws, Indiana missed several scoring chances, and then Michigan center Bill Buntin tipped in a Russell miss to send the game to a second OT. The Wolverines finally prevailed 96-95 on two free throws by Russell in the final minute.

"We just plain blew it, boys," said McCracken afterward in the locker room. "We had them— twice—and kicked it away. We blew it, and it's a shame that a senior team has to lose a great ball game like that, just by giving it away… But keep your chins up, hold your heads high. You're a good ball club. Forget about practice tomorrow and think this one over in your own minds."

After the Michigan loss, the Hoosiers knew that their season was all but over. They bounced back with a 100-87 win over Wisconsin in Bloomington on February 20 but then dropped road games to Purdue (82-70) and Minnesota (100-88). They beat Ohio State 110-90 in Bloomington on March 1. After that game, news leaked out that McCracken had turned in his resigna-tion to Indiana president Elvis Stahr. His last home game was against Purdue on March 6, and his boys sent him out a winner with a 90-79 victory over the Boilermakers. All five members of the starting lineup scored in double figures, and the crowd lingered after the game to give McCracken a large ovation as he was presented with a special plaque for his achievements.

McCracken was sick with the flu and couldn't make the team's final game at Wisconsin on March 8, but his assistant coach, Lou Watson, who had already been chosen as his successor, led the Hoosiers to a 92-73 win that capped off a 19-5 season and gave IU sole possession of fourth place in the Big Ten with a 9-5 conference record.

That spring, Dick Van Arsdale, Tom Van Arsdale and Jon McGlocklin were each selected in the NBA draft, and all three of them went on to successful pro careers.

INDIANA'S RANKING IN THE 1964-65 ASSOCIATED PRESS POLLS

PS	12/8	12/15	12/22	12/29	1/5	1/12	1/19	1/26	2/2	2/9	2/16	2/23	3/2	3/9
—	—	—	—	8	7	2	5	5	9	7	8	7	7	—	—

SEASON STATISTICS
1946-47 TO 1964-65

1946-47

Team Statistics	G	FG/A	PCT	FT/A	PCT	TP	AVG
Indiana	20	433-1435	.302	286-436	.656	1152	57.6
Opponents	20					1004	50.2

Player Statistics	G	FG/A	PCT	FT/A	PCT	TP	AVG
Hamilton	20	109-325	.335	49-74	.662	267	13.4
Ritter	20	65-230	.283	48-65	.738	178	8.9
Williams	19	46-200	.230	61-81	.753	153	8.1
Wallace	18	59-195	.303	18-29	.621	136	7.6
Watson	18	44-170	.259	27-45	.600	115	6.4
Hermann	19	29-90	.322	41-54	.759	99	5.2
Meyers	18	26-75	.347	19-39	.487	71	3.9
Lollar	3	4-12	.333	3-3	1.00	11	3.7
Armstrong	10	12-40	.300	3-4	.750	27	2.7
Kravolansky	16	18-52	.346	7-16	.438	43	2.7
Mendenhall	12	11-24	.458	4-6	.667	26	2.2
Walker	11	8-16	.500	5-16	.313	21	1.9
Jensen	2	1-2	.500	0-2	.000	2	1.0
Mehl	4	1-4	.250	1-1	1.00	3	0.8
Brown	2	0-0	.000	0-0	.000	0	0.0
Cowan	2	0-0	.000	0-1	.000	0	0.0
Herman	2	0-0	.000	0-0	.000	0	0.0
Krupa	2	0-0	.000	0-0	.000	0	0.0
Stuteville	1	0-0	.000	0-0	.000	0	0.0

1947-48

Team Statistics	G	FG/A	PCT	FT/A	PCT	TP	AVG
Indiana	20	418-1407	.297	277-454	.610	1113	55.7
Opponents	20					1051	52.6

Player Statistics	G	FG/A	PCT	FT/A	PCT	TP	AVG
D. Ritter	20	100-337	.297	75-105	.714	275	13.8
Watson	16	70-216	.324	30-49	.612	170	10.6
Meyer	20	62-163	.380	32-66	.485	156	7.8
Williams	19	49-145	.338	46-63	.730	144	7.6
Schwartz	20	33-124	.266	25-40	.625	91	4.6
Armstrong	20	32-108	.296	11-27	.407	75	3.8
J. Stuteville	17	22-79	.278	17-27	.630	61	3.6
Lollar	15	20-61	.328	12-23	.522	52	3.5
Hermann	19	16-71	.225	16-25	.640	48	2.5
Wallace	4	4-16	.250	0-2	.000	8	2.0
Mendenhall	9	5-30	.167	4-6	.667	14	1.6
Brown	7	1-20	.050	6-11	.545	8	1.1
Farris	2	1-6	.167	0-1	.000	2	1.0
Chestnut	2	1-4	.250	0-0	.000	2	1.0
Jensen	8	2-27	.074	3-9	.333	7	0.9

1948-49

Team Statistics	G	FG/A	PCT	FT/A	PCT	TP	AVG
Indiana	22	424-1697	.250	346-564	.613	1194	54.3
Opponents	22					1090	49.5

Player Statistics	G	FG/A	PCT	FT/A	PCT	TP	AVG
Garrett	22	73-277	.264	74-103	.718	220	10.0
Watson	22	80-278	.288	56-88	.636	216	9.8
Tosheff	22	73-265	.275	36-50	.720	182	8.3
Stuteville	19	41-137	.299	41-64	.641	123	6.5
Ritter	22	38-154	.247	41-67	.612	117	5.3
Schwartz	21	35-189	.185	41-65	.631	111	5.3
Ring	22	45-201	.224	19-55	.345	109	5.0
Buck	17	20-72	.278	15-20	.750	55	3.2
Robbins	7	4-25	.160	8-11	.727	16	2.3
Meyer	16	9-57	.158	8-21	.381	26	1.6
Armstrong	10	3-26	.115	5-8	.625	11	1.1
Lukemeyer	12	3-17	.176	2-11	.182	8	0.7

1949-50

Team Statistics	G	FG/A	PCT	FT/A	PCT	TP	AVG
Indiana	22	519-1820	.285	382-614	.622	1420	64.5
Opponents	22	445-1516	.294	352-584	.603	1242	56.5

Player Statistics	G	FG/A	PCT	FT/A	PCT	TP	AVG
Garrett	22	98-344	.285	87-128	.680	283	12.9
Watson	21	102-325	.314	52-94	.553	256	12.2
Stuteville	22	83-228	.364	95-149	.638	261	11.9
Tosheff	22	65-240	.271	34-53	.642	164	7.5
Miranda	22	48-210	.229	22-36	.611	118	5.4
Masters	22	34-142	.239	21-41	.512	89	4.1
Ring	22	27-113	.239	26-48	.542	80	3.6
Hill	22	30-85	.353	15-23	.652	75	3.4
Buck	16	14-56	.250	10-12	.833	38	2.4
Meyers	19	15-51	.294	12-21	.571	42	2.2
Christie	1	1-1	1.00	0-0	.000	2	2.0
Robbins	9	1-11	.091	7-8	.875	9	1.0
Schwartz	3	1-6	.167	1-1	1.00	3	1.0
Vieau	2	0-5	.000	0-0	.000	0	0.0
Luft	1	0-0	.000	0-0	.000	0	0.0
Summers	1	0-3	.000	0-0	.000	0	0.0

1950-51

Team Statistics	G	FG/A	PCT	FT/A	PCT	TP	AVG
Indiana	22	518-1741	.298	384-579	.663	1420	64.5
Opponents	22	387-1389	.279	399-681	.586	1173	53.3
Player Statistics	**G**	**FG/A**	**PCT**	**FT/A**	**PCT**	**TP**	**AVG**
Garrett	22	95-291	.326	99-137	.723	289	13.1
Tosheff	22	78-230	.339	54-67	.806	210	9.6
Miranda	22	85-266	.320	37-46	.804	207	9.4
Ring	22	71-230	.309	42-72	.583	184	8.4
Masters	20	39-138	.283	52-74	.703	130	6.5
Brown	22	55-186	.296	30-50	.600	140	6.4
Buck	20	31-109	.284	12-17	.706	74	3.7
Dobson	15	14-41	.341	18-33	.545	46	3.1
Hill	21	27-106	.255	9-22	.409	63	3.0
Robbins	20	5-38	.132	12-20	.600	22	1.1
Luft	17	5-28	.179	5-17	.294	16	0.9
Vieau	13	5-23	.217	3-12	.250	12	0.9
Schooley	14	2-32	.063	8-11	.727	12	0.9
Baumgartner	6	1-3	.333	2-3	.667	4	0.7
Summers	3	1-2	.500	0-0	.000	2	0.7
McDermond	4	0-4	.000	0-0	.000	0	0.0
Case	1	0-2	.000	0-0	.000	0	0.0

1951-52

Team Statistics	G	FG/A	PCT	FT/A	PCT	TP	AVG
Indiana	22	586-1723	.340	449-691	.650	1621	73.7
Opponents	22	522-1698	.307	426-688	.619	1470	66.8
Player Statistics	**G**	**FG/A**	**PCT**	**FT/A**	**PCT**	**TP**	**AVG**
Schlundt	22	131-289	.453	114-171	.667	379	17.1
Leonard	22	131-369	.355	57-81	.704	319	14.5
Farley	22	70-193	.363	55-88	.625	195	8.9
Masters	22	63-206	.306	66-92	.717	192	8.7
Esposito	22	48-129	.372	59-84	.702	155	7.1
Miranda	22	60-234	.256	20-23	.870	140	6.4
Kraak	21	32-75	.427	29-55	.527	93	4.4
Wood	13	10-39	.256	17-31	.548	37	2.9
Scott	21	18-74	.243	15-36	.417	51	2.4
Baumgartner	7	6-18	.333	4-6	.667	16	2.3
Vieau	15	7-32	.219	8-11	.727	22	1.5
Hill	17	7-35	.200	4-7	.571	18	1.1
DeaKyne	11	3-8	.375	1-2	.500	7	0.6
Schooley	11	0-11	.000	0-2	.000	0	0.0
Swan	5	0-10	.000	0-2	.000	0	0.0
Dobson	1	0-0	.000	0-0	.000	0	0.0

1953-54

Team Statistics	G	FG/A	PCT	FT/A	PCT	TP	AVG
Indiana	24	611-1666	.367	591-907	.652	1813	75.5
Opponents	24	550-1794	.307	496-844	.588	1613	67.2
Player Statistics	**G**	**FG/A**	**PCT**	**FT/A**	**PCT**	**TP**	**AVG**
Schlundt	24	177-354	.500	229-296	.774	583	24.3
Leonard	23	138-432	.319	79-123	.642	355	15.4
Farley	24	77-176	.438	96-153	.627	250	10.4
B. Scott	24	59-151	.391	54-90	.600	172	7.2
Kraak	24	60-187	.321	40-77	.519	160	6.7
Choice	20	37-102	.363	35-60	.583	109	5.5
White	21	27-107	.252	18-27	.667	72	3.4
L. Scott	14	10-48	.208	12-26	.462	32	2.3
Phipps	8	6-20	.300	6-13	.462	18	2.3
Fisher	6	5-16	.313	2-4	.500	12	2.0
Poff	16	6-33	.182	9-13	.692	21	1.3
DeaKyne	8	3-8	.375	2-8	.250	8	1.0
Byers	22	6-26	.231	9-15	.600	21	1.0
Barley	3	0-3	.000	0-0	.000	0	0.0
Williamson	3	0-3	.000	0-2	.000	0	0.0

1954-55

Team Statistics	G	FG/A	PCT	FT/A	PCT	TP	AVG
Indiana	22	590-1553	.380	563-870	.647	1743	79.2
Opponents	22	553-1649	.335	563-784	.784	1669	75.9
Player Statistics	**G**	**FG/A**	**PCT**	**FT/A**	**PCT**	**TP**	**AVG**
Schlundt	22	169-377	.448	234-299	.783	572	26.0
Choice	22	105-270	.389	107.142	.754	317	14.4
Scott	21	64-221	.290	73-107	.682	201	9.6
Barley	18	52-178	.292	45-58	.776	149	8.3
Hodson	13	31-93	.333	26-36	.722	88	6.8
Bryant	20	32-112	.286	17-21	.810	81	4.1
White	13	19-75	.253	5-11	.455	43	3.3
Poff	17	24-93	.258	7-14	.500	55	3.2
Wood	12	12-37	.324	14-18	.778	38	3.2
Baumgartner	13	12-43	.279	10-17	.588	34	2.6
Fisher	8	9-39	.231	3-7	.429	21	2.6
Neal	14	10-43	.233	8-20	.400	28	2.0
Stemle	1	1-1	1.00	0-0	.000	2	2.0
Williamson	17	8-29	.276	9-20	.450	25	1.5
Phipps	6	3-12	.250	0-1	.000	6	1.0
Byers	12	2-23	.087	5-11	.455	9	0.8
Maetschke	3	0-3	.000	0-2	.000	0	0.0
Skeeters	1	0-0	.000	0-0	.000	0	0.0

1955-56

Team Statistics	G	FG/A	PCT	FT/A	PCT	R	PTS	AVG
Indiana	22	643-1665	.386	513-720	.713	34.5	1799	81.8
Opponents	22	623-1789	.348	718-669	.669		1726	78.5
Player Statistics	**G**	**FG/A**	**PCT**	**FT/A**	**PCT**	**R**	**PTS**	**AVG**
Choice	22	148-290	.510	167-235	.711	6.8	463	21.0
Dees	22	140-332	.422	103-127	.811	11.5	383	17.4
Brown	12	68-169	.402	41-61	.672	7.0	177	14.8
Bryant	21	114-321	.355	74-89	.831	2.0	302	14.4
Thompson	22	76-167	.455	36-65	.554	4.2	188	8.6
Hodson	17	30-111	.270	48-59	.814	1.2	108	6.4
Obremsky	21	45-164	.274	22-44	.500	3.0	112	5.3
Ball	9	5-18	.278	10-13	.769	2.1	20	2.2
Fisher	8	6-23	.261	4-7	.571	2.8	16	2.0
Phipps	5	3-10	.300	2-5	.400	0.8	8	1.6
Neal	6	3-14	.214	3-5	.600	0.5	9	1.5
Gee	2	1-3	.333	0-0	.000	0.0	2	1.0
Lumpkin	12	4-34	.118	3-6	.500	0.4	11	0.9
Barley	8	0-8	.000	0-4	.000	0.5	0	0.0
Custer	2	0-0	.000	0-0	.000	0.0	0	0.0
Williamson	2	0-1	.000	0-0	.000	0.0	0	0.0

1956-57

Team Statistics	G	FG/A	PCT	FT/A	PCT	R	PTS	AVG
Indiana	22	633-1634	.387	436-597	.730	42.1	1702	77.4
Opponents	22	639-1762	.363	327-559	.585		1605	73.0
Player Statistics	**G**	**FG/A**	**PCT**	**FT/A**	**PCT**	**R**	**PTS**	**AVG**
Dees	22	187-440	.425	176-209	.842	14.4	550	25.0
Neal	19	90-185	.486	58-91	.637	8.2	238	12.5
Bryant	22	94-281	.335	56-70	.800	4.4	244	11.1
Hodson	22	73-179	.408	48-60	.800	2.7	194	8.8
Thompson	20	65-150	.433	26-39	.667	4.2	156	7.8
Obremsky	20	56-183	.306	33-58	.569	5.3	145	7.3
Hayes	15	25-90	.278	13-20	.650	0.7	63	4.2
Hinds	11	17-45	.378	9-13	.692	4.3	43	3.9
Schofield	3	4-10	.400	3-10	.300	4.0	11	3.7
Flowers	17	18-51	.353	9-15	.600	1.3	45	2.7
Balch	5	2-7	.286	1-2	.500	1.0	5	1.0
Aldridge	6	1-5	.200	3-8	.375	2.2	5	0.8
Gee	8	1-5	.200	1-2	.500	0.0	3	0.4
Doninger	5	0-3	.000	0-0	.000	0.2	0	0.0

1957-58

Team Statistics	G	FG/A	PCT	FT/A	PCT	R	PTS	AVG
Indiana	24	742-1859	.399	431-619	.696	47.0	1915	79.8
Opponents	24	716-1874	.382	450-686	.656	47.0	1882	78.4
Player Statistics	**G**	**FG/A**	**PCT**	**FT/A**	**PCT**	**R**	**PTS**	**AVG**
Dees	24	230-480	.479	153-186	.823	14.4	613	25.5
Obremsky	23	117-320	.366	55-92	.598	7.7	289	12.6
Thompson	23	110-261	.421	47-77	.610	7.2	267	11.6
Wilkinson	23	91-253	.360	55-80	.688	3.7	237	10.3
Gee	18	57-152	.375	48-54	.889	2.6	162	9.0
Radovich	23	62-143	.434	27-49	.551	6.6	151	6.6
Hinds	16	29-94	.309	14-20	.700	4.1	72	4.5
Schlegelmilch	23	31-90	.344	13-28	.464	1.3	75	3.3
Hill	11	10-40	.250	13-20	.650	2.1	33	3.0
Flowers	5	3-17	.176	5-9	.556	2.2	11	2.2
Witte	2	1-3	.333	0-0	.000	1.5	2	1.0
Ball	4	1-4	.250	1-2	.500	0.5	3	0.8
Aldridge	4	0-2	.000	0-2	.000	0.5	0	0.0

1958-59

Team Statistics	G	FG/A	PCT	FT/A	PCT	R	PTS	AVG
Indiana	22	690-1684	.410	369-543	.680	56.6	1749	79.5
Opponents	22	626-1713	.365	434-655	.663	49.1	1686	76.6
Player Statistics	**G**	**FG/A**	**PCT**	**FT/A**	**PCT**	**R**	**PTS**	**AVG**
Bellamy	22	148-289	.512	86-141	.610	15.2	382	17.4
Lee	22	128-356	.360	43-48	.741	3.9	299	13.6
Radovich	22	112-248	.452	51-73	.699	10.1	275	12.5
Long	21	66-162	.407	57-77	.740	2.4	189	9.0
Johnson	16	61-143	.427	22-35	.629	6.3	144	9.0
Wilkinson	12	35-103	.340	26-39	.667	3.8	96	8.0
Flowers	21	62-163	.380	34-51	.667	4.3	158	7.5
Horn	22	47-127	.370	24-34	.706	4.9	118	5.4
Schlegelmilch	16	16-50	.320	5-9	.556	1.6	37	2.3
Witte	8	6-10	.600	5-7	.714	2.8	17	2.1
Gamble	1	1-1	1.00	0-0	.000	1.0	2	2.0
Butte	9	5-14	.357	7-9	.778	1.1	17	1.9
Balch	2	0-1	.000	3-4	.750	1.0	3	1.5
Aldridge	6	2-11	.182	4-4	1.00	0.8	8	1.3
Reinhart	3	1-2	.500	2-2	1.00	0.0	4	1.3
Williams	3	0-4	.000	0-0	.000	0.3	0	0.0

1959-60

Team Statistics	G	FG/A	PCT	FT/A	PCT	R	PTS	AVG
Indiana	24	809-1824	.444	379-554	.684	51.7	1997	83.2
Opponents	24	672-1763	.381	410-598	.686	45.0	1754	73.1
Player Statistics	**G**	**FG/A**	**PCT**	**FT/A**	**PCT**	**R**	**PTS**	**AVG**
Bellamy	24	212-396	.535	113-161	.702	13.5	537	22.4
Radovich	24	142-291	.488	70-94	.745	11.9	354	14.8
Wilkinson	24	110-258	.426	44-70	.629	2.8	264	11.0
Lee	22	101-236	.428	31-44	.705	3.3	233	10.6
Bass	21	63-140	.450	34-46	.739	1.0	160	7.6
Johnson	19	48-140	.343	20-31	.645	2.8	116	6.1
Hall	24	59-148	.399	21-39	.538	5.3	139	5.8
Long	23	33-71	.465	32-40	.800	1.3	98	4.3
Reinhart	6	3-8	.375	5-6	.833	0.5	11	1.8
Mickey	18	13-50	.260	2-8	.250	3.0	28	1.6
Schlegelmilch	6	3-7	.429	3-5	.600	0.7	9	1.5
Altman	13	8-29	.276	1-4	.250	1.3	17	1.3
Wilhoit	13	8-25	.320	1-1	1.00	1.2	17	1.3
Witte	11	5-19	.263	2-5	.400	2.2	12	1.1
Butte	7	1-6	.167	0-0	.000	1.3	2	0.3

1960-61

Team Statistics	G	FG/A	PCT	FT/A	PCT	R	PTS	AVG
Indiana	24	718-1786	.402	376-589	.638	56.8	1812	75.5
Opponents	24	652-1738	.375	409-637	.642	47.7	1713	71.4
Player Statistics	**G**	**FG/A**	**PCT**	**FT/A**	**PCT**	**R**	**PTS**	**AVG**
Bellamy	24	195-389	.501	132-204	.647	17.8	522	21.8
Bolyard	24	155-365	.425	61-99	.616	9.1	371	15.5
Long	24	111-256	.434	59-90	.656	2.8	281	11.7
Bass	23	76-196	.388	34-45	.756	2.0	186	8.1
Hall	24	58-191	.304	31-46	.674	7.5	147	6.1
Rayl	20	34-112	.304	11-22	.500	0.7	79	4.0
Wilhoit	22	28-85	.329	21-33	.636	1.5	77	3.5
Mickey	21	19-64	.297	15-24	.625	5.7	53	2.5
Pavy	18	21-56	.375	3-11	.273	0.7	45	2.5
Porter	16	13-43	.302	8-12	.667	3.1	34	2.1
Fairfield	12	5-15	.333	0-1	.000	1.7	10	0.8
Altman	9	2-3	.667	0-0	.000	0.6	4	0.4
Granger	7	1-7	.143	1-2	.500	0.9	3	0.4
Prickett	1	0-1	.000	0-0	.000	0.0	0	0.0
Roush	1	0-3	.000	0-0	.000	2.0	0	0.0

1961-62

Team Statistics	G	FG/A	PCT	FT/A	PCT	R	PTS	AVG
Indiana	24	810-1939	.418	469-641	.732	54.7	2089	87.0
Opponents	24	754-1852	.407	604-866	.697	54.3	2112	88.0
Player Statistics	**G**	**FG/A**	**PCT**	**FT/A**	**PCT**	**R**	**TP**	**AVG**
Rayl	24	254-580	.438	206-247	.834	3.5	714	29.8
Bolyard	24	184-415	.415	79-111	.712	9.5	447	18.6
Bass	24	117-296	.395	52-79	.658	3.3	286	11.9
Hall	24	92-227	.405	31-59	.525	10.2	215	9.0
Sparks	20	49-121	.405	22-28	.786	6.7	120	6.0
Mickey	22	26-66	.394	28-41	.683	6.2	80	3.6
Porter	22	28-70	.400	18-26	.692	2.8	74	3.4
Altman	14	18-38	.474	9-14	.643	1.6	45	3.2
Wilhoit	24	30-77	.390	13-18	.722	2.6	73	3.0
Fairfield	14	11-36	.306	7-13	.538	4.3	29	2.1
Granger	10	1-12	.083	4-5	.800	1.6	6	0.6
Sutton	2	0-1	.000	0-0	.000	0.5	0	0.0
Holland	1	0-0	.000	0-0	.000	0.0	0	0.0
Roush	1	0-0	.000	0-0	.000	0.0	0	0.0

1962-63

Team Statistics	G	FG/A	PCT	FT/A	PCT	R	PTS	AVG
Indiana	24	764-1769	.432	504-702	.718	48.4	2032	84.7
Opponents	24	801-1885	.425	413-612	.675	51.8	2015	84.0
Player Statistics	**G**	**FG/A**	**PCT**	**FT/A**	**PCT**	**R**	**TP**	**AVG**
Rayl	24	215-516	.417	178-204	.873	3.4	608	25.3
Bolyard	24	192-402	.478	97-139	.698	7.5	481	20.0
T. Van Arsdale	24	122-274	.445	55-100	.550	9.3	299	12.5
D. Van Arsdale	24	95-225	.422	102-142	.718	8.9	292	12.2
Redenbaugh	23	45-113	.398	33-42	.786	3.7	123	5.4
McGlocklin	22	47-115	.409	8-18	.444	3.5	102	4.6
Harden	21	24-48	.500	8-19	.421	1.4	56	2.7
Granger	6	6-12	.500	1-2	.500	0.3	13	2.2
Fairfield	6	4-10	.400	3-5	.600	4.3	11	1.8
Peyser	10	7-17	.412	4-9	.444	2.2	18	1.8
Porter	21	7-33	.212	15-22	.682	2.6	29	1.4
Pease	3	0-4	.000	0-0	.000	0.7	0	0.0
Sutton	2	0-0	.000	0-0	.000	0.0	0	

1963-64

Team Statistics	G	FG/A	PCT	FT/A	PCT	R	PTS	AVG
Indiana	24	793-1925	.412	446-602	.741	52.0	2032	84.7
Opponents	24	779-1858	.419	455-665	.684	53.4	2013	83.9

Player Statistics	G	FG/A	PCT	FT/A	PCT	R	TP	AVG
D. Van Arsdale	24	178-396	.449	179-220	.814	12.4	535	22.3
T. Van Arsdale	24	196-452	.434	120-177	.678	12.3	512	21.3
McGlocklin	24	165-359	.460	46-59	.780	5.7	376	15.7
Redenbaugh	24	101-266	.380	29-41	.707	4.8	231	9.6
Cooper	19	51-116	.440	18-27	.667	4.3	120	6.3
Pfaff	11	24-67	.358	12-15	.800	1.4	60	5.5
Harden	24	35-102	.343	13-24	.542	1.5	83	3.5
Grieger	18	18-57	.316	20-25	.800	1.4	56	3.1
Sutton	2	2-3	.667	0-0	.000	0.0	4	2.0
Walker	17	14-55	.255	3-4	.750	0.9	31	1.8
Peyser	14	9-38	.237	5-8	.625	2.9	23	1.6
Campbell	2	0-5	.000	1-2	.500	2.0	1	0.5
Pease	3	0-7	.000	0-0	.000	0.0	0	0.0
Turpen	1	0-2	.000	0-0	.000	0.0	0	0.0

1964-65

Team Statistics	G	FG/A	PCT	FT/A	PCT	R	PTS	AVG
Indiana	24	868-1895	.458	464-604	.768	46.8	2200	91.7
Opponents	24	721-1725	.418	472-689	.685	51.3	1914	79.8

Player Statistics	G	FG/A	PCT	FT/A	PCT	R	TP	AVG
T. Van Arsdale	24	173-369	.469	95-138	.688	8.5	441	18.4
D. Van Arsdale	24	146-327	.446	121-142	.852	8.7	413	17.2
McGlocklin	23	166-306	.542	63-70	.900	4.1	395	17.2
Redenbaugh	24	127-289	.439	44-60	.733	5.4	298	12.4
Peyser	24	67-155	.432	42-55	.764	4.4	176	7.3
Cooper	24	70-157	.446	25-36	.694	3.8	165	6.9
Harden	24	59-134	.440	40-53	.755	1.8	158	6.6
Grieger	21	24-57	.421	20-30	.667	1.6	68	3.2
Inniger	12	10-23	.435	6-6	1.00	1.1	26	2.2
Dickerson	9	6-15	.400	1-2	.500	0.7	13	1.4
Johnson	15	10-21	.476	0-1	.000	1.5	20	1.3
Russell	11	5-19	.263	4-7	.571	0.6	14	1.3
Walker	14	5-23	.217	3-4	.750	0.6	13	0.9
McMains	1	0-0	.000	0-0	.000	0.0	0	0.0
Turpen	1	0-0	.000	0-0	.000	0.0	0	0.0

1965-66

OVERALL RECORD: 8-16

CONFERENCE RECORD: 4-10 (NINTH PLACE)

The 1965-66 team. First row (left to right): Vern Payne, Erv Inniger, Gary Grieger, Ken Newsome, Butch Joyner, Frank Everett; Second row: head coach Lou Watson, Gary Leinberger, Jack Johnson, Rich Schrumpf, Ron McMains, assistant coach Don Luft; Third row: assistant coach Tom Bolyard, Larry Turpen, Vern Pfaff, Bill Russell, Max Walker, manager Bill Fortner. IU Archives

When coach Branch McCracken retired in 1965, he didn't exactly leave his successor, Lou Watson, with a cupboard full of talent. The top seven scorers (including all five starters) from the 1964-65 team were all seniors. That included Tom and Dick Van Arsdale and Jon McGlocklin, who all went on to successful NBA careers. Their graduation left Watson without any experienced players to build around. Plus, the NCAA probation that had dogged the Indiana athletic department from 1961 to 1964 had severely hurt basketball recruiting, which meant that there also wasn't much up-and-coming talent for Watson to bank on.

There was plenty of speculation at the time that McCracken had seen the writing on the wall and knew that IU wasn't going to be very good once the 1965 seniors graduated, and that he chose to retire when he did for that reason. In reality, McCracken's declining health was the primary factor in his retirement. Nevertheless, the timing was good, because the Hoosiers were unmistakably terrible in the 1965-66 season. There were some bright spots, especially during the final nine games, but the Hoosiers also got taken behind the woodshed and whipped by several opponents.

On opening night, December 1, tiny St. Joseph's College (from Rensselaer, Indiana) came to

Bloomington and dead-locked the Hoosiers 35-35 at the half. Sophomore guard Vern Payne triggered a 17-3 Indiana run to start the second half and the Hoosiers went on to a 76-62 victory. The IU squad took its first road trip on Saturday, December 4, when they traveled to Norman, Oklahoma, and led the Oklahoma Sooners by five points at halftime before losing an 83-82 squeeker. Indiana then returned to Bloomington and dropped two home games to Detroit (78-75) and Kansas State (103-76). During the Kansas State game, the Indiana crowd alternatively booed and cheered various substitutions that Coach Watson made, and then bombarded the court with crumpled-up game programs late in the second half when the Hoosiers were struggling on both ends of the court.

On December 17-18, the 1-3 Hoosiers went to Lexington to play in the Kentucky Invitational. In the first game, Indiana beat California 71-64, led by 16 points from senior guard Max Walker and 13 from Payne. In the championship game of the tournament, Adolph Rupp's undefeated Kentucky Wildcats mercilessly thumped the Hoosiers 91-56. However, Indiana bounced back and showed some fight three days after the Kentucky game when the Hoosiers ran to an 80-58 win over Notre Dame.

Then, on December 31, IU played No. 3 Bradley on the neutral floor of Chicago Stadium. IU unexpectedly dominated the game, leading by 11 at halftime and running up a 104-87 victory over the previously undefeated Braves. Sophomore forward Butch Joyner poured in 28 points for IU, while senior forward Gary Grieger added 24. The Bradley win improved IU's record to 4-4. But then the Hoosiers came back to Bloomington on January 3, and were badly outplayed by Loyola Chicago in a 91-68 loss to close out the preconference season. The Loyola game also featured a bench-clearing brawl between the highly frustrated Hoosiers and the aggressive Ramblers.

In their Big Ten opener against Illinois on January 8 in Bloomington, the Hoosiers had five players score in double figures but still didn't have enough firepower to keep up with the Fighting Illini, who prevailed 98-84. The Indiana guards shot the ball well on January 10 against Michigan, but Indiana couldn't stop the Wolverines in an 88-68 loss in Ann Arbor. Payne scored 25 for the Hoosiers and Walker

1965-66 TEAM ROSTER

Head coach: Lou Watson
Assistant coaches: Don Luft, Tom Bolyard

No.	Player	Hometown	Class	Position	Height
32	Frank Everett	Williamston, NC	So	C	6-6
43	Gary Grieger (Capt.)	Evansville, IN	Sr	F	6-4
42	Erv Inniger	Berne, IN	Jr	G	6-3
32	Jack Johnson	Greenfield, IN	Jr	F	6-6
34	Butch Joyner	New Castle, IN	So	F	6-4
45	Gary Leinberger	St. Louis, MO	So	F	6-7
35	Ron McMains	Frankfort, IN	Jr	F	6-5
25	Ken Newsome	Ohoskie, NC	So	F	6-5
23	Vern Payne	Michigan City, IN	So	G	5-10
24	Vern Pfaff	Ellettsville, IN	Jr	G	5-8
22	Bill Russell	Columbus, IN	Jr	G	6-0
30	Rich Schrumpf	Galien, MI	So	C	6-9
40	Larry Turpen	Shawswick, N	Jr	G	6-1
41	Max Walker	Milwaukee, WI	Sr	G	6-1

SEASON RESULTS 1965-66

Date	Court	Opponent	Result	Score
12/1/1965	H	St. Josephs (IN)	W	76-62
12/4/1965	A	Oklahoma	L	82-83
12/6/1965	H	Detroit	L	75-78
12/13/1965	H	Kansas State	L	76-103
12/17/1965	N1	California	W	71-64
12/18/1965	A	Kentucky	L	56-91
12/21/1965	N2	Notre Dame	W	80-58
12/31/1965	N3	Bradley	W	104-87
1/3/1966	H	Loyola Chicago	L	68-91
1/8/1966	H	Illinois	L	84-98
1/10/1966	A	Michigan	L	68-88
1/15/1966	A	Minnesota	L	82-91
1/17/1966	H	Iowa	W	73-61
2/1/1966	A	DePaul	L	79-100
2/5/1966	H	Michigan	L	76-93
2/7/1966	A	Wisconsin	L	78-79
2/12/1966	A	Illinois	W	81-77
2/14/1966	H	Ohio State	W	81-61
2/19/1966	H	Northwestern	L	82-83
2/21/1966	A	Purdue	L	68-77
2/26/1966	A	Michigan State	L	63-69
2/28/1966	H	Minnesota	L	90-96
3/5/1966	H	Michigan State	W	86-76
3/7/1966	A	Iowa	L	77-82

1 Lexington, KY
2 Fort Wayne, IN
3 Chicago, IL

1965-66 BIG TEN STANDINGS

	W	L	PCT
Michigan	11	3	.786
Michigan St.	10	4	.714
Iowa	8	6	.571
Illinois	8	6	.571
Minnesota	7	7	.500
Northwestern	7	7	.500
Wisconsin	6	8	.429
Ohio State	5	9	.357
Indiana	4	10	.286
Purdue	4	10	.286

added 18. Indiana then dropped its third straight conference game on January 15, in Minneapolis, where the Minnesota Golden Gophers used a late surge to win 91-82. Two nights later, the Hoosiers finally grabbed their first conference win as Payne and Walker combined for 40 points to power IU to a 73-61 win over Iowa in Bloomington.

After the two-week semester break, Indiana went up to Chicago and played DePaul in a nonconference game on February 1. Butch Joyner broke loose for 25 points to lead IU, but the Blue Demons raced to an easy 100-79 victory. Indiana returned to conference play on Saturday, February 5, when No. 9 Michigan came to Bloomington and bludgeoned the Hoosiers 93-76. The following Monday, Indiana went up to Wisconsin and lost a 79-78 heartbreaker when Badger guard Mike Carlin, an Indiana native, buried a short jumper in the lane in the final seconds. The loss put the Hoosiers at 1-5 in league play and in sole possession of last place.

The following week, IU showed some pride by pulling out two surprise victories. The first came on February 12, when the Hoosiers upset Illinois 81-77 in Champaign. Max Walker scored 18 of his game-high 27 points in the second half to carry IU to the win. Back in Bloomington on February 14, six Hoosiers scored in double figures as Indiana blew away Ohio State 81-61 and vacated the conference cellar with a 3-5 record. IU nearly made it a three-game winning streak on February 19, in Bloomington, but Northwestern's Jim Cummins buried two free throws in the final minute to give the Wildcats an 83-82 victory. Payne scored a game-high 31 points for IU, but Max Walker badly twisted his ankle in the middle of the second half and had to be carried off the floor. He had 17 points at the time. He ended up missing the Hoosiers' next game at Purdue.

IU dropped its next three games: 77-68 at Purdue on February 21; 69-63 at Michigan State on February 26; and 96-90 against Minnesota in Bloomington on February 28. Then, Big Ten title contender Michigan State came to Bloomington on March 5, with hopes of a victory that would set up a winner-take-all battle for the conference title with Michigan two days later in East Lansing. However, the Hoosiers wrecked their plans by knocking off the Spartans 86-76, led by 25 points apiece from Walker and Payne. Indiana closed out the season on March 7, in Iowa City, where the Hoosiers aggressively fought a tough Iowa team down to the wire before falling 82-77. That loss dropped Indiana to 4-10 on the season and put the Hoosiers in a tie with Purdue for last place in the Big Ten.

For the season, IU finished 8-16. Lightning-quick guards Max Walker and Vern Payne put on a show with their speed, shooting and ball-hawking defense, and forward Butch Joyner emerged as a steady contributor and a rising star. A lot of players gained valuable experience and since Walker and forward Gary Greiger were the only seniors on the team, Hoosier fans remained optimistic that IU could return to the upper division of the conference the following season. However, they had no idea just how far the Hoosiers would climb.

INDIANA'S RANKING IN THE 1965-66 ASSOCIATED PRESS POLLS

PS	12/7	12/14	12/21	12/28	1/4	1/11	1/18	1/25	2/1	2/8	2/15	2/22	3/1	3/8
—	—	—	—	—	—	—	—	—	—	—	—	—	—	—

1966-67

OVERALL RECORD: 18-8

CONFERENCE RECORD: 10-4 (FIRST PLACE)

TEAM HONORS:

BIG TEN CO-CHAMPION

INDIVIDUAL HONORS:

BUTCH JOYNER—ALL-BIG TEN (FIRST TEAM)

The 1966-67 team. First row (left to right): head coach Lou Watson, Bill Russell, Vern Payne, Bill DeHeer, Butch Joyner, Jack Johnson; Second row: assistant coach Don Luft, Harold Curdy, Erv Inniger, Bill Stenberg, Rich Schrumpf, Gary Leinberger, assistant coach Tom Bolyard; Third row: trainer Warren Ariail, Vern Pfaff, Earl Schneider, Gabe Oliverio, Larry Turpen, manager Dave Power.
IU Archives

Indiana entered the 1966-67 season with two experienced juniors ready to lead the team back to respectability in the Big Ten, after a last-place finish the season before. Flashy point guard Vern Payne and steady forward Butch Joyner headlined a group of returning lettermen that were eager to help IU bounce back from the dismal 1965-66 campaign. They were also joined by a promising group of soph-

omores led by sturdy 6'8" center Bill DeHeer, who quickly earned a starting spot. Coach Lou Watson felt that this team could challenge for a spot in the upper division of the Big Ten, but he didn't anticipate that the Hoosiers would pull off one of the greatest season-to-season turnarounds in league history.

Indiana started slow against a gutsy DePaul team in the season opener on Saturday, December 3, but

1966-67 TEAM ROSTER

Head coach: Lou Watson
Assistant coaches: Don Luft, Tom Bolyard

No.	Player	Hometown	Class	Position	Height
20	Mike Bedree	Fort Wayne, IN	So	G	6-3
21	Harold Curdy	Marion, IN	So	F	6-4
31	Bill DeHeer	Maplewood, MO	So	C	6-8
32	Jim Houlihan	Bluffton, IN	Jr	G	6-3
42	Erv Inniger	Berne, IN	Sr	G	6-3
33	Jack Johnson (Capt.)	Greenfield, IN	Sr	F	6-6
34	Butch Joyner	New Castle, IN	Jr	F	6-4
45	Gary Leinberger	St. Louis, MO	Jr	C	6-7
43	John Muirhead	Danville, IL	So	C	6-7
25	Ken Newsome	Ohoskie, NC	Jr	F	6-5
41	Gabe Oliverio	Annandale, VA	So	G	6-2
24	Vern Pfaff	Ellettsville, IN	Sr	G	5-10
23	Vern Payne	Michigan City, IN	Jr	G	5-10
22	Bill Russell	Columbus, IN	Sr	G	6-0
44	Earl Schneider	Evansville, IN	So	F	6-4
30	Rich Schrumpf	Galien, MI	Jr	C	6-9
35	Bill Stenberg	Rockford, IL	So	F	6-7
40	Larry Turpen	Bedford, IN	Sr	G	6-1

SEASON RESULTS 1966-67

Date	Court	Opponent	Result	Score
12/3/1966	H	DePauw	W	84-71
12/5/1966	H	Missouri	W	77-65
12/7/1966	H	Ohio	L	90-91
12/12/1966	A	Kansas State	L	69-82
12/17/1966	A	Loyola Chicago	W	83-73
12/20/1966	N1	Notre Dame	W	94-91
12/27/1966	N2	Oregon State	W	71-60
12/29/1966	N2	Washington	L	79-81
12/30/1966	N2	Oregon	W	102-64
1/7/1967	A	Iowa	L	73-84
1/9/1967	H	Minnesota	W	83-68
1/14/1967	A	Ohio State	W	81-80
1/30/1967	H	DePaul	W	72-70
2/4/1967	A	Minnesota	W	82-81
2/6/1967	H	Michigan State	W	82-77
2/11/1967	H	Wisconsin	W	93-81
2/13/1967	A	Michigan State	L	77-86
2/18/1967	A	Northwestern	W	81-79
2/20/1967	H	Illinois	W	96-81
2/25/1967	H	Iowa	L	74-75
2/27/1967	A	Michigan	W	98-96
3/4/1967	A	Illinois	L	70-80
3/6/1967	H	Michigan	W	96-90
3/11/1967	H	Purdue	W	95-82

NCAA Tournament

Date	Court	Opponent	Result	Score
3/17/1967	N3	Virginia Tech	L	70-79
3/18/1967	N3	Tennessee	W	51-44

1 Fort Wayne, IN
2 Portland, OR
3 Evanston, IL

1966-67 BIG TEN STANDINGS

	W	L	PCT
Indiana	10	4	.714
Michigan St.	10	4	.714
Iowa	9	5	.643
Wisconsin	8	6	.571
Purdue	7	7	.500
Northwestern	7	7	.500
Ohio State	6	8	.429
Illinois	6	8	.429
Minnesota	5	9	.357
Michigan	2	12	.143

the Hoosiers eventually found their rhythm and put away the Tigers 84-71 at the IU Fieldhouse. Joyner led Indiana with 19 points while Payne chipped in 18. A couple of nights later the Hurryin' Hoosiers' running attack kicked into a higher gear against Missouri and the result was a 77-65 Indiana victory in Bloomington. Then, Ohio University came to town on December 7, and dealt the Hoosiers a sour 91-90 upset when the Bobcats' John Schroeder sank a hook shot in the final seconds of overtime.

Next, the Hoosiers split a pair of road games, losing at Kansas State 82-69 on December 12 but winning 83-73 at Loyola Chicago on December 17. Joyner led IU with 17 points against Kansas State and 26 against Loyola. On December 20, Indiana played Notre Dame at the Fort Wayne Coliseum, a neutral floor located a couple of hours away from both campuses. The Irish held Joyner to six points, but five other Hoosiers scored in double figures and IU prevailed 94-91. Indiana finished up the preconference season with a trip to the Far West Classic in Portland, Oregon. The Hoosiers defeated Oregon State 71-60 on December 27, lost to Washington 81-79, and crushed Oregon 102-64 on December 30.

With a 6-3 run through the preconference schedule, the Hoosiers appeared to be an improved team but they still didn't have the look of a Big Ten title contender. That didn't change in the conference opener at Iowa. The Hoosiers played the Hawkeyes tough, but lost 84-73. After the Iowa game, IU had a five-game stretch of conference contests in which they played a mix of two road games against mediocre teams and three home games in Bloomington. The Hoosiers would win all five and catapult to the top of the Big Ten race. The first of those wins came against Minnesota, 83-68, on January 9, in Bloomington. Joyner led all scorers with 23 points. On January 14, IU barely clipped Ohio State 81-80 in Columbus, led by 22 points from Joyner and 19 from senior guard Erv Inniger.

After the semester break, IU notched a nonconference win over DePaul, 72-70, on January 30. The Hoosiers were powered by a 16-point, 10-rebound, four-block performance from center Bill DeHeer. Next, IU nabbed its second conference road win with an 82-81 come-from-behind victory at Minnesota on February 4. The Hoosiers did it with balanced scoring once again, as DeHeer scored 17 points and three other IU players each scored 16 points: Joyner, Inniger and senior Jack Johnson. IU kept the winning streak alive by returning to Bloomington and beating two straight Big Ten contenders. On February 6, Michigan State came to the IU Fieldhouse and grabbed a five-point halftime lead, but Indiana stormed back and won 82-77. Inniger had a game-high 24 points, but he was tossed out of the game on a controversial call in the second half when he collided with an MSU player. On February 11, six Hoosiers scored in double figures as IU toppled Wisconsin 93-81 to complete the five-game winning streak. Indiana was 5-1 and tied with Northwestern for the Big Ten lead.

Michigan State put an end to the winning streak on February 23, when the Spartans overpowered the Hoosiers 86-77. That put MSU, Indiana and Northwestern in a three-way tie for first place at 5-2. However, Indiana went to Northwestern on February 18, and knocked off the Wildcats 81-79. IU was led by an invaluable 20 points from guard Bill Russell, who filled in as a starter for the injured Inniger (the Hoosiers' third leading scorer). Back in Bloomington, the Hoosiers defeated Illinois 96-81 on February 20, but lost a 75-74 cliffhanger to Iowa in overtime on February 25.

Butch Joyner's clutch basket in the final minute delivered a 98-96 win over Michigan in Ann Arbor on February 27. That put Indiana one game ahead of Michigan State in the conference race with only three games remaining. Next, Indiana played at Illinois on February 20, and fell behind by 28 points halfway through the second half. The Hoosiers came roaring

Junior forward Butch Joyner averaged 18.5 PPG and 10.5 RPG as a junior to lead an upstart Hoosier squad to a surprising Big Ten championship. IU Archives

back but couldn't make up enough ground and lost 80-70 to fall into a first-place tie with MSU, with three other teams only a game behind.

Indiana's final two games were played in Bloomington against last-place Michigan and middle-of-the-pack Purdue. Against the Wolverines, IU trailed by four points at the half, came back and took the lead, and then stalled down the stretch to squeak by with a 96-90 win. That set up a season finale against Purdue, the hottest team in the league (having won five of their previous seven conference games). IU needed a victory to clinch a piece of the conference title, and the Boilermakers would have liked nothing better than to keep their archrival from winning the championship. It was a two-point game at the half, but the Hoosiers pulled away for a 95-82 victory. All five Indiana starters scored in double figures, led by 22 points from Joyner and 18 from Russell.

Michigan State tied Indiana for the conference title with a 10-4 conference record. In the case of a tie, the Big Ten policy at the time was for the team that had been to the NCAA tournament more recently to be eliminated from getting the bid. That meant that Indiana drew the NCAA bid and they ended up playing Virginia Tech in the Mideast Regional Semifinals on March 17, in Evanston, Illinois. The Hoosiers fell behind in the first half, took the lead with 11 minutes remaining in the game, but faltered down the stretch and fell to the Hokies 79-70. Indiana was doomed by shooting only 14-29 (48 percent) from the free throw line. The Hoosiers came back the next day and beat Tennessee 51-44 in the consolation game to close the season at 18-8.

INDIANA'S RANKING IN THE 1966-67 ASSOCIATED PRESS POLLS

PS	12/6	12/13	12/20	12/27	1/3	1/10	1/17	1/24	1/31	2/7	2/14	2/21	2/28	3/7
–	–	–	–	–	–	–	–	–	–	–	–	–	–	–

Despite the disappointing loss in the NCAA tournament, the Hoosiers put together an outstanding season by epitomizing the team concept. Butch Joyner, who earned all-conference honors and emerged as the Hoosiers' leader, said, "This has been the greatest year I've ever had. The guys have been great. We're all unselfish and we played together."

Coach Lou Watson agreed. He simply stated, "We won because everyone put the team ahead of himself, working together and getting the ball to the open man."

1967-68

OVERALL RECORD: 10-14

CONFERENCE RECORD: 4-10 (NINTH PLACE)

After a surprise run to capture the 1967 Big Ten title, the IU basketball squad returned its three marquee players—Butch Joyner, Vern Payne and Bill DeHeer—and was tabbed as the team to beat in the Big Ten for the 1967-68 season.

"If these boys play with the same unselfish team spirit of last year and blend together, we'll have a good club," said Coach Lou Watson. "One thing we won't be able to do this year is sneak up on anyone, since we won a year ago. It's also very possible we could be just as strong a team, or even stronger, and still not do as well in the league. This was a sophomore-junior league last year, and nearly everyone had good freshman teams. With one or two exceptions, everyone looks stronger."

Watson was right. The Big Ten was much stronger from top to bottom in 1967-68. But the Hoosiers weren't nearly as good as they had been the year before, and as a result, IU plummeted back to the bottom of the conference standings.

However, for the first three weeks of December, the Hoosiers looked like they were going to be a powerhouse as they piled up six consecutive victories to start the season. They opened with a ragged 71-65 win over Northern Illinois on December 2, in Bloomington. Vern Payne and Earl Schneider, a 6'9"

1967-68 TEAM ROSTER

Head coach: Lou Watson
Assistant coaches: Don Luft, Tom Bolyard

No.	Player	Hometown	Class	Position	Height
42	Rick Atkinson	Evansville, IN	So	G	6-3
22	Joe Cooke	Toledo, OH	So	G	6-3
31	Bill DeHeer	Maplewood, MO	Jr	C	6-9
40	John Isenbarger	Muncie, IN	So	G	6-3
33	Ken Johnson	Anderson, IN	So	C	6-6
34	Butch Joyner (Capt.)	New Castle, IN	Sr	F	6-4
24	Bobby Kent	Unionville, IN	So	G	5-8
45	Gary Leinberger	St. Louis, MO	Sr	F	6-7
43	John Muirhead	Danville, IL	Jr	C	6-7
25	Ken Newsome	Ohoskie, NC	Sr	F	6-5
20	Mike Niles	Warsaw, IN	So	G	6-4
32	Mike Noland	Indianapolis, IN	So	F	6-6
41	Gabe Oliverio	Annandale, VA	Jr	G	6-2
23	Vern Payne	Michigan City, IN	Sr	G	5-10
44	Earl Schneider	Evansville, IN	Jr	F	6-9
30	Rich Schrumpf	Galien, MI	Sr	C	6-9
35	Bill Stenberg	Rockford, IL	Jr	C	6-7

SEASON RESULTS 1961-62

Date	Court	Opponent	Result	Score
12/2/1967	H	Northern Illinois	W	71-65
12/4/1967	A	Missouri	W	78-69
12/9/1967	H	Ohio	W	89-63
12/11/1967	H	Kansas State	W	89-83
12/16/1967	A	North Carolina State	W	101-97
12/19/1967	N1	Notre Dame	W	96-91
12/28/1967	N2	Western Kentucky	L	91-110
12/29/1967	N2	Southern Methodist	L	84-91
1/2/1968	A	Detroit	L	93-99
1/6/1968	H	Minnesota	W	74-59
1/9/1968	A	Illinois	W	61-60
1/13/1968	H	Northwestern	L	81-86
1/16/1968	A	Purdue	L	60-89
1/29/1968	A	DePaul	L	78-79
2/3/1968	A	Minnesota	L	75-82
2/5/1968	H	Ohio State	L	77-78
2/10/1968	A	Wisconsin	L	83-95
2/17/1968	H	Michigan	W	98-92
2/20/1968	A	Michigan State	L	70-75
2/24/1968	H	Iowa	L	70-78
2/27/1968	A	Northwestern	L	66-73
3/2/1968	A	Ohio State	L	93-107
3/5/1968	H	Wisconsin	W	93-85
3/9/1968	H	Purdue	L	64-68

1 Fort Wayne, IN
2 Dallas, TX

1967-68 BIG TEN STANDINGS

	W	L	PCT
Ohio State	10	4	.714
Iowa	10	4	.714
Purdue	9	5	.643
Northwestern	8	6	.571
Wisconsin	7	7	.500
Michigan St.	6	8	.429
Illinois	6	8	.429
Michigan	6	8	.429
Indiana	4	10	.286
Minnesota	4	10	.286

The 1967-68 team. First row (left to right): Bobby Kent, Gabe Oliverio, Rick Atkinson, Vern Payne, Butch Joyner, Joe Cooke, Mike Niles; Second row: head coach Lou Watson, Bill Stenberg, Earl Schneider, Mike Noland, Ken Johnson, John Isenbarger; Third row: assistant coach Don Luft, Gary Leinberger, Rich Schrumpf, Bill DeHeer, John Muirhead, trainer Warren Ariail. IU Archives

junior forward, led IU with 19 points apiece. On December 4, IU went to Missouri and beat the Tigers 78-69, powered by 25 points from center Bill DeHeer. The following week, IU notched home wins over Ohio (89-63) and Kansas State (89-83). Team captain Butch Joyner missed both games because of a calf injury, but Earl Schneider led the Hoosiers by scoring 26 points in each of the two contests. Ninth-ranked IU then took to the road on December 16, when the team went to Raleigh, North Carolina, and grabbed a thrilling 101-97 overtime victory against the previously undefeated N.C. State Wolfpack. Six different IU players scored in double figures, led by sophomore Joe Cooke with 27 points.

The Hoosiers used another well-balanced scoring attack on December 19, to outpace Notre Dame 96-91. All five IU starters scored in double figures. It was the Hoosiers' sixth straight win and their fourth game in a row without Joyner, the team's leading scorer from the previous season. Indiana's first signs of trouble showed up on December 28-29, when IU went down to Dallas, Texas, and played in the All-Sports

Classic. Keyed-up Western Kentucky shocked No. 3 Indiana in the opener with a convincing 110-91 Hilltopper victory. To add insult to injury, SMU (which was 0-8 on the season) toppled the Hoosiers 91-84 in the consolation game. IU then returned to the Midwest for a final preconference tuneup against Detroit in the Motor City on January 2. Joyner returned for IU and scored 14 points, but the Hoosiers lost 99-93.

Indiana finished the preconference season with a 6-3 record, an identical mark to the one they posted during the preconference a year earlier. However, while the Hoosiers relied on an early five-game winning streak to push them into the position of conference contender in 1966-67, an early five-game losing streak dashed their hopes for a conference crown in 1967-68. The Hoosiers opened with two solid victories over Minnesota and Illinois. IU beat the Golden Gophers 74-59 in Bloomington on January 6, and defeated the Fighting Illini 61-60 in overtime in Champaign on January 9. The Hoosiers shot the ball poorly in both games, but their defense kept them in both contests. Unfortunately, the cold shooting continued, and Indiana lost their next six games, including five against conference opponents.

The first loss came in teeth-gnashing style to Northwestern on January 13, in Bloomington. The Hoosiers led 62-46 with 14:16 left in the game, but only made five field goals the rest of the game and lost 86-81. Then, on January 16, Indiana went to West Lafayette and got massacred by Purdue 89-60. Rick Mount led the Boilermakers with 33 points. Not a single Hoosier scored in double figures. After the semester break, Indiana went to Chicago and got beat by DePaul 79-78, as a huge second-half comeback from the Hoosiers came up just short. All five IU starters scored in double figures against the Blue Demons.

The Hoosiers dropped to 2-3 in Big Ten play with an 82-75 loss at Minnesota on February 3. Two nights later in Bloomington, IU led Ohio State for most of the game, but Buckeye reserve Dan Andreas drained a 15-footer at the buzzer to give OSU a 78-77 victory. On February 10, Indiana went up to Wisconsin and led the Badgers 49-44 at the half, but surrendered a 10-point second-half lead on the way to a 95-83 loss. Indiana finally stopped the bleeding with a 98-92 win over Michigan on February 17, in the IU Fieldhouse, as Joyner led the Hoosiers with 25 points, Payne added 23, and Schneider dropped in 21. Rudy Tomjanovich led the Wolverines with a game-high 30 points.

Despite the Michigan win, Indiana was 3-5 in conference play and out of the race for the title. On the court, the deflated Hoosiers didn't look like they had much to play for as they lost their next four games: 75-70 at Michigan State on February 20; 78-70 against Iowa on February 24 in Bloomington; 73-66 at Northwestern on February 27; and 107-93 at Ohio State on March 2. IU salvaged a little pride by beating Wisconsin 93-85 in Bloomington on March

5. Joyner had a game-high 27 points to go with eight rebounds, while DeHeer had 23 points and a game-high 15 rebounds. On the final day of the season, the once-mighty Hoosiers closed out a disappointing campaign by committing the unforgivable sin of losing to Purdue 68-64 in Bloomington. The Boilermakers stole the game with free throws in the final minutes. The loss dropped the Hoosiers to 4-10, which earned them a last-place tie with Minnesota in the Big Ten standings. After the game, a frustrated Watson said, "We played like we did all year. We had them beat, and then we gave the game back to them by our own mistakes."

While the 1966-67 team found ways to win close games, the 1967-68 squad seemed to find ways to lose them. Thus, after going from last place to first place from 1965-66 to 1966-67, the Hoosiers returned to the cellar in 1967-68. That was a bitter pill to swallow for a team that had once been ranked third in the nation after winning its first six games, and Coach Watson could find few answers to explain the team's precipitous free fall.

INDIANA'S RANKING IN THE 1967-68 ASSOCIATED PRESS POLLS

PS	12/5	12/12	12/19	12/26	1/2	1/9	1/16	1/23	1/30	2/6	2/13	2/20	2/27	3/5	3/12
—	—	9	5	3	—	—	—	—	—	—	—	—	—	—	—

1968-69

OVERALL RECORD: 9-15

CONFERENCE RECORD: 4-10 (TENTH PLACE)

The 1968-69 team. First row (left to right): Jeff Stockdale, Rick Atkinson, Larry Gipson, Kevin Bass, Gabe Oliverio, Joe Cooke; Second row: head coach Lou Watson, Bill Stenberg, Bill DeHeer, Mike Branaugh, Mike Szymanczyk, John Muirhead, assistant coach Jerry Oliver; Third row: manager Don Knapp, Mike Niles, Earl Schneider, Mike Noland, Ken Morgan, Ken Johnson, Ben Niles, assistant coach Tom Bolyard. IU Archives

After rising to No. 3 in the country in the pre-conference season and then falling to last place in the Big Ten in 1967-68, coach Lou Watson and the Hoosiers were looking for some redemption in the 1968-69 season. The team lost its top two players, Vern Payne and Butch Joyner, to graduation. That left senior center Bill DeHeer, a two-year starter, to steady the ship. Two juniors who had shown great promise as sophomores, Joe Cooke and Ken Johnson, were also expected to be important contributors. That also meant that a group of mostly sophomores and juniors had to step into new roles and provide stronger play than the team had gotten the season before.

"This will be a rebuilding year for us," said Coach Watson. "I'm looking for more staying power this year. We'd play well most of the time last year but would then make late mistakes which cost us games. I know our players want to bounce back with a winning year, and we have a group of men who will give us everything they have. But we're going to have to hustle, eliminate mistakes, and play well together in order to win."

The team showed plenty of hustle and determination, but teamwork was lacking at times—at both ends of the floor—and the Hoosiers' shooting percentage for the season ended up being atrocious. As a result, the Hoosiers struggled to another losing season.

On Tuesday, December 3, IU opened in Athens, Ohio, for the dedication game of the Ohio Bobcats' new stadium. In the second half, the Hoosiers showed great generosity to their hosts by surrendering a 13-

1968-69 TEAM ROSTER

Head coach: Lou Watson
Assistant coaches: Jerry Oliver, Tom Bolyard

No.	Player	Hometown	Class	Position	Height
42	Rick Atkinson	Evansville, IN	Jr	G	6-3
40	Kevin Bass	Morristown, IN	So	G	5-10
45	Mike Branaugh	Toledo, OH	Jr	C	6-8
22	Joe Cooke	Toledo, OH	Jr	G	6-3
31	Bill DeHeer (Capt.)	Maplewood, MO	Sr	C	6-9
23	Larry Gipson	Michigan City, IN	So	G	5-10
33	Ken Johnson	Anderson, IN	Jr	C	6-6
24	Ken Morgan	Indianapolis, IN	So	F	6-6
43	John Muirhead	Danville, IL	Sr	C	6-7
34	Ben Niles	Warsaw, IN	So	G	6-5
20	Mike Niles	Warsaw, IN	Jr	G	6-4
32	Mike Noland	Indianapolis, IN	Jr	F	6-6
41	Gabe Oliverio	Annandale, VA	Sr	G	6-2
44	Earl Schneider	Evansville, IN	Sr	F	6-9
35	Bill Stenberg	Rockford, IL	Sr	C	6-7
25	Jeff Stockdale	Lima, OH	So	F	6-4
54	Mike Szymanczyk	Lansing, IL	So	C	6-8

SEASON RESULTS 1968-69

Date	Court	Opponent	Result	Score
12/3/1968	A	Ohio	L	70-80
12/7/1968	H	Missouri	W	58-51
12/9/1968	A	Kansas State	L	83-87
12/14/1968	H	North Carolina State	W	77-62
12/16/1968	H	Loyola Chicago	W	88-83
12/21/1968	A	Notre Dame	L	94-104
12/27/1968	N1	Niagara	W	86-83
12/28/1968	N1	LaSalle	L	88-108
12/30/1968	N1	St. Joseph's (PA)	L	72-80
1/4/1969	H	Ohio State	L	82-90
1/7/1969	A	Michigan	L	87-89
1/11/1969	A	Iowa	L	72-91
1/14/1969	H	Northwestern	W	87-70
1/27/1969	H	DePaul	W	87-66
2/1/1969	H	Michigan State	W	79-76
2/4/1969	A	Wisconsin	W	65-63
2/8/1969	H	Minnesota	L	83-89
2/15/1969	A	Northwestern	L	88-91
2/18/1969	H	Purdue	L	95-96
2/22/1969	A	Minnesota	L	79-83
2/25/1969	H	Wisconsin	W	101-84
3/1/1969	H	Illinois	L	64-77
3/4/1969	A	Ohio State	L	86-108
3/8/1969	A	Purdue	L	76-120

1 Philadelphia, PA (The Palestra)

1968-69 BIG TEN STANDINGS

	W	L	PCT
Purdue	13	1	.929
Illinois	9	5	.643
Ohio State	9	5	.643
Michigan	7	7	.500
Northwestern	6	8	.429
Minnesota	6	8	.429
Michigan St.	6	8	.429
Iowa	5	9	.357
Wisconsin	5	9	.357
Indiana	4	10	.286

point halftime lead and giving away an 80-70 win. Then the IU squad returned to Bloomington and beat Missouri 58-51 on December 7. The Hoosiers only shot 30 percent from the field, but DeHeer had 17 points and 11 rebounds to lead IU to its first win. On December 9, at Kansas State, IU came back from 13 down at halftime to send the game into overtime, but lost to the Wildcats 87-83 in OT. Cooke had 19 points and 10 rebounds. The next week, IU crept back over the .500 mark with two wins in Bloomington: 77-62 over N.C. State on December 14, and 88-83 over Loyola Chicago on December 16.

On December 21, the Hoosiers went to South Bend to take on No. 7 Notre Dame. IU jumped out to a 51-49 lead at the half, but the Irish ran away with a 104-94 victory. Five Hoosiers scored in double figures, led by 31 points from Cooke. The loss put Indiana at 3-3. The IU squad closed out the preconference schedule by playing in the Quaker City Tournament in Philadelphia on December 27-30. In the first game, 5'10" superstar Calvin Murphy scored 47 points against the Hoosiers, but IU beat his Niagara Purple Eagles 86-83 on December 27. The next night, No. 17 LaSalle jumped out to a big lead in the first half and steamrolled Indiana 108-88. Then, St. Joseph's (Pennsylvania) came from behind and took an 80-72 win from the Hoosiers on December 30, to drop IU to 4-5 on the season.

Riding a two-game losing streak, things looked bleak for the Hoosiers heading into conference play, and their fortunes looked much worse when they dropped their first three Big Ten games. In the opener, Ohio State came into the IU Fieldhouse on January 4, and leapt out to a 54-36 halftime lead. The Hoosiers hustled their way back into the game in the second half, cutting the lead to a single point, but still lost 90-82. Then the Hoosiers went on the road and lost at Michigan (89-87 in OT) and Iowa (91-72).

The Iowa loss put Indiana at 4-8 overall and 0-3 in Big Ten play, and led to a closed-door meeting among the players the next day. In their next game, against No. 17 Northwestern in Bloomington on January 14, the Hoosiers came out aggressive and finally found the range on offense, shooting a season-high 49 percent from the field and won 87-70. Cooke dropped in 32 points and Johnson had 21. In a non-conference game on January 27, against DePaul, the Hoosiers dispatched the Blue Demons 87-66, as

Cooke led all scorers with 24. On February 1, Indiana grabbed its third straight home win by beating Michigan State 79-76, behind 24 points from Cooke and 23 from Johnson, whose eight-footer in the final minute sealed the game for IU. The suddenly resurgent Hoosiers then went on the road and stole a 65-63 win at Wisconsin on February 4. That evened IU's season record at 8-8 and conference record at 3-3.

However, the Hoosiers' poor shooting finally caught up with them again, as they lost their next four games: 89-83 against Minnesota in Bloomington on February 8; 91-88 at Northwestern on February 15; 96-95 against No. 9 Purdue in Bloomington on February 18; and 83-79 at Minnesota on February 22. The Indiana squad briefly plugged the dam on February 25, when they raced by Wisconsin 101-88 in Bloomington, led by 24 points and 13 rebounds from Johnson. But then the Hoosiers dropped their final three games of the season. They lost to No. 15 Illinois, 77-64, in the IU Fieldhouse on March 1; they got pummeled 108-86 by Ohio State on March 4, in Columbus; and Purdue's Rich Mount shot down IU with 40 points in a 120-76 Boilermaker massacre on March 8 in West Lafayette.

After improving to 8-8 and 3-3, IU lost seven of its final eight games and finished the season at 9-15 overall and 4-10 in the conference, which earned them an undisputed place in the Big Ten cellar. Coach Lou Watson chalked up the Hoosiers' struggles to a couple of key factors.

"[This] team recovered more rebounds than any other Big Ten team, took more shots than any other and was third in field goals—but last in shooting percentage. That, I believe, resulted from a lack of team play and forcing shots," Watson said. "We played well most of the time … but would then make late mistakes which cost us games. We lost four conference games by a total of ten points."

1969-70

OVERALL RECORD: 7-17

CONFERENCE RECORD: 3-11 (TENTH PLACE)

Despite having some respectable talent, the Hoosiers earned a second straight finish in the Big Ten cellar in the 1968-69 season. However, for the 1969-70 season, they returned their top two scorers in power forward Ken Johnson and shooting guard Joe Cooke (the No. 4 and No. 5 scorers in the Big Ten in 1968-69), and the team desperately wanted to return IU to the place of honor it was accustomed to holding in the Big Ten.

"These young men want to pick themselves up and get back into the thick of Big Ten play," said coach Lou Watson. "We feel as they do—that with a just a little more desire and determination they can become a fine ball club. I can sense this feeling in this squad, and I am sure it will bounce back in great shape."

Despite having two high scorers in Johnson and Cooke, one of the things the Hoosiers needed to improve the most was their shooting. As a team, they shot an abysmal 39 percent from the field in 1968-69. Watson attributed that primarily to selfishness and forcing up bad shots. On the flip side of the coin, the Hoosiers had led the Big Ten in rebounding and looked to be outstanding on the backboards once again, with Johnson leading the way. The other area that IU needed to improve was its defense. The previous season, the Hoosiers simply couldn't get defense

INDIANA'S RANKING IN THE 1968-69 ASSOCIATED PRESS POLLS

PS	12/3	12/10	12/17	12/24	12/31	1/7	1/14	1/21	1/28	2/4	2/11	2/18	2/25	3/4
–	–	–	–	–	–	–	–	–	–	–	–	–	–	–

The 1969-70 team. First row (left to right): head coach Lou Watson, Ken Johnson, Jeff Stocksdale, Rick Atkinson, Mike Niles, Joe Cooke, assistant coach Jerry Oliver; Second row: assistant coach Tom Bolyard, Joby Wright, Mike Branaugh, Mike Szymanczyk, Ken Morgan, Ben Niles; Third row: Tom Boone, Jim Harris, Rick Ford, Larry Gipson, John Hickey. IU Archives

stops when they needed them in close games, and they surrendered far too many points to be able to beat good teams.

Perhaps the biggest challenge that Indiana faced in the 1969-70 season was the just-wait-until-next-year mentality, because Indiana had put together one of the most distinguished recruiting classes in the nation in 1969. It included 6'8" man-child George McGinnis, one of the best prep players in the country and one of the best in Indiana high school history, along with 6'8" center Steve Downing, 6'5" guard/forward John Ritter, flashy point guard Bootsie White and several others. However, those players wouldn't join the varsity until 1970-71. "We are not looking ahead to 1971 with the fine freshman group we now have. We intend to make the move this year," said Watson.

Unfortunately, as the 1969-70 season unfolded and IU's shooting woes continued (and the defense was worse than ever), the running joke on the Indiana campus was that IU's varsity squad was the third best team on campus, behind the Indiana freshman team led by Ritter and an intramural team led by McGinnis and Downing (who were ineligible to compete on the freshman squad while they got their academics in order).

Just before the season started for the IU varsity, Coach Watson went down with a back ailment. Assistant coach Jerry Oliver took over for what was supposed to be a few games until Watson returned. However, Watson ended up needing back surgery and missed the rest of the season, and Oliver functioned as the interim coach.

The Hoosier varsity squad looked promising in winning three of its first four games. IU opened with an 89-81 win over Northern Illinois on December 1, in Bloomington. Then the Hoosiers went on the road and split two games, winning 100-95 at Loyola

Chicago, but losing 109-96 at Missouri. On December 8, Indiana beat Kansas State 102-95 back in Bloomington. In those four games, Cooke and Johnson picked up right where they left off the previous season by scoring at will. However, the Hoosiers also got valuable contributions from two newcomers. Sophomore center Joby Wright and JUCO transfer Jim "Bubbles" Harris both scored in double figures in all four contests.

After jumping out to a 3-1 start, the Hoosiers then dropped three straight games, all against ranked opponents. Against No. 1 Kentucky in Lexington on December 13, IU fell 109-92. No. 19 Ohio University came to Bloomington on December 15, and pulled out an 89-83 win with a strong second-half comeback that kept the Bobcats' record unblemished. No. 6 Notre Dame then came to town on December 20, and used a late surge in the final minutes to steal an 89-88 win from the Hoosiers. Indiana closed out the preconference season by playing in the Bruin Classic on December 27-29, in Los Angeles. The Hoosiers split a pair of games, losing to Princeton 82-76, but beating Georgia Tech 87-65. That put Indiana at 4-5 heading into Big Ten play.

Conference play started ominously as Michigan State's Ron Gutkowski scored on a rebound basket at the buzzer to give the Spartans an 85-84 win over the Hoosiers in a half-filled IU Fieldhouse on January 3. The IU squad then went on the road and suffered consecutive losses to Illinois (94-74) and Minnesota (77-65) before a two-week lull in the season for the semester break. When the Hoosiers returned to action with a nonconference game at DePaul on January 27, they did it without leading scorer Joe Cooke, who was declared academically ineligible for the second semester. IU lost to the Blue Demons 75-70, despite a game-high 33 points from Bubbles Harris.

Indiana traveled to Iowa City to take on No. 20 Iowa, the Big Ten leader at 4-0, on January 31. The Hoosiers led 45-44 at the half, but Iowa was too much down the stretch and prevailed 100-93. On February 3, Indiana finally scratched out a conference win with an 80-78 triumph over Northwestern, a team the Hoosiers were battling for last place. Five IU players scored in double figures, led by senior guard Rick Atkinson with 17. After that brief ray of sunshine, things got bleak again as IU went on a three-game losing stint. The Hoosiers suffered defeats to

1969-70 TEAM ROSTER

Head coaches: Lou Watson, Jerry Oliver (interim)
Assistant coach: Tom Bolyard

No.	Player	Hometown	Class	Position	Height
42	Rick Atkinson (Capt.)	Evansville, IN	Sr	G	6-3
40	Tom Boone	Louisville, KY	So	G	5-10
45	Mike Branaugh	Toledo, OH	Sr	C	6-8
22	Joe Cooke	Toledo, OH	Sr	G	6-3
43	Rick Ford	Cloverdale, IN	So	F	6-5
23	Larry Gipson	Michigan City, IN	Jr	G	5-10
30	Jim Harris	Lorain, OH	Jr	G	6-0
21	John Hickey	Indianapolis, IN	So	G	5-10
33	Ken Johnson	Anderson, IN	Sr	C	6-6
34	Ben Niles	Warsaw, IN	Jr	G	6-5
20	Mike Niles	Warsaw, IN	Sr	G	6-4
24	Ken Morgan	Indianapolis, IN	Jr	F	6-6
25	Jeff Stocksdale	Lima, OH	Jr	F	6-4
54	Mike Szymanczyk	Lansing, IL	Jr	C	6-8
44	Joby Wright	Savannaugh, GA	So	C	6-8

SEASON RESULTS 1969-70

Date	Court	Opponent	Result	Score
12/1/1969	H	Northern Illinois	W	89-81
12/3/1969	A	Loyola Chicago	W	100-95
12/6/1969	A	Missouri	L	96-109
12/8/1969	H	Kansas State	W	102-95
12/13/1969	A	Kentucky	L	92-109
12/15/1969	H	Ohio	L	83-89
12/20/1969	H	Notre Dame	L	88-89
12/27/1969	N1	Princeton	L	76-82
12/29/1969	N1	Georgia Tech	W	87-65
1/3/1970	H	Michigan State	L	84-85
1/6/1970	A	Illinois	L	74-94
1/10/1970	A	Minnesota	L	65-77
1/27/1970	A	DePaul	L	70-75
1/31/1970	A	Iowa	L	93-100
2/3/1970	H	Northwestern	W	80-78
2/7/1970	H	Iowa	L	89-104
2/10/1970	A	Purdue	L	80-98
2/14/1970	H	Ohio State	L	83-100
2/17/1970	H	Wisconsin	W	89-77
2/21/1970	A	Michigan State	L	66-78
2/24/1970	H	Michigan	W	102-93
2/28/1970	A	Northwestern	L	66-75
3/3/1970	H	Illinois	L	75-85
3/7/1970	A	Michigan	L	99-108

1 Los Angeles

1969-70 BIG TEN STANDINGS

	W	L	PCT
Iowa	14	0	1.000
Purdue	11	3	.786
Ohio State	8	6	.571
Illinois	8	6	.571
Minnesota	7	7	.500
Michigan	5	9	.357
Wisconsin	5	9	.357
Michigan St.	5	9	.357
Northwestern	4	10	.286
Indiana	3	11	.214

Iowa (104-89 in Bloomington), Purdue (98-80 in West Lafayette), and Ohio State (100-83 in Bloomington). Indiana stood at 1-7 in conference play and 5-12 overall.

Still, the Hoosiers gathered their pride and won two of their next three games. They beat Wisconsin 89-77 on February 17, in Bloomington, then lost to Michigan State 78-66 in East Lansing on February 21, and then defeated Michigan 102-93 on February 24. Against the Badgers, Harris scored a game-high 24 points and Wright had 23 points and 16 rebounds. Against the Wolverines, Wright led IU with 24 points, while Harris and Johnson scored 22 apiece. IU then secured lone ownership of the conference cellar by losing its final three games—75-66 at Northwestern, 85-75 against Illinois in Bloomington, and 108-99 at Michigan.

The patience of Hoosier fans and the IU administration had worn thin as Indiana finished last in the conference for the third straight season and for the fourth time in five years. What made those disappointing finishes even more distasteful was that during the 1968-69 and 1969-70 seasons, the Hoosiers appeared to have the talent necessary to compete for the Big Ten title. With the stellar class of 1969 set to join the varsity as sophomores for the 1970-71 season, Indiana would have one of the most talented groups of players in the country, and the pressure was on to return IU basketball to its traditional role as a championship contender.

1970-71

OVERALL RECORD: 17-7
CONFERENCE RECORD: 9-5 (FOURTH PLACE)
INDIVIDUAL HONORS:
GEORGE MCGINNIS—ALL-AMERICA,
ALL-BIG TEN (FIRST TEAM)
JOHN RITTER—ACADEMIC ALL-BIG TEN

For the third straight season, Indiana had floundered in cellar of the Big Ten in 1969-70. Nevertheless, there were some prognosticators sho made the Hoosiers the favorite to win the conference during the 1970-71 campaign. While the IU squad returned two potent scorers in junior center Joby Wright and senior guard Jim "Bubbles" Harris, the main reason for the optimism surrounding the Hoosiers' prospects was because of the arrival of 6'8" sophomore wunderkind George McGinnis. McGinnis was being tabbed as a potential All-American before he had even played a collegiate game, and for good reason. The summer before his sophomore year, he had led the U.S. amateur team (which was full of college stars) in scoring and rebounding during a European tour that included the World University Games in Italy. In high school, he won two state championships and broke the Indiana high school career scoring record set by the legendary Oscar Robertson.

Entering the season, McGinnis was almost immediately penciled into the IU starting lineup, and it was expected that other sophomores would join him. His sophomore class included prep stars such as powerful 6'8" center Steve Downing (a high school

INDIANA'S RANKING IN THE 1969-70 ASSOCIATED PRESS POLLS

PS	12/9	12/16	12/23	12/30	1/6	1/13	1/20	1/27	2/3	2/10	2/17	2/24	3/3	3/10
—	—	—	—	—	—	—	—	—	—	—	—	—	—	—

The 1970-71 team. First row (left to right): Steve Downing, George McGinnis, Joby Wright, Jerry Memering, Ken Morgan; Second row: assistant coach Lou Watson, Jeff Stocksdale, Ed Daniels, John Ritter, Ben Niles, Rick Ford, assistant coach Tom Bolyard; Third row: assistant coach Jerry Oliver, Larry Gipson, Kim Pemberton, Frank Wilson, Jim Harris, Bootsie White, manager Bob Shelby. IU Archives

teammate of McGinnis), 6'4" guard Ed Daniels, 6'5" guard/forward John Ritter, and 5'10" sparkplug Bootsie White.

"We will be a young ball club with very good talent," said Coach Lou Watson. "This group of athletes has more ability than any other group I've had since I've been head coach at Indiana. It is up to [assistant coach] Jerry Oliver and me to put this talent together and mold it into a winning combination… The squad has an excellent attitude. The players are highly aware of Indiana's poor record over the last three seasons, and they are determined to win and bring Indiana basketball back to the prestige and recognition it normally commands."

In the season opener on Tuesday, December 1, in Bloomington, the Hoosiers easily rolled by Eastern Michigan 99-82 in front of a capacity crowd that eagerly wanted to see its new sophomore stars. McGinnis didn't disappoint as he scored a game-high 26 points and collected 11 rebounds. However,

Watson wasn't completely impressed. "George can play much better," Watson remarked after the game. "He made way too many errors and did not rebound like he should."

On December 5, the Hoosiers went to Manhattan, Kansas, and snapped Kansas State's 17-game home winning streak with a 75-72 win over the Wildcats. Early in the second half, McGinnis scored 7 straight points to give IU a 49-40 lead, and IU never trailed again. McGinnis finished with 26 points and 10 rebounds, even though he had to sit out a long stretch of the second half because of foul trouble. No. 3 Kentucky came to Bloomington on December 12, and the Hoosiers looked as if they had pulled the upset when John Ritter swished a 55-foot desperation shot at the buzzer of regulation and appeared to give IU a thrilling 82-80 victory. Unfortunately, just before Ritter released his shot, McGinnis called timeout so that IU could set up a play. The referee awarded the timeout, waved off the shot, and Ritter missed

1970-71 TEAM ROSTER

Head coach: Lou Watson
Assistant coaches: Jerry Oliver, Tom Bolyard

No.	Player	Hometown	Class	Position	Height
55	Ed Daniels	Savannaugh, GA	So	G	6-4
32	Steve Downing	Indianapolis, IN	So	C	6-8
43	Rick Ford	Cloverdale, IN	Jr	F	6-5
23	Larry Gipson	Michigan City, IN	Sr	G	5-10
30	Jim Harris (Capt.)	Lorain, OH	Sr	G	6-0
35	George McGinnis	Indianapolis, IN	So	F	6-8
33	Jerry Memering	Vincennes, IN	So	F	6-7
24	Ken Morgan	Indianapolis, IN	Sr	F	6-6
24	Kim Pemberton	Osgood, IN	So	G	6-4
42	John Ritter	Goshen, IN	So	F	6-5
25	Jeff Stocksdale	Lima, OH	Sr	F	6-4
22	Bootsie White	Hammond, IN	So	G	5-8
20	Frank Wilson	Bluffton, IN	So	G	6-3
44	Joby Wright	Savannaugh, GA	Jr	C	6-8

SEASON RESULTS 1970-71

Date	Court	Opponent	Result	Score
12/1/1970	H	Eastern Michigan	W	99-82
12/5/1970	A	Kansas State	W	75-72
12/8/1970	H	Australian All-Stars (Exhib.)	W	80-72
12/12/1970	H	Kentucky	L	93-95
12/15/1970	A	Notre Dame	W	106-103
12/18/1970	H	Ohio	W	87-88
12/22/1970	H	Butler	W	111-94
12/26/1970	N1	Washington State	L	80-83
12/29/1970	N1	San Jose State	W	86-76
12/30/1970	N1	Ohio State	W	85-77
1/9/1971	A	Northwestern	W	101-90
1/12/1971	H	Minnesota	W	99-73
1/16/1971	A	Michigan	L	81-92
2/1/1971	H	Northern Illinois	W	113-112
2/6/1971	H	Purdue	L	81-85
2/9/1971	A	Michigan State	W	71-70
2/13/1971	A	Iowa	W	86-84
2/16/1971	H	Michigan State	W	90-76
2/20/1971	A	Illinois	W	88-86
2/23/1971	H	Michigan	W	88-79
2/27/1971	H	Northwestern	W	97-74
3/2/1971	A	Wisconsin	L	87-94
3/6/1971	H	Iowa	W	104-88
3/9/1971	H	Ohio State	L	75-91
3/13/1971	H	Illinois	L	87-103

1 Portland, OR

1970-71 BIG TEN STANDINGS

	W	L	PCT
Ohio State	13	1	.929
Michigan	12	2	.857
Purdue	11	3	.786
Indiana	9	5	.643
Illinois	5	9	.357
Minnesota	5	9	.357
Michigan St.	4	10	.286
Iowa	4	10	.286
Wisconsin	4	10	.286
Northwestern	3	11	.214

a second chance at the game-winner. Kentucky won 95-93 in overtime. McGinnis scored 38 points and grabbed 20 rebounds, although he shot only 13 of 31 from the field.

After the Kentucky loss, the Hoosiers rattled off three straight victories over No. 7 Notre Dame (106-103), Ohio (88-87), and Butler (111-94). In all three contests, the one-two punch of bruisers George McGinnis and Joby Wright simply overwhelmed opponents. Next, Indiana went to Portland, Oregon, to play in the Far West Classic on December 26-30. IU lost its opener to Washington State 83-80. After trailing by 23 points at the half, Bubbles Harris led a furious IU comeback that came up just short. In the second round, Indiana rolled by San Jose State 86-76, led by a sizzling 41 points from McGinnis. Then the Hoosiers claimed fourth place (out of eight teams) in the tourney by knocking off Big Ten rival Ohio State 85-77.

With a preconference record of 7-2, IU remained one of the Big Ten favorites as the team prepared to begin league play on January 9, at Northwestern. The Hoosiers wrestled a 101-90 win away from the Wildcats, as McGinnis scored 38 points and pulled down 23 rebounds. Next, the Hoosiers easily whipped Minnesota 99-73 in Bloomington on January 12. But then they went up to Ann Arbor on January 16, and got beat 92-81 by the Michigan Wolverines, one of their chief rivals for the conference crown. That dropped the Hoosiers to 2-1 conference play as IU took its annual break for semester exams.

Following the semester break, Indiana scrambled by Northern Illinois 113-112 as five Hoosiers scored in double figures, led by 45 points and 20 rebounds from McGinnis. On February 6, conference play resumed when Purdue came to Bloomington and used a deliberate attack to completely control the game and pull out an 85-81 win over the Hoosiers. After falling back to 2-2 in the Big Ten, the IU squad pulled it together and grabbed two important road wins over Michigan State (71-70) and Iowa (86-84). Then the Hoosiers returned home and battered Michigan State 90-76 on February 16, to improve to 5-2 in league p;ay. Against the Spartans, McGinnis topped all scorers with 37 points and thrilled the Bloomington crowd with several nifty passes.

On February 20, IU renewed its road magic by knocking off Illinois 88-86 in Champaign. Next, IU pulled off its biggest win of the season by toppling

No. 12 Michigan 88-79 in Bloomington on February 23. The loss was the first of the Big Ten season for the Wolverines, who fell to 8-1, while the Hoosiers improved to 7-2. McGinnis led the way with 33 points, while Downing had 28 points, 17 rebounds, and 10 blocked shots—the first ever "triple-double" in the IU record books (and still the only one).

On February 27, Indiana grabbed its sixth straight win by crushing Northwestern 97-74. At 8-2, the IU squad was tied for second place in the Big Ten with Michigan (which lost to league-leader Ohio State the same night IU beat Northwestern). The surging Hoosiers looked well-positioned for a run at the title, since three of their final four games were going to be played in Bloomington, and their one road game was against bottom-dweller Wisconsin. Instead, Indiana's season quickly unraveled and the team imploded.

The first disaster struck on March 2, in Madison, Wisconsin. IU led the Wisconsin Badgers 71-65 with 5:07 remaining, but the Hoosiers went scoreless for the rest of the game (including three missed free throws), and Wisconsin tied the contest and sent it to overtime. After two overtimes, the Badgers prevailed 94-87. The Hoosiers fell to 8-3 and were all but eliminated from the conference race since Ohio State still had only one loss with just three games remaining. IU returned to Bloomington and hosted Iowa on Saturday, March 6. The Hoosiers used a big second-half surge to beat Iowa 104-88, but Ohio State beat Northwestern the same night and officially eliminated IU from the race. During the game, IU fans showed their disappointment and frustration with the team by displaying anti-Watson signs that said things such as "Lose Lou, We'll Win 'Em All" and "Watch Lou Beat IU", as reported by the *Indianapolis Star* the next day.

Following the Iowa game, several Indiana players met with IU professor Dr. John Brown to air some dirty laundry. They leveled a number of nasty charges against

Sophomore wunderkind George McGinnis gets ready to take his defender off the dribble. The 6'8" forward averaged 29.9 PPG and 14.9 RPG to lead the Big Ten during the 1970-71 season. All-Big Ten and All-America honors were awarded to Big George, and his scoring average remains the single-season IU record. IU Archives

Watson, including not teaching them enough about basketball, having a lack of team discipline, and showing favoritism toward John Ritter and George McGinnis. Then, on March 9, No. 12 Ohio State came to Bloomington and clinched the Big Ten title on IU's home floor by beating the Hoosiers 91-75. After the game, Dr. Brown approached the IU staff about the charges that some of the players had made. The next day, a meeting was convened with athletic director Bill Orwig, IU president John Ryan, Coach Watson, and the Indiana players. At the meeting, Watson, who had already been considering retirement and was deeply hurt by the diatribes of the fans and the machinations of his players, resigned. The resignation was effective immedi-

INDIANA'S RANKING IN THE 1970-71 ASSOCIATED PRESS POLLS

PS	12/8	12/15	12/22	12/29	1/5	1/12	1/19	1/26	2/2	2/9	2/16	2/23	3/2	3/9	3/16
16	11	13	11	14	12	11	18	—	—	—	—	—	18	—	—

ately and was done "for the best interest of the team, the university, and my family," said Watson. "I am proud of my 22 years as a player and a coach," he said. "I will do all in my power to help my successor and wish him and each member of the squad every success."

The Hoosiers still had one more game to play that Saturday. Assistant coach Jerry Oliver coached the final contest, but the IU squad looked dazed and confused and fell 103-87 to Illinois in the IU Fieldhouse. McGinnis scored a season-low 17 points and fouled out of the game in the middle of the second half. The same Hoosier team that had been on a six-game tear just two weeks earlier and looked destined for an NCAA or NIT berth had completely disintegrated and plummeted to a 17-7 overall record and a fourth-place finish in the Big Ten with a 9-5 mark. There were no invitations for the postseason.

Despite the winning record, the bitter conclusion to the 1970-71 season was one of the darkest and most infamous hours in the long history of Indiana basketball. Fortunately, a ray of light was about to shine in the form of an obscure 31-year-old disciplinarian who was about to be handed the reins to one of the most storied programs in college basketball.

SEASON STATISTICS
1965-66 TO 1970-71

1965-66

Team Statistics	G	FG/A	PCT	FT/A	PCT	R	PTS	AVG
Indiana	24	717-1725	.416	422-559	.755	43.5	1856	77.3
Opponents	24	725-1724	.421	498-680	.732	51.1	1948	81.2
Player Statistics	G	FG/A	PCT	FT/A	PCT	R	PTS	AVG
Walker	23	157-336	.467	66-82	.805	6.6	380	16.5
Payne	24	139-328	.424	62-79	.785	2.8	340	14.2
Joyner	24	114-294	.388	70-101	.693	7.9	298	12.4
Grieger	22	87-182	.478	67-82	.817	4.5	241	11.0
Johnson	24	81-205	.395	46-65	.708	6.5	208	8.7
Russell	22	48-126	.381	40-51	.784	2.1	136	6.2
Schrumpf	17	28-60	.467	31-38	.816	3.4	87	5.1
Inniger	22	33-99	.333	21-29	.724	1.8	87	4.0
Leinberger	9	9-19	.474	3-9	.333	3.3	21	2.3
Everett	16	15-57	.263	6-14	.429	3.4	36	2.3
Pfaff	9	4-12	.333	6-7	.857	0.3	14	1.6
Turpen	12	2-7	.286	4-4	1.00	0.4	8	0.7
Newsome	2	0-0	.000	0-0	.000	0.5	0	0.0

1966-67

Team Statistics	G	FG/A	PCT	FT/A	PCT	R	PTS	AVG
Indiana	26	846-1975	.428	431-647	.666	51.4	2123	81.7
Opponents	26	743-1878	.396	525-773	.679	50.3	2011	77.3
Player Statistics	G	FG/A	PCT	FT/A	PCT	R	PTS	AVG
Joyner	26	192-383	.501	97-140	.693	10.5	481	18.5
Payne	26	160-393	.407	87-132	.659	2.5	407	15.7
Inniger	17	102-198	.515	26-33	.788	5.1	230	13.5
DeHeer	26	96-242	.397	44-90	.489	10.0	236	9.1
Johnson	26	90-223	.404	53-62	.855	6.3	233	9.0
Russell	26	87-204	.426	56-84	.667	3.5	230	8.9
Schneider	24	50-130	.385	27-44	.614	3.6	127	5.3
Stenberg	23	34-99	.343	23-33	.697	3.7	91	4.0
Pfaff	17	22-52	.423	10-16	.625	0.6	54	3.2
Leinberger	1	0-0	.000	2-2	1.00	0.0	2	2.0
Schrumpf	14	10-22	.455	2-3	.667	1.8	22	1.6
Turpen	9	2-8	.250	4-7	.571	0.6	8	0.9
Oliverio	6	1-11	.091	0-1	.000	0.7	2	0.3
Cordy	4	0-4	.000	0-0	.000	0.5	0	0.0
Houlihan	2	0-2	.000	0-0	.000	0.5	0	0.0
Muirhead	2	0-4	.000	0-0	.000	2.5	0	0.0

1967-68

Team Statistics	G	FG/A	PCT	FT/A	PCT	R	PTS	AVG
Indiana	24	753-1860	.405	429-629	.682	50.8	1935	80.6
Opponents	24	728-1728	.421	518-764	.678	51.3	1974	82.3
Player Statistics	G	FG/A	PCT	FT/A	PCT	R	PTS	AVG
Payne	24	136-354	.384	82-111	.739	2.3	354	14.8
Joyner	18	102-241	.423	47-83	.566	8.3	251	13.9
Schneider	24	119-288	.413	90-117	.769	6.2	328	13.7
DeHeer	24	118-234	.504	78-124	.629	10.4	314	13.1
Cooke	24	127-319	.398	54-71	.761	6.0	308	12.8
Noland	20	53-130	.408	15-22	.682	4.2	121	6.1
Johnson	22	43-136	.316	44-66	.667	6.5	130	5.9
Atkinson	22	23-60	.383	10-16	.625	1.4	56	2.6
Niles	12	14-36	.389	0-3	.000	0.9	28	2.3
Stenberg	18	16-41	.390	8-11	.727	1.4	40	2.2
Isenbarger	3	1-6	.167	0-1	.000	0.3	2	0.7
Oliverio	9	1-5	.200	0-1	.000	0.3	2	0.2
Shrumpf	6	0-8	.000	1-3	.333	1.2	1	0.2
Kent	1	0-2	.000	0-0	.000	0.0	0	0.0

1968-69

Team Statistics	G	FG/A	PCT	FT/A	PCT	R	PTS	AVG
Indiana	24	761-1947	.391	425-648	.656	56.4	1947	81.1
Opponents	24	755-1719	.439	521-733	.711	49.0	2031	84.6

Player Statistics	G	FG/A	PCT	FT/A	PCT	R	PTS	AVG
Cooke	24	213-511	.417	97-128	.758	7.7	523	21.8
Johnson	24	154-346	.445	129-187	.690	12.2	137	18.2
DeHeer	22	104-255	.408	65-119	.546	9.0	273	12.4
Noland	22	78-218	.358	35-52	.673	5.4	191	8.7
Gipson	24	57-159	.358	27-45	.600	2.9	141	5.9
Schneider	22	51-134	.381	16-24	.667	3.3	118	5.4
Branaugh	20	34-76	.447	27-45	.600	3.6	95	4.8
Stocksdale	22	26-97	.268	11-16	.688	2.3	63	2.9
Morgan	12	11-29	.379	2-5	.400	1.5	24	2.0
B. Niles	16	13-33	.394	4-9	.444	1.6	30	1.9
Atkinson	19	10-50	.200	11-17	.647	1.3	31	1.6
M. Niles	12	6-27	.222	1-1	1.00	0.8	13	1.1
Stenberg	7	4-10	.400	0-0	.000	0.1	8	1.1
Bass	3	0-1	.000	0-0	.000	0.0	0	0.0
Muirhead	2	0-1	.000	0-0	.000	0.0	0	0.0

1970-71

Team Statistics	G	FG/A	PCT	FT/A	PCT	R	A	TP	AVG
Indiana	24	889-1924	.462	402-625	.643	54.5	16.9	2180	90.8
Opponents	24	820-1749	.469	427-591	.723	42.7		2067	86.1

Player Statistics	G	FG/A	PCT	FT/A	PCT	R	A	TP	AVG
McGinnis	24	283-615	.460	153-249	.614	14.7	2.8	719	29.9
Wright	24	189-396	.477	44-77	.571	8.6	1.3	422	17.6
Harris	24	116-248	.468	58-76	.763	4.0	3.0	290	12.1
Downing	23	102-202	.505	16-43	.372	9.0	1.1	220	9.6
Ritter	24	60-129	.465	44-54	.815	3.7	2.8	164	6.8
Ford	21	49-103	.476	38-48	.792	3.4	1.2	136	6.5
Daniels	24	55-125	.440	19-35	.543	1.3	2.9	129	5.4
Wilson	22	27-63	.429	14-19	.737	1.3	1.5	68	3.1
White	13	4-19	.211	11-16	.688	0.4	1.2	19	1.5
Memering	9	2-10	.200	2-3	.667	1.2	0.0	6	0.7
Pemberton	6	2-5	.400	0-0	.000	0.7	1.2	4	0.7
Stocksdale	5	0-3	.000	2-4	.500	0.4	0.2	2	0.4
Morgan	3	0-2	.000	1-1	1.00	1.3	0.0	1	0.3
Gipson	4	0-4	.000	0-0	.000	0.5	0.0	0	0.0

1969-70

Team Statistics	G	FG/A	PCT	FT/A	PCT	R	PTS	AVG
Indiana	24	799-1833	.436	430-614	.700	46.0	2028	84.5
Opponents	24	841-1613	.521	430-614	.708	43.4	2141	89.2

Player Statistics	G	FG/A	PCT	FT/A	PCT	R	PTS	AVG
Cooke	12	109-227	.480	50-65	.769	6.6	268	22.3
Harris	24	176-394	.447	82-107	.766	4.8	434	18.1
Johnson	24	138-304	.454	76-122	.623	10.5	352	14.7
Wright	24	148-314	.471	56-107	.523	8.4	352	14.7
Ford	20	50-117	.427	68-77	.883	4.2	168	8.4
Atkinson	24	61-158	.386	34-40	.850	1.9	156	6.5
Gipson	24	48-121	.397	27-39	.692	1.9	123	5.1
M. Niles	18	24-64	.375	11-12	.917	1.6	59	3.3
Branaugh	7	7-22	.318	9-16	.563	3.6	23	3.3
Stocksdale	16	19-53	.358	9-15	.600	1.9	47	2.9
Morgan	16	13-31	.419	5-9	.556	1.5	31	1.9
B. Niles	9	6-17	.353	3-5	.600	1.2	15	1.7
Boone	5	0-4	.000	0-0	.000	0.0	0	0.0

1971-72

OVERALL RECORD: 17-8

CONFERENCE RECORD: 9-5 (THIRD PLACE)

TEAM HONORS:

OLD DOMINION INVITATIONAL CHAMPION

INDIVIDUAL HONORS:

JOBY WRIGHT—ALL-BIG TEN (FIRST TEAM)

JOHN RITTER—ACADEMIC ALL-BIG TEN

FRANK WILSON—ACADEMIC ALL-BIG TEN

The 1971-72 Team. First row (left to right): Bootsie White, Steve Heiniger, Dave Shepherd, Frank Wilson; Second row: Jerry Memering, Steve Downing, Joby Wright, John Ritter, Kim Pemberton, Rick Ford; Third row: assistant coach Dave Bliss, assistant coach Bob Weltlich, head coach Bob Knight, graduate assistant Frank Radovich, assistant coach John Hulls, graduate assistant Charley Harrison, graduate assistant Chuck Williams, [unknown]. IU Archives

When coach Bob Knight arrived in Bloomington, he brought a completely different offensive and defensive system than the full-court pressing, fast-breaking style that had been Indiana's trademark for three decades. While the IU administration chose to confront the dissen- sion that ruined the promising 1970-71 season by replacing Lou Watson with a strong disciplinarian (and it would have been difficult to find a coach who rwas more disciplined than Knight), the IU fans were very skeptical about Knight's reputation for running a deliberate offense and for focusing heavily on an exclusive man-to-man defense that typically resulted in low-scoring games.

Knight was keenly aware of the prevailing skepticism. Before the season started, he commented, "Our emphasis on defense does not mean that we won't fast break. We'll run when the opportunity presents itself. In fact, the better the defense, the more opportunity there is for the fast break. In other words, we're going to try to control the game—the more control you have, the better chance you have of winning."

While the Hoosiers weren't as flush with basketball talent as they had been the year before, Knight still had a decent roster to work with for the 1971-72 season. George McGinnis had bolted for the ABA, Ed Daniels transferred to Marquette and Bubbles Harris had graduated. However, the IU squad still had a pair of 6'8" big men, Joby Wright and Steve Downing, to handle the interior, and John Ritter, a solid scorer on the wing. Guards Bootsie White and Frank Wilson and forward Rick Ford were also experienced players who had shown some flashes of good play in previous seasons. The Hoosiers were far from being the Big Ten favorite, but they weren't expected to be a doormat either.

That season also marked the long-awaited opening of Indiana's new basketball palace, Assembly Hall. IU opened the season with a game in its new home on Wednesday, December 1, against Ball State. Powered by the interior play of Downing and Wright and clutch free throws from Ritter down the stretch, Indiana prevailed 84-77, in front of a wary crowd of 14,853 (Assembly Hall seated 16,666 that first season). Downing pulled down 26 rebounds, an Assembly Hall record that still has never been surpassed.

Three nights later, the Hoosiers beat Miami of Ohio, the defending MAC champs, 65-50 in Bloomington, but suffered a tough break when Downing sprained his knee in the second half. No. 14 Kansas, which had been to the Final Four in 1971, was the next visitor to Assembly Hall on December 6. Indiana played a sloppy game, with 27 turnovers, but still beat Kansas 59-56 in front of a home crowd of 11,736. Downing played through his knee injury and scored a game-high 22 points.

The Hoosiers were 3-0, but on December 11, Knight did more to endear himself to IU fans than those first three victories combined. That day, he took

1971-72 ROSTER

Head coach: Bob Knight
Assistant coaches: Dave Bliss, John Hulls, Bob Weltlich

No.	Player	Hometown	Class	Position	Height
32	Steve Downing	Indianapolis, IN	Jr	C	6-8
43	Rick Ford	Cloverdale, IN	Sr	F	6-5
23	Steve Heiniger	Fort Wayne, IN	So	G	5-10
33	Jerry Memering	Vincennes, IN	Jr	C	6-7
54	Kim Pemberton	Osgood, IN	Jr	G	6-3
42	John Ritter	Goshen, IN	Jr	F/G	6-5
24	Dave Shepherd	Carmel, IN	So	G	5-11
22	Bootsie White	Hammond, IN	Jr	G	5-8
20	Frank Wilson	Bluffton, IN	Jr	G	6-3
44	Joby Wright (Capt.)	Savannah, GA	Sr	F	6-8

SEASON RESULTS 1971-72

Date	Court	Opponent	Result	Score
12/1/1971	H	Ball State	W	84-77
12/4/1971	H	Miami of Ohio	W	65-50
12/6/1971	H	Kansas	W	59-56
12/11/1971	N1	Kentucky	W	90-89
12/15/1971	A	Ohio	L	70-79
12/18/1971	H	Notre Dame	W	94-29
12/22/1971	A	Butler	W	85-74
12/28/1971	N2	Brigham Young	W	61-50
12/29/1971	N2	Old Dominion	W	88-86
1/4/1972	A	Northern Illinois	L	71-85
1/8/1972	A	Minnesota	L	51-52
1/15/1972	H	Wisconsin	L	64-66
1/22/1972	A	Ohio State	L	74-80
1/29/1972	A	Michigan State	L	73-83
2/5/1972	H	Michigan State	W	83-69
2/8/1972	H	Minnesota	W	61-42
2/12/1972	A	Wisconsin	W	84-76
2/19/1972	H	Iowa	W	86-79
2/22/1972	A	Illinois	W	90-71
2/26/1972	A	Purdue	L	69-70
2/29/1972	H	Michigan	W	79-75
3/4/1972	H	Ohio State	W	65-57
3/7/1972	A	Northwestern	W	72-67
3/11/1972	H	Purdue	W	62-48
National Invitation Tournament (NIT)				
3/18/1972	N3	Princeton	L	60-68

1 Louisville, KY
2 Norfolk, VA
3 New York, NY

1971-72 BIG TEN STANDINGS

	W	L	PCT
Minnesota	11	3	.786
Ohio State	10	4	.714
Indiana	9	5	.643
Michigan	9	5	.643
Wisconsin	6	8	.428
Michigan St.	6	8	.428
Purdue	6	8	.428
Illinois	5	9	.357
Iowa	5	9	.357
Northwestern	3	11	.214

Former Ohio State guard Bob Knight took over the reins of the IU program as a 31-year-old upstart with a reputation as a disciplinarian and a defensive-minded coach. He had already led the U.S. Military Academy (Army) to several successful seasons, but he would end up making an indelible mark on the sport during his long career at Indiana.
IU Archives

his squad down to Louisville's Freedom Hall and beat Adolph Rupp's No. 7 Kentucky Wildcats 90-89 in double overtime. Downing, still hobbled by a knee injury, put on one of the greatest performances in school history with 47 points and 25 rebounds, as he played every minute of regulation and both overtimes against one of the Hoosiers' most bitter rivals.

Four days after the emotional Kentucky win, IU went to Athens, Ohio, and dropped its first game of the season, 79-70, to Ohio University, which had also recently defeated nationally ranked Ohio State. The Hoosiers returned to Bloomington and demolished Notre Dame 94-29 in the official dedication game for Assembly Hall on December 18. John Ritter poured in a game-high 31 points to outscore Digger Phelps's Fighting Irish squad by himself. Next, the Hoosiers improved to 6-1 and rose to No. 7 in the nation with an 85-74 win over Butler on December 22, in Indianapolis. Then IU went to Norfolk, Virginia, and won the Old Dominion Invitational by beating No. 8 BYU 61-50 on December 28, and defeating tournament host Old Dominion 88-86 on December 29. It was Indiana's first tournament championship of any kind since 1964-65. The Hoosiers, who had now risen to No. 5 in the polls, closed out the preconference season by going to DeKalb, Illinois, and getting trounced 86-71 by the Northern Illinois Huskies. That loss dropped Indiana to 8-2 heading into league play.

IU had the unenviable task of opening the conference schedule with three of its first four games on the road. Knight coached his first Big Ten game on January 8, at Minnesota, where Williams Arena had a capacity crowd of 19,121 for the first time since 1955. The Gopher fans witnessed a typically intense—and sometimes rough—Big Ten affair. Plus, the game had some added spice because Minnesota's new coach Dick Musselman had called Knight a "born loser" before the game and said that there was no way Knight's Hoosiers were going to beat his Gophers in

Minneapolis. The Hoosiers led 51-46 in the final minutes, but faltered down the stretch as Minnesota closed the game on a 6-0 run and prevailed 52-51. Indiana returned to Bloomington and hosted Wisconsin on January 15. IU led 60-59 and had control of the ball in the final minute, but committed two turnovers and fouled the Badgers' Kim Hughes at the buzzer. Hughes made one of two free throws to send the game into overtime, where Wisconsin won 66-64. The Hoosiers had fallen to 0-2 in league play and had lost in Assembly Hall for the first time. It would take five years for another Big Ten opponent to come into Bloomington and beat the Hoosiers in their new arena.

After the Wisconsin loss, Indiana went to Columbus, Ohio, on January 22 to take on Big Ten leader and defending conference champion Ohio State (also Knight's alma mater). The Hoosiers played well, but the Buckeyes were too much, as OSU's Alan Hornyak scored 36 points and Ohio State won 80-74. The abyss deepened on January 29, when Indiana lost to Michigan State 83-73 in East Lansing and fell into last place in the Big Ten with a 0-4 record.

However, just when it looked like the Hoosiers might languish at the bottom of conference, they turned things around and jumpstarted their season. It began with an 83-69 throttling of Michigan State in Bloomington on February 2. Four of Indiana's five starters scored in double figures against the Spartans, led by 24 from Wright. Next, Minnesota came to town and the resurgent Hoosiers handed out a 61-42 drubbing to the first-place Gophers. After the buzzer sounded, Minnesota coach Dick Musselman, who had demeaned Knight in the press before the first IU-Minnesota game, took a step toward the Indiana bench to shake Knight's hand but saw that Knight was already walking toward the Indiana locker room.

On January 12, the Hoosiers grabbed their first Big Ten road win by beating Wisconsin 84-76 in

INDIANA'S RANKING IN THE 1971-72 ASSOCIATED PRESS POLLS

PS	12/7	12/14	12/21	12/28	1/4	1/11	1/18	1/25	2/1	2/8	2/15	2/22	2/29	3/7	3/14
—	—	12	8	7	5	17	—	—	—	—	—	—	—	20	17

overtime. Then IU returned home and defeated Iowa 86-79 on February 19, to even its conference record at 4-4. Downing reinjured his knee against the Hawkeyes, but Ritter carried the Hoosiers with 32 points and IU sank 34 out of 37 free throws (92 percent). On January 22, Indiana continued its winning streak with an emphatic 90-71 win over Illinois in Champaign. The Hoosiers hit 26 of 29 free throws (88 percent) against the Fighting Illini.

While free throws were a key to the Iowa and Illinois victories, they proved to be part of Indiana's undoing against Purdue on February 26, in West Lafayette. IU jumped out to a 43-33 lead at the half and held a nine-point advantage with 13:11 remaining, but Purdue grabbed the momentum and made all the big plays down the stretch to win 70-69. The Hoosiers made only 11 of 21 free throws (52 percent) for the game, and dropped to 5-5 in conference play.

After the loss to the Boilermakers, Indiana closed the conference season with four straight wins. IU rattled off home victories over Michigan (79-75) and conference co-leader Ohio State (65-57). Then the Hoosiers went up to Northwestern on March 7, and beat the Wildcats 72-67. Finally, the Indiana squad closed out the Big Ten schedule by exacting some revenge on Purdue with a convincing 62-48 win over the Boilermakers in Assembly Hall.

The Hoosiers finished the Big Ten campaign at 9-5, which put them in a tie for third place. It also earned them an invitation to take part in the post-season National Invitational Tournament. The Hoosiers were matched up against Pete Carril's Princeton Tigers, who were riding a nine-game winning streak. It was the first ever NIT appearance for both schools. The game tipped on March 18, in Madison Square Garden. The Hoosiers took an early 12-4 lead, but Princeton controlled the game after that and pulled away at the end for a 68-60 victory.

Indiana had put together a solid season with an upper-division finish in the Big Ten and a postseason conference berth. The loss that haunted Coach Bob Knight the most was the season opener, which the Hoosiers gave away to Minnesota in the final minutes. If IU had pulled out that win, then the conference title would have been split between Minnesota, Ohio State and Indiana. Instead, Minnesota won the crown outright.

Nevertheless, Knight converted the IU players—and many of the IU fans—to his philosophy of working the ball for a good shot on offense and playing an aggressive man-to-man defense. In the years that followed, he would provide ample proof that his system could produce winning basketball.

1972-73

FOR THE COMMENTARY AND STATISTICS FOR THE 1972-73 SEASON, PLEASE SEE CHAPTER 9, "1972-73: KNIGHT CRASHES THE FINAL FOUR."

1973-74

OVERALL RECORD: 23-5

CONFERENCE RECORD: 12-2 (FIRST PLACE)

TEAM HONORS:

BIG TEN CHAMPION, CCA TOURNAMENT CHAMPION

INDIVIDUAL HONORS:

STEVE GREEN—ALL-AMERICA, ALL-BIG TEN (FIRST TEAM), ACADEMIC ALL-AMERICA, ACADEMIC ALL-BIG TEN

QUINN BUCKNER—ALL-BIG TEN (FIRST TEAM)

KENT BENSON—CCA TOURNAMENT MVP

JOHN LASKOWSKI—ACADEMIC ALL-BIG TEN

Optimism and excitement reigned in Bloomington after the Hoosiers' surprising rally to win the 1973 Big Ten title and a subsequent a run to the NCAA Final Four. However, the Hoosiers lost their two senior leaders—John Ritter and Steve Downing—to graduation and entered the 1973-74 season with no seniors on the roster. IU returned three starters in forward Steve

The 1973-74 team. First row (left to right): Scott May, Kent Benson, Don Noort, Tom Abernathy, Steve Green; Second row: trainer Bob Young, Trent Smock, Doug Allen, Bob Wilkerson, John Laskowski, Craig Morris, Jim Crews; Third row: head coach Bob Knight, assistant coach Bob Donewald, John Kamstra, Steve Ahlfeld, Quinn Buckner, assistant coach Dave Bliss, assistant coach Bob Weltlich. IU Archives

Green and guards Quinn Buckner and Jim Crews, and a key reserve in guard/forward John Laskowski, but the team would have to rely primarily on 6'10" freshman Kent Benson, the 1973 Indiana Mr. Basketball, to fill Downing's spot at center. IU was also going to rely on another newcomer, sophomore Scott May (who sat out as a freshman in order to become fully academically eligible) to fill Ritter's spot at forward. What the Hoosiers lacked in senior experience they made up for in depth, as the roster went 14-deep and included a number of highly regarded young players fighting for reserve minutes. As a result, Indiana was ranked third in the nation in the preseason.

The 1973-74 schedule tipped off on Saturday, December 1, against The Citadel in Bloomington. IU had trouble with the Bulldogs' full-court press, which led to 34 Indiana turnovers, but the Hoosiers still overwhelmed their opponents 74-55, led by 14 points from May. Indiana looked much sharper on December 5, when the Hoosiers whipped the Kansas

Jayhawks 72-59 in Assembly Hall, led by 22 points from Steve Green. On December 8, the Indiana squad went down to Louisville and fell behind No. 10 Kentucky 44-39 at the break. In the second half, coach Bob Knight went with a smaller, more versatile lineup with Bobby Wilkerson and John Laskowski at the guards, Green and May at the forwards, and 6'7" Tom Abernathy at center. The IU defense tightened up and Laskowski got hot. IU won 77-68, behind 23 points from "Laz" and 18-22 (82 percent) field goal shooting by the team in the second half.

On December 11, in Bloomington, No. 4 Indiana collided with No. 6 Notre Dame in front of a record-setting crowd of 17,463 (the largest basketball crowd in Indiana state history at the time). Notre Dame played a stronger game and controlled the lead nearly wire to wire on the way to a 73-67 Irish victory. IU bounced back by crushing Ball State 87-62 on December 15, in Muncie, led by 15 points apiece from Green and Laskowski, and 14 each from Benson and Crews. Back in Bloomington, the Hoosiers beat

1973-74 TEAM ROSTER

Head coach: Bob Knight
Assistant coaches: Dave Bliss, Bob Donewald, Bob Weltlich

No.	Player	Hometown	Class	Position	Height
33	Tom Abernathy	South Bend, IN	So	F	6-7
24	Steve Ahlfeld	Wabash, IN	Jr	G	6-0
25	Doug Allen	Champaign, IL	Jr	F	6-6
54	Kent Benson	New Castle, IN	Fr	C	6-10
21	Quinn Buckner (Capt.)	Phoenix, IL	So	G	6-3
45	Jim Crews	Normal, IL	So	G	6-5
34	Steve Green (Capt.)	Sellersburg, IN	Jr	F	6-7
30	John Kamstra	Frankfort, IN	Jr	G	6-1
31	John Laskowski	South Bend, IN	Jr	G/F	6-5
42	Scott May	Sandusky, OH	So	F	6-7
23	Craig Morris	DeGraff, OH	So	G	6-4
43	Don Noort	Worth, IL	So	C	6-8
22	Trent Smock	Richmond, IN	So	F	6-5
20	Bob Wilkerson	Anderson, IN	So	G/F	6-6

SEASON RESULTS 1973-74

Date	Court	Opponent	Result	Score
12/1/1973	H	Citadel	W	74-55
12/5/1973	H	Kansas	W	72-59
12/8/1973	N1	Kentucky	W	77-68
12/11/1973	H	Notre Dame	L	67-73
12/15/1973	A	Ball State	W	87-62
12/22/1973	H	South Carolina	W	84-71
12/26/1973	N2	Brigham Young	W	96-52
12/28/1973	N2	Oregon State	L	48-61
12/29/1973	N2	Oregon	W	56-47
1/5/1974	A	Michigan	L	71-73
1/8/1974	A	Miami of Ohio	W	71-58
1/12/1974	H	Wisconsin	W	52-51
1/14/1974	H	Northwestern	W	72-67
1/19/1974	A	Iowa	W	55-51
1/26/1974	A	Northwestern	W	82-53
2/2/1974	H	Iowa	W	85-50
2/9/1974	H	Illinois	W	107-67
2/11/1974	A	Wisconsin	W	81-63
2/16/1974	H	Michigan	W	93-81
2/18/1974	A	Illinois	W	101-83
2/23/1974	A	Minnesota	W	73-55
2/25/1974	H	Michigan State	W	91-85
3/2/1974	A	Ohio State	L	79-85
3/9/1974	H	Purdue	W	80-79
3/11/1974	N3	(#16) Michigan	L	67-75
CCA Tournament				
3/15/1974	N4	Tennessee	W	73-71
3/17/1974	N4	Toledo	W	73-72
3/18/1974	N4	USC	W	85-60

1 Louisville, KY
2 Portland, OR
3 Champaign, IL
4 St. Louis, MO

1973-74 BIG TEN STANDINGS

	W	L	PCT
Indiana	12	2	.857
Michigan	12	2	.857
Purdue	10	4	.714
Wisconsin	8	6	.571
Michigan St.	8	6	.571
Minnesota	6	8	.429
Iowa	5	9	.357
Ohio State	4	10	.286
Northwestern	3	11	.214
Illinois	2	12	.143

No. 14 South Carolina 84-71, led by 21 points from Quinn Buckner. Next, the 5-1 Hoosiers set off for Portland, Oregon, to play in the Far West Classic. No. 7 Indiana, which was the favorite to win the tournament, pummeled Brigham Young 96-52 in the opening round on December 26. IU led 54-20 at the break, and the Hoosier reserves played most of the second half. However, two nights later, the Oregon State Beavers came out in an aggressive zone defense that befuddled the listless Hoosiers and held them to 18 points in the first half. IU never recovered, and Oregon State won 61-48. The next night, Indiana beat the Oregon Ducks 57-47 to claim third place in the tournament and finish the preconference season at 7-2.

With the start of Big Ten play, IU regrouped and invaded Chrisler Arena in Ann Arbor, Michigan, on January 5. The Hoosiers raced to 41-26 lead at half-time, but backpedaled in the second half as the Wolverines surged back into the game and pulled out a 73-71 victory. Three nights later, the Hoosiers traveled to Miami of Ohio for a nonconference game, and Knight benched four of his five starters, as Steve Green was the only regular to start the game. IU trailed 33-30 at the half, but the Hoosiers' first string entered the game and led a huge second-half run as Indiana came away with a 71-58 win.

IU got back to Big Ten play with a slim 52-51 win over Wisconsin on January 12, at Assembly Hall. Laskowski, who led Indiana with 14 points, hit the game-winning free throws with 0:27 remaining. Next, Northwestern came to town on January 14 and nearly pulled the upset. Buckner and May each missed the front end of a one-and-one in the final 1:05, but Laskowski and Abernathy each buried two free throws in the final minute to give Indiana a 72-67 win. Then, on January 19, the Hoosiers gutted out another ugly win by beating the struggling Iowa Hawkeyes 55-51 in Iowa City.

At 3-1, the Hoosiers were still in the thick of the Big Ten race, but they had been playing uninspired basketball and were struggling to beat inferior teams. The IU offense had been particularly abysmal, averaging only 62.5 points in Big Ten play. Knight decided to tweak the offense by having the players look for longer, slightly riskier outlet passes and push the ball up the court. Plus, Knight added a different wrinkle to the fast break by having his sharp-shooting wing players—May, Green and Lazkowski—run to the 10-20-foot range on the wings rather than filling the lanes. This provided a plethora of spot-up jump shots off of the fast break. The strategy worked. IU crushed a shell-shocked Northwestern team 82-53 in Evanston on January 26. Next the Hoosiers rolled to easy home wins over Iowa (85-50) and Illinois (107-67), and then went up to Wisconsin and drubbed the Badgers 81-63, as five different Hoosiers scored in double figures.

On February 16, IU hosted first-place Michigan in a rematch of their conference opener. The Hoosiers used their new high-octane attack to run away with a 93-81 victory, as Green exploded for a game-high 37 points. When the dust settled after the Michigan win, Indiana was alone in first place in the Big Ten at 8-1, a half-game ahead of the Wolverines. Indiana soon improved to 11-1 after notching road wins over Illinois (101-83) and Minnesota (73-55), and then barely holding off Michigan State 91-85 in Assembly Hall. In the MSU game, "Super Sub" John Laskowski came off the bench and scored 13 points in the second half to carry the Hoosiers to their 12th straight victory overall.

The IU squad now controlled its own destiny. If Indiana could win its final two conference games, the team would be guaranteed of repeating as the outright Big Ten champs. Unfortunately, the Indiana squad stumbled on March 2, in Columbus, Ohio, as the Ohio State Buckeyes, who were fighting to get out of the conference cellar, upset the Hoosiers 85-79 and dropped them into a tie for the Big Ten lead with Michigan. IU returned to Bloomington for a season-ending showdown with arch-rival Purdue on Saturday, March 9. With a victory, the Boilermakers could tie the Hoosiers with a league record of 11-3 and have an outside chance at a share of the conference title if Michigan lost at Michigan State. The Hoosiers and the Boilermakers engaged in an epic see-

"Super Sub" John Laskowski celebrates Indiana's 80-79 victory over Purdue in Assembly Hall on March 9, 1974. Laskowski hit a pair of free throws with eight seconds left to deliver the win for the Hoosiers.
IU Archives

saw battle, but Laskowski confidently stroked in two free throws with 0:08 remaining to give IU a thrilling 80-79 win.

While IU was taking care of business against Purdue, Michigan went to East Lansing and defeated its arch-rival Michigan State 103-87. That put both Indiana and Michigan at 12-2 for the season and gave them each a share of the Big Ten title. However, since

INDIANA'S RANKING IN THE 1973-74 ASSOCIATED PRESS POLLS

PS	12/4	12/11	12/18	12/25	1/2	1/8	1/15	1/22	1/29	2/5	2/12	2/19	2/26	3/5	3/12	3/19	FN
3	3	3	7	7	8	13	12	11	12	12	12	10	9	13	10	11	9

the two teams had split their season series, a playoff game was devised to decide which team would get the Big Ten's berth in the NCAA tournament. The game was played on a neutral floor in Champaign, Illinois, on March 11. Both teams battled with the intensity of champions, but Michigan made the big plays in the second half and won 75-67. "Without any question, the Wolverines deserved to win and represent the Big Ten in the NCAA," said Knight afterwards.

Knight had hoped for a chance at the NIT championship, but the IU administration committed the Hoosiers to play in the new Conference Commissioners Association (CCA) tournament in St. Louis, which was designed as an alternative venue for the top teams that didn't make it to the NCAA. Knight was not happy about having to play in the tournament and everyone knew it. However, when he got on the IU plane to fly to St. Louis, Knight told the team, "If we have got to go, then let's win the damned thing." They did. The Hoosiers weren't very impressive in squeaking by Tennessee (73-71) and Toledo (72-71 in OT), but they woke up in time to crush an excellent USC team 85-60 in the championship game. The Trojans were 24-4 entering the contest and had been consistently ranked in the top 10. The CCA tournament was the coming out party for IU center Kent Benson, who averaged 16.3 points and 11.3 rebounds and was named MVP of the tournament.

The Hoosiers had played some outstanding basketball during their 11-game winning streak in the Big Ten and during their blowout of USC in the CCA tournament. With all their starters and key reserves returning, the Hoosiers would translate that strong play into more consistent success in 1974-75. As it turned out, after the playoff loss to Michigan on March 11, it would be over a full calendar year before IU would lose again.

1974-75

FOR THE COMMENTARY AND
STATISTICS FOR THE 1974-75 SEASON,
SEE CHAPTER 3, "1974-75:
THE MOST DOMINANT TEAM IN IU HISTORY."

1975-76

FOR THE COMMENTARY AND
STATISTICS FOR THE 1975-76 SEASON,
PLEASE SEE CHAPTER 1, "1975-76:
TOUGHNESS, GREATNESS, AND PERFECTION."

1976-77

OVERALL RECORD: 16-11
CONFERENCE RECORD: 11-7 (FOURTH PLACE)
TEAM HONORS:
INDIANA CLASSIC CHAMPION
INDIVIDUAL HONORS:
KENT BENSON—ALL-AMERICA,
ALL-BIG TEN (FIRST TEAM), ACADEMIC ALL-BIG
TEN, ACADEMIC ALL-AMERICA

To say that 1976-77 was a rebuilding year for Indiana basketball would have been an understatement of epic proportion. Gone were All-Americans Scott May and Quinn Buckner, and along with them went Bobby Wilkerson, Tom Abernathy and Jim Crews. Those five had been the nucleus of IU teams that won four consecutive Big Ten championships and an NCAA title. The only returning starter was senior center Kent Benson. All of the other positions were up for grabs. Junior guard Jim Wisman and junior forward Wayne Radford had been valuable reserves in the past and looked like strong candidates to earn a spot in the starting lineup. Other than that, three unseasoned sophomores and a talented group of six freshmen battled for the remaining spots in the rotation.

"We're looking for a lot of things," said coach Bob Knight. "We have to find scoring, on-the-floor leadership, a defensive player capable of playing the best offensive player on the other team... Certain players are going to have to emerge in certain areas if we hope to be competitive."

The 1976-77 team. First row (left to right): Wayne Radford, Rich Valavicius, Kent Benson, Trent Smock, Jim Wisman; Second row: Bill Cunningham, Scott Eells, Butch Carter, Derek Holcomb, Glen Grunwald, Mike Woodson; Third row: assistant coach Bob Donewald, trainer Bob Young, Jim Roberson, Mike Miday, assistant coach Harold Andreas, head coach Bob Knight. IU Archives

One freshman who emerged early and earned a spot in the starting lineup was 6'5" Mike Woodson from Indianapolis. Woodson wore uniform number 42, which had been worn by Scott May during the previous three seasons, and there were times when opponents were probably scratching their heads wondering if May had graduated or not, because Woodson flashed some of the same athletic ability and mid-range shooting form that had characterized May's game.

On opening night, the Hoosiers looked a lot like the teams that had gone 63-1 over the previous two seasons, as IU steamrolled South Dakota 110-64 on November 27, in Bloomington. Five IU players scored in double figures, led by Radford with 18, Benson with 17, and Woodson with 16. However, reality struck on December 1, when the Hoosiers went to Toledo and got beat 59-57 in the dedication game for the Rockets' new basketball stadium. That broke the Hoosiers' 33-game winning streak. On December 6, No. 5 Kentucky overwhelmed the Hoosiers 66-51 in Bloomington. That loss broke Indiana's 34-game win-

ning streak in Assembly Hall. The reality check continued on December 14, when IU went to South Bend and lost to No. 4 Notre Dame 78-65.

At that point, the Hoosiers were 1-3 and had suffered their first three-game losing streak in five years. They responded by winning four in a row. On Friday, December 17, Knight sent out his fifth different starting lineup in five games as the Hoosiers grinded out a 50-42 win over DePaul in Market Square Arena in Indianapolis. Benson led all scorers with 18 points. "I'm tickled for the kids who have struggled so hard and finally won," said Knight after the game. "I seldom talk about winning to [this team], but two days ago, I told them how important it was for them to be rewarded with a victory for all the hard work they'd done."

Next, in the third annual Indiana Classic in Bloomington, Indiana captured the championship by beating Utah State 79-71 and Miami of Ohio 76-55. Woodson broke loose for 26 points against Utah State, while Benson paced the Hoosiers with 26 against Miami. After improving its record to 4-3,

1976-77 TEAM ROSTER

Head coach: Bob Knight
Assistant coaches: Harold Andreas, Bob Donewald,
Tom Miller, Ted Chidster

No.	Player	Hometown	Class	Position	Height
54	Kent Benson (Capt.)	New Castle, IN	Sr	C	6-11
41	Butch Carter	Middletown, OH	Fr	G/F	6-5
20	Bill Cunningham	Phoenix, AZ	Fr	G	6-4
31	Scott Eells	Hoopeston, IL	So	F	6-9
40	Glen Grunwald	Franklin Park, IL	Fr	F	6-9
44	Derek Holcomb	Peoria, IL	Fr	C	6-11
45	Mike Miday	Canton, OH	Fr	F	6-8
22	Wayne Radford	Indianapolis, IN	Jr	G/F	6-3
43	Jim Roberson	Rochester, NY	So	F/C	6-9
33	Trent Smock	Richmond, IN	Sr	G/F	6-5
34	Rich Valavicius	Hammond, IN	So	F	6-5
23	Jim Wisman	Quincy, IL	Jr	G	6-2
42	Mike Woodson	Indianapolis, IN	Fr	G/F	6-5

SEASON RESULTS 1976-77

Date	Court	Opponent	Result	Score
11/27/1976	H	South Dakota	W	110-64
12/1/1976	A	Toledo	L	57-59
12/6/1976	H	Kentucky	L	51-66
12/14/1976	A	Notre Dame	L	65-78
12/17/1976	N1	DePaul	W	50-42
12/20/1976	H	Utah State	W	79-71
12/21/1976	H	Miami of Ohio	W	76-55
12/29/1976	N2	Georgia	W	74-52
12/30/1976	N2	Cincinnati	L	43-52
1/6/1977	H	Purdue	L	63-80
1/8/1977	H	Illinois	W	80-60
1/13/1977	A	Northwestern	W	78-53
1/15/1977	A	Wisconsin	W	79-64
1/17/1977	H	Michigan State	L	60-61
1/22/1977	A	Ohio State	W	79-56
1/27/1977	H	Minnesota	L*	60-79
1/29/1977	H	Iowa	W	81-65
2/3/1977	A	Michigan	L	84-89
2/5/1977	A	Michigan State	W	81-79
2/13/1977	H	Michigan	W	73-64
2/15/1977	A	Minnesota	L*	61-65
2/17/1977	A	Illinois	L	69-73
2/20/1977	A	Purdue	L	78-86
2/24/1977	H	Wisconsin	L	64-66
2/26/1977	H	Northwestern	W	69-54
2/28/1977	A	Iowa	L	73-80
3/5/1977	H	Ohio State	W	75-69

1 Indianapolis, IN
2 New Orleans, LA
* These two games were later forfeited to Indiana.

1976-77 BIG TEN STANDINGS

	W	L	PCT
Michigan	16	2	.889
Purdue	14	4	.778
Iowa	12	6	.667
Indiana	11	7	.611
Michigan St.	9	9	.500
Illinois	8	10	.444
Wisconsin	7	11	.389
Northwestern	7	11	.389
Ohio State	4	14	.222
Minnesota1	0	18	.000

1 NCAA declared all games forfeited

Indiana closed the preconference schedule by traveling to New Orleans and playing in the Sugar Bowl Classic on December 29-30. The Hoosiers opened with a 74-52 win over Georgia, but fell to the undefeated Cincinnati Bearcats 52-43 in the championship game. Against Cincinnati, which was ranked No. 5 in nation, the Hoosiers shot an anemic 33 percent from the field.

With its success in the previous two seasons, Indiana was riding an unprecedented 36-game conference winning streak entering Big Ten play in 1977. The Hoosiers also hadn't lost a Big Ten game in Assembly Hall in five years. Both of those streaks came to an abrupt end on January 6, when Purdue came to Bloomington and gave IU an 80-63 lashing in the Hoosiers' conference opener. Two days later, IU earned its first conference win by clobbering Illinois 80-60 in Bloomington, led by 24 points from Woodson. The following week, the Hoosiers went on the road and secured two solid wins over Northwestern and Wisconsin to improve to 3-1 in conference play.

Back in Bloomington on January 17, the Hoosiers hosted Michigan State and led the Spartans by seven points with under eight minutes remaining. But MSU's full-court press unnerved IU down the stretch and Michigan State stole a 61-60 victory. Next, the Hoosiers played one of their best games of the season in beating the Ohio State Buckeyes 79-56 in Columbus, led by 29 points from Benson and 22 from Woodson. Then they returned home and dropped another game in Assembly Hall as Minnesota came in and rolled to a 79-60 victory, led by 35 points from Gophers center Mychal Thompson. Two days later, IU gained some home court redemption by beating Iowa 81-65, as Woodson poured in a game-high 27 points.

The next week, Indiana continued its strong play on the road. The Hoosiers went to Ann Arbor on February 3, and barely fell to No. 7 Michigan 89-84, as the Wolverines closed the game on a 10-5 run. Woodson and Michigan's Rickey Green each scored 32 points. On February 5, Indiana went to East Lansing and stole an 81-79 win over Michigan State. IU was powered by a 35-point, nine-rebound, four-block performance from Benson, who was fighting an ailing back. The Hoosiers returned from their two-game road trip and played host to Michigan on

Sunday, February 13, in front of a capacity crowd at Assembly Hall and a national television audience. The Hoosiers toppled the fifth-ranked, league-leading Wolverines 73-64, as Woodson scored a game-high 26 points and Benson dropped in 24. IU trailed by three at the intermission, but opened the second half with an 8-0 run and controlled the game the rest of the way.

The Michigan upset improved IU to 7-4 as the squad embarked on a three-game road trip. Unfortunately, the Hoosiers couldn't recreate the magic they had shown in earlier road wins and they dropped three straight—65-61 at Minnesota, 73-69 at Illinois, and 86-78 at Purdue—to drop back to 7-7. In the Purdue game, Benson aggravated his back injury in a collision with the Boilermakers' Joe Barry Carroll. He would end up missing the final four games of the season.

In their first game without Benson, the Hoosiers fell to Wisconsin 66-64 when the Badgers' Bob Falk drilled a baseline jumper in the final seconds in Assembly Hall on February 24. Next, Northwestern came to town on February 26, and grabbed a two-point halftime lead, but Indiana responded with a big second half and pulled away for a 69-54 win. Radford and Woodson scored 24 points apiece and Woodson yanked down a game-high 13 rebounds.

On February 28, Indiana embarked on its final road game of the year against Iowa, and fell to the Hawkeyes 80-73. Woodson led all scorers with 34 points, but he was the only Hoosier in double figures. In their final game of the season, the Hoosiers out-dueled Ohio State 75-

Senior center Kent Benson (54) and freshman forward Mike Woodson (42) team up to go for a tip-in. Benson averaged 19.8 PPG for the season, while Woodson totaled 18.5 PPG. IU Archives

69, as 6'11" freshman Derek Holcomb filled in at center and recorded 23 points, 15 rebounds, and six blocked shots. The win preserved Indiana from having a losing season as the IU squad finished with a 9-9 record in the Big Ten and a 14-13 mark overall (NCAA violations later forfeited Minnesota's wins, including two over IU, and so the official records now have Indiana at 16-11 overall and 11-7 in the conference).

After five straight trips to postseason tournaments during Knight's tenure, the Hoosiers stayed home in March for the first time since the 1970-71 season. However, in addressing the crowd after the Ohio State game, Knight said, "That's not because these kids didn't play their [butts] off for you." He also added, "And a few of those people who jumped off the bandwagon will probably be just as quick jumping back on."

1976-77 ended up being the only season in Bob Knight's 29 years at Indiana that the Hoosiers didn't get an invitation to a postseason tournament.

1977-78

OVERALL RECORD: 21-8

CONFERENCE RECORD: 12-6 (SECOND PLACE)

TEAM HONORS:

GATOR BOWL CLASSIC CHAMPION, INDIANA

CLASSIC CHAMPION

INDIVIDUAL HONORS:

WAYNE RADFORD—ACADEMIC ALL-BIG TEN,

ACADEMIC ALL-AMERICA

For the second straight year, uncertainty reigned in Bloomington as coach Bob Knight prepared his Indiana squad for the 1977-78 campaign. All-American Kent Benson had graduated and took his 19.8 ppg and 10.5 rpg with him to the NBA. Sophomore Mike Woodson returned from an outstanding season in which he scored more points in Big Ten play than any freshman in the history of the conference, but he also needed to improve his defense. Benson's backup at center, 6'11" Derrick Holcomb, had flashed some tremendous potential as a freshman but decided to transfer to Illinois (he was from Peoria). Seniors Jim Wisman and Wayne Radford took over the mantle of leadership, but it was a heavy burden to carry since there were only four upperclassmen on the roster. Most of the positions on the team were available for the taking.

"This is a team that from both an individual and a team concept, almost nothing is solidified," said Knight prior the season. "About the only exception to that is that I think you'd have to say that we're counting on Mike Woodson being a good scorer… I really have no idea what kind of team we'll be. Only time will tell."

INDIANA'S RANKING IN THE 1976-77 ASSOCIATED PRESS POLLS

PS	11/30	12/7	12/14	12/21	12/28	1/4	1/11	1/18	1/25	2/1	2/8	2/15	2/22	3/1	3/8	3/15
5	4	13	16	—	—	—	—	—	—	—	—	—	—	—	—	—

The 1977-78 team. First row (left to right): Bill Cunningham, Tommy Baker, Wayne Radford, Jim Wisman, Butch Carter, Phil Isenbarger; Second row: Steve Risley, Glen Grunwald, Scott Eells, Ray Tolbert, Mike Woodson, Eric Kirchner, Jim Roberson; Third row: trainer Bob Young, [unknown], assistant coach Jim Crews, assistant coach Tom Miller, assistant coach Bob Donewald, head coach Bob Knight. IU Archives

In the season opener on November 26, against East Carolina, Knight used all 13 players on his roster and tried a variety of combinations before a group of mostly second-string players led a second-half charge that carried Indiana to a 75-59 win. Junior forward Scott Eells was a part of the group that triggered the second-half surge, and he finished with a team-high 14 points. After the East Carolina win, IU had over a week to prepare for a game with No. 1 Kentucky in Lexington on December 6. The Hoosiers went into Rupp Arena and battled the Wildcats, but couldn't keep up as Kentucky prevailed 78-64. Woodson led Indiana with 20 points, but fouled out midway through the second half. Indiana freshman forward Steve Risley added 10 points, all in the second half.

On December 10, Indiana crushed a visiting Murray State team 85-61, as Woodson scored 21 and Risley added 16. Next, No. 2 Notre Dame came to town on Wednesday, December 14. Knight's Hoosiers and Digger Phelps's Fighting Irish engaged in another one of their regular nip-and-tuck affairs, as both teams struggled to gain an advantage throughout the contest. With 0:04 on the clock, Wayne Radford

missed his first free throw but buried the second one to deliver a 67-66 upset for the Hoosiers. Then IU upped its record to 4-1 by edging out SMU 56-51 in Indianapolis on December 17. Woodson had a game-high 22 points against the Mustangs, and freshman center Ray Tolbert chipped in 14.

For the fourth straight year, Indiana won its own tournament—the Indiana Classic—on December 20-21. The Hoosiers pummeled Bowling Green 89-52 and then outlasted No. 18 Alabama 66-57 in the championship game. Radford, who scored 24 against Alabama, earned tournament MVP honors. Next, Indiana traveled to Jacksonville, Florida, to play in the Gator Bowl Classic on December 27-28. IU opened with a 69-59 victory over the host Jacksonville Dolphins, and then held off the Florida Gators 73-60 to win the tournament. Radford, who scored a game-high 21 points in the title game, collected his second MVP award in as many tournaments.

Entering Big Ten play, the Hoosiers were on a seven-game winning streak and were ranked 11th in the nation. However, they came out in the conference opener against Iowa on January 5, in Bloomington

1977-78 TEAM ROSTER

Head coach: Bob Knight
Assistant coaches: Bob Donewald, Tim Miller, Jim Crews

No.	Player	Hometown	Class	Position	Height
25	Tommy Baker	Jeffersonville, IN	Fr	G	6-1
41	Butch Carter	Middletown, OH	So	G/F	6-5
20	Bill Cunningham	Phoenix, IL	So	G	6-4
31	Scott Eells	Hoopeston, IL	Jr	F	6-9
40	Glen Grunwald	Franklin Park, IL	So	F	6-9
44	Phil Isenbarger	Muncie, IN	Fr	F	6-8
33	Eric Kirchner	Edelstein, IL	Fr	F	6-7
22	Wayne Radford (Capt.)	Indianapolis, IN	Sr	G/F	6-3
34	Steve Risley	Indianapolis, IN	Fr	F/C	6-8
43	Jim Roberson	Rochester, NY	Jr	F/C	6-9
45	Ray Tolbert	Anderson, IN	Fr	C	6-9
23	Jim Wisman (Capt.)	Quincy, IL	Sr	G	6-2
42	Mike Woodson	Indianapolis, IN	So	G/F	6-5

SEASON RESULTS 1977-78

Date	Court	Opponent	Result	Score
11/26/1977	H	East Carolina	W	75-59
12/5/1977	A	Kentucky	L	64-78
12/10/1977	H	Murray State	W	85-61
12/14/1977	H	Notre Dame	W	67-66
12/17/1977	N1	SMU	W	56-51
12/20/1977	H	Bowling Green	W	89-52
12/21/1977	H	Alabama	W	66-57
12/27/1977	A	Jacksonville	W	69-59
12/28/1977	N2	Florida	W	73-60
1/5/1978	H	Iowa	W	69-51
1/7/1978	H	Illinois	L	64-65
1/12/1978	A	Minnesota	L	62-75
1/14/1978	A	Wisconsin	L	65-78
1/19/1978	H	Ohio State	W	77-63
1/21/1978	A	Purdue	L	67-77
1/26/1978	A	Michigan	L	73-92
1/28/1978	H	Michigan State	W	71-66
2/2/1978	A	Northwestern	W	86-70
2/4/1978	A	Michigan State	L	59-68
2/9/1978	H	Purdue	W	65-64
2/11/1978	H	Northwestern	W	86-62
2/16/1978	A	Ohio State	W	83-70
2/18/1978	H	Michigan	W	71-59
2/23/1978	H	Wisconsin	W	58-54
2/25/1978	H	Minnesota	W	68-47
3/2/1978	A	Illinois	W	77-68
3/4/1978	A	Iowa	W	71-55
NCAA Tournament				
3/12/1978	N3	Furman	W	63-62
3/17/1978	N4	Villanova	L	60-61

1 Indianapolis, IN
2 Jacksonville, FL
3 Charlotte, NC
4 Providence, RI

1977-78 BIG TEN STANDINGS

	W	L	PCT
Michigan St.	15	3	.833
Indiana	12	6	.667
Minnesota	12	6	.667
Michigan	11	7	.611
Purdue	11	7	.611
Ohio State	9	9	.500
Illinois	7	11	.389
Iowa	5	13	.278
Northwestern	4	14	.222
Wisconsin	4	14	.222

and shot an abysmal 33 percent from the field. Fortunately, the Hoosiers' defense held the Hawkeyes to 35 percent, and Indiana had a large advantage from the free throw line that translated into a 69-51 IU win. Illinois came to Bloomington a couple of days later and escaped with a 65-64 upset—the Fighting Illini's first ever win in Assembly Hall—that dropped IU to 9-2 overall and 1-1 in league play.

A week later, Indiana traveled north for a doubleheader on the road against Minnesota and Wisconsin, and came home with a pair of losses. Minnesota used a 16-0 run in the middle of the game to cruise by Indiana 75-62. Then, Wisconsin pressured Indiana's guards into key turnovers in the second half, and the Badgers came away with a 78-65 win.

IU ended its three-game losing streak by upending Ohio State 77-63 on January 19, in Bloomington, as Ray Tolbert scored 24 points and grabbed eight rebounds. However, the Hoosiers went back on the road and dropped two more games—77-67 at Purdue and 92-73 at Michigan—and that left the Hoosiers with a 2-5 record in the Big Ten and virtually no chance at challenging for the conference crown. The Hoosiers' next opponent was No. 7 Michigan State, which was undefeated in league play and riding a 13-game winning streak. The Spartans, who were led by a flashy freshman named Earvin "Magic" Johnson, jumped out to a 34-31 lead at the half, but Indiana came out of the locker room and hit MSU with an 8-0 run to recapture the lead. IU never looked back on the way to a 71-66 upset. Radford had 23 points, five rebounds, five assists, and two steals, plus the 6'3" Radford worked tirelessly on the defensive end to slow down the Spartans' 6'9" Johnson.

Northwestern came to Bloomington on February 2, and the Hoosiers, who were trying to avoid a letdown after the Michigan State win, rolled by the Wildcats 86-70, led by 22 points from Radford and 21 from Woodson. Next, the Hoosiers traveled up to East Lansing on February 4, and attempted to complete a season sweep of Michigan State. IU raced to a 37-32 lead at the half, but Michigan State came out of the intermission with a sense of urgency and Magic Johnson rallied them to a 68-59 win.

The Michigan State loss dropped Indiana, which was ranked in the top twenty at the start of Big Ten play, to 4-6 in the conference and 12-7 overall. The Hoosiers were scheduled to play five of their final eight conference games at home, so they still had a chance at putting together a respectable record. They did better than just respectable. They won all eight of their final Big Ten games.

The first win came against Big Ten co-leader Purdue on February 9, in Bloomington. Seniors Wayne Radford and Jim Wisman buried key free throws in the final minute to lock up a 65-64 Indiana win. After that cliffhanger, IU racked up three consecutive easy wins: 86-62 over Northwestern; 83-70 over Ohio State; and 71-59 over Michigan. Next, Indiana pulled out an ugly 58-54 win over Wisconsin on February 23, in Assembly Hall. Two nights later, the Hoosiers neutralized Minnesota big men Mychal Thompson and Kevin McHale in a 68-47 thrashing of the Golden Gophers in IU's final home game of the season. The red-hot Hoosiers took their six-game winning streak on the road and claimed two more victories—77-68 at Illinois and 71-55 at Iowa. Radford scored a career-high 31 points against the Illini, while Woodson hit for a season-high 31 against the Hawkeyes, including a perfect 9-9 from the field in the second half.

Indiana's furious rally to win its final eight games gave the team a 12-6 conference record (20-7 overall) and a tie for second place in the Big Ten. That was good enough to earn an at-large bid in the NCAA tournament. IU was placed in the East Regional and was paired against Furman in Charlotte, North Carolina, in the first round on March 12. Furman outhustled the Hoosiers, but IU had just enough firepower to pull out a 63-62 win. Two days later in Providence, Rhode Island, Villanova derailed the Hoosiers' nine-game winning streak when guard Rory Sparrow buried the game-winning field goal with 0:15 remaining to give Villanova a 61-60 triumph.

After an 8-1 run through the pre-conference season, followed by an awful start in Big Ten play that

Team captains Wayne Radford and Jim Wisman share the microphone on Senior Day. Both of them played well during their final season in Bloomington and demonstrated excellent leadership. IU Archives

appeared to doom Indiana's season, the young Hoosier squad pulled off a remarkable turnaround in accomplishing a runner-up finish in the conference and an NCAA berth. It was the leadership and strong play of seniors Jim Wisman and Wayne Radford that steadied the team and made all the difference during the Hoosiers' stretch run.

INDIANA'S RANKING IN THE 1977-78 ASSOCIATED PRESS POLLS

PS	11/29	12/6	12/13	12/20	12/27	1/3	1/10	1/17	1/24	1/31	2/7	2/14	2/21	2/28	3/6	3/13
–	–	–	–	–	–	15	11	18	–	–	–	–	–	–	–	13

1978-79

OVERALL RECORD: 22-12
CONFERENCE RECORD: 10-8 (FIFTH PLACE)
TEAM HONORS:
NIT CHAMPION, INDIANA CLASSIC CHAMPION
INDIVIDUAL HONORS:
MIKE WOODSON—ALL-AMERICA,
ALL-BIG TEN (FIRST TEAM)

The 1978-79 team. First row (left to right): Mike Woodson, Steve Risley, Scott Eells, Landon Turner, Phil Isenbarger, Randy Wittman; Second row: Steve Reish, Ray Tolbert, Eric Kirchner, Butch Carter, Ted Kitchel, Glen Grunwald; Third row: assistant coach Ray Bates, head coach Bob Knight, assistant coach Jim Crews, assistant coach Tom Miller, assistant coach Jene Davis, trainer Bob Young, assistant coach Gerry Gimelstob. IU Archives

Sophomores and freshmen once again dominated the Hoosier roster for the 1978-79 season. Eight spots on the team's 14-man roster were filled by underclassmen, and the team's only two seniors—Scott Eells and Jim Roberson—were reserves who had mostly seen limited action in the past. Junior Glen Grunwald was going to miss the season as a medical redshirt to rehabilitate after knee surgery. Junior for-

ward Mike Woodson and sophomore center Ray Tolbert were the only regular starters that returned for the Hoosiers. IU lost playmaker Jim Wisman and all-around forward Wayne Radford to graduation, and their departure left an obvious leadership void. Coach Bob Knight named Woodson, a two-year starter, as the team's captain in the hope that he would step up and fill that void. The Hoosiers had talent, but they also had a lot of questions to answer, and they had to get their act together in a hurry because they faced one of the toughest preconference schedules in school history.

"I really don't know what kind team this will be," Knight admitted in the preseason. "I would like to think, though, that we can improve in three areas. I would hope that we can play better defense, that we have better board play, and that we can get some consistent scoring from others besides Woodson." The Hoosiers did improve on some of those areas, but as Knight quickly discovered, the season itself was an emotional roller coaster, filled with unfathomable lows and endearing highs.

Indiana kicked off the campaign by playing in the Sea Wolf Classic in Anchorage, Alaska, on November 24-26. In the opener, the tenth-ranked Hoosiers were stunned by the Pepperdine Waves 59-58 when Ricardo Brown sank a 22-footer with 0:07 remaining to give Pepperdine the win. IU committed five turnovers in the final two minutes to practically give the game away. To add insult to injury, the next night, Texas A&M used its full-court press to force 20 Hoosier turnovers and handed IU its second consecutive loss, 54-49. Knight benched Woodson at the start of the Texas A&M game, and the 6'5" forward didn't enter the contest until there were seven minutes remaining in the first half. Woodson was never able to get on track as he finished with four points and five turnovers and eventually fouled out. In their third game in Alaska, the Hoosiers finally nabbed a win, 86-65 over Penn State.

In the home opener in Bloomington on December 2, Indiana evened its record at 2-2 by demolishing Morehead State 80-37, led by Ray Tolbert with 20 points and seven rebounds. On Wednesday, December 6, IU played No. 20 Georgetown in Landover, Maryland, at the Capital Centre. The undefeated Hoyas slid by the Hoosiers 60-54, led by 21 points from Eric Floyd. Knight was dismayed by his team's play and sensed that something was wrong. On the plane ride home he paced up and down the aisle of the team's plane telling the players that he knew something was going on and that he wanted to know what it was. He didn't get any answers.

The following Saturday, after the Hoosiers beat Bradley 80-64 in Indianapolis, Knight found out exactly what was going on. A bunch of the IU players

1978-79 TEAM ROSTER

Head coach: Bob Knight
Assistant coaches: Gerry Gimelstob, Tom Miller, Jim Crews

No.	Player	Hometown	Class	Position	Height
25	Tommy Baker	Jeffersonville, IN	So	G	6-2
41	Butch Carter	Middletown, OH	Jr	G	6-5
23	Don Cox	Indianapolis, IN	So	G/F	6-6
31	Scott Eells	Hoopeston, IL	Sr	F	6-9
44	Phil Isenbarger	Muncie, IN	So	F	6-8
40	Glen Grunwald	Franklin Park, IL	Jr	F	6-9
30	Ted Kitchel	Galveston, IN	Rs	F	6-8
33	Eric Kirchner	Edelstein, IL	So	F	6-7
22	Steve Reish	Union City, IN	Fr	G	6-2
34	Steve Risley	Indianapolis, IN	So	F	6-8
43	Jim Roberson	Rochester, NY	Sr	C	6-9
45	Ray Tolbert	Anderson, IN	So	C	6-9
32	Landon Turner	Indianapolis, IN	Fr	F/C	6-9
24	Randy Wittman	Indianapolis, IN	Fr	G	6-5
42	Mike Woodson (Capt.)	Indianapolis, IN	Jr	F	6-5

SEASON RESULTS 1978-79

Date	Court	Opponent	Result	Score
11/24/1978	N1	Pepperdine	L	58-59
11/25/1978	N1	Texas A&M	L	49-54
11/26/1978	N1	Penn State	W	86-65
12/2/1978	H	Morehead State	W	80-37
12/6/1978	N2	Georgetown	L	54-60
12/9/1978	N3	Bradley	W	80-64
12/16/1978	H	Kentucky	W	68-67
12/18/1978	H	Davidson	W	101-64
12/19/1978	H	Washington	W	73-56
12/27/1978	N4	Washington	W	71-57
12/28/1978	N4	Oregon	W	68-60
12/30/1978	N4	Michigan State	L	57-74
1/4/1979	H	Illinois	L	61-65
1/6/1979	H	Purdue	W	63-54
1/11/1979	A	Minnesota	L	63-80
1/13/1979	A	Iowa	L	61-90
1/18/1979	A	Michigan State	L	58-82
1/20/1979	H	Northwestern	W	74-45
1/25/1979	H	Wisconsin	W	82-61
1/27/1979	A	Ohio State	L	63-66
2/1/1979	H	Michigan	W	68-62
2/3/1979	H	Ohio State	W	70-62
2/8/1979	A	Northwestern	W	82-57
2/10/1979	A	Michigan	L	59-60
2/15/1979	H	Michigan State	W	47-59
2/17/1979	A	Wisconsin	W	68-62
2/22/1979	H	Iowa	W	64-62
2/24/1979	H	Minnesota	W	71-46
3/1/1979	A	Purdue	L	48-55
3/3/1979	A	Illinois	W	72-60
National Invitation Tournament (NIT)				
3/8/1979	A	Texas Tech	W	78-59
3/12/1979	H	Alcorn State	W	73-69
3/19/1979	N5	Ohio State	W	64-55
3/21/1979	N5	Purdue	W	53-52

1 Anchorage, AK
2 Landover, MD
3 Indianapolis, IN
4 Portland, OR
5 New York, NY

1978-79 BIG TEN STANDINGS

	W	L	PCT
Michigan St.	13	5	.722
Purdue	13	5	.722
Iowa	13	5	.722
Ohio State	12	6	.667
Indiana	10	8	.556
Michigan	8	10	.444
Illinois	7	11	.389
Wisconsin	6	12	.333
Minnesota	6	12	.333
Northwestern	2	16	.111

Landon Turner and Butch Carter walk off the floor of Madison Square Garden as champions, following the Hoosiers' thrilling 53-52 win over Purdue in the NIT championship game. Carter nailed the game-winning shot. IU Archives

had smoked marijuana during the Alaska tournament. Knight confronted the players about it, and the following Monday made the decision to dismiss three players and put the rest of those involved on probation (with frequent testing and the threat of immediate dismissal if they were caught again).

With a reduced roster and a shaken morale, the Hoosiers played host to No. 6 Kentucky on Saturday, December 16, in Assembly Hall, and pulled off an unexpected 68-67 upset in overtime. Woodson, who scored a game-high 27 points, buried two free throws with 0:05 remaining in OT to seal the win. "I've never been happier for a bunch of kids," said Knight. "This was a day for our players. This was a day they earned after all the heartaches and soul-searching [of the past week]."

Next, the Hoosiers captured the championship of the Indiana Classic by whipping Davidson 101-64 and Washington 73-56. Then, the IU squad traveled to Portland, Oregon, for the Far West Classic from December 27-30. In the opener, IU played the same Washington team that it had beaten the previous week in Bloomington. The result was nearly identi-

cal—Indiana 71, Washington 57. The next night, IU knocked off Oregon 68-60 as Woodson set a new career-high with 36 points. That set up a championship game featuring two Big Ten teams—Indiana and Michigan State. In fact, when the Hoosiers went out to the court for the semifinal game with Oregon, Michigan State had already defeated Washington State in the other semifinal, and the Spartans' Magic Johnson greeted the IU players on their way to the court and was slapping backs and encouraging the Hoosiers to make it an all-Big Ten title game. After the Hoosiers pulled out the win, IU and MSU played in the championship game on December 30. Michigan State captured the title by pulling away in the second half for an easy 74-57 win, as Johnson was named the tournament MVP. Afterwards, Knight joked to Johnson, "No wonder you were wanting us to get there!"

The MSU loss in the Far West Classic ended the Hoosiers' six-game winning streak, but IU had still pulled out an 8-4 pre-conference record despite the team's adversity and a grueling schedule. However, just as they had done the previous season, the

Hoosiers dug themselves an early hole in Big Ten play. IU lost four of its first five conference games, including a 65-61 home loss to No. 4 Illinois in the conference opener and three straight road losses to Minnesota (80-63), Iowa (90-61), and No. 6 Michigan State (82-58). The only win came against Purdue, 63-54, in the second game of league play on January 6, in Assembly Hall.

After falling to 1-4, Indiana bounced back and won five of its next six games. Back in Bloomington, the Hoosiers trounced Northwestern 74-45 and crushed Wisconsin 82-61. Then, on January 27, in Columbus, Ohio, Indiana led No. 10 Ohio State by 9 points with 2:12 left in the game. The Buckeyes, who were undefeated in Big Ten play, took advantage of missed free throws from IU to tie the game at the end of regulation and won 66-63 in overtime. The following week, the Hoosiers returned to Assembly Hall and defeated Michigan 68-62 on February 1, and Ohio State 70-62 on February 3. Against the Wolverines, freshman forward Landon Turner sparked the Hoosiers with a new career-high 21 points, and against the Buckeyes, all five Indiana starters scored in double figures. Next, Indiana went up to Evanston, Illinois, and routed Northwestern 82-57 to improve to 6-5 in conference play.

On February 10, in Ann Arbor, Indiana lost to Michigan 60-59 on a 22-foot buzzer-beater by the Wolverines' Marty Bodnar. On February 15, IU slid back to 6-7 in the Big Ten by dropping its second straight game, this time at the hands of Michigan State, which charged into Assembly Hall and snatched away a 59-47 win. Indiana bounced back once again and won its next three games—68-62 at Wisconsin, 64-62 versus Iowa, and 71-46 versus Minnesota—to improve to 9-7 on the season. However, IU's postseason hopes seemed to go down the drain when the Hoosiers fell to Purdue 55-48 in West Lafayette on March 1. But then came one of the most magnificent performances in IU history. In the season finale against Illinois in Champaign, Mike Woodson canned 18 of 27 field goals and 12 of 14 free throws to ring up 48 points against an Illinois team that was No. 1 in the nation in field goal defense. The Hoosiers won 72-60 to finish 10-8 in league play and 18-12 overall.

Indiana's impressive win over Illinois earned the Hoosiers some last-minute consideration for an NIT berth. IU squeaked into the field and was assigned to play Texas Tech in Lubbock, Texas, on March 8. The Red Raiders, led by coach Gerald Myers, had already beaten Michigan, Texas and Arkansas that season. Tech's David Little declared, "We can beat anybody down here… I think we can beat Indiana." It was wishful thinking. IU won 78-59, as Woodson scored 30.

In the second round, Indiana beat a stubborn Alcorn State team 73-69 on March 12, in Bloomington. That sent the Hoosiers to New York City for the NIT finals in Madison Square Garden. In the semifinals, Indiana dispatched Ohio State 65-55, which led to a showdown with archrival Purdue in the championship game on March 21. The Boilermakers jumped out to a 29-25 halftime lead and held a 52-51 advantage in the final minutes. With 0:21 remaining, Purdue center Joe Barry Carroll missed the front end of a one-and-one, then with 0:06 on the clock, IU's Butch Carter buried the game-winning shot from the top of the key. Purdue's Jerry Sichting had a good look at a potential game-winner for the Boilermakers but he missed it, and Indiana escaped with the title.

Knight, who was a big fan of the NIT (his Army teams made it to the NIT semifinals three times), said after the Purdue win, "I've never had a bigger ambition than to win the NIT. This is as satisfying as the NCAA title [in 1976]."

INDIANA'S RANKING IN THE 1978-79 ASSOCIATED PRESS POLLS

PS	11/28	12/5	12/12	12/19	12/26	1/2	1/9	1/16	1/23	1/30	2/6	2/13	2/20	2/27	3/6	3/13
10	20	—	—	—	—	—	—	—	—	—	—	—	—	—	—	—

1979-80

OVERALL RECORD: 21-8

CONFERENCE RECORD: 13-5 (FIRST PLACE)

TEAM HONORS:

BIG TEN CHAMPION, CABRILLO CLASSIC CHAMPION,

INDIANA CLASSIC CHAMPION

INDIVIDUAL HONORS:

BOB KNIGHT—BIG TEN COACH OF THE YEAR

MIKE WOODSON—ALL-AMERICA, BIG TEN MVP

ISIAH THOMAS—ALL-BIG TEN (FIRST TEAM)

The 1978-79 team. First row (left to right): Mike Woodson, Glen Grunwald, Butch Carter, Ray Tolbert; Second row: Isiah Thomas, Steve Risley, Landon Turner, Eric Kirchner, Tony Brown; Third row: Phil Isenbarger, Randy Wittman, Chuck Franz, Ted Kitchel, Steve Bouchie, Jim Thomas. IU Archives

The Hoosier squad that captured the 1979 NIT championship not only returned all five starters for the 1979-80 season, but also added Glen Grunwald and Ted Kitchel (who both returned from red-shirt seasons) along with a five-man freshman class headlined by Isiah Thomas, one of the most coveted basketball recruits in the nation. "We have some good returning players and some good kids coming in," admitted coach Bob Knight before the season began.

Of the returnees, the standout was 6'5" senior forward Mike Woodson, who had led Indiana in scoring during his sophomore and junior seasons. For his senior year, Woodson was on track to become the all-time leading scorer in IU and Big Ten history. He needed 402 points to surpass Don Schlundt for the

Indiana record and 322 points during league play to overtake Minnesota's Mychal Thompson for the Big Ten mark. Woodson and senior guard Butch Carter, who had hit the game-winning shot in the NIT title game, had been named co-captains of the 1979-80 team and had embraced their leadership role in a way that pleased Coach Knight.

"Woodson and Carter ... have been extremely good in helping the younger players prepare for the season," said Knight. "I think they both matured a lot last year. They have an excellent understanding of what all it takes to have a good team."

Entering the campaign, Indiana was ranked No. 1 in the nation and was the preseason favorite for the national championship. The 1980 Final Four was scheduled to be played in Indianapolis, so it appeared that destiny may have been winking at the Hoosiers. Unfortunately, a cruel twist of fate would eventually throw destiny's plans into disarray.

On December 1, the Hoosiers opened their schedule with an 80-52 shellacking of Miami of Ohio in Assembly Hall. However, much to Knight's chagrin, the Hoosiers only led by a point at the half, before the squad woke up and kicked its attack into high gear. Five different Hoosiers scored in double figures, led by Woodson with 14 and Isiah Thomas with 12 in his collegiate debut. Next, the Hoosiers swept the Indiana Classic with blowouts over Xavier, 92-66, and UTEP, 75-43, on December 7-8. The competition stepped up a notch on December 11, when No. 16 Georgetown came to Assembly Hall. In a well-played game that featured hot shooting from both teams, the Hoosiers survived with a 76-69 win.

After a solid 4-0 start, the Hoosiers slammed headlong into disaster on December 15, in Lexington, Kentucky, against the No. 5 Kentucky Wildcats. The first half went deceivingly well as the Hoosiers jumped out to an early 13-point lead and then held on for a 39-36 advantage at the break. But early in the second half, sophomore guard Randy Wittman, who had led IU in minutes played the previous season, limped off the court in pain and did not return (he ended up missing the entire season with a stress fracture in his foot). Then things got worse. Woodson hurt his back. He stayed in the game but simply wasn't himself, as he went 0-8 from the field in the second half. Soon, IU point guard Isiah Thomas landed himself in foul trouble and was confined to

1979-80 TEAM ROSTER

Head coach: Bob Knight
Assistant coaches: Gerry Gimelstob, Tom Miller, Jim Crews, Jene Davis

No.	Player	Hometown	Class	Position	Height
54	Steve Bouchie	Washington, IN	Fr	F	6-8
31	Tony Brown	Chicago, IL	Fr	G	6-2
41	Butch Carter (Capt.)	Middletown, OH	Sr	G	6-5
23	Chuck Franz	Clarksville, IN	Fr	G	6-2
40	Glen Grunwald	Franklin Park, IL	Sr	F	6-9
44	Phil Isenbarger	Muncie, IN	Jr	F	6-8
30	Ted Kitchel	Galveston, IN	So	F	6-8
34	Steve Risley	Indianapolis, IN	Jr	F	6-8
11	Isiah Thomas	Chicago, IL	Fr	G	6-1
20	Jim Thomas	Fort Lauderdale, FL	Fr	G	6-3
45	Ray Tolbert	Anderson, IN	Jr	F/C	6-9
32	Landon Turner	Indianapolis, IN	So	F/C	6-10
24	Randy Wittman	Indianapolis, IN	So	G	6-6
42	Mike Woodson (Capt.)	Indianapolis, IN	Sr	F	6-5

SEASON RESULTS 1979-80

Date	Court	Opponent	Result	Score
12/1/1979	H	Miami of Ohio	W	80-52
12/7/1979	H	Xavier	W	92-66
12/8/1979	H	UTEP	W	75-43
12/11/1979	H	Georgetown	W	76-69
12/15/1979	A	Kentucky	L	58-69
12/18/1979	N1	Toledo	W	80-56
12/22/1979	H	North Carolina	L	57-61
12/28/1979	N2	Tennessee	W	70-68
12/29/1979	N2	Brown	W	61-52
1/3/1980	A	Ohio State	L	58-59
1/5/1980	A	Wisconsin	L	50-52
1/10/1980	H	Michigan	W	63-61
1/12/1980	H	Michigan State	W	72-64
1/17/1980	H	Iowa	W	81-69
1/19/1980	A	Northwestern	W	81-72
1/24/1980	A	Minnesota	L	47-55
1/26/1980	H	Purdue	W	69-58
1/31/1980	H	Illinois	W	60-54
2/2/1980	A	Purdue	L	51-56
2/7/1980	H	Northwestern	W	83-69
2/9/1980	A	Illinois	L	68-89
2/14/1980	A	Iowa	W	66-55
2/16/1980	H	Minnesota	W	67-54
2/21/1980	A	Michigan State	W	75-72
2/23/1980	A	Michigan	W	65-61
2/28/1980	H	Wisconsin	W	61-52
3/2/1980	H	Ohio State	W	76-73
NCAA Tournament				
3/9/1980	N3	Virginia Tech	W	68-59
3/13/1980	N4	Purdue	L	69-76

1 Indianapolis, IN
2 San Diego, CA
3 Bowling Green, KY
4 Lexington, KY

1979-80 BIG TEN STANDINGS

	W	L	PCT
Indiana	13	5	.722
Ohio State	12	6	.667
Purdue	11	7	.611
Iowa	10	8	.556
Minnesota	10	8	.556
Illinois	8	10	.444
Michigan	8	10	.444
Wisconsin	7	11	.389
Michigan St.	6	12	.333
Northwestern	5	13	.278

the bench for long stretches before fouling out with 6:42 remaining. The end result was 26 percent shooting in the second half for IU and a 69-58 Wildcat victory.

IU returned to the Hoosier state and whipped Toledo 80-56 in Indianapolis on December 18 to improve to 5-1 on the season. Woodson led all scorers with 19 points, but afterwards his back was causing him a lot of pain, and he was diagnosed with a herniated disk that would require surgery. The surgery was soon arranged, and Woodson was sidelined indefinitely to rehabilitate. Indiana had hopes that he could return by the end of the season, but his status remained a question mark. No. 8 North Carolina took advantage of the ailing Hoosiers by coming into Assembly Hall on December 22 and stealing a 61-57 win that dropped IU to 5-2.

Indiana then closed out the preconference season by playing in the Cabrillo Classic in San Diego on December 28-29. Isiah Thomas carried the undermanned Hoosiers to wins over Tennessee (70-68) and Brown (61-50) to wrap up the title. Thomas was named the tournament MVP, but he had 17 turnovers in the two games and drew the ire of Knight for his carelessness with the ball. With Woodson out, it was clear that Thomas was now the focal point of the Hoosiers, and the freshman was now being held to a higher standard by his coach.

After a 7-2 preconference showing, the Hoosiers hobbled into Big Ten play with four players sidelined by injuries. Phil Isenbarger and Ted Kitchel had joined Wittman and Woodson in street clothes for Indiana's conference opener against No. 5 Ohio State in Columbus. Indiana was a surprise five-point leader at halftime, but OSU freshman Clark Kellogg sank two free throws with 0:07 remaining to lift the Buckeyes to a 59-58 win.

After the tough loss to his alma mater, Knight said, "I thought my kids played extremely hard. I was

very proud of them. There were three or four times when they could have let this game get away, but they kept hanging in there, coming back. It all came down to a couple of plays and we didn't get them. But we can't ask for anything more than what the kids gave tonight."

Two nights after the Ohio State loss, Indiana played Wisconsin in Madison, and the Hoosiers blew several opportunities down the stretch in a 52-50 loss to the Badgers. Fortunately, the crippled Hoosiers then returned to Assembly Hall, where they won three straight games—63-61 over Michigan in OT, 72-64 over Michigan State, and 81-69 over Iowa. On January 19, Isiah Thomas returned home to the Chicago area and scored a new career-high 28 points to lead Indiana to an important road win over Northwestern 81-72. On January 24, the Hoosiers dropped a 55-47 contest at Minnesota, but bounced back and won two more games at Assembly Hall: 69-58 over Purdue and 60-54 over Illinois. That put Indiana at 6-3 in league play and in a four-way tie for first place. Plus, it was starting to look like Woodson might be able to return to action before the end of Big Ten play.

Unfortunately, the Hoosiers then staggered a little bit, losing two of the next three games. Both losses came on the road. IU fell 56-51 at Purdue on February 2, and 89-68 at Illinois on February 9. In between those two games, Indiana clobbered Northwestern 83-69 in Bloomington (that win was also the 300th of Knight's career, making him the youngest coach to ever reach that milestone). Indiana stood at 7-5, but was only one game out of first place with six games remaining. That's when the miracle began.

As the five Hoosier starters walked out to center court for the opening tip of their February 14 matchup against No. 20 Iowa in Iowa City, all eyes were on the 6'5" guy in the red No. 42 jersey. Mike

INDIANA'S RANKING IN THE 1979-80 ASSOCIATED PRESS POLLS

PS	12/4	12/11	12/18	12/26	1/2	1/8	1/15	1/22	1/29	2/5	2/12	2/19	2/26	3/4
1	1	1	5	10	11	19	19	16	18	20	—	19	13	7

Woodson was back in the lineup for Indiana. Most observers looked at Woodson with a wary eye and doubted that he could be very effective after missing two months while rehabilitating from major surgery. However, a minute into the game, Woodson peeled off a screen, caught the ball in rhythm and buried his first jump shot. Then he buried his second shot. Moments later he drained his third straight jumper. He eventually scored 18 points and helped carry the Hoosiers to a huge 66-55 win over one of their main rivals for the conference title. Next, Indiana buried Minnesota 67-54 in Assembly Hall, as Woodson scored a game-high 24 points. The following week, the Hoosiers went on the road and stole two games in the state of Michigan. They went to East Lansing and beat Michigan State 75-72 on February 21, as all five IU starters scored in double figures, and then they went to Ann Arbor on February 23, and defeated Michigan 65-61, as Woodson dropped in 24 points. Back in Bloomington on February 28, Indiana survived a 61-52 win over Wisconsin. It was IU's fifth straight victory, and it put the 13th-ranked Hoosiers at 12-5 in Big Ten play and tied with No. 9 Ohio State for first place. That set up the perfect showdown, as OSU was scheduled to play Indiana in Bloomington on the final day of the Big Ten season.

On Sunday, March 2, the Buckeyes and the Hoosiers clashed in a winner-take-all battle for the conference crown. Ohio State grabbed an early 10-3 lead, but Indiana led 37-34 at the half. With eight minutes remaining, the Buckeyes surged to a 59-51 advantage, but the Hoosiers put on a 6-0 run to keep pace. IU senior Butch Carter calmly nailed two free throws in the final seconds to send the game into overtime, where Indiana finally triumphed 76-73 to capture the title and send the tense Assembly Hall crowd into a jubilant frenzy.

When the dust settled after Indiana's amazing comeback run to clinch the Big Ten championship, the Hoosiers discovered that they were the No. 2 seed in the Midwest Regional of the NCAA Tournament. That gave IU a first-round bye and matched up with Virginia Tech in Bowling Green, Kentucky, on March 9. Indiana controlled the game and won 68-59. However, on March 13 in Lexington, Kentucky—the same floor where Woodson and Wittman got hurt at the beginning of the season—Purdue gained its revenge for the defeat to IU in the 1979 NIT final by

knocking the Hoosiers out of the 1980 NCAA tournament with a 76-69 Boilermaker win. Purdue went on to the Final Four.

In the end, the energy it took for Woodson and the Hoosiers to rally for the Big Ten title left IU and its courageous star without much fuel in the tank for a run in the NCAA Tournament. However, Woodson's miraculous six-game comeback earned him Big Ten MVP honors and the 1979-80 Hoosiers won the conference title with one of the most dramatic and exciting three-week stretches of basketball in IU history.

1980-81

FOR THE COMMENTARY AND STATISTICS FOR THE 1980-81 SEASON, PLEASE SEE CHAPTER 5, "1980-81: THE BEST DEFENSE IN COLLEGE BASKETBALL."

1981-82

OVERALL RECORD: 19-10
CONFERENCE RECORD: 12-6 (SECOND PLACE)
TEAM HONORS:
INDIANA CLASSIC CHAMPION
INDIVIDUAL HONORS:
TED KITCHEL—ALL-AMERICA, ALL-BIG TEN (FIRST TEAM)
RANDY WITTMAN—ACADEMIC ALL-AMERICA, ACADEMIC ALL-BIG TEN
LANDON TURNER—ALL-AMERICA (HONORARY)

In a perfect world, the 1981-82 Indiana basketball team would have entered the season as one of the top-ranked teams in college basketball and would have been favored to defend the national championship that it had earned in Philadelphia in the spring of 1981. Of course, this is not a perfect world, but one that is often filled with heartbreaks, accidents and

The 1981-82 team. First row (left to right): Tony Brown, Chuck Franz, Dan Dakich, Winston Morgan, Rick Rowray, Jim Thomas; Second row: Ted Kitchel, Mike LaFave, John Flowers, Uwe Blab, Steve Bouchie, Randy Wittman. IU Archives

cold realities. For the Indiana basketball team, that meant losing its top two returnees for the 1981-82 team. Isiah Thomas, who would have been a junior, declared "hardship" and left IU for the 1981 NBA draft (it should be noted that in Isiah's case, the hardship was legitimate as his mother was struggling to provide for a large family in Chicago). Landon Turner, who was one of the key factors in IU's 1981 NCAA Tournament run and who would have been a senior on the 1981-82 squad, suffered a tragic auto accident during the summer of 1981 that left him paralyzed from the waist down.

Without a single senior on the roster, the leadership of the IU squad fell to juniors Ted Kitchel and Randy Wittman. They were the top two returning scorers and both had redshirted for one season due to injuries, so they were both seniors academically and were entering their fourth season as part of the IU basketball program. Other key returnees included juniors Steve Bouchie and Tony Brown, and sophomore Jim Thomas, who was named to the All-Final Four team in 1981 for his terrific all-around perform-

ance. The loss of Turner also meant that IU had to look for contributions from two freshmen big men: 6'9" John Flowers and 7'2" Uwe Blab, the tallest player ever to play for the Hoosiers.

The defending national champs tipped off the season on November 28, by barely slipping by Miami of Ohio 71-64, as Kitchel carried the Hoosiers with a game-high 24 points. As a result of IU's lackluster performance, Knight benched four starters, including Wittman and Kitchel, when No. 12 Indiana hosted Notre Dame on December 1. The pair came off the bench and sparked the Hoosiers to a 69-55 win. Kitchel scored 22 points and Wittman chipped in 15. Freshman John Flowers, who started in place of Kitchel, also contributed 11 points and seven rebounds, while Notre Dame's John Paxson had game-high honors with 24 points.

On December 8, IU went down to Rupp Arena in Lexington, Kentucky, and got whipped 85-69 by the Kentucky Wildcats, as 1980 Indiana Mr. Basketball Jim Master burned IU for 17 points. The 2-1 Hoosiers went back to Bloomington and roasted a couple sacrificial lambs in the Indiana Classic on December 11-12—Colorado fell 82-41 and Penn State went down 80-51. IU followed those two wins with victories over Tulane (77-59) and Kansas State (58-49) to improve to 6-1. Next, the Indiana squad went to New York City and played in the ECAC Holiday Festival on December 28-29. In the opening game, the 11th-ranked Hoosiers led No. 20 Villanova for most of the game, but Wildcat freshman Ed Pinckney caught fire in the second half and lifted Villanova to a 63-59 win. In the consolation game, Kansas outdueled Indiana 71-61, led by 32 points from David Magley, the 1978 Indiana Mr. Basketball.

The Hoosiers, who were suddenly struggling at 6-3, began Big Ten play with two road games, and lost them both. The first came when IU traveled to East Lansing on January 7, and turned the ball over 24 times in losing to the Michigan State Spartans 65-58. Then, on January 9, Northwestern took advantage of 30 IU turnovers to clobber the Hoosiers 75-61 in Evanston. It was the first time an Indiana team had lost to the Wildcats during Bob Knight's tenure at IU. Four straight losses put IU at 6-5 overall and 0-2 in conference play.

On January 14, in Assembly Hall, IU finally stemmed the tide on the losing streak with a convincing 81-51 victory over Michigan, which entered the game 1-9 for the season. Kitchel had 18 and 10 rebounds, while IU point guard Tony Brown had 15 points, eight rebounds, and eight assists. Next, on January 16, in Bloomington, the Hoosiers pulled out a 66-61 win over Ohio State, snapping the Buckeyes' nine-game winning streak. Indiana continued its winning streak by taking the next three games: 54-53 at Illinois on January 21; 77-55 against Purdue in Bloomington on January 23; and 62-56 at Wisconsin on January 28. Indiana's five-game winning streak, which had improved the Hoosiers to 11-5 overall and 5-2 in the conference, came to an end on January 30, when No. 10 Minnesota came into Assembly Hall and snatched a 69-62 win.

To make matters worse, the Hoosiers' next two games were on the road at Iowa and Minnesota, the top two teams in the Big Ten. On February 4, at Iowa, the fifth-ranked Hawkeyes ran IU out of Iowa City with a 61-40 beating. Then, on February 6, Indiana went into Williams Arena in Minneapolis and unveiled a new weapon in 7'2" center Uwe Blab.

1981-82 TEAM ROSTER

Head coach: Bob Knight
Assistant coaches: Jim Crews, Jene Davis, Kohn Smith, Joby Wright

No.	Player	Hometown	Class	Position	Height
33	Uwe Blab	Munich, Germany	Fr	C	7-2
54	Steve Bouchie	Washington, IN	Jr	F	6-8
31	Tony Brown	Chicago, IL	Jr	G	6-2
25	Cam Cameron	Terre Haute, IN	Jr	G	6-2
11	Dan Dakich	Merrillville, IN	Fr	G/F	6-5
42	John Flowers	Fort Wayne, IN	Fr	F/C	6-9
23	Chuck Franz	Clarksville, IN	Jr	G	6-2
30	Ted Kitchel (Capt.)	Galveston, IN	Jr	F	6-8
43	Mike LaFave	Indianapolis, IN	So	F	6-9
21	Winston Morgan	Anderson, IN	Fr	G/F	6-5
44	Rick Rowray	Muncie, IN	Fr	G	6-6
20	Jim Thomas	Fort Lauderdale, FL	Jr	G/F	6-3
32	Landon Turner (Capt.)	Indianapolis, IN	Sr	F/C	6-10
24	Randy Wittman	Indianapolis, IN	Jr	G	6-6

SEASON RESULTS 1981-82

Date	Court	Opponent	Result	Score
11/28/1981	H	Miami of Ohio	W	71-64
12/1/1981	H	Notre Dame	W	69-55
12/8/1981	A	Kentucky	L	69-85
12/11/1981	H	Colorado State	W	82-41
12/12/1981	H	Penn State	W	80-51
12/14/1981	N1	Tulane	W	77-59
12/19/1981	H	Kansas State	W	58-49
12/28/1981	N2	Villanova	L	59-63
12/29/1981	N2	Kansas	L	61-71
1/7/1982	A	Michigan State	L	58-65
1/9/1982	A	Northwestern	L	61-75
1/14/1982	H	Michigan	W	81-51
1/16/1982	H	Ohio State	W	66-61
1/21/1982	A	Illinois	W	54-53
1/23/1982	H	Purdue	W	77-55
1/28/1982	A	Wisconsin	W	62-56
1/30/1982	H	Minnesota	L	62-69
2/4/1982	A	Iowa	L	40-62
2/6/1982	A	Minnesota	W	58-55
2/11/1982	H	Illinois	W	73-60
2/13/1982	H	Iowa	W	73-58
2/18/1982	H	Wisconsin	W	88-57
2/20/1982	A	Purdue	L	65-76
2/25/1982	A	Ohio State	L	65-68
2/27/1982	A	Michigan	W	78-70
3/4/1982	H	Northwestern	W	79-49
3/6/1982	H	Michigan State	W	74-58
NCAA Tournament				
3/11/1982	N3	Robert Morris	W	94-62
3/13/1982	N3	UAB	L	70-80

1 Indianapolis, IN
2 New York, NY
3 Nashville, TN

1981-82 BIG TEN STANDINGS

	W	L	PCT
Minnesota	14	4	.778
Iowa	12	6	.667
Ohio State	12	6	.667
Indiana	12	6	.667
Purdue	11	7	.611
Illinois	10	8	.556
Michigan St.	7	11	.389
Michigan	7	11	.389
Northwestern	5	13	.278
Wisconsin1	0	18	.000

1 NCAA declared all games forfeited

The 1981-82 season was overshadowed by the tragic car accident suffered by Landon Turner. Turner would have been a senior and was expected to be one of the best forwards in college basketball after a strong finish to his junior season. He was named an honorary captain of the Hoosiers and was also an honorary All-American. IU Archives

Knight inserted Blab into the starting line-up to match up against Minnesota's 7'3" Randy Breuer, one of the best centers in Big Ten. Blab disrupted Breuer into a nine-point, five-rebound performance, while Blab surprised everyone with 18 points and eight rebounds of his own. IU also got a big boost from Randy Wittman, who broke out of a terrible shooting slump by sinking three straight baskets down the stretch to push Indiana into the lead, and he eventually clinched a 58-55 Indiana win with three key free throws. The crucial victory put Indiana at 6-4 in conference play, while the Gophers dropped back to 7-3.

After the Minnesota win, the Hoosiers returned to Bloomington for a three-game homestand and mowed down three opponents in a row. Kitchel broke loose for 34 points as Indiana clobbered Illinois 73-60 on February 11. First-place Iowa came to town on February 13, and the Hoosiers annihilated the No. 5 Hawkeyes 73-58. Then last-place Wisconsin came to Assembly Hall on February 18, and got throttled 88-57. However, after upping their record to 9-4, the high-flying Hoosiers came back to earth when they took their final road swing of the year and dropped two out of three games to fall out of contention for the Big Ten title. The losses came at Purdue, 76-65 on February 20, and Ohio State, 68-65 on February 25. IU salvaged one more road win by beating Michigan 78-70 on February 27, in Ann Arbor, as Kitchel scored a game-high 28 points.

Playing for a postseason berth, the IU squad closed out its schedule by rallying for

INDIANA'S RANKING IN THE 1981-82 ASSOCIATED PRESS POLLS

PS	12/1	12/8	12/15	12/22	12/29	1/5	1/12	1/19	1/26	2/2	2/9	2/16	2/23	3/2	3/9
12	12	10	13	11	11	—	—	—	—	—	—	20	—	—	—

convincing wins over Northwestern (79-49) and Michigan State (74-58) in Assembly Hall. In both games, the Hoosiers showed great scoring balance, with four starters in double figures against the Wildcats and all five in double figures against the Spartans. IU finished league play with a 12-6 record (18-9 overall), which earned the Hoosiers a three-way tie for second place in the Big Ten. That was also good enough to secure an at-large berth in the NCAA tournament, where Indiana was awarded a No. 5 seed in the Mideast Regional.

In the opening round, Indiana demolished 12th-seeded Robert Morris 94-62. The second round was a different story, however, as fourth seed Alabama-Birmingham (whom IU had beaten in the second round a year earlier) jumped all over the Hoosiers from the outset and took a 40-22 lead into the break. That was enough of a cushion for UAB to hold on for an 80-70 win that knocked the defending champs out of the NCAA tournament.

After a 6-5 start, including 0-2 in the Big Ten, this team looked like it was headed for a dismal season. Somehow, Coach Bob Knight was able to pull his players together and turn them into a dangerous team that challenged for the Big Ten championship and earned an NCAA tournament berth. With the entire team set to return for another season, IU fans wondered what Knight could accomplish with these Hoosiers now that they had a year's worth of experience together.

1982-83

OVERALL RECORD: 24-6

CONFERENCE RECORD: 13-5 (FIRST PLACE)

TEAM HONORS:

BIG TEN CHAMPION, HOOSIER CLASSIC CHAMPION, INDIANA CLASSIC CHAMPION

INDIVIDUAL HONORS:

RANDY WITTMAN—ALL-AMERICA, BIG TEN MVP, ALL-BIG TEN (FIRST TEAM), ACADEMIC ALL-AMERICA, ACADEMIC ALL-BIG TEN

TED KITCHEL—ALL-AMERICA, ALL-BIG TEN (FIRST TEAM)

UWE BLAB—ACADEMIC ALL-BIG TEN

The Indiana Hoosiers returned virtually the entire roster from the senior-less squad that had earned a Big Ten runner-up finish in 1981-82. Plus, IU added three excellent freshmen in 6'8" forward Mike Giomi, 6'1" guard Stew Robinson, and 6'4" forward Tracy Foster. Still, the best thing the 1982-83 Indiana team had going for it was a strong group of five seniors—Randy Wittman, Ted Kitchel, Jim Thomas, Tony Brown and Steve Bouchie—who had been through the rigors of championship seasons with previous teams. Naturally, Hoosier fans were very optimistic about IU's chances for the 1982-83 campaign. However, coach Bob Knight was apt to point out that the 1981-82 team had some key weaknesses and deficiencies that needed to be addressed. Plus, the players on the team hadn't actually won anything on their own, without the help of previous Hoosiers such as Mike Woodson, Isiah Thomas and Ray Tolbert.

"Our team is unproven," said Knight in the preseason. "I really don't know how good our team can be. Even though we have everyone back, we have to show improvement in a lot of areas if we are to become a good team."

On opening night, Randy Wittman stole the show in IU's 91-75 trouncing of Ball State in Assembly Hall on November 27. The 6'5" senior guard poured in a new career-high 28 points and

The 1982-83 team. First row (left to right): [unknown manager], Randy Wittman, Jim Thomas, Ted Kitchel, Tony Brown, Steve Bouchie, [unknown manager]; Second row: team physician Dr. Brad Bomba, Chuck Franz, Winston Morgan, Dan Dakich, Stew Robinson, Cam Cameron, Mike Giomi, trainer Tim Garl; Third row: head coach Bob Knight, assistant coach Kohn Smith, assistant coach Joby Wright, Uwe Blab, Tracy Foster, assistant coach Jim Crews, assistant coach Royce Waltman. IU Archives

blanketed the Cardinals' 5'9" Ray McCallum, one of the top shooters in the country. Wittman held him to 13 points and kept him from taking advantage of the new three-point line (which the Big Ten was experimenting with that season) to get some extra mileage from his outside shots. On November 29, Wittman upped the ante on his career shooting night by hitting for 31 points and boosting the Hoosiers to a 75-59 win at Miami of Ohio. Next, the eighth-ranked Hoosiers recorded easy wins over UTEP, 65-54 in Assembly Hall, and Notre Dame, 68-52 in South Bend, to improve to 4-0 on the season.

On December 11-12, IU steamrolled through the Indiana Classic, beating Eastern Michigan 85-48 and Wyoming 78-65. Wittman earned tournament MVP honors after scoring 30 against Wyoming in the title game. On December 18, Indiana went to Manhattan, Kansas, and barely escaped with a 46-44 win against Kansas State, thanks to clutch free throw shooting from Tony Brown and Winston Morgan. Next, on December 22, the 7-0 Hoosiers, ranked No.

5 in the country, played host to the 7-0 Kentucky Wildcats, ranked No. 2. Indiana took a 32-27 lead at the half and made the plays down the stretch to pull out a 62-59 win that drew a small fist-pump from Knight as the buzzer sounded. Wittman had 17 points and 12 rebounds, and Jim Thomas chipped in 15 points and 10 rebounds.

Indiana finished the preconference season with the Hoosier Classic in Market Square Arena in Indianapolis on December 29-30. IU protected its perfect record by sweeping both games. The No. 1-ranked Hoosiers blitzed Grambling 110-62 in the first game, and then walloped Nebraska 67-50 in the championship game.

The undefeated, top-ranked Hoosiers faced the stern challenge of opening Big Ten play with three road games. On January 8, IU traveled to Columbus, Ohio, and engaged in a spirited battle with the Ohio State Buckeyes that featured 14 first-half lead changes. OSU led 34-32 at the break and stayed a step ahead of Indiana for most of the second half on the way to a 70-67 Buckeye victory. It was the fourth time in five years that the Hoosiers had dropped their Big Ten opener.

IU responded to the OSU loss by going to Illinois on January 13, and blasting the Fighting Illini 69-55 with a big second-half run. Wittman scored a game-high 27 points while Kitchel added 20. Then, on January 15, the Indiana squad went into West Lafayette and pounced on Big Ten co-leader Purdue, leading the Boilermakers 36-16 late in the first half. Purdue put together a furious rally in the second half, but IU held them off and claimed an 81-78 triumph. Down the stretch, visions of lost leads at Mackey Arena from previous years—especially 1981—were on Ted Kitchel's mind.

"We had been up here before, played well and lost," said Kitchel. "That's gone through my mind a lot, losing that 16-point lead [in 1981]. That shouldn't have happened, not with that team." Kitchel found some redemption by leading Indiana to its first win in Mackey Arena since 1976.

The next week, the Hoosiers sped to home wins over Michigan State, 89-85, and Michigan, 93-76, to improve their conference record to 4-1. Then the Hoosiers went back on the road for a two-game swing. On January 26, second-ranked IU held off a determined Northwestern team 78-73. On January 29, the Hoosiers traveled to Iowa City and grabbed a two-point halftime lead over No. 14 Iowa. Four minutes into the second half, IU led 33-31, but then the Hawkeyes caught fire and went on a 32-15 run to close the game. Iowa won 63-48 and dropped Indiana to 5-2 and out of its undisputed spot at the top of the Big Ten standings. Afterwards, Coach Knight simply said, "We're going to have to regroup. We did a lot of things wrong."

IU bounced back by winning its next four games. The Hoosiers hosted Wisconsin on February 3, and No. 17 Minnesota on February 5. IU beat the Badgers 83-73, led by 29 points from Kitchel and 12 points and 12 rebounds from center Uwe Blab, and then overwhelmed the Golden Gophers 76-51, as Kitchel posted 20 points, eight rebounds, and four assists. The following week, Indiana duplicated that two-game feat by making a northern road swing to Minnesota and Wisconsin and coming back with two wins. On February 10, Indiana squeezed by No. 19 Minnesota 63-59 in Williams Arena, despite being

1982-83 TEAM ROSTER

Head coach: Bob Knight
Assistant coaches: Jim Crews, Kohn Smith,
Royce Waltman, Joby Wright

No.	Player	Hometown	Class	Position	Height
33	Uwe Blab	Munich, Germany	So	C	7-2
54	Steve Bouchie	Washington, IN	Sr	F	6-8
31	Tony Brown	Chicago, IL	Sr	G	6-2
25	Cam Cameron	Terre Haute, IN	Sr	G	6-2
11	Dan Dakich	Merrillville, IN	So	G	6-5
42	John Flowers	Fort Wayne, IN	So	F/C	6-9
40	Tracy Foster	Fort Wayne, IN	Fr	F	6-4
23	Chuck Franz	Clarksville, IN	Rs	G	6-2
41	Mike Giomi	Newark, OH	Fr	F	6-8
30	Ted Kitchel (Capt.)	Galveston, IN	Sr	F	6-8
21	Winston Morgan	Anderson, IN	So	G/F	6-5
22	Stew Robinson	Anderson, IN	Fr	G	6-1
20	Jim Thomas (Capt.)	Fort Lauderdale, FL	Sr	G	6-3
24	Randy Wittman (Capt.)	Indianapolis, IN	Sr	G/F	6-6

SEASON RESULTS 1982-83

Date	Court	Opponent	Result	Score
11/27/1982	H	Ball State	W	91-75
11/29/1982	A	Miami of Ohio	W	75-59
12/4/1982	H	UTEP	W	65-54
12/7/1982	A	Notre Dame	W	68-52
12/10/1982	H	Eastern Michigan	W	85-48
12/11/1982	H	Wyoming	W	78-65
12/18/1982	A	Kansas State	W	48-46
12/22/1982	H	Kentucky	W	62-59
12/29/1982	N1	Grambling	W	110-62
12/30/1982	N1	Nebraska	W	67-50
1/8/1983	A	Ohio State	L	67-70
1/13/1983	A	Illinois	W	69-55
1/15/1983	A	Purdue	W	81-78
1/20/1983	H	Michigan State	W	89-85
1/22/1983	H	Michigan	W	93-76
1/26/1983	A	Northwestern	W	78-73
1/29/1983	A	Iowa	L	48-63
2/3/1983	H	Wisconsin	W	83-73
2/5/1983	H	Minnesota	W	76-51
2/10/1983	A	Minnesota	W	63-59
2/12/1983	A	Wisconsin	W	75-56
2/16/1983	H	Iowa	L	57-58
2/19/1983	H	Northwestern	W	74-65
2/24/1983	A	Michigan	L	56-69
2/26/1983	A	Michigan State	L	54-62
3/3/1983	H	Purdue	W	64-41
3/5/1983	H	Illinois	W	67-55
3/12/1983	H	Ohio State	W	81-60
NCAA Tournament				
3/20/1983	N2	Oklahoma	W	63-49
3/24/1983	N3	Kentucky	L	59-64

1 Indianapolis, IN
2 Evansville, IN
3 Knoxville, TN

1982-83 BIG TEN STANDINGS

	W	L	PCT
Indiana	13	5	.722
Iowa	11	7	.611
Purdue	11	7	.611
Ohio State	11	7	.611
Illinois	11	7	.611
Minnesota	9	9	.500
Michigan St.	9	9	.500
Northwestern	8	10	.444
Michigan	7	11	.389
Wisconsin1	0	18	.000

1 NCAA declared all games forfeited

As a senior, 6'8" forward Ted Kitchel earned All-America honors for the second straight season. However, a late-season back injury brought a premature end to Kitchel's Indiana career. IU Archives

outrebounded by the Gophers 40-26. Two days later, Wittman poured in 26 points and Blab had 14 points and 11 rebounds to lift the Hoosiers past Wisconsin 75-56 in Madison.

Indiana, which had returned to No. 1 in the UPI poll, stood at the top of the Big Ten with a 9-2 record —a full two games ahead of the closest competitor. With five of their final seven contests scheduled to be played in Assembly Hall, the Hoosiers appeared well-positioned to run away with the conference crown. However, someone forgot to tell that to the sixteenth-ranked Iowa Hawkeyes, who came to Bloomington on February 26, and snuck out of town with a 58-57 win. Wittman was the only Hoosier in double figures with 33 points.

After the Iowa setback, IU got back on track with a tense 74-65 win over Northwestern in Assembly Hall. However, after the Northwestern win, the Hoosiers faced a two-game road swing in the state of Michigan, and the trip turned into a disaster. On February 24, in Ann Arbor, Ted Kitchel left the game in the opening minutes because of back spasms. Kitchel never returned, and the young Michigan Wolverines built a tidal wave of momentum in the second half that carried them to a 69-56 win. Next, Indiana went to East Lansing on February 26, and squared off with Michigan State. Without Kitchel, who had returned to Indiana to get medical attention for his ailing back, the Hoosiers' offense sputtered and the Spartans prevailed 62-54. At 10-5, IU had fallen back into a tie for first place with Ohio State, and with Kitchel's status uncertain, Indiana's Big Ten title hopes were suddenly in jeopardy—even though IU was set to play its final three conference games in Bloomington.

On March 3, Indiana's senior experience showed through, as the veteran Hoosiers showed some championship heart in routing third-place Purdue 64-41. After the game, Purdue coach Gene Keady gave a

INDIANA'S RANKING IN THE 1982-83 ASSOCIATED PRESS POLLS

PS	11/30	12/7	12/14	12/21	12/28	1/4	1/11	1/18	1/25	2/1	2/8	2/15	2/22	3/1	3/8	3/15
9	8	6	5	5	1	1	4	2	2	6	4	2	4	11	7	5

grudging nod to Bob Knight's game plan. "They did exactly what I thought they'd do," said Keady. "They went back to their early days of ball control and great defense when they didn't have great shooters."

That strategy worked for the Hoosiers again on March 5, when IU dispatched Illinois 67-55. That put Indiana at 12-5, with 11-6 Ohio State coming to Bloomington on March 12. The Buckeyes had a chance to earn a share of the Big Ten title if they could beat the Hoosiers, who were still without Kitchel (his back injury had ended his season). However, Ohio State never had a chance. With Wittman leading the way, the Hoosiers burst out of the gates, led by 20 points at the half, and steamrolled the Buckeyes 81-60. Wittman, who was later named the Big Ten MVP, scored a game-high 24 points, and his fellow seniors —Steve Bouchie, Tony Brown and Jim Thomas—also stepped up and had big performances. Bouchie had 10 points, six rebounds and four assists, Brown had nine points and eight assists, and Thomas had 17 points, five rebounds, and five assists. Sophomore Uwe Blab also gave IU a boost by playing on a sprained ankle and scoring 14 points. The win gave Indiana its third undisputed Big Ten championship in four seasons.

In the NCAA tournament the Hoosiers were awarded the No. 2 seed in the Mideast Regional, which gave them a first-round bye. In the second round, Indiana matched up with No. 7 seed Oklahoma, which was led by freshman forward Wayman Tisdale. The All-American Tisdale scored 14 points, but IU won 63-49. In the Regional Semifinals, No. 12 Kentucky got revenge for its December loss to the Hoosiers by knocking IU out of the tournament with a 62-59 Wildcat victory in Knoxville, Tennessee.

Losing Kitchel down the stretch was a heavy blow to the Hoosiers. It caused them to scramble to pull out the Big Ten championship, and it kept them from playing at full strength during the NCAA tournament. Still, the senior-led squad salvaged an excellent 24-6 season. However, with the graduation of Kitchel, Wittman, Thomas, Brown and Bouchie, IU would have to start over again in 1983-84.

1983-84

OVERALL RECORD: 22-9

CONFERENCE RECORD: 13-5 (THIRD PLACE)

TEAM HONORS:

HOOSIER CLASSIC CHAMPION,

INDIANA CLASSIC CHAMPION

INDIVIDUAL HONORS:

STEVE ALFORD—ALL-BIG TEN (FIRST TEAM)

UWE BLAB—ACADEMIC ALL-BIG TEN

After graduating five seniors who had been part of three Big Ten titles in four years, coach Bob Knight had to reconstruct his 1983-84 Hoosier squad from the ground up. The only returning starter was junior center Uwe Blab, who had started 19 of 30 games the previous season. The only senior on the team was reserve guard Chuck Franz, who had seen very little action during his IU career. That left Coach Knight with Blab and some up-and-coming juniors and sophomores—such as Dan Dakich, Mike Giomi and Stew Robinson—to build around.

In addition, the Hoosiers had one of the best incoming freshman classes in the country in Daryl Thomas, Todd Meier, Marty Simmons and Steve Alford. Another addition to the roster was junior college transfer Courtney Witte (the first JUCO player of the Knight era). The challenge for Knight was that all of his players, except Blab, had either minimal or no experience in college basketball.

That lack of experience showed on November 26, when IU dropped its opener 63-57 to Miami of Ohio. The upset-minded Redskins were led by 6'6" sophomore Ron Harper, who burned the Hoosiers for 26 points and 13 rebounds. The key to the game was that Miami shot 52 percent from the field against Indiana, which had been ranked first in the Big Ten in field-goal percentage defense for three straight seasons. After the pulling off the upset, Harper, who did most of the damage for the Redskins, said, "I was shocked it was that easy to score on them." For IU, two freshmen came off the bench and gave important contributions against Miami: Marty Simmons had 15 points, nine rebounds, and seven assists and Steve Alford scored 12 points.

The 1983-84 team. First row (left to right): Dan Dakich, Tracy Foster, Cam Cameron, Chuck Franz, Steve Alford, Stew Robinson; Second row: Courtney Witte, Daryl Thomas, Winston Morgan, Uwe Blab, Mike Giomi, Todd Meier, Marty Simmons. IU Archives

On November 29, in Bloomington, Knight started three freshmen—Simmons, Alford, and Todd Meier—against Notre Dame. Simmons scored a game-high 22 points and Alford chipped in 14 as the Hoosiers beat the Fighting Irish 80-72. Then, on Saturday, December 3, the Hoosiers traveled to Lexington, Kentucky, to play the No. 1 Kentucky Wildcats on national TV. Indiana shocked the Rupp Arena crowd by taking a 32-31 halftime lead. Kentucky fought back, led by star forward Kenny Walker and freshman James Blackmon, an Indiana native. Simmons and Alford kept the Hoosiers in the game, but Kentucky made several key plays in the final minutes to pull out a 59-54 win. Simmons scored a game-high 19 points while Alford scored 17.

IU split its next two games, beating Tennessee Tech 81-66 in Bloomington, but losing to a strong UTEP team 65-51 in Texas. That put the Hoosiers on unsteady ground at 2-3, but they responded by winning their final five preconference games. On December 16-17, they cruised through the Indiana Classic with wins over Texas A&M (73-48) and Illinois State (54-44). Then, on December 21, senior guard Chuck Franz stepped up and made the game-winning three-point play in the final seconds of over-

time to deliver a 56-53 Indiana win over Kansas State. Finally, on December 29-30, Indiana capped off its preconference schedule by winning the Hoosier Classic at Market Square Arena in Indianapolis. In the first game, IU bludgeoned Ball State 86-43, behind 28 points and 11 rebounds from Blab. In the title game, the Hoosiers toppled No. 12 Boston College 72-66, led by 21 points and nine rebounds from Simmons, who was named the tournament MVP. After a wobbly start, the Hoosiers had improved to 7-3.

In the conference opener on January 7, the youthful Hoosiers went into St. John Arena in Columbus, Ohio, and opened up a 19-point lead on Ohio State. The Buckeyes eventually closed the gap, but IU still prevailed 73-62, as Alford and Blab combined for 43 points and 15 rebounds. IU was impressive once again on January 11, in Bloomington, beating No. 9 Illinois 73-68 in overtime. Alford had a game-high 29 points, while Chuck Franz scored 20 (on 7-7 shooting from the field and 6-7 from the line). Purdue was the next visitor to Assembly Hall on January 14, and the Hoosiers looked like they were on their way to another victory as they opened up a 33-21 lead in the waning minutes of the first half. But from that point on, Purdue outscored IU 53-33 and captured a 74-66 win—the Boilermakers' first in Bloomington since 1977. With the victory, Purdue claimed sole ownership of first place in the Big Ten at 4-0, while IU dropped back to 2-1.

The next week, Indiana went north and split its two-game road swing in the state of Michigan, beating Michigan State 70-62 in overtime in East Lansing, but falling to Michigan 55-50 in Ann Arbor. With a 3-2 league record, the Hoosiers were only a game out of first place, but questions remained as to whether the young, inconsistent IU squad could really challenge for the conference title. Indiana answered the call by winning their next seven games. The first two wins came at home over Northwestern (57-44) and Iowa (54-47). Then came wins at Minnesota (67-54) and Wisconsin (81-67), followed by trips to Assembly Hall from Wisconsin, which fell 74-64, and Minnesota, which IU beat 74-72 in overtime. The final win of the streak came on February 16, at Iowa, where IU barely slipped by the Hawkeyes 49-45 to improve to 10-2 in conference play. However, that merely enabled the Hoosiers to keep pace with Big Ten frontrunners Purdue and Illinois, who were also 10-2.

Unfortunately, in the stretch run of the conference race, the inconsistency bug started biting the Hoosiers. Northwestern brought Indiana's seven-game win streak to an end on February 18, in Evanston by handing IU a 63-51 setback. Not a single Indiana player scored in double figures, and the Hoosiers got outrebounded by the Wildcats 41-27. Indiana responded on February 23, in Bloomington by clobbering the Michigan Wolverines 72-57, led by Alford's 18 points and six assists. However, the Hoosiers faltered when Michigan State, which was tied for last place in the conference, came into Assembly Hall on February 26, and stole a 57-54 win. Alford scored 30 points and dished out five assists, but the rest of the IU squad played terribly.

Of course, just when it looked like the Hoosiers were out of the Big Ten race, they went into West Lafayette on February 29, and completely dismantled No. 11 Purdue 78-59, as Stew Robinson broke out for a career-high 22 points off the bench. Then, on March 4, in Champaign, Illinois, Indiana's title hopes finally suffered a fatal blow when Illinois buried the Hoosiers 70-53. Then, on the final day of the season,

1983-84 TEAM ROSTER

Head coach: Bob Knight
Assistant coaches: Jim Crews, Kohn Smith, Royce Waltman, Joby Wright

No.	Player	Hometown	Class	Position	Height
12	Steve Alford	New Castle, IN	Fr	G	6-2
33	Uwe Blab	Munich, Germany	Jr	C	7-2
11	Dan Dakich (Capt.)	Merrillville, IN	Jr	G	6-5
40	Tracy Foster	Fort Wayne, IN	So	F	6-4
23	Chuck Franz	Clarksville, IN	Sr	G	6-2
41	Mike Giomi	Newark, OH	So	F	6-8
30	Todd Meier	Oshkosh, WI	Fr	F	6-8
21	Winston Morgan	Anderson, IN	Rs	G/F	6-5
22	Stew Robinson	Anderson, IN	So	G	6-1
50	Marty Simmons	Lawrenceville, IL	Fr	G/F	6-5
24	Daryl Thomas	Westchester, IL	Fr	F	6-7
52	Courtney Witte	Vincennes, IN	Jr	F	6-8

SEASON RESULTS 1983-84

Date	Court	Opponent	Result	Score
11/26/1983	H	Miami of Ohio	L	57-63
11/29/1983	H	Notre Dame	W	80-72
12/3/1983	A	Kentucky	L	54-59
12/6/1983	H	Tennessee Tech	W	81-66
12/10/1983	A	UTEP	L	61-65
12/16/1983	H	Texas A&M	W	73-48
12/17/1983	H	Illinois State	W	54-44
12/21/1983	H	Kansas State	W	56-53
12/29/1983	N1	Ball State	W	86-43
12/30/1983	N1	Boston College	W	72-66
1/7/1984	A	Ohio State	W	73-62
1/11/1984	H	Illinois	W	73-68
1/14/1984	H	Purdue	L	66-74
1/19/1984	A	Michigan State	W	70-62
1/21/1984	A	Michigan	L	50-55
1/26/1984	H	Northwestern	W	57-44
1/28/1984	H	Iowa	W	54-47
2/2/1984	A	Minnesota	W	67-54
2/4/1984	A	Wisconsin	W	81-67
2/9/1984	H	Wisconsin	W	74-64
2/11/1984	H	Minnesota	W	74-72
2/16/1984	A	Iowa	W	49-45
2/18/1984	A	Northwestern	L	51-63
2/23/1984	H	Michigan	W	72-57
2/26/1984	H	Michigan State	L	54-57
2/29/1984	A	Purdue	W	78-59
3/4/1984	A	Illinois	L	53-70
3/10/1984	H	Ohio State	W	53-49
NCAA Tournament				
3/17/1984	N2	Richmond	W	75-67
3/22/1984	N3	North Carolina	W	72-68
3/24/1984	N3	Virginia	L	48-50

1 Indianapolis, IN
2 Charlotte, NC
3 Atlanta, GA

1983-84 BIG TEN STANDINGS

	W	L	PCT
Illinois	15	3	.833
Purdue	15	3	.833
Indiana	13	5	.722
Michigan	11	7	.611
Michigan St.	9	9	.500
Ohio State	8	10	.444
Northwestern	7	11	.389
Minnesota	6	12	.333
Iowa	6	12	.333
Wisconsin1	0	18	.000

1 NCAA declared all games forfeited

Freshman Steve Alford arrived in Bloomington and surprised a lot of people with his effective play. He wasn't considered an outstanding college prospect because of his lack of height, strength, and quickness. However, Alford quickly broke into the starting lineup and led the Hoosiers in scoring at 15.5 PPG. IU Archives

Indiana blew a big lead but held on for a 53-49 win over Ohio State in Bloomington. That gave IU a 20-8 overall record and a 3-5 conference mark (the same record that had won the conference the year before). Unfortunately, Purdue and Illinois tied for the conference crown with identical 15-3 records, while IU earned sole possession of third place.

Indiana's strong play led to an NCAA berth and the fourth seed in the East Regional. That gave the Hoosiers a first-round bye. They were set to play the winner of 12th-seed Richmond and fifth-seed Auburn, led by future NBA stars Charles Barkley and Chuck Person. The Richmond Spiders pulled the upset and IU squared off with Richmond on March 17, in Charlotte, North Carolina. The Hoosiers used a terrific team effort to hold off the pesky Spiders for a 75-67 win and a berth in the Sweet Sixteen.

Unfortunately, Indiana's opponent in the Regional Semifinal was top-seed North Carolina, the No. 1 team in the nation. Coach Dean Smith's Tar Heels were loaded with talent, including Michael Jordan, Kenny Smith, Sam Perkins and Brad Daugherty, who were all future NBA players. From the time the Hoosiers began preparing for the Tar Heels, Coach Knight told his squad, "We're going to beat North Carolina, and here's how it's going to be done." Part of the plan was to have 6'5" Dan Dakich guard Jordan, the two-time defending college player of the year. When Dakich first found out about the plan, he said that he went back to his room and vomited. However, Dakich did a phenomenal job, holding Jordan to six of 14 from the field and just 13 points, while IU's Steve Alford had 27 points, six rebounds, and three assists. IU controlled the game from the start, opened up a few big leads, and held on for a 72-68 triumph to pull off one of the biggest upsets in NCAA Tournament history.

Two nights after upsetting North Carolina, the Hoosiers suffered their own upset in the Elite Eight,

INDIANA'S RANKING IN THE 1983-84 ASSOCIATED PRESS POLLS

PS	11/29	12/6	12/13	12/20	12/27	1/3	1/10	1/17	1/24	1/31	2/7	2/14	2/21	2/28	3/6	3/13
19	—	—	—	—	—	—	—	—	—	—	—	17	—	—	—	—

falling 50-48 to seventh-seeded Virginia (which had already knocked off Arkansas and Syracuse). Nevertheless, Indiana finished at 22-9 for the season, and although the young squad played with maddening inconsistency at times, they certainly overachieved for the season as a whole, and treated IU fans to several big wins over highly ranked teams.

1984-85

The youthful Indiana team that surprised the Big Ten and the college basketball world during the 1983-84 season returned with virtually its entire roster intact for the 1984-85 campaign. The players were a year older and had the experience of a strong showing in the Big Ten race and a run to the Elite Eight in the NCAA tournament. Plus, the Hoosiers had some valuable additions to the roster. After a medical redshirt season, Winston Morgan returned, and the 6'5" guard/forward was once again expected to be one of the Hoosiers' most versatile performers. The Hoosiers also added a stellar six-man freshman class, led by 6'4" guard Delray Brooks, who was the Indiana Mr. Basketball and the *USA Today* high school player of the year. The only player lost from the active roster was reserve guard Chuck Franz who graduated. The key returnees were senior center Uwe Blab and sophomore guard Steve Alford, who had spent the summer of 1984 winning the Olympic gold medal on the U.S. team coached by Bob Knight. All of that added up to make IU one of the most highly touted teams in the nation and ranked in the top five in most preseason polls.

However, Knight was skeptical. He told his players, "We snuck up on a lot of teams last year. This year they'll be ready for us." He also offered special counsel to Alford, saying, "You've got a target on you now. You're an Olympic gold medallist, and every guard you face is going to try to make a name for himself by trying to shut you down."

On November 24, the IU squad found out exactly what Knight was talking about when the Hoosiers dropped their season opener in Assembly Hall for the second straight season. Playing in front of a sellout crowd and a national television audience, No. 4 Indiana coughed up 25 turnovers and lost 75-64 to the Louisville Cardinals. After the game, Knight mocked his team's high ranking, saying, "I told them a long time ago that there may be 20 really good basketball teams in the United States, but that we're not one of them."

The Hoosiers notched their first win on December 1, by trouncing the Ohio Bobcats 90-73, as Alford poured in 23 points and three other Hoosiers joined him in double figures. Then, on December 4, against Notre Dame in South Bend, Alford found out what it meant to have a target on his back. The Fighting Irish played a box-and-one defense with four Irish defenders playing zone and guard Scott Hicks dogging Alford's steps no matter where he went. It worked. Alford went one of six from the field, scored four points, and had only two rebounds and two assists. Meanwhile, Notre Dame's freshman guard David Rivers broke loose for 23 points and five assists, and the Irish won 74-63.

Next, Kentucky came to Assembly Hall on December 8. Knight inserted Delray Brooks into the starting lineup, and the freshman guard responded by handing out 10 assists, committing zero turnovers, and playing excellent defense on the Kentucky guards. Brooks played all 40 minutes and the Hoosiers won 81-68. Alford was terrific, too, with 27 points, seven assists, and six rebounds. IU also got great contributions from Uwe Blab and Mike Giomi on the front line, and from Winston Morgan off the bench. Afterwards, Knight said, "We've tried to work this week on each guy who gets in the game making a positive contribution. That's what we got today—a positive contribution in every case."

Indiana used the Kentucky game as a springboard to win the final six games on its preconference

The 1984-85 team. First row (left to right): Marty Simmons, Delray Brooks, Steve Alford, Dan Dakich, Uwe Blab, Stew Robinson, Joe Hillman, Winston Morgan; Second row: [unknown], Todd Meier, Daryl Thomas, Mike Giomi, Brian Sloan, Steve Eyl, Kreigh Smith, Magnus Pelkowski. IU Archives

schedule. That included road wins over Iowa State (69-67) and Kansas State (70-58) and two victories each in the Indiana Classic (80-57 over Western Kentucky and 81-44 over St. Joseph's) and the Hoosier Classic (77-72 over Miami of Ohio and 80-63 over Florida). During the seven-game winning streak, the Hoosiers started looking like the quality team everyone had expected them to be. IU finished the preconference schedule at 8-2 and ranked No. 12 in the nation.

Indiana was unquestionably one of the Big Ten favorites, along with Illinois and Michigan, and the Hoosiers looked like a potent force on January 2, when they went into Chrisler Arena and spanked No. 18 Michigan 87-62—the worst loss a Michigan team had suffered in Ann Arbor in 23 years. IU did it by shooting 67 percent from the field, while holding Michigan to a paltry 35 percent. The key matchup was IU's Uwe Blab against Michigan's Roy Tarpley. Blab made 13-17 shots and scored 31 points, while holding Tarpley to 4-15 and 12 points (nine below his season average).

Unfortunately, the old menace of inconsistency from the previous season reared its ugly head on January 5, when the Hoosiers went to East Lansing, Michigan, and played a Michigan State team that was far less talented than the Michigan squad that IU handily defeated three days earlier. The Spartans controlled the game for most of the second half and toppled the Hoosiers 68-61. After that loss, IU came back to Bloomington and clobbered Northwestern (77-50) and Wisconsin (90-68) to improve to 3-1 in league play and 11-3 overall. The Hoosiers were tied with Michigan for the Big Ten lead. However, over the next seven weeks, Indiana went into a bewildering free fall as the team lost 10 of its final 14 conference games.

The first loss came on January 19, when Ohio State beat IU 86-84 in Columbus. Center Uwe Blab scored a career-high 33 points, but his 10-foot hook shot at the buzzer came up just short. After the OSU loss, Coach Knight was so upset with the play of Mike Giomi and Winston Morgan, two of IU's best rebounders, that he benched them for the entire game against Purdue on January 24. The Boilermakers out-rebounded the Hoosiers 37-20 and came away with a 62-52 victory. That led to Knight benching nearly all of his top players—Alford, Morgan, Giomi, Todd Meier, Marty Simmons, Daryl Thomas, Delray Brooks, Stew Robinson and Dan Dakich—for Indiana's game at No. 6 Illinois on January 27. The Fighting Illini won 52-41. Knight's move scandalized some IU fans, who claimed that Knight had essentially given away an important conference to one of Indiana's chief rivals for the Big Ten title. At 3-4, the Hoosiers were almost out of the race before it had even gotten started.

Controversy and confusion swirled over which players Knight would use in the Hoosiers' next game against Iowa on January 31, at Assembly Hall. The IU regulars returned to the floor—all except Mike Giomi, who was dismissed from the team by Knight for missing class. Unfortunately, IU was out of sync against Iowa, and the Hawkeyes won 72-59. However, with the starters back in the lineup, and the team adjusting to life without Giomi, IU won its next three games—89-66 against Minnesota, 58-54 at Wisconsin, and 78-59 at Northwestern. That evened Indiana's conference record at 6-6 and it looked like the Hoosiers were ready to turn things around.

Then things got much worse. The Hoosiers dropped an unprecedented three consecutive games in Assembly Hall—72-63 to Ohio State, 66-50 to No. 16 Illinois, and 72-63 to Purdue. The loss to the Boilermakers was the infamous "chair game" in which Knight flung a chair across the floor in disgust. The Hoosier coach was subsequently ejected from the game and suspended for one contest by the Big Ten.

IU stopped the losing streak by beating Minnesota 79-68 in Minneapolis on February 28. Then, the Hoosiers traveled to Iowa on March 3, and lost to the Hawkeyes 70-50 (that was the game Knight served his one-game suspension). Next, Indiana returned to Bloomington and lost its fourth straight game in Assembly Hall, 68-58 to Michigan State.

During the Hoosiers' conference downturn, Alford had been suffering through the worst shooting slump of his career. However, in the season finale against No. 7 Michigan, the sophomore guard finally righted the ship, scoring 22 points on 11-16 shooting. He also added six rebounds and four assists. IU played

1984-85 TEAM ROSTER

Head coach: Bob Knight
Assistant coaches: Jim Crews, Kohn Smith, Royce Waltman, Joby Wright

No.	Player	Hometown	Class	Position	Height
12	Steve Alford	New Castle, IN	So	G	6-2
33	Uwe Blab (Capt.)	Munich, Germany	Sr	C	7-2
23	Delray Brooks	Michigan City, IN	Fr	G	6-4
11	Dan Dakich (Capt.)	Merrillville, IN	Sr	G	6-5
32	Steve Eyl	Hamilton, OH	Fr	F	6-6
41	Mike Giomi	Newark, OH	Jr	F	6-8
44	Joe Hillman	Glendale, CA	Fr	G	6-2
30	Todd Meier	Oshkosh, WI	So	F	6-8
21	Winston Morgan	Anderson, IN	Jr	G/F	6-5
14	Magnus Pelkowski	Bogota, Columbia	Fr	C	6-10
22	Stew Robinson	Anderson, IN	Jr	G	6-1
50	Marty Simmons	Lawrenceville, IL	So	G/F	6-5
45	Brian Sloan	McLeansboro, IL	Fr	F	6-8
42	Kreigh Smith	Tipton, IN	Fr	F	6-7
24	Daryl Thomas	Westchester, IL	So	F	6-7
52	Courtney Witte	Vincennes, IN	Rs	F	6-8

SEASON RESULTS 1984-85

Date	Court	Opponent	Result	Score
11/24/1984	H	Louisville	L	64-75
12/1/1984	H	Ohio	W	90-73
12/4/1984	A	Notre Dame	L	63-74
12/8/1984	H	Kentucky	W	81-68
12/11/1984	A	Iowa State	W	69-67
12/14/1984	H	Western Kentucky	W	80-57
12/15/1984	H	St. Joseph's (PA)	W	81-44
12/22/1984	A	Kansas State	W	70-58
12/29/1984	N1	Miami of Ohio	W	77-72
12/30/1984	N1	Florida	W	80-63
1/2/1985	A	Michigan	W	87-62
1/5/1985	A	Michigan State	L	61-68
1/10/1985	H	Northwestern	W	77-50
1/12/1985	H	Wisconsin	W	90-68
1/19/1985	A	Ohio State	L	84-86
1/24/1985	A	Purdue	L	52-62
1/27/1985	A	Illinois	L	41-52
1/31/1985	H	Iowa	L	59-72
2/2/1985	H	Minnesota	W	89-66
2/7/1985	A	Wisconsin	W	58-54
2/9/1985	A	Northwestern	W	78-59
2/14/1985	H	Ohio State	L	63-72
2/21/1985	H	Illinois	L	50-66
2/23/1985	H	Purdue	L	63-72
2/28/1985	A	Minnesota	W	79-68
3/3/1985	A	Iowa	L	50-70
3/7/1985	H	Michigan State	L	58-68
3/10/1985	H	Michigan	L	73-71
National Invitation Tournament (NIT)				
3/15/1985	H	Butler	W	79-57
3/19/1985	H	Richmond	W	75-53
3/27/1985	H	Marquette	W	94-82
3/27/1985	N2	Tennessee	W	74-67
3/29/1985	N2	UCLA	L	62-65

1 Indianapolis, IN
2 New York, NY

1984-85 BIG TEN STANDINGS

	W	L	PCT
Michigan	16	2	.889
Illinois	12	6	.667
Purdue	11	7	.611
Ohio State	11	7	.611
Iowa	10	8	.556
Michigan St.	10	8	.556
Indiana	7	11	.389
Minnesota	6	12	.333
Wisconsin	5	13	.278
Northwestern	2	16	.111

The first seven-footer in IU history, center Uwe Blab had a breakout season as a senior when he averaged 16.0 PPG and earned all-conference honors. IU Archives

well and never trailed against the Wolverines until Gary Grant grabbed a deflected pass and scored at the buzzer to give Michigan a 73-71 victory. It was the Hoosiers' fifth straight home loss and it gave them a 7-11 conference record (15-13 overall) and a seventh-place finish in the Big Ten.

Despite IU's struggles during the Big Ten season, the squad still received an invitation to play in the postseason NIT. Knight was reluctant at first, because he didn't think his team had earned it, but he eventually decided to accept and told the team, "You can still get something out of this season. And we can build something for next year." Led by a renewed Alford, Indiana swept through its first three games, beating Butler (79-57), Richmond (75-53), and Marquette (94-82). Then the Hoosiers went to New York City to play the final rounds in Madison Square Garden. In the semifinals, IU dispatched Tennessee 74-67, but in the championship game, UCLA beat IU 65-62, led by sharp-shooting guard Reggie Miller.

During the 1984-85 season, and for years afterward, the question has often been asked, "What went wrong?" One of the common explanations was that Knight and Alford were both exhausted from their experience in the Olympics in the summer of 1984. Another common refrain was that the team never developed adequate on-court leadership. Others have suggested that Knight couldn't find the right buttons to push, and that some of the buttons he did push backfired on him and led to some players losing their confidence and struggling on the court. There's probably some truth to all of those explanations. In the end, it showed that even a great basketball mind such as Bob Knight doesn't always know the right buttons to push to make a team successful. The 1984-85 season ended up being one of only two seasons that Knight's teams finished with a losing conference record during his 29-year tenure at Indiana.

INDIANA'S RANKING IN THE 1984-85 ASSOCIATED PRESS POLLS

PS	11/27	12/4	12/11	12/18	12/25	1/1	1/8	1/15	1/22	1/29	2/5	2/12	2/19	2/26	3/5	3/12
4	12	11	16	16	15	12	11	8	13	—	—	—	—	—	—	—

1985-86

OVERALL RECORD: 21-8

CONFERENCE RECORD: 13-5 (SECOND PLACE)

TEAM HONORS:

HOOSIER CLASSIC CHAMPIONSHIP,

INDIANA CLASSIC CHAMPIONSHIP

INDIVIDUAL HONORS:

STEVE ALFORD—ALL-AMERICA,

ALL-BIG TEN (FIRST TEAM)

The 1985-86 team. First row (left to right): Todd Meier, Courtney Witte, Stew Robinson, Winston Morgan, Steve Alford, Kreigh Smith, Joe Hillman, Delray Brooks; Second row: Jeff Oliphant, Magnus Pelkowski, Ricky Calloway, Steve Eyl, Daryl Thomas, Todd Jadlow, Andre Harris, Brian Sloan. IU Archives

Indiana's 1985-86 season will forever be linked with John Feistein's book *A Season on the Brink.* Coach Bob Knight agreed to give Feinstein access to the most confidential parts of Indiana's basketball program—team practices, locker room conversations, pregame and postgame talks and coaches' meetings— throughout the 1985-86 campaign. As a result, the players, assistant coaches, and other individuals who played a part in Indiana basketball that season have been forever immortalized in the slice of history covered in *A Season on the Brink,* which went on to become one of the best-selling sports books of all time. Knight agreed to do the book because he wanted to show that a college basketball program could win championships while following the rules and requiring its players to go to class.

It ended up being a good season for Feinstein to observe the Indiana program and see Knight's crafti-

1985-86 TEAM ROSTER

Head coach: Bob Knight
Assistant coaches: Ron Felling, Kohn Smith,
Royce Waltman, Joby Wright

No.	Player	Hometown	Class	Position	Height
12	Steve Alford (Capt.)	New Castle, IN	Jr	G	6-2
23	Delray Brooks	Michigan City, IN	So	G	6-4
20	Ricky Calloway	Cincinnati, OH	Fr	G/F	6-6
32	Steve Eyl	Hamilton, OH	So	F	6-6
34	Andre Harris	Grand Rapids, MI	Jr	F	6-6
44	Joe Hillman	Glendale, CA	Rs	G	6-2
11	Todd Jadlow	Salina, KS	So	F/C	6-9
30	Todd Meier	Oshkosh, WI	Jr	F/C	6-8
21	Winston Morgan (Capt.)	Anderson, IN	Sr	G/F	6-5
35	Jeff Oliphant	Lyons, IN	Rs	G	6-5
14	Magnus Pelkowski	Bogota, Columbia	Rs	C	6-10
22	Stew Robinson (Capt.)	Anderson, IN	Sr	G	6-1
45	Brian Sloan	McLeansboro, IL	Rs	F/C	6-8
42	Kreigh Smith	Tipton, IN	Rs	F	6-7
24	Daryl Thomas	Westchester, IL	Jr	F/C	6-7
52	Courtney Witte	Vincennes, IN	Sr	F/C	6-8

SEASON RESULTS 1985-86

Date	Court	Opponent	Result	Score
11/30/1985	H	Kent State	W	89-73
12/3/1985	H	Notre Dame	W	82-67
12/7/1985	A	Kentucky	L	58-63
12/10/1985	H	Kansas State	W	78-71
12/13/1985	H	Louisiana Tech	W	84-63
12/14/1985	H	Texas Tech	W	74-59
12/18/1985	A	Louisville	L	63-65
12/21/1985	H	Iowa State	W	86-65
12/27/1985	N1	Idaho	W	87-57
12/28/1985	N1	Mississippi State	W	74-73
1/2/1986	H	Michigan	L	69-74
1/5/1986	H	Michigan State	L	74-77
1/11/1986	A	Northwestern	W	102-65
1/15/1986	H	Ohio State	W	69-66
1/23/1986	H	Purdue	W	71-70
1/25/1986	H	Illinois	W	71-69
1/30/1986	A	Iowa	L	69-79
2/1/1986	A	Minnesota	W	62-54
2/6/1986	H	Wisconsin	W	78-69
2/8/1986	H	Northwestern	W	77-52
2/16/1986	A	Ohio State	W	84-75
2/20/1986	A	Illinois	W	61-60
2/23/1986	A	Purdue	L	68-85
2/27/1986	H	Minnesota	W	95-63
3/2/1986	H	Iowa	W	80-73
3/5/1986	A	Michigan State	W	97-79
3/8/1986	A	Michigan	L	52-80
NCAA Tournament				
3/13/1986	N2	Cleveland State	L	79-83

1 Indianapolis, IN
2 Syracuse, NY

1985-86 BIG TEN STANDINGS

	W	L	PCT
Michigan	14	4	.778
Indiana	13	5	.722
Michigan St.	12	6	.667
Illinois	11	7	.611
Purdue	11	7	.611
Iowa	10	8	.556
Ohio State	8	10	.444
Minnesota	5	13	.278
Wisconsin	4	14	.222
Northwestern	2	16	.111

ness as a coach, as well as his legendary temper and his unflinching integrity. After the debacle of 1984-85 when a deep, talented, and highly ranked IU team went into a free fall in the Big Ten and suffered the worst conference record in Knight's Indiana career, there were a lot of question marks entering the 1985-86 season. The biggest question was who would play center. Uwe Blab graduated in 1985 and left a gaping hole in the Hoosier lineup. Knight decided that 6'7" junior Daryl Thomas was his best candidate. Thomas was a wing player who had usually liked to play facing the basket. During both his freshman and sophomore years he was listed as a guard/forward in the IU media guide. Knight was convinced he could turn Thomas into a forward/center by teaching how to use his quickness and strength against bigger players, and by enhancing his back-to-the-basket game. This experiment got some early seasoning when the Hoosiers went on a five-country world tour during the summer of 1985.

When the Hoosiers reported to practice in the fall of 1985, Daryl Thomas was already penciled in as Indiana's starting center after his performance on the summer tour. The other key returnees for IU were Steve Alford, Delray Brooks, Winston Morgan and Stew Robinson. Plus, the Hoosiers added a very athletic 6'6" freshman swingman named Rick Calloway and two JUCO players in 6'6" Andre Harris and 6'9" Todd Jadlow.

On November 30, Indiana won its season opener for the first time in three years by defeating Kent State 89-73. Five Hoosiers scored in double figures, led by Alford with 24 and Calloway with 23 off the bench. On December 3, Digger Phelps's Notre Dame squad came to Bloomington and IU upset the tenth-ranked Fighting Irish 82-67 as Alford poured in 32 points and Calloway added 18 points and nine rebounds.

No. 19 Indiana suffered its first loss on December 7, in Lexington, Kentucky, as the ninth-ranked Kentucky Wildcats edged the Hoosiers 63-58. Alford sat out the contest because of a one-game NCAA suspension for appearing in a sorority calendar that was done to help raise money for a camp for handicap kids. National columnists and sports commentators wrote at length about the irony of Alford, from the squeaky-clean Indiana program, being suspended for a game for inadvertently breaking a rule to help a charity, and then having to sit out the game against

Kentucky, whose players at that time were known for the expensive goods they had reportedly received from Wildcat boosters (a 1989 NCAA investigation eventually documented this and led to probation for the Kentucky program).

Following the Kentucky loss, Indiana won six of its final seven preconference games. That included home wins over Kansas State (78-71) and Iowa State (86-65) and sweeps of both the Indiana Classic (84-63 over Louisiana Tech and 74-59 over Texas Tech) and the Hoosier Classic (87-57 over Idaho and 74-43 over Mississippi State). The only loss came to No. 16 Louisville 65-63 in Freedom Hall on December 18. The Cardinals went on to win the NCAA championship that season.

IU entered Big Ten play with an 8-2 record. That was the same mark the Hoosiers brought into conference action the year before, when they got hammered by teams from top to bottom in the league. In the conference opener, No. 15 Indiana got an excellent chance to measure its progress by hosting No. 2 Michigan at Assembly Hall on January 2. The bigger, stronger Wolverines used a 26-5 advantage from the free throw line to defeat the Hoosiers 74-69. Three days later, the Michigan State Spartans came to Bloomington. With Daryl Thomas out of the lineup with a sprained ankle, the MSU front line feasted on IU and the Spartans won 77-71. Those defeats were Indiana's sixth and seventh consecutive conference losses in Assembly Hall going back to the previous season. That fact must have hit home very hard for Knight, who remorsefully told his players after the Michigan State game, "I never thought I would see the day when Indiana basketball was in the state it's in right now."

The next week, Indiana went on the road and captured important wins over Northwestern (102-65) and Wisconsin (80-69). Alford burned the Badgers for 38 points, even though he was fighting a virus. After that, IU returned home and got back to business as usual in Bloomington by pulling out three straight wins in Assembly Hall. Ohio State was the first victim, falling 69-66 on January 15. Next, No. 15 Purdue came to town on January 23, and led 69-64 in the final minutes, before IU rallied to tie the game and then beat the Boilermakers 71-70 in overtime. Two days later, IU beat Illinois 71-69 for the

Daryl Thomas came to Indiana as a wing player, but the Hoosiers lacked an inside presence for the 1985-86 season and so Coach Knight gave the 6'7" Thomas an opportunity at center. Thomas filled the role capably and was IU's second leading scorer for the season at 14.5 PPG. IU Archives

Hoosiers' fifth straight victory. One of the keys to the three-game winning streak in Assembly was the return of Daryl Thomas, who had 15 points and eight rebounds against Ohio State and 10 points and seven rebounds against Purdue. Then Thomas exploded in the Illinois contest with a game-high 30 points.

At that point, Indiana was 5-2 and tied with Michigan for the conference lead. However, the Hoosiers didn't stay in first for long. They went to Iowa City on January 30, and dropped a 79-69 game to a tough Iowa Hawkeye squad. Iowa guard Doug Moe, an Indianapolis native, burned the Hoosiers with 24 points and seven assists. But then Indiana caught fire in February, winning five straight games. The Hoosiers beat Minnesota 62-54 in "The Barn" in Minneapolis on February 1. Back in Bloomington the next week, they beat Wisconsin 78-69 and Northwestern 77-52. Then they went on the road and snatched two important wins, beating Ohio State 84-75 in Columbus and Illinois 61-60 in Champaign. That put IU at 10-3, a half-game ahead of Michigan (10-4) for the Big Ten lead.

Purdue made its presence felt in the conference race by manhandling IU 85-68 on February 23, in Mackey Arena. That dropped Indiana into a first place tie with Michigan at 10-4, while Purdue was now only a half-game back at 10-5. Next, Indiana held serve at home, beating Minnesota 95-63 and Iowa 80-73. IU and Michigan were now tied for the league lead at 12-4, Michigan State emerged as a challenger at 11-5, while Purdue had fallen back to 10-6.

Indiana, now ranked 16th in the country, gave itself a chance for the conference crown by going into East Lansing on March 5, and pummeling No. 17 Michigan State 97-79. Alford led the way with 31 points, while Ricky Calloway had 19 points, Daryl Thomas had 14 points and five rebounds, and Andre Harris chipped in 10 points and six rebounds. That set up a nationally televised showdown with Michigan in Chrisler Arena on the final day of the season. It was a winner-take-all battle for the undisputed Big Ten crown. It was never a contest. Michigan jumped out to a 19-point lead at the half and never looked back. The final score was 80-52. Michigan's powerful front line pulverized the puny Hoosiers on the boards with a 47-29 rebounding advantage.

After the Michigan loss, Knight told his team, "Don't even think about it. It's over. ... Now we've got a tournament to play. We can still get the job done there. All of you know we're capable of it." However, the Hoosiers confidence had been badly shaken by the beating they had taken in Ann Arbor. In the NCAA tournament, the Hoosiers were assigned the No. 3 seed in the East Regional and were paired against No. 14 seed Cleveland State, a running, pressing team that was 27-3 and playing in the NCAA tourney for the first time. The Vikings came out hungry and aggressive and used their depth and quickness to wear down the Hoosiers and eventually secure an 83-79 upset. Cleveland State ended up making it to the Sweet Sixteen, where David Robinson's Navy squad barely edged out the Vikings 71-70.

Ending the season with two very disappointing losses was a bitter pill. Nevertheless, IU had finished 21-8 overall and had restored the Hoosier tradition of excellence in the Big Ten with a 13-5 mark in league play. That success ended up being an important stepping stone to much greater things the following season.

INDIANA'S RANKING IN THE 1985-86 ASSOCIATED PRESS POLLS

PS	11/26	12/3	12/10	12/17	12/24	12/31	1/7	1/14	1/21	1/28	2/4	2/11	2/18	2/25	3/4	3/11
—	—	19	18	17	17	15	—	—	—	15	18	16	15	16	16	16

1986-87

FOR THE COMMENTARY AND STATISTICS FOR

THE 1986-87 SEASON, PLEASE SEE CHAPTER 4,

"1986-87: A TEAM THAT REFUSED TO LOSE."

1987-88

OVERALL RECORD: 19-10

CONFERENCE RECORD: 11-7 (FIFTH PLACE)

TEAM HONORS:

HOOSIER CLASSIC CHAMPION,

INDIANA CLASSIC CHAMPION

INDIVIDUAL HONORS:

DEAN GARRETT—ALL-BIG TEN (FIRST TEAM)

JAY EDWARDS—BIG TEN FRESHMAN

OF THE YEAR

JOE HILLMAN—ACADEMIC ALL-BIG TEN

MAGNUS PELKOWSKI—ACADEMIC ALL-BIG TEN

When Keith Smart's jump shot trickled through the net in the Louisiana Superdome in the final seconds of the 1987 national championship game, his name immediately became associated with one of college basketball's great moments that will be celebrated and remembered long after Keith Smart himself is no longer around. Coach Bob Knight certainly never begrudged Smart for that. In fact, Knight lavishly lauded Smart's play during the final 12 minutes in New Orleans. However, during the 1987-88 season, Knight also had plenty of times that he wished another player had made that shot or that Smart had been a senior rather than a junior when he hit the game-winner. The reason was that Smart got so much attention from that shot, and it created so much in the way

of expectations that Knight believed it affected Smart's play during his senior year.

Smart, Dean Garrett and Ricky Calloway were all returning starters from the 1987 championship team. Gone were Steve Alford, Daryl Thomas, and Steve Meier. Those three seniors had each provided excellent leadership during their senior season. With the addition of freshman phenoms Jay Edwards and Lyndon Jones, the 1987-88 team was stacked with some talented players—probably more talented players than the 1986-87 team that won the championship. However, the 1987-88 team badly missed the leadership from Alford, Thomas and Meier. Without that leadership, many of the players had a difficult time understanding and accepting their roles on the team. The team still played well, but didn't meet the standard of the previous season, and didn't quite live up to its full potential.

The defending national champions looked terrific on opening night, when they blistered Miami of Ohio 90-65 on November 28 in Bloomington. Garrett led the way with 25 points, while Smart had 17 points and seven assists. Next, the Hoosiers wiped out Notre Dame 76-59. Smart had 18 points and 10 assists, but freshman Jay Edwards was the catalyst in the second half as he came off the bench and scored 12 points in 10 minutes. On Saturday, December 5, No. 5 Indiana faced off against No. 2 Kentucky in the Hoosier Dome as part of the Big Four Classic (Louisville and Notre Dame played in the other game). IU and Kentucky staged an excellent battle that eventually went to overtime, where the Wildcats' Rex Chapman hit a back-breaking three-pointer that eventually lifted Kentucky to an 82-76 victory.

Smart, who had played poorly against Kentucky with five points and six turnovers, got to watch most of the next game—against Vanderbilt—from the bench. However, Smart came off the bench in the second half and scored four straight points in the final minutes to turn a one-point deficit into a three-point lead with 1:11 left on the clock. The Hoosiers won 63-61. The other hero was reserve Magnus Pelkowski, who came in and scored 15 first-half points. The Vanderbilt win improved IU to 3-1 Next, the Hoosiers beat James Madison 84-52 and Washington State 63-56 to win the Indiana Classic, and then crushed Eastern Kentucky 103-75 on December 15, in Bloomington. Louisville handed IU its second loss

The 1987-88 team. First row (left to right): Ricky Calloway, Todd Jadlow, Steve Eyl, Dean Garrett, Keith Smart, Kreigh Smith, Joe Hillman; Second row: Lyndon Jones, Jay Edwards, Dave Minor, Magnus Pelkowski, Brian Sloan, Jeff Oliphant, Mark Robinson. IU Archives

of the season, 81-69 on December 19 in Freedom Hall. Finally, IU closed out the preconference slate in the Hoosier Classic in Indianapolis, where Indiana beat Pennsylvania 94-54 and Stanford 83-73.

At 8-2, Indiana was ranked 12th and was considered one of the leading challengers for the Big Ten crown heading into league play. On January 6, IU opened the conference season against No. 16 Iowa in Iowa City. It was only the second time the Hoosiers had played in a hostile environment during the season, and the result was nearly identical to the first time (against Louisville); IU played a great first half, but got trampled after halftime. In this case, IU led Iowa 33-26 at the break, but lost 84-70. Hawkeye point guard B.J. Armstrong led all scorers with 27 points. Things got worse for the defending Big Ten champs on January 11, when they went to Evanston and got upset by Northwestern 66-64. Indiana natives Terry Buford and Jeff Grose hit the deciding free throws down the stretch to give the Wildcats the victory.

The Hoosiers finally scratched out their first conference win on January 14, in Assembly Hall, where IU came from behind to beat Wisconsin 55-53, led by 18 points and 11 rebounds from Garrett. Jay Edwards came off the bench to score six points in nine minutes, in his first game back after missing five games because of academic problems. On January 16, IU's road problems continued as the Hoosiers lost 75-74 in overtime to the Michigan State Spartans, who had lost five straight games before Indiana arrived. Things didn't get any better when Indiana returned to Bloomington and hosted No. 7 Michigan the following week. The Wolverines came in and beat the Hoosiers 72-60, led by 21 points and eight rebounds from Glen Rice. It was the Hoosiers' fourth loss in five Big Ten contests. After the game, a despondent Keith Smart admitted, "At 1-4 in the Big Ten you can only become a spoiler. The championship is beginning to fade away."

For IU's January 27 game at Ohio State, Coach Knight benched veterans Ricky Calloway and Keith

Smart and started three guards—Joe Hillman, Lyndon Jones, and Jay Edwards—along with Dean Garrett and Magnus Pelkowski in the front court. With the new lineup, IU's offense clicked into gear and the Hoosiers beat the Buckeyes 75-71, led by 22 points from Garrett and 21 from Jones. Next, No. 2 Purdue, the Big Ten frontrunner at 6-0, came to Bloomington on January 30. The Hoosiers roared to a 52-37 halftime lead, but the Boilermakers got back in the game with a big second-half surge. However, Dean Garrett clinched an 82-79 Indiana win by burying a 10-footer with 0:06 left on the clock. Garrett finished with a game-high 31 points along with 10 rebounds, and Jay Edwards chipped in 22 points.

After upsetting Purdue, IU rolled to three straight wins. The Hoosiers clobbered Minnesota 92-63 in Bloomington on February 4. They slipped by Illinois 75-74 in Champaign on February 6, led by 24 second-half points from Edwards. Then the Hoosiers, who had returned to the rankings at No. 19, avenged an earlier loss to Northwestern by walloping the Wildcats 74-45 in Assembly Hall. That was the Hoosiers' fifth straight win, and it improved IU to 6-4 in conference play. Unfortunately, Indiana had to play three of its next four games on the road and the Hoosiers went 2-2, losing at Michigan 92-72 and Purdue 95-85, but winning against Michigan State 95-58 and at Wisconsin 84-74.

On February 29, IU fell to 8-7 in league play with a 75-65 loss to Illinois, despite 29 points from Edwards. Then, the Hoosiers showed some pride and made their case for an NCAA berth by closing the season with three straight wins. The first one came against Ohio State, 85-77 in Bloomington on March 5. Next, IU beat Minnesota 91-85 in Minneapolis, where Jay Edwards poured in 36 points (including eight three-pointers) and Keith Smart added 24. On the final day of the season, Indiana bombed Iowa 116-89, led by seniors Smart and Garrett. Smart had 32 points, seven rebounds, and five assists, while Garrett had 26 points and nine rebounds.

Indiana finished the regular season at 19-9 overall and 11-7 in the Big Ten. The defending NCAA champs were awarded a No. 4 seed in the East Regional for the NCAA tournament. In the first round, IU matched up against the 13th-seeded Richmond Spiders. Richmond took a 44-38 halftime lead, but IU grabbed a 65-62 advantage with 6:44

1987-88 TEAM ROSTER

Head coach: Bob Knight
Assistant coaches: Dan Dackich, Ron Felling, Joby Wright, Taylor Locke

No.	Player	Hometown	Class	Position	Height
20	Ricky Calloway	Cincinnati, OH	Jr	G/F	6-6
3	Jay Edwards	Marion, IN	Fr	G/F	6-4
32	Steve Eyl (Capt.)	Hamilton, OH	Sr	F	6-6
22	Dean Garrett (Capt.)	San Clemente, CA	Sr	C	6-10
44	Joe Hillman	Glendale, CA	Jr	G	6-2
11	Todd Jadlow	Salina, KS	Jr	F/C	6-9
4	Lyndon Jones	Marion, IN	Fr	G	6-1
35	Jeff Oliphant	Lyons, IN	So	G	6-5
14	Magnus Pelkowski	Bogota, Columbia	Jr	C	6-10
10	Mark Robinson	Van Nuys, CA	Rs	F	6-5
45	Brian Sloan	McLeansboro, IL	Jr	F/C	6-8
23	Keith Smart (Capt.)	Baton Rouge, LA	Sr	G	6-1
42	Kreigh Smith	Tipton, IN	Jr	G/F	6-7

SEASON RESULTS 1987-88

Date	Court	Opponent	Result	Score
11/28/1987	H	Miami of Ohio	W	90-65
12/1/1987	H	Notre Dame	W	76-59
12/5/1987	N1	Kentucky	L	76-82
12/8/1987	H	Vanderbilt	W	63-61
12/11/1987	H	James Madison	W	84-52
12/12/1987	H	Washington State	W	63-56
12/15/1987	H	Eastern Kentucky	W	103-75
12/19/1987	A	Louisville	L	69-81
12/28/1987	N1	Pennsylvania	W	94-54
12/29/1987	N1	Stanford	W	83-73
1/6/1988	A	Iowa	L	70-84
1/11/1988	A	Northwestern	L	64-66
1/14/1988	H	Wisconsin	W	55-53
1/16/1988	A	Michigan State	L	74-75
1/24/1988	H	Michigan	L	60-72
1/27/1988	A	Ohio State	W	75-71
1/30/1988	H	Purdue	W	82-79
2/4/1988	H	Minnesota	W	92-63
2/6/1988	A	Illinois	W	75-74
2/11/1988	H	Northwestern	W	74-45
2/13/1988	A	Michigan	L	72-92
2/18/1988	H	Michigan State	W	95-58
2/21/1988	A	Purdue	L	85-95
2/24/1988	A	Wisconsin	W	84-74
2/29/1988	H	Illinois	L	65-75
3/5/1988	H	Ohio State	W	85-77
3/10/1988	A	Minnesota	W	91-85
3/12/1988	H	Iowa	W	116-89
NCAA Tournament				
3/18/1988	N2	Richmond	L	69-72

1 Indianapolis, IN
2 Hartford, CT

1987-88 BIG TEN STANDINGS

	W	L	PCT
Purdue	16	2	.889
Michigan	13	5	.722
Iowa	12	6	.667
Illinois	12	6	.667
Indiana	11	7	.611
Ohio State	9	9	.500
Wisconsin	6	12	.333
Michigan St.	5	13	.278
Minnesota	4	14	.222
Northwestern	2	16	.111

During the 1987-88 season, senior Dean Garrett set the IU single-season record with 99 blocked shots. A junior college transfer, the 6'10" Garrett averaged 3.0 blocks per game during his two seasons in Bloomington.
IU Archives

remaining. IU led 69-68 in the waning minutes when Richmond's Rodney Rice drained an 18-footer with Smart hanging all over him and gave the Spiders a 70-69 advantage. Keith Smart had a chance to reclaim the lead for Indiana in the final minute, but he couldn't recreate the magic from the previous season as his final jump shot was off the mark. Richmond then scored on a break away layup and IU guard Joe Hillman missed a three-pointer to tie the game in the final seconds. Richmond won 72-69. The Spiders also went on to upset No. 5 seed Georgia Tech to earn a spot in the Sweet Sixteen.

It was a rebuilding year in Bloomington, even with such outstanding seniors as Keith Smart and Dean Garrett. Freshmen Lyndon Jones and Jay Edwards had emerged as solid college players that each had an opportunity for an excellent career. Plus, one of the subplots of the 1987-88 season was the chemistry that Jones, Edwards and Hillman had displayed at times in a three-guard lineup. That combination would develop championship potency the next season.

INDIANA'S RANKING IN THE 1987-88 ASSOCIATED PRESS POLLS

PS	12/1	12/8	12/15	12/22	12/29	1/5	1/12	1/19	1/26	2/2	2/9	2/16	2/23	3/1	3/8	3/15
6	5	6	5	13	13	12	15	—	—	—	19	—	—	—	—	—

1988-89

FOR THE COMMENTARY AND STATISTICS FOR THE 1988-89 SEASON, PLEASE SEE CHAPTER 10, "1988-89: THE LITTLE TEAM THAT STOLE THE BIG TEN."

1989-90

OVERALL RECORD: 18-11

CONFERENCE RECORD: 8-10 (SEVENTH PLACE)

TEAM HONORS:

HOOSIER CLASSIC CHAMPION,

INDIANA CLASSIC CHAMPION

Indiana high schools were loaded with basketball talent for the high school class of 1989. That was good news for IU basketball coach Bob Knight, who usually landed any high school kid he recruited in the state of Indiana. That was because the Indiana University basketball program had a reputation of greatness and a storied tradition that took on mythic proportions for the citizens of the Hoosier state. For over a half-century, since IU had burst into national prominence by winning its first NCAA championship in 1940, nearly every kid in the state who had played basketball had dreamed of playing for IU. With Coach Knight's tremendous success during the 1970s and 1980s, that dream grew even stronger, because going to IU also meant having an opportunity to win championships year in and year out.

From the class of 1989, five very talented kids from the state of Indiana—Pat Graham, Greg Graham, Chris Lawson, Calbert Cheaney and Todd Leary—chose to accept scholarships to IU. Chris Reynolds from Peoria, Illinois, and highly touted Lawrence Funderburke from Columbus, Ohio, also joined them to make a seven-man recruiting class that some commentators at the time were calling the best in the history of college basketball. When those

1989-90 TEAM ROSTER

Head coach: Bob Knight
Assistant coaches: Dan Dakich, Don Donoher,
Ron Felling, Joby Wright

No.	Player	Hometown	Class	Position	Height
32	Eric Anderson	Chicago, IL	So	F/C	6-9
40	Calbert Cheaney	Evansville, IN	Fr	G/F	6-6
34	Lawrence Funderburke	Columbus, OH	Fr	F	6-8
20	Greg Graham	Indianapolis, IN	Fr	G	6-3
33	Pat Graham	Floyd Knobs, IN	Fr	G	6-5
4	Lyndon Jones	Marion, IN	Jr	G	6-2
54	Chris Lawson	Bloomington, IN	Fr	F/C	6-9
30	Todd Leary	Indianapolis, IN	Fr	G	6-2
23	Jamal Meeks	Freeport, IL	So	G	6-0
24	Matt Nover	Chesterton, IN	Fr	F	6-8
35	Jeff Oliphant (Capt.)	Lyons, IN	Sr	G	6-5
21	Chris Reynolds	Peoria, IL	Fr	G	6-1
10	Mark Robinson	Van Nuys, CA	Sr	F	6-5

SEASON RESULTS 1989-90

Date	Court	Opponent	Result	Score
11/25/1989	H	Miami of Ohio	W	77-66
11/28/1989	H	Kent State	W	79-68
12/2/1989	N1	Kentucky	W	71-69
12/5/1989	H	Notre Dame	W	81-72
12/8/1989	H	South Alabama	W	96-67
12/9/1989	H	Long Beach State	W	92-75
12/16/1989	A	UTEP	W	69-66
12/23/1989	H	Iowa State	W	115-66
12/27/1989	N1	Wichita State	W	75-54
12/28/1989	N1	Texas A&M	W	94-66
1/4/1990	A	Ohio State	L	67-69
1/8/1990	H	Michigan	W	69-67
1/11/1990	A	Northwestern	W	77-63
1/13/1990	H	Purdue	L	79-81
1/18/1990	A	Iowa	W	83-79
1/24/1990	H	Michigan State	L	57-75
1/28/1990	A	Minnesota	L	89-108
2/1/1990	H	Wisconsin	W	85-61
2/4/1990	A	Illinois	L	65-70
2/8/1990	A	Michigan	L	71-79
2/10/1990	H	Northwestern	W	98-75
2/17/1990	H	Iowa	W	118-71
2/19/1990	A	Purdue	L	49-72
2/25/1990	A	Michigan State	L	66-72
3/1/1990	H	Minnesota	L	70-75
3/3/1990	A	Wisconsin	W	70-68
3/8/1990	H	Ohio State	W	77-66
3/10/1990	H	Illinois	L	63-69
NCAA Tournament				
3/15/1990	N2	California	L	63-65

1 Indianapolis, IN
2 Hartford, CT

1989-90 BIG TEN STANDINGS

	W	L	PCT
Michigan St.	15	3	.833
Purdue	13	5	.722
Michigan	12	6	.667
Illinois	11	7	.611
Minnesota	11	7	.611
Ohio State	10	8	.556
Indiana	8	10	.444
Wisconsin	4	14	.222
Iowa	4	14	.222
Northwestern	2	16	.111

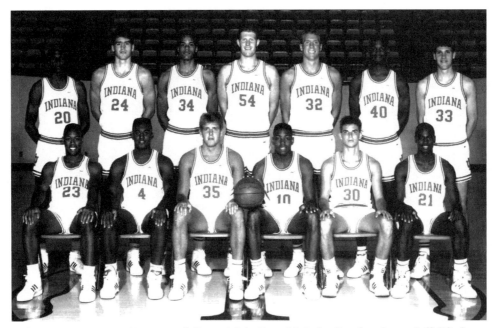

The 1989-90 team. First row (left to right): Jamal Meeks, Lyndon Jones, Jeff Oliphant, Mark Robinson, Todd Leary, Chris Reynolds; Second row: Greg Graham, Matt Nover, Lawrence Funderburke, Chris Lawson, Eric Anderson, Calbert Cheaney, Pat Graham.
IU Archives

recruits joined the Hoosier squad for the 1989-90 season, they joined top returnees Eric Anderson, Lyndon Jones and Jamal Meeks and redshirt freshman Matt Nover to form a young but supremely talented team. The key departures were Joe Hillman, who graduated, and Jay Edwards, who declared for the NBA draft.

"I think there are some physical qualities with this group of kids we have that we might not have had a year ago," said Knight before the season began. "This team potentially has good ability, good athletes and smart kids. Those are all things that I enjoy having. Consequently, I have to feel that it will be a group I will enjoy having around." As it turned out, Knight saw a lot to enjoy in December, but then his young pups got mauled by the big dogs in conference play.

Based on the team's surprise run to the Big Ten title the year before, along with the stellar group of freshmen now wearing cream and crimson uniforms, the Hoosiers entered the season ranked 14th in the country. On opening night, November 25, in Assembly Hall, Knight started two freshmen against Miami of Ohio. One of the starters, Lawrence

Funderburke, wasn't much of a surprise. The other starter, Calbert Cheaney, was definitely a surprise, since Cheaney was one of the lesser regarded members of the recruiting class. However, Cheaney scored a game-high 20 points (on nine-for-11 shooting from the field) and IU won 77-66. Funderburke also had a strong game with 10 points, eight rebounds, and five assists. Next, Knight started two sophomores and three freshmen against Kent State on November 28, in Bloomington. One of the starters was freshman guard Greg Graham, who broke loose for a game-high 24 points, along with six rebounds and four assists. The Hoosiers beat the Golden Flashes 79-68.

On December 2, in the Hoosier Dome, Indiana edged out a probation-decimated Kentucky team 71-69 in front of a crowd of over 40,000 fans in the Big Four Classic in Indianapolis. Five different Hoosiers scored in double figures and Funderburke and Eric Anderson combined for 28 points and 20 rebounds on the Hoosier front line. Next, No. 19 Notre Dame came to Bloomington for an intrastate showdown with 14th-ranked IU on December 5. The Fighting

Irish started four seniors while the Hoosiers started four freshmen. Youth prevailed as Indiana rolled to an 81-72 win, led by a game-high 20 points from Cheaney. To help the cause, freshmen guards Chris Reynolds and Greg Graham teamed up for 30 points and 13 assists.

Led by its youth movement, Indiana was off to a 4-0 start, but the Hoosiers didn't stop there. They won their final six preconference games. That included two wins in the Indiana Classic over South Alabama 96-67 and Long Beach State 92-75. On December 16, the 11th-ranked Hoosiers went down to Texas and edged UTEP 69-66, led by 16 second-half points from Cheaney. A week later, IU bombarded Iowa State 115-66, led by 16 points and 16 rebounds from Eric Anderson and 13 points and 16 rebounds from freshman big man Chris Lawson. Then, in the Hoosier Classic in Indianapolis, Indiana steamrolled Wichita State 75-54 and Texas A&M 94-66 to finish the pre-conference schedule with a 10-0 record. The only loss of the preconference season was Lawrence Funderburke, who quit the team in mid-December and eventually decided to transfer.

Now ranked ninth in the nation, IU opened conference play against Ohio State in Columbus on January 4. The teams fought to a 36-36 tie at the half, but OSU led 69-61 with only 1:12 remaining. That's when IU freshman guard Todd Leary went to work. Leary buried a three pointer and then assisted on a three-point play by Greg Graham that cut the lead to 69-67. However, in the final seconds, Leary missed a three-pointer that could have tied the game, and the Buckeyes escaped with the victory. Ohio State was led by their freshman sensation Jim Jackson, who had 19 points, five rebounds, and seven assists. Then, on January 8, in Bloomington, the Hoosiers fell behind No. 3 Michigan, the defending national champs, by 14 points at the half. However, IU reeled off a torrid 17-0 run during the second half and eventually pulled out a 69-67 victory to the delight of a raucous crowd in Assembly Hall. Junior guard Lyndon Jones led Indiana with 20 points, including 14 in the second half.

The next week, Indiana beat Northwestern 77-63 in Evanston on January 11, but then on January 13, the team committed one of the cardinal sins of Hoosier basketball by losing to Purdue in Bloomington. In that game, the 13th-ranked

Freshman Pat Graham collects a rebound against Iowa State. Graham was the 1989 Indiana Mr. Basketball and was a McDonald's All-American. Pat was one of the marquee members of Indiana's widely glorified 1989 recruiting class. IU Archives

Hoosiers controlled the action early, but coughed up a double-digit halftime lead and fell 81-79 in overtime. Tony Jones led the Boilermaker attack with 21 points and six assists, while Eric Anderson was the only Hoosier in double figures with 30 points. The Purdue loss dropped IU to 2-2 in conference play. The Hoosiers split their next four games. They won 83-79 at Iowa, but then got manhandled 75-57 by Michigan State in Assembly Hall. They lost 108-89 to No. 21 Minnesota in "The Barn" in Minneapolis, but then came back home and drilled Wisconsin 85-61.

The Hoosiers were 4-4 in league play and had fallen to No. 22 in the Associated Press poll. Four of the team's next six games were on the road, and all four of those road opponents were ranked. IU ended up losing all four of those road games. The first two losses came against No. 11 Illinois 70-65 and No. 7 Michigan 79-71. Then the Hoosiers won two home games—98-75 over Northwestern and 118-71 over Iowa. The next two road losses came at No. 12 Purdue 72-49 and No. 15 Michigan State 72-66. That put IU at 6-8 in conference play with only four games remaining, and three of those would be played at Assembly Hall. The young squad gathered up its wounded pride and split the final four games. No. 17 Minnesota came into Bloomington and stole a 75-70 win on March 1. Then IU scratched out a road win by beating Wisconsin 70-68 in Madison. In that game, Calbert Cheaney hit the game-wining 18-footer with 0:03 left on the clock. Back in Bloomington, IU beat Ohio State 77-66 in March 8 but lost its season finale to No. 20 Illinois 69-63 on March 10.

Indiana finished the regular season with an 18-10 record overall, but with a disappointing 8-10 mark in conference play, which left the Hoosiers in seventh place in the Big Ten. Nevertheless, because the Hoosiers had a strong overall record with several wins over ranked teams, and because the Big Ten itself was so strong that season, IU earned an NCAA berth. The Hoosiers got shipped off to the East Regional as a No. 8 seed and were paired against No. 9 seed California in Hartford, Connecticut, in the opening round. The game against California was a typical NCAA tournament battle with lots of lead changes and shifts in momentum. IU led by eight points with 15 minutes remaining, but Cal stormed ahead and led 62-56 with five minutes left. The Hoosiers fought back with a 7-1 run that tied the game at 63 with only 0:05 left to play. The Bears' Keith Smith beat Greg Graham off the dribble and with 3.8 seconds on the clock was fouled by Eric Anderson. Smith buried both free throws and IU missed a desperation heave at the buzzer. Cal won 65-63.

This young squad learned a sometimes-painful lesson about the kind of effort and concentration that are required to win, both during the Big Ten season and in the NCAA tournament. Those lessons would be put to good use over the next three seasons.

INDIANA'S RANKING IN THE 1989-90 ASSOCIATED PRESS POLLS

PS	11/27	12/5	12/12	12/19	12/26	1/2	1/9	1/16	1/23	1/30	2/6	2/13	2/20	2/27	3/6	3/13
14	14	14	11	11	10	9	13	14	12	22	25	—	25	—	—	—

1990-91

OVERALL RECORD: 29-5

CONFERENCE RECORD: 15-3 (FIRST PLACE)

TEAM HONORS:

BIG TEN CHAMPION, HOOSIER CLASSIC CHAMPION,

INDIANA CLASSIC CHAMPION

INDIVIDUAL HONORS:

CALBERT CHEANEY—ALL-AMERICA, ALL-BIG TEN (FIRST TEAM)

ERIC ANDERSON—ALL-BIG TEN (FIRST TEAM)

DAMON BAILEY—BIG TEN FRESHMAN OF THE YEAR

The 1990-91 team. First row (left to right): Todd Leary, Jamal Meeks, Lyndon Jones, Damon Bailey, Chris Reynolds, Greg Graham; Second row: Pat Knight, Calbert Cheaney, Chris Lawson, Eric Anderson, Matt Nover, Pat Graham.
IU Athletics

Coach Bob Knight's freshman-heavy 1989-90 team returned from its jarring 8-10 introduction to Big Ten play with the resolve to make IU a Big Ten contender again during the 1990-91 campaign. However, before the season began, Knight cautioned, "We need to see how and if this team has improved from last season. This is not a team that is just going to be better because it's older." Most notably, the team needed to improve its performance in the final five minutes of close games. During the previous season, eight of the team's ten conference losses had come by eight points or less. A key to turning that around was with better team defense so that the Hoosiers could make stops down the stretch.

Knight also felt this group had the potential for excellence. He said, "I believe that if these players are willing to pay the price past players and teams have paid, that some time in the future, this team will have an opportunity to be thought of along with the other great players and teams that we have had at Indiana."

1990-91 TEAM ROSTER

Head coach: Bob Knight
Assistant coaches: Dan Dakich, Norm Ellenberger, Ron Felling

No.	Player	Hometown	Class	Position	Height
32	Eric Anderson	Chicago, IL	Jr	F/C	6-9
22	Damon Bailey	Heltonville, IN	Fr	G	6-3
40	Calbert Cheaney	Evansville, IN	So	G/F	6-6
20	Greg Graham	Indianapolis, IN	So	G	6-4
33	Pat Graham	Floyd Knobs, IN	So	G	6-5
4	Lyndon Jones (Capt.)	Marion, IN	Sr	G	6-2
25	Pat Knight	Bloomington, IN	Fr	F	6-6
54	Chris Lawson	Bloomington, IN	So	F/C	6-9
30	Todd Leary	Indianapolis, IN	Rs	G	6-3
23	Jamal Meeks	Freeport, IL	Jr	G	6-0
24	Matt Nover	Chesterton, IN	So	F	6-8
21	Chris Reynolds	Peoria, IL	So	G	6-1

SEASON RESULTS 1990-91

Date	Court	Opponent	Result	Score
11/23/1990	N1	Northeastern	W	100-78
11/24/1990	N1	Santa Clara	W	73-69
11/25/1990	N1	Syracuse	L	74-77
11/28/1990	A	Notre Dame	W	70-67
12/1/1990	N2	Louisville	W	72-52
12/4/1990	A	Vanderbilt	W	84-73
12/7/1990	H	Niagara	W	101-64
12/8/1990	H	San Diego	W	91-64
12/15/1990	H	Western Michigan	W	97-68
12/18/1990	H	Kentucky	W	87-84
12/21/1990	A	Iowa State	W	87-76
12/27/1990	N1	Marshall	W	91-67
12/28/1990	N1	Ohio	W	102-64
1/2/1991	H	Illinois	W	109-74
1/5/1991	H	Northwestern	W	99-58
1/14/1991	A	Purdue	W	65-62
1/19/1991	A	Iowa	W	99-79
1/21/1991	H	Ohio State	L	85-93
1/24/1991	A	Michigan	W	70-60
1/26/1991	H	Michigan State	W	97-63
1/30/1991	H	Wisconsin	W	73-57
2/3/1991	A	Minnesota	W	77-66
2/7/1991	A	Northwestern	W	105-74
2/10/1991	H	Purdue	W	81-63
2/17/1991	A	Ohio State	L	95-97
2/21/1991	H	Iowa	L	79-80
2/24/1991	H	Michigan	W	112-79
2/28/1991	A	Michigan State	W	62-56
3/2/1991	A	Wisconsin	W	74-61
3/7/1991	H	Minnesota	W	75-59
3/10/1991	A	Illinois	W	70-58
NCAA Tournament				
3/14/1991	N3	Coastal Carolina	W	79-69
3/16/1991	N3	Florida State	W	82-60
3/21/1991	N3	Kansas	L	65-83

1 Indianapolis, IN
2 Maui, HI
3 Louisville, KY
4 Charlotte, NC

1990-91 BIG TEN STANDINGS

	W	L	PCT
Ohio State	15	3	.833
Indiana	15	3	.833
Illinois	11	7	.611
Michigan St.	11	7	.511
Iowa	9	9	.500
Purdue	9	9	.500
Wisconsin	8	10	.444
Michigan	7	11	.389
Minnesota	5	13	.278
Northwestern	0	18	.000

In addition to the six sophomores who formed the core of the Indiana squad, the Hoosiers added a highly coveted freshman guard named Damon Bailey, who was already a legend in Indiana before he even set foot in Bloomington. Bailey had led his Bedford North Lawrence High School team to three state finals in four years, and during his senior year, they won a state championship in front of a record 40,000 fans in the Hoosier Dome for the championship game. Bailey's accomplishments were even more impressive because he functioned under intense media scrutiny during his entire high school career after John Feinstein's book *A Season on the Brink* publicized the fact that Coach Knight went to watch Bailey play as an eighth grader and was very impressed. As a result of that publicity, Bailey's very first high school practice drew a crowd of reporters and television cameras—and they followed him for the next four years. When Bailey came to IU, he joined a very talented roster of players, but he made an immediate impact as a freshman.

On November 23-25, the Hoosiers kicked off the season at the Maui Classic, where they beat Northeastern 100-78 and Santa Clara 73-69, but fell to No. 13 Syracuse 77-74 in the championship game. After the defeat in the Maui title game, it would be almost two months before the Hoosiers would lose again. The jet-lagged, tenth-ranked IU squad played at Notre Dame on November 28, and fell behind by 10 points at the half. However, junior point guard Jamal Meeks came off the bench to spark Indiana in the second half, and the Hoosiers prevailed 70-67. IU then played No. 25 Louisville on December 1, in the Big Four Classic in Indianapolis, where the Hoosiers handed Louisville a 72-52 loss. The Cardinals' 52 points was their lowest scoring output in three years. Next, Calbert Cheaney's 30 points led No. 7 IU to an 84-73 win at Vanderbilt. At that point, the Hoosiers were 5-1 and they had yet to play a game at home.

Indiana played its next four games in Assembly Hall. The IU squad collected two Indiana Classic wins over Niagara (101-64) and San Diego (91-64). Then the Hoosiers beat Western Michigan 97-68 and No. 18 Kentucky 87-84. Against Kentucky, Cheaney's three-point play in the final minute was the key play that lifted the Hoosiers to the win. Cheaney finished with 23 points and nine rebounds, while Damon Bailey added 16 points and five assists. Next, the Hoosiers won 87-76 at Iowa State and then grabbed the Hoosier Classic title with wins over Marshall (91-67) and Ohio (102-64). With a 12-1 record and a No. 5 national ranking, Indiana was ready to enter league play and prove that they could compete in the Big Ten.

IU got off to a great start in their Big Ten opener by crushing Illinois 109-74 in Assembly Hall. Cheaney led the way with 30 points, while Eric Anderson chipped in 20 points and 10 rebounds. Three days later, Indiana pummeled Northwestern 99-58 in Bloomington. Then the Hoosiers did something that they had a problem doing the previous season—they won a close game on the road, as third-ranked Indiana went into West Lafayette and beat Purdue 65-62 on January 14. Later that week, Indiana notched another road win by clobbering Iowa 99-79 in Iowa City.

After a 4-0 start and 14 straight wins overall, the third-ranked Hoosiers hosted No. 4 Ohio State (which was 5-0 in conference play) in Assembly Hall on January 21, in a game with huge implications for the Big Ten race. IU was mysteriously flat in the first half as the Buckeyes roared to a 48-29 halftime lead. In the second half, the Hoosiers made a huge surge to cut the lead to 82-79 with 1:40 remaining, but Ohio State kept its composure and pulled out a 93-85 win. Afterwards, Knight was very complimentary to the OSU team, saying, "They have two things that I think good teams really have to have. They're athletic and tough-minded."

Following the Ohio State loss, the Hoosiers kept pace with the Buckeyes in the conference race by winning their next six games. They outlasted Michigan 70-60 in Ann Arbor on Jan 24, and then came back to Bloomington and rallied for big wins over No. 22 Michigan State 97-63 and Wisconsin 73-57. After that, the Hoosiers snagged two more road wins by beating Minnesota 77-66 and Northwestern 105-74. Then, on February 10, IU swept the season series with Purdue by beating the Boilermakers 81-63 in Assembly Hall. That put IU at 10-1, only a half-game behind the 11-1 Buckeyes, and set up the second Indiana-Ohio State showdown of the year.

The second Indiana-Ohio State game was staged in Columbus, Ohio, and it turned out to be a thriller on national TV. The second-ranked Buckeyes came from behind to tie the game in the final minute and

Junior guard Jamal Meeks led IU with 4.9 assists per game during the 1990-91 season. For his career, Meeks ended up leading the Hoosiers in assists for three straight seasons. IU Archives

send it into overtime. Without Calbert Cheaney, who fouled out with 0:20 left in regulation, Damon Bailey carried the Hoosiers in the first and, eventually, the second overtime. The game was decided when OSU's Treg Lee buried a six-foot baseline jumper with 0:04 remaining to lift Ohio State to a 97-95 win. Buckeye sophomore Jim Jackson scored a career-high 30 points and pulled down 11 rebounds, while the Hoosiers' Bailey scored a career-high 32 points (including 12 in the overtime periods).

Four days after the emotional Ohio State loss, Indiana's Big Ten title hopes took another hit when No. 24 Iowa came into Assembly Hall and swiped an 80-79 win on a tip-in at the buzzer by Hawkeye forward James Moses. IU blew a 16-point lead during the final 15 minutes of that game. The Hoosiers responded on February 24, by blistering Michigan 112-79 in Bloomington, and then went on the road and seized two important wins over Michigan State (62-56) and Wisconsin (74-61). Then the Big Ten race got interesting. IU's arch-rival Purdue did the Hoosiers a favor by upsetting Ohio State, while Indiana stomped Minnesota 75-59 on March 7, in Assembly Hall. That put Indiana at 14-3 and Ohio State at 15-2 with one game remaining and both teams playing on the road on the final day of the season. On Sunday, March 10, Indiana recorded a convincing 70-58 win over Illinois in Champaign, and later that afternoon, Iowa upset Ohio State in Iowa City. Thus, the Hoosiers and the Buckeyes shared the Big Ten title with identical 15-3 records in conference play.

In the NCAA tournament, the Buckeyes were awarded the No. 1 seed in the Midwest Regional, while third-ranked Indiana was given a No. 2 seed in the Southeast Regional. Fortunately for the Hoosiers, they got to play in Louisville, Kentucky, which is just a couple of hours down I-69 from Bloomington. In the first round, IU easily dispatched Coastal Carolina 79-69, led by 22 points from Eric Anderson and 17 points and 14 rebounds from Calbert Cheaney. In the second round, Indiana fell behind Florida State 36-25 late in the first half. However, from that point on, it was all Indiana. The Hoosiers cruised to an 82-60 victory as five IU players scored in double figures, led by Cheaney with 24 points (in addition to 10 rebounds). In the Sweet Sixteen, third-seed Kansas sped out to a 21-4 lead and had the Hoosiers down 49-27 at the half. Indiana never recovered, and the 12th-ranked Jayhawks went on to an 83-65 victory. Kansas eventually made it all the way to the national championship game, where the Jayhawks got edged out for the NCAA title by the Duke Blue Devils.

The IU players were bitterly disappointed after the Kansas loss. Calbert Cheaney said, "They came out ready to play, and we didn't. They were hungry and we weren't." Chris Reynolds added, "They had more determination. It's embarrassing to say that after you work as hard as we have. ... All we can do now is try to get better and learn from those mistakes."

For a team that struggled to an 8-10 conference record and got beat in the first round of the NCAA tournament the previous year, Knight was pleased with his team's progress for the season. He said, "I'm really, really proud of this team and what they've been able to come back from. We are right where we ought to be. We got beat right where we ought to get beat. So we got a great improvement, and that was our objective."

INDIANA'S RANKING IN THE 1990-91 ASSOCIATED PRESS POLLS

PS	11/27	12/4	12/11	12/18	12/25	1/1	1/8	1/15	1/22	1/29	2/5	2/12	2/19	2/26	3/5	3/12
8	10	7	7	6	5	5	3	3	3	4	4	4	4	5	3	3

1991-92

OVERALL RECORD: 27-7

CONFERENCE RECORD: 14-4 (SECOND PLACE)

TEAM HONORS:

NCAA FINAL FOUR, HOOSIER CLASSIC CHAMPION,

INDIANA CLASSIC CHAMPION

INDIVIDUAL HONORS:

BOB KNIGHT—BIG TEN COACH OF THE YEAR

CALBERT CHEANEY—ALL-AMERICA, ALL-BIG TEN (FIRST TEAM)

The 1991-92 team. First row (left to right): Chris Reynolds, Damon Bailey, Eric Anderson, Jamal Meeks, Todd Leary, Greg Graham; Second row: Matt Nover, Calbert Cheaney, Todd Lindeman, Alan Henderson, Brian Evans, Pat Knight, Pat Graham. IU Athletics

After an 8-10 conference mark in the 1989-90 season, Indiana took the Big Ten by surprise in 1990-91 by pulling out a 15-3 record and winning the Big Ten title. The Hoosiers also finished 29-5 overall and were ranked No. 3 in the nation at the end of the regular season. "I don't know if we can get back to the kind of numbers we had last season, even though I think we're going to be a better basketball team," said coach Bob Knight prior to the 1991-92 campaign.

IU returned all five starters and its top seven scorers from a squad that was one of the most productive offensive teams in Indiana history, with averages of 84.8 points per game and a 53.4 percent field-goal percentage. The key returnees were leading scorer Calbert Cheaney, guards Damon Bailey and Greg Graham, and forward Eric Anderson. The only losses were reserve guard Lyndon Jones, who graduated, and reserve center Chris Lawson, who transferred to Vanderbilt. To help on the interior, 6'9" freshman

1991-92 TEAM ROSTER

Head coach: Bob Knight
Assistant coaches: Dan Dakich, Norm Ellenberger, Ron Felling

No.	Player	Hometown	Class	Position	Height
32	Eric Anderson (Capt.)	Chicago, IL	Sr	F/C	6-9
22	Damon Bailey	Heltonville, IN	So	G	6-3
40	Calbert Cheaney	Evansville, IN	Jr	F	6-6
34	Brian Evans	Terre Haute, IN	Rs	F	6-8
20	Greg Graham	Indianapolis, IN	Jr	G	6-4
33	Pat Graham	Floyd Knobs, IN	Rs	G	6-5
44	Alan Henderson	Carmel, IN	Fr	F/C	6-9
25	Pat Knight	Bloomington, IN	Rs	G	6-5
30	Todd Leary	Indianapolis, IN	So	G	6-3
50	Todd Lindeman	Channing, MI	Fr	C	7-0
23	Jamal Meeks (Capt.)	Freeport, IL	Sr	G	6-0
24	Matt Nover	Chesterton, IN	Jr	F/C	6-8
21	Chris Reynolds	Peoria, IL	Jr	G	6-1

SEASON RESULTS 1991-92

Date	Court	Opponent	Result	Score
11/15/1991	N1	UCLA	L	72-87
11/30/1991	H	Butler	W	97-73
12/3/1991	H	Notre Dame	W	78-46
12/7/1991	N2	Kentucky	L	74-76
12/10/1991	H	Vanderbilt	W	88-51
12/13/1991	H	Boston University	W	88-47
12/14/1991	H	Central Michigan	W	99-52
12/21/1991	N3	St. John's	W	82-77
12/27/1991	N2	Texas Tech	W	86-69
12/28/1991	N2	Indiana State	W	94-44
1/4/1992	A	Cincinnati	W	81-60
1/9/1992	H	Minnesota	W	96-50
1/11/1992	A	Wisconsin	W	79-63
1/14/1992	H	Ohio State	W	91-83
1/18/1992	A	Northwestern	W	96-62
1/21/1992	H	Michigan	W	89-74
1/28/1992	H	Purdue	W	106-65
2/1/1992	A	Michigan State	L	60-76
2/4/1992	A	Illinois	W	76-65
2/9/1992	H	Iowa	W	81-66
2/12/1992	A	Minnesota	L	67-71
2/15/1992	H	Northwestern	W	91-60
2/19/1992	H	Michigan State	W	103-73
2/23/1992	A	Ohio State	W	86-80
3/1/1992	H	Illinois	W	76-70
3/4/1992	A	Iowa	W	64-60
3/8/1992	A	Michigan	L	60-68
3/12/1992	H	Wisconsin	W	66-41
3/15/1992	A	Purdue	L	59-61
NCAA Tournament				
3/19/1992	N4	Eastern Illinois	W	94-55
3/21/1992	N4	Louisiana State	W	89-79
3/26/1992	N5	Florida State	W	85-74
3/28/1992	N5	UCLA	W	106-79
4/4/1992	N6	Duke	L	78-81

1 Springfield, MA
2 Indianapolis, IN
3 New York, NY
4 Boise, ID
5 Albuquerque, NM
6 Minneapolis, MN

1991-92 BIG TEN STANDINGS

	W	L	PCT
Ohio State	15	3	.833
Indiana	14	4	.778
Michigan1	11	7	.611
Michigan St.	11	7	.611
Iowa	10	8	.556
Purdue	8	10	.444
Minnesota	8	10	.444
Illinois	7	11	.389
Wisconsin	4	14	.222
Northwestern	2	16	.111

1 Due to NCAA sanctions, Michigan vacated the records from the 1992 Final Four and the 1992-93 season.

Alan Henderson joined the team and was expected to make an immediate impact. In the preseason, IU was ranked No. 2 in country.

The Hoosiers launched the season on November 15, in Springfield, Massachusetts, in the Hall of Fame Tip-Off Classic. Surprisingly, the 11th-ranked UCLA Bruins drilled the Hoosiers 87-72. IU star Calbert Cheaney struggled with multiple turnovers and shot only 2-9 from the field, while Alan Henderson led the Hoosiers with 20 points and eight rebounds in his collegiate debut. After the UCLA thrashing, Indiana raced to a pair of blowouts in Assembly Hall over cross-state rivals Butler (97-73) and Notre Dame (78-46). That set up a Hoosier Dome battle between No. 9 Indiana and No. 14 Kentucky on December 7. The Wildcats prevailed 76-74 when Greg Graham's buzzer-beating three-pointer missed the mark. Kentucky freshman Jamal Mashburn led the way with 21 points and eight rebounds. The loss dropped Indiana to 2-2 and it was the team's third straight defeat against a ranked opponent, going back to the season-ending loss to Kansas in the 1991 NCAA tournament.

On December 10, Coach Knight benched Cheaney, Anderson and Bailey when the Hoosiers hosted Vanderbilt in Assembly Hall. The trio didn't make an appearance until the second half, but IU still won easily, 88-51. On December 13-14, Indiana walloped Boston University 88-47 and Central Michigan 99-52 to capture the Indiana Classic in Bloomington. Then, the Hoosiers ended their losing streak against ranked teams by going into Madison Square Garden in New York City and beating 10th-ranked St. John's 82-77, led by 25 points from Cheaney. IU held the Redmen to 31 percent shooting from the field, but gave up 26 offensive rebounds and turned the ball over 18 times to allow St. John's to keep the game close. Next, IU swept the Hoosier Classic by beating Texas Tech 86-69 and Indiana State 94-44. Finally, Indiana closed out its preconference schedule by winning 81-60 against the Cincinnati Bearcats, a team that would eventually make a run all the way to the Final Four. The Hoosiers were 9-2 and ready to start conference play as one of the favorites for the league title.

On January 9, in Bloomington, Indiana made a statement by opening the Big Ten season with a 96-50 clobbering of Minnesota—the worst defeat in the history of Golden Gopher basketball. Alan Henderson led IU with 20 points and nine rebounds in his first Big Ten game, while Chris Reynolds handed out 10 assists for the Hoosiers. Two days later, IU scored another blowout at Wisconsin, beating the Badgers 79-63, led by 17 points from Greg Graham. That set up an early-season showdown between Big Ten favorites, No. 4 Ohio State and No. 5 Indiana on January 14, in Bloomington. The game marked the return to Bloomington of Lawrence Funderburke, who transferred to OSU after leaving IU during his freshman year. Funderburke was booed heartily by the Indiana fans while the Hoosiers pulled out a 91-83 victory. After beating Ohio State, IU rolled to three more victories: 96-62 over Northwestern in Evanston; 89-74 over No. 16 Michigan in Bloomington; and 106-65 over Purdue in Bloomington. That gave Indiana 13 consecutive wins and a 6-0 record atop the Big Ten.

No. 13 Michigan State brought an end to the Hoosiers' victory spree on February 1, by pounding the ball into the post and overpowering IU for a 76-60 Spartan win. MSU's big center Mike Peplowski (at 6'11" and 270 lbs.) led the Spartans with 16 points and 11 rebounds. Greg Graham led Indiana with 23 points in a losing effort. The Hoosiers bounced back by winning eight of their next nine games. That included home wins over Iowa (81-66), Northwestern (91-60), No. 11 Michigan State (103-73), and Illinois (76-70). It also included road wins over Illinois (76-65), No. 6 Ohio State (86-80), and Iowa (64-60). The lone defeat during that stretch came at Minnesota, 71-67 on February 12.

After that stretch, Indiana was 22-4 overall and ranked No. 2 in country. The Hoosiers were also 13-2 in conference play, a game ahead of Ohio State, whom they had already defeated twice. With three games remaining, IU only needed two wins to capture at least a share of the conference crown, and three victories would win it outright. The Hoosiers' margin of error shrunk on March 8, when 18th-ranked Michigan toppled IU 68-60. Led by five freshmen in the starting lineup, the Wolverines outrebounded IU 47-35, led by 18 rebounds from forward Chris Webber. Back in Bloomington on March 12, the Hoosiers turned in another subpar performance, but pulled out a 66-41 win over Wisconsin. Cheaney, IU's

Senior forward Eric Anderson struggled with his shooting at the end of the 1991-92 regular season, but he bounced back and provided a nice lift for the Hoosiers during IU's run to the 1992 Final Four.
IU Athletics

leading scorer, struggled through a 1-10 performance from the field and scored only four points.

That left fourth-ranked Indiana with one game remaining on March 15, in West Lafayette against a Purdue team that it had beaten by 41 points in January. For the Hoosiers, it was clear what was at stake. A victory over the Boilermakers would clinch at least a tie for the Big Ten crown (or an outright title if Ohio State lost its season finale) and a likely No. 1 seed in the NCAA tournament. However, once the ball was tipped in Mackey Arena, it soon became clear that this was going to be a traditional IU-Purdue battle. The Hoosiers used a late first-half surge to take a

34-29 lead into the locker room. Indiana opened up a 10-point lead in the second half and it looked like the Hoosiers were going to pull away. But then Purdue's Woody Austin got hot. He scored 10 straight points and the Boilers grabbed a 46-45 lead. Then, in the final minutes, Purdue's Cuonzo Martin drained a key jump shot and made several other clutch plays to lift Purdue to a 61-59 upset. Meanwhile, Ohio State won at Minnesota and finished 15-3 to claim the undisputed Big Ten title over the 14-4 Hoosiers. Knight was so disappointed in the loss that he demoted seniors Eric Anderson and Jamal Meeks from their role as team co-captains.

Indiana's fizzling finish in the Big Ten also relegated the Hoosiers to a No. 2 seed in the West Regional of the NCAA tournament. The Hoosiers, who were ranked No. 5 in the final AP poll, looked like an excellent candidate for an early upset since the team had struggled mightily down the stretch of the conference season, shooting 38 percent from the field over the final four games (as opposed to its 50 percent average for the season). Then, a light bulb kicked on and Indiana came to life in the tournament. Playing in Boise, Idaho, on March 19, the Hoosiers shot a torrid 62 percent from the field and blasted Eastern Illinois 94-55 in the first round. Alan Henderson's 19 points and 11 rebounds led the way. That set up a showdown two days later with Louisiana State and its 7'1", 295-pound All-America center Shaquille O'Neal. In a fiercely fought contest, IU's Eric Anderson and Matt Nover did everything they could to slow down O'Neill, but it was useless as the big man posted 36 points, 12 rebounds, five blocked shots, and two steals. However, the Hoosiers carved up the LSU zone with 54 percent shooting from the field. Damon Bailey hit the biggest shot of the game in the final minutes when he buried a three-pointer as the shot clock expired to turn a three-point lead into

six points. IU went on to an 89-79 win. Cheaney led IU with 30 points and seven rebounds.

In the regional semifinals in Albuquerque, New Mexico, Indiana eliminated Florida State from the tourney for the second straight year with an 85-74 win over the Seminoles as Calbert Cheaney and Greg Graham combined for 36 points and 18 rebounds. Next, in the Elite Eight, came a rematch with the UCLA squad that had convincingly trounced the Hoosiers in the season opener. However, this time a berth in the Final Four was at stake. It was never much of a contest as a charged-up IU squad sprang to a 15-point halftime lead and ended up winning 106-79, led by 23 points from Cheaney and 22 from Bailey. The loss was the most lopsided ever for UCLA in the NCAA tournament.

The Final Four ended up being a mentor-pupil showdown between Bob Knight and Mike Krzyzewski, who played for Knight at Army and was later one of the Knight's assistants. Krzyzewski's Duke Blue Devils, who were the defending NCAA champs and the top ranked team in the country, advanced to the Final Four on an improbable full-court pass and turnaround jump shot from Christian Laettner in the final seconds of a 104-103 overtime win against Kentucky in the Elite Eight. The Hoosiers and the Blue Devils locked horns in the marquee matchup of the Final Four on Saturday, April 4, in the Minneapolis Metrodome. Indiana got off to a great start and built a 12-point lead, and then settled for a 42-37 advantage at the break. However, Duke showed its championship mettle in the second half by surging to a 13-point lead while Indiana's top four scorers—Cheaney, Greg Graham, Bailey and Henderson—all got saddled with foul trouble and eventually fouled out. The Blue Devils led by nine points with a minute to go. That's when IU guard Todd Leary came off the bench for the most phenomenal one-minute perform-

INDIANA'S RANKING IN THE 1991-92 ASSOCIATED PRESS POLLS

PS	11/25	12/2	12/9	12/16	12/23	12/30	1/6	1/13	1/20	1/27	2/3	2/10	2/17	2/24	3/2	3/9	3/16
2	10	9	13	14	10	10	10	5	4	4	6	4	7	2	2	4	5

ance in school history. He buried three straight three-pointers within a span of 24 seconds to get the Hoosiers back into the game. On the final possession, Indiana had a chance to tie but couldn't get the ball to Leary, and so Jamal Meeks attempted a game-tying three-pointer, but it missed the mark and IU lost 81-78. Indiana had contained Laettner, Duke's All-America forward, who scored only eight points in the game. However, Blue Devil point guard Bobby Hurley broke loose for 26 points, including six of nine three-pointers, and forward Grant Hill added 14 points, six rebounds, and six assists. Two nights after slipping by Indiana, the Blue Devils blew out Michigan in the title game to capture their second straight NCAA title.

During the regular season, the Hoosiers slipped a bit from the season before. The team didn't show the same intensity and consistency that it had shown during the 1990-91 campaign. As a result, the IU squad let the Big Ten championship slip away down the stretch. IU's leading scorer, Cheaney, also slipped a little bit. After an All-America sophomore season in which he averaged 21.6 points per game, Cheaney became the focal point of opposing defenses during his junior year, and his production dropped to 17.6 points per game. However, both Cheaney and the Hoosiers played with renewed intensity in the NCAA tournament and put together a fantastic run. In the end, it took a team as good as Duke—which was playing in its fifth consecutive Final Four—to put a stop to the streaking Hoosiers, who had won their previous four tournament games by an average of 22 points.

1992-93

FOR THE COMMENTARY AND STATISTICS FOR
THE 1992-93 SEASON,
PLEASE SEE CHAPTER 8, "1992-93:
THE CULMINATION OF A THREE-YEAR RUN."

SEASON STATISTICS
1971-72 TO 1992-93

1971-72

Team Statistics	G	FG%	FT%	R	A	PF	PTS	PPG
Indiana	25	.454	.696	46.2	13.1	18.8	1840	73.6
Opponents	25	.398	.646	42.9	9.8	19.6	1678	67.1
Player Statistics	G-GS	FG%	FT%	R	A	PF	PTS	PPG
Wright	25-25	.463	.569	9.3	0.8	3.2	498	19.9
Downing	25-25	.425	.551	15.1	0.9	3.2	437	17.5
Ritter	25-25	.510	.873	5.0	2.4	3.0	350	14.0
Wilson	24-23	.456	.708	3.1	2.0	2.8	178	7.4
White	24-21	.432	.778	3.0	4.3	3.5	159	6.6
Shepherd	11-3	.469	.895	0.8	0.9	1.5	63	5.7
Pemberton	16-2	.545	.744	1.5	2.4	1.3	53	3.3
Memering	23-1	.404	.682	2.6	0.7	0.9	53	2.3
Ford	21-0	.391	.710	1.1	0.2	1.2	40	1.9
Heiniger	12-0	.231	.750	0.6	0.3	0.3	9	0.8

1972-73

PLEASE SEE CHAPTER 9

1973-74

Team Statistics	G	FG%	FT%	R	A	TO	PF	PTS	PPG
Indiana	28	.484	.686	43.5	17.1	18.7	21.0	2154	76.9
Opponents	28	.442	.662	36.4	10.5	22.2	18.4	1827	65.3
Player Statistics	G-GS	FG%	FT%	R	A	TO	PF	PTS	PPG
Green	28-28	.545	.688	5.4	1.7	2.5	3.1	467	16.7
May	28-27	.492	.768	5.4	1.5	2.4	3.4	351	12.5
Laskowski	28-3	.507	.774	3.9	1.8	1.9	1.6	350	12.5
Bensen	27-25	.504	.600	7.9	0.9	2.0	3.0	250	9.3
Buckner	28-27	.377	.561	3.8	5.4	3.8	3.6	229	8.2
Abernathy	28-1	.549	.750	3.6	0.7	1.0	1.2	160	5.7
Wilkerson	28-4	.402	.545	2.6	1.2	1.5	1.8	102	3.6
Ahlfeld	22-12	.547	.588	0.9	1.5	0.9	1.2	68	3.1
Crews	22-9	.456	.692	1.7	2.5	1.3	1.0	61	2.7
Kamstra	14-0	.563	.600	0.0	0.1	0.7	0.2	24	1.7
Smock	18-2	.364	.500	1.7	0.6	1.0	0.8	29	1.6
Noort	18-1	.367	.750	1.6	0.2	0.6	0.9	28	1.6
Morris	14-1	.429	.714	0.4	0.6	0.7	0.6	22	1.6
Allen	12-0	.462	.500	0.6	0.3	0.3	0.4	13	1.1

1974-75

PLEASE SEE CHAPTER 3

1975-76

PLEASE SEE CHAPTER 1

1976-77

Team Statistics	G	FG%	FT%	R	A	TO	PF	PTS	PPG
Indiana	27	.479	.693	41.4	16.3	18.3	20.9	1912	70.8
Opponents	27	.426	.683	37.2	11.5	17.3	20.0	1782	66.0
Player Statistics	G-GS	FG%	FT%	R	A	TO	PF	PTS	PPG
Benson	23-23	.503	.750	10.5	1.3	2.7	2.7	456	19.8
Woodson	27-25	.521	.792	6.7	1.6	3.6	3.3	500	18.5
Radford	27-14	.503	.604	2.7	1.8	2.1	1.9	249	9.2
Smock	1-0	.750	.500	2.0	1.0	2.0	1.0	7	7.0
Wisman	26-21	.486	.767	1.7	5.0	2.1	2.7	163	6.3
Miday	3-1	.643	.000	3.7	1.0	1.0	2.0	18	6.0
Cunningham	19-8	.476	.739	2.4	2.3	1.6	2.1	97	5.1
Holcomb	22-4	.447	.567	4.9	0.6	0.8	1.8	85	3.9
Grunwald	26-12	.375	.450	2.2	2.2	1.9	2.3	93	3.6
Valavicious	23-4	.413	.636	1.6	0.8	1.0	1.5	76	3.3
Roberson	23-4	.414	.667	3.5	0.3	1.4	2.0	70	3.0
Carter	23-13	.391	.609	2.2	1.4	1.9	2.0	68	3.0
Eells	21-1	.345	.667	1.6	0.7	1.2	1.0	30	1.4

1977-78

Team Statistics	G	FG%	FT%	R	A	TO	PF	PTS	PPG
Indiana	29	.500	.702	36.7	15.0	18.6	20.3	2039	70.3
Opponents	29	.420	.698	37.7	10.9	18.2	22.1	1850	63.8
Player Statistics	G-GS	FG%	FT%	R	A	TO	PF	PTS	PPG
Woodson	29-28	.524	.769	5.4	1.4	3.3	2.7	577	19.9
Radford	29-25	.579	.770	4.0	2.1	2.2	2.6	453	15.6
Tolbert	29-28	.450	.649	6.9	0.7	2.1	3.2	292	10.1
Risley	28-11	.477	.480	4.0	0.6	1.5	1.8	146	5.2
Wisman	29-22	.462	.746	1.4	4.0	1.7	2.2	142	4.9
Eells	22-6	.571	.828	1.2	0.5	1.2	1.5	96	4.4
Baker	28-7	.423	.583	1.6	2.6	3.1	2.1	87	3.1
Carter	29-6	.508	.677	1.3	2.2	1.9	1.4	83	2.9
Grunwald	24-11	.443	.600	1.8	1.0	1.0	1.7	60	2.5
Isenbarger	16-0	.478	.548	1.4	0.3	0.7	1.0	39	2.4
Cunningham	8-0	.357	.571	0.8	0.6	0.6	1.0	14	1.8
Roberson	26-1	.389	.739	1.9	0.1	0.4	1.1	45	1.7
Kirchner	12-0	.333	.500	0.9	0.0	0.3	0.5	5	0.4

1978-79

Team Statistics	G	FG%	FT%	R	A	TO	S	B	PF	PTS	PPG
Indiana	34	.504	.722	35.6	16.0	16.8	6.1	2.4	18.1	2287	67.3
Opponents	34	.422	.703	34.9	12.1	16.6	6.3	2.0	20.1	2080	61.2
Player Statistics	G-GS	FG%	FT%	R	A	TO	S	B	PF	PTS	PPG
Woodson	34-33	.498	.763	5.7	2.9	3.5	1.6	0.4	2.9	714	21.0
Tolbert	34-32	.544	.696	7.1	1.1	2.5	0.6	1.3	2.9	407	12.0
Carter	33-29	.513	.742	3.0	4.6	2.8	0.9	0.1	2.5	281	8.5
Wittman	34-32	.532	.736	2.6	4.5	2.1	0.9	0.2	2.3	241	7.1
Risley	32-15	.463	.750	3.5	0.5	1.4	0.6	0.0	2.3	210	6.6
Baker	6-5	.417	.857	1.8	4.2	1.8	1.3	0.0	2.8	36	6.0
Turner	33-13	.542	.538	3.4	0.3	1.8	0.5	0.3	2.3	182	5.5
Roberson	6-4	.400	.900	3.8	0.5	1.5	0.5	0.2	2.0	21	3.5
Eells	34-4	.459	.679	1.9	1.0	1.1	0.4	0.1	1.1	114	3.4
Isenbarger	21-2	.414	.731	1.0	0.8	1.0	0.3	0.0	1.0	43	2.1
Reish	11-0	.400	.778	0.6	0.5	0.7	0.3	0.0	0.9	19	1.7
Cox	6-1	.500	.750	0.3	0.2	0.8	0.2	0.0	0.3	8	1.3
Kirchner	14-0	.300	.417	0.8	0.0	0.4	0.1	0.1	0.7	11	0.8
Kitchel	1-0	.000	.000	0.0	0.0	2.0	1.0	0.0	0.0	0	0.0

1979-80

Team Statistics	G	FG%	FT%	R	A	TO	S	B	PF	PTS	PPG
Indiana	29	.490	.705	35.7	16.3	16.0	6.8	3.0	20.1	1979	68.2
Opponents	29	.441	.703	34.6	11.7	17.8	6.2	2.9	20.0	1796	61.9
Player Statistics	G-GS	FG%	FT%	R	A	TO	S	B	PF	PTS	PPG
Woodson	14-14	.453	.835	3.5	2.6	2.4	1.0	0.6	2.3	270	19.3
I. Thomas	29-29	.510	.772	4.0	5.5	4.7	2.1	0.2	3.5	423	14.6
Carter	29-23	.547	.760	3.5	3.1	2.1	1.2	0.2	2.4	323	11.1
Tolbert	29-28	.527	.613	7.2	1.5	1.7	0.7	1.1	2.8	300	10.3
Turner	26-12	.485	.708	4.4	0.5	1.9	0.5	0.4	2.8	192	7.4
Bouchie	22-16	.496	.629	3.7	0.8	1.2	0.3	0.4	2.8	142	6.5
Wittman	5-5	.464	.750	1.4	2.4	1.2	1.6	0.0	1.0	29	5.8
Isenbarger	24-5	.400	.625	1.6	0.8	0.6	0.2	0.3	1.3	67	2.8
J. Thomas	21-2	.455	.615	1.6	0.6	0.6	0.4	0.0	0.8	56	2.7
Risley	27-3	.587	.647	1.6	0.3	0.3	0.1	0.1	0.7	65	2.4
Kitchel	22-4	.320	.583	1.3	0.7	0.7	0.3	0.1	1.1	39	1.8
Grunwald	26-4	.439	.467	1.1	0.6	0.7	0.2	0.1	1.7	43	1.7
Brown	17-0	.318	.300	1.0	0.8	1.1	0.3	0.0	0.7	17	1.0
Franz	20-0	.400	.250	0.6	1.0	0.6	0.1	0.0	0.7	13	0.7

1980-81

PLEASE SEE CHAPTER 5

1981-82

Team Statistics	G	FG%	FT%	R	A	TO	S	B	PF	PTS	PPG
Indiana	29	.492	.736	37.6	17.2	15.6	5.7	2.4	18.7	2004	69.1
Opponents	29	.435	.688	32.5	13.0	14.3	5.8	2.3	19.7	1778	61.3
Player Statistics	G-GS	FG%	FT%	R	A	TO	S	B	PF	PTS	PPG
Kitchel	29-28	.530	.874	4.9	1.9	2.5	0.6	0.3	3.1	568	19.6
Wittman	29-26	.482	.756	3.2	3.5	1.5	1.1	0.2	1.9	347	12.0
Thomas	29-25	.520	.855	6.2	3.6	2.7	1.3	0.2	2.3	267	9.2
Blab	24-10	.556	.586	3.7	0.5	2.2	0.1	0.7	2.2	179	7.5
Bouchie	29-17	.455	.636	4.6	1.0	1.2	0.5	0.5	2.1	185	6.4
Brown	29-12	.439	.700	2.5	2.0	1.5	0.7	0.0	1.4	135	4.7
Flowers	29-8	.455	.469	3.6	0.3	1.0	0.3	0.6	2.2	135	4.7
Dakich	29-10	.515	.667	1.9	2.1	1.3	0.7	0.0	1.6	88	3.0
Morgan	24-8	.396	.645	2.0	1.9	1.6	0.2	0.1	1.4	58	2.4
Rowray	1-0	.000	.500	0.0	1.0	0.0	0.0	0.0	0.0	2	2.0
Cameron	15-0	.375	.722	0.6	0.1	0.4	0.2	0.0	0.5	25	1.7
Franz	21-1	.250	.563	0.6	1.0	0.7	0.2	0.0	1.1	15	0.7

1982-83

Team Statistics	G	FG%	3FG%	FT%	R	A	TO	S	B	PF	PTS	PPG
Indiana	30	.522	.566	.746	34.4	16.8	13.1	5.4	2.7	17.0	2146	71.5
Opponents	30	.436	.415	.672	33.0	11.7	14.2	5.0	2.5	20.7	1832	61.1
Player Statistics	G-GS	FG%	3FG%	FT%	R	A	TO	S	B	PF	PTS	PPG
Wittman	30-30	.543	.444	.824	4.5	2.9	1.6	0.3	0.1	1.8	569	19.0
Kitchel	24-23	.511	.656	.860	4.1	2.2	2.3	1.3	0.0	2.4	415	17.3
Thomas	30-28	.523	.000	.753	5.3	2.7	1.9	1.2	0.0	2.4	307	10.2
Blab	30-19	.518	.000	.567	4.9	0.3	1.6	0.3	1.3	2.7	283	9.4
Bouchie	30-15	.543	.000	.787	3.5	0.8	1.1	0.5	0.4	2.1	188	6.3
Brown	29-18	.524	.000	.821	2.3	4.0	1.9	0.7	0.2	1.5	152	5.2
Flowers	8-2	.542	.000	.000	2.3	0.5	0.5	0.1	1.1	1.9	26	3.3
Morgan	27-5	.533	1.00	.604	1.7	1.8	1.1	0.6	0.2	1.7	78	2.9
Giomi	19-0	.545	.000	.636	1.7	0.1	0.4	0.2	0.2	1.1	43	2.3
Robinson	26-9	.400	.000	.778	1.1	2.7	1.6	0.5	0.0	1.6	49	1.9
Dakich	17-1	.364	.000	.632	1.1	0.6	0.9	0.5	0.0	0.6	28	1.7
Cameron	15-0	.500	.000	.571	0.2	0.1	0.1	0.1	0.0	0.1	8	0.5
Foster	2-0	.000	.000	.000	.05	0.5	0.0	0.0	0.0	0.5	0	0.0

1983-84

Team Statistics	G	FG%	FT%	R	A	TO	S	B	PF	PTS	PPG
Indiana	31	.522	.717	28.8	14.8	12.2	5.1	2.9	18.7	2018	65.1
Opponents	31	.436	.710	30.7	10.8	12.6	5.0	2.0	21.3	1833	59.1
Player Statistics	G-GS	FG%	FT%	R	A	TO	S	B	PF	PTS	PPG
Alford	31-27	.592	.913	2.6	3.2	2.0	1.5	0.1	1.9	479	15.5
Blab	31-27	.528	.635	6.1	0.5	1.7	0.5	1.3	2.9	366	11.8
Simmons	31-26	.476	.661	4.2	2.6	1.7	0.7	0.1	2.2	290	9.4
Giomi	27-15	.487	.724	4.7	0.4	1.3	0.6	0.2	3.3	234	8.7
Robinson	30-15	.536	.773	1.5	3.5	1.8	0.6	0.0	1.2	238	7.9
Morgan	6-2	.621	.800	3.3	2.8	2.0	0.3	0.0	3.2	40	6.7
Dakich	24-4	.545	.623	1.2	2.0	0.8	0.2	0.0	2.0	93	3.9
Franz	27-10	.463	.767	0.7	2.0	1.1	0.4	0.0	1.9	99	3.7
Meier	26-7	.547	.567	1.7	0.7	1.1	0.3	0.0	1.2	75	2.9
Thomas	25-6	.462	.538	1.8	0.3	0.8	0.6	0.1	1.6	69	2.8
Foster	6-0	.333	.600	1.5	0.5	1.5	0.5	0.0	1.2	16	2.7
Witte	20-1	.429	.538	1.0	0.0	0.1	0.1	0.2	0.5	19	1.0

1984-85

Team Statistics	G	FG%	FT%	R	A	TO	S	B	PF	PTS	PPG
Indiana	33	.528	.713	31.7	17.9	13.0	5.7	3.1	19.2	2349	71.2
Opponents	33	.456	.693	32.1	12.2	13.6	5.1	2.6	18.8	2163	65.5
Player Statistics	G-GS	FG%	FT%	R	A	TO	S	B	PF	PTS	PPG
Alford	32-31	.538	.921	3.2	2.7	1.5	1.4	0.0	1.6	580	18.1
Blab	33-31	.565	.714	6.3	1.4	2.2	0.5	2.2	3.0	529	16.0
Giomi	15-11	.637	.565	5.3	1.1	1.4	0.5	0.4	3.1	143	9.5
Robinson	29-14	.466	.692	2.2	4.6	1.9	0.7	0.1	2.1	177	6.1
Thomas	21-10	.551	.659	2.6	0.3	0.8	0.4	0.4	2.1	115	5.5
Dakich	28-11	.535	.735	2.0	2.7	0.9	0.5	0.0	1.4	147	5.3
Morgan	21-11	.545	.667	3.4	3.1	1.8	0.6	0.0	2.6	110	5.2
Eyl	29-14	.500	.649	2.6	1.0	0.9	0.3	0.1	1.3	138	4.8
Simmons	23-9	.529	.591	1.7	1.1	1.1	0.5	0.1	1.6	85	3.7
Brooks	32-12	.443	.732	1.2	1.7	1.0	0.6	0.0	1.7	116	3.6
Smith	23-1	.596	.600	0.8	0.5	0.9	0.2	0.0	0.4	71	3.1
Meier	30-8	.468	.538	2.5	0.9	0.8	0.6	0.2	1.9	79	2.6
Hillman	21-1	.361	.625	0.9	1.0	0.6	0.1	0.0	0.6	31	1.5
Pelkowski	15-0	.500	.400	1.1	0.0	0.1	0.0	0.1	0.6	14	0.9
Sloan	17-1	.250	.333	0.9	0.4	0.7	0.1	0.1	1.2	14	0.8

1983-84

Team Statistics	G	FG%	FT%	R	A	TO	S	B	PF	PTS	PPG
Indiana	29	.537	.737	31.4	15.1	13.4	6.2	2.8	19.1	2213	76.3
Opponents	29	.468	.701	32.2	12.4	14.5	5.3	2.3	19.8	1968	67.9
Player Statistics	G-GS	FG%	FT%	R	A	TO	S	B	PF	PTS	PPG
Alford	28-28	.556	.871	2.7	2.8	1.8	1.8	0.0	1.6	630	22.5
Thomas	26-26	.561	.760	4.8	0.5	2.0	1.0	0.3	3.3	377	14.5
Calloway	29-27	.544	.671	4.9	1.7	2.5	0.7	0.3	2.4	403	13.9
Harris	29-25	.507	.648	5.6	1.0	2.0	0.6	1.7	3.4	243	8.4
Morgan	29-21	.510	.739	3.6	4.6	2.5	0.7	0.2	3.1	192	6.6
Robinson	28-8	.480	.830	1.8	3.0	0.9	0.6	0.1	1.4	166	5.9
Smith	3-1	.500	.500	1.3	1.3	0.7	0.0	0.0	0.3	12	4.0
Jadlow	22-2	.511	.522	1.5	0.3	0.9	0.3	0.2	1.8	58	2.6
Brooks	11-1	.647	.571	1.0	2.0	0.6	0.4	0.0	1.8	26	2.4
Meier	25-3	.522	.667	1.8	0.4	0.5	0.2	0.2	1.3	42	1.7
Witte	14-1	.643	.714	1.6	0.1	0.1	0.3	0.0	0.4	23	1.6
Eyl	27-1	.531	.368	2.1	0.3	0.4	0.3	0.0	1.0	41	1.5

1986-87

PLEASE SEE CHAPTER 4

1987-88

Team Statistics	G	FG%	3FG%	FT%	R	A	TO	S	B	PF	PTS	PPG
Indiana	29	.515	.467	.738	33.0	16.9	13.2	6.0	4.5	18.7	2284	78.8
Opponents	29	.452	.486	.689	34.2	12.2	15.0	6.8	1.9	18.8	2057	70.9
Player Statistics	G-GS	FG%	3FG%	FT%	R	A	TO	S	B	PF	PTS	PPG
Garrett	29-28	.535	.000	.697	8.5	0.4	1.2	0.6	3.4	2.8	467	16.1
Edwards	23-15	.449	.536	.908	2.2	3.2	1.9	0.7	0.3	2.4	358	15.6
Smart	29-21	.518	.321	.870	3.0	3.1	2.3	0.9	0.1	2.3	383	13.2
Calloway	26-19	.489	.000	.658	4.3	2.2	1.9	1.0	0.1	2.3	306	11.8
Hillman	27-16	.576	.200	.841	2.6	3.9	1.2	0.9	0.0	2.1	192	7.1
Jadlow	28-10	.527	.000	.812	3.2	0.2	0.9	0.3	0.3	2.4	154	5.5
Jones	27-15	.505	.600	.632	1.2	2.7	2.0	0.7	0.0	1.0	133	4.9
Eyl	28-14	.627	.000	.429	2.6	1.5	1.4	0.8	0.1	1.7	119	4.3
Pelkowski	20-3	.563	.667	.429	2.4	0.3	0.4	0.3	0.2	1.6	62	3.1
Smith	18-0	.552	.500	.600	1.1	0.4	0.6	0.2	0.0	0.7	44	2.4
Sloan	19-3	.413	.000	.500	1.3	0.6	0.7	0.3	0.2	1.4	41	2.2
Oliphant	12-1	.500	.500	.000	0.8	0.6	0.3	0.3	0.0	0.5	25	2.1

1988-89

PLEASE SEE CHAPTER 10

1989-90

Team Statistics	G	FG%	3FG%	FT%	R	A	TO	S	B	PF	PTS	PPG
Indiana	29	.514	.437	.733	33.4	16.0	14.4	5.2	2.6	18.4	2265	78.1
Opponents	29	.455	.349	.679	32.9	12.1	14.4	6.0	2.7	21.9	2054	70.8
Player Statistics	G-GS	FG%	3FG%	FT%	R	A	TO	S	B	PF	PTS	PPG
Cheaney	29-29	.572	.490	.750	4.6	1.7	1.8	0.8	0.6	2.7	495	17.1
Anderson	29-28	.537	.286	.728	7.0	0.8	2.2	0.3	0.6	2.8	473	16.3
Funderburke	6-3	.491	.000	.519	6.7	1.3	2.0	0.2	1.0	2.0	70	11.7
G. Graham	29-16	.471	.387	.778	2.6	2.0	1.9	0.8	0.4	1.9	281	9.7
P. Graham	29-4	.504	.479	.838	1.6	1.5	1.6	0.5	0.0	1.7	224	7.7
Jones	22-12	.449	.423	.848	1.7	2.5	1.8	0.5	0.0	1.1	135	6.1
Nover	26-14	.527	.000	.732	3.4	0.5	1.1	0.2	0.5	2.3	137	5.3
Meeks	28-13	.487	.600	.861	2.3	3.8	1.5	0.4	0.0	1.8	111	4.0
Lawson	27-7	.474	.000	.650	3.1	0.6	0.6	0.2	0.3	1.9	98	3.6
Reynolds	28-12	.483	1.00	.544	1.7	1.9	1.2	0.9	0.1	1.5	90	3.2
Robinson	21-5	.542	.000	.375	2.1	0.3	0.4	0.8	0.0	1.0	67	3.2
Oliphant	13-0	.632	.417	.800	0.8	0.7	0.5	0.0	0.0	0.2	33	2.5
Leary	22-2	.347	.296	.692	0.6	1.1	0.6	0.2	0.0	0.5	51	2.3

1990-91

Team Statistics	G	FG%	3FG%	FT%	R	A	TO	S	B	PF	PTS	PPG
Indiana	34	.534	.408	.729	34.0	18.7	14.2	7.3	3.3	18.6	2882	84.8
Opponents	34	.433	.427	.655	34.0	13.2	18.5	4.9	2.2	21.6	2352	69.2
Player Statistics	G-GS	FG%	3FG%	FT%	R	A	TO	S	B	PF	PTS	PPG
Cheaney	34-34	.596	.473	.801	5.5	1.4	2.3	1.0	0.4	2.9	734	21.6
Anderson	34-34	.507	.250	.697	7.1	1.1	1.6	0.8	1.5	2.6	466	13.7
Bailey	33-14	.506	.434	.692	2.9	2.9	1.6	1.2	0.3	2.3	373	11.4
G. Graham	34-13	.510	.241	.694	2.6	1.6	1.6	1.0	0.2	1.9	296	8.7
P. Graham	34-4	.500	.342	.850	1.6	1.6	1.2	0.5	0.1	1.5	251	7.4
Nover	34-26	.540	.000	.677	3.9	0.4	1.2	0.4	0.5	2.4	234	6.9
Reynolds	33-4	.541	.000	.675	1.7	2.2	1.2	1.0	0.1	1.7	136	4.1
Jones	34-10	.500	.462	.741	1.4	1.9	0.9	0.4	0.0	0.8	134	3.9
Lawson	27-5	.580	.000	.630	1.7	0.3	0.7	0.3	0.3	1.2	97	3.6
Meeks	34-26	.514	.333	.745	2.0	4.9	1.5	1.0	0.0	1.3	120	3.5
Knight	22-0	.410	.000	.700	1.0	0.9	0.9	0.2	0.0	0.5	39	1.8

1991-92

Team Statistics	G	FG%	3FG%	FT%	R	A	TO	S	B	PF	PTS	PPG
Indiana	34	.502	.422	.732	37.3	17.4	12.4	7.4	3.6	18.0	2837	83.4
Opponents	34	.407	.391	.701	32.8	12.1	16.3	4.6	3.0	23.1	2238	65.8
Player Statistics	G-GS	FG%	3FG%	FT%	R	A	TO	S	B	PF	PTS	PPG
Cheaney	34-32	.522	.384	.800	4.9	1.4	1.9	1.1	0.2	2.5	599	17.6
G. Graham	34-16	.502	.427	.741	4.0	2.6	1.7	1.4	0.3	2.1	436	12.8
Bailey	34-27	.497	.471	.765	3.6	3.1	2.2	0.8	0.0	2.0	422	12.4
Henderson	33-26	.508	.250	.661	7.2	0.5	1.0	1.0	1.5	2.5	383	11.6
Anderson	34-24	.472	.429	.807	5.1	1.4	1.2	0.8	1.1	2.8	372	10.9
Nover	34-16	.544	1.00	.714	3.2	0.1	1.2	0.3	0.4	1.9	221	6.5
Reynolds	33-24	.452	.188	.595	2.2	3.8	1.2	1.5	0.0	1.6	141	4.3
Leary	22-1	.588	.542	.846	0.9	0.9	0.8	0.1	0.0	0.7	84	3.8
Meeks	32-4	.431	.382	.714	2.3	4.2	1.4	1.0	0.0	1.5	115	3.6
Lindeman	20-0	.457	.000	.667	2.0	0.0	0.5	0.1	0.3	1.3	64	2.0

1992-93

PLEASE SEE CHAPTER 8

CHAPTER 19

TWILIGHT OF AN ERA: 1993-94 TO 1999-2000

The toughest challenge that Bob Knight faced during his final seven years in Bloomington may have been living up to the impossibly high standard of excellence that he had set during his first 22 seasons. Make no mistake; Coach Knight had some very competitive teams during his final years at Indiana. They never won fewer than 19 games, they made the NCAA tournament every season, and they made several spirited runs at the Big Ten title against some excellent conference opponents. At most schools—and for most other coaches—those accolades would have been a strong record of success. But for Bob Knight and the Indiana program, they didn't quite live up to expectations because Indiana didn't win any Big Ten championships, never made it past the second round of the NCAA tournament, and never did better than 23 victories in a season during Knight's last seven years at IU.

On the heels of the successful 1992-93 season, Indiana brought in two highly-touted recruiting classes in the fall of 1993 and 1994 that were supposed to provide the core players of Indiana's next generation of championship teams. The 1994 group, which included two McDonald's All-Americans, was considered one of the best recruiting classes in IU history. However, of the ten recruits who came in as part of the 1993 and 1994 classes, only four of them— Robbie Eggers, Richard Mandeville, Andrae Patterson and Charlie Miller—ended up completing their careers at Indiana. And Eggers and Mandeville were

never more than reserve role players for the Hoosiers. The six players who left Indiana did so for various reasons, including academic problems, personal issues, and/or playing time concerns. In the late 1990s, Knight also had two McDonald's All-Americans who transferred: Jason Collier and Luke Recker.

That exodus of talent made it difficult for Coach Knight to replicate the same kind of success he had demonstrated during his first 22 years at the helm of the IU program and led to some restlessness among Indiana fans. However, many IU fans were angered by the way that Knight was treated in the investigation that followed charges of abuse by former IU player Neil Reid in the spring of 2000. During the investigation, allegations from Reid and others were widely publicized while Knight wasn't able to defend himself and tell his side of the story. Then Knight was publicly reprimanded and fined by IU president Myles Brand and put under a zero tolerance policy, which Brand eventually deemed that Knight violated and dismissed him as the IU coach.

Knight's unceremonious firing, along with his final seven seasons without any significant championships, was a tough way for The General to end his legendary Indiana career, which had seen its share of controversy, but which had also witnessed a far greater measure of successful student-athletes and some of the most well-played basketball ever seen in the college ranks.

1993-94

OVERALL RECORD: 21-9

CONFERENCE RECORD: 12-6 (THIRD PLACE)

TEAM HONORS:

HOOSIER CLASSIC CHAMPION, INDIANA CLASSIC CHAMPION

INDIVIDUAL HONORS:

DAMON BAILEY—ALL-AMERICA, ALL-BIG TEN (FIRST TEAM)

TODD LINDEMAN—ACADEMIC ALL-BIG TEN

The 1993-94 team. First row (left to right): Alan Henderson, Damon Bailey, Todd Leary, Pat Graham, Pat Knight; Second row: Steve Hart, Robbie Eggers, Brian Evans, Richard Mandeville, Todd Lindeman, Sherron Wilkerson, Rob Foster.
IU Athletics

After three years of playing in the shadow of star forward Calbert Cheaney, Damon Bailey emerged as the Hoosiers' undisputed floor leader for the 1993-94 season, and the team definitely became Damon's team. Bailey wasn't a flashy player, but he was athletic, versatile, and had a high basketball IQ. Indiana's other returning starter was power forward Alan Henderson, who was returning from off-season knee surgery. He now stabilized the interior while Bailey took care of the perimeter. In addition, sophomore Brian Evans, a sharp-shooting 6'8" for-

ward, returned from a solid freshman campaign that saw him make big plays in several important games, while fifth-year seniors Pat Graham and Todd Leary, who were both sharp-shooting guards, also returned for one final run.

Calbert Cheaney, Greg Graham, Matt Nover and Chris Reynolds all graduated. They were replaced by two new Indiana recruits—Sherron Wilkerson and Steve Hart—and a trio of out-of-state recruits—Robbie Eggers, Richard Mandeville and Rob Foster. Wilkerson, Hart and Foster were all athletic guards,

1993-94 TEAM ROSTER

Head coach: Bob Knight
Assistant coaches: Dan Dakich, Norm Ellenberger, Ron Felling

No.	Player	Hometown	Class	Position	Height
22	Damon Bailey (Capt.)	Heltonville, IN	Sr	G	6-3
32	Robbie Eggers	Cuyahoga Falls, OH	Rs	F	6-10
34	Brian Evans	Terre Haute, IN	So	F	6-8
12	Rob Foster	Los Angeles, CA	Fr	G	6-4
33	Pat Graham (Capt.)	Floyd Knobs, IN	Sr	G	6-5
53	Ross Hales	Elkhart, IN	Sr	F	6-7
23	Steve Hart	Terre Haute, IN	Fr	G	6-3
44	Alan Henderson	Indianapolis, IN	Jr	F	6-9
25	Pat Knight	Bloomington, IN	Jr	G	6-6
30	Todd Leary (Capt.)	Indianapolis, IN	Sr	G	6-3
50	Todd Lindeman	Channing, MI	So	C	7-0
21	Richard Mandeville	LaCanada, CA	Fr	C	7-0
20	Sherron Wilkerson	Jeffersonville, IN	Fr	G	6-4

SEASON RESULTS 1993-94

Date	Court	Opponent	Result	Score
11/27/1993	A	Butler	L	71-75
12/4/1993	N1	(#1) Kentucky	W	96-84
12/7/1993	H	Notre Dame	W	101-82
12/10/1993	H	Tennessee Tech	W	117-73
12/11/1993	H	Washington State	W	79-64
12/18/1993	H	Eastern Kentucky	W	91-80
12/22/1993	A	(#6) Kansas	L	83-86
12/27/1993	N1	Texas Christian	W	81-65
12/28/1993	N1	(#25) Western Kentucky	W	65-55
1/8/1994	H	Penn State	W	80-72
1/11/1994	A	Iowa	W	89-75
1/16/1994	H	(#10) Michigan	W	82-72
1/18/1994	A	(#12) Purdue	L	76-83
1/22/1994	H	Northwestern	W	81-76
1/26/1994	H	(#16) Minnesota	W	78-66
1/30/1994	A	Illinois	L	81-88
2/2/1994	H	Ohio State	W	87-83
2/5/1994	A	Penn State	W	76-66
2/8/1994	A	(#11) Michigan	L	67-91
2/12/1994	H	Iowa	W	93-91
2/19/1994	H	(#9) Purdue	W	82-80
2/24/1994	A	Northwestern	W	81-74
2/27/1994	A	(#20) Minnesota	L	56-106
3/1/1994	H	Illinois	W	82-77
3/6/1994	A	Ohio State	L	78-82
3/9/1994	A	Michigan State	L	78-94
3/12/1994	H	Wisconsin	W	78-65
NCAA Tournament				
3/18/1994	N2	Ohio	W	84-72
3/20/1994	N2	(#12) Temple	W	67-58
3/25/1994	N3	Boston College	L	68-77

1 Indianapolis
2 Landover, MD
3 Miami, FL

1993-94 BIG TEN STANDINGS

	W	L	PCT
Purdue	14	4	.778
Michigan	13	5	.722
Indiana	12	6	.667
Minnesota*	0	0	.000
Michigan St.	10	8	.556
Illinois	10	8	.556
Wisconsin	8	10	.444
Penn State	6	12	.333
Ohio State	6	12	.333
Northwestern	5	13	.278
Iowa	5	13	.278

* NCAA voided all games for Minnesota

while Eggers and Mandeville were both big-man projects. The other addition to the Indiana rotation was 7'0" sophomore Todd Lindeman, who was coming off a redshirt season.

"With the players we have coming back and the players we have coming in, I think we have as good a blend of basketball talent and athletic ability as maybe we've ever had," said coach Bob Knight in the fall of 1993. The big advantage the Hoosiers had over the previous season was depth, especially in the frontcourt. The 1993-94 squad had five players at 6'8" or taller. In fact, they had so many big men that Knight decided to redshirt Robbie Eggers.

Nevertheless, with the loss of four seniors and the team's top two scorers, the Hoosiers needed some players to step up and emerge as team leaders. Bailey and Henderson would meet the challenge. Henderson, a junior, bounced back from his knee injury to become a major force in the paint and one of the top forwards in the Big Ten. After averaging 11.1 points and 8.1 rebounds as a sophomore, he upped those numbers to 17.8 points and 10.3 rebounds for his junior season. Bailey came to Indiana as a prolific scorer (the all-time leading scorer in Indiana high school history), but he averaged only 11.3 PPG over the course of his first three seasons at IU and served mostly as a playmaker and distributor of the basketball. He scored in bunches when the team needed it, like when he scored 32 points at Ohio State in 1991, but other players such as Calbert Cheaney, Greg Graham and Eric Anderson usually handled the bulk of the scoring. That changed during the 1993-94 season when Bailey became a big-time scorer once again—because that's what the team needed. He averaged 19.6 PPG and carried the IU squad to several victories almost by himself.

Bailey and the Hoosiers opened their season with a pair of games in Indianapolis. The first was against Butler in legendary Hinkle Fieldhouse on November 27. The Bulldogs harassed IU into 41 percent shooting from the field, while Butler guard Travis Trice buried seven three-pointers and led his team to a 75-71 upset. Bailey led IU with 23 points while Alan Henderson pulled down a game-high 14 rebounds. After an intense week of practice following the Butler loss, IU squared off with top-ranked Kentucky in the Hoosier Dome on December 4, in front of a national television audience and a raucous crowd evenly divided between blue and red. Indiana roared to a 15-8 lead but then fell behind 33-26 before Bailey took over and pushed the Hoosiers to a 55-44 lead at the half. After the break, Bailey suffered from leg cramps but made all the key plays on both ends of the floor to carry IU to a 96-84 win. Bailey's 29-point, six-rebound, five-assist performance led Kentucky coach Rick Pitino to say, "Damon Bailey was the dominant player [today]. He was the best player on the court."

After toppling Kentucky, the IU squad rolled to four easy home wins over Notre Dame, Tennessee Tech, Washington State and Eastern Kentucky to improve to 5-1. Then they went to Lawrence, Kansas, where the 12th-ranked Hoosiers took on No. 6 Kansas on December 22. Jayhawk guard Jacques Vaughn sank a three-pointer with 4.2 seconds remaining in overtime to lift Kansas to an 86-83 victory. Bailey was magnificent again, scoring 36 points, including 21 in the second half and nine in overtime. Kansas coach Roy Williams said, "Damon Bailey was sensational, and I told him that was one of the most sensational performances I have ever seen."

Indiana closed out the preconference season with double-digit wins over Texas Christian and Western Kentucky in the Hoosier Classic in Indianapolis. That put IU at 7-2 and ranked 14th in the country as the Hoosiers prepared to defend their Big Ten title.

Playing without injured Hoosiers Todd Leary and Brian Evans, IU opened league play on January 8, by defeating Penn State 80-72 in Bloomington, as Bailey and Graham teamed up for 49 points. Then Evans returned and scored 21 points to lead the Hoosiers to an 89-75 win at Iowa on January 11. Leary came back the next game against No. 10 Michigan in Bloomington and sparked IU with 16 points in an 82-72 Indiana victory. Alan Henderson dominated the paint against the Wolverines with 19 points and 16 rebounds.

Next, Henderson collided with his old rival Glen Robinson when eighth-ranked Indiana took on 12th-ranked Purdue in West Lafayette on January 18. Henderson had 24 points and 12 rebounds, but Purdue pulled away in overtime for an 83-76 win, as Robinson poured in a game-high 33 points. The Hoosiers returned home and beat Northwestern and No. 16 Minnesota to up their conference record to 5-1 and take a half-game lead over Purdue for the top spot in the Big Ten. Then, on January 30, IU lost 88-81 at Illinois to fall into a three-way tie for the conference lead with Purdue and Michigan.

Things looked ominous for IU in the next game when Evans reinjured his shoulder in the opening minute against Ohio State and then Knight got ejected a few minutes later after picking up two technicals. The Buckeyes, who were 2-5 in league play entering the game, pushed the Hoosiers to the limit and had the Assembly Hall crowd sitting on its hands. However, Pat Graham came through with a career-high 29 points, including six of seven three-pointers, to propel Indiana to an 87-83 win in overtime. Then, led by 20 points and 16 rebounds from Henderson, the Hoosiers beat Penn State 76-66 on February 5, to keep pace with Michigan atop the Big Ten at 7-2. That set up a showdown between the two league leaders on February 8, in Ann Arbor. Unfortunately, the Hoosiers were without Evans and center Todd Lindeman because of injuries, and the Wolverines feasted on IU's front line in a 91-67 Michigan rout.

The banged-up Hoosiers gutted out three straight wins over Iowa, Purdue and Northwestern to up their record to 10-3 and keep within striking distance of Michigan (12-2). Then the Hoosiers' season began to slip away. It started in Minneapolis on February 27, when the Minnesota Golden Gophers handed IU its worst loss in 89 years in a 106-56 humiliation of the Hoosiers. Minnesota led 56-24 at the half, and Knight chose to simply rest Bailey, Henderson and Evans in the second half. Voshon Lenard led the Gophers with 35 points on 13-17 shooting from the field. Two days later, Indiana responded by pulling out an 82-77 win over Illinois, as senior guards Bailey, Leary and Graham combined for 52 points and 14 assists. However, Indiana fell out of the Big Ten race by dropping its next two games on the road to Ohio State and Michigan State. Against the Spartans, Henderson put up 41 points and 13 rebounds in a losing effort.

That left only a final home game against Wisconsin on March 12, for Indiana to close out the regular season. For IU fans, the contest was largely talked about as "Damon's last game in Assembly Hall." A series of nagging injuries had slowed Bailey during the final weeks of the Big Ten season to the point that he wasn't even able to practice. Heading into the Wisconsin game, his midsection had to be tightly wrapped so that he could play through a rib injury. Nevertheless, he went out and nearly put up a triple-double with 19 points, eight rebounds, and eight assists, and IU won 78-65.

Afterwards, Knight said, "What did [Bailey] do today? He got a tip-in, he posted, he shot from the outside, he drove, he made a half a dozen passes for baskets. I even saw him guard a guy—twice." Speaking to the crowd as part of the Senior Day ceremonies in Assembly Hall, Knight added, "He played today when most of us would not have been able to walk [with his injuries]."

The Wisconsin game was also the final outing in Assembly Hall for senior guards Todd Leary and Pat Graham, as well as Ross Hales, a big 6'7" walk-on from the football team.

In the NCAA tournament, Indiana got the fifth seed in the East Regional. On March 18, the Hoosiers pulled out an 84-72 first-round win over a gritty Ohio University squad. Alan Henderson led the way with 34 points and 13 rebounds, while Brian Evans did an excellent defensive job on Ohio's high-scoring Gary Trent, holding him to 18 points (he averaged 25 per game). In the second round, Evans scored 18 points to lead Indiana to a 67-58 upset of fourth-seed Temple. However, against the Owls, the injury bug bit the Hoosiers again as reserve guard Sherron Wilkerson's season came to an end when he fractured his left leg. In the Sweet Sixteen, the season came to an end for the rest of the Hoosiers when they let a late lead slip away and lost 77-68 to Boston College, which had upset No. 1 North Carolina in the previous round. Bailey, Leary and Graham all scored in double figures in their final collegiate game.

In a season in which Indiana's top six scorers all suffered through various injuries, the Hoosiers still put together a 21-9 record and were in the Big Ten race until the final two weeks when they lost three of their final five games to finish in third place at 12-6. Bailey earned All-America honors, while Henderson

and Evans stepped up their play and Leary and Graham helped steady the ship with their consistency and experience.

After the Boston College game, Knight admitted, "When the season started, I looked at this team and here was my thinking. If we can do three things: get into the last week playing for the Big Ten championship, get to the regional [NCAA Sweet Sixteen], and win 20 games, I'm going to be pleased with what we've done. Well, we actually did all three."

The team's biggest challenge all season long was on the defensive end, where the Hoosiers surrendered 77.0 points per game—the most ever allowed by a Bob Knight-coached team. Fortunately, IU averaged 80.9 PPG, which was enough to stay ahead of 21 opponents. The Hoosiers were particularly potent from three-point range, where they made 45 percent of their attempts to lead the nation.

The 1993-94 season also had a pair of infamous moments that brought a barrage of criticism upon Coach Knight. In IU's preconference game against Notre Dame in Bloomington, Knight's son Pat threw a lackadaisical pass that got intercepted by the Fighting Irish. Coach Knight called a timeout, grabbed Pat and pushed him down into a chair and read him the riot act. During the outburst, Knight kicked the chair Pat was sitting in. To many spectators it looked like Knight had actually kicked Pat, and the IU fans directly behind the Hoosier bench immediately started booing Coach Knight, who turned around and angrily shouted at the fans. The tirade earned Knight a one-game suspension from the IU administration and a flood of bitter diatribes from sports columnists calling for him to be fired. Later in the season, in a game against Michigan State, Knight kneeled down to look the sitting Sherron Wilkerson face-to-face as he administered a tongue-lashing. However, as he yelled, Knight inadvertently head-butted Wilkerson, which re-ignited all the criticisms

INDIANA'S RANKING IN THE 1993-94 ASSOCIATED PRESS POLLS

PS	11/22	11/29	12/6	12/13	12/20	12/27	1/3	1/10	1/17	1/24	1/31	2/7	2/14	2/21	2/28	3/7	3/14
12	11	21	12	12	12	13	14	11	8	11	14	12	16	12	17	18	18

about Knight's coaching methods. Wilkerson downplayed the incident, saying it was blown out of proportion, while Knight said that it happened because he had been suffering from a bad back that weakened his muscle control. Knight grew frustrated by all of the vilifications of him. When he addressed the crowd on Senior Day, he responded to all of the negative press him by saying that when he died, he wanted to be buried upside down so that all of his critics could kiss his rear end.

While Knight's public image took a bit of hit that season, one of the most popular Indiana players of all-time, Damon Bailey, had only seen his popularity grow. Now he was moving on—but also staying put. After an All-America senior season, Bailey was selected as a second-round NBA draft pick of the Indiana Pacers. Unfortunately for Damon, he had been excelling as a basketball player since grade school and all those years had taken a heavy toll on his young body. Shortly after signing a contract with the Pacers, the team advised Damon to have surgery on both knees and he ended up missing the entire season. The next season, he was one of the last players cut from the Pacers roster. After that, he ended up with the Fort Wayne Fury in the CBA, where he became an All-CBA player but never made it back to the NBA.

1994-95

OVERALL RECORD: 19-12

CONFERENCE RECORD: 11-7 (THIRD PLACE)

TEAM HONORS:

HOOSIER CLASSIC CHAMPION,

INDIANA CLASSIC CHAMPION

INDIVIDUAL HONORS:

ALAN HENDERSON—ALL-AMERICA,

ALL-BIG TEN (FIRST TEAM)

TODD LINDEMAN—ACADEMIC ALL-BIG TEN

ROBBIE EGGERS—ACADEMIC ALL-BIG TEN

When the 1994-95 season dawned, senior Alan Henderson and junior Brian Evans were the only two regulars that remained from Indiana's powerful teams that had ruled the Big Ten in the early 1990s. Those two were also joined by junior center Todd Lindeman and senior guard Pat Knight as the only upperclassmen on the 1994-95 roster, which was dominated by seven freshmen. The heart of that group of rookies was the five-man recruiting class of 1994.

That class was so highly touted that it was being compared to Indiana's two best classes ever—1972 and 1989. The difference was that those earlier classes were made up of a core of Indiana kids surrounded by a few Illinois and Ohio recruits. With the class of 1994, there was a dearth of talent in the state of Indiana, so IU went national, bringing in five top recruits from around the country. It included two McDonald's All-Americans in point guard Neil Reed from Louisiana, and 6'8" man-child Andre Patterson from Texas. It also included two highly versatile 6'7" forwards in Rob Hodgson from New York, and Charlie Miller from Florida. Athletic 6'3" guard Michael Hermon from Chicago was a late addition that rounded out an eye-popping recruiting class that was loaded with basketball talent and athleticism. It was the class that was supposed to take Indiana back to the top of the college basketball world.

However, for the 1994-95 campaign, the rookies stepped back and took their lead from Henderson and Evans. After being one of the key contributors for

The 1994-95 team. First row (left to right): Steve Hart, Brian Evans, Pat Knight, Alan Henderson, Todd Lindeman, Sherron Wilkerson; Second row: Neil Reed, Charlie Miller, Robbie Eggers, Richard Mandeville, Andre Patterson, Rob Hodgson, Michael Hermon.   IU Athletics

Team USA in the Goodwill Games during the summer of 1994, Henderson emerged as one of the top power forwards in college basketball. He combined strong low-post moves with a deadly face-up jump shot that he loved to use along the baseline, and he was one of the most prolific rebounders in the country. Evans, a 6'8" forward from Terre Haute that grew up idolizing IU basketball stars such as Randy Wittman and Ted Kitchel, contributed to the Hoosiers with a versatile inside-outside game on both ends of the floor. As a sophomore, he hit 28-56 (50 percent) of his three-point attempts in conference play to lead the Big Ten.

Even with Henderson and Evans leading way, the Hoosiers had to rely on several freshmen to step in and play key roles. The out-of-state rookies quickly realized the higher level of intensity and focus that is demanded in college basketball—especially when there's a target on the chest that reads "Indiana." Still,

several of the rookies flashed their potential by posting some excellent performances.

The Hoosiers opened the regular season at the Maui Invitational in Hawaii. Utah dropped the 11th-ranked Hoosiers 77-72 in the Maui opener, led by Keith Van Horn, who scored all of his 15 points in the second half to lift the Utes to the win. Henderson led IU with 26 points and 10 rebounds. The next day, Indiana clobbered tiny Chaminade 92-79 as Evans poured in 37 points, Henderson had 28 points and 10 rebounds, and freshman Andre Patterson chipped in 14 points and nine rebounds. In their third and final game in Hawaii, the Hoosiers got pummeled 86-68 by Tulane.

The woes continued for Indiana when the team returned to the mainland. On November 29, in South Bend, IU blew an 11-point halftime lead and lost to Notre Dame 80-79 in overtime. The Indiana faithful were growing restless with the Hoosiers' 1-3 start, but the IU squad eased their pain with an 84-63 blowout of Evansville in the RCA Dome on December 3. Freshman point guard Neil Reed led IU with 23 points and five assists and he didn't have a single turnover. Four days later in Louisville, the Hoosiers fell 73-70 to No. 7 Kentucky and dropped back to 2-4 for the season.

Indiana evened its record at 4-4 with a pair of Indiana Classic wins over Morehead State and Miami of Ohio. Then the Hoosiers hosted the undefeated, third-ranked Kansas Jayhawks on December 17. Roy Williams's Kansas teams had won four straight against Knight and Indiana, and many analysts expected them to have an easy time with the struggling Hoosiers in this game. Instead, Indiana countered every move that the Jayhawks made and burst out to a 48-25 halftime lead. IU got an outstanding effort from nearly every player on the roster on the way to an inspired 80-61 victory. Evans scored a game-high 29 points and Henderson added 22, and the two of them helped Indiana outrebound Kansas 57-40. After the Kansas upset, Indiana cruised to three easy blow outs over Butler, Eastern Kentucky and Arkansas-Little Rock to improve to 8-4 going into conference play.

The surging Hoosiers fell back to earth with a thud on January 3, when the Iowa Hawkeyes bludgeoned Indiana 74-55 in Iowa City. Evans, who was averaging 18.7 points per game, was scoreless in the first half and got benched for the entire second half. He responded later that week with 26 points and 10 rebounds to lead Indiana to a 73-70 win over Wisconsin in Assembly Hall. The next week, Indiana upended No. 11 Michigan State 89-82, despite 40 points from MSU guard Shawn Respert. The win was IU's 50th straight victory in Assembly Hall, dating back four years to a two-point defeat to Ohio State in 1991.

Next, Indiana went on the road and split two games, losing to Illinois but winning at Penn State. Against the Nittany Lions, freshman Michael Hermon came off the bench for 11 points, five rebounds, and five assists, and made a pair of driving baskets in the final minutes to spark IU to the victory. Then, Michigan came to Bloomington on January 24. Although they only had two members of the "Fab Five"—Jimmy King and Ray Jackson—still left in college, the Wolverines had enough to put a defensive

1994-95 TEAM ROSTER

Head coach: Bob Knight
Assistant coaches: Dan Dakich, Norm Ellenberger, Ron Felling

No.	Player	Hometown	Class	Position	Height
32	Robbie Eggers	Cuyahoga Falls, OH	Fr	F	6-10
34	Brian Evans	Terre Haute, IN	Jr	F	6-8
23	Steve Hart	Terre Haute, IN	So	G	6-3
44	Alan Henderson (Capt.)	Indianapolis, IN	Sr	F	6-9
30	Michael Hermon	Chicago, IL	Fr	G	6-3
33	Rob Hodgson	Mastic Beach, NY	Fr	F	6-7
25	Pat Knight (Capt.)	Bloomington, IN	Sr	G	6-6
50	Todd Lindeman	Channing, MI	Jr	C	7-0
21	Richard Mandeville	Pasadena, CA	Rs	C	7-0
3	Charlie Miller	Miami, FL	Fr	G/F	6-7
45	Andre Patterson	Abilene, TX	Fr	F	6-8
22	Jean Paul	Naples, FL	Fr	G	6-2
5	Neil Reed	Metairie, LA	Fr	G	6-2
20	Sherron Wilkerson	Jeffersonville, IN	Rs	G	6-4

SEASON RESULTS 1994-95

Date	Court	Opponent	Result	Score
11/21/1994	N1	Utah	L	72-77
11/22/1994	N1	Chaminade	W	92-79
11/23/1994	N1	Tulane	L	68-86
11/29/1994	A	Notre Dame	L	79-80
12/3/1994	N2	Evansville	W	84-63
12/7/1994	N3	(#7) Kentucky	L	70-73
12/9/1994	H	Morehead State	W	79-62
12/10/1994	H	Miami of Ohio	W	92-77
12/17/1994	H	(#3) Kansas	W	80-61
12/21/1994	H	Butler	W	89-66
12/28/1994	N2	Eastern Kentucky	W	92-49
12/29/1994	N2	Arkansas-Little Rock	W	77-53
1/3/1995	A	Iowa	L	55-74
1/7/1995	H	Wisconsin	W	73-70
1/11/1995	H	(#11) Michigan State	W	89-82
1/14/1995	A	Illinois	L	67-78
1/18/1995	A	Penn State	W	71-69
1/24/1995	H	Michigan	L	52-65
1/28/1995	H	Ohio State	W	90-75
1/31/1995	A	(#25) Purdue	L	66-76
2/4/1995	A	Northwestern	W	88-67
2/8/1995	H	Minnesota	L	54-64
2/12/1995	H	Purdue	W	82-73
2/14/1995	A	Ohio State	W	69-52
2/19/1995	A	Michigan	L	50-61
2/25/1995	H	Penn State	W	73-60
3/2/1995	H	Illinois	W	89-85
3/5/1995	A	(#10) Michigan State	L	61-67
3/8/1995	A	Wisconsin	W	72-70
3/12/1995	H	Iowa	W	110-79
NCAA Tournament				
3/17/1995	N4	(#23) Missouri	L	60-65

1 Maui, HI
2 Indianapolis, IN
3 Louisville, KY
4 Boise, ID

1994-95 BIG TEN STANDINGS

	W	L	PCT
Purdue	15	3	.833
Michigan St.	14	4	.778
Indiana	11	7	.611
Michigan	11	7	.611
Illinois	10	8	.556
Minnesota*	0	0	.000
Penn State	9	9	.500
Iowa	9	9	.500
Wisconsin	7	11	.389
Ohio State	2	16	.111
Northwestern	1	17	.056

* NCAA voided all games for Minnesota

stranglehold on Henderson and Evans and bring the Hoosiers' home-court winning streak to end with a convincing 65-52 win over IU.

The Michigan loss dropped Indiana to 3-3 in league play. The Hoosiers then split their next four games. They beat Ohio State and Northwestern, but fell to Purdue in West Lafayette and dropped another home game by losing to Minnesota on February 8, in Bloomington. At 5-5 (13-9 overall) the Hoosiers were struggling just to gain a spot in upper division of the Big Ten. Then something clicked into place and the IU squad won six of its final eight games.

The first was a payback game against No. 25 Purdue in Bloomington on February 12. Indiana ran away with an 82-73 victory, as freshman Charlie Miller broke out for 21 points on 9-11 shooting from the field. Henderson added 26 points and 10 rebounds in his final game against the Boilermakers. Next, IU knocked off Ohio State in Columbus, but lost to Michigan in Ann Arbor, and then defeated Penn State and Illinois in Bloomington. Tenth-ranked Michigan State barely slipped by the Hoosiers 67-61 in East Lansing on March 5, but IU locked up an NCAA bid by beating Wisconsin 72-70 in Madison, and blistering Iowa 110-79 in Bloomington. In his final game in Assembly Hall, Alan Henderson had 35 points (on 16-19 from the field) and nine rebounds against the Hawkeyes. Evans added 28 points as he hit six of eight threes, and Michael Hermon chipped in 13 points and 10 assists.

Indiana finished the regular season at 19-10 overall and 11-7 in Big Ten play, which earned a third-place finish in the conference. In the NCAA tournament, the Hoosiers got shipped out to the West Regional in Boise, Idaho—the same spot where IU launched its Final Four run in 1992. IU was awarded the ninth seed and was set to face eighth-seed Missouri in the first round. Although the Tigers were ranked 23rd in the nation and owned the higher seed,

they were struggling badly after losing five of their final six games in the regular season. As a result, most analysts were predicting a Hoosier victory and were already anticipating a monumental second-round match-up between IU and UCLA—two of the most storied basketball programs in NCAA tournament history. Missouri was motivated by that and came out with ferocious intensity during the game. After trailing by five at the half, Missouri ran off a 12-2 run to open the second half and claim the lead at 38-33. IU tied it at 39-39 before the Tigers surged ahead again. When Brian Evans sank a three-pointer with 1:12 to go, Indiana trailed 61-60. However, Missouri scored on an offensive rebound and then hit a couple of free throws in the final seconds to pull out a 65-60 win.

"[Missouri] just had better enthusiasm for the game," said coach Bob Knight after the game. "They're the team that deserves to play on Sunday, not us."

Against the Tigers, Alan Henderson grabbed a game-high 10 rebounds in his final collegiate game. For his career, that gave him a total of 1,091 rebounds to barely eclipse the school record of 1,088 held by Walt Bellamy. Plus, Henderson became the fourth player in Big Ten history—joining Herb Williams, Greg Kelser and Joe Barry Carroll—to rack up 2,000 points and 1,000 rebounds in a career. He was also the only player in IU history to finish his career in the school's top five leaders in scoring, rebounding, blocks and steals. For an outstanding senior season in which he averaged 23.5 points and 9.7 rebounds, Henderson earned All-America honors. He was also drafted by the Atlanta Hawks with the 16th selection of the first round in the 1995 NBA draft and ended up having a long and productive career with the Hawks.

Despite the tough first-round NCAA loss—only the fourth time in 19 NCAA appearances that a Knight team had lost in the first round up until that

INDIANA'S RANKING IN THE 1994-95 ASSOCIATED PRESS POLLS

PS	11/21	11/28	12/5	12/12	12/19	12/26	1/3	1/10	1/17	1/24	1/31	2/6	2/13	2/20	2/27	3/6	3/13
9	11	—	—	—	—	24	21	—	—	—	—	—	—	—	—	—	—

point—the Hoosiers could feel good about the fact that they salvaged a sinking season with a great stretch run to earn an upper-division finish in the conference and an NCAA berth. All in all, it was a team plagued by repeated bouts of inconsistency, which was understandable with such a young roster.

"We've just had too many stretches where we haven't played as well as we've been capable," said Knight before the Missouri game. "Don't even ask me why. I wish I knew. That's kind of what our season has been like. Still, the thing I hope our players remember is that regardless of what happens here [in the NCAA tournament], they really had to play their way into the tournament. I was really pleased for them that they were able to do that."

1995-96

OVERALL RECORD: 19-12

CONFERENCE RECORD: 12-6 (SECOND PLACE)

TEAM HONORS:

HOOSIER CLASSIC CHAMPION,

INDIANA CLASSIC CHAMPION

INDIVIDUAL HONORS:

BRIAN EVANS—ALL-AMERICA, BIG TEN MVP,

ALL-BIG TEN (FIRST TEAM)

ROBBIE EGGERS—ACADEMIC ALL-BIG TEN

After the Indiana Hoosiers won a respectable 19 games in 1993-94 and 21 games in 1994-95, IU fans were ready to see their team reclaim the Big Ten title and re-emerge among the top-ranked college basketball teams in the country. Many of them were optimistic that the 1995-96 team was ready to take a big step toward those goals. One of the things that fueled that optimism was the fact that IU's outstanding 1994 recruiting class was now entering its second season on campus. That 1994 class was often compared to IU's 1972 and 1989 recruiting classes, which each won a conference championship during their respective sophomore campaigns.

Of course, those 1972 and 1989 groups were a tough standard to live up to, and the 1994 class was-

n't quite up to the task. Before the 1995-96 season even started, two of the members of that five-man class had already left IU. Forward Rob Hodgson had departed in the middle of the previous season after being disappointed because he was asked to redshirt for the year. He transferred to Rutgers. Lightning-quick guard Michael Hermon started 17 games as a freshman and showed some excellent playmaking ability and defensive potential. However, he left the program after his freshman year and never caught on with another Division I team. That left gritty point guard Neil Reed, athletic swingman Charlie Miller, and 6'8" physical specimen Andrae Patterson. All three became key contributors on the 1995-96 team, but they didn't appear to be blossoming into the kind of outstanding players who were needed to form the nucleus of the next championship team.

For the 1995-96 campaign, the Hoosiers' fortunes centered around 6'8" senior forward Brian Evans. In his three previous seasons, Evans had steadily increased his scoring average from 5.3 points to 11.9 to 17.4. He went from being a key role player off the bench as a freshman on the powerful 1992-93 squad to a fixture in the starting lineup as a sophomore and a junior. He also expanded his game from being primarily a spot-up shooter to being an excellent all-around offensive player who was dangerous both inside and outside. Plus, Evans also became a solid low-post defender—much to coach Bob Knight's satisfaction.

With the graduation of Alan Henderson, Evans was the only returning double-figure scorer, and essentially the only player on the roster with ample experience in Division I basketball. The team's only two other upperclassmen were 7'0" center Todd Lindeman, a fifth-year senior who was still trying to earn regular minutes in the rotation, and Haris Mujezinovic, a 6'9", 260-pound junior who was a JUCO transfer that Knight hoped could add some toughness to the Hoosiers in the paint. Guards Chris Rowles and Lou Moore were also JUCO transfers, but both of them were sophomores with three seasons of eligibility remaining and both were unknown quantities. IU also had 7'0" center Richard Mandeville and 6'4" guard Sherron Wilkerson returning from redshirt seasons. After a promising freshman season, Wilkerson was recovering from his second surgery for a leg injury that he suffered in the 1994 NCAA tour-

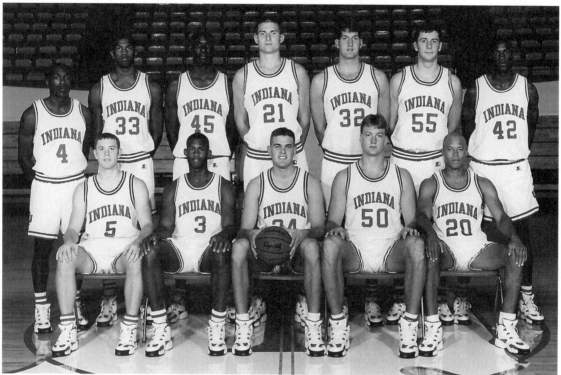

The 1995-96 team. First row (left to right): Neil Reed, Charlie Miller, Brian Evans, Todd Lindeman, Sherron Wilkerson; Second row: Chris Rowles, Larry Richardson, Andre Patterson, Richard Mandeville, Robbie Eggers, Haris Mujezinovic, Lou Moore. IU Athletics

nament. He was now returning as one of eight sophomores on the IU roster.

If this squad was a rock band they probably would have been called "Evans and the Young Pups." As a basketball team, they were one of the favorites to win the Big Ten and were ranked 23rd in the nation in the preseason. Of course, those forecasts were largely based on Knight's past accomplishments in forging championship contenders. As IU fans and the college basketball world soon realized, this team didn't have all the ingredients needed to return the Hoosiers to national prominence.

One of the factors that worked against this team was a grueling nonconference schedule. IU played three top-ten teams—Connecticut, Kentucky and Kansas—and got beat by all three. The Hoosiers also dropped preconference games to Duke and DePaul. The only win over a major conference team came on November 28, against Notre Dame, which was on the way to a disappointing 9-18 season.

The way Indiana opened the season in the Great Alaska Shootout was a bad omen. The Hoosiers scraped by Alaska-Anchorage (a Division II team) 84-79 in their opener, prompting Knight to say, "I'm really embarrassed that we won, because we absolutely in no way deserved to win. …We got outplayed, we got outhustled, we got out-everythinged."

And it only got worse. The Hoosiers dropped their next two games in the Shootout to Duke and Connecticut, before returning to Bloomington later in the week and thumping the Fighting Irish 73-53. Against Notre Dame, Sherron Wilkerson led a balanced IU attack with 14 points, 9 rebounds, and 4 assists, while Evans had 13 points and 14 rebounds. However, the rest of Indiana's preconference wins came over Delaware, Bowling Green, Evansville, Appalachian State and Weber State—not exactly a bunch of basketball powerhouses.

The most disappointing defeat of the preconference season came on December 23, when DePaul drilled a buzzer-beater to upset IU 84-82 in Bloomington. It was the Hoosiers first nonconference loss in Assembly Hall in over a decade, dating back 63 games to November 24, 1984, when Louisville came to Bloomington and stole the season opener.

With a 7-5 record, Indiana limped into Big Ten play. Very few analysts were still talking about the Hoosiers as one of the teams to beat in the conference. But Bob Knight had a trick up his sleeve—and his name was Brian Evans.

IU opened against Michigan State in East Lansing, in Tom Izzo's first Big Ten game as head coach of the Spartans. Evans, who finished with 21 points and five assists, led a big run in the final minutes to put a scare into MSU, but the Hoosiers lost 65-60. "We got hurt as we have all year long with fundamental parts of basketball," said Knight after the game. "We're a team that doesn't know how to win. Until we figure that out … it's going to be very difficult for us."

Indiana started figuring some things out when they returned to Bloomington and ran to convincing wins over Ohio State and Wisconsin. Against the Buckeyes, Andrae Patterson had 26 points and 13 rebounds, which were both career highs. Brian Evans nearly posted a triple-double with 23 points, 11 rebounds, and eight assists. However, Knight saw Evans's high assist total as a double-edged sword because IU's starting guards, Neil Reed and Sherron Wilkerson combined for only four assists. "Evans is our best feeder and our best scorer and that's a bad combination," said Knight.

The 2-1 Hoosiers played their next five conference games against five different Big Ten opponents that were ranked in the top 25, and three of those five games were on the road. During that critical stretch, IU pulled out three victories, while the two losses came against conference leaders Purdue and Penn State on their home courts. Indiana emerged from that stretch at 5-3 and still within striking distance of the Boilermakers and Nittany Lions.

Next, the Hoosiers blew out Northwestern in Assembly Hall and clobbered Minnesota at "The Barn" in Minneapolis to up their record to 7-3 and pull to within a half-game of Purdue and Penn State. With eight conference games remaining, Knight looked like he had done it again by fashioning yet another title contender. Unfortunately, the Hoosiers

1995-96 TEAM ROSTER

Head coach: Bob Knight
Assistant coaches: Dan Dakich, Ron Felling, Craig Hartman

No.	Player	Hometown	Class	Position	Height
32	Robbie Eggers	Cuyahoga Falls, OH	So	F	6-10
34	Brian Evans (Capt.)	Terre Haute, IN	Sr	F	6-8
23	Kevin Lemme	Granger, IN	Sr	G	5-11
50	Todd Lindeman (Capt.)	Channing, MI	Sr	C	7-0
21	Richard Mandeville	Pasadena, CA	So	C	7-0
3	Charlie Miller	Miami, FL	So	G	6-7
42	Lou Moore	Rock Hill, SC	So	G/F	6-7
55	Haris Mujezinovic	Chicago, IL	Jr	C	6-9
45	Andre Patterson	Abilene, TX	So	F	6-8
5	Neil Reed	Metairie, LA	So	G	6-2
33	Larry Richardson	Orange Park, FL	Rs	F	6-8
4	Chris Rowles	Kansas City, MO	So	G	6-1
20	Sherron Wilkerson	Jeffersonville, IN	So	G	6-4

SEASON RESULTS 1995-96

Date	Court	Opponent	Result	Score
11/23/1995	N1	Alaska-Anchorage	W	87-79
11/24/1995	N1	Duke	L	64-70
11/25/1995	N1	(#6) Connecticut	L	52-86
11/28/1995	H	Notre Dame	W	73-53
12/2/1995	N2	(#1) Kentucky	L	82-89
12/8/1995	H	Delaware	W	85-68
12/9/1995	H	Bowling Green	W	78-67
12/16/1995	N3	(#1) Kansas	L	83-91
12/20/1995	A	Evansville	W	76-48
12/23/1995	H	DePaul	L	82-84
12/29/1995	N2	Appalachian State	W	103-59
12/30/1995	N2	Weber State	W	82-62
1/4/1996	A	Michigan State	L	60-65
1/6/1996	H	Ohio State	W	89-67
1/10/1996	H	Wisconsin	W	81-55
1/13/1996	A	(#21) Illinois	W	85-71
1/16/1996	A	(#17) Purdue	L	69-74
1/23/1996	H	(#20) Michigan	W	99-83
1/27/1996	A	(#22) Penn State	L	68-82
1/30/1996	H	(#16) Iowa	W	76-73
2/4/1996	H	Northwestern	W	95-61
2/6/1996	A	Minnesota	W	81-66
2/11/1996	A	(#19) Iowa	L	50-76
2/14/1996	H	(#9) Penn State	W	72-54
2/18/1996	A	Michigan	L	75-80
2/25/1996	H	(#7) Purdue	L	72-74
2/28/1996	H	Illinois	W	76-64
3/2/1996	A	Wisconsin	W	76-68
3/6/1996	A	Ohio State	W	73-56
3/10/1996	H	Michigan State	W	57-53
NCAA Tournament				
3/15/1996	N4	Boston College	L	51-64

1 Anchorage, AK
2 Indianapolis, IN
3 Kansas City, MO
4 Orlando, FL

1995-96 BIG TEN STANDINGS

	W	L	PCT
Purdue1	15	3	.833
Penn State	12	6	.667
Indiana	12	6	.667
Iowa	11	7	.611
Michigan2	10	8	.556
Minnesota3	0	0	.000
Michigan St.	9	9	.500
Wisconsin	8	10	.444
Illinois	7	11	.389
Ohio State	3	15	.167
Northwestern	2	16	.111

1 Doesn't reflect 18 forfeited and two vacated games
2 Records later vacated due to NCAA sanctions
3 NCAA voided all games for Minnesota

Lefty forward Brian Evans carried a young Hoosier team to a second-place finish in the Big Ten in 1996. Evans led the conference in scoring and was named the Big Ten MVP. IU Athletics

A couple of days later, Andrae Patterson, Neil Reed and Todd Lindeman all came down with the flu prior to Indiana's big game with Penn State on February 14, in Bloomington. Led by 32 points from Evans and a 36-19 second-half advantage, IU steam-rolled the ninth-ranked Nittany Lions 72-54. Charlie Miller stepped up with 13 points and nine rebounds and Neil Reed fought through the flu and dished out eight assists. Evans, Miller and Reed each played all 40 minutes. However, the gutsiest performance of the night was delivered by Lindeman, who probably had the worst case of the flu, but came off the bench for 12 points and 11 rebounds.

After that big win over the Nittany Lions, Michigan put a damper on Indiana's title hopes by beating the Hoosiers 80-75 in Ann Arbor. Then, Purdue put the nail in the Hoosiers' coffin by coming to Bloomington on February 25, and pulling out a 74-72 win on a Chad Austin three-pointer with 13.7 seconds left. Prior to the seventh-ranked Boilermakers' victory, Indiana had defeated 14 straight nationally ranked teams in Assembly Hall. The loss also dropped IU to 8-6 in league play and put the team's postseason prospects in jeopardy.

Over the final four games of the regular season, Indiana's seniors stepped up and led the Hoosiers to four straight victories. Evans averaged 21.3 points and 9.5 rebounds during those four games, while Todd Lindeman (who averaged 5.9 points over his four years) played the best basketball of his career, averaging 17.3 points, including a career-high 28 at Ohio State on March 6. That final surge tied Indiana with Penn State at 12-6 for second place in the Big Ten.

IU got a sixth seed in the NCAA tournament and was assigned to the Southeast Regional in Orlando, Florida. Jim O'Brien's Boston College team, an eleventh seed, met them there. The Eagles keyed on Brian Evans and harassed him into a 2-14 shooting performance. None of the other Hoosiers were able to

suffered some tough breaks and lost three of their next four games. In Iowa City on February 10, the Hoosiers' hotel had a gas leak that caused the team to change lodging in the middle of the night. Indiana played Iowa in an early Sunday afternoon game the next day and the sluggish Hoosiers got trampled 76-50.

INDIANA'S RANKING IN THE 1995-96 ASSOCIATED PRESS POLLS

PS	11/20	11/27	12/4	12/11	12/18	12/25	1/2	1/9	1/16	1/22	1/29	2/5	2/12	2/19	2/26	3/4	3/11
23	23	—	—	—	—	—	—	—	—	—	—	—	—	—	—	—	—

step up and fill the void, and IU lost 64-51. It was Indiana's second straight first-round NCAA defeat and it was the second time in three years that the Hoosiers had lost to BC in the tournament.

Against Boston College, the Hoosiers shot only 37 percent from the field and were also plagued by 18 turnovers. Poor shooting and not taking care of the ball were two weaknesses that haunted Indiana all year long. The 1995-96 Indiana team had more turnovers than its opponents for only the seventh time in Bob Knight's 25 seasons at IU. The team's 47 percent field goal shooting was the worst for an Indiana team since 1971-72—Knight's first year in Bloomington.

Throughout the season, as in the Boston College game, it was clear just how much the Hoosiers relied on Brian Evans. He was incredibly consistent, scoring in double figures in all but two games, and he carried IU to several wins. However, IU was at its best when other players stepped up to give him some help, and unfortunately that didn't happen often enough. Patterson and Reid both scored in double figures for the season, with 11.5 and 10.3 points per game, respectively, and Lindeman averaged a career-high 9.8 points, but Evans ended up leading the Hoosiers in nearly every offensive and defensive category—points (21.2), rebounds (7.1), steals (1.4), and blocks (2.1)—and he was second to Reed in assists (4.1). He became the first player in the Knight era to lead the Big Ten in scoring, and his excellent all-around performance earned him the Big Ten MVP award.

In June, the Orlando Magic selected Evans with the 27th pick of the first round of the NBA draft. He ended up playing four seasons in the NBA for Orlando, New Jersey, and Minnesota, and then continued his pro career overseas.

1996-97

OVERALL RECORD: 22-11

CONFERENCE RECORD: 9-9 (SIXTH PLACE)

TEAM HONORS:

PRESEASON NIT CHAMPION, HOOSIER CLASSIC

CHAMPION, INDIANA CLASSIC CHAMPION

INDIVIDUAL HONORS:

A.J. GUYTON—BIG TEN FRESHMAN OF THE

YEAR

ROBBIE EGGERS—ACADEMIC ALL-AMERICA

With the graduation of Brian Evans, a chapter in Hoosier basketball came to a close. Evans was the final link to Indiana's great teams of the early 1990s, and he was the last player who had remained from Indiana's last Big Ten championship team in 1993. After a brilliant senior season, he joined several of his former classmates in the NBA, while at IU the torch was officially passed to the next generation of basketball players to see if they could return the Hoosiers to championship form.

"In '92 and '93, I really didn't think that there was anyone in the country that we couldn't beat," said coach Bob Knight. "In the last three years ... we just haven't been, night after night, as competitive as I want us to be. Over most of the time that I have been here, we have been pretty nationally competitive and that's obviously what we want to get back to."

Coach Knight also knew the key ingredient that his team was missing. "We've got to be a tougher-minded team," he said. "We've got to be a team that is really, really tough to beat. Other teams we have had here have found a way to win and we really haven't had that recently."

Andrae Patterson, Neil Reed and Charlie Miller were the top three returning scorers for IU. The three of them came to Indiana together as part of the 1994 recruiting class. They were now juniors and were expected to step forward and form the nucleus of the team. Two other juniors were also expected to step up and contribute: 7'0" Richard Mandeville and 6'10"

The 1996-97 team. First row (left to right): Neil Reed, Robbie Eggers, Haris Mujezinovic, Richard Mandeville, Andre Patterson; Second row: A.J. Guyton, Charlie Miller, Jason Collier, Larry Richardson, Luke Jimenez, Michael Lewis. IU Athletics

Robbie Eggers. Both of them had come to IU a year before Patterson, Reed and Miller, but both had taken redshirt seasons during their careers to assist in their development. Much of the team's leadership fell to these five juniors because IU's only senior was Haris Mujezinovic, a 6'9" JUCO transfer in his second season in Bloomington.

Coach Knight also expected the program to get a nice shot in the arm from a group of four freshmen. At the head of that recruiting class was 7'0" Jason Collier, one of the most highly coveted big men in the country. Collier averaged 24 points, 14 rebounds, four assists, and four blocks as a senior in high school

and was selected as a McDonald's All-American and Ohio Mr. Basketball. In addition to a variety of low-post skills, Collier was also unique because he possessed an excellent jump shot that extended out to three-point range.

Joining Collier in the 1996 recruiting class were three guards: Michael Lewis, Luke Jimenez and A.J. Guyton. All three were expected to get a chance for immediate playing time because three sophomore guards (Lou Moore, Chris Rowles and Sherron Wilkerson) from the 1995-96 team were no longer part of the IU program. Lewis was the leading scorer in Indiana as a senior and was recruited to play point guard. Jimenez was an all-state guard from Minnesota that turned down scholarship offers from other schools to join IU as a walk-on. Guyton was a highly athletic 6'1" combo guard from Peoria, Illinois. He wasn't a highly rated prospect, but he ended up being the biggest contributor of the four freshmen.

On November 15, freshmen Collier, Guyton and Lewis were all in the starting lineup on opening night when the Hoosiers scratched and clawed their way to a 68-61 win over Connecticut in the RCA Dome. Neil Reed led IU with 20 points while Collier chipped in 12 points and 10 rebounds in his collegiate debut. "I don't think anybody played exceptionally well, but it was really gutsy effort," said Knight afterwards. "For me, playing like that was better than anything else we could have had."

Next, IU grabbed national attention by winning four straight games to capture the Preseason NIT championship. Andrae Patterson earned the tournament MVP award with 20 points and a game-winning turnaround jumper at the buzzer against Evansville in the semifinals, along with a dominating 39-point performance in an 85-69 win over sixth-ranked Duke in the finals. During the tournament, freshman A.J. Guyton also emerged as a consistent scoring threat, averaging 14 points over the four games. After winning the NIT, the Hoosiers, which had been unranked in the preseason, bolted to No. 8 in the AP poll.

The following week, Indiana struggled but beat Notre Dame 76-75 in South Bend. Patterson hit the game-winner—a short jumper in the lane with 0:19 remaining. Then, Indiana faced No. 6 Kentucky in a highly anticipated matchup between the longtime rivals who both ranked among the top teams in the country. It was expected to be one of the most competitive games of the preseason in college basketball. Instead, on a neutral floor in Louisville, the Wildcats devoured the Hoosiers, forcing them into 28 turnovers and running away with a 99-65 victory.

Following the Kentucky debacle, the Hoosiers showed some resilience by bouncing back and winning their final seven preconference games to amass a 13-1 record heading into Big Ten play. The 12th-ranked IU squad kept that momentum going in the first half of its Big Ten opener against Michigan State, as Indiana jumped out to a 43-23 lead going into the locker room. The Spartans battled back and pulled to

1996-97 TEAM ROSTER

Head coach: Bob Knight
Assistant coaches: Dan Dakich, Ron Felling, Craig Hartman

No.	Player	Hometown	Class	Position	Height
40	Jason Collier	Springfield, OH	Fr	F/C	7-0
32	Robbie Eggers	Cuyahoga Falls, OH	Jr	F	6-10
25	A.J. Guyton	Peoria, IL	Fr	G	6-1
12	Luke Jimenez	Redwood Falls, MN	Fr	G	6-3
24	Michael Lewis	Jasper, IN	Fr	G	6-1
21	Richard Mandeville	Pasadena, CA	Jr	C	7-0
3	Charlie Miller	Miami, FL	Jr	G/F	6-7
55	Haris Mujezinovic	Chicago, IL	Sr	C	6-9
23	Jean Paul	Naples, FL	Jr	G	6-2
45	Andre Patterson	Abilene, TX	Jr	F	6-8
5	Neil Reed	Metairie, LA	Jr	G	6-2
33	Larry Richardson	Orange Park, FL	Fr	F	6-8

SEASON RESULTS 1996-97

Date	Court	Opponent	Result	Score
11/15/1996	N1	Connecticut	W	68-61
11/20/1996	H	Princeton	W	59-49
11/22/1996	H	Saint Louis	W	70-54
11/27/1996	N2	Evansville	W	74-73
11/29/1996	N2	(#6) Duke	W	85-69
12/2/1996	A	Notre Dame	W	76-75
12/7/1996	N3	(#6) Kentucky	L	65-99
12/10/1996	N4	DePaul	W	74-57
12/13/1996	N1	Louisiana Tech	W	74-57
12/14/1996	N1	Santa Clara	W	86-74
12/21/1996	N1	Evansville	W	75-57
12/23/1996	H	Butler	W	89-84
12/27/1996	N1	Colgate	W	63-48
12/28/1996	N1	Valparaiso	W	72-51
1/2/1997	H	Michigan State	W	77-65
1/4/1997	A	Wisconsin	L	58-71
1/8/1997	H	(#11) Minnesota	L	91-96
1/15/1997	A	Northwestern	W	66-63
1/18/1997	A	Purdue	L	53-70
1/21/1997	H	(#13) Michigan	W	72-70
1/26/1997	A	Penn State	W	70-55
1/30/1997	A	Ohio State	L	67-73
2/2/1997	H	Illinois	L	71-78
2/4/1997	A	(#25) Iowa	L	67-75
2/8/1997	H	Ohio State	W	93-76
2/11/1997	H	Penn State	W	81-57
2/16/1997	A	(#14) Michigan	W	84-81
2/18/1997	H	Purdue	L	89-87
2/22/1997	H	Northwestern	W	64-49
3/1/1997	A	(#2) Minnesota	L	72-75
3/5/1997	H	Wisconsin	W	70-66
3/8/1997	A	Michigan State	L	60-63
NCAA Tournament				
3/13/1997	N5	(#24) Colorado	L	62-80

1 Indianapolis, IN
2 New York, NY
3 Louisville, KY
4 Chicago, IL (United Center)
5 Winston-Salem, NC

1996-97 BIG TEN STANDINGS

	W	L	PCT
Minnesota[1]	16	2	.889
Iowa	12	6	.667
Purdue	12	6	.667
Illinois	11	7	.611
Wisconsin	11	7	.611
Michigan[2]	9	9	.500
Indiana	9	9	.500
Michigan St.	9	9	.500
Ohio State	5	13	.278
Penn State	3	15	.167
Northwestern	2	16	.111

1 NCAA voided all games for Minnesota
2 Records later vacated due to NCAA sanctions

within a single point midway through the second half before IU pulled away for a 77-65 win. Playing in their first Big Ten game, Collier and Guyton led the Hoosiers to the win. Collier had 25 points and eight rebounds, while Guyton had 16 points on 6-8 shooting from the field and 4-4 from the line.

The Hoosiers' eight-game winning streak ended when the team lost three of its next four games, including double-digit road losses at Wisconsin and Purdue and a heartbreaking home defeat to Minnesota in overtime. The only win during that stretch was a 66-63 nail-biter over Northwestern in Evanston, in which a demoted Neil Reed came off the bench to score 18 second-half points.

Next, as IU prepared to host 13th-ranked Michigan on January 21, Patterson injured his knee in practice and ended up missing the game against the Wolverines, while Collier was hobbled with a back injury that limited him to 11 minutes. Still, the Hoosiers pulled together and raced out to a big lead against Michigan, and then held on for a 72-70 win in a nationally televised game on ESPN. Then, IU improved its Big Ten record to 4-3 with a 70-55 win at Penn State. After that, things turned bleak. IU lost three games in row for the first time in seven years and dropped back to 4-6 in league play (ninth place), which all but eliminated Indiana from contention in the Big Ten race.

The team gamely responded by blowing out Ohio State and Penn State in Assembly Hall. A.J. Guyton scored 24 points and 21 points, respectively, in those two games, but he saved his best for Indiana's rematch with No. 14 Michigan in Ann Arbor on February 16. That day, Indiana rallied from a 20-point second-half deficit before Guyton sent the game into overtime with two consecutive three pointers in the final minute. Then, with 0:26 left in OT, Guyton used a great ball fake to shake off his Michigan defender, square up, and softly drop in a 15-foot

jump shot to seal an 84-81 Indiana victory. "That's as good a play as I've ever had under pressure, except maybe Keith Smart's shot [in the 1987 NCAA title game]," said Knight. Guyton finished with a game-high 31 points including seven three-pointers.

Two days later, Guyton scored 31 again during another overtime game. This time, it was against Purdue in Assembly Hall, but the end result was just the opposite as the Boilermakers' Chad Austin nailed an 18-footer in the final seconds to lift Purdue to an 89-87 win. It was practically an instant replay from the previous season when Austin sank a three-pointer with 13.7 seconds remaining to lift Purdue to a 74-72 win in Bloomington.

After the heartbreaking loss to the Boilermakers, Indiana split its final four games of the regular season and finished with a Big Ten record of 9-9 and a tie for sixth place in the conference. With the Hoosiers' 13-1 preconference record, the team had an overall mark of 22-10, which merited a berth in the NCAA tournament. In the East Regional in Winston-Salem, North Carolina, eighth-seeded Indiana collided with ninth-seeded Colorado. The Hoosiers never matched the intensity of the Buffalos and got whipped 80-62, as Colorado's Chauncey Billups dominated the game with 24 points and some aggressive defense that disrupted the IU guards.

It was the third straight season that Indiana had suffered a first-round loss in the NCAA tournament, and it was a bitterly disappointing end to a season that had started out 14-1. Following that hot start, the Hoosiers went 8-10 the rest of the way. For the season, Indiana shot 43.8 percent from the field—the lowest shooting percentage for any of Knight's teams in his 26 seasons at IU. Despite that low percentage, Indiana was still one of the top scoring teams in the Big Ten by averaging 72.6 points per game. However, the Hoosiers also gave up 68.1 points per game, which ranked them among the worst defensive teams

INDIANA'S RANKING IN THE 1996-97 ASSOCIATED PRESS POLLS

PS	11/19	11/25	12/2	12/9	12/16	12/23	12/30	1/6	1/13	1/20	1/27	2/3	2/10	2/17	2/24	3/3	3/10
—	22	20	8	12	13	13	12	15	17	21	17	24	—	24	22	25	—

in the league. The Indiana team also recorded fewer assists than turnovers for the first time since the 1978-79 season.

After the Colorado loss, the Indiana players blamed the team's poor play down the stretch on lack of concentration, selfishness and lack of effort on the court. Senior Haris Mujezinovic blasted his fellow upperclassmen, saying, "How can you not play as hard as you can when everything's on the line? ...These juniors, I hope they learned their lesson. They've had three years of this now. It's time they woke up and lived up to their expectations."

One of those juniors—Neil Reed—became the lightning rod for criticism about selfishness and disunity among the IU players. As a result, Reid, the former McDonald's All-American, left the Indiana program and transferred to Southern Mississippi in a highly publicized split with Coach Knight.

The bright spot of the season was the play of lightning-quick guard A.J. Guyton, who was voted the Big Ten's Freshman of the Year. He averaged 13.6 points per game—second only to Patterson's 13.7—and led the team with 3.9 assists per game, even though he played shooting guard. Guyton also became only the eighth player in Indiana history to record 400 points, 100 assists, and 100 rebounds in the same season. Isiah Thomas was the only other freshman to accomplish that feat. Plus, Guyton's fellow freshmen Jason Collier, Michael Lewis and Luke Jimenez had all played key roles on the team and developed into solid college players in their own right, and the future of the program appeared to be passing into their hands.

1997-98

OVERALL RECORD: 20-12

CONFERENCE RECORD: 9-7 (FIFTH PLACE)

TEAM HONORS:

HOOSIER CLASSIC CHAMPION,

INDIANA CLASSIC CHAMPION

INDIVIDUAL HONORS:

A.J. GUYTON—ALL-BIG TEN (FIRST TEAM)

ROBBIE EGGERS—ACADEMIC ALL-BIG TEN

Was this the year Indiana would return to the top of the college basketball world? That was the question that Hoosiers fans had on their minds at the beginning of the 1997-98 season. The IU faithful had an itch for a Big Ten title and a deep NCAA run that hadn't been scratched in five years.

Coach Bob Knight, a tireless competitor, was also eager to lead Indiana back to championship-level basketball. Prior to the 1997-98 campaign he said, "I haven't been satisfied with our play [in recent years]. I have just not felt that we've had the kind of basketball here that we have to have, or should have, or that we want to have. It hasn't been the kind of basketball that our teams have usually played. So to that end we tried to make some changes."

Those changes involved bringing in two JUCO transfers—6'8" forward William Gladness and 6'4" guard Rob Turner—and hiring two new assistant coaches—Mike Davis and John Treloar. Another change was the transfer of guard Neil Reed to Southern Mississippi.

With the departure of Reed, only Andrae Patterson and Charlie Miller remained from the once-ballyhooed five-man recruiting class of 1994 that was expected to be the core of Indiana's new generation of champions. Patterson and Miller were now seniors, and they were joined by fifth-year seniors Robbie Eggers and Richard Mandeville for their last campaign in a Hoosier uniform. Patterson still had the potential to become one of the top players in the country. The 6'8", 230-pound power forward had

The 1997-98 team. First row (left to right): Luke Jimenez, Charlie Miller, Richard Mandeville, Robbie Eggers, Andrae Patterson, Luke Recker; Second row: A.J. Guyton, Tom Geyer, Larry Richardson, Jason Collier, William Gladness, Kirk Haston, Rob Turner, Michael Lewis. IU Athletics

breathtaking physical gifts—quickness, strength and agility—and had shown potential for greatness, such as his 39-point MVP performance against Duke in the 1996 Preseason NIT title game, but he had never put it all together for a full season. His senior year would be no different. He didn't become the superstar many expected him to be. Nevertheless, he was a solid contributor in the paint and a constant low-post threat who helped create space for other players.

Indiana's fortunes rested on the perimeter, where ultra-quick 6'1" guard A.J. Guyton returned for his sophomore campaign. Guyton, the Big Ten's Freshman of the Year in 1997, was joined by fellow sophomores Michael Lewis and Luke Jimenez in the backcourt. Lewis prepared to take over IU's point guard duties, while Jimenez looked to provide a spark off the bench with his high-percentage outside shooting. In addition to JUCO transfer Rob Turner, another important new perimeter player was joining the Hoosiers: 1997 Indiana Mr. Basketball Luke Recker. A 6'6" wing player, Recker, who committed to

Indiana after his sophomore year of high school, averaged 27 points and seven rebounds as a senior and was selected as a McDonald's All-American. Recker could play up to four different positions on the court, provide strong outside shooting and athleticism, and could create his own shot off the dribble.

Two other freshmen joined Recker in the Hoosiers' 1997 recruiting class—6'10" Kirk Haston from Lobelville, Tennessee, and 6'8" Tom Geyer, a walk-on from Indianapolis. Both of those big men ended up being redshirted because of Indiana's depth in the frontcourt. Next to Patterson, the Hoosiers' top returnee up front was 7'0" sophomore Jason Collier. The highly coveted recruit averaged a respectable 9.4 points and 5.7 rebounds as a freshman, but had a difficult time adjusting to the physical post play in college basketball. He also had a difficult time adjusting to Knight's demanding, high-intensity coaching style. Nine games into the 1997-98 season, Collier would end up leaving IU, and he eventually transferred to Georgia Tech.

Knight had a deep and versatile team to work with, but finding the right mix of players on the floor and developing the team's chemistry was a struggle early on. In fact, the team suffered its first setback before the season officially began. On November 6, IU got beat 94-77 by Athletes in Action in an exhibition game in Bloomington. Considering the fact that between the mid-1980s and the mid-1990s, Indiana had gone over a decade without losing to a non-conference opponent in Assembly Hall; losing to a bunch of former mid-major players who usually got throttled by schools of all sizes during the exhibition season was quite an embarrassment for the Hoosiers.

Things didn't get much better once the season officially began, as IU lost two of its first three games. The Hoosiers dropped their opener to Temple 59-53 at The Spectrum in Philadelphia, as the Owls set a school record with 19 steals. The IU squad responded by beating UAB in Alabama, but then fell to Hawaii 82-65 in Honolulu in the United Airlines Classic. At 1-2, Indiana had already lost more games than it did during the preconference season the year before when the Hoosiers raced to a 13-1 record.

IU won its next two games to improve to 3-2 before meeting seventh-ranked Kentucky on December 6, in the RCA Dome in Indianapolis. The Wildcats controlled the lead for most of the game, but could never shake off the Hoosiers, who made a run in the final minutes and had several opportunities to tie the game or take the lead, but fell short in a 75-72 loss. Rob Turner stepped up for the Hoosiers with a game-high 25 points in the losing effort, while A.J. Guyton added 19 points and eight rebounds. It was Indiana's fourth straight defeat to its border rival. Fortunately, after that loss, Indiana's schedule got much easier, and the IU squad won its final six non-conference games to salvage a 9-4 record heading into conference play.

The Big Ten schedule looked a little different for the 1998 season as the number of games that each team played was decreased from 18 to 16 in order to accommodate the Big Ten's newly established conference tournament at the end of the season. Knight wasn't a proponent of the conference tournament, but he was out-voted on the issue by the other coaches in the league.

Coach Knight felt that with a shortened schedule it was even more important to get off to a good start

1997-98 TEAM ROSTER

Head coach: Bob Knight
Assistant coaches: Mike Davis, Craig Hartman, John Treloar

No.	Player	Hometown	Class	Position	Height
40	Jason Collier	Springfield, OH	So	C	7-0
32	Robbie Eggers	Cuyahoga Falls, OH	Sr	F	6-10
53	Tom Geyer	Indianapolis, IN	Rs	F	6-8
30	William Gladness	West Memphis, AR	Jr	F	6-8
25	A.J. Guyton	Peoria, IL	So	G	6-1
35	Kirk Haston	Lobelville, TN	Rs	F/C	6-10
12	Luke Jimenez	Redwood Falls, MN	So	G	6-3
24	Michael Lewis	Jasper, IN	So	G	6-1
21	Richard Mandeville	Pasadena, CA	Sr	C	7-0
3	Charlie Miller	Miami, FL	Sr	F	6-7
45	Andrae Patterson	Abilene, TX	Sr	F	6-8
4	Luke Recker	Auburn, IN	Fr	G/F	6-6
33	Larry Richardson	Orange Park, FL	So	F	6-8
23	Rob Turner	Wilmington, DE	Jr	G	6-4

SEASON RESULTS 1997-98

Date	Court	Opponent	Result	Score
11/14/1997	N1	(#24) Temple	L	53-59
11/20/1997	A	UAB	W	80-64
11/28/1997	N2	Hawaii	L	65-82
11/30/1997	N2	Northeast Louisiana	W	103-69
12/3/1997	H	Notre Dame	W	91-80
12/6/1997	N3	(#7) Kentucky	L	72-75
12/9/1997	H	Evansville	W	85-73
12/12/1997	H	Wisconsin-Green Bay	W	72-58
12/13/1997	H	South Alabama	W	64-56
12/22/1997	N4	San Francisco	W	65-52
12/27/1997	N3	SW Missouri State	W	78-66
12/28/1997	N3	Western Michigan	W	70-63
12/31/1997	H	(#14) Iowa	L	76-89
1/3/1998	A	Illinois	L	72-74
1/6/1998	H	(#17) Michigan	W	80-62
1/10/1998	H	Ohio State	W	83-66
1/14/1998	A	Northwestern	W	76-58
1/18/1998	H	(#12) Purdue	W	94-88
1/25/1998	A	Wisconsin	W	69-59
1/28/1998	A	(#22) Michigan State	L	66-84
1/31/1998	H	Minnesota	W	95-82
2/4/1998	H	Penn State	W	95-76
2/10/1998	A	(#8) Purdue	L	89-94
2/14/1998	H	Northwestern	W	73-55
2/19/1998	A	Ohio State	W	74-72
2/22/1998	A	(#22) Michigan	L	64-112
2/24/1998	H	(#23) Illinois	L	72-82
2/28/1998	A	Iowa	L	72-82
Big Ten Tournament				
3/5/1998	N5	Ohio State	W	78-71
3/6/1998	N5	(#9) Purdue	L	71-76
NCAA Tournament				
3/12/1998	N6	Oklahoma	W	94-87
3/14/1998	N6	(#6) Connecticut	L	68-78

1 Philadelphia, PA (The Spectrum)
2 Honolulu, HI
3 Indianapolis, IN
4 Oakland, CA
5 Chicago, IL
6 Washington, DC

1997-98 BIG TEN STANDINGS

	W	L	PCT
Michigan St.	13	3	.813
Illinois	13	3	.813
Purdue	12	4	.750
Michigan1	11	5	.688
Iowa	9	7	.563
Indiana	9	7	.563
Penn State	8	8	.500
Minnesota2	0	0	.000
Wisconsin	3	13	.188
Northwestern	3	13	.188
Ohio State	1	15	.063

1 Due to NCAA sanctions, Michigan has vacated these records
2 NCAA voided all games for Minnesota

Powerful forward Andrae Patterson showed flashes of brilliance during his IU career but put up modest numbers of 11.3 PPG and 5.7 RPG over four years. Nevertheless, he provided a number of colorful contributions to the highlight reel. IU Athletics

William Gladness) and it resulted in more fast-break opportunities and better overall team play.

However, if the Hoosiers were playing well, then Iowa was playing great. The 14th-ranked Hawkeyes (11-1) came into Assembly Hall for the Big Ten opener and ran away with an 89-76 victory as all five Iowa starters scored in double figures, led by freshman guard Ricky Davis with 22 points. IU freshman Luke Recker led the Hoosiers with 19 points. Later in the week, Indiana lost 74-72 at Illinois to drop to 0-2 in conference play for the first time since 1988.

Indiana jumped back into the thick of the conference race by winning its next five games using a balanced offensive attack and a re-energized defense. Back in Assembly Hall, the Hoosiers thumped No. 17 Michigan 80-62 and clobbered Ohio State 83-66. Then they went up to Evanston and beat Northwestern 76-58 as Recker and Guyton each scored 22 points. The most satisfying win of the streak was a 94-88 triumph over archrival Purdue in Bloomington. The Boilermakers had won two straight in Assembly Hall on clutch shots in the final minute, and overall, IU hadn't beaten Purdue since 1995. Indiana-native Luke Recker posted career highs of 27 points and 12 rebounds against the Boilermakers. Then, led by 23 points and 12 rebounds from Andrae Patterson, Indiana beat Wisconsin 69-59 in Madison to improve to 5-2 in conference play. The Hoosiers also re-entered the national rankings at No. 25.

No. 22 Michigan State defended its home court and its top spot in the conference by beating Indiana 84-66 on January 28. Sophomore Mateen Cleeves sparked MSU with 10 points and 13 assists. After losing to the Spartans, Knight had the Hoosiers focus even more on using their quickness to push the ball up the court and take advantage of fast-break opportunities. The strategy worked, as IU stayed in the conference race by winning four of its next five games. The only loss in those five games came against No. 8 Purdue in West Lafayette on February 10. The Boilermakers barely escaped with a 94-89 win. For the Hoosiers, the final contest of that five-game stretch was also the most dramatic. Against Ohio State on February 19, in Columbus, the game was tied in the final minute, and the Buckeyes were working for the last shot. When they tried to get the ball to their leading scorer, Michael Redd, IU's Luke

in conference play, and the Hoosiers had a good opportunity to do that with three of their first four Big Ten games being played in Assembly Hall. IU was also riding a six-game winning streak and, after center Jason Collier left the team in mid-December, the Hoosiers went with a smaller, quicker lineup with three guards (Michael Lewis, A.J. Guyton and Luke Recker) and two forwards (Andrae Patterson and

Recker stepped into the passing lane and stole the ball, and then raced down the court for the game-winning dunk to give Indiana a stunning 74-72 victory.

With the Ohio State win, Indiana sat at 9-4 with three games left in conference play and still had an outside chance at the conference crown if they could win all three games and get some help from other teams. Those hopes were squelched on February 22, when 22nd-ranked Michigan bombarded Indiana with a psyche-bruising 112-64 defeat. The shell-shocked Hoosiers then stumbled to two more losses against Illinois and Iowa to close the season with three straight defeats. The end result was a 9-7 conference record and a fifth-place finish.

In the first ever Big Ten tournament, Indiana opened with a 78-71 win over Ohio State, led by 25 points from Patterson and 23 from Guyton. In the second round, Indiana and Purdue staged a fiercely contested battle that the Boilermakers eventually won 76-71. Patterson had 24 points and eight rebounds for IU, which stood at 19-12 and in danger of not getting invited to the NCAA tournament. The Hoosiers had to sweat it out, but when the selections were announced, Indiana made the field as a No. 7 seed in the East Regional.

IU's first-round opponent was Oklahoma, and for the first time in four years, the Hoosiers pulled out a first-round NCAA victory by beating the Sooners 94-87—but it wasn't easy. Indiana had a 12-point lead with 7:20 to go, but Oklahoma made a 21-6 run to send the game to overtime. Indiana showed some toughness by turning things around in OT and pulling out a 94-87 win. The Hoosiers were led by three 20-point scorers: Patterson (26), Guyton (23), and Recker (21). In the second round, Indiana jumped out to a surprising 41-36 halftime lead over No. 2 seed Connecticut, but the Huskies, who were ranked sixth in the country, got a big second-half performance from its star guard Richard Hamilton and pulled out a 78-68 win.

The 1997-98 Hoosiers dramatically improved their shooting percentage from the season before, raising it from 44 percent (the worst of the Bob Knight era) to 49 percent (the best in the Big Ten that season). It was a team that won its share of games and put together some good performances, but they could never quite get over the hump and win the big game needed to step up to the next level of success. It was a disappointing end for seniors Patterson, Miller, Mandeville and Eggers, who had been recruited to come to Indiana on the heels of the team's great success in the early 1990s, and were expected to be part of the next wave of championships. They became some of Knight's first graduates to ever leave without having won a single conference title.

INDIANA'S RANKING IN THE 1997-98 ASSOCIATED PRESS POLLS

PS	11/16	11/23	12/1	12/8	12/15	12/22	12/29	1/4	1/11	1/18	1/25	2/2	2/9	2/16	2/23	3/1	3/6
17	23	21	—	—	—	—	—	—	—	—	25	—	—	—	—	—	—

1998-99

OVERALL RECORD: 23-11

CONFERENCE RECORD: 9-7 (THIRD PLACE)

TEAM HONORS:

HOOSIER CLASSIC CHAMPION, INDIANA CLASSIC CHAMPION

INDIVIDUAL HONORS:

LUKE RECKER—ACADEMIC ALL-AMERICA, ACADEMIC ALL-BIG TEN

The 1998-99 team. First row (left to right): Dane Fife, Larry Richardson, William Gladness, Rob Turner, Michael Lewis, Lynn Washington; Second row: A.J. Guyton, Luke Recker, Tom Geyer, Kirk Haston, Jarrad Odle, Kyle Hornsby, Luke Jimenez. IU Athletics

Indiana returned seven lettermen and four starters for the 1998-99 season, but the team lost a lot of height in the frontcourt with the graduation of Andre Patterson (6'8"), Charlie Miller (6'7"), Robbie Eggers (6'10"), and Richard Mandeville (7'0"). Plus, Jason Collier (7'0") transferred to Georgia Tech. Fortunately, redshirt freshman Kirk Haston, a 6'10"

center from Lobelville, Tennessee, turned out to be a pleasant surprise and helped fill the gap. He joined 6'8" senior William Gladness, 6'8" junior Larry Richardson, and 6'7" junior Lynn Washington (a newcomer as a JUCO transfer) to form a serviceable front line. However, the Hoosiers' heart and soul were undoubtedly on the perimeter where they had depth, talent and toughness. A.J. Guyton, Michael Lewis and Luke Recker comprised Coach Bob Knight's three-guard lineup that returned completely intact for a new season.

Michael Lewis, a 6'1" junior, had been a big-time scorer in high school but adjusted well to his role as a floor leader that was primarily responsible for setting up his teammates at IU. Plus, Lewis played with a hard-nosed style that Coach Knight liked. Meanwhile, Lewis's fellow junior and running mate, A.J. Guyton, was coming off an All-Big Ten season as a sophomore and had helped Team USA win the gold medal in the 1998 Goodwill Games. The lithe 6'1" Guyton came to Indiana as a fleet-footed guard who could slash to the basket, but during his sophomore season, he greatly improved his shooting touch as well, upping his field goal percentage from 43 percent as a freshman to 47 percent as sophomore (and his three-point percentage went from 39 percent to 44 percent). Entering his junior season, Guyton was now included on several preseason All-America teams, although he was still a year away from true national prominence. The other returning starter from the three-headed backcourt was Luke Recker, a 6'6" wing player who technically played small forward, but definitely played it with the ball-handling and shooting skills of a guard. Recker had come to Indiana with high expectations as a McDonald's All-American and had delivered with an excellent freshman season in which he was the second leading scorer on the team (behind Guyton), shot 49.8 percent from the field, and grabbed 3.9 rebounds per game. Beyond the numbers, Recker showed great poise and basketball savvy on the court and was expected to be even better with a season at IU under his belt.

As potent as those three guards were, IU had three more coming off the bench who were also dangerous. Luke Jimenez, a 6'3" junior and former walk-on, was an excellent outside shooter. He shot 53 percent from the field as a sophomore and 49 percent from three-point land. Senior Rob Turner also provided additional firepower. The athletic 6'4" senior was a JUCO transfer in his second season at IU. After averaging 20 PPG as a sophomore in junior college, he averaged 7.3 PPG (on 50 percent field-goal shooting) in a reserve role at IU as a junior. He showed the ability to put up points in a hurry, as demonstrated by his 19 points in the first half against Kentucky. The other

1998-99 TEAM ROSTER

Head coach: Bob Knight
Assistant coaches: Mike Davis, Pat Knight, John Treloar

No.	Player	Hometown	Class	Position	Height
11	Dane Fife	Clarkston, MI	Fr	G	6-4
53	Tom Geyer	Indianapolis, IN	Fr	F	6-8
30	William Gladness	West Memphis, AR	Sr	F	6-8
25	A.J. Guyton (Capt.)	Peoria, IL	Jr	G	6-1
35	Kirk Haston	Lobelville, TN	Fr	F/C	6-10
32	Kyle Hornsby	Anacoco, LA	Rs	G/F	6-5
12	Luke Jimenez	Redwood Falls, MN	Jr	G	6-3
24	Michael Lewis	Jasper, IN	Jr	G	6-1
43	Jarrad Odle	Swayzee, IN	Fr	F	6-8
10	Antwaan Randle El	Riverdale, IL	Fr	G	5-11
4	Luke Recker	Auburn, IN	So	G/F	6-6
33	Larry Richardson	Orange Park, FL	Jr	F	6-8
23	Rob Turner	Wilmington, DE	Sr	G	6-4
44	Lynn Washington	San Jose, CA	Jr	F	6-7

SEASON RESULTS 1998-99

Date	Court	Opponent	Result	Score
11/7/1998	N1	Seton Hall	W	83-69
11/8/1998	N1	South Carolina	W	76-55
11/14/1998	H	Indiana State	W	76-70
11/18/1998	H	UAB	W	94-54
11/23/1998	N2	Kansas State	W	71-70
11/24/1998	N2	(#18) Utah	W	52-49
11/25/1998	N2	(#19) Syracuse	L	63-76
12/1/1998	A	Notre Dame	W	76-72
12/5/1998	H	(#10) Temple	W	63-62
12/8/1998	N3	(#5) Kentucky	L	61-70
12/11/1998	H	Boise State	W	90-66
12/12/1998	H	Bowling Green	W	81-55
12/20/1998	H	San Francisco	W	106-54
12/27/1998	N1	Drake	W	102-46
12/28/1998	N1	Ball State	W	72-62
12/31/1998	A	(#21) Iowa	L	52-67
1/3/1999	H	Illinois	W	62-53
1/5/1999	A	Michigan	L	70-82
1/9/1999	A	Ohio State	L	56-73
1/13/1999	H	Northwestern	W	81-78
1/16/1999	A	(#13) Purdue	W	87-76
1/24/1999	H	(#11) Michigan State	L	59-73
1/26/1999	A	(#19) Minnesota	L	83-90
1/31/1999	A	Penn State	W	98-95
2/3/1999	H	(#11) Wisconsin	W	71-60
2/9/1999	H	(#21) Purdue	L	81-86
2/13/1999	A	Northwestern	W	69-62
2/17/1999	H	(#11) Ohio State	L	67-69
2/21/1999	H	Michigan	W	73-71
2/24/1999	A	Illinois	W	70-64
2/27/1999	H	(#18) Iowa	W	88-81
Big Ten Tournament				
3/5/1999	N4	Illinois	L	66-82
NCAA Tournament				
3/11/1999	N5	George Washington	W	108-88
3/13/1999	N5	(#9) St. John's	L	61-86

1 Indianapolis, IN
2 Lahaina, HI
3 Louisville, KY
4 Chicago, IL
5 Orlando, FL

1998-99 BIG TEN STANDINGS

	W	L	PCT
Michigan St.	15	1	.938
Ohio State	12	4	.750
Wisconsin	9	7	.563
Indiana	9	7	.563
Iowa	9	7	.563
Minnesota1	0	0	.000
Purdue	7	9	.438
Northwestern	6	10	.400
Michigan2	5	11	.313
Penn State	5	11	.313
Illinois	3	13	.188

1 NCAA voided all games for Minnesota
2 Due to NCAA sanctions, Michigan has vacated these records

backcourt reserve was 6'4" freshman Dane Fife, a McDonald's All-American and Michigan Mr. Basketball in 1998. He averaged 26 points, five rebounds, and five assists as a high school senior, and Knight wooing him to Indiana was viewed as a serious coup, since both Fife's father and brother had both played for the University of Michigan. "Fife is a tough kid," said Knight. "Before you can talk about his skills, you have to talk about how tough the kid is. He wants to win. We need what this kid can bring to our program."

In addition to Fife, two other new recruits joined the Indiana squad. Jarrad Odle, a 6'8" forward, had been one of the top scorers in the state of Indiana both as a junior and a senior in high school. He was a tough inside player who could also step out and hit the mid-range jumper. Kyle Hornsby, a 6'5" guard from Louisiana, was a three-time all-state selection in high school and an amazingly accurate jump shooter. As senior he shot 70 percent from the floor, including 60 percent from three-point range. He was also a longtime fan of Indiana basketball. However, because of Indiana's crowded backcourt, Hornsby ended up redshirting. Fife, Odle and Hornsby would all eventually make their mark on the IU program, but it would take a couple of years.

For the 1998-99 campaign, the Hoosiers had an unprecedented seven games scheduled in November. They opened with four straight wins over Seton Hall, South Carolina, Indiana State and Alabama-Birmingham. Recker and Guyton picked up where they left off by leading the Hoosiers in scoring, but the biggest surprise was Kirk Haston. He and Recker were the only IU players to score in double figures in each of the first four games, and Haston put together an outstanding 18-point, 16-rebound performance in a come-from-behind win against the Indiana State Sycamores.

After jumping out to a 4-0 start, 21st-ranked Indiana traveled to the Maui Classic in Hawaii on November 23-25. In the opener, Indiana rallied back from a 16-point halftime deficit to beat Kansas State 71-70, and then squeaked by 18th-ranked Utah 52-49 in a defensive struggle. Against the Utes, Haston had 10 points and 10 rebounds in his first career start at center. In the championship game, IU lost to No. 19 Syracuse 76-63, despite getting 24 points and 10 rebounds from power forward William Gladness.

Against the Orangemen, A. J. Guyton was held scoreless for the first time in his collegiate career.

After returning from Hawaii, Indiana beat Notre Dame 76-72 in overtime in South Bend, as Luke Recker scored a game-high 27 points. Then, the Hoosiers shot down No. 10 Temple 63-62 in Assembly Hall on a Guyton three-pointer with seven seconds remaining. In their next game on December 8, against No. 5 Kentucky in Louisville's Freedom Hall, the Hoosiers once again used the three-pointer as a potent weapon. IU trailed the Wildcats 51-42 with 1:23 to go, but Luke Recker drilled two straight threes to cut the lead to 51-48. After forcing Kentucky into a shot-clock violation, Indiana got the ball back with 13.2 seconds left on the clock. With time ticking down, freshman Dane Fife got the ball on the wing, faked his Kentucky defender into the air, took one dribble, and released a three-pointer that poured through the net with 1.7 seconds remaining and sent the game into overtime. Having spent all of their energy on that thrilling comeback, the Hoosiers bowed 70-61 in overtime. After that tough stretch, Indiana cruised to five straight double-digit victories, which put the team's record at 13-2 at the end of the pre-conference schedule. The Hoosiers had also risen to No. 8 in the AP poll as they prepared to open Big Ten play.

The 21st-ranked Iowa Hawkeyes hosted Indiana on New Year's Eve for the conference opener. Iowa's zone defense gave IU fits, and the Hawkeyes prevailed 67-52, as Recker and Guyton combined to shoot 5-21 from the field. The duo bounced back and teamed up to score 37 points on January 3, when the Hoosiers beat Illinois 62-53 in Bloomington. But then Indiana went on the road and dropped two more games to Michigan and Ohio State. The Hoosiers were 1-3 in league play and had practically dealt themselves out of the conference race before it even started heating up.

Indiana got back in the win column by holding on for an 81-78 win over Northwestern in Bloomington on January 13. Michael Lewis had 14 points and 11 assists and Recker notched a game-high 28 points. Next, the Hoosiers notched their biggest win of the year by beating 13th-ranked Purdue 87-76 in West Lafayette. All five Indiana starters scored in double figures for the first time that season. Center William Gladness and power forward Larry

Richardson both had double-doubles. Recker and Guyton had 24 points and 21 points, respectively, and Michael Lewis had 11 points and nine assists. IU shot 53 percent from the floor, while limiting Purdue to 40 percent shooting. It was an outstanding team effort and IU's first victory in West Lafayette in six years. It also lifted the Hoosiers' conference record back to 3-3.

With the win at Purdue, Indiana had begun to establish itself as a dangerous team. However, the competition in the Big Ten was brutal. In the Hoosiers' next seven games, five of their conference opponents were ranked in the top 25. IU lost four of those games, including three in Assembly Hall to Michigan State, Purdue and Ohio State. The other defeat was a 90-83 overtime loss at Minnesota, in a game that the Hoosiers led for the first 38 minutes. The most exciting win during that stretch was a 98-95 double overtime cliffhanger at Penn State in which A.J. Guyton exploded for a career-high 33 points. The other key win in that seven-game stretch was a 71-60 triumph over No. 11 Wisconsin. Against the Badgers, Knight inserted Rob Turner as a starter to form a four-guard lineup. Turner responded with 22 points and 8-11 shooting from the field.

Unfortunately, after those seven games, the Hoosiers stood at 6-7 in league play and 19-9 overall. With three games remaining, they needed to pull out at least another win or two in order to lock up an NCAA berth and assure a decent seed in the Big Ten tournament. IU also had the potential to vie for a high seed in the NCAA tournament if it could finish strong. For the first time that season, Indiana put together a three-game conference winning streak by sweeping all three of its final games. The first was a 73-71 nail-biter over Michigan in Bloomington. Recker hit 22-25 free throws and finished with a game-high 24 points. Then the Hoosiers played their seventh overtime game of the season in a 70-64 OT

victory against Illinois in Champaign. Finally, on senior night, IU closed its conference season at 9-7 by knocking off No. 18 Iowa 88-81 on February 27. The Hoosiers earned the third seed in Big Ten conference tournament at the United Center in Chicago, but in their first game, they got upset by Illinois 82-66. The difference in the game was that the Fighting Illini emasculated the Hoosiers on the boards with a 51-26 rebounding advantage.

Still, the Hoosiers received a respectable sixth seed in the NCAA tournament. IU was placed in the South Regional in Orlando, Florida. It was nearly identical to Indiana's situation in the 1996 tournament when IU was a sixth seed in the Southeast Regional in Orlando and got upset by 11th-seed Boston College in the first round. This time, the Hoosiers easily got out of the first round by steam-rolling George Washington 108-88, behind 27 points and nine rebounds from Kirk Haston and 20 points from Luke Recker. IU shot a sizzling 66 percent from the floor. Unfortunately, in the second round, IU collided with an excellent St. John's team (a third seed), led by Erick Barkley and Ron Artest. The Redmen took advantage of their athleticism and size to wallop the Hoosiers 86-61—the worst NCAA defeat in IU history.

As disappointing as the St. John's loss was, Indiana suffered an even bigger setback a month later when sophomore Luke Recker, IU's leading scorer, announced that he had decided to leave Indiana. Recker said that he wasn't happy with his development as a basketball player, but he thanked Coach Knight for giving him the opportunity to fulfill his childhood dream of playing for IU. In his two years in Bloomington, Recker's hustling plays and his clutch scoring made him a crowd favorite—he may have been the most popular Indiana player since Damon Bailey. The fact that he was an in-state high school star who chose to play for IU and lobbied

INDIANA'S RANKING IN THE 1998-99 ASSOCIATED PRESS POLLS

PS	11/17	11/24	12/1	12/8	12/15	12/22	12/29	1/5	1/12	1/19	1/26	2/2	2/9	2/16	2/23	3/2	3/9
22	21	17	16	11	10	10	8	13	23	18	20	21	17	19	20	17	19

other top in-state players to stay at home and play for Coach Knight also helped endear him to the Hoosier faithful. That made his announcement even more of a shock. His roommate Dane Fife said, "Luke Recker, in a sense, is Indiana basketball, like Steve Alford and Damon Bailey. We are sure going to miss him." Recker eventually transferred to Arizona, but after a life-threatening car accident, he decided to move closer to home and transferred to Iowa for his final two seasons of eligibility.

In addition to Recker's departure, the IU team nearly lost its No. 2 scorer, junior A.J. Guyton. When the season ended, Guyton considered entering the NBA draft. However, the day of Recker's jolting announcement, Guyton declared that he intended to stay at Indiana and play out his senior year.

1999-2000

OVERALL RECORD: 20-9

CONFERENCE RECORD: 10-6 (FIFTH PLACE)

TEAM HONORS:

HOOSIER CLASSIC CHAMPIONSHIP

INDIVIDUAL HONORS:

A.J. GUYTON—ALL-AMERICA, BIG TEN PLAYER OF THE YEAR (MEDIA), ALL-BIG TEN (FIRST TEAM)

TOM GEYER—ACADEMIC ALL-BIG TEN

KIRK HASTON—ACADEMIC ALL-BIG TEN

KYLE HORNSBY—ACADEMIC ALL-BIG TEN

With the transfer of leading scorer and former home-state golden boy Luke Recker the previous spring, IU fans had low expectations entering the 1999-2000 season. In fact, expectations were lower than at any point during the previous decade. Not since the 1988-89 season did the Hoosiers appear to have so little chance of competing for the Big Ten championship (of course, that season, IU pulled a surprise and won the conference title going away). On a national level, the forecast for the Indiana squad was equally reserved. For only the

second time in eleven seasons, the Hoosiers were unranked in the preseason AP poll.

While fans and prognosticators outside the Indiana program had their doubts about this squad, coach Bob Knight and the people on the inside were quietly optimistic about the team's chances. Nine lettermen returned, including five seniors. While both Ohio State and Purdue also returned five seniors, each of the other eight Big Ten teams had an average of only two seniors. That gave the Hoosiers a definite advantage, especially since three of IU's seniors were guards—A.J. Guyton, Michael Lewis and Luke Jimenez. Guyton was the Hoosiers' top returning scorer, Lewis had led IU in assists for two straight seasons, and Jimenez had been a solid contributor off the bench in each of his first three seasons. The other two seniors occupied the frontcourt: 6'8" Larry Richardson and 6'7" Lynn Washington. That leadership and experience made this team the kind of team that Bob Knight preferred to have. And with no juniors on the roster, the rest of the team was full of sophomores and freshmen so that made the senior leadership even more critical.

One of the younger players who helped inspire optimism in this team's chances was 6'10" sophomore Kirk Haston, who had surprisingly led Indiana with 6.5 rebounds per game during the 1998-99 season and chipped in 9.9 points per game as well. He also posted seven double-doubles during his freshman campaign. Haston was expected to get help up front from Richardson and Washington, as well as sophomore Jarrad Odle and freshman Jeffrey Newton, a thin 6'9" forward from Atlanta that possessed a variety of quick post moves and a decent mid-range jump shot. As a senior in high school, Newton had averaged 22 points, nine rebounds, and three blocks per game and had been ranked among the top 100 recruits in the nation. Another freshman big man, 6'11" George Leach, was forced to redshirt because he was only a partial qualifier academically.

In addition to those young pups in the front court, Dane Fife, Kyle Hornsby and Tom Coverdale added some youth to the backcourt. The 6'4" Fife was a sophomore and a former McDonald's All-American. After averaging 26 points per game as a senior in high school, Fife had struggled offensively as a freshman at IU, averaging only 3.3 PPG. However, he had quickly become IU's best defensive player. Hornsby was a

The 1999-2000 team. First row (left to right): Lynn Washington, Dane Fife, A.J. Guyton, Michael Lewis, Luke Jimenez, Tom Coverdale; Second row: Tom Geyer, Larry Richardson, Kirk Haston, George Leach, Jeffrey Newton, Jarrad Odle, Kyle Hornsby. IU Athletics

6'5" sharp-shooter whom a lot of people in Bloomington were comparing to Pat Graham. After redshirting his first season, Hornsby was now ready to see action as a freshman. Tom Coverdale, a hard-nosed 6'2" guard, was the 1998 Indiana Mr. Basketball and was coming off a year of seasoning at prep school in New England. Of the three young guards, only Fife averaged significant minutes since the IU backcourt was dominated by seniors Guyton, Lewis and Jimenez.

The key to the IU's fortunes rested primarily with Guyton. The ultra-quick shooting guard had been a streaky scorer for three seasons. Some nights he would catch fire, while other nights he quietly slid into the background. Although he had achieved success and recognition as a first-team All-Big Ten selec-

tion as a sophomore and a preseason All-American as a junior, Guyton arguably became the most improved player in the Big Ten as a senior. The biggest difference in his game was consistency. After averaging 15.5 points per game over his first three seasons, Guyton upped that mark to 19.7 points per game as a senior and on many nights he carried the Hoosiers on his diminutive back.

Indiana's preconference schedule, which was one of the toughest in the nation, quickly provided an opportunity for the Hoosiers to see what kind of team they had. They opened against Texas Tech in Lubbock, Texas, on November 19, in Texas Tech's brand new United Spirit Arena. Red Raiders center Andy Ellis burned Indiana for 30 points and 10 rebounds, but IU held the Red Raiders to 32 percent

1999-2000 TEAM ROSTER

Head coach: Bob Knight
Assistant coaches: Mike Davis, Pat Knight, John Treloar

No.	Player	Hometown	Class	Position	Height
3	Tom Coverdale	Noblesville, IN	Fr	G	6-2
11	Dane Fife	Clarkston, MI	So	G	6-4
53	Tom Geyer	Indianapolis, IN	So	F	6-8
25	A.J. Guyton (Capt.)	Peoria, IL	Sr	G	6-1
35	Kirk Haston	Lobelville, TN	So	F/C	6-10
32	Kyle Hornsby	Anococo, LA	Fr	G/F	6-5
12	Luke Jimenez	Redwood Falls, MN	Sr	G	6-3
5	George Leach	Charlotte, NC	Rs	C	6-11
24	Michael Lewis	Jasper, IN	Sr	G	6-1
50	Jeffrey Newton	Atlanta, GA	Fr	F	6-9
43	Jarrad Odle	Swayzee, IN	So	F	6-8
33	Larry Richardson	Orange Park, IL	Sr	F	6-8
44	Lynn Washington	San Jose, CA	Sr	F	6-7

SEASON RESULTS 1999-2000

Date	Court	Opponent	Result	Score
11/19/1999	A	Texas Tech	W	68-60
11/26/1999	N1	(# 5) Temple	W	67-59
11/30/1999	H	Notre Dame	W	81-64
12/4/1999	N2	(#13) Kentucky	W	83-75
12/7/1999	A	Missouri	W	73-68
12/10/1999	H	Buffalo	W	106-55
12/11/1999	H	Indiana State	L	60-63
12/18/1999	H	Wyoming	W	99-80
12/21/1999	N3	(#6) North Carolina	W	82-73
12/27/1999	N4	Canisius	W	95-53
12/28/1999	N4	Holy Cross	W	79-44
1/5/2000	H	Wisconsin	W	71-67
1/8/2000	A	Penn State	W	85-78
1/11/2000	A	(#11) Michigan State	L	71-77
1/15/2000	H	Minnesota	W	86-61
1/18/2000	H	Iowa	W	74-71
1/22/2000	A	Purdue	L	77-83
1/25/2000	H	Michigan	W	85-50
2/2/2000	H	Penn State	W	87-77
2/5/2000	A	Northwestern	W	89-67
2/9/2000	A	Minnesota	L	75-77
2/13/2000	A	Michigan	W	86-65
2/19/2000	H	(#7) Ohio State	L	71-82
2/22/2000	A	Illinois	L	63-87
2/26/2000	H	(#5) Michigan State	W	81-79
2/29/2000	H	(#20) Purdue	W	79-65
3/5/2000	A	Wisconsin	L	53-56
Big Ten Tournament				
3/10/2000	N5	(#25) Illinois	L	69-72
NCAA Tournament				
3/17/2000	N6	Pepperdine	L	57-77

1 Springfield, MA
2 Louisville, KY
3 East Rutherford, NJ
4 Indianapolis, IN
5 Chicago, IL
6 Buffalo, NY

1999-2000 BIG TEN STANDINGS

	W	L	PCT
Michigan St.	13	3	.813
Ohio State	13	3	.813
Purdue	12	4	.750
Illinois	11	5	.688
Indiana	10	6	.625
Wisconsin	8	8	.500
Michigan	6	10	.375
Iowa	6	10	.375
Penn State	5	11	.313
Minnesota	4	12	.250
Northwestern	0	16	.000

shooting from the floor and took away a 68-60 victory, led by 22 points from Guyton. Next, Indiana played No. 5 Temple in the Tip-Off Classic in Springfield, Massachusetts. In the birthplace of basketball, the Hoosiers put on a clinic in how to blow holes in a zone defense and upset the Owls 67-59 as Guyton scored 22 points for the second straight game and Kirk Haston added 20 points and nine rebounds.

The Hoosiers followed up those two quality wins with victories over traditional rivals Notre Dame and Kentucky. Against the Fighting Irish, Guyton scored eight of his 20 points in overtime as Indiana won 84-64 by outscoring Notre Dame 19-2 in the extra period in Bloomington. Then on December 4, in the RCA Dome in Indianapolis, the IU squad beat Kentucky for the first time in six years by holding the Wildcats to 40 percent shooting from the floor, while the Hoosiers shot 55 percent. Led by a combined 38 points and 11 assists from Guyton and Lewis, IU prevailed 83-75 and inspired a bear hug between Bob Knight, his assistant coach and son Pat Knight, as the Hoosiers jogged off the floor in triumph.

On December 7, IU grinded out its second tough road win of the season, beating Missouri 73-68 and improving to 5-0 on the season. The Hoosiers then opened the Indiana Classic by dismantling Buffalo 106-55. However, in the championship game, the Hoosiers lost for the first time in the 25-year history of the tournament when the Indiana State Sycamores toppled the 15th-ranked Hoosiers 63-60. Guyton suffered through a 4-21 shooting night that included 16 straight misses during one long stretch. In the next game, Guyton bounced back with 29 points to lead IU to a 99-80 win over Wyoming in Assembly Hall.

The Hoosiers took to the road again to play on another neutral floor in the Jimmy V Classic in East Rutherford, New Jersey, and their opponent was No. 6 North Carolina. Indiana broke open a 63-63 tie by closing the game on a 19-10 run over the final six minutes to earn an 82-73 win over the Tar Heels, who would eventually make a run to the Final Four at the end of the season. Guyton buried seven three-pointers and scored a game-high 31 points. Indiana ended the preconference season by pummeling Canisius and Holy Cross to win the Hoosier Classic in Indianapolis. That put IU at 10-1 and included upsets of three top 15 teams. After practically being written off in the preseason, the Hoosiers entered Big Ten play as the highest ranked team in the conference at No. 10, with Michigan State (No. 11) and Ohio State (No. 13) right on their heels.

After opening league play with wins over Wisconsin in Bloomington and at Penn State, Indiana faced its first big game of the year when the Hoosiers went up to East Lansing on January 11, to take on Big Ten favorite Michigan State, which also started the conference at 2-0. IU led by six points with a minute and a half to play. The Spartans rallied back, but Haston sank two free throws with 15.2 seconds left to put Indiana up 62-59. In the final seconds, MSU forward Morris Peterson (a lefty) caught the ball fading to his right, made a quick spin, and launched a high, looping three-pointer that hit the bottom of the net and sent the game into overtime. In the extra session, the Spartans scored the first five points and never let the game out of control after that on the way to a 77-71 victory. Guyton led all scorers with 28 points, while guard Charlie Bell led MSU with 22 points.

Following the heart-breaker in East Lansing, Indiana routed Minnesota 86-61 in Assembly Hall and then hosted the Iowa Hawkeyes, which were now coached by former IU All-American Steve Alford. The Hawkeyes played an excellent game and led by seven points with eight minutes remaining, but down the stretch Guyton and Haston carried Indiana to a 74-71 win. Haston led IU with 25 points and 12 rebounds. On January 22, the Hoosiers lost 83-77 at Purdue to drop back to 4-2 in Big Ten play. After the Purdue loss, Indiana renewed its hopes for a shot at the conference title by steamrolling Michigan and Northwestern in Bloomington and then convincingly beating Northwestern in Evanston to improve to 7-2.

However, the Hoosiers lost four of their final seven games. The first of those losses—and the turning point of Indiana's season—came on February 9, at Minnesota. IU led the Golden Gophers 69-61 with 3:22 left on the clock. Minnesota then repeatedly pounded the ball into sophomore center Joel Przybilla who kept scoring inside until he tied the game at 75-75 with 0:39 to go. After IU center Kirk Haston missed a couple of shots, the Gophers went back to Przybilla again and he scored inside with 3.9 seconds remaining to give Minnesota the lead. Guyton missed a desperation 25-footer at the buzzer, and IU lost 77-

Senior guard A.J. Guyton stepped up his game in his final season as IU, averaging 19.7 PPG and leading Indiana to a spirited and unexpected run at the conference title. Guyton was named an All-American and also received the Big Ten Player of the Year award from the media. IU Athletics

75. The Minnesota defeat started a stretch in which the Hoosiers lost three out of four games and fell to 8-5 in league play, eliminating any hopes of a Big Ten title with only three games left in conference play.

Still, the Indiana squad managed a couple more big wins. The Hoosiers upset No. 5 Michigan State

81-79 in overtime on February 26, in Bloomington. Guyton scored a game-high 34 points but air-balled a long attempt to win the game in overtime. Fortunately, Lynn Washington grabbed the ball and stuck it in the basket to give IU the win. Freshman Kyle Hornsby also came off the bench to give Indiana a big spark. He played 26 minutes and contributed 10 points, five rebounds, two assists, two steals, and some floor burns from diving after loose balls. "Hornsby had a heart about as big as lion today. ... He did a hell of a job," said Michigan State coach Tim Izzo afterwards.

Next, the Hoosiers buried Purdue 79-65 on Senior Day in Assembly Hall. The loss denied Purdue a share of the conference crown, while Indiana improved its record to 20-6 overall. Knight joked with the Senior Day crowd, "We haven't won as many games as we'd like to have at this point, but we've won a helluva lot more than some people thought." What Knight and the Assembly Hall crowd did not anticipate was that it would be Indiana's last win of the season.

IU dropped its final game of the regular season, 56-53 at Wisconsin, in a game the Badgers badly needed to solidify their NCAA tournament hopes (not only did they make the tournament, but they went all the way to the Final Four). Then, IU got knocked out in its first game of the Big Ten tournament by Illinois when Cory Bradford buried a three-pointer with 1.3 seconds remaining to give the Fighting Illini a 72-69 victory.

Nevertheless, IU was awarded the sixth seed in the East Regional for the NCAA tournament, and the Hoosiers were optimistic about their chances of mak-

ing a run. Unfortunately, two days before the Hoosiers opened the tourney against the Pepperdine Waves in Buffalo, CNN/*SI* released story in which former IU guard Neil Reed accused Coach Knight of once choking him during a practice, as well as other verbal and physical abuse. Former and current players spoke out on Knight's behalf, denying the charges, but the publicity engulfed the team and became a major distraction. The allegations triggered a series of events that eventually spiraled out of control and led to Knight's dismissal six months later. In the Pepperdine game, the Hoosiers lost second-leading scorer Kirk Haston in the opening minutes when he sprained his right knee. That allowed the Waves to completely blanket Guyton with multiple defenders and hold him to only two shot attempts for the game. Pepperdine led by 20 at the half and cruised to a 77-57 upset of the 22nd-ranked Hoosiers.

Although the Pepperdine game provided a disappointing end to the career of Indiana's five seniors, there were still some accomplishments worth noting. In his final game as a Hoosier, Michael Lewis passed Quinn Buckner to become Indiana's career leader in assists with 545. Meanwhile, Guyton finished his IU career with 2,100 points to move into fourth place on the school's all-time scoring list, trailing only Calbert Cheaney, Steve Alford and Don Schlundt. Guyton's magnificent senior year also earned him All-American and All-Big Ten honors, and he was named the Big Ten Player of the Year by the media. In June, the Chicago Bulls selected Guyton in the second round of the NBA draft with the 32nd second overall pick, and A.J. ended up playing two full seasons with the Bulls before moving on to stints in the NBDL and Europe.

INDIANA'S RANKING IN THE 1999-2000 ASSOCIATED PRESS POLLS

PS	11/15	11/22	11/29	12/6	12/13	12/20	12/27	1/3	1/10	1/17	1/24	1/31	2/7	2/14	2/21	2/28	3/7	3/14
—	—	—	23	15	21	20	12	10	9	11	14	11	10	10	16	14	18	22

SEASON STATISTICS
1993-94 TO 1999-2000

1993-94

Team Statistics	G	FG%	3FG%	FT%	R	A	TO	S	B	PF	PTS	PPG
Indiana	30	.484	.454	.750	38.1	17.4	15.9	6.1	4.2	18.4	2428	80.9
Opponents	30	.423	.371	.634	36.0	15.5	13.6	7.3	2.7	21.8	2311	77.0
Player Statistics	G-GS	FG%	3FG%	FT%	R	A	TO	S	B	PF	PTS	PPG
Bailey	30-30	.481	.423	.802	4.3	4.3	3.3	1.5	0.2	2.5	589	19.6
Henderson	30-29	.531	.333	.657	10.3	1.2	2.0	1.3	1.9	3.0	534	17.8
Evans	27-24	.448	.457	.793	6.8	2.2	1.9	1.4	0.5	2.1	321	11.9
Graham	28-15	.516	.569	.893	2.3	2.4	2.4	0.3	0.1	1.9	331	11.8
Leary	28-12	.487	.459	.855	2.3	3.5	1.7	0.5	0.0	1.4	231	8.3
Lindeman	29-18	.548	.000	.600	3.9	0.3	1.4	0.7	0.8	3.0	162	5.6
Hart	30-5	.500	.444	.667	2.0	1.1	1.5	0.6	0.5	1.6	118	3.9
Wilkerson	28-12	.359	.294	.686	2.3	2.0	1.1	0.5	0.4	2.0	90	3.2
Mandeville	24-3	.353	.000	.500	1.8	0.1	0.5	0.0	0.0	1.4	27	1.1
Knight	27-2	.267	1.00	.714	0.7	1.1	0.7	0.1	0.0	0.4	22	0.8
Hales	13-0	.167	.000	.500	0.3	0.0	0.2	0.1	0.1	0.4	3	0.2

1994-95

Team Statistics	G	FG%	3FG%	FT%	R	A	TO	S	B	PF	PTS	PPG
Indiana	31	.484	.360	.666	37.8	15.7	15.4	5.9	4.7	18.4	2345	75.6
Opponents	31	.410	.335	.680	35.1	12.5	15.5	6.4	2.3	21.5	2158	69.6
Player Statistics	G-GS	FG%	3FG%	FT%	R	A	TO	S	B	PF	PTS	PPG
Henderson	31-31	.597	.200	.633	9.7	1.7	2.9	1.4	2.1	3.1	729	23.5
Evans	31-30	.462	.417	.783	6.7	3.3	2.3	0.8	0.5	2.5	538	17.4
Patterson	28-20	.494	.500	.689	3.9	0.8	1.8	0.6	0.6	2.9	203	7.3
Hermon	28-17	.418	.231	.659	3.1	3.4	2.5	1.3	0.0	2.6	167	6.0
Reed	30-18	.383	.310	.667	1.7	2.5	1.2	0.6	0.0	1.6	176	5.9
Miller	31-12	.467	.533	.621	2.8	0.8	1.4	0.3	0.2	1.2	175	5.7
Lindeman	30-10	.492	.000	.569	3.1	0.4	1.2	0.3	1.0	2.5	147	4.9
Hart	30-14	.460	.231	.694	2.3	1.4	1.3	0.5	0.3	1.6	142	4.7
Knight	31-3	.268	.250	.750	1.2	1.9	1.2	0.3	0.0	0.6	45	1.5
Paul	10-0	.333	.333	.750	0.1	0.0	0.1	0.1	0.0	0.5	8	0.8
Eggers	24-0	.316	.000	.214	1.1	0.1	0.2	0.1	0.1	0.5	15	0.6

1995-96

Team Statistics	G	FG%	3FG%	FT%	R	A	TO	S	B	PF	PTS	PPG
Indiana	31	.472	.391	.703	37.0	16.3	15.1	6.2	3.6	18.3	2349	75.8
Opponents	31	.409	.334	.679	34.9	13.5	14.9	6.9	2.6	22.2	2142	69.1

Player Statistics	G-GS	FG%	3FG%	FT%	R	A	TO	S	B	PF	PTS	PPG
Evans	31-31	.447	.392	.847	7.1	4.1	2.3	1.4	0.6	1.8	658	21.2
Patterson	31-29	.461	.351	.737	6.2	1.5	2.4	0.9	1.4	3.3	350	11.3
Reed	31-28	.455	.455	.802	2.4	4.4	2.4	1.2	0.1	2.0	327	10.5
Lindeman	24-12	.618	.000	.576	4.1	0.5	1.6	0.3	0.9	2.8	235	9.8
Miller	31-25	.469	.314	.693	4.0	2.1	2.0	0.6	0.4	2.1	254	8.2
Wilkerson	17-13	.387	.323	.673	3.5	3.2	2.3	0.9	0.1	2.3	127	7.5
Mujezinovic	30-10	.583	.000	.514	3.8	0.3	1.2	0.5	0.1	2.6	195	6.5
Mandeville	29-4	.425	.375	.846	2.6	0.4	0.7	0.3	0.1	1.8	82	2.8
Eggers	29-3	.482	.476	.273	1.9	0.4	0.5	0.4	0.5	0.7	67	2.3
Rowles	24-0	.417	.125	.563	1.5	1.3	1.1	0.3	0.0	0.8	40	1.7
Moore	3-0	.200	.000	.500	0.7	0.7	1.0	0.7	0.0	1.0	3	1.0
Lemme	16-0	.600	.500	.750	0.2	0.1	0.3	0.1	0.0	0.4	11	0.7

1996-97

Team Statistics	G	FG%	3FG%	FT%	R	A	TO	S	B	PF	PTS	PPG
Indiana	33	.438	.374	.766	35.8	13.9	15.4	6.4	4.0	18.0	2397	72.6
Opponents	33	.422	.333	.688	35.2	13.5	15.2	6.7	2.7	22.5	2247	68.1

Player Statistics	G-GS	FG%	3FG%	FT%	R	A	TO	S	B	PF	PTS	PPG
Patterson	30-25	.470	.256	.758	6.7	1.4	2.6	1.1	1.3	3.0	410	13.7
Guyton	33-29	.435	.386	.851	3.3	3.9	2.2	1.2	0.5	1.3	450	13.6
Reed	33-26	.415	.404	.854	2.9	2.2	1.8	0.6	0.1	1.6	417	12.6
Collier	33-27	.434	.462	.684	5.7	0.7	2.2	0.5	1.0	2.3	310	9.4
Miller	33-17	.463	.360	.730	4.2	0.9	1.7	0.8	0.5	2.0	264	8.0
Lewis	33-14	.369	.316	.798	2.2	2.9	2.1	0.8	0.0	1.7	189	5.7
Mandeville	32-7	.471	.364	.844	2.1	0.3	0.8	0.3	0.2	2.3	113	3.5
Mujezinovic	32-15	.476	.000	.660	2.6	0.5	1.1	0.3	0.2	2.3	111	3.5
Jimenez	28-2	.405	.455	.833	0.6	0.9	0.4	0.5	0.0	0.7	55	2.0
Richardson	22-1	.550	.667	.643	1.2	0.1	0.6	0.1	0.2	0.7	42	1.9
Eggers	30-3	.351	.250	.438	2.0	0.3	0.3	0.3	0.1	0.8	36	1.2
Paul	11-0	.000	.000	.000	0.6	0.0	0.4	0.3	0.0	0.2	0	0.0

1997-98

Team Statistics	G	FG%	3FG%	FT%	R	A	TO	S	B	PF	PTS	PPG
Indiana	32	.491	.380	.731	33.7	17.8	15.3	7.3	3.3	18.3	2457	76.8
Opponents	32	.446	.341	.675	34.8	15.7	15.5	7.6	2.3	19.6	2346	73.3

Player Statistics	G-GS	FG%	3FG%	FT%	R	A	TO	S	B	PF	PTS	PPG
Guyton	32-30	.468	.439	.766	3.5	3.7	2.5	1.2	0.3	1.9	537	16.8
Recker	32-30	.498	.362	.781	3.9	2.8	2.3	1.5	0.4	2.6	408	12.8
Patterson	32-27	.495	.278	.793	5.8	1.4	2.1	0.9	0.9	3.0	402	12.6
Collier	9-7	.563	.000	.667	5.2	1.0	2.1	0.7	1.0	2.0	96	10.7
Gladness	32-26	.542	.000	.577	5.1	1.1	1.6	1.3	0.6	2.1	275	8.6
Turner	28-10	.503	.328	.571	2.8	1.8	1.3	0.3	0.1	0.9	204	7.3
Lewis	32-20	.490	.375	.832	2.5	4.7	2.5	0.9	0.1	2.2	197	6.2
Miller	31-5	.365	.227	.735	2.4	0.7	0.6	0.3	0.3	1.4	117	3.8
Jimenez	30-3	.526	.488	.600	1.0	1.4	0.6	0.4	0.0	1.1	89	3.0
Richardson	28-0	.500	.000	.656	1.3	0.1	0.9	0.1	0.3	1.9	81	2.9
Mandeville	27-1	.438	.167	.714	1.3	0.1	0.4	0.1	0.1	1.1	34	1.3
Eggers	19-0	.368	.000	.429	1.2	0.2	0.2	0.4	0.1	0.5	17	0.9

1998-99

Team Statistics	G	FG%	3FG%	FT%	R	A	TO	S	B	PF	PTS	PPG
Indiana	34	.469	.361	.697	35.3	16.6	14.9	7.6	3.4	17.3	2565	75.4
Opponents	34	.419	.346	.703	36.8	15.0	16.8	6.9	3.8	20.1	2366	69.6
Player Statistics	G-GS	FG%	3FG%	FT%	R	A	TO	S	B	PF	PTS	PPG
Recker	34-33	.428	.364	.747	4.0	2.6	2.3	1.7	0.3	2.4	546	16.1
Guyton	34-34	.455	.406	.755	3.4	2.6	2.3	0.6	0.4	1.2	543	16.0
Haston	34-13	.514	.000	.753	6.5	0.9	1.6	0.6	0.8	2.3	336	9.9
Gladness	33-24	.563	.500	.642	5.4	1.6	1.7	1.3	0.2	2.0	259	7.8
Lewis	33-13	.518	.349	.789	1.8	4.5	2.1	0.7	0.1	1.9	202	6.1
Turner	33-13	.483	.313	.767	2.3	0.9	0.9	0.3	0.2	1.0	182	5.5
Richardson	29-14	.505	.000	.588	2.5	0.3	1.0	0.3	0.8	1.8	130	4.5
Washington	30-14	.441	.000	.579	3.2	0.5	0.8	0.6	0.5	1.8	123	4.1
Fife	33-11	.450	.243	.683	2.1	1.5	1.4	1.0	0.1	1.8	109	3.3
Odle	21-1	.382	.333	.538	1.7	0.2	0.6	0.2	0.1	1.4	65	3.1
Randle El	11-0	.368	.286	.000	0.7	1.0	0.8	0.6	0.0	0.5	16	1.5
Jimenez	32-0	.368	.333	.471	0.8	1.0	0.6	0.4	0.0	0.6	45	1.4
Geyer	9-0	.333	.000	.750	0.7	0.3	0.1	0.0	0.0	0.1	9	1.0

1999-2000

Team Statistics	G	FG%	3FG%	FT%	R	A	TO	S	B	PF	PTS	PPG
Indiana	29	.478	.378	.709	38.9	16.1	14.6	7.5	4.9	18.1	2253	77.7
Opponents	29	.388	.332	.687	36.9	21.0	13.5	6.9	3.5	21.0	1985	68.4
Player Statistics	G-GS	FG%	3FG%	FT%	R	A	TO	S	B	PF	PTS	PPG
Guyton	29-29	.459	.419	.789	2.8	2.3	2.4	1.0	0.4	0.9	570	19.7
Haston	29-27	.496	.000	.730	8.3	1.4	2.1	0.8	1.2	2.9	444	15.3
Lewis	29-19	.519	.379	.774	3.9	5.3	2.5	1.3	0.1	2.7	299	10.3
Washington	29-21	.553	.000	.688	4.8	0.9	0.4	0.8	0.4	2.1	200	6.9
Newton	29-17	.460	1.00	.538	3.8	1.1	1.6	0.4	1.8	1.8	198	6.8
Richardson	28-4	.521	.000	.529	3.6	0.2	1.3	0.3	0.6	2.3	158	5.6
Fife	27-22	.455	.227	.800	3.0	2.0	1.3	1.8	0.2	2.7	133	4.9
Hornsby	24-1	.458	.346	.704	2.1	0.9	0.5	0.4	0.0	1.1	82	3.4
Odle	27-2	.449	.000	.682	2.3	0.5	0.8	0.3	0.1	1.0	77	2.9
Jimenez	29-3	.357	.300	.857	1.4	1.6	0.8	0.5	0.0	0.9	70	2.4
Geyer	10-0	.300	.000	.000	1.0	0.2	0.1	0.2	0.0	0.2	12	1.2
Coverdale	10-0	.375	.600	.500	1.0	0.7	0.1	0.0	0.0	0.4	10	1.0

CHAPTER 20

Mike Davis could hardly have taken over the Indiana head coaching job under more difficult and divisive circumstances. Although many Hoosier fans had begun to resign themselves to the fact that it might be time for legendary coach Bob Knight to retire during the late 1990s, the way Knight was ignominiously dismissed led to widespread anger throughout the Hoosier state. When Davis, one of Knight's assistants, stepped into the role of interim coach after Knight's firing, he immediately became a lightning rod for many of the ill feelings that Indiana fans had toward the IU administration and the way Knight's dismissal was handled. Plus, Davis had to fill the shoes of one of the greatest coaches in the history of the game. Plus, he was the first black coach in Indiana's history. All of that added up to put Davis in a very tough spot.

As a player, Davis had been the 1979 Alabama Mr. Basketball and then played four seasons for the Alabama Crimson Tide. He won Alabama's Hustle Award for four straight seasons and became known as a defensive stopper, while also averaging 10.1 PPG for his career. After playing in Europe and the CBA for several years, Davis got a CBA assistant coaching job under John Treloar and then served as an assistant coach at his alma mater Alabama for two seasons. Then, prior the 1997-98 season, both Treloar and Davis joined Knight's staff at Indiana. When Knight was fired in the fall of 2000, the Indiana players threatened a mass exodus unless the IU administration turned over the team to Davis and Treloar. On an interim basis for one season, Indiana hired Davis as the head coach and Treloar as the associate head coach, and at the end of the season, the administra-tion expected to make a national search for a new coach.

However, Davis pulled off a surprise by leading a young team with no seniors to 21 wins (a record for a first-year coach at Indiana), upsets over two top-five teams, and an NCAA berth. In some circles, Davis was given consideration as the national coach of the year. When the season was over, Indiana removed the interim tag from Davis's title. The next season, the Hoosiers captured the Big Ten crown and made an unexpected run to the NCAA Final Four. Those accomplishments re-ignited the IU faithful and shed the national spotlight on the Indiana basketball program. Many Hoosier fans began to believe that Coach Davis was the man to lead IU back to elite status in the college basketball world.

Unfortunately, Davis's next two seasons in Bloomington were not nearly as successful. Due in part to the recruiting fallout from Knight's firing and in part from some recruiting problems, the Indiana roster became depleted of big men, which became a major factor in leading to two disappointing seasons. In the 2002-03 season, the Hoosiers started out 8-0 and rose to No. 6 in the national polls, but stumbled in the second half of the season and finished sixth in the Big Ten. The 2003-04 season was even worse, as Indiana plummeted to 14-15 overall, the worst record for a Hoosier team in 34 years. Those struggles led to a lot of angry finger-pointing directed toward Coach Davis and his staff. Yet Davis had a highly regarded group of recruits that were coming to the IU campus in the fall of 2004, and there was optimism that they could help turn the situation around.

2000-01

OVERALL RECORD: 21-13

CONFERENCE RECORD: 10-6 (FOURTH PLACE)

TEAM HONORS:

HOOSIER CLASSIC CHAMPION, INDIANA CLASSIC CHAMPION

INDIFIDUAL HONORS:

KIRK HASTON—ALL-AMERICA, ALL-BIG TEN
(FIRST TEAM), ACADEMIC ALL-BIG TEN

JARED JEFFRIES—BIG TEN FRESHMAN OF THE YEAR

KYLE HORNSBY—ACADEMIC ALL-BIG TEN

JARRAD ODLE—ACADEMIC ALL-BIG TEN

The 2000-01 team. First row (left to right): Tom Coverdale, A.J. Moye, Dane Fife, Andre Owens, Kyle Hornsby; Second row: Jeffrey Newton, Kirk Haston, George Leach, Mike Roberts, Jared Jeffries, Jarrad Odle. IU Athletics

As the 2000-01 season dawned, dark storm clouds of controversy and turmoil overshadowed the Indiana basketball program. The storm broke just before the Hoosiers played in the 2000 NCAA tournament the previous spring. In a suspiciously timed article that was released by CNN/*SI* on March 15, just two days before Indiana played Pepperdine in the first round of the NCAA tournament, former IU guard Neil Reed accused coach Bob Knight of verbal and physical abuse, including choking him during a team practice. The IU administration launched its own investigation in response to the charges and unearthed additional complaints that led the university to eventually fine Knight $30,000, suspend him for three games of the 2000-01 season, and put him under a "zero tolerance" policy in which any inappropriate behavior would result in his dismissal as basketball coach. Knight stewed all summer under what he felt was an undefined policy of zero tolerance that made it unclear what his boundaries were as the Indiana head coach. Plus, he felt that he never really got the chance to defend himself against what he viewed as unfair accusations made against him. The situation came to a climax on September 7, when Knight grabbed a student by the arm and reprimanded him after the student spoke disrespectfully to Knight outside of Assembly Hall. Three days later, on September 10, IU president Myles Brand fired Knight for what Brand called multiple violations of the zero tolerance policy culminating in the incident with the student outside of Assembly Hall.

Following Knight's dismissal, several large student rallies occurred to show support for Knight and disdain for the way the IU administration had treated him. After hearing the news that Knight was leaving, several members of the basketball team declared their intention to leave Indiana, unless the administration retained assistant coaches John Treloar and Mike Davis. Privately, IU offered to make Treloar and Davis the co-head coaches on an interim basis, but Treloar stepped forward and said that Davis deserved the job because he had been working so hard to land a head coaching job. IU acceded by naming Davis interim head coach and Treloar interim associate head coach.

With Knight assistants Davis and Treloar retained, all of the Indiana scholarship players decided to stick around. However, even if Coach Knight had still been around to guide this team, its preseason prospects would have been viewed as highly unpredictable. The Hoosiers lost five seniors—A.J. Guyton, Michael Lewis, Luke Jimenez, Lynn Washington and Larry Richardson—and did not have a single senior on the roster for the 2000-01 campaign. Plus, they only had three juniors—Kirk Haston, Dane Fife and Jarrad Odle. That meant the remaining eight roster spots were all filled with freshmen and sophomores, and many of them would have to be counted on to play key roles for the IU squad. Indiana went from being one of the most experienced teams in the Big Ten in 1999-2000, to the youngest and least-experienced squad in the conference in 2000-01. Plus, the Hoosiers were now being led by an interim head coach that had never before held a head coaching job

at any level of basketball. Expectations for the Indiana team were predictably low.

Junior center Kirk Haston was Indiana's top returning scorer at 15.3 PPG, and he was also the top returning rebounder in the conference at 8.3 RPG. The lean 6'10" Haston was a bit of a throw-back center. He complemented a variety of inside post moves with a traditional hook shot that he could hit with deadly accuracy. He could also step out and knock down jump shots facing the basket. While Haston anchored the frontcourt, junior guard Dane Fife was the top returnee in the backcourt. Fife had started 33 out of 60 games during his first two seasons in Bloomington and had become Indiana's best perimeter defender. After averaging over 25 PPG as a senior in high school, Fife only averaged 4.0 PPG during his two years at IU, and Coach Davis wanted Fife to be more aggressive on the offensive end. Other returnees that had shown flashes of strong play the previous season were junior Jarrad Odle and sophomores Jeffrey Newton and Kyle Hornsby.

They were joined by a stellar freshman class headed by Jared Jeffries and A.J. Moye, two of the top recruits in the country. Jeffries, a highly versatile 6'10" forward, was a hometown kid from Bloomington. He was Indiana's Mr. Basketball in 2000, a McDonald's All-American, and the Gatorade National Player of the Year. He selected IU over Duke when the time came for his college choice (although he also considered going straight to the NBA out of high school). A.J. Moye was a stocky 6'3" guard from Atlanta and was Georgia's Mr. Basketball in 2000 and a Parade All-American. He averaged 31 PPG and 14 RPG as a senior and led his high school team to a 33-0 record and a state title during his junior season.

With Haston, Jeffries, Newton and Odle, along with freshmen Mike Roberts and George Leach (who was coming off a redshirt season), Indiana's frontcourt was arguably deeper and more talented than any Hoosier frontcourt had been in over a decade. The team's talent was such that Coach Knight had spent part of the summer designing new wrinkles on offense to take advantage of the athletic new frontcourt. "I had a set-up with this team offensively that would have allowed us to have more defined movements and at the same time enable us to do a lot of new things," said Knight in the weeks after he was fired. With Knight's departure, Coach Davis scrapped the motion

2000-01 TEAM ROSTER

Head coach: Mike Davis (interim)
Assistant coaches: John Treloar, Julius Smith, Dan Panaggio

No.	Player	Hometown	Class	Position	Height
3	Tom Coverdale	Noblesville, IN	So	G	6-2
11	Dane Fife (Capt.)	Clarkston, MI	Jr	G	6-4
35	Kirk Haston (Capt.)	Lobleville, TN	Jr	F/C	6-10
32	Kyle Hornsby	Anacoco, LA	So	G/F	6-5
1	Jared Jeffries	Bloomington, IN	Fr	F	6-10
5	George Leach	Charlotte, NC	Fr	F/C	6-11
2	A.J. Moye	Atlanta, GA	Fr	G	6-3
50	Jeffrey Newton	Atlanta, GA	So	F	6-9
43	Jarrad Odle (Capt.)	Swayzee, IN	Jr	F	6-8
20	Andre Owens	Indianapolis, IN	Fr	G	6-2
33	Mike Roberts	Eugene, OR	Fr	F	6-9

SEASON RESULTS 2000-01

Date	Court	Opponent	Result	Score
11/14/2000	H	Pepperdine	W	80-68
11/17/2000	H	South Alabama	W	70-62
11/22/2000	N1	(#25) Temple	L	61-69
11/24/2000	N1	Texas	L	58-70
11/29/2000	A	Indiana State	L	58-59
12/2/2000	H	Southern Illinois	W	85-63
12/5/2000	A	(#10) Notre Dame	W	86-78
12/8/2000	H	Western Michigan	W	87-59
12/9/2000	H	Ball State	W	65-50
12/16/2000	H	(#24) Charlotte	W	76-72
12/18/2000	H	Missouri	L	63-68
12/22/2000	N2	Kentucky	L	74-88
12/28/2000	N3	Northeastern	W	103-65
12/29/2000	N3	Valparaiso	W	63-60
1/4/2001	A	(#12) Wisconsin	L	46-49
1/7/2001	H	(#1) Michigan State	W	59-58
1/9/2001	A	Michigan	L	64-70
1/17/2001	H	Penn State	W	77-69
1/20/2001	A	Minnesota	L	74-78
1/23/2001	H	Purdue	W	66-55
1/27/2001	A	(#17) Iowa	L	66-71
1/31/2001	A	Ohio State	W	70-67
2/3/2001	A	Penn State	W	85-78
2/11/2001	H	Michigan	W	72-59
2/14/2001	H	Northwestern	W	78-54
2/17/2001	H	(#4) Illinois	L	61-67
2/20/2001	A	(#5) Michigan State	L	57-66
2/24/2001	H	(#17) Wisconsin	W	85-55
2/28/2001	H	Minnesota	W	89-53
3/3/2001	A	Purdue	W	74-58
Big Ten Tournament				
3/9/2001	N4	(#21) Wisconsin	W	64-52
3/10/2001	N4	(#4) Illinois	W	58-56
3/11/2001	N4	Iowa	L	61-63
NCAA Tournament				
3/15/2001	N5	Kent State	L	73-77

1 New York, NY
2 Louisville, KY
3 Indianapolis, IN
4 Chicago, IL
5 San Diego, CA

2000-01 BIG TEN STANDINGS

	W	L	PCT
Michigan St.	13	3	.813
Illinois	13	3	.813
Ohio State	11	5	.688
Indiana	10	6	.625
Wisconsin	9	7	.563
Iowa	7	9	.438
Penn State	7	9	.438
Purdue	6	10	.375
Minnesota	5	11	.313
Michigan	4	12	.250
Northwestern	3	13	.188

offense because he wasn't well-versed in the complicated version of the motion that Knight ran, and in its place, Davis implemented a simpler offense that relied more on spacing the floor and inside-out passing, and less on screening and movement. On the defensive side of the ball, Davis kept Knight's tradition of using a man-to-man defense almost exclusively.

The Hoosiers opened against the same team that had ended their season the previous spring in the NCAA tournament—the Pepperdine Waves. This time IU hosted Pepperdine in Assembly Hall as part of the Preseason NIT. After a shaky first half, Indiana broke loose in the second half for an 80-68 victory. Haston had a game-high 28 points and 14 rebounds, and Jeffries chipped in 15 points, five rebounds, and four assists in his first college game. However, the key for the Hoosiers was Tom Coverdale, who came off the bench for seven points and eight assists. Davis had been struggling throughout the preseason to find a point guard to run the IU offense. Against Pepperdine, Indiana was stagnant and out of sync on offense in the first half until Coverdale came in and started directing traffic and getting the ball to the right spots. "If we didn't have Tom Coverdale tonight we would probably have lost the game," Davis said afterward. He had found his point guard.

Next, Indiana mowed down South Alabama 70-62 to advance to the NIT semifinals in New York City. In the Big Apple, IU was handed consecutive defeats from Temple and Texas to drop to 2-2 for the season. After the NIT, IU returned to the Hoosier state for a tough road game in Terre Haute on November 29, against the Indiana State Sycamores, who had beaten the Hoosiers in Assembly Hall the year before. Sycamore guard Michael Menser hit two three-pointers in the final 8.5 seconds to deliver a stunning 59-58 upset for ISU. After falling to 2-3, the IU squad won its next five games, including victories over 10th-ranked Notre Dame and 24th-ranked Charlotte. Against the Fighting Irish, Coverdale had 30 points and six assists to power Indiana to an 86-78 win in South Bend.

IU followed up its five-game winning streak with two lackluster efforts that resulted in losses to Missouri, 68-63 in Assembly Hall, and Kentucky, 88-74 at Freedom Hall in Louisville. "Maybe the guy they bring here next year will get [these guys] to play hard. I can't do it," said a frustrated Mike Davis after the Kentucky game. "I can't coach this team. What buttons do I push? No way they'll keep me for this job."

After those two setbacks, Indiana crushed Northeastern 103-65 and slipped by Valparaiso 63-60 to win the Hoosier Classic. Against Valpo, Coverdale led IU with 17 points and hit consecutive three-pointers at the end to lift the Hoosiers to victory. Indiana stood at 9-5 entering conference play, where things were expected to get a lot of tougher for the young, inexperienced IU squad.

The veteran Wisconsin Badgers, ranked 12th in the country, gave the Hoosiers a taste of Big Ten basketball in a hostile road environment as Wisconsin came from behind to win 49-46 in front of 17,000 fans in the Kohl Center in Madison. Things didn't get any easier on January 7, when IU hosted No. 1 Michigan State in Bloomington. The Spartans were 12-0 for the season and were the reigning NCAA champions. IU and MSU engaged in the rough defensive struggle on a Sunday afternoon in front of capacity crowd in Assembly Hall and a national television audience on CBS. Michigan State led 58-56 with under 10 seconds left in the game. Indiana ran one final play in which Kirk Haston set a screen, flared out to the wing, caught a pass from Kyle Hornsby and squared up just in time to bury a three-pointer that delivered a thrilling 59-58 Hoosier victory and sent Assembly Hall into a frenzied melee. Haston finished with a game-high 27 points, while Jared Jeffries added 16 points, eight rebounds, and four assists.

Predictably, the young team suffered a letdown after the emotional win over Michigan State. IU lost three of its next five games, with each of the losses coming on the road—to Michigan, Minnesota and Iowa. Against the Golden Gophers and the Hawkeyes, Indiana frittered away double-digit second-half leads. The game against 17th-ranked Iowa on January 27, was especially bitter because the Hoosiers led 43-26 at the half, and the Iowa player who led the second half charge was former Hoosier Luke Recker, who finished with a game-high 27 points. He burned his former teammates down the stretch after Dane Fife got in foul trouble. The Iowa loss put IU at 3-4 in league play and cast a shadow over the team's chances of making the NCAA tournament for the 15th consecutive season.

All-American forward Kirk Haston became one of the Big Ten's most potent big men during the 2000-01 season. The 6'10" Haston showed that he could play both inside and outside and he helped IU put together another surprisingly successful season. IU Athletics

On January 31, in Columbus, Ohio, Kirk Haston made a timely steal and then scored in the lane to lift Indiana to a 70-67 road win over Ohio State. Haston and Coverdale shared game-high honors with 18 points each, while Jeffries had 16 points and eight rebounds. A few days later, Indiana squandered a 20-point lead but notched another road win by beating Penn State 85-78. Then the Hoosiers returned to Bloomington and rolled to easy wins over Michigan and Northwestern to improve their Big Ten record to 7-4. That also moved IU into third place in the conference and renewed the team's postseason hopes. Those hopes were dimmed when No. 4 Illinois beat the Hoosiers 67-61 in Bloomington, and then IU lost 66-57 at Michigan State. However, the IU squad finished strong, whipping No. 17 Wisconsin 85-55 and Minnesota 89-53, and then the Hoosiers went to West Lafayette and trounced archrival Purdue 74-58. IU finished with a Big Ten record of 10-6, the same mark the Hoosiers had earned the season before with a veteran team dominated by five seniors.

In the Big Ten tournament in Chicago, Indiana opened with a 64-52 win over 17th-ranked Wisconsin as the IU frontline of Haston, Newton and Jeffries combined for 44 points and 22 rebounds. In the Hoosiers' next game against fourth-ranked Illinois in the semifinals, the guards moved to the forefront. Coverdale and Fife blanketed Illinois's Frank Williams and exchanged in some animated trash talk with the Big Ten MVP. Williams suffered through a 5-16 shooting night, while Coverdale led all scorers with 17 points. Williams still had a chance to redeem himself when Coverdale missed two free throws with 8.9 seconds left, and Williams got the ball and raced the full length of the court. He leapt from the free throw line and scooped the ball right at the rim, but Haston came out of nowhere and swatted the ball away to assure a 58-56 Indiana win. The next day, Indiana nearly controlled the lead from start to finish in the championship game against Iowa, but freshman guard Brody Boyd (and Indiana native) got hot for the Hawkeyes down the stretch and buried several crucial three-pointers that gave Iowa a 63-61 triumph.

Despite the Iowa loss, Indiana had won five games in a row leading up to that contest and seven of their final ten games overall, including three wins over ranked teams. In the AP poll following the Big Ten tournament, Indiana entered the poll for the first time in the season at No. 20. IU was also awarded with a No. 4 seed in the West Regional of the NCAA tournament, where the Hoosiers were matched up

against MAC champion Kent State, the 11th seed. The streaking Hoosiers were considered a dangerous team and they were viewed as one of the potential sleepers of the tournament by many prognosticators. The IU players were eager to bounce back from the embarrassing 77-57 upset to Pepperdine the year before. Nevertheless, the game against undersized Kent State played out very similar to the title game of the Big Ten tournament against Iowa. IU controlled the lead for much of the contest, but let it slip away down the stretch. Kent State point guard Trevor Huffman took over the game in the final minutes, while Indiana point guard Tom Coverdale injured his hip and then fouled out. He could only watch helplessly as his Hoosier teammates let the game slip away 77-73. IU's two best defensive players, Fife and Jeffries, also struggled with foul trouble in the second half.

The loss to Kent State was Indiana's fifth first-round exit in the NCAA tournament in seven years. Prior to the tournament, many Indiana fans and college basketball analysts had called upon the IU administration to take the interim tag away from Mike Davis's title in order to reward him for leading the Hoosiers to a successful season. However, school officials remained steadfast in their determination to wait until the season was over before making a decision about the head coaching job, which helped fuel speculation that they were going to go after a higher profile coach, such as Rick Pitino, Rick Majerus, or former IU All-American Steve Alford, the head coach at Iowa. Less than a week after Indiana was ousted from the tournament, the IU administration announced that Davis would become the permanent head coach by signing a new four-year contract.

It was a season that began with the cataclysmic firing of Bob Knight and witnessed a talented but inexperienced Hoosier team struggle through the nonconference season and the beginning of Big Ten

INDIANA'S RANKING IN THE 2000-01 ASSOCIATED PRESS POLLS

PS	11/13	11/20	11/27	12/4	12/11	12/18	12/25	1/1	1/8	1/15	1/22	1/29	2/5	2/12	2/19	2/26	3/5	3/12
—	—	—	—	—	—	—	—	—	—	—	—	—	—	—	—	—	—	20

play. However, IU came on strong at the end of the conference schedule and also played some of their best basketball in the Big Ten tournament. Of course, the NCAA tournament upset to Kent State was frustrating, but the general sentiment in the Hoosier state seemed to be that it was a successful season.

Kirk Haston emerged as one of the top big men in the conference, averaging 19.0 points and 8.7 rebounds to earn All-America and first-team All-Big Ten honors. Freshman Jared Jeffries started every game, averaged 13.8 points and 6.9 rebounds, and was named Big Ten Freshman of the Year. Tom Coverdale, after being relegated to the end of the bench as a freshman, earned the starting job at point guard as a sophomore and averaged 10.7 points and 4.8 assists. With no seniors and only three juniors, the Indiana squad looked like it was going to enter the 2001-02 season as one of the top-ranked teams in the country. Unfortunately, Indiana's prospects changed when Haston decided to enter his name in the NBA draft. The Charlotte Hornets selected him with the 16th pick of the first round. He ended up spending a couple of seasons on the bench for the Hornets before being released.

2001-02

FOR THE COMMENTARY AND STATISTICS FOR THE 2001-02 SEASON, PLEASE SEE CHAPTER 7, "2001-02: A RETURN TO THE INDIANA TRADITION."

2002-03

OVERALL RECORD: 21-13

CONFERENCE RECORD: 8-8 (SIXTH PLACE)

TEAM HONORS:

MAUI INVITATIONAL CHAMPION

INDIVIDUAL HONORS:

JEFF NEWTON—ALL-BIG TEN (FIRST TEAM)

KYLE HORNSBY—BIG TEN MEDAL OF HONOR, ACADEMIC ALL-BIG TEN

JASON STEWART—ACADEMIC ALL-BIG TEN

Coming off a season in which IU won its first Big Ten title in nine years and made a phenomenal postseason run to finish as the runner-up in the 2002 NCAA tournament, a buoyant attitude prevailed in Bloomington heading into the 2002-03 season. The Hoosiers' upset of No. 1 Duke and berth in the 2002 Final Four had shined the national spotlight on the Indiana program and heightened expectations for the future. And the Hoosier fans weren't the only ones who were excited. Indiana's returning lettermen had gotten a taste for success and hungered for another helping. They hit the gym hard in their self-motivated summer workouts in order to prepare for another successful season.

"When you have the year that we did last year, the worst thing that can happen is for a team to get complacent," said coach Mike Davis, before the start of the 2002-03 season. "Our guys have worked so hard this summer, lifting and staying in shape. With the schedule that we have coming up, we had better be ready."

Leading the charge in the weight room and individual workouts were the team's three seniors: Kyle Hornsby, Tom Coverdale, and Jeff Newton. All three had stepped up and starred during key moments in the Hoosiers' NCAA tournament run. Hornsby was named to the Final Four all-tournament team. Coverdale was the MVP of the East Regional after leading IU to wins over Duke and Kent State. Newton had 19 points and six rebounds to spur the Hoosiers past Oklahoma in the Final Four. Those three were joined by two juniors, A.J. Moye and

The 2002-03 team. First row (left to right): A.J. Moye, Marshall Strickland, Ryan Tapak, Kyle Hornsby, Tom Coverdale, Donald Perry, Mark Johnson, Bracey Wright; Second row: Sean Kline, Jason Stewart, Daryl Pegram, Jeff Newton, George Leach, Mike Roberts, Joe Haarman, Roderick Wilmont. IU Athletics

George Leach, who had also provided key contributions during the NCAA run. Moye, a 6'3" small forward, provided a huge spark off the bench in the upset of Duke, including an instantly legendary block of Duke's 6'8" Carlos Boozer in the second half that helped preserve a pivotal Hoosier rally. At the end of the first half against Oklahoma, the 6'11" Leach had played six critical minutes in which he threw down a thunderous dunk and blocked two shots to help keep IU in the game heading into halftime.

Those holdovers were also bolstered by a highly ranked recruiting class, led by 6'3" Bracey Wright and 6'2" Marshall Strickland, two of the most widely coveted guards in the country. Both were excellent athletes, high scorers and strong outside shooters. Wright was recruited as a shooting guard, while Strickland was groomed to be Indiana's point guard of the future. Their arrival gave Indiana a lot of talent and depth in the backcourt. They joined Coverdale, Hornsby, and Moye to give Coach Davis five quality guards to rotate in his three-guard lineup. However,

the one guard that Indiana lost was graduating senior Dane Fife, who was the Big Ten's Defensive Player of the Year in 2002. Fife had been IU's go-to guy on the defensive end, as he almost always matched up against the other team's best perimeter player. The Indiana squad ended up badly missing Fife's defensive presence in the backcourt.

In the frontcourt, IU lost both its starters. Jarrad Odle, the Hoosiers' third leading scorer, graduated, while Jared Jeffries, Indiana's leading scorer and rebounder and the 2002 Big Ten MVP, made the jump to the NBA after his sophomore season. Defensively, Jeffries was to the frontcourt what Fife was to the backcourt, and on the offensive end, the Hoosiers often ran things through Jeffries, who could utilize a variety of post moves or adeptly pass out of the post when he was double-teamed. IU's frontcourt duties now fell to Newton and Leach, as well as two players that were coming off redshirt seasons: sophomore Mike Roberts and freshman Sean Kline. Although Newton would step up and have an excellent senior season, the loss of Jeffries ended up being a heavy blow to the Indiana offense, which would never find the same kind of rhythm that it had demonstrated with Jeffries in the post the season before.

Nevertheless, Indiana was ranked 21st in the nation in the preseason and was favored, along with Michigan State, for the top spot in the Big Ten. The Hoosiers tipped off the season in Hawaii at the Maui Invitational. George Leach dominated the paint with 19 points, 16 rebounds, and four blocks as IU dominated UMass 84-71 in the Maui opener. All five Hoosier starters scored in double figures. The next night, Indiana built a 17-point second-half lead over 20th-ranked Gonzaga and then held on for a 76-75 win. In the championship game, the Hoosiers played their third game in three days, and several of the veterans showed signs of fatigue. However, in the second half, Indiana's freshmen carried the team to a 70-63 win over Virginia. Marshall Strickland came off the bench to score 15 points, all in the second half, while Bracey Wright scored a game-high 21 points and was named tournament MVP. It was only the second time in the history of the tournament that a freshman had received that honor.

Back in Bloomington on December 1, Indiana smothered North Texas 84-58 as Wright scored 21 points for the second straight game. Next, in a rematch of the 2002 NCAA title game, 10th-ranked Indiana faced No. 9 Maryland in Conseco Fieldhouse in Indianapolis as part of the Big Ten-ACC Challenge. Both teams struggled with their shooting, but the game had the intensity of a tournament matchup in March. Coverdale took over the game in the final minutes of regulation and in the overtime period, hit several big three-pointers and orchestrated low-post opportunities for Jeff Newton and Sean Kline as IU prevailed 80-74 in OT. Coverdale had 30 points, six rebounds, and five assists. Newton had 13 points and 14 rebounds, and Wright added 19 points, seven rebounds, and six assists. Strickland came off the bench for four points and six assists and Kline had 10 points and five rebounds in a reserve role, including some important free throws late in the game.

After the Maryland game, IU steamrolled both Illinois-Chicago and Vanderbilt in Assembly Hall. Then, the Hoosiers played the Purdue Boilermakers on December 14, at the RCA Dome in Indianapolis.

2002-03 TEAM ROSTER

Head coach: Mike Davis
Assistant coaches: John Treloar, Jim Thomas, Ben McDonald

No.	Player	Hometown	Class	Position	Height
3	Tom Coverdale (Capt.)	Noblesville, IN	Sr	G	6-2
32	Kyle Hornsby (Capt.)	Anacoco, LA	Sr	G/F	6-5
21	Mark Johnson	Oregon, WI	So	G	6-2
23	Sean Kline	Huntington, IN	Fr	F	6-8
5	George Leach	Charlotte, NC	Jr	C	6-11
2	A.J. Moye	Atlanta, GA	Jr	G/F	6-3
50	Jeff Newton (Capt.)	Atlanta, GA	Sr	F	6-9
31	Daryl Pegram	Los Angeles, CA	Fr	F	6-9
12	Donald Perry	Tallulah, LA	So	G	6-2
33	Mike Roberts	Eugene, OR	So	F	6-9
40	Jason Stewart	Edwardsport, IN	Jr	F	6-8
22	Marshall Strickland	Winfield, MD	Fr	G	6-2
34	Ryan Tapak	Indianapolis, IN	So	G	6-2
10	Roderick Wilmont	Miramar, FL	Rs	G	6-4
4	Bracey Wright	The Colony, TX	Fr	G	6-3

SEASON RESULTS 2002-03

Date	Court	Opponent	Result	Score
11/25/2002	N1	Massachusetts	W	84-71
11/26/2002	N1	(# 20) Gonzaga	W	76-75
11/27/2002	N1	Virginia	W	70-63
12/1/2002	H	North Texas	W	84-58
12/3/2002	N2	(#9) Maryland	W	80-74
12/7/2002	H	Illinois-Chicago	W	91-62
12/9/2002	H	Vanderbilt	W	73-56
12/14/2002	N2	Purdue	W	66-63
12/21/2002	N3	(#18) Kentucky	L	64-70
12/28/2002	A	Temple	L	64-71
12/31/2002	A	Ball State	W	76-62
1/4/2003	H	Charlotte	W	70-60
1/8/2003	H	Penn State	W	78-65
1/11/2003	A	Ohio State	L	69-81
1/15/2003	H	Northwestern	W	71-57
1/18/2003	H	(#8) Illinois	W	74-66
1/21/2003	H	Ohio State	W	69-51
1/25/2003	A	Purdue	L	47-69
1/28/2003	A	Michigan State	L	54-61
2/1/2003	A	(#8) Louisville	L	76-95
2/5/2003	A	Northwestern	L	61-74
2/8/2003	H	Michigan State	L	62-67
2/12/2003	H	Michigan	W	63-49
2/15/2003	A	Wisconsin	L	59-71
2/19/2003	A	Iowa	W	79-63
2/25/2003	A	(#18) Illinois	L	54-80
3/1/2003	H	Iowa	W	91-88
3/4/2003	H	Minnesota	W	74-70
3/8/2003	A	Penn State	L	66-74
Big Ten Tournament				
3/13/2003	N4	Penn State	W	77-49
3/14/2003	N4	Michigan	W	63-56
3/15/2003	N4	(#13) Illinois	L	72-73
NCAA Tournament				
3/21/2003	N5	Alabama	W	67-62
3/23/2003	N5	(#4) Pittsburgh	L	52-74

1 Lahaina, Hawaii
2 Indianapolis, IN
3 Louisville, KY
4 Chicago, IL
5 Boston, MA

2002-03 BIG TEN STANDINGS

	W	L	PCT
Wisconsin	12	4	.750
Illinois	11	5	.688
Michigan State	10	6	.625
Purdue	10	6	.625
Michigan	10	6	.625
Indiana	8	8	.500
Minnesota	8	8	.500
Iowa	7	9	.438
Ohio State	7	9	.438
Northwestern	3	13	.188
Penn State	2	14	.125

For three seasons, point guard Tom Coverdale played the role of Indiana's primary catalyst. When the book closed on Cov's career at the end of the 2002-03 season, he finished as one of the most effective floor leaders in school history. IU Athletics

It was an unorthodox nonconference game that was being played because the traditional archrivals were only set to play each other once during the Big Ten conference season. Newton recorded his fifth straight double-double with 16 points and 12 rebounds to lead seventh-ranked Indiana to a 66-63 victory. Leach chipped in 11 points and 14 rebounds as the Hoosiers beat the Boilermakers on the glass 49-35.

A week after the in-state rivalry game with Purdue, the Hoosiers went down to Louisville to face 18th-ranked Kentucky in the annual border war with the Wildcats. In a fierce struggle with multiple second-half lead changes and momentum shifts, IU took the lead 64-63 with 0:25 remaining on a rebound

basket from Wright off of a missed free throw. Kentucky's Marquis Estill scored inside with 12 seconds to go to give the lead back to Kentucky 65-64. IU ran an isolation play for Wright, who got mobbed by Wildcats on the baseline and missed a jumper in the final seconds. Davis thought Wright was fouled and rushed onto the court to argue his point with the referees. That earned him two quick technical fouls and an ejection. When the dust had settled and all the free throws were shot, the final score was Kentucky 70, Indiana 64. It was the Hoosiers' first loss of the season after eight straight victories.

IU finished out the preconference season by losing a tough 71-64 game at Temple, beating Ball State 76-62 in Muncie, and outlasting Charlotte 70-60 in Assembly Hall. As a result, Indiana entered Big Ten play with a 10-2 record and ranked 15th in the county. The Hoosiers won two of their first three conference games, beating bottom-feeders Penn State and Northwestern in Assembly Hall, but falling to Ohio State in Columbus. That set up IU's first big game of the conference season as the 18th-ranked Hoosiers hosted No. 8 Illinois on January 18, in Bloomington. IU was without Bracey Wright, who had aggravated an old back injury in the Ohio State game. However, Jeff Newton put the Hoosiers on his back and carried them to a 74-66 win with 28 points, eight rebounds, and five blocked shots. Meanwhile, Newton's counterpart, Illinois forward Brian Cook (the leading scorer in the conference at the time) fouled out with 15 points on 7-17 shooting.

The Hoosiers followed the Illinois win with a 69-51 triumph over Ohio State on January 21, in Assembly Hall, as Marshall Strickland came off the bench to lead IU with 15 points. The win over OSU gave Indiana a conference record of 4-1 and an overall record of 14-3, and the Hoosiers were ranked 14th in country. That was the pinnacle of the season. Indiana would go 7-10 the rest of the way, including 4-7 in the team's remaining Big Ten games.

After the Ohio State game, the Hoosiers faced its most brutal stretch of the league schedule with seven of their next nine games on the road. It started with an embarrassing 69-47 loss to Purdue in West Lafayette. It was the first time the Boilermakers had beaten the Hoosiers since 1999. Next, Indiana went to Michigan State and took the Spartans down to the wire, but for the second straight year, Indiananative

Adam Ballinger hit a late three-pointer in East Lansing to clinch a win for MSU. The final score was 61-54. Bracey Wright returned to the IU lineup for the first time against the Spartans, but scored only four points. Next, Indiana faced the daunting task of taking on No. 8 Louisville, one of the hottest teams in the country with 14 straight wins, in a nonconference game in Louisville. IU led 43-35 at the half and controlled the game and the tempo for the first 32 minutes, but when the game slipped away, it happened quickly and with tremendous force. The Cardinals (who shot just 29 percent from the field in the first half) caught fire down the stretch and turned up the heat with their full-court press to finish the game on a 17-0 run that led to a 95-76 victory.

The Purdue, Michigan State and Louisville games were all contests that the Hoosiers weren't expected to win, although Coach Davis had hoped to steal at least one or two of those games. However, the Hoosiers followed up those three losses by dropping two games that they were supposed to win. Northwestern whipped Indiana 74-61 in Evanston. It was the Wildcats first win over the Hoosiers since 1988. Then IU returned to Bloomington and dropped a 67-62 cliffhanger to Michigan State in overtime. The five-game skid dropped IU to 14-8 overall and 4-5 in league play, and robbed the Hoosiers of the confident swagger they had shown early in the season.

The Hoosiers recovered a little pride by going 4-3 over their remaining seven conference games, but that stretch also included a humiliating 80-54 loss at Illinois and a disappointing 74-66 defeat to lowly Penn State in the final game of the regular season, which left Indiana with an 8-8 Big Ten record and a sixth-place finish in the conference. Senior guards Tom Coverdale and Kyle Hornsby struggled terribly during the Big Ten season and drew a lot of heat for Indiana's disappointing finish. Coverdale shot 36 per-

cent from the field during the 2003 Big Ten season (compared to 45 percent during the 2002 Big Ten season), while Hornsby shot 39 percent during the 2003 campaign (compared to 46 percent during 2002). Hornsby also lost his starting job to freshman Marshall Strickland in the middle of the conference season.

Fighting for an NCAA tournament berth, Indiana showed some renewed life during the Big Ten tournament in Chicago. Coverdale and Newton sparked IU to a 77-49 blowout over Penn State in the first round; Newton led all scorers with 23 points. In the second round, A.J. Moye exploded for 18 points, while Newton and Coverdale chipped in 15 apiece, in a 63-56 win over Michigan. In the semifinals, Coverdale led a late charge and finished with 21 points, but the Hoosiers lost 73-72 to 13th-ranked Illinois, the eventual champion of the league tournament.

Indiana's 20-12 record resulted in a No. 7 seed in the NCAA tournament, and in the first round, the Hoosiers were matched up against Davis's alma mater, Alabama, which like IU, had started the season strong but faltered during February and March. Playing in Boston, the Crimson Tide opened a 35-24 lead at the half, but Coverdale led IU back into the game in the second half. IU led 55-51 with 3:55 remaining when A.J. Moye invoked images of his Carlos Boozer block against Duke in the 2002 tournament by rejecting an inside basket from Alabama's 6'8" Erwin Dudley. When Alabama missed a potential game-tying three-pointer with only 0:23 remaining, Coverdale grabbed the rebound and a Moye dunk on the other end sealed a 67-62 Indiana victory. Coverdale had 23 points and eight assists. Two days later, Indiana got manhandled by a big, strong Pittsburgh team, the No. 2 seed, and lost 74-52. The Panthers, who were ranked fourth, keyed on Coverdale, whom they viewed as the catalyst of the Hoosier attack, and held him to just six points.

INDIANA'S RANKING IN THE 2002-03 ASSOCIATED PRESS POLLS

PS	11/19	11/26	12/3	12/10	12/17	12/24	12/31	1/7	1/14	1/21	1/28	2/4	2/11	2/18	2/25	3/4	3/11	3/18
21	22	19	10	7	6	10	17	15	18	14	19	—	—	—	—	—	—	—

In the press conference following the loss to Pittsburgh, Coach Davis went back to when the team was 8-0 in December and said that was when the problems began to creep in. He said the team began hearing how good they were and it ruined some of the young players and began to foster an attitude of selfishness on the team, which Davis cited as the main factor in the team's eventual demise.

In his final press conference of the season, Davis also took a moment to tip his hat to his floor leader from his first three seasons at IU. "It has been a great pleasure to coach Tom Coverdale," said Davis. "Tom had a slump this year that he went through for about a month, but other than that, he has fought his heart out playing basketball. And some nights if it wasn't for Tom Coverdale, we probably wouldn't have scored at all." Coverdale finished his career as one of the most effective point guards in Indiana history. Even though he didn't hardly play at all his freshman year, he ended up third among the school's all-time assist leaders, behind only four-year players Michael Lewis and Quinn Buckner. He also finished 28th (and Newton finished 29th) on Indiana's all-time career scoring list, which put him ahead of fellow point guards Buckner and Lewis.

2003-04

OVERALL RECORD: 14-15

CONFERENCE RECORD: 7-9 (SEVENTH PLACE)

The Indiana basketball program entered its 104th season with a mixed bag of emotions. During the summer of 2003, coach Mike Davis had put together a group of five recruits that was arguably the best recruiting class in college basketball, including three outstanding players from the state of Indiana. Unfortunately, none of those five players would be arriving on the IU campus until the fall of 2004 and Indiana's immediate prospects for the 2003-04 season were fairly dim. The Hoosiers were generally expected to be relegated to the second division of the Big Ten. The conference's preseason media rankings predicted a seventh-place finish for IU. There was some optimism in Bloomington among the players and the coaches that the team could do better than that, but any predictions involved a lot of "ifs" and required that a lot of players step up to do things they hadn't done in the past.

The biggest question mark for Indiana was in the frontcourt. Over the previous three seasons, Indiana had lost Kirk Haston and Jared Jeffries to the NBA draft and Jeff Newton to graduation. That left senior center George Leach as the only experienced big man left on the Hoosiers' roster, and Leach had yet to show that he could be a consistent force in the paint. He started 30 out of 32 games as a junior and played 22.5 minutes per game, but only averaged 6.5 points and pulled down 5.5 rebounds per game despite having a well-sculpted 6'11" frame and a long wingspan. Leach's specialty had been blocked shots, as he had averaged 1.8 blocks per game during his first three years in Bloomington. However, his post defense was a problem at times, since he often allowed opponents to catch the ball deep in the lane and then went for the block, which landed him with frequent foul trouble. Nevertheless, Leach had been a solid frontcourt role player, but as a senior, he would have to be Indiana's primary inside presence on both sides of the floor, and that made a lot of IU fans nervous.

Junior Mike Roberts and sophomore Sean Kline were expected to battle for the other starting frontcourt spot. Both had seen minimal time on the floor the previous season so they were both unknown entities. Roberts lacked athleticism but had shown good fundamentals and toughness. Kline had once been a top recruit. He ran the floor well and possessed good offensive skills around the basket, but his post defense was a big question mark because he was foul-prone and not very good at denying the ball.

In addition to Leach, Roberts and Kline, the IU frontcourt was expected to get some help from two new freshmen recruits—Patrick Ewing, Jr. (the son of former NBA superstar Patrick Ewing) and Jessan Gray-Ashley. Knowing that the Hoosiers were going to be thin up front for the 2003-04 season, Coach Davis had searched far and wide for several frontcourt recruits during the summer and fall of 2002. He came close to landing a couple of blue-chippers such as

The 2003-04 team. First row (left to right): Errek Suhr, Marshall Strickland, George Leach, A.J. Moye, Ryan Tapak, Donald Perry, Mark Johnson; Second row: Bracey Wright, Patrick Ewing, Jr., Jason Stewart, Jessan Gray-Ashley, Mike Roberts, Roderick Wilmont, Sean Kline. IU Athletics

Luol Deng and Charlie Villanueva. However, when those two (as well as a few other high school and JUCO big men) decided to go elsewhere, Indiana ended up signing Gray-Ashley in the fall and Ewing, Jr. the following spring. Both were big man projects with a large upside down the road. Neither was expected to provide a lot of immediate help, but Ewing was expected to get an opportunity for some minutes because of his outstanding athleticism and energy. One other Hoosier who was expected to help in the frontcourt was senior A.J. Moye. Although best suited to play small forward, the 6'3" Moye was a strong, stocky player who had filled in at power forward the previous season and was expected to see some additional minutes as that spot again. By the start of the Big Ten season, Moye would be the Hoosiers' starting power forward and would play that role almost exclusively throughout the rest of the season.

If the frontcourt was the Hoosiers' biggest weakness, then the backcourt was supposed to be Indiana's greatest strength. Although IU lost Tom Coverdale

and Kyle Hornsby to graduation, sophomores Bracey Wright and Marshall Strickland returned. Wright had started every game he played in as a freshman and had led the Hoosiers in scoring at 16.2 PPG and was the team's third leading rebounder as 5.0 RPG. He entered the 2003-04 campaign as the top returning scorer in the Big Ten and was considered to be one of the best shooting guards in college basketball. After having off-season back surgery, Wright was also expected to regain his full explosiveness, which meant that he could be a threat to create off the dribble in addition to his forte as an outside shooter.

Wright's backcourt running mate Strickland had become a starter midway through his freshman year and had been a solid guard that played within himself, hit the open shot, and showed good poise on the floor. With Coverdale gone, Strickland was the heir apparent at point guard. Other guards that rounded out the deep backcourt were redshirt freshman Roderick Wilmont, a 6'4" shooting guard that was an outstanding athlete, juniors Ryan Tapak and Mark Johnson, two sharp-shooters who were former walk-

2003-04 TEAM ROSTER

Head coach: Mike Davis
Assistant coaches: John Treloar, Ben McDonald, Thad Fitzpatrick

No.	Player	Hometown	Class	Position	Height
3	Patrick Ewing, Jr.	Marietta, GA	Fr	F	6-8
44	Jessan Gray-Ashley	Davenport, IA	Fr	F/C	6-10
21	Mark Johnson	Oregon, WI	Jr	G	6-2
23	Sean Kline	Huntington, IN	So	F	6-8
5	George Leach (Capt.)	Charlotte, NC	Sr	C	6-11
2	A.J. Moye (Capt.)	Atlanta, GA	Sr	G/F	6-3
12	Donald Perry	Tallulah, LA	Jr	G	6-2
33	Mike Roberts	Eugene, OR	Jr	F	6-9
40	Jason Stewart	Edwardsport, IN	Sr	F	6-8
11	Errek Suhr	Bloomington, IN	Fr	G	5-8
22	Marshall Strickland	Winfield, MD	So	G	6-2
34	Ryan Tapak	Indianapolis, IN	Jr	G	6-2
10	Roderick Wilmont	Miramar, FL	Fr	G	6-4
4	Bracey Wright	The Colony, TX	So	G	6-3

SEASON RESULTS 2003-04

Date	Court	Opponent	Result	Score
11/21/2003	H	UNC-Greenboro	W	71-63
11/24/2003	A	Vanderbilt	L	60-73
11/29/2003	N1	Xavier	W	80-77
12/2/2003	A	Wake Forest	L	67-100
12/6/2003	H	(#4) Missouri	L	58-63
12/10/2003	A	Notre Dame	W	66-63
12/13/2003	H	Butler	W	62-50
12/20/2003	N1	(#2) Kentucky	L	41-80
12/23/2003	H	Morehead State	W	77-57
12/29/2003	A	North Texas	W	79-70
1/3/2004	H	Temple	L	50-59
1/6/2004	A	Wisconsin	L	45-79
1/11/2004	A	Michigan	W	59-57
1/17/2004	H	Northwestern	W	73-62
2/20/2004	A	Ohio State	W	69-61
1/24/2004	A	Minnesota	W	86-81
1/27/2004	H	(#21) Purdue	W	63-58
1/31/2004	A	Michigan State	L	84-72
2/3/2004	H	Illinois	L	49-51
2/7/2004	H	Iowa	L	82-84
2/11/2004	A	Penn State	W	75-56
2/14/2004	A	Purdue	L	56-71
2/18/2004	H	Minnesota	L	71-73
2/21/2004	H	Ohio State	L	56-59
2/25/2004	A	Northwestern	L	59-63
3/3/2004	H	Michigan	W	61-56
3/6/2004	H	(#17) Wisconsin	L	50-72
Big Ten Tournament				
3/11/2004	N1	Ohio State	W	83-69
3/12/2004	N1	(#12) Illinois	L	59-71

1 Indianapolis, IN

2003-04 BIG TEN STANDINGS

	W	L	PCT
Illinois	13	3	0.813
Wisconsin	12	4	0.750
Michigan State	12	4	0.750
Iowa	9	7	0.563
Michigan	8	8	0.500
Northwestern	8	8	0.500
Purdue	7	9	0.438
Indiana	7	9	0.438
Ohio State	6	10	0.375
Minnesota	3	13	0.188
Penn State	3	13	0.188

ons, and Errek Suhr, a 5'8" freshman walk-on who was a hard-nosed competitor and a heady point guard.

For the fifth straight season, Indiana played one of the most challenging preconference schedules in the nation. And this time the schedule included four tough road games and two neutral site appearances. The Hoosiers opened the season by winning two of their first three games. They surrendered a 17-point second-half lead but hung on to beat UNC-Greensboro 71-64 as Wright and Strickland combined for 40 points. They got drubbed 73-60 by Vanderbilt down in Memorial Gymnasium—a very tough venue to steal a road game. The Commodores' Matt Freije became the first of many inside players to have a career night against the Hoosiers as he posted 32 points and 13 rebounds. Next, the Hoosiers played Xavier in the Wooden Tradition at Conseco Fieldhouse in Indianapolis. The Musketeers, who are based in Cincinnati, had five Indiana natives on their roster (IU only had four) including 2003 Indiana Mr. Basketball Justin Cage, and they were ranked 26th in the AP poll. Bracey Wright shot down the Musketeers with 27 points in an 80-77 IU victory in overtime. Wright scored 13 of his points in the final minutes of regulation and OT. However, Indiana suffered a key setback in the Xavier game as George Leach injured his left knee and would end up missing IU's next nine games.

In their first three contests, Indiana had 28 assists and 45 turnovers. It was blatantly apparent just how much the Hoosiers missed point guard and floor leader Tom Coverdale, and it also appeared that sophomore Marshall Strickland wasn't quite ready to pick up where Coverdale left off. Over the next eight games, coach Mike Davis experimented with four different players as the starting point guard—Strickland, Wright, Ryan Tapak and Donald Perry.

Without Leach in lineup, the Hoosiers went 4-4 in their remaining preconference games. The only win over a high-quality opponent was a 66-63 victory at Notre Dame in which Tapak came off the bench and scored eight points including the game-winning three-pointer. Unfortunately, that eight-game stretch also included a 100-67 blowout at the hands of No. 18 Wake Forest in Winston-Salem, North Carolina, and an even more embarrassing 80-41 whipping from No. 2 Kentucky (No. 1 in ESPN/USA Today Coaches

Poll) in the RCA Dome in Indianapolis. Plus, it included Assembly Hall losses to No. 4 Missouri and unranked Temple (who was 4-5 at the time). Against Missouri, IU blew a big second-half lead as the Tigers finished the game on a 15-0 run and prevailed 63-58. Against Temple, in the final game of the preconference schedule, the Hoosiers stood outside and launched 39 three-pointers (and made only eight) over the Temple zone. The Owls controlled the game from start to finish and won 59-50.

The Temple loss gave the Hoosiers a 6-5 overall record and put them in a position where they had to post an excellent Big Ten record if they wanted to have a shot at an at-large bid in the NCAA tournament. Heading into conference play, Davis said that his goal was to win the Big Ten. The quest didn't start well. Defending champion Wisconsin destroyed IU 79-45 in Madison on January 6, as Bracey Wright (who was averaging 22 PPG at the time) was held to just seven points on 2-15 shooting from the field. The Hoosiers, now 6-6 overall, were getting killed in the paint, and Davis was still struggling to find a floor leader who could make the offense run in rhythm. Plus, after taking three beatings by over 30 points, the team had developed a severe confidence problem. Indiana's prospects looked bleak, and the Hoosier faithful had begun to turn on Davis, blaming him for Indiana's lackluster play.

"The pressure is always on at Indiana—all the time, every game," said Davis. "[IU fans] live and die with every game. …Every time we lose it's my fault. That's part of the job. …When you take a position like this, it's a part of it, and you have to understand that."

However, just when it looked like Indiana's season was going down the drain, the team miraculously bounced back and won five straight games, including three on the road. George Leach returned to the lineup and at least provided some size and experience on the inside, Bracey Wright started sharing the ball more, and Marshall Strickland broke out of his season-long shooting slump and began contributing some solid performances. The first win was a 59-57 triumph at Michigan sparked by a 14-point, five-rebound, and five-assist performance from Strickland and big efforts from Rod Wilmont and Sean Kline off the bench. Next, Indiana beat Northwestern 73-62 in Assembly Hall as 10 different Hoosiers scored in the

game. Then IU went back on the road and beat Ohio State and Minnesota. Against the Golden Gophers, the IU squad blew an 18-point lead but pulled out an 86-81 win in overtime as five Hoosiers scored in double figures, led by Wright with 22 and Moye with 20. Next, IU capped off the five-game winning streak by beating archrival Purdue, ranked 21st in the country, in Bloomington. Wright drove to the basket and dished to Wilmont for two consecutive three-pointers in the final minute to lift Indiana to a 63-58 victory. The win put Indiana in first place in the Big Ten at 5-1 and with three conference road wins under their belt and six of their final ten games being played at home, the Hoosiers suddenly found themselves in the catbird seat in the Big Ten race. Three weeks earlier, Indiana fans were calling for Mike Davis's head, and now he was the leading candidate in the early race for the Big Ten Coach of the Year.

Unfortunately, Indiana's remarkable turnaround didn't last. The team would only win two more conference games the rest of the season. Michigan State brought the winning streak to an end with an 84-72 win over IU in East Lansing, as Spartan center Paul Davis went off with 32 points. Then Indiana blew second-half leads against both Illinois and Iowa and lost to both teams by two points in Assembly Hall. The Hoosiers momentarily stopped the carnage by winning 75-56 at Penn State. Next, IU lost four straight, including defeats at Purdue and Northwestern and two more close losses in Assembly Hall to second-division teams Ohio State and Minnesota. In both of those games, the Hoosiers once again gave away leads in the final minutes. Also, during the Purdue game, Sean Kline suffered a season-ending knee injury, which struck another blow to Indiana's already-thin frontcourt.

IU salvaged a 61-56 win over Michigan on March 3, but 17th-ranked Wisconsin came to Bloomington three days later and crushed IU 72-50 to give the Hoosiers a 7-9 conference record and a seventh place finish in the Big Ten. It was only the third time in 34 years that Indiana finished with a losing record in the conference. The Hoosiers also ended the regular season with a 13-14 overall record, which was the first time since 1969-70 that an Indiana team had a losing record overall.

Indiana's only hope for keeping the school's streak of 18 consecutive NCAA appearances alive was to win the Big Ten Tournament, which was being staged in Indianapolis. If they couldn't win the conference tournament, then they needed to win at least two games to boost their overall record back to the .500 mark in order to be eligible for the NIT. Otherwise, the Hoosiers wouldn't play in a postseason tournament for the first time since 1976-77. In the first round, Indiana played Ohio State and stumbled to a 31-20 deficit with 6:29 remaining in the first half. That's when Ryan Tapak, Mark Johnson and Mike Roberts took over. They joined A.J. Moye and Marshall Strickland in the lineup and helped the Hoosier offense find a rhythm that had been missing all season. They sparked a 21-4 run that gave IU a 41-35 lead at the break. It was more of the same in the second half as IU prevailed 83-69. Tapak finished the game with 11 assists (tying a Big Ten Tournament record) and Mark Johnson had 13 points. A.J. Moye had 19 points and eight rebounds, while Bracey Wright led Indiana with 20 points—most of them coming in the second half when Tapak kept setting him up for mid-range jump shots. The next day, Johnson sparked the Hoosiers again with a flurry of three-pointers to bring Indiana to a 54-54 tie with Big Ten champion Illinois with only 5:44 left in the game. However, Deron Williams sparked the Illini to a 71-59 victory that put an end to Indiana's season.

The 2003-04 season started with a lot of "ifs" and it ended with a bunch of "ifs" as well. If the Hoosiers had found a way to pull out wins over Missouri and Temple (two preconference games they should have won at home), and if they hadn't squandered those late leads in four Big Ten games in

Assembly Hall, then they would have been looking at a 20-win season and would have made the annual pilgrimage to the NCAA tournament. As it turned out, the team finished 14-15 and played some of the worst basketball that had been seen in Bloomington in a long time. The statistics tell part of the tale about how ugly it really was. For the season, Indiana's field goal percentage was .397, the worst for an Indiana squad since the 1968-69 team shot .391. The Hoosiers averaged 64.9 points per game, the lowest point production for an IU team since the 1950-51 squad averaged 64.5. IU averaged only 11.9 assists per game, which was the lowest number ever recorded since the Hoosiers started tracking their assists in the 1970-71 season. All of these numbers only served as further evidence of what ended up being the most dismal season of Indiana basketball in three and a half decades.

Many IU fans clung to the hope that the Hoosiers' highly regarded incoming recruits could help turn things around. Others blamed Coach Davis for Indiana's disastrous season and called for his dismissal even though he was only two years removed from a trip to the Final Four and had four seasons remaining on his contract. However, at the end of the season, the IU president Adam Herbert gave Davis a public vote of confidence, saying, "I want to make it clear that Mike Davis will be the coach of the Indiana Hoosiers next year and for years to come."

Athletic director Terry Clapacs added, "Basketball is important at Indiana University, as it is to the entire state. And I'm sure with the recruiting class that Coach Davis has assembled, we'll be [back] on the right track immediately."

INDIANA'S RANKING IN THE 2003-04 ASSOCIATED PRESS POLLS

PS	11/24	12/1	12/8	12/15	12/22	12/29	1/5	1/12	1/19	1/26	2/2	2/9	2/16	2/23	3/1	3/8	3/15
—	—	—	—	—	—	—	—	—	—	—	—	—	—	—	—	—	—

SEASON STATISTICS
2000-01 TO 2003-04

2000-01

Team Statistics	G	FG%	3FG%	FT%	R	A	TO	S	B	PF	PTS	PPG
Indiana	34	.453	.362	.636	37.3	15.1	14.6	6.8	5.2	19.1	2408	70.8
Opponents	34	.394	.331	.715	35.2	11.8	14.9	7.5	3.2	20.5	2186	64.3
Player Statistics	G-GS	FG%	3FG%	FT%	R	A	TO	S	B	PF	PTS	PPG
Haston	33-28	.469	.377	.687	8.7	1.2	2.4	1.1	1.2	2.8	626	19.0
Jeffries	34-34	.442	.245	.620	6.9	2.4	2.9	0.9	1.2	2.9	469	13.8
Coverdale	34-32	.454	.356	.663	3.4	4.8	2.6	1.6	0.1	2.6	363	10.7
Hornsby	29-11	.432	.426	.710	2.0	1.0	1.0	0.6	0.1	1.7	199	6.9
Newton	33-24	.517	.000	.529	4.8	1.2	1.4	0.6	1.7	2.3	200	6.1
Fife	34-34	.374	.306	.629	2.8	3.2	2.0	1.4	0.2	3.0	173	5.1
Owens	30-4	.453	.389	.742	1.4	0.7	1.1	0.4	0.2	1.2	140	4.7
Moye	30-0	.466	.444	.737	2.4	0.4	0.6	0.3	0.2	1.3	100	3.3
Odle	26-3	.484	.444	.588	2.8	0.4	0.7	0.2	0.1	1.4	86	3.3
Leach	20-0	.375	.000	.478	1.5	0.2	0.7	0.1	1.1	1.3	35	1.8
Roberts	10-0	.417	.000	.467	1.3	0.1	0.0	0.1	0.1	0.8	17	1.7

2001-02
PLEASE SEE CHAPTER 7

2002-03

Team Statistics	G	FG%	3FG%	FT%	R	A	TO	S	B	PF	PTS	PPG
Indiana	34	.426	.349	.718	36.3	13.8	11.5	4.3	5.1	18.0	2376	69.9
Opponents	34	.416	.294	.717	35.9	12.1	10.4	6.3	3.5	20.0	2280	67.1
Player Statistics	G-GS	FG%	3FG%	FT%	R	A	TO	S	B	PF	PTS	PPG
Wright	30-30	.433	.375	.752	5.0	2.1	2.1	0.8	0.6	2.0	486	16.2
Newton	34-34	.432	.297	.748	8.2	2.0	2.3	0.7	1.5	2.9	507	14.9
Coverdale	34-34	.380	.349	.821	3.6	4.5	1.9	0.8	0.1	2.0	405	11.9
Hornsby	34-21	.385	.380	.647	2.7	1.6	0.6	0.5	0.1	1.8	225	6.6
Leach	32-30	.552	.000	.633	5.5	0.4	1.3	0.3	2.5	2.4	208	6.5
Strickland	34-13	.389	.355	.738	2.4	2.0	1.2	0.6	0.1	1.9	207	6.1
Moye	33-7	.545	.286	.641	3.9	0.8	0.9	0.4	0.3	2.6	181	5.5
Kline	27-1	.429	.000	.467	1.9	0.4	0.6	0.2	0.1	2.0	75	2.8
Perry	24-0	.310	.269	.731	0.8	0.4	0.8	0.3	0.0	0.6	52	2.2
Roberts	18-0	.313	.000	.727	1.3	0.1	0.3	0.2	0.1	1.3	26	1.4
Tapak	10-0	.143	.000	.000	0.2	0.2	0.1	0.1	0.1	0.0	2	0.2
Pegram	2-0	1.00	.000	.000	1.0	0.5	0.5	0.0	0.0	1.0	2	1.0
Johnson	6-0	.000	.000	.000	0.3	0.0	0.0	0.0	0.0	0.2	0	0.0
Stewart	3-0	.000	.000	.000	0.3	0.0	0.0	0.0	0.3	0.0	0	0.0
Haarman	1-0	.000	.000	.000	2.0	0.0	1.0	0.0	0.0	1.0	0	0.0

2003-04

Team Statistics	G	FG%	3FG%	FT%	R	A	TO	S	B	PF	PTS	PPG
Indiana	29	.397	.330	.724	35.2	11.9	12.4	5.1	3.5	18.5	1881	64.9
Opponents	29	.425	.334	.730	36.4	12.3	12.1	6.0	3.6	17.8	1961	67.6
Player Statistics	G-GS	FG%	3FG%	FT%	R	A	TO	S	B	PF	PTS	PPG
Wright	29-29	.374	.343	.789	5.4	2.4	2.3	0.9	0.5	1.6	536	18.5
Strickland	29-26	.359	.367	.772	3.2	2.7	1.9	1.1	0.2	2.1	314	10.8
Moye	29-22	.467	.378	.727	6.4	1.5	1.9	0.7	0.1	3.2	291	10.0
Leach	20-20	.486	.000	.694	5.5	0.5	1.3	0.4	2.3	2.9	181	9.1
Kline	22-12	.500	.000	.717	4.0	0.8	1.5	0.3	0.4	3.3	156	7.1
Johnson	9-0	.455	.429	1.00	0.1	0.3	0.2	0.2	0.0	0.4	37	4.1
Tapak	20-5	.311	.288	.571	2.5	2.0	1.2	0.9	0.3	1.8	67	3.4
Perry	28-13	.280	.278	.667	1.7	2.4	1.4	0.5	0.0	1.3	93	3.3
Wilmont	27-6	.292	.258	.400	2.5	0.3	0.5	0.3	0.1	1.0	89	3.3
Ewing	28-9	.525	1.00	.481	3.6	0.2	0.9	0.5	0.6	2.3	78	2.8
Roberts	22-3	.484	.000	.417	0.9	0.1	0.4	0.1	0.0	1.5	35	1.6
Gray-Ashley	7-0	.500	.000	.000	0.6	0.0	0.4	0.0	0.1	0.7	4	0.6
Suhr	4-0	.000	.000	.000	0.3	0.5	0.5	0.0	0.0	0.3	0	0.0
Stewart	4-0	.000	.000	.000	0.3	0.0	0.0	0.0	0.3	0.5	0	0.0

PART III

THE HOOSIER TRADITION

ASSEMBLY HALL

1901-1917

TEAM RECORD: 61-43 (.587)

IU's first basketball home was the original Assembly Hall. As the time, it was known simply as the Men's Gymnasium and it was a small multi-purpose building that was used to host indoor sports and other campus activities. IU Archives

By modern standards, the first home of Indiana basketball looked more like a large house than a sporting arena. It was a wood frame structure that was built in 1896 at a cost of $12,000 to host a variety of Indiana University activities including indoor sports and physical education classes. It was known simply as the Men's Gymnasium at that time, and it wasn't equipped to handle big crowds. Its seating capacity was about 600, but more than that stuffed into the gym in later years when basketball started gaining popularity. It was located on the east side of Owen Hall. On the IU campus today, this site is now a small "A" parking lot that sits adjacent to the south side of the Indiana Memorial Union building.

On February 21, 1901, the first intercollegiate basketball game was played in the gym when IU hosted Butler and lost 24-20 to the Bulldogs. However, Indiana got its first home win on March 8, when the Hoosiers trounced Wabash 26-17.

In March 1911, the IU gym played host to the finals of the first ever Indiana high school basketball

tournament. At that time, the tournament was actually hosted by the IU Boosters Club rather than the IHSAA. The Boosters Club wanted to bring the best high school teams to Bloomington in hopes of exposing more high school players to Indiana University and attracting the top talent to play for the IU varsity.

Shortly after IU began serving as the annual host for the high school finals, it became clear that the school has outgrown the facility, and many students, alumni and boosters began to petition school officials to erect a new and improved indoor sporting facility. The students even went so far as to characterize the gym as a public menace and a health risk in the student-run *Indiana Daily Student* newspaper. Finally, when the funds became available, construction on a new gym was begun during 1916. On January 13, 1917, the Hoosiers played their final game in their original gym, beating Iowa State 29-13. After the new facility was built, this structure was mostly used for hosting meetings, and at some unknown point was renamed "Assembly Hall." The building was torn down in 1938.

MEN'S GYMNASIUM

1917-1928

TEAM RECORD: 86-31 (.735)

In 1917, the Hoosiers moved into the new Men's Gymnasium, which included the first true basketball court that was meant to accommodate spectators. As this photo shows, parking was an issue even back then, when the automobile was in its infancy. IU Archives

On January 19, 1917, the Hoosiers christened their new Gothic basketball cathedral by beating Big Ten rival Iowa 12-7. Apparently both teams had trouble adjusting to the new baskets in the arena. Indiana's 12 points remains the least that a Hoosier team has ever scored in a winning ball game.

The new facility was built from Indiana limestone, and the price tag for the completed structure ended up being $250,000. It included an indoor track, a pool, locker rooms, offices for athletics and physical education staff, and a trophy room. But the centerpiece was the 2,400-seat basketball arena on the second floor. It was simply called the new Men's Gymnasium, and for a first few years it was often just referred to as the "New Gym."

One of the most significant features of the New Gym was that it may have been the first in the country to utilize glass backboards. After the first couple of years in the New Gym, spectators seated behind the backboards complained that they couldn't see all of the action because of the opaque wooden backboards.

Thus, the Nurre Mirror Plate Company in Bloomington was employed to create new backboards that contained one-and-a-half-inch-thick plate glass so that fans could see the game without having their view obstructed.

The IU basketball program and the New Gym played host to the school's first All-American in 1921, when center Everett Dean roamed the floor as the Hoosiers' high-scoring center. Four years later, Dean returned to his alma mater to become the first great Indiana head coach. In Dean's second season at the helm in 1925-26, he led the Hoosiers to the school's first conference championship. That year, IU used an 8-2 record in the Men's Gym as the springboard for capturing the league crown.

Two years later, in the 1927-28 campaign, IU went 11-0 in the Men's Gym on the way to a 15-2 season and the school's second conference crown. That ended up being the last season in the Men's Gym. The growth of the university and the surging popularity of IU basketball triggered the need for a basketball theater on a larger scale.

Today, the Men's Gymnasium is still in use as part of the complex for Indiana's School of Health, Physical Education, and Recreation (HPER).

Inside the new Men's Gymnasium, the crowd nuzzled in very close to the court. This photo is from Indiana's game against Purdue on February 4, 1925.
IU Archives

THE FIELDHOUSE

1928-1960

TEAM RECORD: 234-74 (.760)

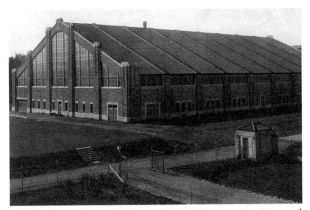

By the late 1920s, Indiana University was growing and the interest in basketball was accelerating. As a result, IU built a new 8,000-seat Fieldhouse to host home basketball games. IU Archives

The IU basketball program got a significant upgrade for the 1928-29 season when the team moved into its new "Fieldhouse," which was built adjacent to the Men's Gymnasium. The Fieldhouse was Indiana's first true basketball stadium, and it would go on to become one of the classic venues in college basketball during its time. The stadium could seat up to 8,000 spectators (later extended to 10,000), provided extensive lighting of the floor and the baskets, and had at center court a press box that could seat 35 journalists and included 10 built-in telegraph wires. The structure cost $350,000 and it was paid for with construction bonds, as well as a $2.00 fee levied against each Indiana student.

The arena was just barely completed in time for the Hoosiers' season opener against the Washington (Missouri) Bears on December 8, 1928. Coach Everett Dean's troops were upset 31-30 by the Bears. However, in the dedication game for the Fieldhouse on December 13, the Hoosiers pulled out an impressive 34-26 victory over a powerful Pennsylvania Quakers team. The dedication game itself was a gala event with a capacity crowd that included Indiana's Governor-Elect Harry Leslie and Big Ten Commissioner John Griffith.

The first point that Indiana put on the scoreboard in the Fieldhouse came from a free throw by junior center Branch McCracken, who went on to earn All-America honors the next season. In 1938-39, McCracken returned to Bloomington and succeeded Dean as Indiana's head coach. During the 1940s and 1950s, McCracken's fast-breaking basketball teams treated Fieldhouse audiences to a lot of exciting games, as well as four conference titles and two NCAA championships. The Fieldhouse was also the home court for 20 different Hoosier All-Americans during its 32 seasons of hosting the IU basketball program.

The final game in the Fieldhouse was played on February 29, 1960, when an IU squad led by Walt Bellamy completely dominated the Big Ten champion Ohio State Buckeyes in a 99-83 IU victory. Ohio State went on to win the NCAA championship.

Today, the Fieldhouse is still a living legend. It has been converted into the Wildemuth Intramural Center with several rows of basketball courts that see a continuous stream of action. Because the facility is attached to the School of Health, Physical Education, and Recreation (HPER), the courts are often simply referred to as "The Hyper," and they host some of the most competitive pickup basketball games that you'll find anywhere in the country.

In addition to a larger seating capacity, the Fieldhouse included much better lighting and a larger floor, as seen in this photo from the Hoosiers' first game in the new arena on December 8, 1928.
IU Archives

NEW FIELDHOUSE

1960-1971

TEAM RECORD: 85-41 (.675)

Meant to be purely an interim solution until IU's premium basketball facility could be built, the "New Fieldhouse" ended up hosting the Hoosiers for 11 seasons because of tough financial times for the athletic department in the 1960s. IU Archives

Because of a variety of issues in the Fieldhouse including parking, lighting and seating, by the mid-1950s, the Indiana administration began to extensively research plans and options for building a grand, state-of-the-art modern basketball arena. However, because those plans were taking so long to come to fruition, because the money still had to be raised, and because it was decided to build the new football stadium first, an interim solution was devised for basketball.

IU built a $1.7 million indoor practice facility out on the new athletic department grounds on 17th Street, where the football stadium was built and where the eventual basketball arena was to be constructed. The interim facility was rudimentary and not much of an upgrade from the old Fieldhouse, except in the areas of lighting and parking. It was simply called the "New Fieldhouse," and it had a floor of dirt and sawdust, and no air conditioning.

The Hoosiers were only supposed to play there for a few seasons and then the facility would be turned over to other sports for primary use as a practice facility. However, because of the Indiana's NCAA

probation (due to football violations) handed down in 1960, the IU sports programs took a heavy setback financially. And then, after Coach Branch McCracken retired at the end of the 1964-65 season, the basketball team fell on hard times with losing seasons in four of the next six years. As a result, IU's long-awaited basketball palace faced innumerable delays and IU ended up playing 11 seasons in the New Fieldhouse.

IU All-Americans Walt Bellamy, Jimmy Rayl, Tom and Dick Van Arsdale and George McGinnis called it home during their playing days at IU. The New Fieldhouse was also host to the two greatest scoring games in IU history when Jimmy Rayl poured in 56 points against Minnesota on January 27, 1962, and then hit for another 56 against Michigan State on February 23, 1963. The first game in the New Fieldhouse was an 80-53 blowout of Indiana State on December 3, 1960, and the last game was a 103-87 season-ending loss to Illinois on March 13, 1971.

In 1997, the facility was renamed the "Gladstein Fieldhouse" and was resurfaced for the IU track and field team. It has hosted the Big Ten's indoor track and field championships on multiple occasions.

ASSEMBLY HALL

1971-PRESENT

TEAM RECORD: 389-60 (.866)

Indiana's long-envisioned state-of-the-art basketball theater was finally completed for the 1971-72 season, which coincided with the arrival of a new 31-year-old coach named Bob Knight. Since then, Assembly Hall has become one of the most recognizable icons of college basketball. IU Archives

IU's dream to build a modern basketball wonder finally bore fruit in 1971. After decades of planning and four years of construction, the new "Assembly Hall"—named in honor of IU's first basketball arena—was completed in time for the beginning of the 1971-72 season. The goal was to build an aesthetically pleasing, large-capacity basketball theater that would have all of the modern conveniences and cater to Indiana's burgeoning mass of basketball fans, and IU spent $12.2 million to make those dreams come true.

In order to make the arena an ideal place to watch a game, the IU officials were intent on having the vast majority of seats on the sides, with only a small number of seats behind the baskets. The end result was that in order to get the 17,000+ seats into the arena, the sides had to be very steep, and the two balconies were up so high that they felt very far away from the court. Nevertheless, the arena soon began filling up with Hoosier fans, and IU has consistently

been one of college basketball's attendance leaders every year since Assembly Hall was built.

While Indiana fans have long been crazy about IU basketball, the Hoosiers' consistent attendance has also been tied to the fact that the opening of Assembly Hall coincided with the arrival of highly successful coach Bob Knight. From his arrival that first season, Knight coached 29 straight winning teams, including 11 conference champions and three NCAA champions. Knight's legendary teams are the primary reason that IU has achieved a staggering winning percentage of .866 in Assembly Hall. As a result, Assembly Hall has become one of the most recognizable and intimidating arenas in all of college basketball.

The first game was played in the new arena on December 1, 1971, when IU defeated Ball State 84-77. That night, IU center Steve Downing collected 26 rebounds—an Assembly Hall record that still stands. The official dedication game for the Hall came on December 18, when IU annihilated Notre Dame 94-

The steep inclines on both sides of the court give the impression of the Assembly Hall crowd hanging right over the floor. This has been part of the intimidation factor that has made Assembly Hall one of the toughest places in college basketball for visitors to snare a victory. IU Archives

29. IU's John Ritter finished with 31 points to outscore the Fighting Irish all by himself. Also, at that dedication game, the Assembly Hall floor was officially commemorated as the "Branch McCracken Memorial Basketball Floor."

Since the mid-1990s, Hoosier fans and the IU administration have debated which direction to take with Assembly Hall. In order to meet the demand for tickets, IU clearly needs an arena that can seat over 20,000 fans. The big question has been whether to renovate Assembly Hall or build a new arena. However, without the funds to do either of those options, no serious plans have been pursued.

Meanwhile, Assembly Hall continues to provide one of the greatest home-court advantages in sports.

CHAPTER 22
THE ALL-TIME INDIANA TEAM

Comparing athletes of different eras is extremely difficult, and often unfair. But of course, it's something that sports fans love to do. IU has been blessed with great athletes, outstanding shooters, and numerous All-Americans over a period of eleven different decades. That makes it a monumental challenge to select 15 players to comprise an all-time Indiana team. Here, the author provides his selections for a first team and a second team of all-time Indiana performers.

IU Archives

FIRST TEAM
BOB KNIGHT, COACH

Bob Knight is the Big Ten's all-time winningest coach, both overall (.734) and in conference play (.700). He led the Hoosiers to 11 league titles, five trips to the Final Four, and three NCAA championships. He did all of that while running a clean program and demanding that his players go to class. As a coach, Knight was a brilliant tactician and motivator, and his motion offense and pressure defense greatly influenced other Big Ten teams to adopt a more precise, defensive-oriented style of play. Of course, Knight was also known for his intense, demanding personality that accepted nothing less than excellence, and occasionally led to some controversial flare-ups. That was all part of the Knight legend at Indiana, and for nearly three decades, he reigned as one of the most popular and recognizable figures in the Hoosier state.

WALT BELLAMY, CENTER

Walt Bellamy came to IU in 1957 as an athletically gifted 6'11" big man with basketball skills that were still under development. With coach Branch McCracken's eager tutelage, Bellamy left Indiana four years later as an All-American, a star in the 1960 Olympics, and one of the best centers in the history of college basketball. He possessed excellent speed for running the floor and often beat his defender down the court for easy dunks. By the time he was an upperclassman, he also developed a potent hook shot that could provide reliable scoring in the half-court offense. But above all, Bellamy was a tenacious rebounder. His career average of 15.5 rebounds per game is still an IU record—and it is one that may never be eclipsed. Bellamy also went on to a highly successful NBA career and was elected to the Basketball Hall of Fame in 1993.

KENT BENSON, CENTER

As a high school player, Kent Benson was one of the most widely coveted big men in the country, and IU was, in many ways, the surprise winner in a recruiting battle that also featured Notre Dame, Purdue, Kentucky and other schools. Still, as a freshman, Benson struggled to learn the Indiana system and adjust to Coach Knight's demanding approach. He even considered leaving the team that first year. To his credit, he stuck it out. He wasn't a terrific athlete, but he made up for that with well-rounded basketball skills and a steadfast work ethic that enabled him to become a three-time All-American and one of the most accomplished centers in the history of college basketball. He was also one of the key components of Indiana's fabled 1975-76 team. A year later, the Milwaukee Bucks made him the No. 1 pick in the 1977 NBA draft.

ARCHIE DEES, CENTER

DON SCHLUNDT, CENTER

Wedged in between the years when pivot man Don Schlundt rewrote the record books in Bloomington and when Walt Bellamy became an IU legend, the center position of the Hoosiers' offense was in the capable hands of 6'8" Archie Dees. In 1956-57 and 1957-58, Dees led the Hoosiers to consecutive conference championships and earned Big Ten MVP honors in both of those seasons. On the offensive end, Dees was a model of consistency with a career scoring average of 22.7 PPG; however, he was far more than just a scorer. Dees was one of the most versatile and complete basketball players in Indiana history. Agile and athletic, he was a strong rebounder, an excellent free throw shooter, a crafty defender, and he possessed a deadly jump shoot. When Dees graduated in 1958, he trailed only Schlundt on Indiana's all-time scoring list.

Due to the Korean War waiver (which allowed freshmen to compete in varsity athletics because of the dearth of young men on college campuses), 6'9" Don Schlundt became eligible to play for the Hoosiers during his first year and he immediately began shattering scoring records. He used a deadly hook shot, which he could shoot with either hand, to score at will against most opponents. He was very coordinated for a player his size, but he got pushed around a lot on defense as a freshman. However, he took advantage of his freshman experience to become a force on both ends of the floor as a sophomore, and that year, he helped the Hoosiers make a brilliant run all the way to the 1953 NCAA title. By the end of his sophomore year, Schlundt was already Indiana's all-time leading scorer, and by the end of his senior year he had amassed 2,192 points—an IU record that would stand for over two decades. At the end of his college career, Schlundt decided to go into the insurance business instead of signing an NBA contract with the Syracuse Nationals.

IU Archives

IU Archives

CALBERT CHEANEY, FORWARD

The name of Calbert Cheaney was easily overlooked among the high profile group of high school stars that coach Bob Knight brought to Indiana as part of his 1989 recruiting class. But once the ball was tipped in their first practice, it became readily apparent that the 6'7" swingman Cheaney was the best prospect of the bunch. The smooth left-hander could do it all. He had quickness and strength. He could shoot, rebound, defend, pass and score off the dribble. He had a phenomenal mid-range game, and in Knight's motion offense, he was able to find a lot of scoring opportunities. He remains the all-time leading scorer in Indiana and Big Ten history. His teams won two Big Ten championships and went to the Final Four in 1992. During his senior season, 1992-93, he was the consensus national player of the year. After graduation, he went on to a long career in the NBA.

ALAN HENDERSON, FORWARD

On Hoosier teams dominated by perimeter players in the early 1990s, Alan Henderson served as an anchor in the interior. The 6'9" Henderson wasn't an awe-inspiring athlete like his teammates Calbert Cheaney and Greg Graham, but Henderson was tough, smart, and very competitive. He was an excellent rebounder and low post defender and could also score inside, as well as face up and bury mid range jump shots. He led the Hoosiers in rebounding all four years, and in his final game at Indiana, he broke Walt Bellamy's career rebounding record. Henderson finished his career among IU's top-five all-time in four different categories: scoring, rebounding, blocked shots and steals. He suffered a debilitating knee injury at the end of the 1992-93 season, and without him at full strength, the top-ranked Hoosiers lost to Kansas in the Elite Eight. In the 1995 NBA draft, the Atlanta Hawks selected Henderson in the first round, and he went on to a successful career that included the 1997-98 NBA Most Improved Player Award.

IU Archives

SCOTT MAY, FORWARD

IU Archives

GEORGE McGINNIS, FORWARD

Forward Scott May's value to Indiana was made manifest during the 1974-75 season, when a deep and dominant Hoosier team lost the 6'7" May to a broken arm during the final weeks of the regular season. The undefeated IU squad kept winning, but the margins were much slimmer, and fate caught up with them in the regional finals when Kentucky upset Indiana 92-90. May was IU's leading scorer when he went down, but more than his scoring, IU really missed his defense. May and the Hoosiers got their redemption the next season by going 32-0 to capture a fourth straight Big Ten title along with the NCAA championship. May, who was an excellent athlete and an outstanding shooter, was the consensus 1976 college player of the year. After the season ended, he starred on the 1976 U.S. Olympic basketball team that swept its way to the gold medal. That fall, he joined the Chicago Bulls, who had drafted him with the second pick of the 1976 NBA draft.

When you talk about the most dominant players in IU history, it's difficult find anyone more impressive than 6'8" forward George McGinnis, who was also one of the biggest recruits that Indiana has ever landed. When Big George broke in as a sophomore during the 1970-71 season, he was already a man among boys. With broad shoulders, meat hooks for arms, and the quickness of a guard, McGinnis was a powerful force—and virtually unstoppable—on offense and on the boards. He averaged 29.9 PPG and 14.9 RPG to lead the Big Ten. He helped the Hoosiers improve from 7-17 in 1969-70 to 17-7 in 1970-71, his first season on the varsity. However, with the talent IU had, that wasn't enough to satisfy Hoosier fans, and at the end of the season, coach Lou Watson resigned. Bob Knight was hired as Watson's successor, but McGinnis decided to go pro and quickly became a superstar for the Indiana Pacers in the ABA.

IU Archives

MIKE WOODSON, FORWARD

Mike Woodson arrived at Indiana as a freshman for the 1976-77 season, the year after Scott May departed. Woodson took on May's jersey number 42, and took up his starting spot at forward. With a prolific mid-range game, Woodson also averaged 18.5 PPG to take up much of the scoring slack from May's departure. Even though Woodson was a couple of inches shorter than May, there were probably at least a few opponents that saw Woodson's number 42 and wondered, "Hasn't that guy graduated yet?" Unfortunately, those opponents had to face another four years of getting hammered into submission by jumpers from number 42. If it weren't for an injury that caused Woodson to miss over half of his senior year, he would have easily surpassed Don Schlundt as Indiana's all-time leading scorer if he simply scored at his regular career pace of 19.8 PPG during the games that he missed. Nevertheless, the highlight of Woodson's career came during his senior season when he returned from back surgery to spark IU to six straight wins to capture the 1980 Big Ten title. Although he only played in those six conference games, he was still selected as the Big Ten MVP. Woodson eventually went on to a prolific NBA career.

IU Archives

STEVE ALFORD, GUARD

Although he was highly regarded as a high school player, there were a lot of doubts as to whether 6'2" guard Steve Alford could compete at the collegiate level. He was not fleet of foot, nor very tall or strong. He was a shooting guard that couldn't really create his own shot. However, Alford was the quintessential Indiana gym rat and Bob Knight's motion offense was the perfect system to provide Alford with plenty of open jump shots. It didn't take long for Alford to foil his detractors. He led the Hoosiers in scoring for four straight seasons, was named as an All-American in 1986 and 1987, was the 1987 Big Ten MVP, and capped off his career by leading IU to the 1987 NCAA championship. When he graduated, he held the school's career record for points, steals and free throw percentage. He was, quite simply, one of the greatest outside shooters in the history of college basketball.

IU Archives

QUINN BUCKNER, GUARD

IU Archives

BOB LEONARD, GUARD

In the days before media attention and NBA defections turned college basketball recruiting into the circus event that it is today, Quinn Buckner was a widely publicized, highly coveted recruit who put off his signing until the very last minute—and then he chose Indiana. Even with all of his advanced billing, Buckner, who also played football for IU in his first two seasons, didn't disappoint. From his first day of practice (even after joining the team late because of football), Buckner became the Hoosiers' floor leader. He put up solid numbers throughout his Indiana career, but those numbers don't show the full value of Buckner's presence on the court. His leadership, defense and toughness don't show up on a stat sheet, nor does the fact that he was an intense competitor, an excellent team player and a winner. In his four years at IU, Buckner led the Hoosiers to four Big Ten championships, two Final Fours and one NCAA title. He also went on to become only the second basketball player in history to win championships in high school, college and the NBA, as well as an Olympic gold medal. The other was Jerry Lucas, and Magic Johnson joined them in 1993.

On Indiana's 1953 NCAA championship team, Don Schlundt was characterized as "Mr. Inside" while Bob Leonard was "Mr. Outside." Schlundt and Leonard were arguably the best one-two punch in IU history. Schlundt drew a lot of double-teams, which opened up shots for the hot shooting Leonard. Meanwhile, Leonard helped keep opposing defenses from collapsing too intently on Schlundt by providing a constant shooting threat on the perimeter. Leonard, whose scoring marks would have rewritten the IU record books if it weren't for Schlundt, was also an excellent floor general and passer. He became adept at feeding the ball to Schlundt in positions where the big guy could score, and thus, Leonard played a big role in helping Schlundt become such a prolific scorer. Leonard earned All-Big Ten and All-America honors during both 1953 and 1954, and he went on to both play and coach professional basketball.

IU Archives

JIMMY RAYL, GUARD

IU Archives

ISIAH THOMAS, GUARD

If there was one player who could rival Steve Alford as the best outside shooter in IU history, it was Jimmy Rayl. Short, skinny and baby-faced, Rayl certainly didn't have the look of a player who could strike fear into the hearts of his opponents. But once the ball was tipped, IU foes quickly learned that you had better locate Rayl, because as soon as he crossed over half-court, he was a threat to shoot the ball the moment he found an opening. Rayl possessed uncanny shooting accuracy that extended out to 35 feet from the basket. Rayl's 29.8 PPG in 1961-62 stood as the IU record for scoring average until McGinnis broke it in the 1970-71 season. However, Rayl still holds the school's single-game scoring record with 56 points. He hit that mark twice—against Minnesota in 1962 and against Michigan State in 1963. No other player has ever broken 50. Plus, Rayl did that in the days before the three-point shot. Since he made the majority of his baskets beyond 20 feet, if those long ones had counted as threes, as they do today, then Rayl would have probably broken 70.

Another one of Indiana's greatest recruiting victories was Bob Knight's wooing of Chicago's prized high school phenom Isiah Thomas. Blessed with breathtaking quickness and athletic ability, Thomas also possessed basketball savvy, hard-nosed toughness and an indomitable will. Isiah's resolve and his basketball prowess were put through the crucible of adversity during his freshman season, when IU's star player, senior Mike Woodson, went down with a back injury and the burden of carrying the Hoosiers fell on Thomas's young shoulders. Isiah helped IU stay in contention until Woodson returned, and then Indiana swept its remaining conference games to capture the 1980 Big Ten championship. The next season, the team got off to a slow start, but Thomas led the resurgent Hoosiers to a dominating run through the NCAA Tournament to win the 1981 national championship. In the NCAA championship game against North Carolina, Thomas scored a game-high 23 points and was named the Most Outstanding Player of the Final Four. He was also voted All-Big Ten in both 1980 and 1981. After his sophomore year, Thomas entered the NBA draft and the Detroit Pistons selected him with the No. 2 overall pick. He went on to become one of the NBA's greatest players and won world championships with the Pistons in 1989 and 1990.

IU Archives

DAMON BAILEY, GUARD

No player ever came to Indiana carrying a greater burden of expectations than Damon Bailey. Knight had scouted Bailey since the eighth grade, and that fact became nationally known when the book *Season on the Brink* was released in 1986. As a result, Bailey spent his entire high school career under intense media scrutiny. Nevertheless, he led his team to the state finals three times, won the 1990 state championship, and became the all-time leading scorer in Indiana high school history. He was a legend in the Hoosier state before he ever set foot on the IU campus for his freshman year. The consummate team player, Bailey took a back seat to teammates Calbert Cheaney and Greg Graham in the scoring department during his first three seasons, but did whatever the Hoosiers needed to help win basketball games—pass, rebound, defend, shoot threes ... whatever was needed. However, as a senior, Bailey returned to his high school roots and became a big time scorer once again, averaging 19.6 PPG. Bailey was a good—but not

spectacular—athlete; however, his greatest strengths were his high basketball IQ, his unselfishness, and his will to win. During his four years in Bloomington, the Hoosiers won 108 games (an average of 27 wins per season), including 11 victories in NCAA tournament play, four straight trips to the Sweet Sixteen, and a Final Four berth in 1992.

SECOND TEAM

BRANCH McCRACKEN, COACH

Branch McCracken pioneered a running, pressing, aggressive style of basketball that later spread throughout the Big Ten and also became the standard in most Indiana high schools. McCracken's teams won national championships in 1940 and 1953 and almost always challenged for the Big Ten title, winning four conference championships and placing second eight times. What may have endeared McCracken to the IU faithful more than anything else was the fact that his teams dominated Purdue with a 28-15 record against the Boilermakers during his 24 seasons at the helm.

STEVE DOWNING, CENTER

Overshadowed by his illustrious teammate George McGinnis, during high school and during their sophomore season on the Indiana varsity, Steve Downing became a force in the paint during his junior and senior seasons, averaging 18.9 PPG and 12.7 RPG over his final two seasons. In 1973, he was an All-American and the Big Ten MVP. Against Michigan as a sophomore, he delivered Indiana's only recorded triple-double with 28 points, 17 rebounds, and 10 blocks.

EVERETT DEAN, CENTER

In 1921, Indiana's 6'0" senior center Everett Dean became the school's first All-American in basketball. Dean led IU in scoring in each of his three seasons on the varsity. He was a versatile performer who could score in a variety of ways inside and outside, and he became the most prolific scorer that Indiana had ever seen during that era. Later, he returned to IU and became the school's first great coach.

DEAN GARRETT, CENTER

When junior college transfer Dean Garrett arrived in Bloomington for the 1986-87 season, he immediately filled Indiana's pressing need for another inside scoring threat as well as for a big man that could protect the basket on defense. The 6'10" Garrett was a solid scorer and rebounder, but above all else, he was a phenomenal shot blocker. For his career, he averaged 3.0 blocks per game. His inside presence was a crucial factor for Indiana's 1987 NCAA title team.

BILL GARRETT, FORWARD/CENTER

The first African-American basketball recruit in Big Ten history, Bill Garrett broke the color barrier with the same type of grace that Jackie Robinson exhibited. But beyond that, he was a phenomenal basketball player. Fast, lithe, athletic and crafty, Garrett was a natural for the forward position in college basketball, but usually played center because the Hoosiers lacked a true big man during his years in Bloomington. Playing against bigger opponents, he was still an All-American in 1951 and led IU to a stellar 19-3 record.

BRIAN EVANS, FORWARD

A versatile 6'8" forward, Evans improved tremendously during the course of his career. He went from a spot-up shooter as a freshman to a guy that could play both inside and outside on offense and defense as a senior. He also became an All-American and the 1996 Big Ten MVP. Evans also became the first player to lead the Big Ten in scoring during the Bob Knight era.

STEVE GREEN, FORWARD

Steve Green was Bob Knight's first recruit and he didn't disappoint his mentor. Green ended up being a three-year starter and a two-time All-American (1974, 1975). He was a deadly shooter that made 53 percent of his field goal attempts for his career. He was also a calm, confident performer who often delivered in the clutch. IU won Big Ten titles in each of his three seasons on the varsity.

JARED JEFFRIES, FORWARD

Like Isiah Thomas, the multi-skilled 6'10" Jared Jeffries only played two seasons in Bloomington, but

he made them memorable. In his sophomore year, Jeffries carried the Hoosiers to their first Big Ten title in nine seasons and then the team made an underdog run all the way to the NCAA championship game. Along the way, Jeffries picked up the Big Ten MVP award and All-American honors.

TED KITCHEL, FORWARD

Much like Steve Green before him, 6'8" Ted Kitchel was a tall forward with a deadly shooting touch. Also like Green, Kitchel was a two-time All-American (1982, 1983). Over his final two seasons, Kitchel averaged 18.5 PPG on 52 percent field-goal shooting. During Kitchel's five years in Bloomington (which included a redshirt season in 1979-80), the Hoosiers captured three conference titles and the 1981 NCAA championship.

DICK VAN ARSDALE, FORWARD

Branch McCracken's last great recruiting victory was landing Dick Van Arsdale and his twin brother Tom in 1961. Both of them became three-year starters at IU. A 6'5" forward, Dick was rugged, agile and competitive. He could take the ball to the basket or shoot from the outside, and he was an aggressive rebounder. Dick was a first team All-Big Ten selection in 1964. He was also an All-American in 1965 and an Academic All-American in both 1964 and 1965.

TOM VAN ARSDALE, FORWARD

Not surprisingly, Tom Van Arsdale played almost exactly like his brother Dick. The two of them finished their college careers with almost identical statistics. Tom averaged 17.4 PPG and 10.0 RPG, while Dick averaged 17.2 PPG and 10.0 RPG. The one big difference was on the free throw line. Tom didn't go to the free throw line as often and shot a lower percentage (65 percent for Tom and 79 percent for Dick). In 1965, Tom joined Dick as an All-American and an Academic All-American. Both of them went on to long and productive NBA careers.

JAY EDWARDS, GUARD

Jay Edwards was a smooth 6'4" shooting guard who bounced back from a rocky freshman year off the court to have a stellar sophomore campaign in which he led IU to an unexpected Big Ten title in 1989 and was voted the Big Ten Player of the Year by the media. His clutch shots against Purdue, Michigan and Illinois during the 1988-89 season are still widely remembered by IU fans.

A.J. GUYTON, GUARD

Quick, high-scoring guard A.J. Guyton was a four-year starter who improved tremendously as a senior to become an All-American in 2000. He finished his career fourth on the all-time IU scoring list. He was also voted by the media as the Big Ten Player of the Year in 2000.

VERN HUFFMAN, GUARD

One of the great athletes in the history of IU sports, Vern Huffman is the only Hoosier that has ever earned All-America honors in both football and basketball. In 1936, his leadership, all-around play and toughness spurred coach Everett Dean's IU squad to an 18-2 record and a Big Ten title.

LOU WATSON, GUARD

One of IU's first four-year starters (he got to play as a freshman following his service in World War II), Lou Watson was a big guard at 6'5" and quickly earned a became the floor leader for Coach McCracken's fast-breaking attack. He was the team's MVP as a junior and senior and an All-American in 1950.

RANDY WITTMAN, GUARD

A deadly sniper from the outside, 6'5" Randy Wittman was one of the best shooters in IU history. As a sophomore, his clutch shooting helped lead IU to the 1981 NCAA championship. His senior year, he helped carry IU to a conference title and was awarded the Big Ten MVP and named All-American.

BIBLIOGRAPHY

Alford, Steve and John Garrity. *Playing for Knight: My Six Seasons with Coach Knight.* New York: Simon and Schuster, 1989.

Angotti, Art. Knight Before the Game: 1992-93. Indianapolis: University Sports Radio Network, 2003.

Arbutus (Indiana University yearbook), 1901-1971.

Bailey, Damon and Wendell Trogdon. *Damon: Beyond the Glory.* Mooresville, IN: Backroads Press, 2003.

Bailey, Damon and Wendell Trogdon. *Damon: Living a Dream.* Mooresville, IN: Backroads Press, 1995.

Berger, Phil. *Bobby Knight: The Truth Behind America's Most Controversial Coach.* New York: Pinnacle Books, 2000.

Big Ten Conference 2003-04 Men's Basketball Media Guide. Peoria, IL: MultiAd Sports, 2003.

Bloomington Courier, miscellaneous issues.

Bloomington Herald-Times, miscellaneous issues.

Bloomington Herald-Telephone, miscellaneous issues.

Byrd, Cecil K. and Ward W. Moore. *Varsity Sports at Indiana University: A Pictorial History.* Bloomington, IN: Indiana University Press, 1999.

Carpenter, Monte. *Quotable General.* Nashville, TN: TowleHouse Publishing, 2001.

Collins, Dorothy C. and Cecil K. Byrd. *Indiana University: A Pictorial History.* Bloomington, IN: Indiana University Press, 1992.

Dean, Everett. *Indiana Basketball.* Self-published, 1932.

Dean, Everett. *Progressive Basketball: Methods and Philosophy.* Englewood Cliffs, NJ: Prentice-Hall, 1950.

DiPrimio, Pete and Rick Notter. *Hoosier Handbook: Stories, Stats and Stuff About IU Basketball.* Wichita, KS, 1995.

Douchant, Mike. *Inside Sports College Basketball Guide.* Detroit: Visible Ink Press, 1998.

Feinstein, John. *A Season on the Brink: A Year with Bob Knight and the Indiana Hoosiers.* New York: Macmillan, 1986.

Fort Wayne Journal-Gazette, miscellaneous issues.

Fort Wayne News-Sentinel, miscellaneous issues.

Gould, Todd. *Pioneers of the Hardwood: Indiana and the Birth of Professional Basketball.* Bloomington, IN: Indiana University Press, 1998.

Gray, Hetty. *Net Prophet: The Bill Garrett Story.* Fairland, IN: Sugar Creek Publishing, 2001.

Hammel, Bob. *A Banner Year at Indiana.* Bloomington, IN: Indiana University Press and *The Herald-Times,* 1993.

Hammel, Bob. *Beyond the Brink with Indiana.* Bloomington, IN: Indiana University Press and *The Herald-Telephone,* 1987.

Hammel, Bob and Larry Crewell. *The Champs '81.* Bloomington, IN: Indiana University Press and The Herald-Telephone, 1981.

Hammel, Bob and Kit Klingelhoffer. *Glory of Old IU: 100 Years of Indiana Athletics.* Champaign, IL: Sports Publishing, 1999.

Hammel, Bob and Rich Clarkson. *Knight with the Hoosiers.* Topeka, KS: Josten's Publications, 1975.

Hammel, Bob and Larry Crewell. *NCAA Indiana: All the Way.* Bloomington, IN: The Herald-Telephone and Indiana University Press, 1976.

Hammel, Bob and Rich Clarkson. *Silver Knight.* Bloomington, IN: The Herald-Times, 1997.

Hoose, Phillip M. Hoosiers: *The Fabulous Basketball Life of Indiana, 2nd Edition.* Indianapolis: Guild Press of Indiana, 1995.

Hosey, Tim and Bob Percival. *Bobby Knight: Countdown to Perfection.* New York: Leisure Press, 1983.

Indiana Daily Student, 1900-1936.

Indiana University Basketball Managers Reports, 1922-23 to 1970-71

Indiana University Basketball Media Guides, 1953-54 to 2003-04.

Indianapolis Journal, miscellaneous issues.

Indianapolis News, miscellaneous issues.

Indianapolis Star, 1936-2004.

Inside Indiana, 2001-2004.

Isenhour, Jack. *Same Knight, Different Channel: Basketball Legend Bob Knight at West Point and Today* Washington, D.C.: Brassey's, 2003.

Knight, Bob with Bob Hammel. *Knight: My Story.* New York: Thomas Dunne Books, 2002.

Lemberger, Louis. *Where Basketball is King—Or Is It Knight?* New York: Vantage Press, 1990.

Louisville Courier-Journal, miscellaneous issues.

McCracken, Branch. *Indiana Basketball.* Englewood Cliffs, NJ: Prentice-Hall, 1955.

McKee, Carl R. *Indiana University Basketball Trivia.* Boston: Quinlan Press, 1987.

Marquette, Ray. *Indiana University Basketball.* New York: Alpine Books, 1975.

Marquette, Ray. *Indiana University Basketball:* The Perfect Season. New York: Alpine Books, 1976.

Marshall, Kerry D. *Two of a Kind: The Tom and Dick Van Arsdale Story.* Indianapolis: Scott Publications, 1992.

Mellen, Joan. *Bob Knight: His Own Man.* New York: Avon Books, 1989.

Official 2002 NCAA Division I Men's Basketball Championship Program. Lexington, KY: Host Communications, 2002.

Official 2004 NCAA Final Four Tournament Records Book. Chicago: Triumph Books, 2004.

Official 2004 Men's NCAA Basketball Records. Chicago: Triumph Books, 2004.

Rappoport, Ken. *The Classic: The History of the NCAA Basketball Championship.* Kansas City: National Collegiate Athletic Association, 1979.

Roberts, Randy. *But They Can't Beat Us: Oscar Robertson and the Crispus Attucks Tigers.* Champaign, IL: Sports Publishing, 1999.

Sports Illustrated, miscellaneous issues.

Sulek, Robert Paul. Hoosier Honor: *Bob Knight and Academic Success at Indiana University.* New York: Praeger Publications, 1990.

Sutton, Stan and John Laskowski. *John Laskowski's Tales from the Hoosier Locker Room.* Champaign, IL: Sports Publishing, 2003.

Tolliver, Melanie. *Indiana University Basketball: For the Thrill of It.* Champaign, IL: Sports Publishing, 2002.

Wells, Herman B. *Being Lucky: Reminiscences and Reflections.* Bloomington, IN: Indiana University Press, 1980.

Wolfe, Rich. *Good Knight/Knightmares.* Self-published, 2001.

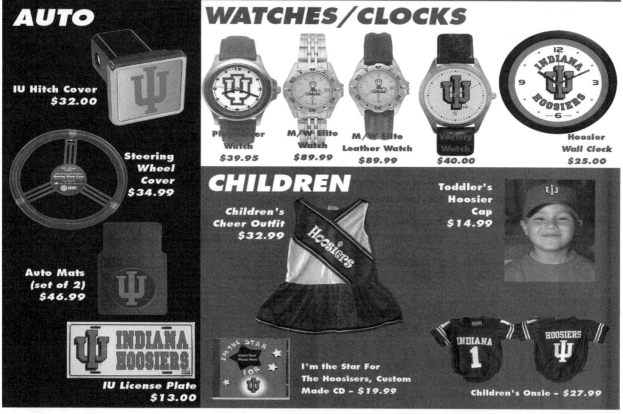